CALIFORNIA REAL ESTATE

Practice

THE GOLD STANDARD

8TH EDITION

Walt Huber & Arlette Lyons

Worthy of Being a Coffee Table Book!

40 Excellent Years!

CALIFORNIA REAL ESTATE

Practice

THE GOLD STANDARD

8TH EDITION

Walt Huber, MBA
Arlette Lyons, CRS, GRI, SRES

CALIFORNIA REAL ESTATE PRACTICE

COPYRIGHT 1974, 1981, 1988, 1994, 2005, 2010, 2012, 2015 - 8th Edition
Educational Textbook Company, Inc.
P. O. Box 3597
Covina, California 91722
(626)339-7733
(626)332-4744 (Fax)
etctextbooks.com or etcbooks.com

Library of Congress Cataloging-in-Publication Data

California Real Estate Practice - Walt Huber and Arlette Lyons

Summary: Covers all material in Real Estate Practice classes with special emphasis on California real estate procedures. Written in very clear and simple language, easy-to-read format with photographs, charts, and graphs. Includes glossary and index. Suitable for students, salespeople, brokers, and teachers seeking information about the practice of real estate in the day-to-day operations of a real estate brokerage. This textbook is designed to fulfill the course requirement necessary to take the California Real Estate Salesperson and Broker Exams.

1. Real estate business - California
2. Real property - California
        I. Walt Huber, II. Arlette Lyons
HD266. C2B644 2005
333.33

ISBN 978-16-2684-252-6

All Rights Reserved

All rights to this real estate textbook are reserved. No part of this text may be reproduced or transmitted in any form, by any means, including electronic or mechanical photocopying, recording, or storing in any retrieval system, or otherwise used without the prior written permission of this publisher.

Printed in the United States of America

This publication is designed to provide accurate and authoritative information in regard to the subject matter covered. It is sold with the understanding that the publisher is not engaged in rendering legal or other professional services. If legal or other expert assistance is required, the services of a competent professional person should be sought. All advice is given as purely anecdotal, and reflects the opinions and experiences of the authors, but is not held out as standard operating procedure. Practice varies throughout the state and brokerage by brokerage.

Forms reprinted with permission, CALIFORNIA ASSOCIATION OF REALTORS®, and forms, logo, and miscellaneous material reprinted with permission, Lyons and Associates, Inc. Endorsement not implied.

Preface

This premium textbook is more worthy of being called a coffee table book than a reference book. It's a keeper!

In honor of Educational Textbook Company's 40 years of excellence, we're putting out this ground-breaking "Gold Standard" 8th Edition of *California Real Estate Practice*.

GOLD STANDARD EDITION

We call this the "Gold Standard" because it is the textbook by which all other Real Estate Practice textbooks will be judged for decades. You'll want it within reach throughout your educational experience as well as professional career. It's meant to be cherished as a must-have, go-to reference book, and even in a world where technology changes daily, the information and hands-on advice in this book will make it timeless. No matter how computers change the industry, this is a people business, and your personal relationships with your clients will forever be enhanced by following the advice in this exceptional, quality book. Priceless person-to-person trust and professionalism can't be replaced by all the digital improvements in the world, but it helps to be well versed in both methods— which is why we've included a brand new chapter on **Online and Technological Advances** in the business that improve but don't replace personal service.

ENHANCEMENTS

Everything you need to know about practicing the fine art of real estate sales is contained in this updated, upgraded, and quality enhanced book! The finely detailed rewrite includes not only the newest forms and the latest information, but also the "tried and true" traditional methods that continue to work. We also include newer methods, like virtual offices, online search engines, MLS sharing opportunities, smartphone and tablet mobile downloads, etc. We combine both the best of old-school personal service with more modern techniques that speed up the buying and selling process and satisfy both file cabinet lovers as well as technology aficionados.

NEW DIGITAL TECHNOLOGY

The real estate industry will forever be changed by the advent of new mobile technology. Smartphones, tablets, Wi-Fi, Apps, downloadable forms, and real estate specific search engines, like Realtor.com and Zillow.com, have sped up the process of buying and selling real estate to lightning speed unbelievable just a few years ago. The MLS shares details previously unavailable to non-licensees. Virtual tours, QR codes, and new website urls ending in .realtor are all sea changes in the industry that are just exploding in popularity. Don't be intimidated… we explain things clearly and simply throughout the book.

If 90% of purchasers start their search online, you and your students need to know how to take advantage of this marketing bonanza. Facebook isn't just for "friends" anymore… ▼

 CALIFORNIA REAL ESTATE PRACTICE

NEW LEARNING TECHNIQUES

Finally, we've added matching vocabulary assignments at the end of each chapter to help you retain definitions of the most important terminology in the chapters. It's a learning method that takes you one step closer to being able to pass your real estate licensing exams and improve your understanding of this fascinating topic. You won't find a better quality textbook on the market and will be proud to see this displayed on your coffee table next to your other high profile impressive books!

LATEST PURCHASE AGREEMENT

The latest version of the CAR® **Residential Purchase Agreement and Joint Escrow Instructions (RPA-CA Revised 11/14)** represents a dramatic change in details required to fill out the form. It is much more specific in terms of dates and time limitations for contingencies and addresses the need for more clarity in the Purchase Agreement form. Not only do we reproduce the latest form, we break it down section by section in simple language, explaining all the newest revisions to one of, if not THE, most important forms in a real estate transaction!

SPECIAL THANKS

The authors would like to express their appreciation to the professionals who helped to make this textbook extraordinary. They include: Rick Lee, prepress and layout editor; Colleen Taber, executive editor; Shelley Geary, supervising editor; Phillip Dockter, art director; Melinda Winters, cover artist; and Troy Stacey, graphic artist.

We'd also like to thank Professor Walt Zozula from Glendale College and Wayne Rapp from Gold Coast Schools for their valuable input. Special thanks to Duane Gomer, a lecturer at Duane Gomer Seminars, Bruce Miller, real estate attorney and owner of American Notary Institute, and Fabiola Torres, Distance Education Coordinator from Glendale College, for their helpful suggestions.

Professor Levin P. Messick, who established the appraisal degree program at Mt. San Antonio College and Glendale College, was instrumental in making this Practice book the exceptional text that it is. Judi Belanger of Accredited Real Estate Schools of Northern California lent her valuable assistance as well.

We can't thank co-author Arlette Lyons enough for being so conscientious and taking yet another pass at this book to make sure we really updated all the vital information that needed to be addressed.

California Association of REALTORS® has been generous enough to provide us with their excellent and frequently used real estate forms. We reprinted them with permission, but no endorsement is implied.

Dedicated to the Millennials (1982-2004)
"The Largest Tech-Savvy Generation"

Dear Millennials:

We dedicate this wealth-building book to you! Your generation is so large that you'll eventually make up over half of our work force. Your sheer numbers alone will cause the "Next Big House Buying Wave"—a trend that will increase the prices of real estate.

As you've grown up with mobile devices and social media, you're already changing how real estate brokerages operate. The future is in your tech-savvy hands.

Whether you plan to purchase a home or become a licensed professional, keep this book on your coffee table as a reference book or reminder of your future goals.

Acknowledgments

This book contains the input of many prominent educators and real estate professionals. Their involvement as contributing advisors has made it possible for us to cover a wide range of material in detail and, at the same time, offer practical perspectives based upon their extensive classroom and industry experience. Their contributions were invaluable and merit our most sincere thanks.

R. Bryant
Allan Hancock College

J. DiRuscio
Allan Hancock College

R. Smith
American River College

Jim Glickman, MAI
American River College

Steve Sodergren
Antelope Valley College

Professor Ballman
Antelope Valley College

Chris Hamilton
Antelope Valley College

Joe Newton
Bakersfield College

Robin Sherman
Cabrillo College

Bruce Southstone, CRB, CRS
Cabrillo College

R. Gable
Canada College

John T. Martinez
Chabot College

Richard McCartney
Chabot College

John A. Culver
Chabot College

Robert Andersen
Chabot College

C. Weeks
Chabot College

J. Brooks
Chabot College

Earl H. Bond
Chaffey College

A. Turner
Chaffey College

J. O. Wright
Chaffey College

Carol Jensen
City College San Francisco

M. Zelaya
City College San Francisco

Leo Bello
City College San Francisco

Hal Bouley
Coastline College

D. Ables
Coastline College

Corina D. Rollins
College of Marin

K. Fowler
College of Marin

Marc Gottlieb
College of San Mateo

R. Vitale
College of The Canyons

Jeff Eddy
College of The Sequoias

Robert Morgan
Compton College

Ronald G. Rueb
Contra Costa College

B. Mnichowicz
Cosumnes River College

Professor Ellerman
Cosumnes River College

Nick Zoumbos
Crafton Hills College

Don Blazej
Cuesta College

Gregory Daunoras
Cuyamaca College

Professor Langager
Diablo Valley College

Dr. Elliott J. Dixon
East Los Angeles College

O. Vasquez Anderson
East Los Angeles College

Roderick Lipscomb
East Los Angeles College

Michael Botello, Esq.
El Camino College

Dr. Donna Grogan, GRI, CPM
El Camino College

Derf Fredericks
El Camino College

Bud Zeller
Folsom Lake College

Charles Krackeler
Foothill College

John E. Roberto, CRS, GRI
Fresno City College

M. Saito
Fresno City College

Dr. Robert J. Bowers
Fullerton College

Charmaine Smith
Fullerton College

Karen Obuljen
Golden West College

Dino Vlachos
Golden West College

W. Gibson
Hartnell College

C. Storey
Imperial Valley College

Frank Pangborn
Irvine Valley College

John Shaw
Lassen Community College

Robert Anderson
Los Angeles City College

Thomas Duffy
Los Angeles City College

M. Eisenberg
Los Angeles City College

Professor Maricich
Los Angeles Harbor College

Kenneth Gunderson
Los Angeles Harbor College

Harold Lerner
Los Angeles Pierce College

L.G. Bellamy
Los Angeles Southwest College

Professor Taylor
Los Angeles Trade-Tech College

Jerry Fish
Los Medanos College

Ignacio Gonzalez
Mendocino College

Harvey Rafel
Merced College

Shirley Jones
Merced College

T. Gee
Merritt College

Edward L. Culbertson
MiraCosta College

Ron Grant
Merritt Colllege

Mike Daniels
MiraCosta College

Frank Diaz
Mission College

J.C. Bawiec
Modesto Junior College

T. Provance
Modesto Junior College

Becky D. Jones
Monterey Peninsula College

Mary Ann Zamel
Mt. San Antonio College

Glenn Vice
Mt. San Antonio College

R. Stephan
Mt. San Antonio College

Paul Guess
Mt. San Jacinto College

S. James
Mt. San Jacinto College

Heli Sairanen
Napa Valley College

G. Daum
Orange Coast College

David Kemp
Palomar College

R. Graves
Palomar College

A. Carmello
Riverside Community College

Bill McGrath
Sacramento City College

Charles D. Brown
Sacramento City College

Paul Grutsis
San Bernardino Valley College

E. Delcoure
San Bernardino Valley College

Michael Durrett
San Bernardino Valley College

Dr. Shad Jefferies
San Diego Mesa College

S. Griger
San Diego Mesa College

D. Stone
San Joaquin Delta College

Janet Truscott
San Joaquin Delta College

R. Hall
San Jose City College

Gary Goldberg, Attorney
Santa Barbara City College

Steve Herndon
Santa Rosa Junior College

Jim Michaelson
Santa Rosa Junior College

Dr. Evelyn D. Winkel
Santiago Canyon College

William Rawlings
Santiago Canyon College

Kim Tyler
Shasta College

Marty Carrick
Shasta College

John Jurivich
Shasta College

M. Wurschmidt
Shasta College

Jo Middleton
Shasta College

Mike Walker
Sierra College

Allan Nuttall
Skyline College

Robert C. Cass
Southwestern College

Ronald E. Loncki
Southwestern College

J.R. Chantengco, CCIM, MBA
Southwestern College

Chris Grover
Victor Valley College

Professor Faz Elahi
West Los Angeles College

George H. Miller
West Valley College

Real Estate Specialists

Charles Ellis
Occidental College

James Short
San Diego State Univ.

Reginald Woolfolk
West Valley Occupational Cntr.

Lorraine Abrams
West Valley Occupational Cntr.

Evan Morris
North Valley Occupational Cntr.

Claudia Wagner
North Valley Occupational Cntr.

Marvin Morris
Academy of Real Estate

Noble Fields, CEO
Noble Fields School of Real Estate

Robin Gifford
Noble Fields School of Real Estate

Kerry Surin
Noble Fields School of Real Estate

Don Kalal, Owner
California Broker's Institute

Jeff Heller
Accelerated Real Estate School

Donald Tram
ischoolmagic Real Estate School

Richard Tamayo
America's Real Estate School

Peter Yip
Golden City Professional Studies

Mary Shoane
Real Estate and Loan School

Paul Nguyen
999 Realty College

Joe Domond
The Executive Learning Center

Richard Leu
Auric Realty Academy

Lee Mench
The Learning Source

Craig Dubron
United Educational Services

Joe Cobb
Realty Experts Training Academy

Robert Gabai
Americana College

Tia J. Shin
Learnet Academy, Inc.

David Schneider
Americas Real Estate and Management
Schools

Blair Black
The Realty Institute

Shane Hunter
Revei Real Estate School

Table of Contents

Chapter 3: The Listing Agreement: How to Secure a Listing 69

Chapter 4: Breakdown of the Listing Agreement: How to Fill It Out 99

Chapter 8: Online Search, Alerts, and Beyond: Constantly Evolving Technology

261

Chapter 9: Finance: Understanding the Finance Process   297

The Salesperson: How to Get Started

I. Enter the Real Estate Salesperson — Becoming a Traditional and Digital Expert

Congratulations on taking this practice course, an important step towards obtaining your real estate license and beginning a career in real estate. Now is the time to set your goals and focus on how to achieve them.

Always put your short-term and long-term goals in writing and review and revise them at least once a year. Where do you want to be in five years? Keep abreast of changes in the industry, like search alerts and advancements in mobile device technology (see Chapter 8).

You need to know what your job description is, what is expected of you, and how to best perform the duties that will lead to a rewarding and successful career in real estate sales.

People will buy and sell real estate in all types of economic conditions, as real estate is cyclical and the only constant is "change."

.Buyers and sellers searching the Internet have not eliminated the need for brokers. They spend on average about 12 weeks researching prices, neighborhoods, and financing before coming to us as professionals to physically show them properties and guide them through the negotiations of buying a property and finalizing the sale through close of escrow.

More than half of listing views are done on mobile devices.

Our brick and mortar offices are generally getting smaller but are still necessary for the image and physical setting to meet face-to-face with clients.

Amazon has killed the brick and mortar bookstores, and iTunes has practically wiped music stores off the planet. But real estate still requires offices (although somewhat smaller than in the past) where buyers and sellers can sit down and interact with a professional in the business. This is where the hand-holding comes in—the Internet has no heart or compassion for the very emotional and potentially process of buying or selling a home.

CHAPTER OUTLINE

As a real estate professional, you have access and experience in filling out the numerous required forms, disclosures, and contracts necessary to fulfill the personal service of taking a purchase from listing to offer to close of escrow.

Without the expert knowledge of a real estate licensee, for example, a buyer could miss one little check box on a form that might cost the buyer or seller thousands of dollars—more than justifying the cost of any commission paid to a broker.

Make no mistake, real estate is a personal service industry that requires the expert knowledge of a trained licensee, and while much of the preliminary footwork is now done online by buyers, brokerages aren't going anywhere.

A. FIRST, GET THE SUPPORT OF YOUR FAMILY

It's important to have the support of family members. Your time will not always be your own. You may have to show property on Sunday afternoon or sit an "Open House" on your listing or some other agent's listing. Many real estate tasks demand evening performances, when both clients are usually home, so your family meals will not always be a "planned gourmet event." Some creative adjustments will need to be made by all.

1. You Should Have Six Months' Savings

It is also extremely important to have saved a little nest egg to meet your financial obligations for approximately six months, as there is frequently a lag time of at least two to three months prior to receiving your first commission. Your clients' needs should be your first priority, not your concerns about paying your personal bills.

If your expectations are realistic, you should be able to enjoy an adequate standard of living while building your new career and wealth.

B. BROKERS KNOW WHEN YOU PASS THE SALESPERSON'S EXAM

When you apply and pass the state real estate examination, you will be inundated by solicitations from various offices wanting to interview you. Some will be franchises and some will be independently-owned offices. Therefore, finding a sponsoring broker—a real estate office in which to hang your license—should not be a problem. However, selecting the right environment for you that complements your knowledge and experience is the most important choice that you're going

to make at this time. Avoid changing from one office to another, as it is often an expensive and emotional transition. Not only will you need to start anew, learn the office procedures, meet new associates, purchase new business cards, and other necessary advertising items, but you'll also need to contact your whole sphere of influence to let your contacts know of your move, and how to reach you. A **SPHERE OF INFLUENCE** *is made up of people you know, including friends, neighbors, family, and business associates that you contact regularly.* Social networking sites like **Twitter, Facebook,** and **LinkedIn** have vastly increased an agent's sphere of influence, as well as sped up the process of putting a listing before the public eye! A *GEOGRAPHICAL FARM is a specific neighborhood, community, or zip code in which you solicit for real estate business.* The idea is to establish and "brand" yourself as the local community expert and develop relationships with potential clients who will choose you over your competition when it comes to buying or selling real estate.

More importantly, while considering a move, it's hard for any agent to be productive, as the move may drain time and energy away from clients' needs. So take your time interviewing and be wise in your selection of a sponsoring broker.

Interview with at least three different brokers. If you need a lot of training or mentoring, your initial commissions will naturally be lower, but you will gain the confidence and experience you lack.

II. The Broker Interview

A. HOW YOU SELECT AN EMPLOYING BROKER

One good broker source is a personal referral from buyers, sellers, or other agents who are pleased with the services rendered to them. Successful agents work for brokers with good reputations—that's where and with whom you want to be associated.

Your reputation as an agent is directly related to the reputation of the broker and other agents with whom you choose to work.

Observe the real estate signs, advertising, and the brokerage websites in the areas you plan to service. If one company overshadows all others, then you may want to interview with its broker or office manager.

The majority of buyers and sellers will have shopped the Internet prior to buying or selling a home.

Another way you can locate a broker in good standing is by calling the local Association of REALTORS®. You may also want to get on the Internet and check out listings from various websites, check the various brokers' presence in the industry and how they represent themselves. In fact, the majority of buyers shop the Internet prior to even contacting an agent and purchasing a property.

B. THE APPOINTMENT

You'll need to make an appointment for approximately one hour with the brokers of your choice, preferably at their place of business, so that you can form an opinion of their facilities and the other agents in the company.

There are numerous local "Association of REALTORS®" that operate under the umbrella of the California Association of REALTORS® (CAR) and the National Association of REALTORS® (NAR) (see **Figure 1-1**). These regional organizations are a force for good and the betterment of their practitioners and the public they serve. The Association may operate a Multiple Listing Service (MLS), wherein REALTORS®, electronically or digitally, place the listings they have for sale for the benefit of the membership and their clients.

A local MLS can now share listing information with numerous sources available to the public, including local and national websites and newspapers. Increasing the exposure of a listing greatly increases the likelihood of a sale.

Figure 1-1   **www.cvar.net**

Be prepared to fill out an application for sales associate (see Figure 1-2).

Remember, first impressions are important, and your goal should be to strive for professionalism.

Remember: You and the broker are interviewing each other!

1. What Questions to Ask

a. What Are Your Startup Costs?

You probably will be considered an independent contractor, and it's important to start off on the right foot. Some brokers charge a monthly desk

Figure 1-2

Application for Sales Associate

Please complete both
pages of this application

Name and Address

Last	First	Middle	Social Security Number
Address			Phone Number (Home)
City	State	Zip	Phone Number (Work)

Real Estate Experience
(Complete this section only if you have previous experience in selling real estate)

Do you have a real estate salesperson's license?　　　Yes ___　No ___
Do you have a broker's license?　　　　　　　　　　　Yes ___　No ___

License ever suspended? _____

Are you or have you been a member of a Board of REALTORS®? _____

Which Board? _____ Dates of membership _____

General Information

Are you familiar with the irregular hours and weekends you will be working?	Yes ___	No ___
And the irregular earnings?	Yes ___	No ___
Are these acceptable to you?	Yes ___	No ___
Are there any problems that might interfere with your work?	Yes ___	No ___

Indicate for how long you are in a position to financially sustain yourself:

___ 3 months　___ 6 months　___ 1 year　___ other

Will you devote full-time to a career in real estate?	Yes ___	No ___
What total earnings do you expect to receive from selling real estate?	$ _____	
Are you willing to devote a reasonable time to learn the basics of the real estate business?	Yes ___	No ___
Will you join the local board of REALTORS® if you are employed by us?	Yes ___	No ___
Have you filed for bankruptcy in the last five years?	Yes ___	No ___

Please insert and additional information or comments which should be considered for evaluating your qualifications: _____

_____

© 2015 ETC., Inc.　　　　　　　**Always list your computer skills!**

Education

Preparatory/High School	Name/Address	Grade Completed/Degree
College/University		
Real Estate Related Courses/Other		

Employment Record

Date Employed	Name of Company and Nature of Business	Address and Telephone	Job Title/Superior	Earnings	Reason for Leaving
from					
to					
from					
to					
from					
to					
from					
to					

References List 4 people willing to provide professional and/or character references (excluding relatives or previous employers).

Name	Telephone	Address	Occupation

Automobile Information

Do you own a car? _____ Make _____ Year _____

Driver's License Number and State of Issuance _____

I authorize investigation and verification of all statements contained in this application. I hereby affirm that my statements and answers to all questions on this application are true and correct.

_____   _____
Signature   Date

© 2015 ETC., Inc.

and telephone fee. These can be minimal, such as $25 per month, all the way to thousands of dollars per month, depending on what's being offered in benefits and your commission split.

There is a substantial annual fee to belong to CAR, NAR, and a local association (approximately $600), plus MLS fees that may cost another $150.

b. Who Pays For Expenses?

You need to know what the broker pays for and what you are expected to pay for:

1. Costs of signs: "For Sale" and "Open House" signs, flags, etc.
2. Cost of having signs put up and taken down
3. Multiple Listing input (most inputs are free and computer generated)
4. Business cards
5. Stationery, literature, brochures
6. Newspaper and magazine advertisements (used less frequently)
7. Telephone charges (including long distance)
8. Desk fees
9. Forms – The California Association of REALTORS® offers zipForm® Plus free to their members. *ZIPFORMS are constantly upgraded CAR contract forms that can be downloaded from the Internet (www.car.org)*
10. Trade magazines
11. Local Chambers of Commerce membership
12. Yellow Page advertisement
13. Internet websites and email addresses (personal and office). Your email should reflect your profession. (You can now use ".realtor" as part of your domain name, like "walthuber.realtor."

A catalog of zipForms® can be downloaded to all your mobile devices (iPad®, iPhone®, Android®, etc.) and your desktop or notebook computers (free with CAR membership).

c. What Are the New Salesperson Requirements?

Brokers expect their agents to have a clean and operable car with adequate insurance to cover any liability while showing property. Most brokers will insist that they also be protected under your policy.

For safety and liability issues, most agents prefer to meet a client at a property.

Professional liability insurance is a must. Most brokers carry **ERRORS AND OMISSION INSURANCE (E&O)**, *which is usually paid for by the salesperson at close of escrow.* It can be paid yearly or on a per transaction basis. The cost of this professional liability insurance depends on the broker's claim history. As with most types of insurance, there usually is a deductible, which can range from $1,000 to $10,000 per claim. When being sued, you can anticipate losing the deductible immediately. Therefore, a low deductible is what you are hoping for.

Errors and Omission (liability) Insurance (E&O) protects real estate agents and their brokers against catastrophic lawsuits.

An owner trying to sell his or her own home will probably not have this insurance; yet another reason they should use a licensed professional to complete a transaction.

Will your broker contribute a reasonable amount should you be found liable in a lawsuit or arbitration judgment? Regulations require that all agents sign a contract with their brokers. See the CAR® **Independent Contractor Agreement (ICA) (Between Broker and Associate-Licensee Contract)** form (see **Figure 1-3**).

Most offices have their own websites where their listings appear with links to other related sites of interest, such as www.realtor.com. Promote your domain name (url) on all your advertisements, yard signs, and mail outs.

Professionalism will lead to a successful real estate career. A genuine care for the clients' needs and goals will go a long way towards goodwill.

d. What Training and Support Will I Receive?

Some companies will send you to a school for a week or so. Others will have an in-house trainer teaching the forms and various closing techniques. Still others will have a seasoned agent as a mentor checking with the new salespeople on a regular basis, answering their questions, making suggestions on how to improve their performances, and accompanying them on appointments.

Practicing on a client can prove expensive for all concerned. Don't let pride stand in the way of asking for your broker's guidance if you need it.

Additionally, there is a wealth of training and seminars at the local Association of REALTORS® offered free, or for a very minimal fee, to their dues-paying members. These classes and seminars address the multifaceted real estate industry's need for technical support and the constant legal changes brought on by this dynamic field. *MENTORING is hands-on experience and mentoring is meant to improve your performance or help you to attain a required level of skill.*

A salesperson must work under the supervision of one broker at a time. The broker owns the listings and pays agents their commissions.

e. What is My Portion of the Commission?

COMMISSION SPLITS detail what percentage belongs to you and what percentage belongs to your broker. You need to know when and how your broker pays your commission. You must remember that not all agents are on the same commission split. Most seasoned agents with a good track record receive a higher percentage than a brand new, untried agent. To encourage higher productivity, many brokers offer a bonus incentive after a certain amount of commission has been earned by the agent. This escalating type of commission benefits both the broker and the agents.

No matter how high your commission, a percentage of nothing is still nothing!

With a *STRAIGHT COMMISSION, the broker usually does not charge a desk fee, but pays the agent a commission based on a percentage of the selling price at close of escrow.* The agents usually pay their own Multiple Listing Service (MLS) fees.

A *100% COMMISSION refers to any commission payment arrangement between a real estate salesperson and the employing broker in which the salesperson handling a real estate transaction receives most of the commission earned by the office.* In this case, the salesperson usually pays the broker a "monthly desk fee" and a proportionate share of the office expenses, such as advertising, clerical and secretarial, telephone, and multiple listing services. The salesperson may pay for all expenses incurred in addition to a flat monthly fee, which may total more than $1,000 per month.

A 100% commission arrangement allows a supervising broker to charge a $750-$1,000 "desk fee" to supervise salespeople. An agent can work for only one broker at a time, and cannot act independently of his or her broker. All fees and commissions are disbursed through your broker.

The 100% commission plan is not appropriate for you as a new agent for the obvious reason that you still have much to learn about the real estate business. You cannot be expected to pay an adequate and proportionate contribution to the company at such an early stage in your career.

f. What Are the Miscellaneous Benefits?

Some brokers provide additional incentives to successful salespeople to assist them in attending educational seminars offered by local, state, and national boards of real estate. Real estate certificates and degrees are available through many community colleges and other educational institutions. The broker may also permit salespeople, or the more successful ones at least, to purchase their own residence without having to pay some part of the commission. Whatever the final compensation plan arranged, you and your broker should avoid any misunderstanding by having these and other details carefully spelled out in writing, and signed in an **Independent Contractor Agreement** (see Figure 1-3).

It's important, at this time, to disclose your past work experiences, how much time and effort you plan to devote to all aspects of your real estate career, including ongoing education, as this may bring about a more favorable split. Let's remember that in order for an office to be successful, there must be a reasonable margin of profit for both the broker and the associates. Presenting a first-class picture to the real estate industry and to the clients bears a cost that should not be overlooked. You may be asked at this time to fill out an **Application for Sales Associate** (refer back to Figure 1-2).

As a new licensee, the most important issue in the interview is to determine the integrity of the broker and the office and your level of comfort and harmony experienced while there.

g. Who Answers the Telephone?

Who answers the telephone in the office? This is an important issue because it determines how you'll give priority to your tasks and budget your time. (See "Floor Time" in Chapter 5.) When an agent answers the office phone, he or she is getting **floor time** to answer buyers' or sellers' inquiries, which may result in new clients.

III. Large vs. Small Offices

Don't forget: Small offices may have a large Internet presence. It pays to do a little research before you interview with a brokerage.

As a new agent, you'll want to examine the size of the company for which you want to work. Keep in mind that a firm's growth potential may be the opposite of what you expect. For example, a corporate-owned business may decide to remain small, while a sole proprietor may choose to go big, opening up a number of branch offices and hiring as many as 60 licensees and more to staff each.

Size invariably determines the types of technical and managerial decisions that confront a firm, as well as training and opportunities provided to new employees.

In general, the small firm tends to remain flexible, thus better able to seize upon opportunities with no need to obtain corporate approval. Its activities are limited primarily to selling. However, to attract buyers, it's important that there be several good listing agents in the company to increase its inventory.

The large firm, by contrast, is diversified, can develop capital more readily, is less flexible, and must carry a higher burden of overhead, including extensive training, with less accurate control of its resources.

It can't hurt to ask about a company's long-range growth plans and how you fit in before deciding where you want to work.

IV. Independent Contractor and Employer Relationships

A salesperson who is actively engaged in professional real estate activities must be employed by a licensed real estate broker. Commissions are only paid to brokers, who then split that commission with their agents, depending on the Independent Contractor Agreement (see Figure 1-3).

In California, all salespeople working under a broker are considered employees for the purposes of administration of the real estate law, even if they act as independent contractors.

An **INDEPENDENT CONTRACTOR** *sells results (and receives commissions) rather than time, and his or her physical conduct is not subject to the control of another.* An **EMPLOYEE**, *on the other hand, works under the direct control (designated hours and breaks) and supervision of the employer.*

The California Bureau of Real Estate (CalBRE) considers a salesperson an employee of the broker for the purpose of administration of the real estate broker law, even if he or she is an independent contractor. This makes the broker responsible for the supervision of the real estate activities of their salespersons.

In most real estate offices the salespeople are hired as independent contractors. They come and go at will, working no fixed hours and paying their own estimated taxes (federal and state income taxes, social security, Medicare, unemployment insurance, and state disability insurance). On the other hand, more strictly supervised (set hours, dress code, etc.) workers, such as secretaries and assistants, are generally considered employees.

The broker is required to carry worker's compensation for salespeople who are independent contractors in the same way that they do for employees.

A. INDEPENDENT CONTRACTOR AGREEMENT HIGHLIGHTS

Here are some highlighted sections of the CAR® Independent Contractor Agreement (Between Broker and Associate-Licensee) (see Figure 1-3).

3. **Independent Contractor Relationship.** This paragraph establishes the associate licensee's status as an independent contractor "to the maximum extent permissible by law."

3G. This advisory warns brokers that failure to carry workman's compensation on associate licensees (even independent contractors) may result in the issuance of stop-work orders and fines up to $1,000 per agent, not to exceed $100,000 per company.

5. **Proprietary Information and Files.** This establishes that the **broker owns all listings, files, leads, transaction documents, and other agreements**; they are taken and performed in the broker's name. ▼

Figure 1-3

CALIFORNIA ASSOCIATION OF REALTORS®

INDEPENDENT CONTRACTOR AGREEMENT
(Between Broker and Associate-Licensee)
(C.A.R. Form ICA, Revised 11/13)

This Agreement, dated _____ , is made between _____
_____ ("Broker") and
_____ ("Associate-Licensee").
In consideration of the covenants and representations contained in this Agreement, Broker and Associate-Licensee agree as follows:

1. **BROKER:** Broker represents that Broker is duly licensed as a real estate broker by the State of California, ☐ doing business as _____ (firm name), ☐ a sole proprietorship, ☐ a partnership, or ☐ a corporation. Broker is a member of the _____ Association(s) of REALTORS®, and a subscriber to the _____ Multiple Listing Service(s). Broker shall keep Broker's license current during the term of this Agreement.

2. **ASSOCIATE-LICENSEE:** Associate-Licensee represents that: **(i)** he/she is duly licensed by the State of California as a ☐ real estate broker, ☐ real estate salesperson, and **(ii)** he/she has not used any other names within the past five years, except _____ Associate-Licensee shall keep his/her license current during the term of this Agreement, including satisfying all applicable continuing education and provisional license requirements.

3. **INDEPENDENT CONTRACTOR RELATIONSHIP:**
   A. Broker and Associate-Licensee intend that, to the maximum extent permissible by law: **(i)** This Agreement does not constitute an employment agreement by either party; **(ii)** Broker and Associate-Licensee are independent contracting parties with respect to all services rendered under this Agreement; and **(iii)** This Agreement shall not be construed as a partnership.
   B. Broker shall not: **(i)** restrict Associate-Licensee's activities to particular geographical areas, or **(ii)** dictate Associate-Licensee's activities with regard to hours, leads, open houses, opportunity or floor time, production, prospects, sales meetings, schedule, inventory, time off, vacation, or similar activities, except to the extent required by law.
   C. Associate-Licensee shall not be required to accept an assignment by Broker to service any particular current or prospective listing or parties.
   D. Except as required by law: **(i)** Associate-Licensee retains sole and absolute discretion and judgment in the methods, techniques, and procedures to be used in soliciting and obtaining listings, sales, exchanges, leases, rentals, or other transactions, and in carrying out Associate-Licensee's selling and soliciting activities; **(ii)** Associate-Licensee is under the control of Broker as to the results of Associate-Licensee's work only, and not as to the means by which those results are accomplished; **(iii)** Associate-Licensee has no authority to bind Broker by any promise or representation; and **(iv)** Broker shall not be liable for any obligation or liability incurred by Associate-Licensee.
   E. Associate-Licensee's only remuneration shall be the compensation specified in paragraph 8.
   F. Associate-Licensee who only performs as a real estate sales agent, shall not be treated as an employee for state and federal tax purposes. However, an Associate-Licensee who performs loan activity shall be treated as an employee for state and federal tax purposes unless the activity satisfies the legal requirements to establish an independent contractor relationship.
   G. The fact the Broker may carry workers' compensation insurance for Broker's own benefit and for the mutual benefit of Broker and licensees associated with Broker, including Associate-Licensee, shall not create an inference of employment.
   (Workers' Compensation Advisory: Even though a Real Estate sales person may be treated as independent contractors for tax and other purposes, the California Labor and Workforce Development Agency considers them to be employees for workers' compensation purposes. According to that Agency: **(i)** Broker must obtain workers' compensation insurance for a Real Estate sales person and **(ii)** Broker, not a Real Estate sales person, must bear the cost of workers' compensation insurance. Penalties for failure to carry workers' compensation include, among others, the issuance of stop-work orders and fines of up to $1,000 per agent, not to exceed $100,000 per company.)

4. **LICENSED ACTIVITY:**
   A. All listings of property, and all agreements, acts or actions for performance of licensed acts, which are taken or performed in connection with this Agreement, shall be taken and performed in the name of Broker. Associate-Licensee agrees to and does hereby contribute all right and title to such listings to Broker for the benefit and use of Broker, Associate-Licensee, and other licensees associated with Broker.

Broker's Initials (_____) (_____)   Associate-Licensee's Initials (_____) (_____)

The copyright laws of the United States (Title 17 U.S. Code) forbid the unauthorized reproduction of this form, or any portion thereof, by photocopy machine or any other means, including facsimile or computerized formats. Copyright © 1990-2013, CALIFORNIA ASSOCIATION OF REALTORS®, INC. ALL RIGHTS RESERVED.

ICA REVISED 11/13 (PAGE 1 OF 4)

Reviewed by _____ Date _____

EQUAL HOUSING OPPORTUNITY

INDEPENDENT CONTRACTOR AGREEMENT (ICA PAGE 1 OF 4)

Agent: WALT HUBER	Phone:	Fax:	Prepared using zipForm® software
Broker: WALT HUBER REALTOR			

Brokers must bear the cost of workman's comp insurance and cannot pass it on to a licensee!

CHAPTER 1

B. Broker shall make available to Associate-Licensee, equally with other licensees associated with Broker, all current listings in Broker's office, except any listing which Broker may choose to place in the exclusive servicing of Associate-Licensee or one or more other specific licensees associated with Broker.

C. Associate-Licensee shall provide and pay for all professional licenses, supplies, services, and other items required in connection with Associate-Licensee's activities under this Agreement, or any listing or transaction, without reimbursement from Broker except as required by law.

D. Associate-Licensee shall work diligently and with his/her best efforts to: **(i)** sell, exchange, lease, or rent properties listed with Broker or other cooperating Brokers; **(ii)** solicit additional listings, clients, and customers; and **(iii)** otherwise promote the business of serving the public in real estate transactions to the end that Broker and Associate-Licensee may derive the greatest benefit possible, in accordance with law.

E. Associate-Licensee shall not commit any unlawful act under federal, state or local law or regulation while conducting licensed activity. Associate-Licensee shall at all times be familiar, and comply, with all applicable federal, state and local laws, including, but not limited to, anti-discrimination laws and restrictions against the giving or accepting a fee, or other thing of value, for the referral of business to title companies, escrow companies, home inspection companies, pest control companies and other settlement service providers pursuant to the California Business and Professions Code and the Real Estate Settlement Procedures Acts (RESPA).

F. Broker shall make available for Associate-Licensee's use, along with other licensees associated with Broker, the facilities of the real estate office operated by Broker at _____
and the facilities of any other office locations made available by Broker pursuant to this Agreement.

G. PROHIBITED ACTIVITIES: Associate-Licensee agrees not to engage in any of the following Real Estate licensed activities without the express written consent of Broker:
☐ Property Management; ☐ Loan Brokerage; ☐ Business Brokerage; ☐ _____
☐ _____
However, if Associate-Licensee has a Real Estate Broker's License, Associate-Licensee may nonetheless engage in the following prohibited activity(ies) only: _____
provided that **(1)** such prohibited activities are not done under the Broker's License, **(2)** no facilities of Broker (including but not limited to phones, fax, computers, and office space) are used for any such prohibited activities, **(3)** Associate-Licensee shall not use any marketing, solicitation or contact information that include Broker's name (including business cards) for such prohibited activities, **(4)** Associate-Licensee informs any actual or intended Principal for whom Associate-Licensee performs or intends to perform such prohibited activities the name of the broker under whose license the prohibited activities are performed, and **(5)** if Associate-Licensee is performing other permitted licensed activity for that Principal under Broker's license, then Associate-Licensee shall inform any actual or intended Principal for whom the prohibited activities are performed that the prohibited activities are not performed under Broker's license.

5. PROPRIETARY INFORMATION AND FILES:
A. All files and documents pertaining to listings, leads and transactions are the property of Broker and shall be delivered to Broker by Associate-Licensee immediately upon request or termination of this Agreement.
B. Associate-Licensee acknowledges that Broker's method of conducting business is a protected trade secret.
C. Associate-Licensee shall not use to his/her own advantage, or the advantage of any other person, business, or entity, except as specifically agreed in writing, either during Associate-Licensee's association with Broker, or thereafter, any information gained for or from the business, or files of Broker.

6. SUPERVISION: Associate-Licensee, within 24 hours (or ☐ _____) after preparing, signing, or receiving same, shall submit to Broker, or Broker's designated licensee: **(i)** all documents which may have a material effect upon the rights and duties of principals in a transaction; **(ii)** any documents or other items connected with a transaction pursuant to this Agreement in the possession of or available to Associate-Licensee; and **(iii)** all documents associated with any real estate transaction in which Associate-Licensee is a principal.

7. TRUST FUNDS: All trust funds shall be handled in compliance with the Business and Professions Code, and other applicable laws.

8. COMPENSATION:
A. TO BROKER: Compensation shall be charged to parties who enter into listing or other agreements for services requiring a real estate license:
☐ as shown in "Exhibit A" attached, which is incorporated as a part of this Agreement by reference, or
☐ as follows: _____

Any deviation which is not approved in writing in advance by Broker, shall be: **(1)** deducted from Associate-Licensee's compensation, if lower than the amount or rate approved above; and, **(2)** subject to Broker approval, if higher than the amount approved above. Any permanent change in commission schedule shall be disseminated by Broker to Associate-Licensee.

Broker's Initials (_____) (_____)   Associate-Licensee's Initials (_____) (_____)

Copyright © 1990-2013, CALIFORNIA ASSOCIATION OF REALTORS®, INC.
ICA REVISED 11/13 (PAGE 2 OF 4)

Reviewed by _____ Date _____

INDEPENDENT CONTRACTOR AGREEMENT (ICA PAGE 2 OF 4)

Untitled

B. TO ASSOCIATE-LICENSEE: Associate-Licensee shall receive a share of compensation actually collected by Broker, on listings or other agreements for services requiring a real estate license, which are solicited and obtained by Associate-Licensee, and on transactions of which Associate-Licensee's activities are the procuring cause, as follows:

☐ as shown in "Exhibit B" attached, which is incorporated as a part of this Agreement by reference, or
☐ other: _____

_____
_____
_____

C. PARTNERS, TEAMS, AND AGREEMENTS WITH OTHER ASSOCIATE-LICENSEES IN OFFICE: If Associate-Licensee and one or more other Associate-Licensees affiliated with Broker participate on the same side (either listing or selling) of a transaction, the commission allocated to their combined activities shall be divided by Broker and paid to them according to their written agreement. Broker shall have the right to withhold total compensation if there is a dispute between associate-licensees, or if there is no written agreement, or if no written agreement has been provided to Broker.

D. EXPENSES AND OFFSETS: If Broker elects to advance funds to pay expenses or liabilities of Associate-Licensee, or for an advance payment of, or draw upon, future compensation, Broker may deduct the full amount advanced from compensation payable to Associate-Licensee on any transaction without notice. If Associate-Licensee's compensation is subject to a lien, garnishment or other restriction on payment, Broker shall charge Associate-Licensee a fee for complying with such restriction.

E. PAYMENT: (i) All compensation collected by Broker and due to Associate-Licensee shall be paid to Associate-Licensee, after deduction of expenses and offsets, immediately or as soon thereafter as practicable, except as otherwise provided in this Agreement, or a separate written agreement between Broker and Associate-Licensee. **(ii)** Compensation shall not be paid to Associate-Licensee until both the transaction and file are complete. **(iii)** Broker is under no obligation to pursue collection of compensation from any person or entity responsible for payment. Associate-Licensee does not have the independent right to pursue collection of compensation for activities which require a real estate license which were done in the name of Broker. **(iv)** Expenses which are incurred in the attempt to collect compensation shall be paid by Broker and Associate-Licensee in the same proportion as set forth for the division of compensation (paragraph 8(B)). **(v)** If there is a known or pending claim against Broker or Associate-Licensee on transactions for which Associate-Licensee has not yet been paid, Broker may withhold from compensation due Associate-Licensee on that transaction amounts for which Associate-Licensee could be responsible under paragraph 14, until such claim is resolved. **(vi)** Associate-Licensee shall not be entitled to any advance payment from Broker upon future compensation.

F. UPON OR AFTER TERMINATION: If this Agreement is terminated while Associate-Licensee has listings or pending transactions that require further work normally rendered by Associate-Licensee, Broker shall make arrangements with another associate-licensee to perform the required work, or Broker shall perform the work him/herself. The licensee performing the work shall be reasonably compensated for completing work on those listings or transactions, and such reasonable compensation shall be deducted from Associate-Licensee's share of compensation. Except for such offset, Associate-Licensee shall receive the compensation due as specified above.

9. **TERMINATION OF RELATIONSHIP:** Broker or Associate-Licensee may terminate their relationship under this Agreement at any time, with or without cause. After termination, Associate-Licensee shall not solicit: **(i)** prospective or existing clients or customers based upon company-generated leads obtained during the time Associate-Licensee was affiliated with Broker; **(ii)** any principal with existing contractual obligations to Broker; or **(iii)** any principal with a contractual transactional obligation for which Broker is entitled to be compensated. Even after termination, this Agreement shall govern all disputes and claims between Broker and Associate-Licensee connected with their relationship under this Agreement, including obligations and liabilities arising from existing and completed listings, transactions, and services.

10. **DISPUTE RESOLUTION:**
Broker and Associate-Licensee agree to mediate all disputes and claims between them arising from or connected in any way with this Agreement before resorting to court action. If any dispute or claim is not resolved through mediation, or otherwise, instead of resolving the matter in court, Broker and Associate-Licensee may mutually agree to submit the dispute to arbitration at, and pursuant to the rules and bylaws of, the Association of REALTORS® to which both parties belong.

11. **AUTOMOBILE:** Associate-Licensee shall maintain automobile insurance coverage for liability and property damage in the following amounts $ _____ /$ _____ . Broker shall be named as an additional insured party on Associate-Licensee's policies. A copy of the endorsement showing Broker as an additional insured shall be provided to Broker.

Broker's Initials (_____) (_____)

Copyright © 1990-2013, CALIFORNIA ASSOCIATION OF REALTORS®, INC.
ICA REVISED 11/13 (PAGE 3 OF 4)

Associate-Licensee's Initials (_____) (_____)

Reviewed by _____ Date _____

EQUAL HOUSING OPPORTUNITY

INDEPENDENT CONTRACTOR AGREEMENT (ICA PAGE 3 OF 4)

Untitled

12. **PERSONAL ASSISTANTS:** Associate-Licensee may make use of a personal assistant, provided the following requirements are satisfied. Associate-Licensee shall have a written agreement with the personal assistant which establishes the terms and responsibilities of the parties to the employment agreement, including, but not limited to, compensation, supervision and compliance with applicable law. The agreement shall be subject to Broker's review and approval. Unless otherwise agreed, if the personal assistant has a real estate license, that license must be provided to the Broker. Both Associate-Licensee and personal assistant must sign any agreement that Broker has established for such purposes.

13. **OFFICE POLICY MANUAL:** If Broker's office policy manual, now or as modified in the future, conflicts with or differs from the terms of this Agreement, the terms of the office policy manual shall govern the relationship between Broker and Associate-Licensee.

14. **INDEMNITY AND HOLD HARMLESS; NOTICE OF CLAIMS:**
   A. Regarding any action taken or omitted by Associate-Licensee, or others working through, or on behalf of Associate-Licensee in connection with services rendered or to be rendered pursuant to this Agreement or Real Estate licensed activity prohibited by this agreement: (i) Associate-Licensee agrees to indemnify, defend and hold Broker harmless from all claims, disputes, litigation, judgments, awards, costs and attorney's fees, arising therefrom and (ii) Associate-Licensee shall immediately notify Broker if Associate-Licensee is served with or becomes aware of a lawsuit or claim regarding any such action.
   B. Any such claims or costs payable pursuant to this Agreement, are due as follows:
   ☐ Paid in full by Associate-Licensee, who hereby agrees to indemnify and hold harmless Broker for all such sums, or
   ☐ In the same ratio as the compensation split as it existed at the time the compensation was earned by Associate-Licensee ☐ Other: _____

   Payment from Associate-Licensee is due at the time Broker makes such payment and can be offset from any compensation due Associate-Licensee as above. Broker retains the authority to settle claims or disputes, whether or not Associate-Licensee consents to such settlement.

15. **ADDITIONAL PROVISIONS:** _____
   _____

16. **DEFINITIONS** As used in this Agreement, the following terms have the meanings indicated:
   A. "Listing" means an agreement with a property owner or other party to locate a buyer, exchange party, lessee, or other party to a transaction involving real property, a mobile home, or other property or transaction which may be brokered by a real estate licensee, or an agreement with a party to locate or negotiate for any such property or transaction.
   B. "Compensation" means compensation for acts requiring a real estate license, regardless of whether calculated as a percentage of transaction price, flat fee, hourly rate, or in any other manner.
   C. "Transaction" means a sale, exchange, lease, or rental of real property, a business opportunity, or a manufactured home, which may lawfully be brokered by a real estate licensee.

17. **ATTORNEY FEES:** In any action, proceeding, or arbitration between Broker and Associate-Licensee arising from or related to this Agreement, the prevailing Broker or Associate-Licensee shall be entitled to reasonable attorney fees and costs.

18. **ENTIRE AGREEMENT:** All prior agreements between the parties concerning their relationship as Broker and Associate-Licensee are incorporated in this Agreement, which constitutes the entire contract. Its terms are intended by the parties as a final and complete expression of their agreement with respect to its subject matter, and may not be contradicted by evidence of any prior agreement or contemporaneous oral agreement. This Agreement may not be amended, modified, altered, or changed except by a further agreement in writing executed by Broker and Associate-Licensee.

Broker: **Associate-Licensee:**

_____   _____
(Brokerage firm name)   (Signature)

By _____
Its ☐ Broker ☐ Office manager (check one)   _____
                            (Print name)

_____   _____
(Print name)   (Address)

_____   _____
(Address)   (City, State, Zip)

_____   _____
(City, State, Zip)   (Telephone)   (Fax)

_____
(Telephone)   (Fax)

THIS FORM HAS BEEN APPROVED BY THE CALIFORNIA ASSOCIATION OF REALTORS® (C.A.R.). NO REPRESENTATION IS MADE AS TO THE LEGAL VALIDITY OR ADEQUACY OF ANY PROVISION IN ANY SPECIFIC TRANSACTION. A REAL ESTATE BROKER IS THE PERSON QUALIFIED TO ADVISE ON REAL ESTATE TRANSACTIONS. IF YOU DESIRE LEGAL OR TAX ADVICE, CONSULT AN APPROPRIATE PROFESSIONAL.

This form is available for use by the entire real estate industry. It is not intended to identify the user as a REALTOR®. REALTOR® is a registered collective membership mark which may be used only by members of the NATIONAL ASSOCIATION OF REALTORS® who subscribe to its Code of Ethics.

Published and Distributed by:
REAL ESTATE BUSINESS SERVICES, INC.
a subsidiary of the California Association of REALTORS®
525 South Virgil Avenue, Los Angeles, California 90020

Reviewed by _____ Date _____

EQUAL HOUSING OPPORTUNITY

ICA REVISED 11/13 (PAGE 4 OF 4)

INDEPENDENT CONTRACTOR AGREEMENT (ICA PAGE 4 OF 4)   Untitled

---

Pay close attention to Box 14. Checking the second box is preferable.

6. **Supervision.** This paragraph focuses on the ways in which the broker will supervise the associate licensee's work, such as the licensee submitting, within 24 hours, certain documents to the broker for review—including documents connected with any transaction in which the associate licensee is a principal, whether or not the property is listed with the broker.

8A. **Compensation to Broker.** In this paragraph, brokers set forth their ordinary commission rates by filling in the blanks or attaching a commission schedule to the contract. Under California Law, all commissions are negotiable between the client and broker. The licensee must obtain the broker's permission to charge a different fee that does not match the broker's rate schedule.

8B. **Compensation to Associate-Licensee.** This paragraph provides that the licensee is entitled to a share of a commission only when the commission has actually been collected by the broker. The broker has a right to enforce payment, but is not obligated to sue the client or otherwise try to enforce the listing agreement. It is important to note that brokers who do not fight to uphold their licensees' rights will quickly lose their agents and their reputation as fair brokers.

8F. **Commission Upon or After Termination.** Both parties agree that the broker owes the licensee his or her share of the commission even if terminated with cause. If the licensee has not completed all work on the transaction prior to termination, the work must be finished by another licensee or the broker. Whoever does the work is entitled to a "reasonable compensation," which is offset from the terminated agent's share of the commission.

9. **Termination of Relationship.** Broker or Associate-Licensee can terminate the relationship at any time, with or without cause.

10. **Dispute Resolution.** Both parties agree to submit to mediation before going to court. If unsuccessful, they may agree to arbitration as an alternative.

14. **Indemnity and Hold Harmless.** This section concerns responsibility for liabilities or expenses the broker incurs as a result of the associate's handling of a transaction. Many brokers will check the first box, leaving the agent with the full responsibility of the liability. Others may share the responsibility proportionately to the extent of their respective share of the commission earned.

V. Your Planning Objectives and Goals

Now that you've carefully selected your office, it's important to set realistic goals; draw a blueprint and follow it. Without defining objectives or charting a course, you're like the sailor without a rudder, haphazardly navigating a sea of confusion. Knowing how much money you need to make per year helps you define your monthly and weekly goals. How many people must you usually contact prior to getting a listing appointment? How many showings do you normally make before writing an offer?

Plan your work and work your plan.

Ideally, goals ought to be in writing because they then have visual impact and are more readily examined and reviewed. Abstract and unreasonable goals will become more apparent if written. Certain real estate activities bring about better results than others. Knowing this, you can be selective and schedule daily business so as to save time and effort.

Write down your yearly goals. Open your drawer or computer files periodically for review and updating. They are just dreams until you put them in writing.

A. SPHERE OF INFLUENCE

Immediately contact your sphere of influence, including friends, relatives, past and present coworkers, trades and service people, etc. On a monthly basis, contact your "geographical farm." You'll always have a healthy harvest of new clients if you cultivate your farm regularly. Be sure to let them know the name of your firm, and how you can be contacted. A personal note asking about family and pets is best, but a preprinted form is also acceptable. Business cards should be included as well as email address and information about your company's website. A short, simple letter of introduction (see **Figure 1-4**) should include your name, the logo, name of the brokerage (and CalBRE license number) for which you are now working, as well as the address, mobile phone number, and website information.

There are many people who make up your "sphere of influence." These people might be members of clubs, church groups, your friends, your neighbors, or organizations to which you belong. The list should continually be adjusted and increased. All contacts should be meaningful to you. Naturally, these people also receive appropriate greetings during the holiday season. Thanksgiving cards are a good way to wish your clients a happy holiday season without any religious connotation.

B. SCHEDULE DAILY ACTIVITIES

Prior to coming into the office, you should write out a schedule of your daily activities. Allow a certain amount of time to return phone calls, develop new leads, and answer emails, texts, and other correspondence. Review all new listings, and edit out sold properties, including MLS and social media site!

In order to be productive, you should start each day with an itinerary, but remain flexible. Take time to answer emails first thing!

C. SOLICITING

Call on past clients, buyers, and sellers. Other sources are open house leads, walk-ins, referrals, door-to-door solicitations, cold calls, warm calls, "For Sale by Owners," and expired listings. *COLD CALLS are telephone calls to people you don't know. **WARM CALLS** are calls to people you already know and are usually more productive.* Always identify yourself as a salesperson when calling, and ask if it's a convenient time to call. *EXPIRED LISTINGS are listings that did not sell within the contract period.* These are good sources of listings, as the owners are probably still motivated to sell. You

Figure 1-4

Lyons and Associates, Inc., Realtor

REAL ESTATE EXCELLENCE

I have great news for you!
I am now associated with

Lyons and Associates, Inc., Realtor
Our goal is to provide excellence

in real estate

If I can be of service to you.

please call anytime

2820 E. Garvey Avenue South, West Covina, CA 91791
(626) 331-0141 • FAX: (626) 331-9772

CalBRE: 00414792   www.lyonsandassociatesrltr.com

must treat them with sensitivity and suggest a new approach for the sale, but never criticize another agent or company!

Before "cold calling" potential clients, it's important to consult the "National Do Not Call Registry." Telemarketers and sellers are required to search the registry at least once every 31 days and drop the phone numbers of registered consumers from their call lists. This includes faxes and mobile phone numbers which means no cold texting either! For more information, see: www.ftc.gov.

Telephone neighbors to inform them about a new listing or sale by using a reverse directory. A **REVERSE DIRECTORY** *is a website or publication, similar to a phone book, where phone numbers are listed by address rather than name.*

Farming works because you constantly advertise to the same group. It assures you that they know your name and you can expect to "harvest" an annual crop of clients. Don't forget to ask for referrals from your contacts!

D. PREVIEWING

You should preview new properties (as well as review older listings) on behalf of potential buyers and for your own information. There may be some important changes, such as condition and price reduction. It is important to let your buyers know that you preview many properties before selecting the best ones for their viewing. Naturally, you'll call the seller prior to previewing. Always leave a card. You must include your CalBRE salesperson license number on your card.

1. The Sales Kit

The SALES KIT is simply an inventory of items or aids that you may need in your daily real estate-related activities. With them, you should be able to handle both the expected and the unexpected opportunities presented to you.

The majority of your "sales kit" will be contained on your mobile device (such as an iPad or tablet), but "hard copy" contracts, addendums, etc., should be kept in a briefcase for easy access.

Your "sales kit" may be stored on your mobile device, which is much more useful.

E. SHOWING PROPERTIES

Although most buyers search the web first, remember that "only direct" personal contacts lead to sales.

Before properties are shown, the buyer should be prequalified by at least one lender. This can be done at your office or at the buyer's home. Do not show more than five houses in any one showing. Have the buyers participate in the process by having them write their comments on a "Buyers' Comment Sheet," with their own rating (found in Chapter 5). Of course, after showing a property, you should keep a list of all the properties your clients have seen and a copy of the buyer's comments for future reference.

> **Send thank-you notes (usually by email) to everyone to whom you showed a listing, including the addresses of the properties and keep them in a computer file. It not only creates goodwill with your buyers, but keeps track of what properties you've shown to clients, which could be important to proving your right to a commission in the Safety Clause (see Chapter 4).**

F. BECOMING AN EXPERT

You should create your own area of expertise by becoming knowledgeable in condo sales, new sales, probates, foreclosures, or property management. The more you know, the more confident you'll be, and this will be reflected in your attitude and conveyed to clients, who will appreciate working with a confident and knowledgeable agent.

If you join NAR, CAR, and a local board of REALTORS®, there are many advanced REALTOR® designations that indicate a higher degree of education and specialty. For example, the Certified Residential Specialist (CRS) designation indicates an agent's advanced training and expertise.

G. ATTRIBUTES OF AN EFFECTIVE SALESPERSON (Real Estate Expert)

Successful salespeople, in general, find their jobs satisfying and rewarding, both emotionally, because of the satisfaction they get helping people buy and sell their homes, and career-wise, because of their financial reward. **Figure 1-5** lists some "factors that lead salespeople to success."

Figure 1-5 **Factors That Salespeople Lead To Success**

1. Ability to think critically and make sound judgments.

2. Interest in advancement toward higher financial rewards.

3. Ambition and the willingness to work hard and long hours.

4. Don't let the mobile world pass you by. Keep abreast of all the wireless technology out there. Learn about it and use it to your advantage!

5. Art of negotiating, being persuasive.

6. A positive attitude toward job, colleagues, clients, employer, and others.

7. A well-running, fairly new vehicle is essential to give the appearance of success, and for comfort and safety, because so much driving of clients is involved.

8. Good salespeople know they cannot operate in a vacuum, they must belong to a team. Creating comradeship in various professional organizations and community betterment groups is a must. Join NAR®, CAR®, etc.

9. Consistency in completing details, even if it's dull paperwork.

10. Courtesy and respect for others encourages the same attitude towards you.

11. Cultivation of good habits; developing sales executive attitude.

12. Good salespeople know that they cannot last long in the business without keeping up with the latest information and changing technology. Take some computer classes and adult education classes, which are available through many community colleges. Keep abreast of changes in the industry — like "green" requirements and mobile technology.

13. Efficiency saves time. Time is well spent getting ready for the office and showings.

14. Empathy for other people. Listen and put yourself in the other person's place.

15. Ethics. The "Golden Rule" is never out of fashion. Be fair to all.

16. Evaluate the competition, and learn from it. What is your competition doing? Learn from their successes, and avoid their failures.

17. Positive goals should be in writing, reviewed and revised. Keep focused.

18. Initiative. Good salespeople are self-starters. They know that wasted time is wasted opportunity.

© 2015 ETC., Inc.

VI. Enter the Broker

While the majority of this text addresses your responsibilities as a salesperson, it eventually transitions into mainly broker's responsibilities. It's only natural, as a successful agent, that you'll eventually aspire to become a broker.

The broker, like the salesperson, acts as an intermediary—a catalyst—in bringing together buyers and sellers. You'll help others in the acquisition, listing, selling, leasing, exchanging, financing, and managing of real property. Some brokers just manage their office and supervise their salespeople, while others also get out there and sell. Some brokers don't want the responsibility of running their own offices, so they work for other brokers.

A. AGENCY REPRESENTATION

The listing agreement establishes a *FIDUCIARY RELATIONSHIP, meaning brokers owe a duty of the highest care and confidentiality to their principals (clients), whose interest they promote even at the cost of some greater benefit to themselves.* Prior to entering into any real estate contracts, there must be full disclosure regarding agency relationships.

1. Disclosure Regarding Agency Relationships

The client that the broker is representing (buyer, seller, or both) must be disclosed to all parties, in writing, prior to entering into a transaction. (See Chapter 3, Disclosure Regarding Real Estate Agency Relationships form, Figure 3-2).

When a broker represents more than one party in the same transaction, it is known as DUAL AGENCY. This must also be approved and disclosed in writing prior to entering into the transaction. All your clients have the expectation of complete confidentiality.

It is unethical for a salesperson (as a broker's representative) to state to the buyer that the "price is soft." Your obligation is to obtain the best possible price and terms for your client.

When two agents from the same office are representing both the buyer and the seller in one transaction, it is also considered a dual agency. This must be approved and disclosed in writing prior to entering into a contract, although each agent may not know the other agent's client.

B. DIRECTING AND SUPERVISING (Requirements of a Broker)

Included in this concept are the supervision and the administration of personnel and the guidance the broker offers the staff in achieving planned objectives.

The *OFFICE POLICY MANUAL, found in many brokerage offices to handle recurring situations, is designed to clarify rules and policies for the staff in their relationships inside and outside the office sphere.* In order for the office to run as a well disciplined team, everyone should adhere to a strict policy regarding the handling of files and clients.

As a broker/manager, you must provide leadership to your salespeople, who should not be expected to learn the principles of salesmanship and supervision without direction. You should encourage questions and be readily available to your staff.

A detailed office **TRANSACTION FILE**, *which includes all property contracts, documents, and disclosures signed or initialed by the principals*, must be approved in writing by you, the broker, or your office manager. In an effort to coordinate these activities, you should use a checklist dated and initialed by you or your office manager, and the real estate agent. To save paper, a **GREEN OFFICE** (*concerned with their immediate and residual impact on the environment*) will digitally scan items in the transaction file. See Chapter 14 for more details concerning transaction files.

Scanned files, which may include digital signatures, must be kept for at least three years.

C. COOPERATING BROKERS

A cooperating broker is a broker who participates in facilitating a real estate transaction with the broker who listed the property.

As often as not, properties are sold by a broker who is not the listing agent. **Compensation to the selling office must be determined at the time the listing is taken and posted on the Multiple Listing form available to all MLS subscribers.** It is unethical to write an offer and renegotiate the commission paid to the selling office. Some brokers are good listing agents, while others excel strictly as selling agents. Both activities require creativity and salesmanship. While obtaining listings renews the office's inventory, it is also important to move them. See **Figure 1-6** for an example of a sample MLS listing. (See MLS information in Chapter 4.)

Obviously, a great deal of cooperation is needed for brokers to function smoothly in the marketing process. *To show property listed by another broker, permission should first be obtained through the seller, if possible, by making a SHOWING APPOINTMENT*. Should there be a cancellation, it goes without saying that the seller would be contacted.

Always ask (or require) agents to leave a business card in an agreed upon location when showing a property. Collect these cards regularly, get feedback from the showing agents, and share this information with the seller. You can also check your lockboxes for this information.

You can check on your lockbox activity online through your computer, smartphone, or tablet to see who has entered the property and in what order. If something is amiss, you know who was the last to enter the home. You should also always close the door after you enter so another broker doesn't just walk in after you without using his or her code and leaving evidence of his or her presence.

D. COMMISSIONS

Most brokers are paid a commission based on a percentage of the sales price they obtain on their transactions. In commercial and industrial transactions, the rate of

Figure 1-6
MLS Listing

ARLETTE A. LYONS, CRS, GRI		Office: 626-331-0141
		Cell: 626-825-0023
Broker-Owner - LYONS & ASSOC., INC. REALTOR		Fax: 626-331-9772
Real Estate Excellence		AALYONS@AOL.COM
		DRE License: 00414792

1147 W Rowland AV, West Covina 91790

						My Ratings:		**My Notes:**
Status:	**Closed Sale**	ML#:	**CV14043049**			Sold Price:		$453,000
List Contract:	03/03/2014	PType:	**Single Family Residence/D**			Orig. Price:		$445,000

1 / 30

Bed:	**4**	APN:	8440026019	YrBuilt:	**1954/ASR**	Area:	669
Bath(F,T,H,Q):	**2,0,0,0**	Zone:		Style:		MB:	
Sqft (Src):	**1,438 (Assessor's Data)**	Ac/LotSqft (Src):	**0.326/14,180 (A)**	Cmplx:		DOM:	10
$/Sqft:	**$315.02**	Lot Dim:		#Units:	**1**	CDOM:	10
Stories:	**One Level**	Land:	**Fee**	HOA:		View:	No
Entry Location	**Ground Level**	Horse:		55+:	**No**	Pool:	Yes
SchDist:		Patio:	**Yes**	Highsch:		FP:	Yes
Elem:		Midsch:					
Sale Type:				Standard			

Directions: North side of Street
LP Includs:
Description: Original owners have lovingly maintained this charmer! This property has a double sized lot with loads of mature fruit trees: apricot, a variety of oranges, persimmon, avocado, pecan, grapefruit. 2 ponds, a huge pool with diving board & cover, the lot just goes on & on, it even has a bomb shelter! Double detached garage with auto door opener, extra long concrete driveway with a security gate and covered parking area. All the bedrooms are spacious and feature cozy built-in cabinetry. Living room with brick frplc, formal dining room & kitchen with breakfast nook all overlook the lush rear yard & massive patio with skylights to bring in even more natural light. Inside laundry room, this home offers ample storage and has block wall fencing all around! It is a true delight!

Features

Fireplace:	**Living Room**	Construction Materials:	
Cooling:	**Central**	Lot Features:	**Back Yard, Front Yard, Landscaped, Lot 10000-19999 Sqft, Lot Shape-Rectangular, Lot-Level/Flat, Sprinkler System, Sprinklers In Front, Sprinklers In Rear**
Heating:	**Central Furnace**		
Laundry:	**Area**		
Interior Features:	**Ceramic Counters**	Community Features:	**Curbs, Gutters, Sidewalks**
Rooms:	**All Bedrooms Down, Entry, Formal Entry, Living Room, Utility**	Style:	
	Dining Room, In Kitchen	Door Features:	**French Doors**
Floor:		Roof:	**Composition**
Accessibility Features:		Exterior Features:	**Koi Pond**
Appliances:	**Dishwasher, Garbage Disposal, Gas Range**	Foundation:	**Raised**
Utilities:		Structural Condition:	
Pool:	**Private, In Ground**	Other Structures:	
Spa:		Window Features:	
Patio:	**Deck, Covered, Concrete**	Security Features:	
Common Walls:	**No Common Walls**	Sewer:	**Sewer Connected**
Direction Faces:	**South**	Water Source:	**District/Public**
View:	**None**	Disclosures:	
		Parking:	
		HOA:	

Sold Price:	$453,000	CurLstPrc:	$453,000	Purchase Contract:	03/12/2014
Sold:	04-15-14	OrgLstPrc:	$445,000		

Customer Full - Residential

ML#: CV14043049

© 2014 CRMLS. Information is believed to be accurate, but shall not be relied upon without verification. Accuracy of square footage, lot size and other information is not guaranteed.

© 2013 CRMLS. Information is believed to be accurate, but shall not be relied upon without verification. Accuracy of square footage, lot size and other information is not guaranteed.

MLS listings are online... Use your smartphone and other mobile devices to show your clients MLS listings.

commission is sometimes based on a **graduated scale**. For example, in the sale of a shopping center, you may be paid five percent on the first $500,000, three percent on the next $300,000, two percent on the next $200,000 and one percent on any amount over $1,000,000.

No matter what plan is being used, all commissions are negotiable between the seller and the listing broker, and determined when the listing agreement is signed, not when an offer is presented.

In some instances, brokers are able to command a fee for their services, similar to the lawyer who establishes the amount of the fee on the basis of the time involved, complexity of the case, economy, and other factors. This fee is usually paid by the person or firm that contracts for your broker's services, be it for the acquisition, disposition, exchange, or lease of property. It is important to stress that all commissions are negotiable between the parties and are regionally influenced.

VII. The Brokerage Firm

As a broker, you'll be heavily involved with the managerial functions of planning, organizing, directing, and controlling all aspects of your brokerage. These functions require a lot of time and energy. Because of these demanding and time-consuming tasks, not all brokers decide to open their own brokerages; some work for other brokers and have more time to devote elsewhere. Nevertheless, as a salesperson, if you want to open your own office, you'll first have to become a broker.

A. GETTING STARTED IN BUSINESS

As a licensed salesperson with aspirations to become a broker and open your own office, you will need to follow a course patterned along the following steps:

1. **Obtain the required real estate broker's license** (see Chapter 15 for licensing information).

2. **Create a domain name.** It should uniquely identify the name of your website. For example, walthuber.realtor.

3. **Secure the necessary capital.** You should have sufficient capital to pay for the initial setup as well as all operative charges and expenses for the first year. In addition, you should have enough money to support your family for a period that will likely not show much profit. Many of the initial charges are non-recurring.

4. **Decide on a location to lease.** The selected office site must be zoned for commercial use, allowing for future expansion. It also should be readily accessible and close to a well-known and widely recognizable point of reference, such as a major shopping center.

5. **Choose a building.** The building must be suitable for present needs and, like the site itself, one that will provide for expansion and convenience of office

CHAPTER 1

layout. For a general brokerage, it's wise to have broad exposure to traffic. Select a building close to the street with large windows for displays. The building should also provide for a reception area and a private "closing" room, which may double as a conference room.

6. **Obtain a business license.** Most cities require that anyone conducting a business obtain a permit from the city or county. If the person's real name or corporate name is not used, a *DOING BUSINESS AS (DBA)* is filed with the clerk of the county where the principal place of business is located. It is also necessary to give notice of the intended DBA by publishing the information in a newspaper of general circulation, in the judicial district in which the business is headquartered, for three weeks (21 days).

7. **Have a telephone and Internet system installed.** A large deposit may be required in order to obtain the initial installation of a business phone, unless you have had previous dealings with the telephone company or can otherwise satisfy them that the business is a good credit risk. High-speed wireless connections are a necessity!

8. **Open a trust account and a regular business checking account.** Trust accounts are not required if you do not accept client funds, but most brokers find them to be an appropriate depository for their clients' funds. (**The maximum amount of personal funds a broker may keep in a trust fund account is $200.**)

9. **Order supplies.** This includes forms, business cards, and other items that are needed in the orderly conduct of the business.

10. **Arrange for newspaper and other credit.** Like the telephone, this item is high on the list of expenditures. Advertising is an absolute must for survival.

11. **Obtain office equipment.** This includes such items as computers, printers, fax machine, copier, typewriters, shredders, and file cabinets. Sometimes these can be leased if you need to conserve capital.

12. **Order signs.** These would be needed for the office building as well as for your listings. Hire a company to install these. Quite often the agents purchase their own "Open House" signs and their own lockboxes.

13. **Hire a receptionist/secretary.** This may, of necessity, be on a part-time basis.

14. **Create a policy manual.**

15. **Create a training program for new licensees.**

16. **Contract for other services.** Custodial or janitorial services need to be obtained.

17. **Establish connections with ancillary companies.** Such companies provide the essential supporting services. Among those you should call on are the local escrow, loan, title insurance, physical inspection, and termite companies.

18. **Join local, state, and national associations of REALTORS®.** By joining you will be allowed the use of the copyrighted designation REALTOR® and enjoy the use of other services provided by virtually every local board. (This is not mandatory.)

The California Association of REALTORS® (CAR) provides the majority of forms used in real estate transactions (zipForms® are free to CAR members).

19. **Announce the firm's establishment.** Send out letters and emails to all those located in the area in which your brokerage is to operate. Advertise your opening everywhere.

20. **Create a website.** Once you've purchased a domain name, you should hire a service to professionally design your website. The better your website looks, the better you look.

Your website is an essential business tool. Not only should it be professionally designed, but maintained on a regular basis. Properties off the market still listed can indicate to a potential client that your brokerage is not reliable.

B. KEEPING UP WITH THE COMPETITION

The office doesn't just start and stop with the walls of your firm's brokerage. Your transaction information should be available anytime and anywhere. Now that's possible thanks to applications available from CAR.

The ***ZIPFORM® MOBILE WEB EDITION*** *lets you connect to your zipForm® online account, allowing you to manage your online transactions "on the go."*

You can use your iPad®, iPhone®, Android®, and other devices to:

1. create a new transaction;

2. list the forms within a transaction;

3. add forms from licensed libraries;

4. list and modify transactions by date and name;

5. fill in all fields with the "edit" feature (and automatically use that information for all transaction file records;

6. generate forms in PDF format; and

7. email forms in PDF format with comments.

C. FORMS OF REAL ESTATE BROKERAGE OWNERSHIP

As a new broker, you must decide what kind of organizational structure is best for your business. This varies with different circumstances and taxes. As conditions change, an entrepreneur will adapt accordingly by changing from one form of ownership to another.

1. Sole Proprietorship

A ***SOLE PROPRIETORSHIP*** *is characterized by an office run by one owner solely responsible for all decisions.* The owner/manager type of organization may operate alone, but typically employs one or more salespeople. This type of real

estate ownership once comprised the bulk of brokerage firms in California, but large corporations are quietly gaining on them. **One disadvantage is the unlimited liability of a sole proprietorship.** Others are the continuous personal supervision and attention required to assure success. The benefits of a sole proprietorship include:

a. **All profits and expenses accrue to the owner.** (Some restrictions may apply due to insufficient capital and a limited ability to raise large sums of capital.)

b. **Ease and low cost of organization with strict control on its operation.** (There are salespeople, however, who prefer to work for larger organizations and the recognition they enjoy.)

c. **Secrecy and flexibility can be maintained.** The methods of doing business can be altered quickly to meet changes in competition, economic condition, income taxes, and so on. The sole proprietorship can readily change to partnership or corporation if desired.

d. **Dissolution.** The business may be dissolved/discontinued with relative ease.

If you use your own name, no DBA is needed. A" Doing Business As (DBA)," *like "CaliRealty.net," requires about $200 for a county record filing of the* *new name (plus the cost of purchasing the website name) so you can create* *a new bank account.*

2. Partnership

Under the Revised Uniform Partnership Act adopted by California, a *PARTNERSHIP is an association of two or more persons as co-owners of a business for profit.* Real estate partnerships are relatively few in number. One partner must be a licensed broker. Like a sole proprietorship, **a major disadvantage of this type of ownership is the unlimited liability of all partners**. Benefits include:

a. **Partners are taxed as individuals**, not as a partnership. There is no requirement for approval by the state.

b. **Relative freedom from government regulations.** (It is the least permanent form of business ownership, however, usually due to lack of resources to buy out deceased or withdrawing partner's interest.)

c. **Additional partners can be invited to join**, creating a new written partnership should the firm want to expand. (Of course, this divided authority can cause managerial difficulties, making decisions more difficult to reach or resolve.)

d. **Retention of valuable salespeople** through new partnership offerings can make a productive salesperson, who has obtained a broker's license, an owner.

e. **Checks and balances system.** Each partner is liable for the others' actions, therefore developing a sense of responsibility in the success of the firm.

f. **Greater stability** is possible than with a sole proprietorship, because the partnership is usually larger, but there must be cooperation on all business activities.

3. Corporation

A *CORPORATION is a legal "artificial being" that conducts business under its California Secretary of State chartered name.* The number of real estate companies that are incorporated is growing. Most of these were motivated to incorporate for any of three reasons: possible income tax benefits, limited liability, and growth into a large-scale operation better suited to the corporate form. *Ownership in a corporation is evidenced by owning shares of STOCK.* Advantages and disadvantages include:

a. **Liability of the owners** is limited only to the amount of their investment, but cost of California incorporation is relatively high ($1000+), including incorporation and charter fees, records books, attorney fees, minimum $800 state income tax, etc.

b. **Transfer of ownership** is easily facilitated by simple endorsement of the stock certificate. Some **disadvantages** are due to governmental requirements, like double taxation (corporate filing and tax on dividends to owners of stock), and decision making made by the board of directors.

c. **Permanency.** Death, disability, or retirement of one of the owners does not lead to dissolution of the corporate entity. The listings remain active until another corporate broker can be found. A corporation is said to have a perpetual existence.

d. **Income tax benefits.** Tax legislation permits brokers to combine into a corporation, but be taxed as a partnership, called a *SUBCHAPTER S CORPORATION, which, in general, does not pay any federal income taxes. Instead, the corporation's income or losses are divided among and passed through to its shareholders. The shareholders must then report the income or loss on their own individual income tax returns.* (The disadvantage of the standard corporation is that income taxes are paid first by the corporation and by the stockholders individually on the paid dividends, usually at a lower rate—double taxation.)

VIII. Record Keeping

A. TRUST FUND RECORDS

All brokerages, regardless of size, are required to keep detailed accounting system records of client funds and other forms.

Brokers are not required to have a trust fund account, but most do, especially if they are involved in property management. A columnar record of all trust funds received and paid out is required. Trust funds must be placed in, or with one of the following, within **three business days** of being received:

1. A neutral escrow depository, also known as the escrow company.
2. A trust fund account.
3. Given to the principal.

It is important that client funds be separate from brokers' business and personal accounts. We recommend different banks be used for the "trust fund accounts" (other people's money).

COMMINGLING *is the illegal mixing of the client's and broker's funds.* **CONVERSION** *is the illegal practice of misappropriation and using the client's money.*

In order not to be accused of commingling, brokers cannot put their personal funds in the trust account, with the exception of $200 to cover bank services.

The law (**Section 10148, Business and Professions Code**) states that a real estate broker must retain for **three years** copies of all **listings, purchase contracts, cancelled checks, trust records**, and any other documents executed in connection with any transaction for which a real estate broker license is required. Records for transactions involving loans under the real property loan law or security dealer transactions must be retained for **four years**. Upon notice, all records must be made available for inspection by auditors or other designated representatives of the Real Estate Commissioner (CalBRE).

CalBRE rules now allow buyers to deposit earnest money directly into escrow themselves (within three days).

B. SALES RECORDS (Keep for Three Years; Four Years if Doing Property Management)

Keep your filing system uncomplicated; everyone in the office should know how to file properly and to which account.

One way to keep a filing system simple is to file the transactions chronologically (according to date), from opening of escrow, with a cross reference to the sellers and buyers. All contracts, even cancelled escrows and rejected offers, are kept in the transaction file along with all the executed disclosures. Agents are encouraged to keep a paper trail of all communications, faxes, emails, text messages, and telephone conversations during the escrow period. They are also encouraged to streamline their operation by discarding all duplications. The transaction files (or digital scans) are kept for a minimum of three years in the office file cabinets (**we recommend at least four years**). For more detailed filing information, see Chapter 14 (Real Estate Assistants).

All files must remain secure in the broker's office or on the office computer.

1. Listings

A "Listing" is an employment contract hiring an agent to facilitate the sale of a property.

Most multiple listing services are now computerized, and the office listing inventory is readily accessible to the broker and the salesperson. You can see at a glance all the active listings, the listings in escrow, and the closed sales.

Keep computer files the same way you would paper—simple and easy to access. Always back up computer files, promptly saving them to a flash drive, external backup drive, or on the cloud. Back up files should be kept at a seperate location.

2. Purchase Contracts and Commissions

The sales contracts, as well as all rejected offers and cancelled escrows, must also be retained in the office for a minimum of three years. Commissions are generally paid through the escrow company usually from the sellers' proceeds to the broker, who, in turn, issues a check to the salesperson in a timely fashion. At this time, there are deductions for miscellaneous agreed-upon shared expenses. After having checked and initialed all contracts and disclosures necessary to close the transaction, the broker pays the salesperson his or her commission, and the records are filed. There is no withholding for tax purposes by the broker because the salespeople are independent contractors.

All closed and pending sales must be reported to the local Association of REALTORS® MLS, within a very short period, usually two days. If this rule is not adhered to, the agent and the broker may be heavily fined, unless the client does not authorize such reporting. Keep information fresh and up-to-date, not stale and outdated.

IX. CHAPTER SUMMARY

Always put your realistic career goals in writing. Review and revise them at least once a year.

The support of family members and a monetary reserve (at least **six months' savings**) at the onset of any career are of utmost importance.

As a new licensee, you may be inundated by solicitations from various offices wanting to interview and possibly hire you. Selecting the office with the right **working environment** is one of the most important decisions you will make at this time. You should interview with at least three brokers.

You can locate potential sponsoring brokers by observing real estate signs and newspaper advertising, as well as checking local Associations of REALTORS® and the Internet.

You should also know what the **start-up costs** are, who pays for expenses, and what training and support you can expect to receive. There are also various possible **commission agreements** of which you should be aware.

You'll want to examine the size of the company for which you want to work. Size invariably determines the types of technical and managerial problems which confront a firm, as well as training and opportunities provided to new employees.

Salespeople working under a broker are considered **employees** for the purposes of administration by the California Bureau of Real Estate (CalBRE), even if the real estate office treats you as an **independent contractor** for other purposes (such as withholding).

After choosing your office, immediately contact friends, relatives, past and present co-workers, trades, and service people, who make up your **sphere of influence**. Become knowledgeable in condo sales, new sales, probates, foreclosures, and property management. Find your niche and work it. The more you know, the more confident you'll become, and it will show!

The listing agreement creates a **fiduciary relationship**, meaning listing brokers owe a duty of the highest care and confidentiality to the sellers. A broker may represent a seller, a buyer, or both, but that relationship must be disclosed to, and approved by, all parties, in writing, **prior** to entering into a transaction.

A **policy manual** is designed to establish rules and policies for a brokerage's staff governing their relationships inside and outside the office (see **Chapter 15**). A broker/manager must supervise his or her salespeople, who should not merely be hired and expected to learn principles of salesmanship without direction.

More often as not, properties are sold by a broker who is not the listing broker (**cooperative sales**). Always be sure to leave a business card or ask other brokers when showing a property.

All **commissions are negotiable** at the time the listing is taken.

As a salesperson, if you want to open your own office, you'll first have to become a broker. There are a number of steps involved in opening an office, including securing the necessary capital and deciding on a location. You will also have to decide what form of business ownership is best suited for you, whether it is a **sole proprietorship**, a **partnership**, or a **corporation**. **Subchapter "S" corporations** do not pay any federal income taxes. Instead, the corporation's income or losses are divided among and passed through to its shareholders. The shareholders must then report the income or loss on their own individual income tax returns.

All offices, regardless of size, are required to keep detailed records of clients' funds and other forms of deposit in a trust account. **Client funds** (other people's money) must be kept separate from the broker's business and personal accounts.

A **trust fund account** is limited to $200 of a broker's money. All clients' funds must be deposited within **three business days** of receipt or acceptance of offer if the agent has written authorization to hold the deposit uncashed. All brokers must keep detailed records of their clients' funds (other people's money).

Sales records must be kept for a minimum of **three years and four years if doing property management**.

X. MATCHING VOCABULARY Fill in the blanks with the correct letter

A. Android®
B. Apple, Inc.
C. CalBRE
D. Cold calls
E. Commingling
F. Commission split
G. Conversion
H. Corporation
I. DBA
J. Domain name
K. Dual agency

L. Employee
M. Errors and Omission Insurance
N. Expired listings
O. Fiduciary relationship
P. Geographical farm
Q. Green Office
R. Independent contractor
S. Office policy manual
T. 100% commission

U. Partnership
V. Reverse directory
W. Sales kit
X. Sole proprietorship
Y. Sphere of influence
Z. Straight commission
AA. Stock
BB. Training
CC. Transaction file
DD. Warm calls
EE. zipForms®

1. _____ A list of prospects that an agent regularly contacts in the hope they will become clients.

2. _____ Most brokers carry this professional liability insurance to protect themselves and their agents against catastrophic lawsuits.

3. _____ The broker usually does not charge a desk fee, but pays the agent based on a set percentage of the selling price at the close of escrow.

4. _____ Hands on experience and mentoring meant to improve your performance or help you attain a required level of skill.

5. _____ This person works under the direct control and supervision of the employer.

6. _____ This person sells results rather than time, and his or her physical conduct is not subject to the control of another.

7. _____ A group of households within a geographical area with whom the agent stays in touch on a regular basis.

8. _____ Calling prospective clients who are not known to the salesperson.

9. _____ A website or publication, similar to a phone book, where numbers are listed by address rather than name.

10. _____ An inventory of items, or aids, that you may need in your daily real estate-related activities.

11. _____ Brokers owe a duty of the highest care and confidentiality to their principals (clients), whose interest they promote even at the cost of some greater benefit to themselves.

12. _____ Listings that did not sell within the contract period.

13. _____ Calls made to people you already know and which are usually more productive.

14. _____ When a broker represents more than one party (i.e, both buyer and seller).

15. _____ Includes all property contracts, documents, and disclosures signed or initialed by the principals (broker must keep for at least three years).

16. _____ An office run by one owner solely responsible for all decisions.

17. _____ A form of ownership considered a legal "artificial being" conducting business under its California chartered name.

18. _____ An association of two or more persons as co-owners of a business for profit.

19. _____ The illegal mixing of the client's and broker's funds.

20. _____ The illegal practice of misappropriation and using the client's money.

21. _____ Owners of a corporation each own shares of this as evidence of ownership.

22. _____ This guide is found in many brokerage offices to help handle recurring situations and is designed to give rules and policies for the staff in their relationships inside and outside the office sphere.

23. _____ The goal here is to create a healthy work environment, conserve energy, and reduce pollution.

24. _____ What percentage that goes to the salesperson and what percentage goes to the broker.

25. _____ Catalog of contract forms widely used in California and available for free to CAR members.

26. _____ Doing Busines As. Ficticious business name.

27. _____ The unique name that identifies a website.

28. _____ A commission system where the broker pays all of the commission to the salesperson but charges the salesperson a desk fee of $750 to $1,000 per month.

29. _____ Maker of such products as the iPhone®, iPad®, and iPod®.

30. _____ Operating system other than Apple®.

31. _____ The California Bureau of Real Estate, which governs all real estate licensing and enforces the California Real Estate Commissioner's Regulations.

See Page 609 for Answers

XI. CHAPTER QUIZ

1. How many brokers may a salesperson work for at one time?
   a. Three
   b. Two
   c. One
   d. Unlimited

2. Which of the following is a way to find a sponsoring broker?
   a. Observe real estate signs.
   b. Check online sites and newspaper advertising in the areas you plan to service.
   c. Call the local Association of REALTORS®.
   d. All of the above.

3. What is the best example of a "sphere of influence"?
   a. Central location of a telecommunication company
   b. People living outside an agent's city
   c. Friends, family, neighbors, and business associates you know and contact regulary
   d. Both b and c

4. A salesperson who is actively engaged in professional real estate activities:
   a. must have his or her own office.
   b. must be employed by a licensed real estate broker.
   c. must pay compensation directly to cooperating agents.
   d. none of the above.

5. A broker is required to have:

  a. a trust account.

  b. an accounting system (disbursement ledger).

  c. an escrow company.

  d. $300 of the broker's personal funds in the trust account.

6. The listing agreement can best be described as a(n):

  a. dual agency.

  b. deposit receipt.

  c. employment contract.

  d. offer to buy.

7. What is Broker's Error and Omission insurance?

  a. Insurance to protect the borrower against foreclosure

  b. Insurance to protect the seller against buyers' claims

  c. Insurance to protect the agent and broker against buyers' and sellers' claims

  d. Buyers' protection against earthquake damages

8. In order to open his or her own office, a real estate agent must:

  a. obtain a broker's license.

  b. secure the necessary capital.

  c. decide on a location.

  d. all of the above.

9. What are cold calls?

  a. Contacting clients late at night.

  b. Contacting people the agent does not know.

  c. Contacting people with whom the agent has done business.

  d. Returning calls for another agent.

10. All deposits from clients must be placed in a broker's trust fund account, given to the principal, or placed in a neutral escrow depository:

  a. within one week.

  b. within 10 days.

  c. minus a small fee.

  d. within three business days from acceptance of offer.

ANSWERS: 1. c; 2. d; 3. c; 4. b; 5. b; 6. c; 7. c; 8. d; 9. b; 10. d

KEVIN & KAZ
Spouses Selling Houses
RE/MAX Execs BROKER ASSOCIATES
310-410-9777
Helping People Move Ahead

CHAPTER 2

Prospecting: How to Market, Advertise, and Promote

I. Prospecting

Communication is the name of the game! Advertising and promotion keeps your name in the public eye, but buyers and sellers want agents who communicate with them quickly via smartphones, email, and text messaging!

A. FINDING SELLERS AND GETTING LISTINGS (Looking for an Agent)

Obtaining new listings (the contractual right to help sell another's property) are the lifeblood of all real estate offices. Listing properties for sale keeps you in business.

1. The Internet

a. Your Company and Personal Website

Your company and personal website are indispensable tools for finding sellers who want to sign a listing agreement (contract) for you to help them sell their property. Your websites should contain as much useful information as possible; including:

1. properties you currently have for sale,
2. properties that have just sold,
3. the prices of both for sale and just sold homes, as well as
4. your biographical information,
5. an attractive photo of yourself and possibly your brokerage offices, and
6. a way for your website visitors to sign up to be on your mailing list. **Don't forget to prominently display your email, phone number and text number so callers have as many options as possible to contact you.**

CHAPTER OUTLINE

Just remember to return a communication by text, email or phone call just as soon as humanly possible after they contact you. Put your smartphone on vibrate so as not to disturb your current meeting, but at the earliest convenience you might excuse yourself for a moment to use the restroom and send an immediate text or quick email telling your caller you are in the middle of a meeting but will call them back ASAP. If you say it's going to be an hour then make it an hour! Don't leave a client hanging on and waiting for your call if you are going to take longer than anticipated!

Most buyers and sellers start their search online.

b. Search Engines

Search Engines like Google are the first place sellers go to find a respectable real estate professional. Make sure your name or brokerage is high on the list when users "Google" certain words like real estate sales, especially in your area or zip code.

c. Email

Email is a fast and efficient way to communicate with clients. If you have a client interested in a neighborhood or particular home, emailing the homeowner who is expressing that interest is a quick method to contact them. There are several ways of getting clients emails which will be discussed soon.

d. Texting

Texting is generally more useful for notifying buyers when a property comes up for sale, however, when looking for sellers, you may consider texting them with a link to a comparative market analysis (CMA) that you've created for them or to notify them of a change in the market in their neighborhood. Be careful your texting list has given you permission to contact them this way as many phone plans charge for text messages and you don't want to annoy potential new clients or charge them for what you find interesting.

e. Referrals

Referrals from past clients and your entire sphere of influence that you contact monthly are rich sources of new clients. Be sure to get their email and text information so you can continue to contact them in the future (with their permission).

1. Online Referral Websites (Like Yelp!)

Yelp! is not just for restaurant reviews anymore. If sellers type in a search for a real estate agent in a particular area, the Yelp! website will pop up and they can read basic contact information for you and your brokerage; but more importantly, they can read real recommendations or poor reviews written by past clients. Your professionalism and personality are being graded by often anonymous Yelp! users, so they can be brutal if they are displeased—just one more reason to keep your clients happy!

f. Social Networking Sites

Social Networking Sites like Facebook are becoming the place to go for sellers to find real prospects that appear between friend posts. Information is gleaned from many sources to pinpoint the appropriate audience to receive ads. You may place your company's ads so they only go out to Facebook users in a general area. You can also create a list just like your personal "friends" list, but "business contacts" that you wish to send messages to or post recent sales or other information that will encourage a potential seller to contact you.

LinkedIn is a professional/social networking site that can be a good source of geographical farming. Put the word out you are looking for fellow members who are contemplating selling their home or business and ask them to pass it on to their other LinkedIn members.

g. Real Estate Search Engines

1. Realtor.com

Realtor.com is associated with the National Association of REALTORS® (NAR), an organization that is trusted by many for a variety of reasons, including the fact that NAR members adhere to a strict Code of Ethics. They have a reputation for being more accurate than other sites and have binding contract agreements. Realtor.com, which is owned by the National Association of Realtors®, also offers a list of REALTORS® by area city, state, or zipcode, making it easy for a potential seller to find the right agent or broker!

Remember that not all real estate agents are REALTORS®. REALTORS® are members of the National Association of REALTORS®. People new to the business often use "REALTOR®" and real estate agent interchangeably, but they are not one and the same. The authors of this book are proud members of NAR!

2. Zillow.com and Trulia.com

Zillow is another very popular real estate website. Sellers will visit this site that uses automated valuation systems to determine the "potential" price of a home. They often use the figures generated by Zillow to help determine a selling price for their own home—although those figures are created by computer averages and do not necessarily reflect comparable market analysis (CMA) numbers.

As a professional it's up to you to help your clients achieve a realistic expectation for the price of their home, as Zillow does not take into consideration the remodeled interior of a home, say, new granite counter tops, or outside improvements such as a new cobblestone driveway or large old trees. It's up to you to incorporate these amenities into the pricing of a seller's home. Zillow also offers "Agent Reviews" that potential sellers may peruse while looking for a selling as well as buying agent!

Trulia.com, owned by Zillow, is an online residential real estate site for homebuyers, sellers, renters, and real estate professionals.

Sellers spend an average of one year contemplating the sale of their home— your name should be the first one they think of when they finally decide to sell. Constantly promoting your "brand" will result in a healthy crop for your geographical farm!

2. Direct Mail (Traditional and New School)

Direct mail is a tried and true method of marketing to your "geographical farm" and your "sphere of influence." It's easier and less expensive than ever with online printers like Vistaprint. Take advantage of the U.S. Postal Service as well as your computer to send direct mail!

a. Postcards

Postcards are very useful way of getting your name out to the public. Without an envelope to open, the recipients can't help but read the contents when they take it out of their mailbox. You can list homes for sale or just sold, you can ask for potential sellers to contact you, you can post a picture of yourself, and/or a list of comparable properties in the neighborhood.

If you're comfortable using a smartphone app like Instagram or Snapseed, you can take a picture of a home and attach them through Postagram app, allowing you to send personalized postcards with a picture of their own home to potential clients. You can also send virtual postcards through email!

Both postcards and flyers can be left on doorsteps or hung on doorknobs (doorhanger), saving the cost of postage.

As an alternative to postcard advertising, a three-fold mail-out, hand addressed and stamped (not metered) has a greater chance of being opened than something that looks like junk mail!

b. Comparative Market Analysis (CMA)

COMPARATIVE MARKET ANALYSIS (CMA) is data that gives the sellers a price range for the home by comparing the details of similar homes (comps) in a particular area that have recently sold. Let potential clients know what the prices are for homes in their neighborhood. How you get the CMAs to new clients, however, is the problem. Direct mail ads, postcards, and emails (once you get their contact information) are all methods of getting those "comps" into sellers' hands.

Even if a recipient is not yet ready to sell, your name may be the first to come to mind if he or she receives regular comp information from you and your brokerage.

3. Expired Listings

Your local MLS has expired Listings that let you know that someone was trying to sell his or her home, but was unsuccessful. All the contact information is available to MLS members, and it's up to you to convince the seller to try again, and why you are capable of selling the home.

Never badmouth another agent! Ultimately, it's bad for business and gives YOU the unsavory reputation. Also, referrals from other areas may be a source of listings for you, but not by a broker or agent about whom you have spoken badly.

4. For Sale By Owners (FSBOs)

Simply hand delivering a Transfer Disclosure Statement (TDS) could illustrate to the seller the complexity of selling a home they may not be aware of, and potentially gain you a new client.

a. Craigslist

Craigslist is an excellent resource for finding FSBOs. After trying to sell their own property, owners may be delighted to hand over the responsibilities and work to a professional such as yourself. You can sell them on your expertise needed to fill out the numerous forms (and disclosures required) and the dangers of not filling them out properly, as well as take the burden of showing their property and prequalifying clients.

b. Bulletin Boards

Bulletin Boards often post homes for sale by their owners.

Don't forget the good old-fashioned telephone call! Most of the FSBOs you will contact will be by phone. Make sure to ask for other contact information once you do reach them by phone, however, and ask permission to keep in touch with them in the future- and then do it! Once you contact them, remind them that you can also help them find a new home after you sell theirs!

c. Yard Signs

Posted signs on yards, in windows or tacked up around the neighborhood are often used by FSBOs. This is great for you as an agent as they have provided you their contact information without being asked. Call them and offer them a Comparative Market Analysis (CMA) or a Transfer Disclosure Statement (TDS) as a gesture of goodwill and a hint at what they may not know about as nonprofessionals.

d. Newspaper Classified Ads

FSBOs frequently place their property for sale in the classified section of the newspaper. When you contact them ask for email and text information so you can let them know immediately if you have an interested client. Add them to your geographical farm!

5. Professional Business Contacts (Sphere of Influence)

a. Title Company

Title Company employees you may be acquainted with can tell you when a home drops out of escrow or when a home goes into foreclosure. They can also let you know how to contact out of state or absentee owners who can be a gold mine for new listing sources. They can also provide mailing lists for any area or neighborhood you would like to "farm."

CHAPTER 2

Foreclosures are a touchy subject, but you may very well be doing a seller a favor by offering to represent them! They have little to lose, and you may help save their credit rating.

b. Probate Attorneys

Probate attorneys deal with heirs to property (who often live out of state). When it comes to selling property, you want to be the first agent they turn to! Probate Attorneys can keep you abreast of litigation whereby a property may be coming up for sale and the need for a listing agent.

c. Divorce Attorneys

Divorce Attorneys, without breaking confidentiality agreements, may be doing their clients a service by referring them to you if a divorcing couple will need to sell their mutual home—which can also mean the possibility of needing to buy one or more new residences! The fact you don't actually know the clients may be to your advantage as both parties will see you as unbiased.

The biggest complaint by sellers and buyers is a lack of communication! Don't fall into that trap. Maintain as frequent contact as your client allows—by phone calls, emails or texts, depending on their preference. Texting is becoming the most requested form of communication between client and agent because it is so quick and they can reveal the details later.

B. OPEN HOUSES (Finds Both Buyers and Sellers)

An **OPEN HOUSE** *is a planned period of time during which a property for sale is held open for public viewing* (see **Figure 2-1**).

An open house is an excellent prospecting tool for finding both buyers and sellers. Signing them in on arrival is recommended

Using "Open House Apps" rather than just a sign-in sheet "captures" your open house viewers' information for further contact. Not only do you get their contact information, often you can find out what specifics they're looking for in a property and provide them the personal service of limiting their efforts to those homes in which they will be interested.

C. FINDING BUYERS (Looking for a Home)

Sellers are looking for an agent whereas buyers are looking for homes. Open houses are great for finding new buyers and sellers!

Because open houses are excellent resources for obtaining both buyers and sellers, it seems appropriate to discuss it here as we transition into the suggestions for finding buyers. More techniques will be discussed in Chapter 5, Finding the Right House

Figure 2-1 **Open House Guidelines**

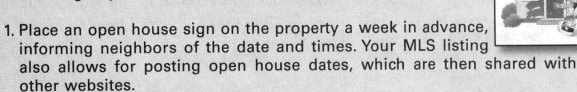

The following steps will insure a good response to the open house:

1. Place an open house sign on the property a week in advance, informing neighbors of the date and times. Your MLS listing also allows for posting open house dates, which are then shared with other websites.

2. Advertise the open house in the local newspaper and the MLS with easy driving instructions included.

3. Contact (mail or email) successful real estate agents and invite them to the open house.

4. Invite at least 25 neighbors in person, by telephone, or with post cards.

5. Half an hour before the open house, visit the neighbors you have invited and remind them of the open house.

6. Place your open house signs in strategic locations to drive-by traffic near your open house. Always ask permission of the property owners beforehand. Although you won't be placing your signs directly on their lawn, it's always a good policy to be courteous. An annoyed property owner can easily destroy or remove your sign.

7. You will need a "guest book" to be signed by everyone entering the property, including a phone number contact and email contact. Again, if possible, convince your viewers to fill out an open house computer application so you both know what they are looking for!

A drawing for a lottery ticket encourages the visitors to accurately sign the guest book. Be sure your new client is not already represented by a broker!

8. If the house is large, there should be two agents on the premises.

9. It's a good idea to have only one group of visitors at a time go through the property.

You can place a sign on the door asking other visitors to wait for a few minutes while you finish showing the home.

10. Hand each visitor a flyer with at least one photograph of the property stating its square footage, lot size, room description, and other amenities. It should also state when it was built, the school districts, and, of course, the price. On the reverse side of the flyer, you should have your résumé or bio, complete with your picture, as well as your website information.

11. It is important to leave the seller's home in neat condition, which means removing extra flyers, disposable coffee cups, miscellaneous trash, etc. Write them a note about the open house including information about how

many people came through and thanking them for preparing their home for showing. You should also send them an email with pertinent information.

12. Naturally, all visitors should be contacted later (usually through email, but if your viewers are not computer literate, make sure you follow through with written notes) and thanked for attending the open house. Get their feedback, and offer your services to them. This is an excellent way of adding to your prospect database!

© 2015 ETC., Inc.

One of the "tricks of the trade" when holding an open house includes baking a fresh batch of cookies in the oven—the delicious aroma is appealing, making the house seem "homier." Plus, you have cookies to offer your prospects! If you are in a hurry, just put cinnamon on an apple and bake it for 10 minutes.

for the Right Buyer, but many of the areas mentioned above for locating sellers cross over into locating buyers as well, so they bear repeating.

1. Open Houses

Have open house visitors fill out a wish list on your mobile tablet or laptop— Your local MLS site has a page where they can pick how many bedrooms they would like, how many bathrooms, swimming pool, carpet or hardwood floors, school district… it is extremely detailed, but you can fill out as little or as much as your potential client feels comfortable. Most importantly, there is an option for auto alerts (see Chapter 3).

Be sure to ask if the client already has a broker – no poaching please!

Again, speed is the name of the game! When a property that meets their criteria comes on the market, call or text your clients right away to let them know you're available to set up a showing at their earliest convenience!

2. Emails and Texts

Once you have the contact information of a potential buyer, don't overwhelm a client who is unfamiliar with mobile technology—still offer them the support and contact by telephone if that makes them the most comfortable. A young couple, on the other hand, may resent constant phone calls, but appreciate a text or "tweet" on Twitter letting them know you have a home to show them! Know your audience.

Once again, communication is the key to a successful real estate career, particularly now as technology evolves so quickly. Keep abreast of all the latest techniques available for your use, and as always be sensitive to the party with whom you are doing business.

3. Internet Search Engines

You want your name to be as close to the top of the list as possible when a potential buyer searches for an agent online.

> *You'll notice that on Google, for example, the top few responses to an Internet search have a slightly colored background or a small box that labeled "Ad" — that's because they are paid for advertisements! You can pay a premium to have your brokerage name moved to a higher spot on the list—and buying an ad can make you top dog. Be sure to budget for this expense though and keep track of whether or not it is paying off for you in the long run! In other words, always ask where the client found the name of your brokerage.*

a. Personal/Business Websites

For the same reasons your website (once found by a search engine) can bring in sellers it can bring in buyers. However, you have the opportunity to show actual listings you currently have for sale on your website. It's terribly important, however, to have your website up-to-date. There is nothing more frustrating for a buyer than to find a house on your site he or she loves only to discover it's no longer available. They may feel you've pulled a "bait and switch" on them and lose their trust.

> *Make sure you have an "opt out" button for your viewers to click so they don't feel uncomfortable worrying that your brokerage will begin to "spam" them if they're not really committed to buying a house yet, and leave them receiving notifications long after they've bought a new house or moved on!*

If you don't know how, or don't have the time, always hire a responsible party to maintain your website. The material available should change regularly so as to bring viewers back to the site to see what you've posted recently. Also, you can have your host provider keep track of who has visited your site.

Potential buyers will probably have visited websites Realtor.com and Zillow.com before contacting you. Studies show that buyers interview an average of three agents in person before choosing the one they hire.

4. Postcards (Glossy Card Stock or Virtually Online)

Like open houses, postcards offer a dual opportunity to bring in both sellers and buyers. On one side of the card you can list information about your brokerage, its reputation and a photo of yourself and your company logo – and on the other a list of current comps for homes in your neighborhood. You can display a home just currently sold to incorporate trust in both buyer and seller that you are good at your job.

Surveys have shown that sellers spend an average of about a year making the decision to sell, but buyers spend about five months making that decision.

If you've been sending out postcards monthly, your brokerage's name will have been in front of them for those entire 5-12 months! Familiarity often nurtures trust, and as they don't have to be opened like junk mail, they can't help but see what you've put on your postcard.

Postcards can be delivered to a doorstep or online!

5. For Sale By Owners (FSBOs)

Once an FSBO's house is sold, he or she will need another home!

As discussed earlier, owners selling their own homes may be glad to give up the headache to a professional. The potential buyers who inquire about that home may not be right for that property, but you can add them to your contact database as you know now they are at least thinking about buying a new home.

Also, the FSBO, once he or she has sold a house, will need another place to dwell—a little double-dipping opportunity for you as a broker to make another sale—or at the very least get a portion of the commission for recommending the seller-turned-buyer to another broker (particularly if not in your area).

a. Craigslist

Craigslist is a good mining source for FSBOs as well as renters looking for a place to live.

Why not contact renters and convince them that buying might be a better option? You can also offer to help them prequalify for a loan, a task by which they may be intimidated, but when they see how well you manage the situation, they may decide you are the agent for them!

b. Newspaper Ads

Newspaper ads as mentioned in the seller section are often placed by FSBOs making them easy for you to contact.

c. Bulletin Boards

Bulletin Boards are also places where a FSBO might place his or her contact information.

6. Referrals – Getting Recommendations

a. Past Clients

If you're doing your job well, you should be able to ask your current and past clients for recommendations (positive feedback). How to get referrals will be covered next in this chapter.

Let satisfied customers know you'd appreciate them letting their friends and family know of the terrific job you did for them either in helping them buy or sell a home. It's the freest form of advertising and often the most trusted!

Don't be a secret agent. Hand out cards and let everyone know how proud you are to be a real estate professional!

b. Professional Business Contacts (Geographical Farm)

As with sellers, title companies, probate attorneys, and divorce attorneys are all legitimate sources for finding potential buyers.

> **As unfortunate as it is, when a couple divorces—one or both of the parties will have to find a new place to live. It could mean the sale of one, two or even three homes! With delicacy you can make the approach not distasteful but a welcome relief from one of the many worries and tasks in front of the separating couple.**

D. THE ART OF DEVELOPING REFERRALS

To build clientele and achieve a high referral business, your buyers and sellers must be kept fully informed every step of the way.

Goodwill is earned by making it known that you always have the client's best interests in mind. But good intentions are not enough; you must be a doer. Explain to the client what you are doing each step of the way. Let them know when you order the termite report and credit report, when you check out the preliminary title report, submit the loan application, order an appraisal report, check out the documentation, get all the necessary final papers signed by all of the parties, etc. Call clients or leave email/text messages at every step of the process.

Stay one step ahead of the game by contacting your escrow officer to find out what clients should expect next! It works both ways—the escrow officer appreciates your attention and your clients are impressed by the fact you're always on top of the situation.

You should also demonstrate interest beyond the close of escrow. You can do this by sending out monthly newsletters. You can help both buyers and sellers in their move by providing helpful information about such items as utility arrangements, address notification to publishers, and so on.

Helping buyers and sellers make the moving process less stressful will insure their gratitude and lead to repeat business and referrals. One way to do this is by providing them with helpful information like a moving checklist, covering many of the details often overlooked in the chaos of moving.

> **If your clients are moving to another area, look up competent agents in the Certified Residential Specialist (CRS) Directory, and refer them to your moving clients with any questions they may have concerning their new neighborhood. Establishing this new relationship may add to that broker's referral database, and encourage him or her to reciprocate by referring clients to you. Referrals often lead to a percentage of the referral to the agent's commission.**

Remember: If you ask for criticism, you're asking a client to find something wrong. Instead, consider asking about what services they most appreciated. The more positive their response, the more open they may be to putting their comments in a written referral.

II. Advertising and Promotion

In spite of the importance and cost involved in advertising, many offices fail to give advertising the time and attention it deserves. The ads get routinely repeated, the job gets done mechanically, and the results may not be rewarding. Advertisements are often written and placed according to how other offices do it, instead of according to sound advertising principles that will motivate the reader to react to this property, reach for the telephone, and contact you—the main purpose for the ad. If the advertisement does not reach the targeted audience or fails to convince prospects to respond, then your time and advertising dollars are wasted.

Remember: An advertisement is both a "listing" tool and a "selling" tool.

Sellers watching the Internet, newspapers or online newspapers, yard signs, and trade magazines may be influenced for good or bad by an office's advertising method. The best results are achieved when one creative and responsible person is put in charge of the advertising program. Agents, office managers, or trusted assistants and other persons in the office should give feedback and suggestions, but one person should be in charge. He or she should be responsible for watching the cost, controlling the volume, scheduling the advertising for the most effective exposure, compiling and interpreting sales data, evaluating the effectiveness of the advertising, and making sure that what actually needs to be done is done. Putting one person in charge eliminates confusion and waste that can result from several people moving in conflicting directions.

Effective salespeople, the "high earners," will often place additional ads in publications, above and beyond the ads placed by the firm. These very successful agents will often create their own websites that can be completely independent of their broker (terms and conditions need to be worked out with the broker).

It is critically important to keep track of the effectiveness and cost of all advertising. If the ad works, then it can be repeated. If it doesn't, then it needs to be improved. To determine this, use a Traffic Sheet/Ad Call Log Book. A **TRAFFIC SHEET/AD CALL LOG BOOK** *is an informative analytical tool that logs in daily calls that specifically gives you a daily and historical review of how effectively your brokerage is advertising and the important caller data* (see **Figure 2-2**). The broker and all salespeople should be reading this traffic sheet daily because it details what properties are "hot," whom they called and for what property, and most importantly, all the ways to contact the prospects so they can be put on the mailing list.

The traffic sheet can be digitized and sent out to all brokers and agents at the end of the day.

Figure 2-2	Traffic Sheet/Ad Call Log Book		
Agent	**Source**	**Property**	**Client's Name and Phone Number**
A. L.	Homes & Land	500 San Jose	Mrs. Beverly Buyer - (818) 555-5555 (Needs 4 BR. & Covina Schools. Also must sell present home in W. Covina located at 1300 Merced.)

© 2015 ETC., Inc.

There are also various "free" advertisement opportunities available to companies that regularly advertise in one medium. If you are overseeing the advertising, you should be on the lookout for good public relation (PR) opportunities. *PUBLIC RELATIONS is taking advantage of free press coverage to promote your firm, especially when someone in your organization has made some admirable social contribution that benefits the community, such as organizing or attending a philanthropic event.* These articles are best written, and more credible, from a third person point of view.

Remember: Writing good advertisements takes time. Be sure to set aside sufficient time for the actual task of designing the ad, reviewing it, and revising it.

Whenever an advertisement is the "first point of contact" with a possible client, you must include your CalBRE license number (on business cards, stationary, and website). As the listing agent, you should send or email a copy to the seller and other clients. Don't be a secret agent. It pays to toot your own horn!

A. REAL ESTATE ADVERTISING

All advertising, whether a specific property or a brokerage's services, serves to advertise the company brand!

Product advertising gives the reader information about the benefits and specific features of a property. The advantages of owning property are always an effective selling point in an ad (see **Figure 2-3**).

B. ADVERTISING MEDIA (Three Current Types)

Advertising is more effective for selling a company's image than for selling just one individual property listing!

Knowing what and how to trigger a positive reaction from the reader is important, but now you need to select the best media for the advertisement. Generally speaking, the size of the company determines the scope and the variety of media to use. Each type of media must be expected to pay for itself in results, just as each property listed and sold must contribute to your firm's productivity.

Figure 2-3

The Advantages of Owning Your Own Home
"The American Dream—Your Nest"

There are many advantages to owning real estate, some of which are listed below and should be brought to the ad reader's attention. Any one or more of the following may be the "sizzle that sells the steak" when advertising property.

1. Inflation protection – Equity build up as each house payment may reduce the loan
2. Small initial investment – Particularly if down payment requirements are low
3. Provides necessity of life – Shelter – Pride of homeownership – **Your nest**
4. Higher return on investment – Less risky than stock market in the long run
5. Loan security – Established fixed or adjusted interest rates
6. Establishes stability – Homeowners are considered stable
7. Security – No rent increase, no 30- or 60-day notice to quit
8. Forced savings – Your equity increases as prices escalate
9. Enduring resources – Homes can be refinanced, money can be pulled out
10. Tax advantages – There are numerous deductions and write-offs available to homeowners that reduce the cost of ownership
11. You can lease out your property for monthly income

© 2015 ETC., Inc.

1. Electronic Media

a. Internet Sites (Constantly Evolving)

The Internet is one of the most important types of advertising media available to real estate companies. It is an arena "ripe for the picking" for companies looking to exploit many creative and unique advertising opportunities.

These sites have become much more technical, with links to other websites, such as those that can calculate mortgages and give school rating information. It must be stressed that your company's website should be professionally designed to attract prospective buyers and sellers. See Chapter 8 for more information, such as the creation of the domain suffix ".realtor."

It's important to constantly update your website! If no one in your office has the expertise to do so, hire an assistant or a web consultant to regularly do this task.

Not only is your personal and broker's website an effective advertising tool, but new technologies are constantly being created to enhance your presence on the Internet. In Chapter 8 you will find more information regarding email websites, MLS sharing of listings, as well as other techniques to put your name and your listings on the Interent for the most effective use of advertising media.

Real estate-related websites like Realtor.com and Zillow.com will be discussed in Chapter 8.

b. Radio and Television

Only high cost limits the use of radio and TV (satellite and cable), as they are especially effective for the multi-office operation looking to promote the company.

Radio (especially during drive time) and television ads (including cable) reach a much larger audience than other advertising forms; they're a better outlet for **promoting your firm and developing good public relations than for marketing specific properties**. The cost may also be justified when you're representing a developer of tracts for homes or subdivisions.

2. Walk or Drive-By Advertising

a. Shopping Guides

Many supermarkets offer their customers free homebuyers' guides that advertise current real estate listings. Be sure to post your website address!

b. Yard Signs on Property

One of the most efficient, yet relatively inexpensive means of advertising, is your firm's own sign, prominently placed on a listed property. It should remain in place until the new owners move in, with riders attached, such as "In Escrow," "Sold," or "Bought." This is concrete proof that you and your firm get results.

"Riders" on your signs can also include the unique website address of the home for sale (see Chapter 8 for more information about creating these websites and a new type of bar code called a Quick Response [QR] box).

c. Billboards and Other Outdoor Advertising

Freestanding signs along streets and large billboards on the outside of buildings are eye-catching. They also keep you and your firm in the public eye, and may, consciously or subconsciously, influence prospects to think of you when they're in need of a real estate professional. Billboards are evolving. No longer just static signs, they now use LED technology and can rotate and change messages.

e. Window Displays

When the advertising is large and accompanied with pictures of properties, the window displays in your office can be particularly effective. The window should not be cluttered—it should be neat and constantly updated. The more walk-by traffic, the more effective the window display.

Prominently displayed office signs outside your brokerage brings in walk-by traffic.

f. Bus, Car, Bench, and Taxi Signs

Transit advertising can be locally productive in getting brief messages to the general public and keeping your name in the public eye.

Ads placed inside public transportation like a bus or taxi allow a client longer viewing time of an ad. There's nothing like being bored in traffic to get commuters to read anything in sight. Taxis often service out-of-towners who may very well be relocating to that city.

3. Paper Media Strategies

a. Newspapers (Online and Paper)

Newspaper advertising can be an effective media for residential (home) sales. They are usually delivered to the residence daily or weekly. Newspaper ads can be subdivided into classified and display ads.

1. Classified Advertising

Classified advertising in newspapers or online newspapers is particularly common in the "For Rent" and "For Sale" sections, usually alphabetically according to area or city. *Designed to advertise a specific property, **CLASSIFIED ADS** enjoy high readership and viewership among those looking for housing.* Advertisements in print newspapers or online are typically short and charge fees. Other print types are Yellow Pages, homebuyers guides, brochures, and flyers.

Classified ads are mostly designed for resale and rental properties.

2. Display Advertising

These ads are outside the classified section of the newspaper or popups on your website. ***DISPLAY ADVERTISING*** *sells through the use of both words and graphic elements, such as pictures, drawings, and maps.* For an example of display advertising, see **Figure 2-4**. They can be in color and much more eye-catching than classified ads.

The main purpose of display advertising is to keep your firm's name before the public, and to attract sellers to list with the company.

These pricier ads may be placed in the classified section to stand out against small ads, or they may be featured in a highly attractive, glossy magazine-type insert in the weekend newspaper. In the *Los Angeles Times*, one of the several inserts is called "View" and is divided into "Properties by Area" so readers can narrow their search to a specific zipcode, county, or region.

Figure 2-4

Lyons
and Associates, Inc., Realtor
REAL ESTATE   EXCELLENCE

http://www.lyonsrealtors.ismyreagent.com • http://www.lyonsandassociatesrltr.com
Like us on Facebook & visit our website for up to date listing info!
Facebook.com/LyonsAndAssociatesRealtors

GORGEOUS VIEW LOT, COVINA HILLS! $98,500

34,511 sqft View lot in highly desired neighborhood of Covina. Built your dream home on this secluded lot. Lot is mostly flat and ready to built. Plans for a 3,400 single family residence plus garage are available. Preliminary geotechnical engineering and engineering geologic investigation report is available.

CHINO HILLS! STANDARD SALE!!! $210,000

2 BR/2 BA ground level unit with a great open floor plan, and a wrap around patio with built in spa & waterfall, outdoor fireplace/BBQ. Inside we have an open living room with cozy fireplace and separate dining area, kitchen with breakfast bar. First bedroom has 2 double doors and access to hallway & 3/4 bathroom. Master bedroom has slider leading out to patio and spa, with full bath and separate sink area. Property sold as is.

LAKEWOOD PROBATE SALE! $299,950

Title shows 3 bedrooms, home has plenty of ceramic tile floors, newer windows, a long 'as is' condition without repairs or warranty.

AZUSA LEASE ! 3BR/2BA $2,100/MO

Spacious well maintained home nestled on a quiet street in North Azusa. Very open floor plan perfect for entertaining. The large formal living room is highlighted by the brick fire place. There is a formal dining area off the kitchen. The newly remodeled kitchen features new cabinets and counter tops and tile floor with room for a breakfast area . The family room offers a wet bar and the sliding door leads to the private back yard. The home offers three bedrooms. The master suite has a private bathroom and a sliding glass door allows access to the back yard. Three car garage and much more. The home is ready for immediate occupancy.

DIAMOND BAR LEASE 2BR/2BA $1700

Property is located in the City of Diamond Bar but has a Walnut address. Located in the Walnut School District. Very quiet complex with lots of green area. Close to the Metrolink station. Water and Trash are included in rent. Garage is very good size for 2 cars plus some space.

2820 E. Garvey Ave. South, West Covina
(626) 331-0141

0010314754 022313

Often " insert" display ads are "prestige" properties out of the price range of the average buyer, but the name of the brokerage, as well as the particular agents may become familiar to them when they go to look for a home in their price range.

b. Magazines

Although more costly than many other options, **TRADE AND GENERAL MAGAZINES** *are an important form of print advertising medium for any brokerage.*

A well-placed ad in an upscale local magazine is expensive, but may draw in well-to-do clients who can afford more expensive homes.

c. Telephone and City Directories

Your company's name in the telephone directory and the yellow pages is a must to facilitate maximum and convenient exposure. Yellowpages.com may be a relatively expensive type of advertisement, but more than cost-effective.

While it costs you money to advertise large ads in a hard-copy yellow page directory, it's delivered free to virtually every home. There are online yellow pages available to advertise in as well.

d. Direct Mail (U.S. Postal Service)

Once you consistently contact a group of people each month, over and over again, your name will become more and more familiar. In real estate, name recognition is priceless.

This form of advertising includes such items as postcards, letters, pamphlets, booklets, brochures, circulars, leaflets, and folders. The cost is relative, depending on the quality of the products, the frequency with which you update them, and the quantity you choose to mail out. Postcards, for example, are less expensive to print and mail than brochures, and people will almost always read them. There are many companies that print and mail your product using bulk rates! Create a code on the advertisement that will let you know what ad callers are responding to.

As with all advertising, keep track of how many responses were generated, including direct mail. Inquire as to which specific mail-out influenced your prospects, then increase that method. Internet Apps can make this process easier and more efficient!

e. Club, Religious, and Institutional Newsletters

Brokers can get name recognition by advertising their firms in these publications. The fact you share some common interests may steer clients in your direction.

f. Business Cards, Letterheads, Company Post Cards, Institutional Folders

These should be consistent and have your company logo, as well as all your other pertinent company information.

Lyons and Associates, Inc., incorporates a stylized blue lion's head in its logo. Over the years, this graphic has become highly recognizable in the community, assuring customers of the firm's stability and success.

g. Giveaways

Items imprinted with your company's logo, such as calendars, maps, notepads, pencils, pens, yardsticks, mouse pads, flash drives, refrigerator magnets, and a variety of small household items are ways to keep your firm's name before the public.

The more useful the specialty item (like a mousepad with your logo), the longer the prospect will keep it. The more visible the item, the more often it subconsciously reinforces your firm's presence—think of something they'll see every day!

C. ADVERTISING POINTERS

There are many points to keep in mind when planning and implementing an advertising program.

1. **Be consistent.** Advertising agencies are in agreement that it takes a long time before advertising makes an impact in the community. Select logo, typography, and slogans with care, as they will be around a long time.

The longer your logo and/or slogan is in the public eye, the more established and reliable your firm will appear to your community. Keep your logo recognizable and put it in front of the public as often as possible.

2. An advertising program must be **thoroughly and carefully coordinated**, every detail and step of a sales campaign supported at every point. All efforts should be totally integrated.

3. Base your advertising and sales campaigns on **market research and buyer-reaction surveys** (tracking how many calls are generated). Measure advertising result!

Thanks to Internet technology, you can track how many potential buyers access the website for a particular property.

4. **Visit every property** to be advertised to learn all you can about the listing before writing the ad. Take photographs with your smartphone for office, ads, and prospects.

5. Put the material in good order; **write the ad from the buyer's viewpoint**, not yours.

6. **Use meaningful words and phrases**, telling the story in as few words as possible. Use language that stirs the imagination and the emotions, but keep it simple. Keep all abbreviations to a minimum, and don't use creative abbreviations that no one understands.

7. **Decide on the audience** for your ad; bear in mind the person who will be reading or viewing it. Use different appeals for different markets. Don't be concerned with crowds, but with individuals.

8. **Write to inspire confidence**, making the copy just long enough to tell your story. Don't oversell, and don't exaggerate.

Resist the temptation to overstate a home's appeal. A property should be at least as attractive (as it is in the ad) when the buyer sees it.

9. **Include benefits**; advertise not what the property is so much as what it will do for the buyer. "RELAX BY THE POOL" as a headline demonstrates what is referred to as "selling the sizzle, not the steak."

10. **Furnish salespeople with the full facts** about the advertising campaign so they're not in the dark when the telephones begin ringing. Train your staff to ask the right questions—get names, email addresses, and telephone numbers; encourage callers to come in and meet you.

Remember: The purpose of advertising is to meet the clients and bring them into the office to build a rapport with them.

11. **Make the most of all inquiries and prospect leads** brought in by your ads and sales literature. This includes the proper use of the telephone. Illustrate the benefits of having a knowledgeable, thoughtful agent who knows callers' needs in order to find the right property for them.

12. **Budget properly.** "Five to seven percent" of gross commissions earned monthly or annually is a safe amount to expend for advertising. You must maintain cost records to measure the results of the advertising outlay.

In deciding which media to use, keep in mind that the objective is not automatically to reach the largest audience, but to reach the greatest number of potential buyers at the most economical cost.

D. WRITING EFFECTIVE ADS (AIDA)

A time-tested method used in writing ads is the AIDA formula.

AIDA stands for Attention, Interest, Desire, and Action.

Whatever type of advertisement is used, you, the writer, must effectively:

1. **Attract "Attention."** Use a clever heading or opening phrase. Use white space around margins, or bold type to emphasize key ideas or words that can be found in daily newspapers (and online): WRITER'S RETREAT... DIRT CHEAP... DO IT YOURSELF... LOVE AT FIRST SIGHT... ENCHANTMENT FOR SALE.

2. **Arouse "Interest."** Get the readers to continue reading by maintaining interest and curiosity through a flood of ideas in the body of the ad. Invite readers to imagine enjoying the pool in the summertime, entertaining guests on the patio, or secluding themselves in a convertible den used as a study or library.

3. **Stimulate "Desire."** Now that the reader's eye has been caught, the ad must continue with pictures or by words to paint a picture of the house, appealing to the senses and emotions. Tell the reader, in as few words as possible, what he or she wants to know. The language should be clear, concise, and understandable. Your firm's ads will inspire confidence if you consistently give just the facts and avoid exaggeration and overstatements.

4. **Compel "Action."** The close of an effective ad stimulates immediate action, for example, "For inspection, call or text XXX-XXXX now or visit www.walthuber. realtor or www.walthuber.com"

E. BUDGETING FOR ADVERTISING (Includes Internet)

No one makes money on properties that aren't selling. You can't sell a property without some form of advertising, and all advertising costs money.

> *In a very competitive market, you'll find that salespersons' commission splits are higher, resulting in brokers shifting some of the burden of advertising costs to their agents.*

The most successful brokers are the ones best able to appropriately allocate their advertising dollars; you should know where your advertising dollars are best spent.

Learn from your successes and your mistakes. Put more money into advertising that has proven successful to you in the past and rethink the advertisement methods that aren't working for you. Advertising in and of itself will not sell the property. It's only a means by which to get your phones to ring. It takes a combination of factors and forces to produce a completed sale.

How should you budget for advertising? For each dollar of profit, the average real estate business allocates five to seven percent for sales promotion. In other words, **of every dollar of gross commission income, about 5 to 7 cents is paid out in all forms of advertising and promotion.**

As to specific ways in which allocation is made, pick one guideline to determine your advertising budget. If you find a method is not working for you, change it.

Don't forget to budget for web designers and Internet hosting services! Send or email a copy of all advertising to your seller on a regular basis. The average agent spends between $500 and $1,000 a year on real estate technology.

F. KEEP EVALUATING ADVERTISING EFFECTIVENESS

If your advertising program is not producing the results you want, you must make some changes. In order to know the effectiveness of the advertising campaign, you must have an evaluation system to determine which ads work and which ads need help. Offices deal with this check and balance in various ways. One popular method is to have the telephone log maintained by the receptionist or floor person (Traffic Sheet/Ad Call Log Book—Figure 2-2—detailed earlier). Newspaper and magazine ads usually have a code number, making it easy for the person answering the telephone to know which property is involved.

Each call should be entered showing its source (i.e., signs, newspapers, Internet, yellow pages, mail outs) and which agent answered the inquiry. It's important to mention that any inquiry directly resulting from the efforts of another salesperson, such as a mail out, should be referred to that particular agent, no matter who answers the telephone.

You should regularly examine the incoming call log book to determine the impact of any advertising campaign.

G. CONSUMER FINANCE PROTECTION BUREAU (CFPB)

Advertising of real estate credit is under the jurisdiction of the Consumer Finance Protection Bureau (CFPB).

The Truth in Lending Act, or Regulation Z, a part of the federal Consumers Credit Protection Act of 1968, requires disclosure of credit costs as a percent as well as total finance charges. It is enforced by the Consumer Finance Protection Bureau.

If any financing term is mentioned, the ad must also mention the annual percentage rate (APR) and all other financing terms. The APR makes your ability to compare loans more accurate. See the Consumer Finance Protection Bureau regulations.

---

1. Regulations of the Real Estate Commissioner (Regarding Advertising)

As will be covered in Chapter 15, the Real Estate Commissioner can adopt regulations that have the same force and intent as law. Regulations concerning advertising, for example, are covered in the following:

Article 9, 2770. Electronic Communication – Advertising and Dissemination of Information on the Internet.

2770.1. Advertising - License Designation.

Use of the terms broker, agent, Realtor, loan correspondent or the abbreviations bro., agt., or other similar terms or abbreviations, is deemed sufficient identification to fulfill the designation requirements. ▼

2773. Disclosure of License Identification Number on Solicitation Materials – First Point of Contact with Consumers.

(a) A real estate broker or salesperson, when engaging in acts for which a license is required, shall disclose its, his or her eight (8) digit real estate license identification number on all solicitation materials intended to be the first point of contact with consumers. If the name of more than one licensee appears in the solicitation, the license identification number of each licensee shall be disclosed. The license numbers of employing brokers or corporate brokers whose names or logos or trademarks appear on solicitation materials along with the names and license numbers of licensed employees or broker associates do not need to appear on those materials.

Solicitation materials intended to be the first point of contact with consumers, and in which a licensee must disclose a license identification number, include the following:

(1) Business cards;

(2) Stationery;

(3) Websites owned, controlled, and/or maintained by the soliciting real estate licensee; and

(4) Promotional and advertising fliers, brochures, email and regular mail, leaflets, and any marketing or promotional materials designed to solicit the creation of a professional relationship between the licensee and a consumer, or which is intended to incentivize, induce or entice a consumer to contact the licensee about any service for which a license is required. The type size of the license identification number shall be no smaller than the smallest size type used in the solicitation material.

(b) For the purposes of Business and Professions Code Section 10140.6, so solicitation materials do not include the following:

(1) Advertisements in electronic media (including, without limitation, radio, cinema, and television ads, and the opening section of streaming video and audio);

(2) Print advertising in any newspaper or periodical; and

(3) "For Sale" signs placed on or around a property intended to alert the Public the property is available for lease, purchase or trade.

III. CHAPTER SUMMARY

Listings (contractual right to sell another's property for a commission) are the lifeblood of all real estate offices. There are numerous ways to contact potential sellers, including telephone contacts, email, postcards, newsletters, and many more, such as real estate websites like Realtor.com and Zillow.com. Listings may also come from expired listings, foreclosures, FSBOs, and **geographical farms** that consist of a neighborhood where agents cultivate new clients and regularly update their real estate activities and values. **Open houses** are also an excellent way to prospect for both buyers and sellers.

It's important to get **referrals** to increase business. The more helpful an agent is both before, during, and after a sale, the more likely a client is to give referrals. Other agents and brokers can also recommend your services, although you may have to share your commissions with them.

Effective advertising utilizes the **AIDA formula—Attention, Interest, Desire, and Action.**

The purpose of advertising may be to sell a particular property, but more often than not it is a tool to get potential clients into the office and build a relationship with them. **Newspaper ads** are the most commonly used form of print advertising for a brokerage, whereas the Internet is most often used for particular properties.

There are numerous other forms of advertising, including magazines, radio, tv, and social media sites like Facebook, LinkedIn, Twitter, and Yelp!.

The **Internet** is a significant advertising arena, limited only by your imagination and technical expertise. It's important to keep your company's website updated on a regular basis. Buyers who shop through the Internet are more informed and educated and buy faster. Most still want a knowledgeable salesperson to help them finalize a choice of home and details of closing.

The effectiveness of advertising should be tracked through the use of a **traffic sheet** or **ad call logbook**. The more successful the method, the larger the percentage of the advertising budget should be spent on that medium.

The **Consumer Finance Protection Bureau (CFPB)** enforces the **Truth in Lending Act (Regulation Z)** which regulates the advertising of real estate credit. If any financing term is used in an ad, the **annual percentage rate (APR)** must also be included. **Article 9** of the **Regulations of the Real Estate Commissioner** also establishes advertising guidelines and restrictions.

IV. MATCHING VOCABULARY Fill in the blanks with the correct letter

A. AIDA - Attention, Interest, Desire, and Action
B. Classified Ads
C. Comparative Market Analysis CMA)
D. Consumer Finance Protection Bureau (CFPB)

E. Direct mail
F. Door Hangers
G. FSBOs, For Sale by Owners
H. Geographical farm
I. Guaranteed sales plan
J. Newspapers (Print and Online)

K. Open house
L. Public relations
M. Referrals
N. Staging (furniture placement)
O. Statement of identification

1. _____ Data analysis that gives the sellers a price range for their home by comparing it to similar homes that have recently sold.

2. _____ Maximizing first impressions and preparing your home for showing and open houses by moving furniture and dressing up the home.

3. _____ A planned set of hours during which a property for sale is held open for public viewing.

4. _____ A form used by title companies that is filled out by buyers and sellers to verify their identities.

5. _____ A neighborhood in which a real estate agent "cultivates" new clients by contacting its residents up to 12 times a year in order to update them on real estate activities and values.

6. _____ When an owner decides and trys to sell his own property.

7. _____ This type of newspaper advertisement is designed to advertise a specific property and enjoys high readership among those looking for low and medium priced housing.

8. _____ A time-tested step-by-step method used in writing ads; this formula gets the job done.

9. _____ Advertising of real estate credit terms is under this federal organization's jurisdiction.

10. _____ An agreement by the company to purchase the property at a given price after the "holding period of the property."

11. _____ Type of advertising that is sent using the U.S. postal service.

12. _____ Taking advantage of free press coverage to promote your firm, especially when someone in your organization has made some admirable social contribution that benefits the community, such as organizing or attending a philanthropic event.

13. _____ Potential clients received through the agent's good will and treatment of current clients.

14. _____ This type of business promotion fits on front door handles or can be attached by a rubber band.

15. _____ Often considered the most effective way to advertise homes and your brokerage to the public on a daily or weekly basis.

See Page 609 for Answers

CHAPTER 2

V. CHAPTER QUIZ

1. A comparison of one property's value to similar recently sold properties is called a:
   a. cheat sheet.
   b. log book.
   c. comparative market analysis.
   d. none of the above.

2. Open houses are good for:
   a. finding buyers.
   b. finding sellers.
   c. neither a nor b.
   d. both a and b.

3. Why are holding open houses beneficial to you as an agent?
   a. They expose your listing to the buying public and other agents who may not have previously seen your listing.
   b. They demonstrate to your sellers how hard you are working for them to obtain the best price for their home.
   c. You get to meet potential buyers, as well as prospects, who may need to sell prior to purchasing.
   d. All of the above.

4. Which groups should be included in your "sphere of influence"?
   a. Personnel managers
   b. Postal workers
   c. Union officials
   d. All of the above

5. "FSBO" is an abbreviation of:
   a. for sale by operator.
   b. for sale buyer's option.
   c. forced sale by owner.
   d. for sale by owner.

6. Whch of the following is a means of locating buyers looking for homes?
   a. Open Houses
   b. Emails
   c. Internet search engines
   d. All of the above.

7. In general, the most effective media to use in the advertising of homes is:

    a. billboards or bus stop benches.
    b. magazines or shopping guides.
    c. newspapers or Internet.
    d. none of the above.

8. CMA stands for:

    a. comparative market analysis.
    b. computer matching analysis.
    c. competitive member association.
    d. none of the above.

9. The time-tested model used in writing ads is the AIDA formula, which stands for:

    a. always include disclaimers accurately.
    b. actual interest disclosed annually.
    c. artistic, illustrated, desirable, anticipation.
    d. attention, interest, desire, action.

10. When evaluating the effectiveness of the advertising campaign, the broker/manager should:

    a. ignore ad responses.
    b. check the phone call log book/traffic sheet.
    c. rely only on traditional forms of advertising.
    d. none of the above.

ANSWERS: 1. c; 2. d; 3. d; 4. d; 5. d; 6. d; 7. c; 8. a; 9. d; 10. b

CHAPTER 3

The Listing Agreement: How to Secure a Listing

I. Employing an Agent

A *LISTING* is an employment contract between an owner and a licensed real estate broker entered into for the purpose of the broker providing services to find ready, willing, and able persons to buy, rent, or lease a particular property under the terms specified in the contract. It is often called a Residential Listing Agreement (RLA), and the most commonly used CAR® listing form is subtitled "Exclusive Authorization and Right to Sell." An agent holding a listing is bound by the law of agency and owes certain duties of care to his or her principal. The buyer and seller, on the other hand, are two principals, yet not bound by the laws of agency.

"Agency" is the relationship between principal (usually a buyer or seller) and agent (salesperson/broker) wherein the agent is employed by the principal to do certain acts (selling, buying or leasing), like negotiating with third parties.

A listing, then, is a contract of employment to hire an agent (salesperson), wherein a principal hires the services of an agent—who works for a licensed real estate broker—to perform certain prescribed services for a stated period of time. Usually, these involve the selling (or exchanging) of real property of the owner/principal, but the definition can be much wider than this. On occasion, an agent may be employed to represent a potential buyer to purchase a certain (type of) property, to seek out and negotiate a rental or leasehold, or to represent a prospective borrower in obtaining a trust deed-backed loan. As an agent, you may also be called upon to represent a principal in the purchase or sale of a business opportunity, and other services for which you are licensed.

In California, as in almost all other states, employment contracts must be in writing to be enforceable. In real estate, the employment contract is the "listing agreement," but a signed disclosure of agency relationship is also required. "Death of either the seller or broker terminates the listing contract," unless the company is incorporated.

Moreover, the listing agreement (employment contract) must be definite and certain as to the "terms" of the broker's employment (see Figure 3-1). The **fiduciary obligation** owed

CHAPTER OUTLINE

to the principals, discussed in earlier chapters, bears repeating here. In connection with the drafting of the listing agreement, as the licensee, you owe the highest fiduciary duty of care, skill, and diligence in working for the best interests of your principal (client).

Listings are the backbone of sales; that is, you must first be able to "sell the owners" on listing their property before you can "sell a buyer a property." Spending adequate time in listing the property at the right price is extremely important.

"Always give both buyer and seller a copy of any real estate agreement when it is signed." It's the law. Couples who are considered "one legal person" receive one copy. If there are five couples, give five copies.

A. RIGHT TO A COMMISSION

The listing contract is basically a **bilateral (two parties exchange promises) contract** of employment for the purpose of finding a buyer.

The commission is, therefore, earned when you (the broker) have produced a buyer who is "ready, willing, and able" to purchase at the price and under the terms agreed to by both seller and buyer. (Commissions are always negotiable.)

Occasionally the words "ready," "willing," and "able" become subject to legal interpretation. In general, the words "ready and willing" mean that you must produce a buyer with a bona fide offer at a specified or accepted price and terms. The word "able" requires that you have a buyer financially capable of complying with the terms of the sale, including initial cash with down payment and the ability to obtain trust deed financing.

Once such a buyer is produced, you, as the broker, are deemed to have earned the commission. Even if the sellers refused to sign the purchaser's offer, they may be held liable to you, the broker, for a commission. Obviously the general rule is controlling only in the absence of any agreement to the contrary. Modification or variation can be made by the parties' agreement.

Similarly, a seller may be held liable to you, the broker, where, after both buyer and seller have signed a purchase agreement contract, the sale fails to close because of some fault of the seller. For instance, there may be a defective title, or failure to deliver the title, or the sellers may have changed their mind about selling, or be guilty of fraud, in which case you may still be entitled to the commission.

If escrow doesn't close, it is highly unlikely a broker will spend the time and money going to court where it could take years to adjudicate.

B. TYPES OF LISTINGS

Contrary to popular belief, there are only two main types of listings—the exclusive and the open listings. All of the others are variations of these two and represent methods of marketing the property or compensating the agent.

The Residential Listing Agreement (Exclusive Authorization and Right to Sell listing, along with the Seller Advisory form and seller's net proceeds) is one of the few items in the seller's "listing kit" of which the buyer will not receive a copy.

1. Open Listing

An **OPEN LISTING** *is a written contract authorizing one or more brokers (and their salespeople) to act as agent in the sale of the principal's property for a fixed commission.*

Usually, no time limit is specified for the work in an open listing; the owners may withdraw the property from the market whenever they wish. Sale of the property cancels all outstanding listings. It is not necessary to notify each agent. The commission is earned by the broker who is the first to find a buyer ready, willing, and able to meet the terms of the listing, or whose offer is accepted by the seller. If the owners themselves sell the property, they are not liable for commission to the listing agents.

An open listing is little better than no listing at all, as it is not placed on the MLS.

Sometimes brokers take on such listings only when they can't obtain them on an exclusive basis. Consequently, they tend to store them in their "pockets" (not share them with other brokers) until a buyer comes along, or if they already have a "pocket" buyer in mind. A **POCKET BUYER** *is prepared to buy a property before that property is actually listed with a broker.* Meanwhile, the brokers usually expend little or no effort and money in marketing the properties. Some of these listings may be verbal only. However, until reduced to writing, no commission is enforceable.

Open listings are rarely used.

Builders, subdividers, and developers will often utilize this type of listing when they can negotiate a reduced commission from the broker. This is often where "pocket buyers" come in. For example, a couple who is looking to buy into a condominium complex before it's even completed may be considered pocket buyers. Other users are executors and administrators of estates, attorneys, trustees, and owners of industrial and commercial properties.

2. Exclusive Listings (Expiration Date Required)

It is very likely that a licensee other than the listing broker will end up finding a buyer. Cooperation among brokers is the rule, rather than the exception. Cooperative sales are an accepted way of life among licensees. In fact, at least 80% of all properties are sold by cooperating agents ("outsiders"). A **COOPERATING BROKER** *is a non-listing broker with whom the listing broker agrees to share a commission (not necessarily 1/2 and 1/2) if the non-listing broker finds the buyer.*

An "Exclusive Authorization and Right to Sell" listing, posted on an MLS, encourages participation in the sale by numerous brokers, resulting in the most market exposure and the highest possible selling price. Cooperating brokers then share the commission, as agreed. The listing broker must send a 1099 to the selling broker if the selling broker is not incorporated.

The two major categories of the exclusive listing are discussed next. Both must be for a definite time period. Unless a specified termination date is stated in the agreement, you, as a licensee, may become subject to disciplinary action under California Real Estate Law.

Copies of exclusive listing agreements, with a definite expiration date (90 days is typical), must be given to the person signing at the time the signature is obtained.

a. Exclusive Agency Listing

The **EXCLUSIVE AGENCY LISTING** *provides that one agent has the right to be the only person, other than the owner, to sell a property during a specified period.* The owner, however, has the right to independently sell the property without paying a commission to the listing broker. Therefore, the drawback of an exclusive agency listing is that the broker is, or could be, in competition with the owner for the sale.

Rarely is an exclusive agency listing placed with an MLS. Most MLS boards only allow exclusive authorization and right to sell listings.

Frequently, the exclusive agency is created by a provision in the agreement stating that the owner will pay a commission or fee to the listing broker if the property is sold either by the broker or by any other person (except the owner) during the term of the employment, including any extensions thereof. When a cooperating agent sells your listing and that company is not incorporated, the listing broker must send out a 1099 tax form to the unincorporated broker.

Most brokers with an exclusive agency listing will insist that an owner quote the same asking price as the broker.

Carefully document every showing and provide the names of your (and any other broker's) prospects to the seller. This will keep a seller from dealing directly with your buyer and leaving you out of the commission for a specified period.

b. Exclusive Authorization and Right to Sell Listing

Eliminating the pitfalls of the exclusive agency listing, the **EXCLUSIVE AUTHORIZATION AND RIGHT TO SELL LISTING** *entitles the broker to commissions on all sales during the life of his or her agreement with the owner, even when the owners themselves sell the property* (see **Figure 3-1**).

Figure 3-1

CALIFORNIA
ASSOCIATION
OF REALTORS®

RESIDENTIAL LISTING AGREEMENT
(Exclusive Authorization and Right to Sell)
(C.A.R. Form RLA, Revised 11/13)

1. **EXCLUSIVE RIGHT TO SELL:** _____ ("Seller")
hereby employs and grants _____ ("Broker")
beginning (date) _____ and ending at 11:59 P.M. on (date) _____ ("Listing Period")
the exclusive and irrevocable right to sell or exchange the real property in the City of ___*Marina del Rey*___
County of ___*Los Angeles*___ , Assessor's Parcel No. _____
California, described as: ___*123 Sail Avenue*___ ("Property").

2. **ITEMS EXCLUDED AND INCLUDED:** Unless otherwise specified in a real estate purchase agreement, all fixtures and fittings that are attached to the Property are included, and personal property items are excluded, from the purchase price.
ADDITIONAL ITEMS EXCLUDED: _____
ADDITIONAL ITEMS INCLUDED:
Seller intends that the above items be excluded or included in offering the Property for sale, but understands that: **(i)** the purchase agreement supersedes any intention expressed above and will ultimately determine which items are excluded and included in the sale; and **(ii)** Broker is not responsible for and does not guarantee that the above exclusions and/or inclusions will be in the purchase agreement.

3. **LISTING PRICE AND TERMS:**
   A. The listing price shall be: _____
   _____ Dollars ($ _____).
   B. Additional Terms: _____
   _____
   _____

4. **COMPENSATION TO BROKER:**
   Notice: The amount or rate of real estate commissions is not fixed by law. They are set by each Broker individually and may be negotiable between Seller and Broker (real estate commissions include all compensation and fees to Broker).
   A. Seller agrees to pay to Broker as compensation for services irrespective of agency relationship(s), either ☐ _____ percent of the listing price (or if a purchase agreement is entered into, of the purchase price), or ☐ $ _____
   AND _____ , as follows:
   (1) If during the Listing Period, or any extension, Broker, cooperating broker, Seller or any other person procures a ready, willing, and able buyer(s) whose offer to purchase the Property on any price and terms is accepted by Seller, provided the Buyer completes the transaction or is prevented from doing so by Seller. (Broker is entitled to compensation whether any escrow resulting from such offer closes during or after the expiration of the Listing Period, or any extension.)
   OR **(2)** If within _____ calendar days (a) after the end of the Listing Period or any extension; or (b) after any cancellation of this Agreement, unless otherwise agreed, Seller enters into a contract to sell, convey, lease or otherwise transfer the Property to anyone ("Prospective Buyer") or that person's related entity: **(i)** who physically entered and was shown the Property during the Listing Period or any extension by Broker or a cooperating broker; or **(ii)** for whom Broker or any cooperating broker submitted to Seller a signed, written offer to acquire, lease, exchange or obtain an option on the Property. Seller, however, shall have no obligation to Broker under paragraph 4A(2) unless, not later than **3 calendar days** after the end of the Listing Period or any extension or cancellation, Broker has given Seller a written notice of the names of such Prospective Buyers.
   OR **(3)** If, without Broker's prior written consent, the Property is withdrawn from sale, conveyed, leased, rented, otherwise transferred, or made unmarketable by a voluntary act of Seller during the Listing Period, or any extension.
   B. If completion of the sale is prevented by a party to the transaction other than Seller, then compensation due under paragraph 4A shall be payable only if and when Seller collects damages by suit, arbitration, settlement or otherwise, and then in an amount equal to the lesser of one-half of the damages recovered or the above compensation, after first deducting title and escrow expenses and the expenses of collection, if any.
   C. In addition, Seller agrees to pay Broker: _____
   D. Seller has been advised of Broker's policy regarding cooperation with, and the amount of compensation offered to, other brokers.
   (1) Broker is authorized to cooperate with and compensate brokers participating through the multiple listing service(s) ("MLS") by offering to MLS brokers out of Broker's compensation specified in 4A, either ☐ _____ percent of the purchase price, or ☐ $ _____ .
   (2) Broker is authorized to cooperate with and compensate brokers operating outside the MLS as per Broker's policy.
   E. Seller hereby irrevocably assigns to Broker the above compensation from Seller's funds and proceeds in escrow. Broker may submit this Agreement, as instructions to compensate Broker pursuant to paragraph 4A, to any escrow regarding the Property involving Seller and a buyer, Prospective Buyer or other transferee.
   F. **(1)** Seller represents that Seller has not previously entered into a listing agreement with another broker regarding the Property, unless specified as follows: _____
   (2) Seller warrants that Seller has no obligation to pay compensation to any other broker regarding the Property unless the Property is transferred to any of the following individuals or entities: _____
   _____
   (3) If the Property is sold to anyone listed above during the time Seller is obligated to compensate another broker: **(i)** Broker is not entitled to compensation under this Agreement; and **(ii)** Broker is not obligated to represent Seller in such transaction.

© 2013, California Association of REALTORS®, Inc.

Seller's Initials (_____) (_____)

RLA REVISED 11/13 (PAGE 1 OF 5)

Reviewed by _____ Date _____

EQUAL HOUSING OPPORTUNITY

RESIDENTIAL LISTING AGREEMENT - EXCLUSIVE (RLA PAGE 1 OF 5)

Agent: WALT HUBER   Phone: Fax: Prepared using zipForm® software
Broker: WALT HUBER REALTOR

Property Address: 123 Sail Avenue
Marina del Rey, CA 90292 _____ Date: _____

5. MULTIPLE LISTING SERVICE:

A. Broker is a participant/subscriber to _____ Multiple Listing Service (MLS) and possibly others. Unless otherwise instructed in writing the Property will be listed with the MLS(s) specified above. That MLS is (or if checked ☐ is not) the primary MLS for the geographic area of the Property. All terms of the transaction, including sales price and financing, if applicable, (i) will be provided to the MLS in which the property is listed for publication, dissemination and use by persons and entities on terms approved by the MLS and (ii) may be provided to the MLS even if the Property is not listed with the MLS.

BENEFITS OF USING THE MLS; IMPACT OF OPTING OUT OF THE MLS; PRESENTING ALL OFFERS

WHAT IS AN MLS? The MLS is a database of properties for sale that is available and disseminated to and accessible by all other real estate agents who are participants or subscribers to the MLS. Property information submitted to the MLS describes the price, terms and conditions under which the Seller's property is offered for sale (including but not limited to the listing broker's offer of compensation to other brokers). It is likely that a significant number of real estate practitioners in any given area are participants or subscribers to the MLS. The MLS may also be part of a reciprocal agreement to which other multiple listing services belong. Real estate agents belonging to other multiple listing services that have reciprocal agreements with the MLS also have access to the information submitted to the MLS. The MLS may further transmit the MLS database to Internet sites that post property listings online.

EXPOSURE TO BUYERS THROUGH MLS: Listing property with an MLS exposes a seller's property to all real estate agents and brokers (and their potential buyer clients) who are participants or subscribers to the MLS or a reciprocating MLS.

CLOSED/PRIVATE LISTING CLUBS OR GROUPS: Closed or private listing clubs or groups are not the same as the MLS. The MLS referred to above is accessible to all eligible real estate licensees and provides broad exposure for a listed property. Private or closed listing clubs or groups of licensees may have been formed outside the MLS. Private or closed listing clubs or groups are accessible to a more limited number of licensees and generally offer less exposure for listed property. Whether listing property through a closed, private network - and excluding it from the MLS - is advantageous or disadvantageous to a seller, and why, should be discussed with the agent taking the Seller's listing.

NOT LISTING PROPERTY IN A LOCAL MLS: If the Property is listed in an MLS which does not cover the geographic area where the Property is located then real estate agents and brokers working that territory, and Buyers they represent looking for property in the neighborhood, may not be aware the Property is for sale.

OPTING OUT OF MLS: If Seller elects to exclude the Property from the MLS, Seller understands and acknowledges that: **(a)** real estate agents and brokers from other real estate offices, and their buyer clients, who have access to that MLS may not be aware that Seller's Property is offered for sale; **(b)** Information about Seller's Property will not be transmitted to various real estate Internet sites that are used by the public to search for property listings; **(c)** real estate agents, brokers and members of the public may be unaware of the terms and conditions under which Seller is marketing the Property.

REDUCTION IN EXPOSURE: Any reduction in exposure of the Property may lower the number of offers and negatively impact the sales price.

PRESENTING ALL OFFERS: Seller understands that Broker must present all offers received for Seller's Property unless Seller gives Broker written instructions to the contrary.

Seller's Initials _____ / _____   Broker's Initials _____ / _____

B. MLS rules generally provide that residential real property and vacant lot listings be submitted to the MLS within 2 days or some other period of time after all necessary signatures have been obtained on the listing agreement. Broker will not have to submit this listing to the MLS if, within that time, Broker submits to the MLS a form signed by Seller (C.A.R. Form SELM or the local equivalent form).

C. MLS rules allow MLS data to be made available by the MLS to additional Internet sites unless Broker gives the MLS instructions to the contrary. Seller acknowledges that for any of the below opt-out instructions to be effective, Seller must make them on a separate instruction to Broker signed by Seller (C.A.R. Form SELI or the local equivalent form). Specific information that can be excluded from the Internet as permitted by (or in accordance with) the MLS is as follows:

(1) Property Availability: Seller can instruct Broker to have the MLS not display the Property on the Internet.

(2) Property Address: Seller can instruct Broker to have the MLS not display the Property address on the Internet.

Seller understands that the above opt-outs would mean consumers searching for listings on the Internet may not see the Property or Property's address in response to their search.

(3) Feature Opt-Outs: Seller can instruct Broker to advise the MLS that Seller does not want visitors to MLS Participant or Subscriber Websites or Electronic Displays that display the Property listing to have the features below. Seller understands **(i)** that these opt-outs apply only to Websites or Electronic Displays of MLS Participants and Subscribers who are real estate broker and agent members of the MLS; **(ii)** that other Internet sites may or may not have the features set forth herein; and **(iii)** that neither Broker nor the MLS may have the ability to control or block such features on other Internet sites.

(a) Comments And Reviews: The ability to write comments or reviews about the Property on those sites; or the ability to link to another site containing such comments or reviews if the link is in immediate conjunction with the Property.

(b) Automated Estimate Of Value: The ability to create an automated estimate of value or to link to another site containing such an estimate of value if the link is in immediate conjuction with the Property.

Seller's Initials (_____) (_____)

Reviewed by _____ Date _____

EQUAL HOUSING OPPORTUNITY

Property Address: **123 Sail Avenue**
Marina del Rey, CA 90292 _____ Date: _____

6. **SELLER REPRESENTATIONS:** Seller represents that, unless otherwise specified in writing, Seller is unaware of: **(i)** any Notice of Default recorded against the Property; **(ii)** any delinquent amounts due under any loan secured by, or other obligation affecting, the Property; **(iii)** any bankruptcy, insolvency or similar proceeding affecting the Property; **(iv)** any litigation, arbitration, administrative action, government investigation or other pending or threatened action that affects or may affect the Property or Seller's ability to transfer it; and **(v)** any current, pending or proposed special assessments affecting the Property. Seller shall promptly notify Broker in writing if Seller becomes aware of any of these items during the Listing Period or any extension thereof.

7. **BROKER'S AND SELLER'S DUTIES: (a)** Broker agrees to exercise reasonable effort and due diligence to achieve the purposes of this Agreement. Unless Seller gives Broker written instructions to the contrary, Broker is authorized to **(i)** order reports and disclosures as necessary, **(ii)** advertise and market the Property by any method and in any medium selected by Broker, including MLS and the Internet, and, to the extent permitted by these media, control the dissemination of the information submitted to any medium; and **(iii)** disclose to any real estate licensee making an inquiry the receipt of any offers on the Property and the offering price of such offers. **(b)** Seller agrees to consider offers presented by Broker, and to act in good faith to accomplish the sale of the Property by, among other things, making the Property available for showing at reasonable times and, subject to paragraph 4F, referring to Broker all inquiries of any party interested in the Property. Seller is responsible for determining at what price to list and sell the Property. **Seller further agrees to indemnify, defend and hold Broker harmless from all claims, disputes, litigation, judgments attorney fees and costs arising from any incorrect information supplied by Seller, or from any material facts that Seller knows but fails to disclose.**

8. **DEPOSIT:** Broker is authorized to accept and hold on Seller's behalf any deposits to be applied toward the purchase price.

9. **AGENCY RELATIONSHIPS:**
    A. **Disclosure:** If the Property includes residential property with one-to-four dwelling units, Seller shall receive a "Disclosure Regarding Agency Relationships" (C.A.R. Form AD) prior to entering into this Agreement.
    B. **Seller Representation:** Broker shall represent Seller in any resulting transaction, except as specified in paragraph 4F.
    C. **Possible Dual Agency With Buyer:** Depending upon the circumstances, it may be necessary or appropriate for Broker to act as an agent for both Seller and buyer, exchange party, or one or more additional parties ("Buyer"). Broker shall, as soon as practicable, disclose to Seller any election to act as a dual agent representing both Seller and Buyer. If a Buyer is procured directly by Broker or an associate-licensee in Broker's firm, Seller hereby consents to Broker acting as a dual agent for Seller and Buyer. In the event of an exchange, Seller hereby consents to Broker collecting compensation from additional parties for services rendered, provided there is disclosure to all parties of such agency and compensation. Seller understands and agrees that: **(i)** Broker, without the prior written consent of Seller, will not disclose to Buyer that Seller is willing to sell the Property at a price less than the listing price; **(ii)** Broker, without the prior written consent of Buyer, will not disclose to Seller that Buyer is willing to pay a price greater than the offered price; and **(iii)** except for (i) and (ii) above, a dual agent is obligated to disclose known facts materially affecting the value or desirability of the Property to both parties.
    D. **Other Sellers:** Seller understands that Broker may have or obtain listings on other properties, and that potential buyers may consider, make offers on, or purchase through Broker, property the same as or similar to Seller's Property. Seller consents to Broker's representation of sellers and buyers of other properties before, during and after the end of this Agreement.
    E. **Confirmation:** If the Property includes residential property with one-to-four dwelling units, Broker shall confirm the agency relationship described above, or as modified, in writing, prior to or concurrent with Seller's execution of a purchase agreement.

10. **SECURITY AND INSURANCE:** Broker is not responsible for loss of or damage to personal or real property, or person, whether attributable to use of a keysafe/lockbox, a showing of the Property, or otherwise. Third parties, including, but not limited to, appraisers, inspectors, brokers and prospective buyers, may have access to, and take videos and photographs of, the interior of the Property. Seller agrees: **(i)** to take reasonable precautions to safeguard and protect valuables that might be accessible during showings of the Property; and **(ii)** to obtain insurance to protect against these risks. Broker does not maintain insurance to protect Seller.

11. **PHOTOGRAPHS AND INTERNET ADVERTISING:**
    A. In order to effectively market the Property for sale it is often necessary to provide photographs, virtual tours and other media to buyers. Seller agrees (or ☐ if checked, does not agree) that Broker may photograph or otherwise electronically capture images of the exterior and interior of the Property ("Images") for static and/or virtual tours of the Property by buyers and others on Broker's website, the MLS, and other marketing sites. Seller acknowledges that once Images are placed on the Internet neither Broker nor Seller has control over who can view such Images and what use viewers may make of the Images, or how long such Images may remain available on the Internet. Seller further agrees that such Images are the property of Broker and that Broker may use such Images for advertisement of Broker's business in the future.
    B. Seller acknowledges that prospective buyers and/or other persons coming onto the property may take photographs, videos or other images of the property. Seller understands that Broker does not have the ability to control or block the taking and use of Images by any such persons. (If checked) ☐ Seller instructs Broker to publish in the MLS that taking of Images is limited to those persons preparing Appraisal or Inspection reports. Seller acknowledges that unauthorized persons may take images who do not have access to or have not read any limiting instruction in the MLS or who take images regardless of any limiting instruction in the MLS. Once Images are taken and/or put into electronic display on the Internet or otherwise, neither Broker nor Seller has control over who views such Images nor what use viewers may make of the Images.

12. **KEYSAFE/LOCKBOX:** A keysafe/lockbox is designed to hold a key to the Property to permit access to the Property by Broker, cooperating brokers, MLS participants, their authorized licensees and representatives, authorized inspectors, and accompanied prospective buyers. Broker, cooperating brokers, MLS and Associations/Boards of REALTORS® are **not** insurers against injury, theft, loss, vandalism or damage attributed to the use of a keysafe/lockbox. Seller does (or if checked ☐ does not) authorize Broker to install a keysafe/lockbox. If Seller does not occupy the Property, Seller shall be responsible for obtaining occupant(s)' written permission for use of a keysafe/lockbox (C.A.R. Form KLA).

Seller's Initials (_____) (_____)

Reviewed by _____ Date _____

EQUAL HOUSING OPPORTUNITY

123 Sail Avenue
Property Address: Marina del Rey, CA 90292 _____ Date: _____

13. SIGN: Seller does (or if checked ☐ does not) authorize Broker to install a FOR SALE/SOLD sign on the Property.
14. EQUAL HOUSING OPPORTUNITY: The Property is offered in compliance with federal, state and local anti-discrimination laws.
15. ATTORNEY FEES: In any action, proceeding or arbitration between Seller and Broker regarding the obligation to pay compensation under this Agreement, the prevailing Seller or Broker shall be entitled to reasonable attorney fees and costs from the non-prevailing Seller or Broker, except as provided in paragraph 19A.
16. ADDITIONAL TERMS: ☐ REO Advisory Listing (C.A.R. Form REOL) ☐ Short Sale Information and Advisory (C.A.R. Form SSIA)
_____
_____
_____
_____
_____
_____

17. MANAGEMENT APPROVAL: If an associate-licensee in Broker's office (salesperson or broker-associate) enters into this Agreement on Broker's behalf, and Broker or Manager does not approve of its terms, Broker or Manager has the right to cancel this Agreement, in writing, within **5 Days** After its execution.
18. SUCCESSORS AND ASSIGNS: This Agreement shall be binding upon Seller and Seller's successors and assigns.
19. DISPUTE RESOLUTION:
  A. MEDIATION: Seller and Broker agree to mediate any dispute or claim arising between them regarding the obligation to pay compensation under this Agreement, before resorting to arbitration or court action. Mediation fees, if any, shall be divided equally among the parties involved. If, for any dispute or claim to which this paragraph applies, any party (i) commences an action without first attempting to resolve the matter through mediation, or (ii) before commencement of an action, refuses to mediate after a request has been made, then that party shall not be entitled to recover attorney fees, even if they would otherwise be available to that party in any such action. THIS MEDIATION PROVISION APPLIES WHETHER OR NOT THE ARBITRATION PROVISION IS INITIALED. **Exclusions from this mediation agreement are specified in paragraph 19C.**
  B. ARBITRATION OF DISPUTES:
  Seller and Broker agree that any dispute or claim in Law or equity arising between them regarding the obligation to pay compensation under this Agreement, which is not settled through mediation, shall be decided by neutral, binding arbitration. The arbitrator shall be a retired judge or justice, or an attorney with at least 5 years of residential real estate Law experience, unless the parties mutually agree to a different arbitrator. The parties shall have the right to discovery in accordance with Code of Civil Procedure §1283.05. In all other respects, the arbitration shall be conducted in accordance with Title 9 of Part 3 of the Code of Civil Procedure. Judgment upon the award of the arbitrator(s) may be entered into any court having jurisdiction. Enforcement of this agreement to arbitrate shall be governed by the Federal Arbitration Act. Exclusions from this arbitration agreement are specified in paragraph 19C.
  "NOTICE: BY INITIALING IN THE SPACE BELOW YOU ARE AGREEING TO HAVE ANY DISPUTE ARISING OUT OF THE MATTERS INCLUDED IN THE 'ARBITRATION OF DISPUTES' PROVISION DECIDED BY NEUTRAL ARBITRATION AS PROVIDED BY CALIFORNIA LAW AND YOU ARE GIVING UP ANY RIGHTS YOU MIGHT POSSESS TO HAVE THE DISPUTE LITIGATED IN A COURT OR JURY TRIAL. BY INITIALING IN THE SPACE BELOW YOU ARE GIVING UP YOUR JUDICIAL RIGHTS TO DISCOVERY AND APPEAL, UNLESS THOSE RIGHTS ARE SPECIFICALLY INCLUDED IN THE 'ARBITRATION OF DISPUTES' PROVISION. IF YOU REFUSE TO SUBMIT TO ARBITRATION AFTER AGREEING TO THIS PROVISION, YOU MAY BE COMPELLED TO ARBITRATE UNDER THE AUTHORITY OF THE CALIFORNIA CODE OF CIVIL PROCEDURE. YOUR AGREEMENT TO THIS ARBITRATION PROVISION IS VOLUNTARY."
  "WE HAVE READ AND UNDERSTAND THE FOREGOING AND AGREE TO SUBMIT DISPUTES ARISING OUT OF THE MATTERS INCLUDED IN THE 'ARBITRATION OF DISPUTES' PROVISION TO NEUTRAL ARBITRATION."

  Seller's Initials _____ / _____   Broker's Initials _____ / _____

  C. ADDITIONAL MEDIATION AND ARBITRATION TERMS: The following matters shall be excluded from mediation and arbitration: (i) a judicial or non-judicial foreclosure or other action or proceeding to enforce a deed of trust, mortgage or installment land sale contract as defined in Civil Code §2985; (ii) an unlawful detainer action; (iii) the filing or enforcement of a mechanic's lien; and (iv) any matter that is within the jurisdiction of a probate, small claims or bankruptcy court. The filing of a court action to enable the recording of a notice of pending action, for order of attachment, receivership, injunction, or other provisional remedies, shall not constitute a waiver or violation of the mediation and arbitration provisions.

Seller's Initials (_____) (_____)

Reviewed by _____ Date _____

Property Address: *123 Sail Avenue*
Marina del Rey, CA 90292 _____ Date: _____

20. **ENTIRE AGREEMENT:** All prior discussions, negotiations and agreements between the parties concerning the subject matter of this Agreement are superseded by this Agreement, which constitutes the entire contract and a complete and exclusive expression of their agreement, and may not be contradicted by evidence of any prior agreement or contemporaneous oral agreement. If any provision of this Agreement is held to be ineffective or invalid, the remaining provisions will nevertheless be given full force and effect. This Agreement and any supplement, addendum or modification, including any photocopy or facsimile, may be executed in counterparts.

21. **OWNERSHIP, TITLE AND AUTHORITY:** Seller warrants that: (i) Seller is the owner of the Property; (ii) no other persons or entities have title to the Property; and (iii) Seller has the authority to both execute this Agreement and sell the Property. Exceptions to ownership, title and authority are as follows: _____ .

By signing below, Seller acknowledges that Seller has read, understands, received a copy of and agrees to the terms of this Agreement.

Seller _____ Date _____
Address _____ City _____ State _____ Zip _____
Telephone _____ Fax _____ Email _____

Seller _____ Date _____
Address _____ City _____ State _____ Zip _____
Telephone _____ Fax _____ Email _____

Real Estate Broker (Firm) _____ Cal BRE Lic. # _____
By (Agent) _____ Cal BRE Lic. # _____ Date _____
Address _____ City _____ State _____ Zip _____
Telephone _____ Fax _____ Email _____

© 1991-2013, California Association of REALTORS®, Inc. United States copyright law (Title 17 U.S. Code) forbids the unauthorized distribution, display and reproduction of this form, or any portion thereof, by photocopy machine or any other means, including facsimile or computerized formats.

THIS FORM HAS BEEN APPROVED BY THE CALIFORNIA ASSOCIATION OF REALTORS® (C.A.R.). NO REPRESENTATION IS MADE AS TO THE LEGAL VALIDITY OR ACCURACY OF ANY PROVISION IN ANY SPECIFIC TRANSACTION. A REAL ESTATE BROKER IS THE PERSON QUALIFIED TO ADVISE ON REAL ESTATE TRANSACTIONS. IF YOU DESIRE LEGAL OR TAX ADVICE, CONSULT AN APPROPRIATE PROFESSIONAL.

Published and Distributed by:
REAL ESTATE BUSINESS SERVICES, INC.
a subsidiary of the California Association of REALTORS®
525 South Virgil Avenue, Los Angeles, California 90020

Reviewed by _____ Date _____

RLA REVISED 11/13 (PAGE 5 OF 5)

RESIDENTIAL LISTING AGREEMENT - EXCLUSIVE (RLA PAGE 5 OF 5) Untitled

The "exclusive authorization and right to sell" is the most desirable listing from the broker's point of view, eliminating most, if not all, commission misunderstandings.

Because you, as the listing broker, will reap the benefit of a commission regardless of who sells, you and your office coworkers are more likely to expend your full energies in the marketing of the property.

This type of listing often contains a section referred to as a *SAFETY CLAUSE, which is a negotiated period (any agreed time period) after the termination of the listing during which the listing broker may still be entitled to a commission if the property is sold to a buyer who was shown the property during the listing period.* To protect yourself, you must furnish the owner/seller, within three days after expiration of the listing, with a list of persons to whom you, or any cooperating broker, have shown the property during the listing period. If the owner or another broker sells the property to someone on the list within the protected period (usually 90 days), as the original listing broker, you should be entitled to a commission.

Sending a thank-you email with the address of the property you've shown a client creates goodwill as well as written proof that you did indeed show a property and on what date for the purposes of the Safety Clause.

c. Net Listing

Here, the compensation is not definitely determined. A *NET LISTING provides that the agent is to retain all money received in excess of a predetermined net price to the owner.* For example, if the owner stipulates that he or she wants no less than $375,000 out of the deal and you find a buyer for $390,000, your compensation is the difference—$15,000. The terms of the listing might require that the owner is to get no less than a fixed amount after all expenses of sale (other than brokerage) and after paying off all existing liens and encumbrances.

Although acceptable in California, net listings are discouraged as they frequently result in charges of misrepresentation or fraud.

As the agent, you must disclose the full amount of your compensation before the owners bind themselves to accepting an offer. A violation of this real estate law (**Section 10176(g) of the Business and Professions Code**) constitutes grounds for revocation or suspension of your license.

It's imperative that you, as the broker, explain in writing the exact consequence of a net listing, so there is no confusion about any earned commission.

The net listing may be either exclusive or nonexclusive. Thus, we see that there is no pure net listing type of agreement without combining it under either the open, exclusive agency, or exclusive right to sell listing contracts.

3. MULTIPLE LISTING (Multiple Listing Service — MLS)

A *MULTIPLE LISTING SERVICE (MLS)* *is a marketing database of listing of properties for sale, set up by a group of cooperating real estate brokers. It provides details about the property as well as the commission split being offered by the listing broker. Each MLS has its own rules and procedures.* If the membership are all REALTORS®, then the rules are patterned on regulations published by the National Association of REALTORS®.

A Multiple Listing Service (MLS) is an association of real estate brokers who pool their listings, recent sales, and share commissions and information on a regular basis.

The owner gives the listing to a broker, usually (though not necessarily) on an exclusive basis, authorizing him or her to distribute a exclusive authorization and right to sell to members of the MLS.

Ordinarily, if you are the broker who secures the multiple listing, you exercise control over any negotiations and other rights incident to the listing. If you, as the listing broker, "sell the property," you are entitled to the entire commission. On the other hand, if another member/broker "sells the property," the commission is divided between you both in accordance with the pre-negotiated terms in the listing contract between the seller and broker.

For the broker, the assurance of a more concentrated marketing effort provides a greater chance for a faster sale at top price; hence, an easier and larger commission and more money for the seller.

Because of the large number of licensees accessing a MLS, the property gains the advantage of wide exposure.

a. MLS on the Internet

All Multiple Listing Services are on the Internet and are member interactive, allowing retrieval and input from MLS participants.

All pending and sold properties must be updated on an MLS within 48 hours or the association will fine the listing office and/or agent, unless the client prohibits such disclosure.

Internet MLS postings include all the pertinent information about a property found on a listing agreement, plus additional information essential to agents who intend to show and sell the property. This information includes some basics like location, price, physical description, school district, and sewer hookup information, as well as the location and type of lockbox. It also lists contact information, like whether to contact the seller or the listing agent, delineates the commission split, and any other caveats attached to the selling of the property. The fact that the seller has a biting dog, for example, is a piece of valuable information you might find on an MLS posting.

b. Office Exclusive

In the sale of a residence, the most common marketing practice is to give an "exclusive authorization and right to sell" to a member of a multiple listing service, wherein each of the members is deemed to be a cooperating agent. This is, of course, done with approval of the owner. If such consent is not given, an **OFFICE EXCLUSIVE** *is generally obtained, that is, the listing agent, along with members of the same firm only, are given permission to show and to submit offers.* The seller must give this approval in writing, which must be forwarded to notify the MLS association.

Occasionally, clients will make an offer through their own agent after you show them the property. You have done the work, but the other agent reaps the benefits. Always inquire from prospective buyers if they are working with another agent. Some agents ask for a loyalty agreement from their buyers wherein, for a specified period, the buyers agree to transact any offer on the properties shown by their agents.

4. Buyer's Listing (Working for Buyer)

May a broker represent a buyer, or even both parties to a transaction? Yes. In the case of a dual agency, the law provides that a broker may act as agent for both parties to a transaction and can collect compensation from them if there is full disclosure to both, and each agrees in writing to the arrangement. Agency relationships and commission agreements, then, are not restricted solely to sellers.

The CAR® form, **Buyer Representation Agreement (BRE),** can be used to create an agency relationship and commission agreement whereby the buyer pays the commission. It contains a provision for separate compensation to be paid if the agent is successful in obtaining an option on the property that the buyer fails to exercise. Compensation can be based upon commissions, consultation fees, *per diem* charges, or any combination thereof.

5. Whom Does the Broker Represent?

Brokers are ordinarily agents of the parties who first employ them. By law, a listing broker is the agent of the seller of the property in every instance.

There are, however, many complicating factors in applying the law of agency to real estate brokerage transactions. The problem is not one of determining whose agent the broker is with reference to the transaction as a whole, but of determining on whose behalf the broker is acting as to each particular aspect of the transaction. For example, a listing broker who accepts a deposit toward purchase from an offeror holds the deposit as agent for the offeror until there is an acceptance of the offer by the seller.

If, without the knowledge and consent of the principal (seller), the listing broker acts for the prospective buyer, the principal may, when discovering this fact, declare the listing contract void. This is true even though the transaction is

a good one for the seller and even though the buyer acts in good faith and was unaware of the double (dual) agency.

Although brokers owe the utmost duty and loyalty to those who employ them, brokers must deal fairly and honestly with both their clients and their customers/buyers at all times.

> **Be careful! When representing the seller, you should avoid discussing financial terms with a buyer or you may be inadvertently creating a dual agency that you have not disclosed.**

II. Agency Relationship Disclosure Act

Listing and selling agents are required to provide both buyers and sellers with specified written (and oral) agency disclosures. This California law applies to all transactions involving one-to-four residential units for sale or rent and manufactured homes.

A written agency disclosure must be delivered to the seller prior to the signing of the listing contract. As a licensee, you're also required to disclose to the buyer and seller whether you're acting as seller's agent, buyer's agent, or dual agent. The agency relationship must thereafter be confirmed in written form when a contract (purchase agreement or lease) is drafted. The CAR® **Disclosure Regarding Real Estate Agency Relationship (AD)** form can be used to accomplish this disclosure, which is required by our legislature, (see **Figure 3-2**). Additionally, this confirmation is included in the CAR® Purchase Agreement (RPA-CA) contract.

The disclosure form must set forth the agency relationship between the buyers and sellers and you, the licensee, based upon your relationship to the buyer and/or seller.

Only one of two agency relationships is possible.

A. SINGLE AGENCY (Only Buyer's Agent or Seller's Agent)

As a licensee, single agency indicates that you are an agent for only one party, representing **either the seller or the buyer**, but not both. Here the principal (seller or buyer) must specifically authorize you to perform acts on his or her behalf.

The listing agent must represent the seller, but may also represent the buyer with the knowledge and consent of both parties (Dual Agency).

B. DUAL AGENCY (Agent Representing Both Buyer and Seller)

In this case, you, the licensee, represent **both the buying and selling parties**. Being in the delicate position of representing both parties, you must be completely neutral to avoid a conflict of interest. You may be privy to personal information

Figure 3-2

CALIFORNIA
ASSOCIATION
OF REALTORS®

DISCLOSURE REGARDING
REAL ESTATE AGENCY RELATIONSHIP
(Listing Firm to Seller)
(As required by the Civil Code)
(C.A.R. Form AD, Revised 11/12)

☐ (If checked) This form is being provided in connection with a transaction for a leaseholder interest in a dwelling exceeding one year as per Civil Code section 2079.13(j) and (l).

When you enter into a discussion with a real estate agent regarding a real estate transaction, you should from the outset understand what type of agency relationship or representation you wish to have with the agent in the transaction.

SELLER'S AGENT
A Seller's agent under a listing agreement with the Seller acts as the agent for the Seller only. A Seller's agent or a subagent of that agent has the following affirmative obligations:
To the Seller: A Fiduciary duty of utmost care, integrity, honesty and loyalty in dealings with the Seller.
To the Buyer and the Seller:
    (a) Diligent exercise of reasonable skill and care in performance of the agent's duties.
    (b) A duty of honest and fair dealing and good faith.
    (c) A duty to disclose all facts known to the agent materially affecting the value or desirability of the property that are not known to, or within the diligent attention and observation of, the parties. An agent is not obligated to reveal to either party any confidential information obtained from the other party that does not involve the affirmative duties set forth above.

BUYER'S AGENT
A selling agent can, with a Buyer's consent, agree to act as agent for the Buyer only. In these situations, the agent is not the Seller's agent, even if by agreement the agent may receive compensation for services rendered, either in full or in part from the Seller. An agent acting only for a Buyer has the following affirmative obligations:
To the Buyer: A fiduciary duty of utmost care, integrity, honesty and loyalty in dealings with the Buyer.
To the Buyer and the Seller:
    (a) Diligent exercise of reasonable skill and care in performance of the agent's duties.
    (b) A duty of honest and fair dealing and good faith.
    (c) A duty to disclose all facts known to the agent materially affecting the value or desirability of the property that are not known to, or within the diligent attention and observation of, the parties.
An agent is not obligated to reveal to either party any confidential information obtained from the other party that does not involve the affirmative duties set forth above.

AGENT REPRESENTING BOTH SELLER AND BUYER
A real estate agent, either acting directly or through one or more associate licensees, can legally be the agent of both the Seller and the Buyer in a transaction, but only with the knowledge and consent of both the Seller and the Buyer.
In a dual agency situation, the agent has the following affirmative obligations to both the Seller and the Buyer:
    (a) A fiduciary duty of utmost care, integrity, honesty and loyalty in the dealings with either the Seller or the Buyer.
    (b) Other duties to the Seller and the Buyer as stated above in their respective sections.
In representing both Seller and Buyer, the agent may not, without the express permission of the respective party, disclose to the other party that the Seller will accept a price less than the listing price or that the Buyer will pay a price greater than the price offered.
The above duties of the agent in a real estate transaction do not relieve a Seller or Buyer from the responsibility to protect his or her own interests. You should carefully read all agreements to assure that they adequately express your understanding of the transaction. A real estate agent is a person qualified to advise about real estate. If legal or tax advice is desired, consult a competent professional.
Throughout your real property transaction you may receive more than one disclosure form, depending upon the number of agents assisting in the transaction. The law requires each agent with whom you have more than a casual relationship to present you with this disclosure form. You should read its contents each time it is presented to you, considering the relationship between you and the real estate agent in your specific transaction. **This disclosure form includes the provisions of Sections 2079.13 to 2079.24, inclusive, of the Civil Code set forth on page 2. Read it carefully. I/WE ACKNOWLEDGE RECEIPT OF A COPY OF THIS DISCLOSURE AND THE PORTIONS OF THE CIVIL CODE PRINTED ON THE BACK (OR A SEPARATE PAGE).**

☐ Buyer ☐ Seller ☐ Landlord ☐ Tenant _____ Date _____

☐ Buyer ☐ Seller ☐ Landlord ☐ Tenant _____ Date _____

Agent _____ DRE Lic. # _____
      Real Estate Broker (Firm)

By _____ DRE Lic. # _____ Date _____
    (Salesperson or Broker-Associate)

Agency Disclosure Compliance (Civil Code §2079.14):
- When the listing brokerage company also represents Buyer/Tenant: The Listing Agent shall have one AD form signed by Seller/Landlord and a different AD form signed by Buyer/Tenant.
- When Seller/Landlord and Buyer/Tenant are represented by different brokerage companies: (i) the Listing Agent shall have one AD form signed by Seller/Landlord and (ii) the Buyer's/Tenant's Agent shall have one AD form signed by Buyer/Tenant and either that same or a different AD form presented to Seller/Landlord for signature prior to presentation of the offer. If the same form is used, Seller may sign here:

(SELLER/LANDLORD: DO NOT SIGN HERE)   **(SELLER/LANDLORD: DO NOT SIGN HERE)**
Seller/Landlord _____ Date _____   Seller/Landlord _____ Date _____

The copyright laws of the United States (Title 17 U.S. Code) forbid the unauthorized reproduction of this form, or any portion thereof, by photocopy machine or any other means, including facsimile or computerized formats. Copyright © 1991-2010, CALIFORNIA ASSOCIATION OF REALTORS®, INC. ALL RIGHTS RESERVED.

Reviewed by _____ Date _____

EQUAL HOUSING OPPORTUNITY

AD REVISED 11/12 (PAGE 1 OF 2)
DISCLOSURE REGARDING REAL ESTATE AGENCY RELATIONSHIP (AD PAGE 1 OF 2)

Agent: WALT HUBER	Phone:	Fax:	Prepared using zipForm® software
Broker:			

CIVIL CODE SECTIONS 2079.24 (2079.16 APPEARS ON THE FRONT)

2079.13 As used in Sections 2079.14 to 2079.24, inclusive, the following terms have the following meanings:
(a) "Agent" means a person acting under provisions of title 9 (commencing with Section 2295) in a real property transaction, and includes a person who is licensed as a real estate broker under Chapter 3 (commencing with Section 10130) of Part 1 of Division 4 of the Business and Professions Code, and under whose license a listing is executed or an offer to purchase is obtained. **(b)** "Associate licensee" means a person who is licensed as a real estate broker or salesperson under Chapter 3 (commencing with Section 10130) of Part 1 of Division 4 of the Business and Professions Code and who is either licensed under a broker or has entered into a written contract with a broker to act as the broker's agent in connection with acts requiring a real estate license and to function under the broker's supervision in the capacity of an associate licensee. The agent in the real property transaction bears responsibility for his or her associate licensees who perform as agents of the agent. When an associate licensee owes a duty to any principal, or to any buyer or seller who is not a principal, in a real property transaction, that duty is equivalent to the duty owed to that party by the broker for whom the associate licensee functions. **(c)** "Buyer" means a transferee in a real property transaction, and includes a person who executes an offer to purchase real property from a seller through an agent, or who seeks the services of an agent in more than a casual, transitory, or preliminary manner, with the object of entering into a real property transaction. "Buyer" includes vendee or lessee. **(d)** "Dual agent" means an agent acting, either directly or through an associate licensee, as agent for both the seller and the buyer in a real property transaction. **(e)** "Listing agreement" means a contract between an owner of real property and an agent, by which the agent has been authorized to sell the real property or to find or obtain a buyer. **(f)** "Listing agent" means a person who has obtained a listing of real property to act as an agent for compensation. **(g)** "Listing price" is the amount expressed in dollars specified in the listing for which the seller is willing to sell the real property through the listing agent. **(h)** "Offering price" is the amount expressed in dollars specified in an offer to purchase for which the buyer is willing to buy the real property. **(i)** "Offer to purchase" means a written contract executed by a buyer acting through a selling agent which becomes the contract for the sale of the real property upon acceptance by the seller. **(j)** "Real property" means any estate specified by subdivision (1) or (2) of Section 761 in property which constitutes or is improved with one to four dwelling units, any leasehold in this type of property exceeding one year's duration, and mobile homes, when offered for sale or sold through an agent pursuant to the authority contained in Section 10131.6 of the Business and Professions Code. **(k)** "Real property transaction" means a transaction for the sale of real property in which an agent is employed by one or more of the principals to act in that transaction, and includes a listing or an offer to purchase. **(l)** "Sell," "sale," or "sold" refers to a transaction for the transfer of real property from the seller to the buyer, and includes exchanges of real property between the seller and buyer, transactions for the creation of a real property sales contract within the meaning of Section 2985, and transactions for the creation of a leasehold exceeding one year's duration. **(m)** "Seller" means the transferor in a real property transaction, and includes an owner who lists real property with an agent, whether or not a transfer results, or who receives an offer to purchase real property of which he or she is the owner from an agent on behalf of another. "Seller" includes both a vendor and a lessor. **(n)** "Selling agent" means a listing agent who acts alone, or an agent who acts in cooperation with a listing agent, and who sells or finds and obtains a buyer for the real property, or an agent who locates property for a buyer or who finds a buyer for a property for which no listing exists and presents an offer to purchase to the seller. **(o)** "Subagent" means a person to whom an agent delegates agency powers as provided in Article 5 (commencing with Section 2349) of Chapter 1 of Title 9. However, "subagent" does not include an associate licensee who is acting under the supervision of an agent in a real property transaction.
2079.14 Listing agents and selling agents shall provide the seller and buyer in a real property transaction with a copy of the disclosure form specified in Section 2079.16, and, except as provided in subdivision (c), shall obtain a signed acknowledgement of receipt from that seller or buyer, except as provided in this section or Section 2079.15, as follows: **(a)** The listing agent, if any, shall provide the disclosure form to the seller prior to entering into the listing agreement. **(b)** The selling agent shall provide the disclosure form to the seller as soon as practicable prior to presenting the seller with an offer to purchase, unless the selling agent previously provided the seller with a copy of the disclosure form pursuant to subdivision (a). **(c)** Where the selling agent does not deal on a face-to-face basis with the seller, the disclosure form prepared by the selling agent may be furnished to the seller (and acknowledgement of receipt obtained for the selling agent from the seller) by the listing agent, or the selling agent may deliver the disclosure form by certified mail addressed to the seller at his or her last known address, in which case no signed acknowledgement of receipt is required. **(d)** The selling agent shall provide the disclosure form to the buyer as soon as practicable prior to execution of the buyer's offer to purchase, except that if the offer to purchase is not prepared by the selling agent, the selling agent shall present the disclosure form to the buyer not later than the next business day after the selling agent receives the offer to purchase from the buyer.
2079.15 In any circumstance in which the seller or buyer refuses to sign an acknowledgement of receipt pursuant to Section 2079.14, the agent, or an associate licensee acting for an agent, shall set forth, sign, and date a written declaration of the facts of the refusal.
2079.16 Reproduced on Page 1 of this AD form.
2079.17 (a) As soon as practicable, the selling agent shall disclose to the buyer and seller whether the selling agent is acting in the real property transaction exclusively as the buyer's agent, exclusively as the seller's agent, or as a dual agent representing both the buyer and the seller. This relationship shall be confirmed in the contract to purchase and sell real property or in a separate writing executed or acknowledged by the seller, the buyer, and the selling agent prior to or coincident with execution of that contract by the buyer and the seller, respectively. **(b)** As soon as practicable, the listing agent shall disclose to the seller whether the listing agent is acting in the real property transaction exclusively as the seller's agent, or as a dual agent representing both the buyer and seller. This relationship shall be confirmed in the contract to purchase and sell real property or in a separate writing executed or acknowledged by the seller and the listing agent prior to or coincident with the execution of that contract by the seller.
(c) The confirmation required by subdivisions (a) and (b) shall be in the following form.

_____(DO NOT COMPLETE, SAMPLE ONLY)_____ is the agent of (check one): ☐ the seller exclusively; or ☐ both the buyer and seller.
(Name of Listing Agent)

_____(DO NOT COMPLETE, SAMPLE ONLY)_____ is the agent of (check one): ☑ the buyer exclusively; or ☐ the seller exclusively; or
(Name of Selling Agent if not the same as the Listing Agent) ☐ both the buyer and seller.

(d) The disclosures and confirmation required by this section shall be in addition to the disclosure required by Section 2079.14.
2079.18 No selling agent in a real property transaction may act as an agent for the buyer only, when the selling agent is also acting as the listing agent in the transaction.
2079.19 The payment of compensation or the obligation to pay compensation to an agent by the seller or buyer is not necessarily determinative of a particular agency relationship between an agent and the seller or buyer. A listing agent and a selling agent may agree to share any compensation or commission paid, or any right to any compensation or commission for which an obligation arises as the result of a real estate transaction, and the terms of any such agreement shall not necessarily be determinative of a particular relationship.
2079.20 Nothing in this article prevents an agent from selecting, as a condition of the agent's employment, a specific form of agency relationship not specifically prohibited by this article if the requirements of Section 2079.14 and Section 2079.17 are complied with.
2079.21 A dual agent shall not disclose to the buyer that the seller is willing to sell the property at a price less than the listing price, without the express written consent of the seller. A dual agent shall not disclose to the seller that the buyer is willing to pay a price greater than the offering price, without the express written consent of the buyer. This section does not alter in any way the duty or responsibility of a dual agent to any principal with respect to confidential information other than price.
2079.22 Nothing in this article precludes a listing agent from also being a selling agent, and the combination of these functions in one agent does not, of itself, make that agent a dual agent.
2079.23 A contract between the principal and agent may be modified or altered to change the agency relationship at any time before the performance of the act which is the object of the agency with the written consent of the parties to the agency relationship.
2079.24 Nothing in this article shall be construed to either diminish the duty of disclosure owed buyers and sellers by agents and their associate licensees, subagents, and employees or to relieve agents and their associate licensees, subagents, and employees from liability for their conduct in connection with acts governed by this article or for any breach of a fiduciary duty or a duty of disclosure.

Buyer's Initials (_____) (_____)   Seller's Initials (_____) (_____)

Published and Distributed by:
REAL ESTATE BUSINESS SERVICES, INC.
a subsidiary of the CALIFORNIA ASSOCIATION OF REALTORS®
525 South Virgil Avenue, Los Angeles, California 90020

AD REVISED 11/12 (PAGE 2 OF 2)

Reviewed by _____ Date _____

EQUAL HOUSING OPPORTUNITY

DISCLOSURE REGARDING REAL ESTATE AGENCY RELATIONSHIP (AD PAGE 2 OF 2)

Untitled

you can't divulge to the other party, such as a seller's willingness to accept less for a home, or a buyer's intent to offer more. Because an agent, by law, is a fiduciary, you have a duty of utmost care, integrity, honesty, and loyalty to both the buyer and seller, representing their separate interests independently. This task requires a certain amount of diplomacy, but it has some real advantages for you as an agent, not the least of which is control and knowledge of all pertinent information of the transaction from start to finish.

If either party can prove that a "material fact" was not clearly disclosed, you may have breached your required fiduciary duty.

For self-protection, you must inform both parties of your dual representation, and immediately obtain written consent from both parties, and disclose all relevant facts to each.

You may receive more than one agency disclosure form depending upon the number of agents assisting in the transaction. A buyer, seller, landlord, and/or tenant must acknowledge receipt of a signed copy of the agency disclosure form.

1. Broker Relationship

It is important to remember that, by definition and in practice, as a salesperson, you are an agent of your broker.

All listings you obtain are taken in the name of your broker, not your own. Hence, the broker is the agent of the sellers, even if the broker has never met the sellers, because when you took the listing, you were acting on behalf of the broker. By the same token, when you write an offer for a buyer, you are also representing your broker in that transaction.

If you leave the employ of a broker, your listings are owned by your broker and stay with that broker, although the departing agent may retain some rights to any resulting compensation.

III. Preparing for the Listing Appointment

The real estate transaction begins even before the listing interview. A **LISTING INTERVIEW/CONSULTATION** *is an appointment with a prospective seller with the intent of persuading that seller to list a property with you at a fair market price.* You will need to do a market analysis of the area before you call upon the owner with whom you've made an appointment. This research is an absolute must if you're to obtain a salable listing, that is, one that is accepted on the market as being competitive.

An overpriced listing is not much better than no listing at all. Once salespeople know a property is overpriced, it can take months before they will show it again.

As will be seen, the time involved in research can be greatly reduced if you have access to current files. You can also subscribe to various services, such as the multiple listing service in the community, or to agencies that provide sales and other data.

Now, imagine yourself planning to conduct a listing interview. Drive through the area before visiting with the prospective sellers. You'll want to check "just sold" properties in the vicinity of the subject property, determine the type of sale (whether VA, FHA, or conventional), check other brokers' current listings, in addition to those recently expired, determine what "For Sale By Owner (FSBO)" signs are in the area, and be prepared to answer why owners are selling without benefit of a broker. Further, you'll want to get a good feel of the area by observing its appearance, preferably during daylight, and, finally, driving up to the house to determine its **curb appeal**.

"Curb appeal" refers to how a house appears to a passerby, compared to the rest of the neighborhood. Have a picture of the house on the front page of your presentation.

You may want to complete as much of the listing form as possible before leaving your office. It helps to get down on paper many supporting facts and figures, thus conserving valuable time at the listing interview. You'll also impress the owners with your competency and efficiency. You may even compute the **SELLER'S PROCEEDS** *by calculating how much (cash) the seller will receive after payment of all liens and expenses, based upon a predetermined fair market value established through your research.* This allows the seller to focus on the net amount of cash he or she will receive.

You should, of course, arrive at the appointed time, as to be late may cause you to lose a client's confidence even before you start.

Remember: First impressions are the most lasting.

A. MEETING THE LISTING PROSPECT

When meeting prospective sellers at their home, start the conversation on a positive note, finding some feature of the home that you can honestly compliment, such as its cheerful atmosphere or attractive decorating. Be sincere because sellers see through forced compliments.

Ask to see the house and grounds, finding subjects of common interest as you preview the premises. At some time, you might inquire about their plans for relocating after the home is sold. This will aid you in finding out their "true motives for selling," thus helping to direct your efforts more effectively.

For instance, if the husband is being transferred or offered a better position by a competing employer, the sellers are highly motivated. They are likely to be more reasonable in setting the final listing price, supported by market data, which you will present to show the probable selling price. In contrast, the speculator who is simply interested in seeing what kind of profit can be obtained by placing his or her home on the market is going to be a hard bargainer. In the latter case, a long listing period is in order, and the ultimate listing price may be too high.

Maintain a positive frame of mind throughout the interview. Assume from the very beginning that you will be listing and selling the property. Choose emphatic statements, such as: "Once our sign is up ...," "When we get our buyer ...," and "As we progress in the marketing process ... ."

Get the owners involved as you emphasize "we" and "our" problems and solutions.

Even the negative features of the property can be brought up in a way that does not offend the sellers. You can always place the blame on the prospective buyer. Rather than direct criticism, allude to what the typical buyer might say. For example, if the house needs a paint job, you might say, "Mr. and Mrs. Owner, I'm a little concerned that buyers may remark on the number of paint chips and cracks on the house." In this way, you are suggesting that something be done to help show the property at its best.

B. RESEARCH PROCEDURES IN OBTAINING A LISTING

Use title companies (preliminary title report) to obtain the legal description, lot size, zoning, and surrounding streets of the subject property.

Check out ownership from a title company, getting the owner's name.

The California documentary transfer tax paid is based on $.55 per $500, or fraction thereof, of the selling price or fair market value, whichever is higher.

Check out comparable sales, obtainable from closed escrow listings maintained by your MLS. These show how many homes in the area were sold, at what price and terms they sold, and those that did not sell (most probably because they were overpriced). Adjoining streets should be included in the study in addition to the street on which the subject property is located. If you belong to a multiple listing service, their up-to-date information is readily available to you, compiled in multiple summary sheets. Finally, viewing the homes on the market in the area can help you formulate a better picture of the market.

"Comparables" are sold properties that are similar to the subject property in size and amenities, and located preferably within one mile of said property.

Check out other sources of technical data—agencies that answer questions about items that buyers and other brokers are likely to ask. The following city, county, or state agencies are available to help you, since often a simple telephone call is all that's necessary to obtain the kind of information you seek.

Building and Safety Department – to check on certificate of occupancy for improvements made, and to check on building permits. It is important to note that most real estate attorneys recommend that buyers should decide whether or not to require building permits to be evidenced as a condition of the sale.

Always let the buyer check on building permits to limit your liability!

City or County Planning Departments – to check on existing and proposed zoning and to check on applications for zone changes, yard variances, conditional use

permits, and so on. Cases are on file at the planning desks, and copies of their contents can usually be obtained. You need to give the physical location of the property, since planning departments don't necessarily work by legal descriptions or popular street addresses. For example, state that the property is located on the south side of Morrison Street, between Ranchito and Murietta streets, measured as so many feet from major intersections.

Engineering Departments – to check on existing and proposed sewers, connections thereto, assessment bonds, acreage fees, public works projects, and so on. Be prepared with the street address and legal description. For complicated lot splits, or flag lots (lots shaped like flags), or legal boundary descriptions, a personal visit to obtain the information is recommended.

Bureau of Assessments – to check for any street, sewer, or lighting bonds against a property, or to check for the payoff on same. The bond number or legal description is needed. Payoff amounts can make the difference between your seller accepting a particular offer or not. Many agents use a third-party vendor to determine supplementary taxes.

The seller can pay off assessment bonds or the buyer can assume them— as long as they are disclosed. A preliminary title report should disclose such items.

Division of Highways – for information regarding adopted or proposed freeway routes, address inquiries to the public information counter, where you'll need to furnish the name of the freeway on which you want data, major cross streets on either side of the subject property, and the legal description.

Board of Education – to obtain new and old boundaries for elementary, middle, and high school districts, the city, county, or unified board is helpful. All you need to furnish is the street address and the type of school you're calling about.

IV. Closing the Seller

There is no distinct point in time that you start or stop the close, since all of the activities leading to the owners' signatures on the listing agreement form constitute one continuous sales process. If you remain confident and positive throughout, demonstrating that you can do the job of selling the property at a favorable price and under desirable terms, the owner is bound to react favorably.

A planned presentation should be made, using visual aids on your notebook computer or tablet as much as possible.

Sellers are pleasantly surprised when you show them a smartphone or tablet picture of their property on the cover of your Comparative Market Analysis (CMA). Listing presentation software is also available for your laptop computer.

The market data your research has produced will not only be important to help in the close, but also critical in establishing the listing price at which the property should sell. Unfortunately, some agents, in order to get the listing, will over inflate the asking price.

If you're going to get things done, you'll have to "toot your own horn." Tell the prospects about yourself and your accomplishments in the field. Furnish information about your firm, using material that gives a short history of the company, including its achievements in marketing. Show listing and sales volume records, point out the many extras offered by the company and yourself, and explain the post-listing services to help convince the owner to list with you. Letters of recommendation from past clients are important at this stage of the presentation.

Throughout the interview, listen carefully, anticipate any objections, and respond appropriately to questions. As each of the questions or objections is answered, you move nearer and nearer to the final close. A common technique that works well is the assumed consent. With the listing form (and pen) in front of you throughout the interview, be sure to write and get agreement on minor points at appropriate times, such as the way in which title is held, and whether any assessments exist. Another technique that works well is to ask: "Would you prefer a 30-day or two-month escrow?" "Do you have a particular escrow company (or termite company, title company, etc.), or shall we provide you with some choices?" "Is it best to call for showing appointments in the morning, or are afternoons better?"

As a method of gaining consent for a listing, ask if you can use an electronic lockbox key code and display a sign on the property. Some agents present their market analysis online.

Should you want to plunge headlong into the business at hand, you might ask straight-forwardly: "Mr. Seller, if you and I can get together on price and terms, can we place the property on the market tonight?"

A. OVERCOMING OBJECTIONS TO LISTING

It is rare for anyone to phone and ask you to come right out to take a listing, few or no questions asked. After all, you must realize that you're probably dealing with the largest single asset that the seller possesses. Listing property is selling at its most creative and a highly competitive game. You will be confronted with many questions and objections, and you must be ready and able to tactfully respond to and overcome these land mines if you are to successfully accomplish your mission. Listed below are a number of objections that are commonly made and some suggested responses.

Objection 1: "Saving the commission." "Why should we pay you a big commission when we can sell it ourselves?" This is perhaps the single most important reason why owners won't list, even if they don't state it this way. Many replies can be made to this, all of them dramatizing the benefits which accrue to the owners if they list with you, for example, "marketing know-how, saving time, avoiding legal entanglements, negotiations and specialization, financing, peace of mind, and so forth."

Responses to Objection 1:

(1) First, the chief reason you should not sell it yourself and save the commission is that, in reality, you aren't really saving the commission. Technically, while you, the seller, pay the commission, in practice it's always the buyer who pays it—and who saves it—if it's eliminated, since your price reflects a net figure to him or her.

(2) If you try to sell your own house, you avoid paying the commission, but you'll be on call day and night. You'll have to pay for all your own signs and advertising. You'll have to deal with all the problems, inconveniences, hazards, headaches, and legalities that go with selling a house, including the various disclosures and the timely release of all contingencies. Is it really worth it?

Objection 2: "I want to think it over." When sellers say this, it's because they do not fully understand, you have failed to satisfactorily answer questions or objections, or because of fear of the unknown. It's best to ask specifically what they want to think over. Go over the listing agreement, reviewing point by point, getting agreement on each item, that is, the financing, personal property included, taxes, size of lot, and rooms. The listing should contain facts, not fiction, and the review is the golden opportunity to get the owner's commitment so that differences and doubts can be satisfactorily resolved. Maybe the owners are afraid of strangers, parting with a key, or having a sign on the lawn. By persistent questioning you could find out what is troubling them.

Responses to Objection 2:

Is there something that I have not made clear or explained thoroughly? Is it the price? Terms? Down payment? Let's think this over together. There's something that is preventing your making a decision. Let's discuss that first.

In the meantime, interest rates may be going up.

Objection 3: "I want to buy a new (replacement) house before I sell." This objection presents a golden opportunity for the broker who is active in guaranteed trade-in plans or who has dealt with contingent sales. Again emphasize the "we" in the problem-solving process. Get your buyers and yourself into the action.

Responses to Objection 3:

(1) My company has an excellent guaranteed sales program that eliminates any risk or worry for you, Mr. Seller. Now the only problem we face is to find you the home that you're looking for. What exactly are your looking for?

(2) You're in a poor bargaining position if you buy before you sell. Would you want someone to purchase your house in the hopes that maybe he could sell his? If you make your offer without a contingency, you could end up in double jeopardy, with two home

mortgages to pay. You may end up selling in desperation, at a distressed price, and sustaining a loss.

Objection 4: "I have a friend in the business" or "I want to interview several brokers." With so many licenses outstanding in California, the typical owner is bound to know someone with a license. You should never attempt to belittle or downgrade the competitor, suggesting instead that his or her friend can participate in the sales effort in a number of ways. First, through membership in the multiple listing service. Second, though you may have the listing, through the MLS the friend could also show the property to any qualified buyer and share in the commission. Most important of all, stress again the many benefits and services your firm offers to get the job done effectively.

Responses to Objection 4:

I'm sure your friend is well qualified, but it might be difficult for him or her to be completely objective about your property, just as it is difficult for many of us to be impartial about our own homes. Your friend may be reluctant to discuss sensitive issues with you, or you may not wish for him or her to know all about your financial affairs. "He/she might not wish to hurt your feelings," for instance, by suggesting how you could improve the salability of the property. He/she may hesitate about telling you some of the objections raised by prospective buyers that could prove helpful in the marketing.

Objection 5: "I don't want to sign a listing." Here, you will need to explain the adverse consequences of taking a verbal or pocket listing and the many benefits to the owner of signing an exclusive listing, discussed in the early part of this chapter. You may also categorically state that it is office procedure to have all contracts in writing in order to avoid misunderstandings.

Responses to Objection 5:

(1) When a broker accepts an exclusive listing, a strong fiduciary relationship is created, which obligates him or her to expend the maximum time and effort on the seller's behalf. With an exclusive listing, we must provide many more services, including expensive advertising.

(2) The legal pitfalls are so numerous without a written contract that we could not justify working on your property. Your house could not be advertised or merchandised properly.

Objection 6: "We'll only give you a 30-day listing." Many people don't want to tie up their property for long periods of time, so this objection is a reasonable one. Anticipating this, an effective salesperson tries for a three-month listing. If you're doing a good job explaining the many services your company offers, and devote time to explaining the market, the sellers will be more understanding of the need to give you sufficient time to expose the property to the maximum number of qualified buyers at the best possible price.

Responses to Objection 6:

(1) We need time to map our merchandising campaign, including processing, advertising, getting out mailers, caravanning, pitching to other brokers, and all the other things necessary to get it sold.

(2) In a 30-day listing period there are four weekends, representing only eight days in which your property can be effectively shown and sold. Eight days just isn't enough time to reach the largest number of people in order to get the job done.

Objection 7: "Other brokers can get my price." Here, we have the seller who is prepared to list, but who wants to do so only at his or her price; that is, one that is well above market. The best tool is the comparative market analysis (CMA), detailed in Chapter 5. Without reliable data, you may end up with a listing that takes up much time, expense, and energy, but yields no results.

Response to Objection 7:

Anyone with a license can list your property, but do you really want to just list, or do you want to sell? Many brokers sign up a listing at any price, and then bring down the price later. False promises are not in line with our company's policy. We list to sell.

V. Servicing Listings

Service sells listings. Computers are great, but you need a personal touch.

It's up to you to retain the harmonious relationship you set up in the listing appointment, making the seller a partner in the selling process. Explain what the seller can do to help sell, what is going to happen, and what to do, including what to do when strangers stop by.

Keeping in touch on a regular basis helps to keep lines of communication open, avoiding any problems that might arise. You are afforded opportunities to let your clients know what you're doing to earn the agreed-upon commission. All too often, the owner who is not aware of the total services he or she is receiving may begrudge paying you a commission merely for spending an hour or two showing potential buyers the home. A weekly or monthly written report stating all your activities is very effective.

A. STEPS IN SERVICING A LISTING

1. Have owners/sellers sign the listing agreement (give them a copy).
2. Enter the listing and a summary information sheet into the multiple listing service via the Internet (unless an "office only" exclusive is given).
3. Get keys.
4. Install an electronic lockbox.
5. Order "For Sale" signs and riders. *RIDERS are supplemental attachments to signs (like "Three Bedrooms" or website of the agent).*
6. Place signs at the front and/or back and side of the property.
7. Copy of information about the listed property at the front desk.

1. Lockboxes (Electronic)

LOCKBOXES contain the property's keys and greatly facilitate the showing process.

Lockboxes are available through the local Association of REALTORS®. Most of the time, they are placed on the front door (avoid water pipes). It's a good idea to keep a duplicate key code in the office for late inspections or should something happen to the original.

Lockboxes have come a long way from the little metal container that used to sit on top of the front door. Now, most of them are electronic marvels that can chronologically read the code number of anyone entering the premises via the lockbox. They are safer than ever before, but the code should be changed frequently to reduce the risk of someone inadvertently obtaining your secret code. Programmers or keys should never be loaned to anyone.

2. Weekly Summary

Send a thank-you letter to your new clients. Use language that is warm and friendly, such as illustrated in **Figure 3-3**.

Keep a weekly summary from the moment you take a listing to final sale and close of escrow.

Keep in touch weekly with your clients, letting them know what you're doing for them and give expert advice—like the possibility of lowering the listing price if no offer or little interest is being shown in a property.

Figure 3-3

January 5, 20XX

Lyons and Associates, Inc., Realtor
REAL ESTATE EXCELLENCE

Mr. & Mrs. A. Seller
1000 E. Main Street
Anytown, CA 10000

Dear Mr. and Mrs. Seller:

First of all, I want to thank you for listing your lovely home with Lyons and Associates. Please be assured that you will be kept informed of any and all real estate activities, not only on your home, but in your area.

I will be sending you copies of all our ads, and I will be contacting you at least on a weekly basis to evaluate the quality of our showings.

Should you have any question, suggestion or request, please do not hesitate to contact me; I am as near as your telephone.

Best regards,

Arlette A. Lyons, CRS, GRI, SRES
Owner-Broker

2820 E. GARVEY AVENUE SOUTH, WEST COVINA, CA 91791 • (626) 331-0141 • FAX: (626) 331-9772

VI. CHAPTER SUMMARY

A **listing** is a contract of employment by which a principal hires the services of an **agent** (licensed real estate broker) to perform certain prescribed services, usually selling. An **agency** is the relationship between a principal and an agent.

In California, **employment contracts** (listings) are required to be in writing to be enforceable.

Listings are the "backbone" of sales; an agent must be able to sell the seller on the listing before the agent can sell prospective buyers. The two main types of listings are open and exclusive.

An **open listing** is a written contract that allows one or more brokers to act as agent in the sale of the principal's property. In reality, an open listing is little better than no listing at all. **Net listings** are rarely used.

An **exclusive listing** employs a broker, named in the contract, to represent the owner/principal exclusively. There are two categories of exclusive listings. The **exclusive agency listing** provides that only one agent has the right to earn a commission. The drawback to this form of listing is that the broker could be in competition with the owner for the sale.

The **Exclusive Right to Sell** listing entitles the broker to commissions on all sales, during the life of the agreement, even if the owners themselves sell the property.

A **Multiple Listing Service (MLS)** is a marketing database of listings of properties for sale set up by a group of cooperating real estate brokers providing details about the property and the commission split.

A broker may represent a buyer or even both parties to a transaction. When both parties are represented by the same company/agent, it is known as **dual agency**. Such an arrangement is legal only if full disclosure is made to both parties to a transaction and they agree in writing.

Listing and selling agents are required to provide both buyers and sellers (of one-to-four residential units and manufactured homes) with specified written disclosures through the **agency relationship disclosure** form.

There are many reasons for listing with a qualified broker, the most important being to employ a real estate marketing specialist who is knowledgeable in the rules and regulations of real estate transactions.

A commission is earned by the agent when an offer is made by a ready, willing, and able buyer to purchase on the exact price and terms shown in the listing.

VII. MATCHING VOCABULARY **Fill in the blanks with the correct letter**

A. Agency
B. Commission
C. Cooperating broker
D. Employment contracts
E. Exclusive Right to Sell listing

F. Listing
G. Listing interview
H. Lockbox
I. Multiple listing service
J. Net listing
K. Open listing
L. Pocket buyer

M. Riders
N. Safety clause
O. Seller's proceeds

1. _____ A non-listing broker with whom the listing broker agrees to share a commission if the non-listing broker produces a buyer.

2. _____ A negotiated period after the termination of the listing during which the listing broker may still be entitled to a commission if the property is sold to a buyer who was shown the property during the listing period.

3. _____ A group of brokers banding together to share listings and commissions.

4. _____ An appointment with a prospective seller with the intent of persuading that seller to list a property with you at a fair market price.

5. _____ How much cash the seller will receive after payment of all liens and expenses.

6. _____ An employment contract between an owner and a licensed real estate broker entered into for the purpose of the broker providing service to find a ready, willing, and able person to buy, rent, or lease a property.

7. _____ A written contract authorizing one or more brokers to act as agent in the sale of the principal's property for a fixed commission.

8. _____ This person is prepared to buy a property before that property is actually listed with a broker.

9. _____ Entitles the broker to commissions on all sales during the life of his or her agreement with the owner, even when the owners themselves sell the property.

10. _____ This type of listing provides that the agent is to retain all money received in excess of a predetermined net price to the owner.

11. _____ This contains the property's keys and greatly facilitates the showing process.

12. _____ Supplemental attachments to signs, like "Three Bedrooms."

13. _____ The relationship between principal and agent wherein the agent is employed by the principal to do certain acts, like negotiating with third parties.

14. _____ In California, this type of contract must be in writing to be enforceable.

15. _____ This is earned when you have produced a buyer who is "ready, willing, and able" to purchase at the price and under the terms agreed to by both seller and buyer, whether or not escrow closes.

See Page 609 for Answers

VIII. CHAPTER QUIZ

1. A contract by which a principal employs an agent/broker to do certain things for the principal, usually finding a buyer for his or her property, is called a:

   a. court order.
   b. purchase offer.
   c. purchase contract.
   d. listing.

2. In California, a listing agreement:

   a. is an employment contract.
   b. must be in writing to be enforceable.
   c. is both a and b.
   d. is neither a nor b.

3. Although agents ordinarily represent owners and sellers, they may be employed occasionally to represent buyers in:

   a. negotiating leaseholds.
   b. obtaining mortgage loans.
   c. purchasing business opportunities.
   d. all of the foregoing activities.

4. The type of listing in which the owners would be held liable for a commission even if they themselves sold the property is called a(n):

   a. exclusive agency listing.
   b. exclusive right to sell listing.
   c. multiple listing.
   d. open listing.

5. The listing which is most likely to give rise to charges of misrepresentation or fraud is the:

   a. multiple listing.
   b. open listing.
   c. net listing.
   d. exclusive listing.

6. A "pocket buyer" refers to a buyer:

   a. with deep pockets, meaning lots of money.
   b. who is prepared to buy a property before it's listed with a broker.
   c. who is a friend or relative of the broker.
   d. all of the above.

7. A "safety clause" is usually found in the most preferred type of listing, which is the:

   a. Open listing only
   b. Exclusive right to sell listing
   c. Net listing
   d. Multiple listing

8. If you leave the employ of a broker and go to work for another broker:

   a. your listings stay with your old broker.
   b. your listings are your own and go with you to your new brokerage.
   c. you must split your commissions between your old and new broker.
   d. none of the above.

9. A commission is earned by the broker when all terms of the contract have been fulfilled and he or she has produced a buyer who is:

   a. ready to buy.
   b. able to buy.
   c. willing to buy.
   d. all of the above.

10. How a house appears when compared to the rest of the neighborhood is called:

   a. landscape lookability.
   b. curb appeal.
   c. comparative shopping rating.
   d. paint and plaster appeal.

ANSWERS: 1. d; 2. c; 3. d; 4. b; 5. c; 6. b; 7. b; 8. a; 9. d; 10. b

SUNSET BROKERS

Scott Chapin

http://www.bankhomes.com

0/493-4357

Breakdown of the Listing Agreement: How to Fill It Out

I. Breakdown and Analysis of Listing Agreement

Because the listing agreement is usually the first in a series of contracts and documents used in the sale of real property, you must completely understand the form and fill it in accurately and explicitly, leaving no room for doubt. In order to eliminate the possibility of poorly drawn contracts, the California Real Estate Commissioner requires that all agreements prepared by salespeople be approved and initialed by their designated broker or office manager within a reasonable time.

Some salespeople specialize in listing presentations using their notebook computers or tablets.

Each section of the CAR® Residential Listing Agreement (RLA) (Exclusive Authorization and Right to Sell) form is discussed in the following paragraphs, numbered and labeled to correspond with the paragraphs in the CAR® form for our evaluation. (To see the form in its entirety, refer back to Figure 3-1.) There are a wide variety of similar forms written and printed by private companies in use. While the specific language may differ in each, they all have the same basic intent: To create an agency relationship between the licensee and the owner whose property is being listed and to establish the basis for compensation, which, under the Statute of Frauds, must be in writing. Moreover, when properly drafted, a commission may be earned upon an offer to purchase on the exact price and terms shown in the listing, even if the seller does not choose to accept the buyer's offer.

The life blood of the real estate business is listings—convincing sellers to employ you to help them sell their home within a certain period of time, for a stated price.

CHAPTER OUTLINE

The following boxes contain the sections of the Residential Listing Agreement for close analysis.

CALIFORNIA ASSOCIATION OF REALTORS®

RESIDENTIAL LISTING AGREEMENT
(Exclusive Authorization and Right to Sell)
(C.A.R. Form RLA, Revised 11/13)

1. **EXCLUSIVE RIGHT TO SELL:** _____ ("Seller")
hereby employs and grants _____ ("Broker")
beginning (date) _____ and ending at 11:59 P.M. on (date) _____ ("Listing Period")
the exclusive and irrevocable right to sell or exchange the real property in the City of ___*Marina del Rey*___ ,
County of ___*Los Angeles*___ , Assessor's Parcel No. _____ ,
California, described as: ___*123 Sail Avenue*___ ("Property").

START - PAGE 1 OF 5

---

1. **Exclusive Right to Sell:** Enter name(s) of the Seller on the first line. Then, the name of the Broker (not the agent, who signs the form at the end of the contract), followed by the beginning and ending date of the contract (an average of three to six months) concluding at 11:59 P.M. of the last day. The city and county is then identified, followed by the assessor's parcel number and the unique street address of the property. Write out the date rather than using numbers.

Exclusive listings require a definite end time and date.

> **2. ITEMS EXCLUDED AND INCLUDED:** Unless otherwise specified in a real estate purchase agreement, all fixtures and fittings that are attached to the Property are included, and personal property items are excluded, from the purchase price.
> ADDITIONAL ITEMS EXCLUDED: _____ .
> ADDITIONAL ITEMS INCLUDED: _____ .
> Seller intends that the above items be excluded or included in offering the Property for sale, but understands that: **(i)** the purchase agreement supersedes any intention expressed above and will ultimately determine which items are excluded and included in the sale; and **(ii)** Broker is not responsible for and does not guarantee that the above exclusions and/or inclusions will be in the purchase agreement.

2. Items Excluded and Included: The form specifies that all fixtures and fittings that are attached to the property are included, and personal property items are excluded from the purchase price. This is the opportunity to fill in any "Additional Items Excluded and Included" in the listing. This does not preclude a Buyer from asking for excluded items when making an offer, which may or may not be separately accepted by the Seller.

In a listing agreement, as in a purchase contract, any handwritten instructions take precedence over any preprinted instructions.

> **3. LISTING PRICE AND TERMS:**
> **A.** The listing price shall be: _____
> _____ Dollars ($ _____).
> **B.** Additional Terms: _____
> _____ .

3. Listing Price and Terms: This is the price at which the property is offered.

3(A) In section (A) you fill in the amount (e.g., six hundred thousand dollars) followed by the numerical equivalent ($600,000).

3(B) Additional Terms: This is where you include any financing terms, such as down payment amount, all cash, loan assumption, subject to existing loan, and seller carry-back. If your Seller is offering a loan assumption, you will also need to include the amount and terms of the existing loan.

If financial terms are specified, sellers are not obligated to pay a commission when they refuse a full price offer, unless the offer is for all cash with no contigencies.

> **4. COMPENSATION TO BROKER:**
> Notice: The amount or rate of real estate commissions is not fixed by law. They are set by each Broker individually and may be negotiable between Seller and Broker (real estate commissions include all compensation and fees to Broker).

4. Compensation to Broker: The compensation paid to Brokers is always decided by mutual agreement between principal and agent.

A. Seller agrees to pay to Broker as compensation for services irrespective of agency relationship(s), either ☐_____ percent of the listing price (or if a purchase agreement is entered into, of the purchase price), or ☐ $_____, AND _____, as follows:

(1) If during the Listing Period, or any extension, Broker, cooperating broker, Seller or any other person procures a ready, willing, and able buyer(s) whose offer to purchase the Property on any price and terms is accepted by Seller, provided the Buyer completes the transaction or is prevented from doing so by Seller. (Broker is entitled to compensation whether any escrow resulting from such offer closes during or after the expiration of the Listing Period, or any extension.)

OR (2) If within _____ calendar days **(a)** after the end of the Listing Period or any extension; or **(b)** after any cancellation of this Agreement, unless otherwise agreed, Seller enters into a contract to sell, convey, lease or otherwise transfer the Property to anyone ("Prospective Buyer") or that person's related entity: **(i)** who physically entered and was shown the Property during the Listing Period or any extension by Broker or a cooperating broker; or **(ii)** for whom Broker or any cooperating broker submitted to Seller a signed, written offer to acquire, lease, exchange or obtain an option on the Property. Seller, however, shall have no obligation to Broker under paragraph 4A(2) unless, not later than **3 calendar days** after the end of the Listing Period or any extension or cancellation, Broker has given Seller a written notice of the names of such Prospective Buyers.

OR (3) If, without Broker's prior written consent, the Property is withdrawn from sale, conveyed, leased, rented, otherwise transferred, or made unmarketable by a voluntary act of Seller during the Listing Period, or any extension.

4(A) Fill in either the agreed to percentage of listing (or purchase) price or a specific amount of the real estate commission. A percentage is preferable because it automatically adjusts based on the actual selling price.

(1) This simply states that the Seller will pay the Broker a commission if he or she (or any cooperating Broker) sells the property during the listing or extension period, or obtains a buyer who is ready, willing, and able.

(2) **DO NOT CONFUSE SAFETY CLAUSE WITH THE LISTING PERIOD.** As the listing Broker, you and the Seller agree to a specific time period (180 days for example). To protect themselves, Brokers must furnish the Owners with a written notice including the names of prospects to whom they (and any other cooperating licensees) have shown the property or for whom they made an offer, during the listing period. If the owner **OR A NEW LISTING BROKER** sells the property to anyone on the list, which must be provided to the Seller within **three calendar days** of the expiration of the listing, you, as the original Broker, may be entitled to a commission.

(3) If the property is made "unmarketable" by any voluntary act of the Seller during the listing period, the Broker is entitled to his or her commission.

The Safety Clause not only protects your right to earn a commission as an original listing broker, but also protects you, as a secondary broker, from entering into a contract with a seller who is already obligated to another broker. You should ask the seller directly if he or she has, or did have, a previous listing agreement. If the answer is yes, you should stress to your seller the importance of filling out the new Safety Clause honestly, including the list of previous prospects. If it turns out that you were misled, either intentionally or unintentionally, the broker with a legitimate previous claim is still entitled to a commission. You may, however, have grounds to sue the seller for your lost compensation.

> **B.** If completion of the sale is prevented by a party to the transaction other than Seller, then compensation due under paragraph 4A shall be payable only if and when Seller collects damages by suit, arbitration, settlement or otherwise, and then in an amount equal to the lesser of one-half of the damages recovered or the above compensation, after first deducting title and escrow expenses and the expenses of collection, if any.
>
> **C.** In addition, Seller agrees to pay Broker: _____ .

4(B) If completion of the sale is prevented by a party other than the Seller, then the total commission is to be the lesser of the commission due under section 4A, or "one half" of the damages recovered by the Seller after deducting expenses.

4(C) For any additional compensation due the Broker such as MLS fees, advertising expenses, administration fees, etc. Some Brokers do not charge this fee.

> **D.** Seller has been advised of Broker's policy regarding cooperation with, and the amount of compensation offered to, other brokers.
>
> (1) Broker is authorized to cooperate with and compensate brokers participating through the multiple listing service(s) ("MLS") by offering to MLS brokers out of Broker's compensation specified in 4A, either ☐ _____ percent of the purchase price, or ☐ $ _____ .
>
> (2) Broker is authorized to cooperate with and compensate brokers operating outside the MLS as per Broker's policy.

4(D) This indicates the Broker's policy regarding cooperation with other brokers, and the amount of compensation offered to them.

(1) The Seller authorizes the Broker to enter the listing in a multiple listing service (MLS), thereby cooperating with other participating Brokers. The amount of compensation that will be paid to the cooperating Broker is entered as either a percentage or a flat amount. This amount is determined by the listing Broker but approved by the Seller.

(2) This indicates the Broker's cooperation with and compensation to non-MLS members.

> **E.** Seller hereby irrevocably assigns to Broker the above compensation from Seller's funds and proceeds in escrow. Broker may submit this Agreement, as instructions to compensate Broker pursuant to paragraph 4A, to any escrow regarding the Property involving Seller and a buyer, Prospective Buyer or other transferee.

4(E) The Seller agrees to have the escrow pay the Broker's commission directly from the sale proceeds. The Broker will then pay his or her salesperson their agreed to commission.

> **F.** (1) Seller represents that Seller has not previously entered into a listing agreement with another broker regarding the Property, unless specified as follows: _____ .
>
> (2) Seller warrants that Seller has no obligation to pay compensation to any other broker regarding the Property unless the Property is transferred to any of the following individuals or entities: _____
>
> (3) If the Property is sold to anyone listed above during the time Seller is obligated to compensate another broker: **(i)** Broker is not entitled to compensation under this Agreement; and **(ii)** Broker is not obligated to represent Seller in such transaction.

CHAPTER 4

4(F) The Seller "discloses any previous broker's right to commission" here.

(1) This is where the Seller indicates if he or she has any previous agreement with another broker.

(2) This is where the Seller lists the names that entitles a previous broker to the commission for the sale of the property.

(3) This indicates that the current Broker will not be compensated if the property is sold to anyone on that list, and is released from any contractual obligation to the Seller.

Seller's Initials (_____) (_____)

Reviewed by _____ Date _____

EQUAL HOUSING OPPORTUNITY

Seller's and Reviewer's Initials: The bottom of pages 1-3 must be initialed by the Seller and by the Broker or designated office manager, as part of their duty to supervise.

Property Address: *123 Sail Avenue Marina del Rey, CA 90292*   Date: _____

Property Address and Date: The address of the listed property and the date the listing form is being completed must be entered at the top of pages 2 and 3.

---

5. MULTIPLE LISTING SERVICE:
A. Broker is a participant/subscriber to _____ Multiple Listing Service (MLS) and possibly others. Unless otherwise instructed in writing the Property will be listed with the MLS(s) specified above. That MLS is (or if checked ☐ is not) the primary MLS for the geographic area of the Property. All terms of the transaction, including sales price and financing, if applicable, (i) will be provided to the MLS in which the property is listed for publication, dissemination and use by persons and entities on terms approved by the MLS and (ii) may be provided to the MLS even if the Property is not listed with the MLS.

BENEFITS OF USING THE MLS; IMPACT OF OPTING OUT OF THE MLS; PRESENTING ALL OFFERS

WHAT IS AN MLS? The MLS is a database of properties for sale that is available and disseminated to and accessible by all other real estate agents who are participants or subscribers to the MLS. Property information submitted to the MLS describes the price, terms and conditions under which the Seller's property is offered for sale (including but not limited to the listing broker's offer of compensation to other brokers). It is likely that a significant number of real estate practitioners in any given area are participants or subscribers to the MLS. The MLS may also be part of a reciprocal agreement to which other multiple listing services belong. Real estate agents belonging to other multiple listing services that have reciprocal agreements with the MLS also have access to the information submitted to the MLS. The MLS may further transmit the MLS database to Internet sites that post property listings online.

EXPOSURE TO BUYERS THROUGH MLS: Listing property with an MLS exposes a seller's property to all real estate agents and brokers (and their potential buyer clients) who are participants or subscribers to the MLS or a reciprocating MLS.

CLOSED/PRIVATE LISTING CLUBS OR GROUPS: Closed or private listing clubs or groups are not the same as the MLS. The MLS referred to above is accessible to all eligible real estate licensees and provides broad exposure for a listed property. Private or closed listing clubs or groups of licensees may have been formed outside the MLS. Private or closed listing clubs or groups are accessible to a more limited number of licensees and generally offer less exposure for listed property. Whether listing property through a closed, private network - and excluding it from the MLS - is advantageous or disadvantageous to a seller, and why, should be discussed with the agent taking the Seller's listing.

NOT LISTING PROPERTY IN A LOCAL MLS: If the Property is listed in an MLS which does not cover the geographic area where the Property is located then real estate agents and brokers working that territory, and Buyers they represent looking for property in the neighborhood, may not be aware the Property is for sale.

OPTING OUT OF MLS: If Seller elects to exclude the Property from the MLS, Seller understands and acknowledges that: **(a)** real estate agents and brokers from other real estate offices, and their buyer clients, who have access to that MLS may not be aware that Seller's Property is offered for sale; **(b)** Information about Seller's Property will not be transmitted to various real estate Internet sites that are used by the public to search for property listings; **(c)** real estate agents, brokers and members of the public may be unaware of the terms and conditions under which Seller is marketing the Property.

REDUCTION IN EXPOSURE: Any reduction in exposure of the Property may lower the number of offers and negatively impact the sales price.

PRESENTING ALL OFFERS: Seller understands that Broker must present all offers received for Seller's Property unless Seller gives Broker written instructions to the contrary.

Seller's Initials _____ / _____   Broker's Initials _____ / _____

B. MLS rules generally provide that residential real property and vacant lot listings be submitted to the MLS within 2 days or some other period of time after all necessary signatures have been obtained on the listing agreement. Broker will not have to submit this listing to the MLS if, within that time, Broker submits to the MLS a form signed by Seller (C.A.R. Form SELM or the local equivalent form).

C. MLS rules allow MLS data to be made available by the MLS to additional Internet sites unless Broker gives the MLS instructions to the contrary. Seller acknowledges that for any of the below opt-out instructions to be effective, Seller must make them on a separate instruction to Broker signed by Seller (C.A.R. Form **SELI** or the local equivalent form). Specific information that can be excluded from the Internet as permitted by (or in accordance with) the MLS is as follows:

(1) Property Availability: Seller can instruct Broker to have the MLS not display the Property on the Internet.

(2) Property Address: Seller can instruct Broker to have the MLS not display the Property address on the Internet.

Seller understands that the above opt-outs would mean consumers searching for listings on the Internet may not see the Property or Property's address in response to their search.

(3) Feature Opt-Outs: Seller can instruct Broker to advise the MLS that Seller does not want visitors to MLS Participant or Subscriber Websites or Electronic Displays that display the Property listing to have the features below. Seller understands **(i)** that these opt-outs apply only to Websites or Electronic Displays of MLS Participants and Subscribers who are real estate broker and agent members of the MLS; **(ii)** that other Internet sites may or may not have the features set forth herein; and **(iii)** that neither Broker nor the MLS may have the ability to control or block such features on other Internet sites.

(a) Comments And Reviews: The ability to write comments or reviews about the Property on those sites; or the ability to link to another site containing such comments or reviews if the link is in immediate conjunction with the Property.

(b) Automated Estimate Of Value: The ability to create an automated estimate of value or to link to another site containing such an estimate of value if the link is in immediate conjuction with the Property.

5. Multiple Listing Service: This states that all terms of the transaction will be provided to the selected MLS, including additional Internet sites, unless the Broker submits a form signed by the Seller (CAR Seller Instruction to Exclude Listing from MLS (SEL) form or the locally required form) withholding the listing from the MLS.

At least one photo of the front of the property without broker signage must accompany the submission to the MLS for wider Internet distribution.

The Listing Agreement includes a section on the disclosure of the benefits of having the seller's property entered in the Multiple Listing Service. In a sellers' market, the listing company may unethically encourage the sellers to hold the property as an office listing rather than exposing it to the Multiple Listing Service. Having read and initialed this most important box, should encourage the sellers to expose their property to the largest amount of buyers for the highest and best offer. It is the job of the listing agent to educate his or her sellers—it is their fiduciary relationship in action!

6. SELLER REPRESENTATIONS: Seller represents that, unless otherwise specified in writing, Seller is unaware of: **(i)** any Notice of Default recorded against the Property; **(ii)** any delinquent amounts due under any loan secured by, or other obligation affecting, the Property; **(iii)** any bankruptcy, insolvency or similar proceeding affecting the Property; **(iv)** any litigation, arbitration, administrative action, government investigation or other pending or threatened action that affects or may affect the Property or Seller's ability to transfer it; and **(v)** any current, pending or proposed special assessments affecting the Property. Seller shall promptly notify Broker in writing if Seller becomes aware of any of these items during the Listing Period or any extension thereof.

START - PAGE 3 OF 5

6. Seller Representations: This section indicates that the Seller, unless otherwise specified in writing, is unaware of any financial, legal, or physical reasons that would negatively affect the legal transfer of the property. This protects the Broker from liability for damages due to problems with clear title.

> **7. BROKER'S AND SELLER'S DUTIES: (a)** Broker agrees to exercise reasonable effort and due diligence to achieve the purposes of this Agreement. Unless Seller gives Broker written instructions to the contrary, Broker is authorized to **(i)** order reports and disclosures as necessary, **(ii)** advertise and market the Property by any method and in any medium selected by Broker, including MLS and the Internet, and, to the extent permitted by these media, control the dissemination of the information submitted to any medium; and **(iii)** disclose to any real estate licensee making an inquiry the receipt of any offers on the Property and the offering price of such offers. **(b)** Seller agrees to consider offers presented by Broker, and to act in good faith to accomplish the sale of the Property by, among other things, making the Property available for showing at reasonable times and, subject to paragraph 4F, referring to Broker all inquiries of any party interested in the Property. Seller is responsible for determining at what price to list and sell the Property. **Seller further agrees to indemnify, defend and hold Broker harmless from all claims, disputes, litigation, judgments attorney fees and costs arising from any incorrect information supplied by Seller, or from any material facts that Seller knows but fails to disclose.**

7. Broker's and Seller's Duties: The Broker is to use due diligence to market the property in the best manner possible. This also gives authorization to the Broker, unless otherwise instructed by the Sellers in writing, to order all necessary disclosures. The Seller must notify the Broker immediately should there be anticipated legal problems in conveying the property. Furthermore, the Seller is to make the property fully available for showing and takes full responsibility for all information he or she provides to the Broker, and agrees to indemnify the Broker from all claims arising from any incorrect information supplied.

> **8. DEPOSIT:** Broker is authorized to accept and hold on Seller's behalf any deposits to be applied toward the purchase price.

8. Deposit: This is the authorization for the Broker to accept and hold any deposits on the Seller's behalf to be applied toward the purchase.

> **9. AGENCY RELATIONSHIPS:**
> **A. Disclosure:** If the Property includes residential property with one-to-four dwelling units, Seller shall receive a "Disclosure Regarding Agency Relationships" (C.A.R. Form AD) prior to entering into this Agreement.
> **B. Seller Representation:** Broker shall represent Seller in any resulting transaction, except as specified in paragraph 4F.
> **C. Possible Dual Agency With Buyer:** Depending upon the circumstances, it may be necessary or appropriate for Broker to act as an agent for both Seller and buyer, exchange party, or one or more additional parties ("Buyer"). Broker shall, as soon as practicable, disclose to Seller any election to act as a dual agent representing both Seller and Buyer. If a Buyer is procured directly by Broker or an associate-licensee in Broker's firm, Seller hereby consents to Broker acting as a dual agent for Seller and Buyer. In the event of an exchange, Seller hereby consents to Broker collecting compensation from additional parties for services rendered, provided there is disclosure to all parties of such agency and compensation. Seller understands and agrees that: **(i)** Broker, without the prior written consent of Seller, will not disclose to Buyer that Seller is willing to sell the Property at a price less than the listing price; **(ii)** Broker, without the prior written consent of Buyer, will not disclose to Seller that Buyer is willing to pay a price greater than the offered price; and **(iii)** except for (i) and (ii) above, a dual agent is obligated to disclose known facts materially affecting the value or desirability of the Property to both parties.

9. Agency Relationships:

9(A) Disclosure: All agency disclosure forms must be signed prior to entering into the contract.

9(B) Seller Representation: The Broker shall represent the Seller in any resulting transaction, except as specified in paragraph 4F (Names of Reserved Parties).

9(C) Possible Dual Agency With Buyer: This addresses the possibility of the Broker representing both the Buyer and Seller and the need for full disclosure of that relationship. Also, as a dual agent, the Broker is obligated to disclose known facts materially affecting the value and desirability of the property to both parties.

> **D. Other Sellers:** Seller understands that Broker may have or obtain listings on other properties, and that potential buyers may consider, make offers on, or purchase through Broker, property the same as or similar to Seller's Property. Seller consents to Broker's representation of sellers and buyers of other properties before, during and after the end of this Agreement.
>
> **E. Confirmation:** If the Property includes residential property with one-to-four dwelling units, Broker shall confirm the agency relationship described above, or as modified, in writing, prior to or concurrent with Seller's execution of a purchase agreement.

9(D) Other Sellers: The Seller is made aware that the Broker may be listing other similar properties and, therefore, may be representing the buyers purchasing these properties while directly involved in the sale of the Seller's property.

9(E) Confirmation: The appropriate "agency relationship shall be confirmed, in writing, prior to or concurrent with the Seller's execution of a purchase agreement."

> **10. SECURITY AND INSURANCE:** Broker is not responsible for loss of or damage to personal or real property, or person, whether attributable to use of a keysafe/lockbox, a showing of the Property, or otherwise. Third parties, including, but not limited to, appraisers, inspectors, brokers and prospective buyers, may have access to, and take videos and photographs of, the interior of the Property. Seller agrees: **(i)** to take reasonable precautions to safeguard and protect valuables that might be accessible during showings of the Property; and **(ii)** to obtain insurance to protect against these risks. Broker does not maintain insurance to protect Seller.

10. Security and Insurance: The Broker is not responsible for loss or damage to the property. The Seller must take reasonable steps to safeguard any valuables that might be accessible during showings of the property. The Seller agrees to obtain insurance to cover these risks.

> **11. PHOTOGRAPHS AND INTERNET ADVERTISING:**
>
> **A.** In order to effectively market the Property for sale it is often necessary to provide photographs, virtual tours and other media to buyers. Seller agrees (or ☐ if checked, does not agree) that Broker may photograph or otherwise electronically capture images of the exterior and interior of the Property ("Images") for static and/or virtual tours of the Property by buyers and others on Broker's website, the MLS, and other marketing sites. Seller acknowledges that once Images are placed on the Internet neither Broker nor Seller has control over who can view such Images and what use viewers may make of the Images, or how long such Images may remain available on the Internet. Seller further agrees that such Images are the property of Broker and that Broker may use such Images for advertisement of Broker's business in the future.
>
> **B.** Seller acknowledges that prospective buyers and/or other persons coming onto the property may take photographs, videos or other images of the property. Seller understands that Broker does not have the ability to control or block the taking and use of Images by any such persons. (If checked) ☐ Seller instructs Broker to publish in the MLS that taking of Images is limited to those persons preparing Appraisal or Inspection reports. Seller acknowledges that unauthorized persons may take images who do not have access to or have not read any limiting instruction in the MLS or who take images regardless of any limiting instruction in the MLS. Once Images are taken and/or put into electronic display on the Internet or otherwise, neither Broker nor Seller has control over who views such Images nor what use viewers may make of the Images.

11. Photographs and Internet Advertising: The Seller approves or disapproves of the Broker or prospective buyers taking or providing photographs, creating virutal tours or other media, and providing such media to the MLS or other Internet sources.

> *Just because a house is empty doesn't mean it can't be robbed. Expensive-to-replace items like pool equipment, built-in appliances and central air units have been stolen and carpeting used to carry the items out. We no longer take interior pictures. We withhold when possible information that the property is vacant unless we are reassured that the caller is a "real estate agent." Virtual tours may be given to other brokers in a presentation of the property when it is assured that the viewers are indeed, brokers and in an office setting watching the virtual tour.*

---

12. **KEYSAFE/LOCKBOX:** A keysafe/lockbox is designed to hold a key to the Property to permit access to the Property by Broker, cooperating brokers, MLS participants, their authorized licensees and representatives, authorized inspectors, and accompanied prospective buyers. Broker, cooperating brokers, MLS and Associations/Boards of REALTORS® are **not** insurers against injury, theft, loss, vandalism or damage attributed to the use of a keysafe/lockbox. Seller does (or if checked ☐ does not) authorize Broker to install a keysafe/lockbox. If Seller does not occupy the Property, Seller shall be responsible for obtaining occupant(s)' written permission for use of a keysafe/lockbox (C.A.R. Form KLA).

---

12. **Keysafe/Lockbox:** If only one lockbox is on the property, it must be a "Board Authorized Electronic Lockbox" to allow other cooperating agents to show the property. A separate lockbox for handymen and others may also be placed on the property, usually a back door, so that all MLS participants have access to show the house.

---

13. **SIGN:** Seller does (or if checked ☐ does not) authorize Broker to install a FOR SALE/SOLD sign on the Property.

START - PAGE 4 OF 5

13. **Sign:** The Seller agrees/doesn't agree to have a sign placed on the property.

---

14. **EQUAL HOUSING OPPORTUNITY:** The Property is offered in compliance with federal, state and local anti-discrimination laws.

---

14. **Equal Housing Opportunity:** The property is offered in compliance with all laws adhering to anti-discrimination regulations.

---

15. **ATTORNEY FEES:** In any action, proceeding or arbitration between Seller and Broker regarding the obligation to pay compensation under this Agreement, the prevailing Seller or Broker shall be entitled to reasonable attorney fees and costs from the non-prevailing Seller or Broker, except as provided in paragraph 19A.

---

15. **Attorney Fees:** This states that in any lawsuit or arbitration between the Seller and the Broker regarding the obligation to pay compensation, the prevailing party shall be entitled to reasonable attorney costs, except as provided in paragraph 19A.

---

16. **ADDITIONAL TERMS:** ☐ REO Advisory Listing (C.A.R. Form REOL) ☐ Short Sale Information and Advisory (C.A.R. Form SSIA) _____

_____

_____

_____

_____

_____

---

16. Additional Terms: This is an excellent place to insert terms not covered above, such as the Sellers paying for termite clearance and title insurance.

---

17. MANAGEMENT APPROVAL: If an associate-licensee in Broker's office (salesperson or broker-associate) enters into this Agreement on Broker's behalf, and Broker or Manager does not approve of its terms, Broker or Manager has the right to cancel this Agreement, in writing, within **5 Days** After its execution.

18. SUCCESSORS AND ASSIGNS: This Agreement shall be binding upon Seller and Seller's successors and assigns.

---

17. Management Approval: Within five days (or a "reasonable period") from execution of this agreement, the associate licensee's Broker or Manager may disapprove this contract.

"Supervision of salespersons' activities" requires the broker to initial each page of the 5-page listing and, if the broker does not approve of any terms, he or she has the right to cancel the listing within five days.

18. Successors and Assigns: This agreement is binding on the Seller and the Seller's successors and assigns.

---

19. DISPUTE RESOLUTION:

A. MEDIATION: Seller and Broker agree to mediate any dispute or claim arising between them regarding the obligation to pay compensation under this Agreement, before resorting to arbitration or court action. Mediation fees, if any, shall be divided equally among the parties involved. If, for any dispute or claim to which this paragraph applies, any party (i) commences an action without first attempting to resolve the matter through mediation, or (ii) before commencement of an action, refuses to mediate after a request has been made, then that party shall not be entitled to recover attorney fees, even if they would otherwise be available to that party in any such action. THIS MEDIATION PROVISION APPLIES WHETHER OR NOT THE ARBITRATION PROVISION IS INITIALED. **Exclusions from this mediation agreement are specified in paragraph 19C.**

---

19. Dispute Resolution:

19(A) Mediation: This explains that the Seller and the Broker will mediate any dispute arising from this agreement, or any resulting transaction before resorting to arbitration or court action. Exclusions from this mediation agreement are specified in paragraph 19C.

Mediation should tried before arbitration or the courts.

B. ARBITRATION OF DISPUTES:

Seller and Broker agree that any dispute or claim in Law or equity arising between them regarding the obligation to pay compensation under this Agreement, which is not settled through mediation, shall be decided by neutral, binding arbitration. The arbitrator shall be a retired judge or justice, or an attorney with at least 5 years of residential real estate Law experience, unless the parties mutually agree to a different arbitrator. The parties shall have the right to discovery in accordance with Code of Civil Procedure §1283.05. In all other respects, the arbitration shall be conducted in accordance with Title 9 of Part 3 of the Code of Civil Procedure. Judgment upon the award of the arbitrator(s) may be entered into any court having jurisdiction. Enforcement of this agreement to arbitrate shall be governed by the Federal Arbitration Act. Exclusions from this arbitration agreement are specified in paragraph 19C.

"NOTICE: BY INITIALING IN THE SPACE BELOW YOU ARE AGREEING TO HAVE ANY DISPUTE ARISING OUT OF THE MATTERS INCLUDED IN THE 'ARBITRATION OF DISPUTES' PROVISION DECIDED BY NEUTRAL ARBITRATION AS PROVIDED BY CALIFORNIA LAW AND YOU ARE GIVING UP ANY RIGHTS YOU MIGHT POSSESS TO HAVE THE DISPUTE LITIGATED IN A COURT OR JURY TRIAL. BY INITIALING IN THE SPACE BELOW YOU ARE GIVING UP YOUR JUDICIAL RIGHTS TO DISCOVERY AND APPEAL, UNLESS THOSE RIGHTS ARE SPECIFICALLY INCLUDED IN THE 'ARBITRATION OF DISPUTES' PROVISION. IF YOU

REFUSE TO SUBMIT TO ARBITRATION AFTER AGREEING TO THIS PROVISION, YOU MAY BE COMPELLED TO ARBITRATE UNDER THE AUTHORITY OF THE CALIFORNIA CODE OF CIVIL PROCEDURE. YOUR AGREEMENT TO THIS ARBITRATION PROVISION IS VOLUNTARY."

"WE HAVE READ AND UNDERSTAND THE FOREGOING AND AGREE TO SUBMIT DISPUTES ARISING OUT OF THE MATTERS INCLUDED IN THE 'ARBITRATION OF DISPUTES' PROVISION TO NEUTRAL ARBITRATION."

Seller's Initials	/	Broker's Initials	/

19(B) Arbitration of Disputes: This is an explanation of arbitration between the Seller and the Broker. In order to come into effect, both parties must initial it. Do not give advice on how to handle this clause unless you are an attorney. Have the Sellers read the clause and suggest that, if they are unsure on how to proceed, they should consult their legal adviser.

C. **ADDITIONAL MEDIATION AND ARBITRATION TERMS:** The following matters shall be excluded from mediation and arbitration: (i) a judicial or non-judicial foreclosure or other action or proceeding to enforce a deed of trust, mortgage or installment land sale contract as defined in Civil Code §2985; (ii) an unlawful detainer action; (iii) the filing or enforcement of a mechanic's lien; and (iv) any matter that is within the jurisdiction of a probate, small claims or bankruptcy court. The filing of a court action to enable the recording of a notice of pending action, for order of attachment, receivership, injunction, or other provisional remedies, shall not constitute a waiver or violation of the mediation and arbitration provisions.

19(C) Additional Mediation and Arbitration Terms: This lays out what matters will be excluded form the arbitration process.

Never give legal or tax advice to your principals, unless you are an attorney or CPA.

20. **ENTIRE AGREEMENT:** All prior discussions, negotiations and agreements between the parties concerning the subject matter of this Agreement are superseded by this Agreement, which constitutes the entire contract and a complete and exclusive expression of their agreement, and may not be contradicted by evidence of any prior agreement or contemporaneous oral agreement. If any provision of this Agreement is held to be ineffective or invalid, the remaining provisions will nevertheless be given full force and effect. This Agreement and any supplement, addendum or modification, including any photocopy or facsimile, may be executed in counterparts.

START - PAGE 5 OF 5

20. **Entire Agreement:** This agreement "supersedes" all prior discussions, negotiations, and agreements between the Seller and Broker. In other words, the agreement includes only what is in it, and does not include any oral agreements not included in this agreement.

21. **OWNERSHIP, TITLE AND AUTHORITY:** Seller warrants that: (i) Seller is the owner of the Property; (ii) no other persons or entities have title to the Property; and (iii) Seller has the authority to both execute this Agreement and sell the Property. Exceptions to ownership, title and authority are as follows: _____
_____ .

21. **Ownership, Title and Authority:** This is where Sellers acknowledge that they are authorized to convey the property. The fill-in portion asks for exceptions, hence the answer should be NONE.

By signing below, Seller acknowledges that Seller has read, understands, received a copy of and agrees to the terms of this Agreement.

Seller _____ Date _____

Address _____ City _____ State _____ Zip_____

Telephone _____ Fax _____ Email _____

Seller _____ Date _____

Address _____ City _____ State _____ Zip_____

Telephone _____ Fax _____ Email _____

Real Estate Broker (Firm) _____ Cal BRE Lic. # _____

By (Agent) _____ Cal BRE Lic. # _____ Date _____

Address _____ City _____ State _____ Zip_____

Telephone _____ Fax _____ Email _____

All Sellers sign the listing contract and date it, entering their address and pertinent information. As the real estate agent, you enter the firm name, then sign it directly underneath (as a representative of the brokerage firm), including all pertinent information, such as fax number, email address, and license number.

Under Section 10142 of the Real Estate Law, the agent is required to give a copy of the listing agreement to his or her principal(s) (all signing parties) at the time the signature is obtained.

The Sellers' signatures constitute acknowledgment that they received a copy as of the date indicated. In the event they were to protest that they did not know what the contract contained, or what it meant, the agent can refute such allegations. If the owner is married, the signatures of both spouses should be obtained, even if the property is held in the name of one alone. Despite the apparent ownership by one alone, under the community property laws of California, the Buyer may find it impossible to sue for specific performance unless both spouses have signed.

© 1991-2013, California Association of REALTORS®, Inc. United States copyright law (Title 17 U.S. Code) forbids the unauthorized distribu form, or any portion thereof, by photocopy machine or any other means, including facsimile or computerized formats.

THIS FORM HAS BEEN APPROVED BY THE CALIFORNIA ASSOCIATION OF REALTORS® (C.A.R.). NO REPRESENTATION IS MADE ACCURACY OF ANY PROVISION IN ANY SPECIFIC TRANSACTION. A REAL ESTATE BROKER IS THE PERSON QUALIFIED TRANSACTIONS. IF YOU DESIRE LEGAL OR TAX ADVICE, CONSULT AN APPROPRIATE PROFESSIONAL.

Published and Distributed by:
REAL ESTATE BUSINESS SERVICES, INC.
a subsidiary of the California Association of REALTORS®
525 South Virgil Avenue, Los Angeles, California 90020

Reviewed by _____

RLA REVISED 11/13 (PAGE 5 OF 5)

II. Completing the Listing Kit

Once the Listing Agreement has been properly filled out, you will need to supply your seller with additional information, including disclosures and forms to be filled out. These

are all part of a listing kit. A *LISTING KIT is the packet of forms an agent provides to the seller when taking a listing.*

Fortunately, the California Association of REALTORS®, through its subsidiary Real Estate Business Service (REBS), has come up with standardized forms to make fulfilling the sellers' listing requirements easier and more uniform. The following is a list of CAR® forms (available digitally through **zipForms® Plus**) that you should include in the listing kit:

1. Residential Listing Agreement (RLA) (Complete form - see Chapter 3, Figure 3-1) with Seller's Advisory (SA) (**Figure 4-1**) (Buyer does not receive a copy of this form.)

2. Disclosure Regarding Real Estate Agency Relationship (AD) (Chapter 3, Figure 3-2).

3. Seller's Affidavit of Nonforeign Status and/or California Withholding Exemption (AS) (**Figure 4-2**)

> *Instead of providing the buyers with a Seller's Affidavit of Nonforeign Status and/or California Withholding Exemption where the sellers' social security numbers are disclosed, you may choose to use a Qualified Substitute (usually the escrow company) who takes care of this without disclosing this sensitive information.*

4. Lead-Based Paint and Lead-Based Paint Hazards Disclosure, Acknowledgement, and Addendum (FLD) (**Figure 4-3**)

5. Natural Hazard Disclosure Statement (NHD) (**Figure 4-4**)

6. Estimated Seller's Proceeds (ESP) (**Figure 4-5**) (Buyer does not receive a copy of this form.)

7. Home Warranty Application or Waiver (**Figure 4-6**)

8. Water Heater and Smoke Detector Statement of Compliance (WHSD) (**Figure 4-7**)

9. Notice to Buyers and Sellers - Defective Furnances in California (Not reproduced here. **This is not a CAR® form, but rather a broker-generated form**.)

10. Transfer Disclosure Statement (TDS) (See Chapter 7, Figure 7-4.)

11. Sellers' Property Questionnaire

> *A prudent agent should have a template for all transactions. Therefore, with a click of the mouse, you have all the forms necessary for each transaction. However, keep in mind that when a form is updated you must manually remove the old form from the template and replace it with the new one. Distributing a package template to all office salespersons should maintain uniformity and help relieve the broker of some potential liability for missing forms or advisories.*

Figure 4-1

CALIFORNIA
ASSOCIATION
OF REALTORS®

SELLER'S ADVISORY
(C.A.R. Form SA, Revised 11/13)

Property Address: _123 Sail Avenue, Marina del Rey, CA   90292_ ("Property")

1. **INTRODUCTION:** Selling property in California is a process that involves many steps. From start to finish, it could take anywhere from a few weeks to many months, depending upon the condition of your Property, local market conditions and other factors. You have already taken an important first step by listing your Property for sale with a licensed real estate broker. Your broker will help guide you through the process and may refer you to other professionals, as needed. This advisory addresses many things you may need to think about and do as you market your Property. Some of these things are requirements imposed upon you, either by law or by the listing or sale contract. Others are simply practical matters that may arise during the process. Please read this document carefully and, if you have any questions, ask your broker or appropriate legal or tax advisor for help.

2. **DISCLOSURES:**

   A. **General Disclosure Duties:** You must affirmatively disclose to the buyer, in writing, any and all known facts that materially affect the value or desirability of your Property. You must disclose these facts whether or not asked about such matters by the buyer, any broker, or anyone else. This duty to disclose applies even if the buyer agrees to purchase your Property in its present condition without requiring you to make any repairs. If you do not know what or how to disclose, you should consult a real estate attorney in California of your choosing. Broker cannot advise you on the legal sufficiency of any disclosures you make. If the Property you are selling is a residence with one to four units except for certain subdivisions, your broker also has a duty to conduct a reasonably competent and diligent visual inspection of the accessible areas and to disclose to a buyer all adverse material facts that the inspection reveals. If your broker discovers something that could indicate a problem, your broker must advise the buyer.

   B. **Statutory Duties:** (For one-to-four Residential Units):
      (1) You must timely prepare and deliver to the buyer, among other things, a Real Estate Transfer Disclosure Statement ("TDS"), and a Natural Hazard Disclosure Statement ("NHD"). You have a legal obligation to honestly and completely fill out the TDS form in its entirety. (Many local entities or organizations have their own supplement to the TDS that you may also be asked to complete.) The NHD is a statement indicating whether your Property is in certain designated flood, fire or earthquake/seismic hazard zones. Third-party professional companies can help you with this task.
      (2) Depending upon the age and type of construction of your Property, you may also be required to provide and, in certain cases you can receive limited legal protection by providing, the buyer with booklets entitled "The Homeowner's Guide to Earthquake Safety," "The Commercial Property Owner's Guide to Earthquake Safety," "Protect Your Family From Lead in Your Home" and "Environmental Hazards: A Guide For Homeowners and Buyers." Some of these booklets may be packaged together for your convenience. The earthquake guides ask you to answer specific questions about your Property's structure and preparedness for an earthquake. If you are required to supply the booklet about lead, you will also be required to disclose to the buyer any known lead-based paint and lead-based paint hazards on a separate form. The environmental hazards guide informs the buyer of common environmental hazards that may be found in properties.
      (3) If you know that your property is: (i) located within one mile of a former military ordnance location; or (ii) in or affected by a zone or district allowing manufacturing, commercial or airport use, you must disclose this to the buyer. You are also required to make a good faith effort to obtain and deliver to the buyer a disclosure notice from the appropriate local agency(ies) about any special tax levied on your Property pursuant to the Mello-Roos Community Facilities Act, the Improvement Bond Act of 1915, and a notice concerning the contractual assessment provided by section 5898.24 of the Streets And Highways Code (collectively, "Special Tax Disclosures").
      (4) If the TDS, NHD, or lead, military ordnance, commercial zone or Special Tax Disclosures are provided to a buyer after you accept that buyer's offer, the buyer will have 3 days after delivery (or 5 days if mailed) to terminate the offer, which is why it is extremely important to complete these disclosures as soon as possible. There are certain exemptions from these statutory requirements; however, if you have actual knowledge of any of these items, you may still be required to make a disclosure as the items can be considered material facts.

   C. **Death and Other Disclosures:** Many buyers consider death on real property to be a material fact in the purchase of property. In some situations, it is advisable to disclose that a death occurred or the manner of death; however, California Civil Code Section 1710.2 provides that you have no disclosure duty "where the death has occurred more than three years prior to the date the transferee offers to purchase, lease, or rent the real property, or [regardless of the date of occurrence] that an occupant of that property was afflicted with, or died from, Human T-Lymphotropic Virus Type III/Lymphadenopathy-Associated Virus." This law does not "immunize an owner or his or her agent from making an intentional misrepresentation in response to a direct inquiry from a transferee or a prospective transferee of real property, concerning deaths on the real property."

   D. **Condominiums and Other Common Interest Subdivisions:** If the Property is a condominium, townhouse, or other property in a common interest subdivision, you must provide to the buyer copies of the governing documents, the most recent financial statements distributed, and other documents required by law or contract. If you do not have a current version of these documents, you can request them from the management of your homeowner's association. To avoid delays, you are encouraged to obtain these documents as soon as possible, even if you have not yet entered into a purchase agreement to sell your Property.

The copyright laws of the United States (Title 17 U.S. Code) forbid the unauthorized reproduction of this form, or any portion thereof, by photocopy machine or any other means, including facsimile or computerized formats. Copyright © 1991-2013, CALIFORNIA ASSOCIATION OF REALTORS®, INC. ALL RIGHTS RESERVED.

Seller's Initials (_____) (_____)

Reviewed by _____ Date _____

EQUAL HOUSING OPPORTUNITY

SA REVISED 11/13 (PAGE 1 OF 2)

SELLER'S ADVISORY (SA PAGE 1 OF 2)

Agent: WALT HUBER	Phone:	Fax:	Prepared using zipForm® software
Broker: WALT HUBER REALTOR			

123 Sail Avenue
Property Address: Marina del Rey, CA 90292 _____ Date: _____

3. **CONTRACT TERMS AND LEGAL REQUIREMENTS:**
    A. **Contract Terms and Conditions:** A buyer may request, as part of the contract for the sale of your Property, that you pay for repairs to the Property and other items. Your decision on whether or not to comply with a buyer's requests may affect your ability to sell your Property at a specified price.
    B. **Withholding Taxes:** Under federal and California tax laws, a buyer is required to withhold a portion of the purchase price from your sale proceeds for tax purposes unless you sign an affidavit of non-foreign status and California residency, or some other exemption applies and is documented.
    C. **Prohibition Against Discrimination:** Discriminatory conduct in the sale of real property against individuals belonging to legally protected classes is a violation of the law.
    D. **Government Retrofit Standards:** Unless exempt, you must comply with government retrofit standards, including, but not limited to, installing operable smoke detectors, bracing water heaters, and providing the buyer with corresponding written statements of compliance. Some city and county governments may impose additional retrofit standards, including, but not limited to, installing low-flow toilets and showerheads, gas shut-off valves, tempered glass, and barriers around swimming pools and spas. You should consult with the appropriate governmental agencies, inspectors, and other professionals to determine the retrofit standards for your Property, the extent to which your Property complies with such standards, and the costs, if any, of compliance.
    E. **EPA's LEAD-BASED PAINT RENOVATION, REPAIR AND PAINTING RULE:** The new rule requires that contractors and maintenance professionals working in pre-1978 housing, child care facilities, and schools with lead-based paint be certified; that their employees be trained; and that they follow protective work practice standards. The rule applies to renovation, repair, or painting activities affecting more than six square feet of lead-based paint in a room or more than 20 square feet of lead-based paint on the exterior. Enforcement of the rule begins October 1, 2010. See the EPA website at www.epa.gov/lead for more information.
    F. **Legal, Tax and Other Implications:** Selling your Property may have legal, tax, insurance, title or other implications. You should consult an appropriate professional for advice on these matters.
4. **MARKETING CONSIDERATIONS:**
    A. **Pre-Sale Considerations:** You should consider doing what you can to prepare your Property for sale, such as correcting any defects or other problems. Many people are not aware of defects in or problems with their own Property. One way to make yourself aware is to obtain professional home inspections prior to sale, both generally, and for wood destroying pests and organisms, such as termites. By doing this, you then have an opportunity to make repairs before your Property is offered for sale, which may enhance its marketability. Keep in mind, however, that any problems revealed by such inspection reports or repairs that have been made, whether or not disclosed in a report, should be disclosed to the buyer (see "Disclosures" in paragraph 2 above). This is true even if the buyer gets his/her own inspections covering the same area. Obtaining inspection reports may also assist you during contract negotiations with the buyer. For example, if a pest control report has both a primary and secondary recommendation for clearance, you may want to specify in the purchase agreement those recommendations, if any, for which you are going to pay.
    B. **Post-Sale Protections:** It is often helpful to provide the buyer with, among other things, a home protection/warranty plan for the Property. These plans will generally cover problems, not deemed to be pre-existing, that occur after your sale is completed. In the event something does go wrong after the sale, and it is covered by the plan, the buyer may be able to resolve the concern by contacting the home protection company.
    C. **Safety Precautions:** Advertising and marketing your Property for sale, including, but not limited to, holding open houses, placing a keysafe/lockbox, erecting FOR SALE signs, and disseminating photographs, video tapes, and virtual tours of the premises, may jeopardize your personal safety and that of your Property. You are strongly encouraged to maintain insurance, and to take any and all possible precautions and safeguards to protect yourself, other occupants, visitors, your Property, and your belongings, including cash, jewelry, drugs, firearms and other valuables located on the Property, against injury, theft, loss, vandalism, damage, and other harm.
    D. **Expenses:** You are advised that you, not the Broker, are responsible for the fees and costs, if any, to comply with your duties and obligations to the buyer of your Property.
5. **OTHER ITEMS:** _____
    _____
    _____

Seller has read and understands this Advisory. By signing below, Seller acknowledges receipt of a copy of this document.

Seller _____ Date _____
Print Name _____

Seller _____ Date _____
Print Name _____

Real Estate Broker _____ By _____ Date _____
                                                                (Agent)
Address _____ City _____ State _____ Zip _____

Telephone _____ Fax _____ E-mail _____

THIS FORM HAS BEEN APPROVED BY THE CALIFORNIA ASSOCIATION OF REALTORS® (C.A.R.). NO REPRESENTATION IS MADE AS TO THE LEGAL VALIDITY OR ADEQUACY OF ANY PROVISION IN ANY SPECIFIC TRANSACTION. A REAL ESTATE BROKER IS THE PERSON QUALIFIED TO ADVISE ON REAL ESTATE TRANSACTIONS. IF YOU DESIRE LEGAL OR TAX ADVICE, CONSULT AN APPROPRIATE PROFESSIONAL.

This form is available for use by the entire real estate industry. It is not intended to identify the user as a REALTOR®. REALTOR® is a registered collective membership mark which may be used only by members of the NATIONAL ASSOCIATION OF REALTORS® who subscribe to its Code of Ethics.

Published and Distributed by:
REAL ESTATE BUSINESS SERVICES, INC.
a subsidiary of the California Association of REALTORS®
525 South Virgil Avenue, Los Angeles, California 90020

Reviewed by _____ Date _____

SA REVISED 11/13 (PAGE 2 OF 2)   **SELLER'S ADVISORY (SA PAGE 2 OF 2)**   Untitled

This (along with the Listing Agreement) is one of the few forms in the "listing kit" of which the buyer will not receive a copy.

Figure 4-2

CALIFORNIA
ASSOCIATION
OF REALTORS®

**SELLER'S AFFIDAVIT OF NONFOREIGN STATUS
AND/OR CALIFORNIA WITHHOLDING EXEMPTION**
FOREIGN INVESTMENT IN REAL PROPERTY TAX ACT (FIRPTA)
AND CALIFORNIA WITHHOLDING LAW
(Use a separate form for each Transferor)
(C.A.R. Form AS, Revised 4/12)

Internal Revenue Code ("IRC") Section 1445 provides that a transferee of a U.S. real property interest must withhold tax if the transferor is a "foreign person." California Revenue and Taxation Code Section 18662 provides that a transferee of a California real property interest must withhold tax unless an exemption applies.

I understand that this affidavit may be disclosed to the Internal Revenue Service and to the California Franchise Tax Board by the transferee, and that any false statement I have made herein may result in a fine, imprisonment or both.

123 Sail Avenue

1. **PROPERTY ADDRESS** (property being transferred): *Marina del Rey, CA 90292* _____ ("Property")
2. **TRANSFEROR'S INFORMATION:**
   Full Name _____ ("Transferor")
   Telephone Number _____
   Address _____
   (Use HOME address for individual transferors. Use OFFICE address for an "Entity" i.e.: corporations, partnerships, limited liability companies, trusts and estates.)
   Social Security No., or Federal Employer Identification No. _____
   For a corporation qualified to do business in California, California Corporation No. _____
   Note: In order to avoid withholding, IRC Section 1445 (b) requires that the Seller (a) provides this affidavit to the Buyer with the Seller's taxpayer identification number ("TIN"), or (b) provides this affidavit, including Seller's TIN, to a "qualified substitute" who furnishes a statement to the Buyer under penalty of perjury that the qualified substitute has such affidavit in their possession. A qualified substitute may be (i) an attorney, title company, or escrow company (but not the Seller's agent) responsible for closing the transaction, or (ii) the Buyer's agent.
3. **AUTHORITY TO SIGN:** If this document is signed on behalf of an Entity Transferor, THE UNDERSIGNED INDIVIDUAL DECLARES THAT HE/SHE HAS AUTHORITY TO SIGN THIS DOCUMENT ON BEHALF OF THE TRANSFEROR.
4. **FEDERAL LAW:** I, the undersigned, declare under penalty of perjury that, for the reason checked below, if any, I am exempt (or if signed on behalf of an Entity Transferor, the Entity is exempt) from the federal withholding law (FIRPTA).
   ☐ (For individual Transferors) I am not a nonresident alien for purposes of U.S. income taxation.
   ☐ (For corporation, partnership, limited liability company, trust and estate Transferors) The Transferor is not a foreign corporation, foreign partnership, foreign limited liability company, foreign trust or foreign estate, as those terms are defined in the Internal Revenue Code and Income Tax Regulations.
5. **CALIFORNIA LAW:** I, the undersigned, declare under penalty of perjury that, for the reason checked below, if any, I am exempt (or if signed on behalf of an Entity Transferor, the Entity is exempt) from the California withholding law.
   Certifications which fully exempt the sale from withholding:
   ☐ The total sales price for the Property is $100,000 or less.
   ☐ The Property qualifies as my principal residence (or the decedent's, if being sold by the decedent's estate) within the meaning of IRC Section 121 (owned and occupied as such for two of the last five years).
   ☐ The Property was last used as my principal residence (or the decedent's, if being sold by the decedent's estate) within the meaning of IRC Section 121 without regard to the two-year time period.
   ☐ The transaction will result in a loss or zero gain for California income tax purposes. (Complete FTB Form 593-E.)
   ☐ The Property has been compulsorily or involuntarily converted (within the meaning of IRC Section 1033) and Transferor intends to acquire property similar or related in service or use to be eligible for non-recognition of gain for California income tax purposes under IRC Section 1033.
   ☐ Transferor is a corporation (or an LLC classified as a corporation) that is either qualified through the California Secretary of State or has a permanent place of business in California.
   ☐ Transferor is a partnership (or an LLC that is not a disregarded single member LLC, classified as a partnership) and recorded title to the Property is in the name of the partnership or LLC. If so, the partnership or LLC must withhold from nonresident partners or members as required.
   ☐ Transferor is exempt from tax under California or federal law.
   ☐ Transferor is an insurance company, qualified pension/profit sharing plan, IRA or charitable remainder trust.
   Certifications which may partially or fully exempt the sale from withholding:
   ☐ The Property is being, or will be, exchanged for property of like kind within the meaning of IRC Section 1031.
   ☐ Payments for the Property are being made in installments, the transferor is a non-resident seller and withholding will be applied to each principal payment.
   ☐ As a result of the sale of the Property, Seller's tax liability, calculated at the maximum tax rate regardless of Seller's actual rate, will be less than the 3 1/3% withholding otherwise required. Seller will be required to sign a certification, under penalty of perjury, specifying the amount to be withheld. **(Not to be used for sales closing prior to January 1, 2007)**

By _____ Date _____
(Transferor's Signature) (Indicate if you are signing as the grantor of a revocable/grantor trust)

_____   _____
Typed or printed name   Title (If signed on behalf of Entity Transferor)

Buyer's unauthorized use or disclosure of Seller's TIN could result in civil or criminal liability.

Buyer _____ Date _____
(Buyer acknowledges receipt of a Copy of this Seller's Affidavit)
Buyer _____ Date _____
(Buyer acknowledges receipt of a Copy of this Seller's Affidavit)

The copyright laws of the United States (Title 17 U.S. Code) forbid the unauthorized reproduction of this form by any means, including facsimile or computerized formats. Copyright © 1988-2012, CALIFORNIA ASSOCIATION OF REALTORS®, INC. All Rights Reserved.
THIS FORM HAS BEEN APPROVED BY THE CALIFORNIA ASSOCIATION OF REALTORS® (C.A.R.). NO REPRESENTATION IS MADE AS TO THE LEGAL VALIDITY OR ADEQUACY OF ANY PROVISION IN ANY SPECIFIC TRANSACTION. A REAL ESTATE BROKER IS THE PERSON QUALIFIED TO ADVISE ON REAL ESTATE TRANSACTIONS. IF YOU DESIRE LEGAL OR TAX ADVICE, CONSULT AN APPROPRIATE PROFESSIONAL.
This form is available for use by the entire real estate industry. It is not intended to identify the user as a REALTOR®. REALTOR® is a registered collective membership mark which may be used only by members of the NATIONAL ASSOCIATION OF REALTORS® who subscribe to its Code of Ethics.

Published and Distributed by:
REAL ESTATE BUSINESS SERVICES, INC.
a subsidiary of the California Association of REALTORS®
525 South Virgil Avenue, Los Angeles, California 90020

Reviewed by _____ Date _____

AS 4/12 (PAGE 1 OF 2)
SELLER'S AFFIDAVIT OF NONFOREIGN STATUS AND/OR CALIFORNIA WITHHOLDING EXEMPTION (AS PAGE 1 OF 2)

Agent: WALT HUBER	Phone:	Fax:	Prepared using zipForm® software
Broker: WALT HUBER REALTOR			

(Often referred to as FIRPTA.) If all the seller's answers are "no" on this form, there's a good possibility of a tax liability. Advise your seller to consult a tax advisor! Also, make sure the buyer signs a copy of this, as he or she may be responsible for the seller's taxes!

IMPORTANT NOTICE: An Affidavit should be signed by each individual or entity Transferor to whom or to which it applies. Before you sign, any questions relating to the legal sufficiency of this form, or to whether it applies to you or to a particular transaction, or about the definition of any of the terms used, should be referred to an attorney, certified public accountant, or other professional tax advisor, the Internal Revenue Service, or the California Franchise Tax Board. For further information on federal guidelines, see C.A.R. Legal Q & A *"Federal Withholding: The Foreign Investment in Real Property Tax Act,"* and/or IRS Publication 515 or 519. For further information on state guidelines, see C.A.R. Legal Q & A *"California Nonresident Withholding,"* and/or California FTB Pub. 1016.

FEDERAL GUIDELINES

FOREIGN PERSONS DEFINED. The following general information is provided to assist sellers in determining whether they are "foreign persons" for purposes of the Foreign Investment in Real Property Tax Act (FIRPTA), IRC §1445. FIRPTA requires a buyer to withhold and send to the Internal Revenue Service 10% of the gross sales price of a United States (U.S.) real property interest if the seller is a foreign person. No withholding is required for a seller who is a U.S. person (that is, not a foreign person). In order for an individual to be a U.S. person, he/she must be either a U.S. citizen or a U.S. resident alien. The test must be applied separately to each seller in transactions involving more than one seller. Even if the seller is a foreign person, withholding will not be required in every circumstance.

NONRESIDENT ALIEN INDIVIDUAL. An individual whose residence is not within the U.S. **and** who is not a U.S. citizen is a nonresident alien. The term includes a nonresident alien fiduciary. An alien actually present in the U.S. who is not just staying temporarily (i.e., not a mere transient or sojourner), is a U.S. resident for income tax purposes. An alien is considered a U.S. resident and not subject to withholding under FIRPTA if the alien meets either the **green card test** or the **substantial presence test** for the calendar year.

GREEN CARD TEST. An alien is a U.S. resident if the individual was a lawful permanent resident of the U.S. at any time during the calendar year. This is known as the "green card test."

SUBSTANTIAL PRESENCE TEST. An alien is considered a U.S. resident if the individual meets the substantial presence test for the calendar year. Under this test, the individual must be physically present in the U.S. on at least: (1) 31 days during the current calendar year; and (2) 183 days during the current year and the two preceding years, counting all the days of physical presence in the current year but only 1/3 the number of days present in the first preceding year, and 1/6 the number of days present in the second preceding year.

DAYS OF PRESENCE IN THE U.S. TEST. Generally, a person is treated as physically present in the country at any time during the day. However, if a person regularly commutes to work in the U.S. from a residence in Canada or Mexico, or is in transit between two points outside the U.S. and is physically present in the country for less than 24 hours, he/she is not treated as present in the U.S. on any day during the transit or commute. In addition, the individual is not treated as present in the U.S. on any day during which he/she is unable to leave the U.S. because of a medical condition which arose while in the U.S.

EXEMPT INDIVIDUAL. For the substantial presence test, do not count days for which a person is an exempt individual. An exempt individual is anyone in the following categories:

(1) An individual temporarily present in the U.S. because of (a) full-time diplomatic or consular status, (b) full-time employment with an international organization or (c) an immediate family member of a person described in (a) or (b).

(2) A teacher or trainee temporarily present in the U.S. under a "J" visa (other than as a student) who substantially complies with the requirements of the visa. An individual will not be exempt under this category for a calendar year if he/she was exempt as a teacher or trainee or as a student for any two calendar years during the preceding six calendar years.

(3) A student temporarily present in the U.S. under an "F" or "J" visa who substantially complies with the requirements of the visa. Generally, a person will not be exempt as a student for any calendar year after the fifth calendar year for which he/she was exempt as a student, teacher or trainee. However, the individual may continue to be exempt as a student beyond the fifth year if he/she is in compliance with the terms of the student visa and does not intend to permanently reside in the U.S.

CLOSER CONNECTION TO A FOREIGN COUNTRY. Even if an individual would otherwise meet the substantial presence test, that person is not treated as meeting the test for the current calendar year if he/she:

(1) Is present in the U.S. on fewer than 183 days during the current year, and

(2) Has a tax home in a foreign country and has a closer connection to that country than to the U.S.

SPECIAL RULES. It is possible to be both a nonresident alien and a resident alien during the same tax year. Usually this occurs for the year a person arrives in or departs from the U.S. Other special provisions apply to individuals who were U.S. residents for at least three years, cease to be U.S. residents, and then become U.S. residents again.

NONRESIDENT ALIEN INDIVIDUALS MARRIED TO U.S. CITIZENS OR RESIDENT ALIENS may choose to be treated as resident aliens for most income tax purposes. However, these individuals are considered **nonresidents** for purposes of withholding taxes.

A FOREIGN PERSON OR PARTNERSHIP is one that does not fit the definition of a domestic corporation or partnership. A domestic corporation or partnership is one that was created or organized in the U.S., or under the laws of the U.S., or of any U.S. state or territory.

GUAM AND U.S. VIRGIN ISLANDS CORPORATIONS. A corporation created or organized in or under the laws of Guam or the U.S. Virgin Islands is not considered a foreign corporation for the purpose of withholding tax for the tax year if:

(1) at all times during the tax year, less than 25% in value of the corporation's stock is owned, directly or indirectly, by foreign persons, and

(2) at least 20% of the corporation's gross income is derived from sources within Guam or at least 65% of the corporation's income is effectively connected with the conduct of a trade or business in the U.S. Virgin Islands or the U.S. for the 3-year period ending with the close of the preceding tax year of the corporation, or the period the corporation has been in existence if less.

A NONRESIDENT ALIEN TRUSTEE, ADMINISTRATOR OR EXECUTOR of a trust or an estate is treated as a nonresident alien, even though all the beneficiaries of the trust or estate are citizens or residents of the U.S.

Buyer's Initials (_____)(_____)

Seller's Initials (_____)(_____)

Copyright © 1988-2012, CALIFORNIA ASSOCIATION OF REALTORS®, INC.
AS REVISED 4/12 (PAGE 2 OF 2)

Reviewed by _____ Date _____

EQUAL HOUSING OPPORTUNITY

SELLER'S AFFIDAVIT OF NONFOREIGN STATUS AND/OR CALIFORNIA WITHOLDING EXEMPTION (AS PAGE 2 OF 2)

Rather than disclose sensitive information like social security numbers, an escrow company can take care of this, avoiding revealing too much personal information.

Figure 4-3

CALIFORNIA ASSOCIATION OF REALTORS®

LEAD-BASED PAINT AND LEAD-BASED PAINT HAZARDS DISCLOSURE, ACKNOWLEDGMENT AND ADDENDUM
For Pre-1978 Housing Sales, Leases, or Rentals
(C.A.R. Form FLD, Revised 11/10)

The following terms and conditions are hereby incorporated in and made a part of the: ☐ California Residential Purchase Agreement, ☐ Residential Lease or Month-to-Month Rental Agreement, or ☐ Other: _____ _____, dated _____, on property known as: _____123 Sail Avenue, Marina del Rey CA 90292_____ ("Property") in which _____ is referred to as Buyer or Tenant and _____ is referred to as Seller or Landlord.

LEAD WARNING STATEMENT (SALE OR PURCHASE) Every purchaser of any interest in residential real property on which a residential dwelling was built prior to 1978 is notified that such property may present exposure to lead from lead-based paint that may place young children at risk of developing lead poisoning. Lead poisoning in young children may produce permanent neurological damage, including learning disabilities, reduced intelligent quotient, behavioral problems and impaired memory. Lead poisoning also poses a particular risk to pregnant women. The seller of any interest in residential real property is required to provide the buyer with any information on lead-based paint hazards from risk assessments or inspections in the seller's possession and notify the buyer of any known lead-based paint hazards. A risk assessment or inspection for possible lead-based paint hazards is recommended prior to purchase.

LEAD WARNING STATEMENT (LEASE OR RENTAL) Housing built before 1978 may contain lead-based paint. Lead from paint, paint chips and dust can pose health hazards if not managed properly. Lead exposure is especially harmful to young children and pregnant women. Before renting pre-1978 housing, lessors must disclose the presence of lead-based paint and/or lead-based paint hazards in the dwelling. Lessees must also receive federally approved pamphlet on lead poisoning prevention.

EPA'S LEAD-BASED PAINT RENOVATION, REPAIR AND PAINTING RULE: The new rule requires that contractors and maintenance professionals working in pre-1978 housing, child care facilities, and schools with lead-based paint be certified; that their employees be trained; and that they follow protective work practice standards. The rule applies to renovation, repair, or painting activities affecting more than six square feet of lead-based paint in a room or more than 20 square feet of lead-based paint on the exterior. Enforcement of the rule begins October 1, 2010. See the EPA website at www.epa.gov/lead for more information.

1. **SELLER'S OR LANDLORD'S DISCLOSURE**

   I (we) have no knowledge of lead-based paint and/or lead-based paint hazards in the housing other than the following:

   _____
   _____
   _____

   I (we) have no reports or records pertaining to lead-based paint and/or lead-based paint hazards in the housing other than the following, which, previously or as an attachment to this addendum have been provided to Buyer or Tenant:

   _____
   _____
   _____

   I (we), previously or as an attachment to this addendum, have provided Buyer or Tenant with the pamphlet *"Protect Your Family From Lead In Your Home"* or an equivalent pamphlet approved for use in the State such as *"The Homeowner's Guide to Environmental Hazards and Earthquake Safety."*

   For Sales Transactions Only: Buyer has 10 days, unless otherwise agreed in the real estate purchase contract, to conduct a risk assessment or inspection for the presence of lead-based paint and/or lead-based paint hazards.

   I (we) have reviewed the information above and certify, to the best of my (our) knowledge, that the information provided is true and correct.

   _____   _____
   Seller or Landlord   Date

   _____   _____
   Seller or Landlord   Date

The copyright laws of the United States (Title 17 U.S. Code) forbid the unauthorized reproduction of this form, or any portion thereof, by photocopy machine or any other means, including facsimile or computerized formats. Copyright © 1996-2010, CALIFORNIA ASSOCIATION OF REALTORS®, INC. ALL RIGHTS RESERVED.

Buyer's Initials (_____) (_____)

Reviewed by _____ Date _____

EQUAL HOUSING OPPORTUNITY

FLD REVISED 11/10 (PAGE 1 OF 2)

LEAD-BASED PAINT AND LEAD-BASED PAINT HAZARDS DISCLOSURE (FLD PAGE 1 OF 2)

Agent: WALT HUBER	Phone:	Fax:	Prepared using zipForm® software
Broker: WALT HUBER REALTOR			

Property Address: 123 Sail Avenue
Marina del Rey, CA 90292 _____ Date _____

2. LISTING AGENT'S ACKNOWLEDGMENT

Agent has informed Seller or Landlord of Seller's or Landlord's obligations under §42 U.S.C. 4852d and is aware of Agent's responsibility to ensure compliance.

I have reviewed the information above and certify, to the best of my knowledge, that the information provided is true and correct.

_____ By _____
(Please Print) Agent (Broker representing Seller or Landlord)   Associate-Licensee or Broker Signature   Date

3. BUYER'S OR TENANT'S ACKNOWLEDGMENT

I (we) have received copies of all information listed, if any, in 1 above and the pamphlet *"Protect Your Family From Lead In Your Home"* or an equivalent pamphlet approved for use in the State such as *"The Homeowner's Guide to Environmental Hazards and Earthquake Safety."* **If delivery of any of the disclosures or pamphlet referenced in paragraph 1 above occurs after Acceptance of an offer to purchase, Buyer has a right to cancel pursuant to the purchase contract. If you wish to cancel, you must act within the prescribed period.**

For Sales Transactions Only: Buyer acknowledges the right for 10 days, unless otherwise agreed in the real estate purchase contract, to conduct a risk assessment or inspection for the presence of lead-based paint and/or lead-based paint hazards; OR, (if checked) ☐ Buyer waives the right to conduct a risk assessment or inspection for the presence of lead-based paint and/or lead-based paint hazards.

I (we) have reviewed the information above and certify, to the best of my (our) knowledge, that the information provided is true and correct.

_____   _____
Buyer or Tenant   Date   Buyer or Tenant   Date

4. COOPERATING AGENT'S ACKNOWLEDGMENT

Agent has informed Seller or Landlord, through the Listing Agent if the property is listed, of Seller's or Landlord's obligations under §42 U.S.C. 4852d and is aware of Agent's responsibility to ensure compliance.

I have reviewed the information above and certify, to the best of my knowledge, that the information provided is true and correct.

_____ By _____
Agent (Broker obtaining the Offer)   Associate-Licensee or Broker Signature   Date

THIS FORM HAS BEEN APPROVED BY THE CALIFORNIA ASSOCIATION OF REALTORS® (C.A.R.). NO REPRESENTATION IS MADE AS TO THE LEGAL VALIDITY OR ADEQUACY OF ANY PROVISION IN ANY SPECIFIC TRANSACTION. A REAL ESTATE BROKER IS THE PERSON QUALIFIED TO ADVISE ON REAL ESTATE TRANSACTIONS. IF YOU DESIRE LEGAL OR TAX ADVICE, CONSULT AN APPROPRIATE PROFESSIONAL.
This form is available for use by the entire real estate industry. It is not intended to identify the user as a REALTOR®. REALTOR® is a registered collective membership mark which may be used only by members of the NATIONAL ASSOCIATION OF REALTORS® who subscribe to its Code of Ethics.

Published and Distributed by:
REAL ESTATE BUSINESS SERVICES, INC.
a subsidiary of the California Association of REALTORS®
525 South Virgil Avenue, Los Angeles, California 90020

Reviewed by _____ Date _____

FLD REVISED 11/10 (PAGE 2 OF 2)

LEAD-BASED PAINT AND LEAD-BASED PAINT HAZARDS DISCLOSURE (FLD PAGE 2 OF 2)

This form must be filled out (if house was built before 1978) whether or not the seller knows of any lead-based paint used on the property.

Figure 4-4

CALIFORNIA
ASSOCIATION
OF REALTORS®

NATURAL HAZARD DISCLOSURE STATEMENT

(C.A.R. Form NHD, Revised 10/04)

123 Sail Avenue

This statement applies to the following property: *Marina del Rey, CA 90292*

The transferor and his or her agent(s) or a third-party consultant disclose the following information with the knowledge that even though this is not a warranty, prospective transferees may rely on this information in deciding whether and on what terms to purchase the subject property. Transferor hereby authorizes any agent(s) representing any principal(s) in this action to provide a copy of this statement to any person or entity in connection with any actual or anticipated sale of the property.

The following are representations made by the transferor and his or her agent(s) based on their knowledge and maps drawn by the state and federal governments. This information is a disclosure and is not intended to be part of any contract between the transferee and transferor.

THIS REAL PROPERTY LIES WITHIN THE FOLLOWING HAZARDOUS AREA(S):

A SPECIAL FLOOD HAZARD AREA (Any type Zone "A" or "V") designated by the Federal Emergency Management Agency.
Yes _____   No _____   Do not know and information not available from local jurisdiction _____

AN AREA OF POTENTIAL FLOODING shown on a dam failure inundation map pursuant to Section 8589.5 of the Government Code.
Yes _____   No _____   Do not know and information not available from local jurisdiction _____

A VERY HIGH FIRE HAZARD SEVERITY ZONE pursuant to Section 51178 or 51179 of the Government Code. The owner of this property is subject to the maintenance requirements of Section 51182 of the Government Code.
Yes _____   No _____

A WILDLAND AREA THAT MAY CONTAIN SUBSTANTIAL FOREST FIRE RISKS AND HAZARDS pursuant to Section 4125 of the Public Resources Code. The owner of this property is subject to the maintenance requirements of Section 4291 of the Public Resources Code. Additionally, it is not the state's responsibility to provide fire protection services to any building or structure located within the wildlands unless the Department of Forestry and Fire Protection has entered into a cooperative agreement with a local agency for those purposes pursuant to Section 4142 of the Public Resources Code.
Yes _____   No _____

AN EARTHQUAKE FAULT ZONE pursuant to Section 2622 of the Public Resources Code.
Yes _____   No _____

A SEISMIC HAZARD ZONE pursuant to Section 2696 of the Public Resources Code.
Yes (Landslide Zone) _____   Yes (Liquefaction Zone) _____
No _____   Map not yet released by state _____

The copyright laws of the United States (Title 17 U.S. Code) forbid the unauthorized reproduction of this form, or any portion thereof, by photocopy machine or any other means, including facsimile or computerized formats. Copyright © 1998-2004, CALIFORNIA ASSOCIATION OF REALTORS®, INC. ALL RIGHTS RESERVED.
NHD REVISED 10/04 (PAGE 1 OF 2)

Buyer's Initials (_____) (_____)
Seller's Initials (_____) (_____)
Reviewed by _____ Date _____

EQUAL HOUSING OPPORTUNITY

NATURAL HAZARD DISCLOSURE STATEMENT (NHD PAGE 1 OF 2)

Agent: WALT HUBER   Phone: Fax: Prepared using zipForm® software
Broker: WALT HUBER REALTOR

Property Address: 123 Sail Avenue
Marina del Rey, CA 90292 _____ Date: _____

THESE HAZARDS MAY LIMIT YOUR ABILITY TO DEVELOP THE REAL PROPERTY, TO OBTAIN INSURANCE, OR TO RECEIVE ASSISTANCE AFTER A DISASTER.

THE MAPS ON WHICH THESE DISCLOSURES ARE BASED ESTIMATE WHERE NATURAL HAZARDS EXIST. THEY ARE NOT DEFINITIVE INDICATORS OF WHETHER OR NOT A PROPERTY WILL BE AFFECTED BY A NATURAL DISASTER. TRANSFEREE(S) AND TRANSFEROR(S) MAY WISH TO OBTAIN PROFESSIONAL ADVICE REGARDING THOSE HAZARDS AND OTHER HAZARDS THAT MAY AFFECT THE PROPERTY

Signature of Transferor(s) _____ Date _____

Signature of Transferor(s) _____ Date _____

Agent(s) _____ Date _____

Agent(s) _____ Date _____

Check only one of the following:

☐ Transferor(s) and their agent(s) represent that the information herein is true and correct to the best of their knowledge as of the date signed by the transferor(s) and agent(s).

☐ Transferor(s) and their agent(s) acknowledge that they have exercised good faith in the selection of a third-party report provider as required in Civil Code Section 1103.7, and that the representations made in this Natural Hazard Disclosure Statement are based upon information provided by the independent third-party disclosure provider as a substituted disclosure pursuant to Civil Code Section 1103.4. Neither transferor(s) nor their agent(s) (1) has independently verified the information contained in this statement and report or (2) is personally aware of any errors or inaccuracies in the information contained on the statement. This statement was prepared by the provider below:

Third-Party Disclosure Provider(s) _____ Date _____

Transferee represents that he or she has read and understands this document. Pursuant to Civil Code Section 1103.8, the representations made in this Natural Hazard Disclosure Statement do not constitute all of the transferor's or agent's disclosure obligations in this transaction.

Signature of Transferee(s) _____ Date _____

Signature of Transferee(s) _____ Date _____

The copyright laws of the United States (Title 17 U.S. Code) forbid the unauthorized reproduction of this form, or any portion thereof, by photocopy machine or any other means, including facsimile or computerized formats. Copyright © 1998-2004, CALIFORNIA ASSOCIATION OF REALTORS®, INC. ALL RIGHTS RESERVED.

THIS FORM HAS BEEN APPROVED BY THE CALIFORNIA ASSOCIATION OF REALTORS® (C.A.R.). NO REPRESENTATION IS MADE AS TO THE LEGAL VALIDITY OR ADEQUACY OF ANY PROVISION IN ANY SPECIFIC TRANSACTION. A REAL ESTATE BROKER IS THE PERSON QUALIFIED TO ADVISE ON REAL ESTATE TRANSACTIONS. IF YOU DESIRE LEGAL OR TAX ADVICE, CONSULT AN APPROPRIATE PROFESSIONAL.

This form is available for use by the entire real estate industry. It is not intended to identify the user as a REALTOR®. REALTOR® is a registered collective membership mark which may be used only by members of the NATIONAL ASSOCIATION OF REALTORS® who subscribe to its Code of Ethics.

Published and Distributed by:
REAL ESTATE BUSINESS SERVICES, INC.
a subsidiary of the California Association of REALTORS®
525 South Virgil Avenue, Los Angeles, California 90020

Reviewed by _____ Date _____

NHD REVISED 10/04 (PAGE 2 OF 2)

NATURAL HAZARD DISCLOSURE STATEMENT (NHD PAGE 2 OF 2)   Untitled

Figure 4-5

CALIFORNIA
ASSOCIATION
OF REALTORS®

ESTIMATED SELLER PROCEEDS
(C.A.R. Form ESP, Revised 4/06)

SELLER: _____ DATE: _____

PROPERTY ADDRESS: 123 Sail Avenue, Marina del Rey CA 90292 _____

This estimate is based on costs associated with _____ type of financing.

PROJECTED CLOSING DATE: _____ PROPOSED SALE PRICE: $ _____

Current Annual Property Taxes: $ _____ Rate: _____ % Monthly Homeowners Dues, if any: $ _____

CHARGES BY EXISTING LIEN HOLDERS

Interest to payoff date (first loan)	# Days _____	$ _____
Interest (secondary financing)	# Days _____	$ _____
Interest on lines of credit or other financing		$ _____
Prepayment penalty		$ _____
Demand and Reconveyance fees		$ _____
Other lender fees (wire transfers, courier, etc.)		$ _____

ENCUMBRANCES (EXISTING LIENS)

First Loan	Rate: _____%	$ _____
Secondary Financing	Rate: _____%	$ _____
Secured Lines of Credit		$ _____
Bonds, Liens, etc.		$ _____
Other _____		$ _____
TOTAL ENCUMBRANCES		$ _____

ESCROW AND TITLE CHARGES

Escrow Fee ☐ including any Exchange Fees $ _____
Title Insurance Policy $ _____
Drawing, Notary and Recording Fees $ _____

GROSS EQUITY $ _____
(Expected sale price less encumbrances)

ESTIMATED CREDITS

Prorated Property Taxes   # Days _____ $ _____
Prorated Homeowners Dues   # Days _____ $ _____
Other _____ $ _____
Other _____ $ _____

OTHER EXPENSES & PRORATIONS

Brokerage -Listing ☐ Amount $ _____ or ☐ _____ % $ _____
Fee   -Selling ☐ Amount $ _____ or ☐ _____ % $ _____
Transfer Tax-County Rate per $1,000 $ _____ $ _____
      -City   Rate per $1,000 $ _____ $ _____
Property Taxes   # Days _____ $ _____
Homeowners Dues   # Days _____ $ _____
Buyer's Closing Costs $ _____
Natural Hazard Disclosure and/or other Reports $ _____
Wood Destroying Pest and/or other Inspection Fees $ _____
Corrective Work and/or other Repairs $ _____
Home Warranty Program $ _____
Rents and Security Deposits $ _____
VA/FHA Discount Points and Fees $ _____
HOA Transfer and/or Move-Out Fees $ _____
Other _____ $ _____
_____ $ _____
_____ $ _____

TOTAL ESTIMATED CREDITS $ _____

PROCEEDS RECAP

Expected Sale Price $ _____
LESS Total Encumbrances - _____
LESS Total Estimated Expenses - _____
PLUS Total Estimated Credits + _____

ESTIMATED TOTAL SELLER PROCEEDS $ _____

LESS any Note Carried by Seller - _____
LESS any Federal/State Withholding - _____

TOTAL ESTIMATED EXPENSES $ _____   **ESTIMATED SELLER CASH PROCEEDS** $ _____

This estimate, based upon the above sale price, type of financing and projected closing date, has been prepared to assist Seller in estimating costs and proceeds. Amounts will vary depending upon differences between actual and estimated repairs that may occur in the transaction, unpaid loan balances, assessments, liens, impound accounts, charges by lenders, escrow companies, title insurers and other service providers and other items. Not all liens may yet have been identified. Neither Broker nor Agent guarantee these figures represent the actual, or only, amounts and charges.
By signing below Seller acknowledges that Seller has read, understands and received a copy of this Estimated Seller Proceeds.

Seller _____ Date _____
Seller _____ Date _____
Real Estate Broker (Firm) _____ DRE Lic. # _____
By (Agent) _____ DRE Lic. # _____ Date _____
Address _____ City _____ State ____ Zip _____
Telephone _____ Fax _____ E-mail _____

The copyright laws of the United States (Title 17 U.S. Code) forbid the unauthorized reproduction of this form, or any portion thereof, by photocopy machine or any other means, including facsimile or computerized formats. Copyright © 1988-2006, CALIFORNIA ASSOCIATION OF REALTORS®, INC. ALL RIGHTS RESERVED.
THIS FORM HAS BEEN APPROVED BY THE CALIFORNIA ASSOCIATION OF REALTORS® (C.A.R.). NO REPRESENTATION IS MADE AS TO THE LEGAL VALIDITY OR ADEQUACY OF ANY PROVISION IN ANY SPECIFIC TRANSACTION. A REAL ESTATE BROKER IS THE PERSON QUALIFIED TO ADVISE ON REAL ESTATE TRANSACTIONS. IF YOU DESIRE LEGAL OR TAX ADVICE, CONSULT AN APPROPRIATE PROFESSIONAL.
This form is available for use by the entire real estate industry. It is not intended to identify the user as a REALTOR®. REALTOR® is a registered collective membership mark which may be used only by members of the NATIONAL ASSOCIATION OF REALTORS® who subscribe to its Code of Ethics.

Published and Distributed by:
REAL ESTATE BUSINESS SERVICES, INC.
a subsidiary of the California Association of REALTORS®
525 South Virgil Avenue, Los Angeles, California 90020

Reviewed by _____ Date _____

EQUAL HOUSING OPPORTUNITY

ESP REVISED 4/06 (ESP PAGE 1 OF 1)   **ESTIMATED SELLER PROCEEDS (ESP PAGE 1 OF 1)**

Agent: WALT HUBER   Phone: Fax: Prepared using zipForm® software
Broker: WALT HUBER REALTOR

Most sellers forget that they're making mortgage payments in arrears (January's payment is for December's interest), and may therefore be responsible for up to one month's interest at the time of closing. It's important to include a thirty-day interest payment under the estimated cost column. This form is one of the few in the listing kit of which the buyer DOES NOT receive a copy!

Figure 4-6

A home warranty protects the buyer (for up to one year) from failure of built-ins like stoves and dishwashers, as well as big ticket items like roofing, plumbing, and electrical.

Although negotiable, the home warranty is often paid for by the seller as an incentive to the buyer. If the seller refuses to pay for this protection, always offer it to the buyer. If neither is interested, it's necessary for them to sign a waiver stating that the warranty's options were explained and that they declined coverage. Anybody can pay for home warranties—even brokers who want to offer incentives to their clients.

Figure 4-7

CALIFORNIA
ASSOCIATION
OF REALTORS®

**WATER HEATER AND SMOKE DETECTOR
STATEMENT OF COMPLIANCE**
(C.A.R. Form WHSD, Revised 11/10)

Property Address: *123 Sail Avenue, Marina del Rey, CA 90293*

NOTE: A seller who is not required to provide one of the following statements of compliance is not necessarily exempt from the obligation to provide the other statement of compliance.

WATER HEATER STATEMENT OF COMPLIANCE

1. **STATE LAW:** California Law requires that all new and replacement water heaters and existing residential water heaters be braced, anchored or strapped to resist falling or horizontal displacement due to earthquake motion. "Water heater" means any standard water heater with a capacity of no more than 120 gallons for which a pre-engineered strapping kit is readily available. (Health and Safety Code §19211d). Although not specifically stated, the statute requiring a statement of compliance does not appear to apply to a properly installed and bolted tankless water heater for the following reasons: There is no tank that can overturn; Pre-engineered strapping kits for such devices are not readily available; and Bolting already exists that would help avoid displacement or breakage in the event of an earthquake.
2. **LOCAL REQUIREMENTS:** Some local ordinances impose more stringent water heater bracing, anchoring or strapping requirements than does California Law. Therefore, it is important to check with local city or county building and safety departments regarding the applicable water heater bracing, anchoring or strapping requirements for your property.
3. **TRANSFEROR'S WRITTEN STATEMENT:** California Health and Safety Code §19211 requires the seller of any real property containing a water heater to certify, in writing, that the seller is in compliance with California State Law. If the Property is a manufactured or mobile home, Seller shall also file a required Statement with the Department of Housing and Community Development.
4. **CERTIFICATION:** Seller represents that the Property, as of the Close Of Escrow, will be in compliance with Health and Safety Code §19211 by having the water heater(s) braced, anchored or strapped in place, in accordance with those requirements.

Seller/Landlord _____ _____ Date _____
             (Signature)   (Print Name)

Seller/Landlord _____ _____ Date _____
             (Signature)   (Print Name)

The undersigned hereby acknowledges receipt of a copy of this document.

Buyer/Tenant _____ _____ Date _____
           (Signature)   (Print Name)

Buyer/Tenant _____ _____ Date _____
           (Signature)   (Print Name)

SMOKE DETECTOR STATEMENT OF COMPLIANCE

1. **STATE LAW:** California Law requires that (I) every single-family dwelling and factory built housing unit sold on or after January 1, 1986, must have an operable smoke detector, approved and listed by the State Fire Marshal, installed in accordance with the State Fire Marshal's regulations (Health and Safety Code §13113.8) and (II) all used manufactured or mobilehomes have an operable smoke detector in each sleeping room.
2. **LOCAL REQUIREMENTS:** Some local ordinances impose more stringent smoke detector requirements than does California Law. Therefore, it is important to check with local city or county building and safety departments regarding the applicable smoke detector requirements for your property.
3. **TRANSFEROR'S WRITTEN STATEMENT:** California Health and Safety Code §13113.8(b) requires every transferor of any real property containing a single-family dwelling, whether the transfer is made by sale, exchange, or real property sales contract (installment sales contract), to deliver to the transferee a written statement indicating that the transferor is in compliance with California State Law concerning smoke detectors. If the Property is a manufactured or mobile home, Seller shall also file a required Statement with the Department of Housing and Community Development (HCD).
4. **EXCEPTIONS:** Generally, a written statement of smoke detector compliance is not required for transactions for which the Seller is exempt from providing a transfer disclosure statement.
5. **CERTIFICATION:** Seller represents that the Property, as of the Close Of Escrow, will be in compliance with the law by having operable smoke detector(s) (I) approved and listed by the State Fire Marshal installed in accordance with the State Fire Marshal's regulations Health and Safety Code §13113.8 or (II) in compliance with Manufactured Housing Construction and Safety Act (Health and Safety Code §18029.6) located in each sleeping room for used manufactured or mobilehomes as required by HCD and (III) in accordance with applicable local ordinance(s).

Seller/Landlord _____ _____ Date _____
             (Signature)   (Print Name)

Seller/Landlord _____ _____ Date _____
             (Signature)   (Print Name)

The undersigned hereby acknowledge(s) receipt of a copy of this Water Heater and Smoke Detector Statement of Compliance.

Buyer/Tenant _____ _____ Date _____
           (Signature)   (Print Name)

Buyer/Tenant _____ _____ Date _____
           (Signature)   (Print Name)

The copyright laws of the United States (Title 17 U.S. Code) forbid the unauthorized reproduction of this form, or any portion thereof, by photocopy machine or any other means, including facsimile or computerized formats. Copyright © 1991-2010 CALIFORNIA ASSOCIATION OF REALTORS®, INC. ALL RIGHTS RESERVED.
THIS FORM HAS BEEN APPROVED BY THE CALIFORNIA ASSOCIATION OF REALTORS® (C.A.R.). NO REPRESENTATION IS MADE AS TO THE LEGAL VALIDITY OR ADEQUACY OF ANY PROVISION IN ANY SPECIFIC TRANSACTION. A REAL ESTATE BROKER IS THE PERSON QUALIFIED TO ADVISE ON REAL ESTATE TRANSACTIONS. IF YOU DESIRE LEGAL OR TAX ADVICE, CONSULT AN APPROPRIATE PROFESSIONAL.
This form is available for use by the entire real estate industry. It is not intended to identify the user as a REALTOR®. REALTOR® is a registered collective membership mark which may be used only by members of the NATIONAL ASSOCIATION OF REALTORS® who subscribe to its Code of Ethics.

Published and Distributed by:
REAL ESTATE BUSINESS SERVICES, INC.
a subsidiary of the CALIFORNIA ASSOCIATION OF REALTORS®
525 South Virgil Avenue, Los Angeles, California 90020

Reviewed by _____ Date _____

WHSD REVISED 11/10 (PAGE 1 OF 1)

WATER HEATER AND SMOKE DETECTOR STATEMENT OF COMPLIANCE (WHSD PAGE 1 OF 1)

Agent: WALT HUBER	Phone:	Fax:	Prepared using zipForm® software
Broker: WALT HUBER REALTOR			

Owners and landlords must have a smoke alarm that displays the date of manufacture, allow a place for the date of installation to be written, incorporate a hush feature, incorporate an end-of-life warning, and, for battery-operated devices, contain a non-removable 10-year battery. Building permits issued for alterations, repairs, or additions for more than $1,000 must have this type approved and listed by the State Fire Marshal.

You should advise the sellers to have the utility meters read but continue service to avoid a shut down that may cause water heater damage from sediment clogging up the system. The buyers should be given the names and telephone numbers of all utilities so that they may follow up the sellers' request with their own.

III. The Broker's Role in Real Estate Appraisal

Helping a seller determine a home's selling price is the key to getting the seller to set a reasonable listing price.

Just as financing is the key to the typical real estate transaction, valuation is the foundation of real estate sales. If you're looking for an extensive treatment of appraisal, you'll find many excellent texts on the subject through the National Association of Independent Fee Appraisers (NAIFA), local realty boards, colleges, and libraries. **We suggest you read *Real Estate Appraisal*, by Walt Huber, Levin P. Messick, IFAC, and William Pivar, available through Educational Textbook Company (see back of book).**

A. HELPING SELLERS DETERMINE LISTING PRICE

Market value is sometimes referred to as "exchange value" or "value in exchange." It is the value of property as determined by sales in the open market.

MARKET VALUE refers to the amount of cash (or cash equivalent) that is most likely to be paid for a property on a given date in a fair and reasonable open market sale.

A property well listed is a property half sold.

Indeed, much of the listing interview will be concerned with price, since it is unlikely that the seller will arbitrarily accept the suggestion of a sales price without discussion and persuasion. The seller will say something like, "This other salesperson said I could get $480,000," where the house, in this case, is unlikely to go for more than $450,000. As a professional knowledgeable in comparable sales prices, your response should let the seller know that buyers are not usually inclined to pay more than what they would have to pay for a similar property.

As a fiduciary, you owe it to your principal to obtain the best market price, but you also owe it to yourself to get the seller to list at a saleable price.

Most sellers are misinformed about the market, choosing to believe that because of the excellent condition of the carpets and drapes, for example, they should get considerably more. This so-called "subjective value" holds little, if any, credence in the objective marketplace, where in the final analysis the value is established by what buyers are willing to pay in the sale of a property. Sellers usually ask for a much higher selling price than they could ever hope to get. They rely on reputed sales, obtained from hearsay, where, for example, neighbors may have claimed to have sold their homes for higher figures than advertised. The remaining neighbors may be lulled into a false sense of security, believing their property to be worth more than it is.

It's up to you to research the market and come up with a saleable price or market value, derived from a reliable source, usually an MLS.

There are three common approaches to valuation, the most acceptable for residential property is referred to as the **MARKET DATA** or **COMPARATIVE APPROACH**, *where value is indicated by recent sales of comparable properties in the homes sales market.* This approach is the most appropriate, and often used to set the listing price. The second method, called the **COST APPROACH**, *calculates the current cost of replacing or reproducing the improvement less depreciation, and adds the value of the land, which is never depreciated.* The third, useful primarily in income-producing properties (like apartments), is the **NET INCOME** or **CAPITALIZATION APPROACH**, *which capitalizes the net earnings by an appropriate rate.*

Although the last two approaches are important in the appraisal process, and indeed may be the only ones used when no market data is available, **the comparative approach is usually the most valid and reliable for establishing value in the residential market.**

We only address this approach to value since it is here that you, the licensee, will be best equipped to arrive at a realistic probable selling price of the majority of your listings. To further examine the cost and capitalization approaches, we recommend that you take one or more courses in appraisal to fully understand these methods.

The market data approach is based on the assumption that both buyer and seller are fully informed as to: the property and its uses; the state of the market for the particular type of property; the fact that each is willing to buy and to sell without undue pressure (that is, neither is compelled to buy or to sell); and that the property has been exposed in the open market for a reasonable period of time (the listing period).

B. MARKET DATA APPROACH OR COMPARATIVE VALUE

Unfortunately, depending on a full market data appraisal has its limitations. For example: 1) there may be no recent sales with which to compare; 2) no two properties are exactly alike, even if the only difference is location; 3) differences exist in depreciation, maintenance, use, and occupancy; 4) it's hard to compare amenities because of the hard to define nature of views, topography, or the direction the house faces; 5) there may be motivations behind sales that influenced the price; and 6) the decor and appliances contained within each vary a good deal. Thus, adjustments must be made depending on the degree of variation: The more decisions and judgments the evaluator (appraiser) must make, the greater the potential error in accurately comparing values.

The market data approach is usually the most reliable expression of value since it represents the actual homes sales transactions of informed buyers and sellers.

1. Comparative Market Analysis (CMA)

Real estate salespeople depend on the simplicity and availability of information necessary for a comparative market analysis over the complexity and cost of a full appraisal.

The most effective tool at your disposal is the comparative market analysis (CMA) form (see **Figure 4-8**). All computer-generated CMAs differ slightly. It is relatively easy to complete, the information is readily obtainable, and quite often pictures of the comparables are available—making it simple but convincing in presentation. You can present data in logical sequence and develop an accurate and current portrayal of what buyers will pay for property in the local subject area.

Information needed to complete the form is most often secured from the multiple listing summaries available to subscribers on the Internet. Information can also be obtained from company files, other brokers specializing in the area, county records, appraisers, and title companies.

In a CMA, it is important to only select recent sales of properties comparable to the subject property.

The more similar they are, the more readily sellers will accept the data, and the more likely they will be to accept your advice and counsel on the listing price. Moreover, the more comparable the data offered, the more valid and reliable your probable selling price will be.

A basic CMA may be divided into four broad sections. The first section, "**Active Listings**," contains current listings, representing asking prices. It shows the current competition. The information includes the address of the listed properties and the number of bathrooms—which for greater accuracy ought to be broken down into full baths, three-quarter baths (ones containing a stall shower, no tub), and half-baths (containing only bowl and sink). It should also address whether the house has a den or family room, the amount of square footage in the house and lot, and other improvements.

"Active Listings" on a CMA often have inflated asking prices that very few buyers actually expect to pay.

The list price entered and the number of days the property has been on the market are important factors to consider because they will help you explain to potential sellers the probable value of their homes.

If a property has been on the market for, say, 59 days, but the average listing sells in 30 days, it's obvious that the property is overpriced. Other factors could account for the slowness in selling, of course, but the root causes of most slow sales are price, terms, and condition. Now is the time to suggest that the seller reduce the price, secure more generous terms, or both.

The second section lists similar properties that have sold recently. "**Closed Sale Listings**" indicates current pricing and the probable top market price. Here we show not the asking price, but what the sellers actually accepted.

There should be a minimum of three properties in each category. If there is not enough data, then you should increase the time frame to eight or nine months. You may even extend the location up to one mile or more from the subject property.

In addition to the information called for under current listings, the date sold and the amount for which it sold is also included.

Figure 4-8

Comparative Market Analysis

Summary of Comparable Listings

This page summarizes the comparable listings contained in this market analysis.

Active Listings

Address	L/S Price	Bd	Bth	Sqft	$/Sq	Built	ML#	List Date	DOM
4039 Merced AV	$350,000	4	2.00	1,518	$231	1964	A08018892	1/21/08	179
14103 Clark ST	$389,999	2	2.00	1,540	$253	1927	H08021490	2/12/08	157
14022 Rexwood AV	$409,950	4	2.00	1,536	$267	1957	C07144614	10/1/07	291
4009 Kenmore AV	$469,900	4	3.00	1,611	$292	2007	C07130630	9/4/07	318
3359 Athol ST	$480,000	3	2.00	1,345	$357	1948	H08015071	1/31/08	169
	$419,970	**3.0**	**2.20**	**1,510**	**$280**	**1961**			**222.80**

Closed Sale Listings

Address	L/S Price	Bd	Bth	Sqft	$/Sq	Built	ML#	Sold Date	DOM
4258 Jerry AV	$390,000	3	2.00	1,516	$257	1947	C07158945	1/14/08	61
13443 Athol ST	$380,000	2	1.00	1,320	$288	1948	W07145504	12/26/07	85
4234 Baldwin Park BL	$410,000	3	1.00	1,398	$293	1952	M07099805	9/7/07	35
4027 Center ST	$430,000	3	2.00	1,441	$298	1963	I07133034	11/13/07	65
3462 Paddy Lane	$480,000	4	2.00	1,428	$336	1971	I07100207	9/24/07	71
	$418,000	**3.0**	**1.60**	**1,421**	**$295**	**1956**			**63.40**

Withdrawn Listings

Address	L/S Price	Bd	Bth	Sqft	$/Sq	Built	ML#	List Date	DOM
3643 Rhodes LN	$458,000	3	2.00	1,514	$303	1998	C07166353	11/15/07	230
	$458,000	**3.0**	**2.00**	**1,514**	**$303**	**1998**			**230.00**

Expired Listings

Address	L/S Price	Bd	Bth	Sqft	$/Sq	Built	ML#	List Date	DOM
3935 Harlan AV	$390,000	3	2.00	1,488	$262	1956	C07148734	10/10/07	93
3845 Foster AV	$399,900	3	2.00	1,431	$279	1980	K07154263	10/22/07	245
4347 Cutler AV	$400,000	2	1.00	1,372	$292		I07112255	7/31/07	77
3827 Foster AV	$420,000	3	3.00	1,510	$278	1989	H07110767	7/27/07	352
3355 Vineland AV	$429,000	3	2.00	1,380	$311	1950	C07142370	9/27/07	90
3457 Cosbey AV	$448,000	3	1.00	1,492	$300	1950	A07179038	12/21/07	102
13249 Corak St.	$449,000	3	2.00	1,318	$341	1952	C07174488	12/10/07	184
4588 Kenmore AV	$450,000	4	3.00	1,460	$308	1958	C07152990	10/18/07	93
4025 Harlan AV	$452,000	3	2.00	1,344	$336	1961	W08020615	2/8/08	36
13362 Earl AV	$457,000	4	2.00	1,344	$340	1976	C07163452	11/10/07	58
3937 Bresee AV	$479,000	4	3.00	1,664	$288	2004	C07113281	8/1/07	181
3720 Paddy Lane AV#1	$480,000	4	3.00	1,600	$300	2004	C07161629	11/5/07	183
3831 Bresee AV	$498,888	4	3.00	1,591	$314	1988	A07110196	7/26/07	32
3831 Bresee AV	$498,888	4	3.00	1,591	$314	1988	A07128451	8/30/07	27
3831 Bresee AV	$498,888	4	3.00	1,591	$314	1988	A07142588	9/27/07	20
3831 Bresee AV	$498,888	4	3.00	1,591	$314	1988	A07151897	10/17/07	15
3831 Bresee AV	$498,888	4	3.00	1,591	$314	1988	A07159190	11/1/07	14
3831 Bresee AV	$498,888	4	3.00	1,591	$314	1988	A07165395	11/15/07	16
3831 Bresee AV	$498,888	4	3.00	1,591	$314	1988	A07171458	12/2/07	27
3831 Bresee AV	$498,888	4	3.00	1,591	$314	1988	A07180894	12/30/07	14
3831 Bresee AV	$498,888	4	3.00	1,591	$314	1988	A08007560	1/16/08	13
3831 Bresee AV	$498,888	4	3.00	1,591	$314	1988	A08016201	2/3/08	22
	$465,581	**4.0**	**2.50**	**1,514**	**$308**	**1979**			**86.09**

A Comparative Market Analysis

ARLETTE LYONS

How much the similar property sold for and the terms under which it sold have the most impact on what the subject property is worth and how it can best be marketed.

The third section in the CMA is the "**Withdrawn Listing**." These properties have been withdrawn for whatever reason.

The fourth section, "**Expired Listings**," shows those properties which, once listed, failed to sell. These unsold properties might be called "rejected prices," because no sale took place after they had been exposed on the market for as long as four months. The acid test of a good listing is its successful sale.

Perhaps this analysis of the Comparative Market Analysis has convinced you of the many benefits of the well-listed property. Moreover, the listing agent may very well end up losing the listing to a competitor.

There are several computer software programs that interact with the various associations of REALTORS®. These programs download MLS information as well as pictures. This sharing of information is known as "networking."

C. INVENTORY (MLS)

INVENTORY (MLS) is the number of months' supply of home listings "for sale" at a particular time. In an average market there is about a six months' supply of properties for sale.

In a *BUYER'S MARKET (more listings than buyers) there is more inventory of homes for sale than purchasers, so the seller generally has to lower prices to compete with the numerous other listings available.*

In a *SELLER'S MARKET (more buyers than sellers) there are fewer homes for sale, and based on the law of supply and demand the seller can ask for a higher price.*

Even in a seller's market you have to be careful not to overprice listings!

D. PITFALLS IN ACCEPTING OVERPRICED LISTINGS

Do not take a listing when it is overpriced by a relatively large margin, that is, when its probability of selling is negligible. In a sellers' market, some agents will take a listing at any price, hoping to get it reduced during the life of the listing, as well as benefitting from sign value.

Extenuating circumstances, such as a favored client with whom you have other dealings, past or present, may lead you to exercise discretion. However, you should generally reject a listing when the owner is not serious about selling, or is uncooperative and unreasonable.

If you must take a listing at a higher price, inform the sellers that you may need to re-evaluate the price in a month or so. Explain that now is the time to price right. You can otherwise justify taking an overpriced listing only if the price is within reason, if the seller has an urgent reason for selling, or if you are not sure of the value. In short, do not accept any listing wherein you cannot live up to your agency responsibility to perform satisfactorily on behalf of the principal.

Overpriced properties (10% over value) are stigmatized by market-savvy brokers who won't waste their time showing them! Houses on the market for too long, even once the price has been reduced, may be perceived by buyers as having something wrong with them.

E. LICENSED APPRAISERS

A caveat should be observed by all practitioners: As a real estate agent, you should not hold yourself out as a licensed appraiser, unless, of course, you are. California allows sales agents to make unverified or informal appraisals, such as the comparative market analysis, but professional appraisers, whose work is vital for lending, expert testimony in legal proceedings, or taxation matters, must be licensed by the California Office of Real Estate Appraisers.

As a real estate licensee, you should mostly limit your appraisal activities to comparative market studies (CMAs) or market sales analysis.

The recent adoption of the *HOME VALUATION CODE OF CONDUCT (HVCC) says that appraisals must be ordered by third-party appraisal management companies.* What this means is appraisals may no longer be ordered by loan brokers, and both loan and real estate brokers may or may not have access to an appraisal on the property. This has resulted in an explosive growth of *APPRAISAL MANAGEMENT COMPANIES (AMC)*, which now largely control the appraisal process.

Appraisal Management Companies (AMCs) charge high fees but pay their appraisers very little; this is unnecessary regulation that requires borrowers to pay more for appraisals. Many real estate professionals question the purpose of even having AMCs.

IV. CHAPTER SUMMARY

A well-defined listing agreement will eliminate potential disagreements and misunderstandings, and help you earn your commission. The CAR® form for taking a listing is called the **Residential Listing Agreement (Exclusive Authorization and Right to Sell) (RLA)**. An exclusive listing requires a definite end time and date.

In a listing agreement, any **handwritten instructions** take precedence (priority) over any **preprinted instructions**.

Unless terms are specified, sellers are not obligated to pay a commission when they refuse a full price offer, unless the offer is for all cash.

Compensation paid to brokers is always decided by mutual agreement between principal and agent. **There are no commission rates set by law**.

Do not confuse the safety clause with the listing period. The agent and seller agree in a **safety clause** to a specific time period after termination of a listing during which the listing broker may still be entitled to a commission. Brokers must furnish the owners with a written notice, within 3 days, of all the names of prospects to whom the property was shown during that period, either by the broker or a cooperating broker. If the owner, or a new listing broker sells the property to anyone on the list within the safety period, the original broker may be entitled to a commission.

Never give legal or tax advice to your principals, unless you are licensed to do so.

An agent is required to give a copy of any document to his or principals at the time the signatures are obtained.

A **listing kit** is comprised of several forms that complete the listing process, including the: **Residential Listing Agreement and Seller's Advisory, Disclosure Regarding Real Estate Agency Relationships, Seller's Affidavit of Nonforeign Status, Transfer Disclosure Statement**, and **Supplemental Statutory and Contractual Disclosures**, and **Seller's Questionnaire**. The disclosures included in the kit also cover **smoke detectors**, **water heaters**, **lead-based paint**, **natural hazards**, and **defective furnace notices**, when applicable.

Finally, an **Estimated Seller's Proceeds** form is included, as well as a **Home Warranty Application or Waiver** to be signed by sellers and buyers if refusing it.

Market value refers to the amount of cash (or cash equivalent) that is most likely to be paid for a property on a given date in a fair and reasonable open market sale.

There are several approaches to valuation, including the most commonly-used **Market Data** or **Comparative Approach**, where value is indicated by recent sales of comparable properties. The **Cost Approach** is also used for residential property, and the **Net Income** (or **Capitalization**) **Approach** for income-producing properties.

A **Comparative Market Analysis (CMA)** can be compiled by a real estate salesperson, and does not require the expertise of an appraiser. A basic CMA has three sections, including "**Active Listings**," which contains current listings, representing asking prices. The second section is "**Closed Sale Listings**," indicating current pricing and probable top market price. "**Withdrawn Listings**" are properties that have been withdrawn for whatever reason. "**Expired Listings**" show houses that listed but failed to sell.

Real estate licensees are not appraisers. They should limit their appraisal activities to **market studies** or **market sales analysis**.

V. MATCHING VOCABULARY Fill in the blanks with the correct letter

A. Attorney
B. Buyer's Market
C. Cost approach
D. Home warranty
E. Home valuation code of conduct (HVCC)

F. Inventory (MLS)
G. Lead-based paint disclosure
H. Listing kit
I. Market data or Comparative approach

J. Market value
K. Net income or Capitalization approach
L. Seller's Market

1. _____ A packet of forms an agent provides to the seller when taking a listing.

2. _____ The amount of cash to be paid for a property on a given date in a fair and reasonable open market sale.

3. _____ This approach to valuation is one where the value is indicated by recent sales of comparable properties in the market.

4. _____ This valuation method calculates the current cost of replacing or reproducing the improvement less depreciation, and adds the value of the land, which is never depreciated.

5. _____ This method of valuation is useful primarily in income-producing properties.

6. _____ Only give legal or tax advice to your principals if you are a(n):

7. _____ This form must be filled out (if the house was built before 1978) whether or not the seller knows of any lead-based paint used on the property.

8. _____ This warranty protects the buyer for up to one year from failure of built-ins like stoves and dishwashers, as well as big ticket items like roofing, plumbing, and electrical.

9. _____ This code says that appraisals must be ordered by third-party appraisal management companies, not loan or real estate brokers.

10. _____ The housing market situation where there is more inventory of homes for sale than purchasers, so the seller generally has to lower prices to compete with the numerous other listings available.

11. _____ The number of months' supply of home listings "for sale" at a particular time.

12. _____ The housing market situation where there are fewer homes for sale, and, based on the law of supply and demand, the seller can ask for a higher price.

See Page 609 for Answers

VI. CHAPTER QUIZ

1. Which of the following is true concerning listing agreements?

   a. Handwritten instructions takes precedence (priority) over preprinted instructions.
   b. Preprinted instructions take precedence (priority) over handwritten instructions.
   c. Handwritten and preprinted instructions have equal weight.
   d. None of the above.

2. An agent is required to give a copy of the listing agreement to his or her principal:

   a. at the time an offer is presented.
   b. at the time the signature is obtained.
   c. when the principal pays the commission.
   d. all of the above.

3. Which of the following forms is a part of the seller's listing kit?

   a. Estimated Seller's Proceeds
   b. Residential Listing Agreement
   c. Both a and b
   d. None of the above

4. Which of the following is true concerning the adoption of HVCC?

   a. HVCC refers to Home Valuation of Code of Conduct.
   b. Appraisals must be ordered by third-party appraisal management companies.
   c. As a result, AMCs are experiencing a tremendous growth.
   d. All of the above.

5. Exclusive listings require a:

   a. definite end time.
   b. definite date.
   c. both a and b.
   d. neither a nor b.

6. The amount of cash or cash equivalent that is most likely to be paid for a property on a given date in a fair and reasonable open market transaction is referred to as:

   a. market value.
   b. fair guess value.
   c. gross value.
   d. net value.

7. What type of valuation approach involves calculating the current cost of replacing or reproducing the improvement, less depreciation, and adding the value of the land?

   a. Comparative approach
   b. Cost approach
   c. Capitalization approach
   d. All of the above

8. Which of the following can provide information needed to complete a Comparative Market Analysis (CMA)?

   a. Multiple listing summaries
   b. Other brokers
   c. County records
   d. All of the above

9. Lead-based paint disclosure is necessary for homes built:

   a. before 1978.
   b. before 1988.
   c. after 1978.
   d. all of the above.

10. Which of the following is TRUE concerning appraisals in California?

   a. Sales agents are allowed to make professional appraisals.
   b. Sales agents are allowed to make informal appraisals only.
   c. Professional appraisers need not be licensed.
   d. All of the above.

ANSWERS: 1. a; 2. b; 3. c; 4. d; 5. c; 6. a; 7. b; 8. d; 9. a; 10. b

You are

HOMES.COM

gain
adva

Selling:
Finding the Right Buyer

I. The American Dream

As a real estate practitioner, you need to know as much about buying and selling properties as possible, understanding not only the obvious benefits and rewards, but also the drawbacks and risks associated with home ownership. You also need to know all aspects of the real estate business in order to more effectively assist your clientele, including anticipating and answering objections. Buyers and sellers look to you to be their guide.

Think of yourself as a navigator; you should guide your clients through the selling and buying process with a good map and a solid strategy.

II. Shopping for a Home

For most buyers, purchasing a home is the most important financial decision they will ever make, and becomes the largest asset they will ever own as the loan is paid off.

When shopping for a home, buyers ask themselves many questions: Are they buying the right type of house? Are they buying too much or not enough? Are they stretching their resources far enough to prevent another move within a short period of time?

Most property owners move on the average of every six to eight years.

You need to anticipate these concerns and address them before they ever come up. You have to be mindful of the characteristics of all forms of housing. The variety seems endless. You need to know and understand what your client is looking for, realizing that price range and terms are very significant to the client, but by no means the only considerations.

CHAPTER OUTLINE

> **Buyers must realistically select the area in which they can afford to purchase, which may not necessarily be the one in which they would prefer to live. For the first-time homebuyer, that first house is often the one that will make it possible to eventually buy his or her dream home—a step in the right direction.**

Good K-12 schools and commuting are very important to a family, and you should know the various school district boundaries (and specific school boundaries), and verify that information prior to finalizing an offer. For example, Beverly Hills schools are prized and in high demand. Commuting distance to your clients' work is another important time and environmental issue you should prioritize.

A. PURCHASING A HOME: A GENERAL DISCUSSION

The buyers, especially if they are first-time buyers, will have lots of questions regarding their home purchase. It's a good time to get to know them. They may want a large lot, or perhaps this may be a detriment. When looking at a model home, remind your client that it's expensively decorated for display purposes only, and that any upgrades will be added to the price, as well as landscaping and window coverings costs.

1. New Homes

New homes offer the advantages of modern, up-to-date design, construction, plumbing, electrical fixtures, wall and floor outlets, and built-ins, especially in the kitchen. They are more attractive in and out, have a greater useful economic life, and provide more efficient heating and cooling equipment. Moreover, new homes may command larger and longer loans than older houses. Yet, many buyers believe that newer homes are not as well built as the older ones. Finally, land values in California are more likely to increase as the area builds up.

Homes in great school districts sell for a premium price!

2. Older Homes

*Older homes are called **RESALES**.* They offer many advantages over the brand new ones. They are generally located in proven, fully-developed, and established areas. There is often better public transportation and more shopping choices and schools, and they may be closer to employment centers and central business districts. The house has been physically "shaken down." In other words, faulty construction, structural defects, and settling problems are either evident, corrected, or non-existent. Whether or not a house is a "lemon" may not readily be apparent in the new house. Buyers can usually see what they are getting in an older house and in the neighborhood. Landscaping is in place. Finally, more house per square foot can be obtained for the price, with bargain prices often available for "fixer-uppers."

Any insurance claims related to the property made by the seller within the last "five years" must be disclosed to the buyer in the seller questionnaire, as well as the Transfer Disclosure Statement (TDS).

It's important to get a professional inspection (as a condition in the contract) on all real estate purchases, including new houses. This costs around $350, depending on the size of the property and the scope of the inspection. It's usually paid for by the buyer, who gets the report, with a copy going to the seller within a predetermined time frame. Later, sellers being presented with the buyers' "wish list" for repairs may decide to do some of the repairs (or none), at which time the transaction may be rescinded—buyers get their deposit back, and sellers get to put their property back on the market. If the buyers choose not to get an inspection, you must have a signed waiver in your transaction file.

PHYSICAL DEPRECIATION is the normal wear and tear as things need to be repaired or replaced. Garbage disposals, carpets, roofs, and paint jobs just wear out (deteriorate).

The shoppers for the used or older home look for the same things as the new homebuyers, plus many more that are connected with the physical structure itself. Oversized hallways and kitchens, along with high ceilings, also mean extra fuel bills and maintenance. As a salesperson trying to sell an older home, you may be faced with many problems. There may be termite and dry-rot damage, cracked foundations or walls, chipped masonry, worn-out or obsolete electrical wiring, faulty heating and air conditioning, corroded plumbing, and a variety of other problems, including improperly built add-ons.

Additions made without the proper building permits can be a source of problems when selling a property. Most buyers want to be reassured that the home they are purchasing is built up to current codes. An insurance company may deny full fire coverage because of the non-permitted additions or alterations.

The floor plan and design of older homes may suffer from obsolescence. *FUNCTIONAL OBSOLESCENCE is the loss of value due to adverse design factors within a structure that affect the marketability of the property.* It could be a single-car garage, a wall furnace, no bath off the master bedroom, inefficient layout, or utility.

ECONOMIC OBSOLESCENCE is any loss of value due to conditions outside of the property itself (external). These are not considered "curable"—they are beyond the control of the property owner. For example, a noisy freeway built next to your property.

It's obvious that maintenance and repair costs might be significantly higher on an older home. The cost of refurbishing, renovating, or remodeling may more than offset the assumed advantages of lower price and other benefits.

Upgrading a property may be an over-improvement for that neighborhood. The purchasers may not be able to recover the added investment.

B. SOME ADVANTAGES TO OWNING A HOME

1. **Appreciation.** Property values in California have historically increased throughout the years. Although, at times, there have been some economic downturns and flattening of the market, real estate values return and provide a hedge against inflation.

2. **Tax benefits.** These benefits are considerable because interest paid and property taxes are state and federal income tax-deductible items for owner-occupied properties. In addition, the income tax capital gains forgiveness for owner-occupied properties upon resale (up to $500,000 for couples) is a boon for the owner.

There are capital gains income tax forgiveness on the sale of a home up to $250,000 for singles and $500,000 for married people who file a joint return. To qualify, the home must have been the principal residence for a minimum of "two years of the five years" prior to the sale. At least one spouse must be the owner during this time, but both spouses must have lived there for the two-year period.

3. **Equity buildup.** This is payoff of the debt because each monthly housing payment partially repays the loan. In contrast, the residential tenant only gets rent receipts in lieu of a tax deduction and equity buildup he or she would get as an owner.

4. **Cash flow.** Should the owner-residents decide to convert the property to a rental, they may do so, and then are permitted additional business deductions from income taxes. Only landlords can deduct maintenance repairs and depreciation of rentals.

C. SOME DISADVANTAGES TO OWNING A HOME

1. **Loss of Value.** The building and other improvements ultimately wear out or lose value through physical, functional, and economic obsolescence, but land may increrase in value.

2. **Upkeep and maintenance.** Some people, including the aged, who find it too burdensome to maintain a home, find that renting is less demanding.

3. **Liquidity (turning property into cash).** A home investment is not very flexible due to the length of time needed to sell it to get cash. Even in a sellers' market, transfer of title does not formally take place until all of the terms and conditions of the sale have been complied with. A thirty day escrow is usually the shortest time necessary to close a transaction.

4. **Foreclosure.** There is always the possibility of losing a major investment through foreclosure for nonpayment of property taxes, HOA dues, and mortgage payments. The possibility of losing a job or becoming medically disabled can happen to any owner.

D. BUDGETING FOR A HOME

An important question all potential buyers must ask themselves is: How much should I pay for a house? The answer depends on many variables. Personal debt must first be taken into consideration. Many present day lenders realize that a borrower who is debt free is able to afford higher monthly payments than others who have maxed out their credit cards. Housing payments should not exceed 30% of the borrower's gross monthly income. When you include personal debt in addition to the house payment, 38% of a buyer's gross income is usually the maximum.

Monthly Housing Payment
(Principal + Interest + Monthly Taxes and Insurance + HOA dues) =
25% to 30% of Gross Monthly Income

Monthly Housing Payment + Other Long-Term Monthly Debts =
33% to 38% of Gross Monthly Income

It is vital for you to be aware of these ratios in order to qualify buyers and not show them property priced beyond their means. This is a **big mistake** in any situation that will cause the buyer embarrassment and a waste of time for all parties to the transaction.

When first meeting a buyer, you should explain that there are various types of loans currently available to buyers, which can be customized to their unique requirements. It is to their benefit to be prequalified by a lender who has the information on the best loans available—**leave this task to the professionals**.

> *Give your buyers the names of at least two lenders (or mortgage loan brokers) with whom you have successfully worked. Offer to make the appointment for them. Explain how important it is for buyers to be "prequalified" when presenting an offer and, as usual, ask your buyers for their feedback regarding these lenders.*

All things being equal, the seller will choose a qualified buyer over an unqualified one. Being **qualified** is an excellent benefit that the buyers should be made aware of, especially in a hot sellers' market where multiple offers are often received. Not being prequalified can easily cost them their dream home. You should aim to have your buyers prequalified prior to showing properties—this benefits them.

In a "hot sellers' market," you often receive several offers on the same property. The seller, naturally, will consider only the better ones, and having a qualified buyer is one of these valid considerations.

Self-employed individuals quite often have difficulty qualifying for a loan. Lenders usually require these buyers to furnish at least two years' personal or business income tax returns with their loan applications. Again, because lenders have many ways of servicing borrowers, they have different loans for different people.

Buyers who don't make an effort to be prequalified demonstrate a lack of motivation or lack of good credit.

III. Why Buyers Buy

It was found that the typical purchaser paid more for a house than the rules of thumb suggested. Purchasers spent closer to almost three times their annual income for a house. You can draw your own conclusions concerning the reasons for such attitudes. Homebuyers buy with **emotion rather than with an investment point of view**.

It is interesting to note that a large percentage of buyers move less than five miles from their old location. It stands to reason, then, that neighborhood must be uppermost in buyers' minds, with perhaps the need for more space the prime motive for moving.

Buyers often keep buying the same type of house they already own. You should visit the buyers' home and take notice of their style of living in order to eliminate showing houses that don't fit their lifestyle. Buyers will be impressed by your knowledge and thoughtfulness concerning their needs.

People don't buy houses; they buy benefits.

As for selection of the house ultimately purchased, the reasons given are special features—views, fireplaces, landscaping, number of baths and bedrooms, adequate closet space, expandable floor plan, large kitchen, and so on.

Among those buyers who shopped with licensees, most bought through them, yet over half went to more than one brokerage before buying.

> **The busiest time of year for buying and selling is June and July, when parents are free to investigate the housing market while children are not in school. For most people, February is a breathing period, following the heavy spending outlay at Christmas, while March is the time to get ready for tax deadlines in April. Nevertheless, people buy and sell real estate all year long.**

IV. Techniques of Selling

Selling is communicating. Therefore, in order to sell effectively, you must be able to communicate effectively. It's important to remember that communication is a two-way process.

When interacting with clients, listening is at least as important as talking!

We communicate most effectively with those who share our common interests, cultural background, income, and education. Young salespeople, for example, may be more successful when selling to their own age group, because they can communicate best with

their own peers. This is not a hard and fast rule, however, as communication skills vary from person to person. It's essential to know your client and speak appropriately. The more well-rounded you are, the more clients will be able to relate to you.

In order to be most effective, you should communicate on more than one level. It's always helpful to include aids—like mobile devices, charts, photos, and graphs—as well as actually involving your clients in the decision-making process.

A computer generated keynote presentation makes a powerful visual impact!

A. DIRECT CONTACT COMMUNICATIONS (Face-to-Face)

The most effective two-way communication occurs in a face-to-face situation. Inaccuracies and misunderstandings can be resolved by questioning the other party and getting accurate feedback.

Soliciting business on a direct-contact (face-to-face) basis is more effective than by telephone, email, or snail mail.

The second most effective communication occurs in a two-way but not face-to-face situation. An example is the smartphone or telephone call. Feedback is possible, but you don't have the benefit of nonverbal assists such as body language.

The least effective communication is one-way, such as a letter. At this level, neither immediate feedback nor the identification of accompanying nonverbal cues is possible.

The closer you get to the prospect, the better your chances for a sale.

Sending a letter or email to a prospect is fine, so long as it's a pre-approach letter. To be effective, however, you must call for an appointment. Although the telephone is an indispensible device, no one can list or sell by phone. It is merely a tool through which you make arrangements to meet personally with your prospects.

For example, when you're on a listing appointment, getting the prospects to respond with a "yes" to questions puts them in a favorable frame of mind. Having them follow the listing contract with you, line by line, and getting agreement on each item helps to smooth communications. Better still, hand them a pad and pen and directly involve them in the process. Not only will it be easier for them to understand now, but it will lessen the chance of problems arising later. You can fill these items out on zipForms® on your mobile tablet in the presence of your clients.

Repeating or summarizing important points can be an effective method of emphasizing the things you want the prospect to remember.

Your message should be delivered in a clear, articulate, honest, and enthusiastic manner. Remember: It's not so much what you say, but how you say it. Voice inflection, facial expressions, and body language all contribute to the overall impression you leave with a prospect. Even with the best intentions, you can fail to persuade a prospect because of the way you express yourself. Present a professional attitude at all times and avoid irritating mannerisms.

Remember: You were given two ears and one mouth; therefore, you should listen twice as much as you speak.

B. LETTER OR WEBSITE COMMUNICATIONS (One-Way)

As the least effective mode of communication, the letter should be used principally as a pre-conditioner. Make sure your email address and website are highlighted so your clients can go to your site for further information.

Use the letter to offer the prospects your services, suggesting that they call you for help or state that you will call them for something. In other words, use the letter to let the client know that you will follow through by mobile phone or in person. As such, the letter is a potentially powerful tool in the communications channel.

A well-organized letter is similar to the well-organized ad that we discussed in Chapter 3. You will want to state the purpose of the letter, the benefits being offered, your qualifications as an agent, and an invitation to call you. The format of the letter should be similar to the ad, using the AIDA approach.

AIDA stands for Attention, Interest, Desire, and Action.

Suppose, for example, that you have the listing at 743 West Fircroft Avenue, Covina, and you want to interest the neighbors in the property. See **Figure 5-1** for a sample of how such a letter can be drafted. Notice that it attracts attention at the outset—the address spelled out across from the heading immediately alerts the receiver that a neighbor's property is singled out for something. You can spark their interest, because who isn't at least curious about what's happening around his or her property? If the neighbors themselves desire another home or know someone who does, the letter may arouse this desire. Finally, you have invited action by asking the recipient to call, write, or email for further information.

Figure 5-1

Lyons and Associates, Inc., Realtor
REAL ESTATE EXCELLENCE

January 4, 20XX

Re: 743 West Fircroft Avenue

Dear _____:

We have just listed 743 West Fircroft Avenue in your neighborhood. This is a beautiful 3-bedroom, family room, 2-bath home listed for $500,000.

We are very excited about this property, and I will be glad to show it to you or to your friends or relatives interested in moving to your area, giving you a chance to choose your new neighbors.

Please call or email me.

Best Regards,

Arlette Lyons, CRS, GRI
Owner-Broker
License Number: 00414792
(626) 331-0141
aalyons@aol.com
http://LyonsandAssociatesRltr.com

2820 E. GARVEY AVENUE SOUTH, WEST COVINA, CA 91791 • (626) 331-0141 • FAX: (626) 331-9772

Giving a free comparative market analysis to the homeowner is a great gift. In order to address letters personally to the owners adjacent to your listing, check with your favorite title company. Always address letters personally, never to "Occupant." Use a stamp rather than a postage meter.

Some unsolicited letters from a real estate agency will get tossed in the trash unopened, but nobody throws out a postcard without at least turning it over to see what it says. Be sure to include a photograph of the property on the postcard! It's also less expensive because you can print more than one card per page, and the postage costs less for postcards than letters.

C. PHONE COMMUNICATIONS (Two-Way)

If used properly, the telephone can open more doors and result in more sales because it leads to direct contact and saves time. You can reach far more prospects through efficient use of this instrument than you can contact by door-to-door solicitation. It fixes the hour of appointment and is appreciated by the busy prospect. Despite all these benefits, it is too often abused.

Used improperly, the telephone will cost the firm many dollars, sales, listings, and goodwill. Check the "National Do Not Call Registry" regulations before using the phone to solicit business.

1. Proper Use of the Phone

Before telephoning, you should **organize** your schedule to make as many calls as possible at one session. Plan in advance what you're going to say. At all times, have your materials on hand—lists, pen and pad, calendar, and appointment book, incoming call registers, ad switch sheets, and so on.

When making calls, be **natural**. Use your normal speaking voice, and talk to the person on the other end as if he or she were sitting across the desk from you. Be clear in your enunciation and diction and simple in your language. A smile helps, and a sincere, pleasant ring in your voice may get you another listing or selling interview.

You should be **positive**. Avoid being apologetic or timid. Speak with firmness and authority, as if you expect the prospect to say yes.

At the first meeting with potential clients it's important to set up parameters such as how to reach each other and appropriate times for calling. Nobody wants a phone call at 3:00 AM.

No one can sell real estate on the telephone. Stay on the line only long enough to make an appointment so you can meet in person.

2. Incoming Call Register

We've discussed the general guiding principles of good telephone usage, with emphasis on outgoing calls. When the telephone rings in the office, greet the caller with "Lyons Realty, good morning (afternoon, evening), may I help you?" Vary the greeting at holidays. By injecting the firm name first, you've assured the caller that they dialed correctly. By keeping the greeting short, you allow customers more time to speak, which is, after all, why they are calling. Your name should be de-emphasized in the greeting. After establishing a friendly relationship, you can give the caller your name in a way much more likely to be remembered.

One of the most effective time-saving tools you and your broker have to handle telephone calls is the Incoming Call Register. The **INCOMING CALL REGISTER** *provides the salesperson with a series of questions to ask the caller, and furnishes a handy record of calls for follow-up now or later* (see **Figure 5-2**).

Figure 5-2

FILE REF. _____

Incoming Call Register

GOALS: 1. Create a Favorable Image

2. Make an appointment as soon as possible

REMINDER QUESTIONS: Name?   Address?   Phone No.?   What area preferred?   What type home?   What price range?   How many in family?   Ages?   What area of employment?   Will you sell present home?   Any special requirements?   Would you like list of available homes in preferred area?   What is convenient time for appointment?

Ad Reference _____ Date _____

Address of Home in Ad _____

Name of Caller _____

Address _____ Phone _____

Area Desired _____

Special Requirements _____

Type of Home _____ Price Range ____

Type or Place of Employment _____

Family Information _____

Now Owns or Rents _____

♦ Date and Time of Appointment _____

Comments _____

Follow up _____

© 2015 ETC., Inc.

Because most incoming calls will be from people who saw an ad in the newspaper, a sign on the property, or the like, it's a wise policy for your real estate firm to retain the completed forms after the sales associates are through with them. Your company may wish to evaluate the responses to ads, assess the outcome of inquiries, and use those which did not sell for later call-backs.

Record keeping is essential for controlling revenue and expenses and follow-up.

Knowing which ads are pulling in callers, how many calls are needed to produce each sale, and the telephone effectiveness of the salespeople—during and outside of floortime—assists the broker in planning, directing, and controlling operations of the office and sales staff.

FLOOR TIME is the time assigned to an agent to answer the company phone. Any new customers who don't ask for an associate by name become the agent's prospect.

3. Answering Ad Calls (Internet or Newspaper)

You should always be prepared for incoming calls, answering as soon as the phone rings. Nothing turns off a caller faster than to have the telephone

ring six or eight times before receiving a response, or being put on hold for a long period of time. Because many prospects are calling in order to eliminate some of the advertised properties, a slow response to their call may eliminate that property from their list altogether, and you'll have lost a chance for a sale before you even began.

People like to talk to a live person rather than an automated service with a variety of confusing and time-consuming options.

Advertising frequently accounts for the major item of expense in the typical general brokerage office, so the broker can ill afford to lose any calls by ineffective handling.

If the call is for someone who is not in the office, carefully jot down the name and number of the caller and ask about the nature of the call. You may be able to assist the caller. After you hang up, call the salesperson for whom the message was intended if timing is important. You may also be able to forward calls directly to the agent!

Sales associates ought to leave word of where and how they can be contacted and when they expect to return, or make clear under what conditions their cell phone numbers may be given out.

On the other hand, if the salesperson is in the office but is tied up at the moment, inform the caller that the agent is detained but will call right back, or ask whether the party will hold for a few moments. However, never leave someone hanging on the phone indefinitely. Frequently inform the caller that the salesperson is still busy. Otherwise, the caller may hang up.

Always ask permission before putting someone on hold!

Preparation for calls also means knowing the inventory. As the salesperson with floor duty (meaning it's your turn to stay in the office and answer the phones), you should inspect every new listing, as well as review old listings, in order to be familiar with any property people may call about.

To respond with, "I'm happy you called on this particular one—it's a sure winner," will not come off sincerely if you're unable to answer a few basic questions about the property. You need to be aware of the status of your company's listings.

a. When a Neighbor Calls

A large number of ad calls emanate from people who just want to learn the listing price of a property. Look at these callers as opportunities for new business that can be added to your database. They may be toying with the idea of selling their homes and are attempting to get a feel for market prices. Obtain their names and telephone numbers, which they should be eager to provide if they really want some information. Ask if they're familiar with the neighborhood in which the house is located. If they are, tell them what a good buy the house they're calling on is, and add that you wish you had two more like it in the neighborhood.

> **When neighbors call about the listing price of a property, don't assume they're just being nosy. Offer to drop by a free comparative market analysis of their home's value—you may even gain a new listing!**

Most callers will respond honestly to a friendly but direct question, so there's no harm in simply asking them if they live in the neighborhood. If the answer is yes, ask if they are considering selling their own property.

4. From Phone Call to Appointment

Callers ask many questions about ads and signs and raise many objections to meeting an agent in person when they merely want information. To become a successful agent or broker, you need to be aware of these roadblocks and be prepared to overcome them, even if it takes memorizing sets of responses.

New technology on for sale signs eliminate some of these problems. Website domain names with the address of the property can fill them in on all the MLS information plus your contact information.

It will pay off if you have ready answers to the most frequently asked questions. Make up your mind that the next time prospects ask for an address you will convince them they'll be better served if they "visit your office and elect you as their official house hunter."

5. The Switch Sheet

Callers rarely end up buying the properties about which they originally call. Moreover, some advertised homes may sell before the caller inquires about them. Therefore, it's important to be prepared at all times to show similar properties. For this purpose a series of "switch sheets" should be made up in advance. These sheets show the address, price, and so forth, as illustrated in **Figure 5-3**.

A "Switch Sheet" is a quick reference list of properties within a similar price range, school district, size, etc. Computers greatly simplify and speed up this task.

Using switch sheets helps get appointments. They allow you to consider alternative listings before coming under the pressure of an actual call. When there are many calls, and you're the salesperson on the floor, you may not have time to think clearly enough to maintain buyer interest unless you do some homework in advance. Prepare before the calls roll in, and you'll make a more favorable impression on the caller.

Being prepared allows you to be more helpful and confident from the very first phone call and gives you an advantage over less organized agents a caller may have previously contacted.

Often, the newspaper ad about which the prospect is calling is still running, although the property has been sold. You might say, "I'm sorry, the home has just

Figure 5-3

Switch Sheet

Ad Heading: *Covina Charmer*   Property: *743 W. Fircroft Ave.,Covina $425,000*

Other Properties	Listing No.	Price and Room Descripton
1. 834 Shasta, Covina	C20324	$450,000 3 BR, FR, & pool
2. 656 Meadow Road	C56713	$400,000 2 BR, den
3. 754 Calvados	C059304	$410,000 3 BR, Covina schools

Agents taking floortime should be fully prepared for receiving ad calls. Not only should agents know what is being advertised and what signs are out, but they should also have other properties to discuss with the callers. All agents taking floortime need to be informed about their company's and other companies' listings.

sold, but we have a new listing that may be just what you're looking for. Let's hurry and get in right away." Enthusiasm will pay off, especially in light of the speed with which the first property was sold. In any event, the ad switch sheet will expedite the selling process. You may also add that sometimes escrows fall through and offer to keep them posted.

An independent or smaller brokerage may not have other properties that fit the bill, but you can always remind a caller that your brokerage is a member of a multiple listing service, so you have access to many other listings. Ask them to bring a paper with their choices circled, and offer to check out all the houses together. Then, pin down a specific appointment.

If you can't get the appointment, offer to give them information on the circled ads—immediately look up the properties in the MLS and call or email them back with that information.

Remind your callers that by allowing you to look up all the ads they're interested in, they'll have to make fewer phone calls and, more importantly, will only give out their personal information to one agent.

6. The Office Caravan

A switch sheet insures that you'll have access to comparable properties to which you can direct callers if a property is for some reason inappropriate or unavailable. While it's important to review this document daily, an even more efficient habit is that of the office caravan. An **OFFICE CARAVAN** *is a weekly outing whereby all available salespersons from one office preview (together in a van or separately in individual cars) all the newest brokerage listings, as well as other brokerages' listings.*

An "Agent's Comment Sheet" allows agents to critique several properties in comparison with each other. It's helpful to remind the office staff of a property's appeal or lack thereof.

After previewing available properties, each agent is expected to fill out an Agent Comment Sheet (see **Figure 5-4**). Previewing current listings insures that a broker's agents are aware of all new listings and know how to find those listings easily when driving clients around.

One copy of the Agent Comment Sheet is placed in the broker's "master file" and another is kept by the agent. Doing so allows brokers and listing agents an opportunity to suggest improvements to a seller.

Figure 5-4

Agent Comment Sheet

Weekly Office Caravan

AGENT NAME:

319 S La Serena Dr,
Suggested Listing Price

ListPrice $ 455,000
Bedrooms 3   Baths 1.75
Sq. Feet 1,680   Lot Size 12919

Poor (1)   Average (2)   Good (3)   Excellent (4)
Showing Appeal:
Overall Condition:

AGENT COMMENTS:

1

AGENT NAME:

226 S Monte Verde St,
Suggested Listing Price

ListPrice $ 649,000
Bedrooms 3   Baths 2.50
Sq. Feet 1,780   Lot Size 39945

Poor (1)   Average (2)   Good (3)   Excellent (4)
Showing Appeal:
Overall Condition:

AGENT COMMENTS:

2

AGENT NAME:

3577 E Hillhaven Dr,
Suggested Listing Price

ListPrice $ 279,000
Bedrooms 3   Baths 2.00
Sq. Feet 1,322   Lot Size 9557

Poor (1)   Average (2)   Good (3)   Excellent (4)
Showing Appeal:
Overall Condition:

AGENT COMMENTS:

3

Information deemed to be reliable although not guaranteed.

There's no reason you can't create this fill-in form online.

V. The Critical Path of Selling

A sale may be viewed as a five-step process: The pre-approach, the initial contact or greeting, counseling the buyers, showing the property, and the close.

A. STEPS INVOLVED IN A SALE

1. The Pre-Approach

A carefully planned sales presentation is an absolute necessity to effective selling. No matter how knowledgeable and capable you are as a salesperson, you won't make as many sales if you're not armed with a forceful and intelligent sales talk.

Of the three methods of communicating discussed—direct contact, written correspondence, and telephone communications—the most effective is direct contact or face-to-face selling. It's also the most costly, in view of your most expensive commodity, "your time."

Out of approximately 2,000 available working hours in a year, only about half of them are actually spent with prospects.

The remaining time is devoted to necessary, but nonproductive activities and handling mountains of office details, which is why so many successful brokers are hiring professional assistants. (See Chapter 14 for more information regarding real estate assistants.) With or without an assistant, you should always organize your time and talents effectively. Devote time to pre-call planning and specific pre-approach analysis to improve your face-to-face selling.

To maximize the results of selling time, you should develop a lively, intelligent sales presentation. This presentation is a series of short, logical reasons why a prospect should use your services. It shouldn't, however, sound canned or "rehearsed." Your marketing techniques can be outlined in a keynote presentation on your mobile device.

There is no such thing as "canned talk," only a "canned salesperson" delivering the talk. Like courtesy, enthusiasm is contagious.

Breathe life into your presentation. Make it sincere and convincing each time you deliver it. Although the presentation may seem repetitious to you, remember it's new to the prospect. If you're enthusiastic, the prospect will get fired up too.

In short, selling real estate involves preparation. This means being prepared at all times for the expected as well as the unexpected.

As a competent salesperson, you should know how potential buyers initiate action. For example, studies show that typical buyers who check out local newspapers will look first at the back of the paper. Second, buyers mark the ads in which they're interested. Third, they make a decision to call about ads that appeal to them. Because buyers call for information, your efficient use of the telephone is vital. Fourth, buyers go to an office. Which office they choose depends in large measure on the ability of the salesperson who answered the call. Many buyers also check the Internet and follow the same steps.

Once in the office, the question should no longer be whether prospects will buy, but when.

When buyers call about an ad, find out why that particular property appealed to them. Buyers will often respond with something like: "I saw a house with the most beautiful den (yard, dining room, etc.)." The appropriately rehearsed approach to this type of caller is: "Mr. Caller, I have many houses that may interest you. I know how valuable your time is, but I'll match my time with yours. Tell you what I'll do. Why not let me take you and Mrs. Caller out with no pressure to buy? I'd like to show you three or four homes and invite you to critique them. After that, I'll be able to determine what it is you like."

Determine your callers' "hot buttons"—the things they find important. Don't sell price, size, or, for that matter, house. "Sell the interview," and ask for an appointment.

In light of the dangerous times in which we live, agents rarely pick up clients anymore. It's safer to ask them to meet you at your office or a virtual office. After establishing a relationship, it's a good idea to visit clients' homes to get a feel for how they live and what they like.

Terminate the call with the usual close: "Can you be ready for previewing this morning, or would mid-afternoon be better?"

2. The Initial Contact or Greeting

Wherever you have the interview, be on time. It's best to encourage prospective buyers to meet you at your office or a virtual office for safety issues and because you can more effectively control the situation there.

No amount of time spent on the Internet can replace the reassurance of a personal meeting with a professional. This is your chance to show them you know what you're doing and have their best interests at heart. "The Internet has no heart!"

After greeting the buyers, cement the relationship with a warm, firm handshake. Offering a beverage is one of many ways to put your clients at ease. Build confidence by showing your knowledge and interest in them. To make a sale, you must satisfy the buyer's needs. These needs can be summarized into four broad classifications:

a. **The need for trust.** Buyers need to have complete confidence in you and your firm.

b. **The need for information.** You must be knowledgeable and have the ability to communicate information accurately. This means knowing the neighborhood, market conditions, legal aspects, forms, and so forth.

c. **The need for advice.** In your role of counselor and problem solver, you must be familiar with all aspects of real estate. You should have an understanding of human nature so you'll be able to react to the buyer's needs.

d. The need for financing. Because the typical family will invest the bulk of their savings and other assets in a home, you must know the kinds of financing plans available, the costs, and so on. You should also have a list of lenders to recommend and/or websites where buyers can be prequalified.

3. Counseling and Qualifying the Buyers

Before prospects purchase a home, they must have the financial ability, desire, and intent to buy.

The process of reconciling buyers' needs and desires with the reality of their financial capacity is called COUNSELING or QUALIFYING THE BUYER. Determine what your buyers can afford and what they can buy for that amount. Whenever possible, avoid showing properties until after you've counseled your buyers.

Find out why and what your prospects want to buy, what their needs are, and how these needs can be realistically met.

Always attempt to prequalify a prospect before showing a property. It can save you and your client time and energy, not to mention saving your clients embarrassment and disappointment if they can't afford a particular property. A "fully qualified" client is preferred. See Chapter 12 for more information about the difference between prequalified and fully qualified.

You will, no doubt, encounter prospects who are reluctant to get prequalified by a lender, particularly in the early stages of the house-hunting process. Rather than alienate or turn away potential buyers, you should keep in mind that first-time buyers, in particular, will probably be unfamiliar with real estate protocol. They may be "lender shy" only because the process feels like too much commitment too soon. Assure them that prequalification doesn't obligate them in any way to purchase or bind them to a lender.

If prospects refuse to be prequalified, you can give them a ballpark figure of how much they'll need to make in order to afford a particular price range.

A few simple leading questions can help you assess a "lender-shy" buyer's psychological and financial capacity to buy.

1. *How soon do you want (or have) to buy?*

2. *How much of your savings have you designated for a down payment?*

3. *If I show you something you like, are you in a position to make an independent decision today?*

4. *Do you own your own home? If so, do you have to use the equity from your present house in order to buy another home?*

Note that each of these questions is carefully worded to obtain important information without appearing to pry into buyers' private lives. To ask how much they've saved for a down payment may really be asking them to reveal their total savings. Be diplomatic. When asked how much money they have for a down payment, most people hesitate before giving a direct (and therefore candid) answer. If the question is asked in a sincere manner and a somewhat matter-of-fact tone of voice, as if the information is routine, the earnest buyer is more likely to answer honestly. Once you've determined a buyer's sincerity and basic financial potential for home ownership, you should encourage him or her to get prequalifed (see Chapter 9).

Statistics reveal that buying a house is the largest single purchase most people will make in their lifetime, and that nearly all of their savings will be used in the purchase down payment.

a. Credit Rules of Thumb (The Three C's)

Qualifying buyers must include the evaluation of their credit by the institutional lender who will be asked to make a loan commitment. Chapter 9 covers what lenders look for before they commit themselves to a long-term loan. The willingness of creditors to lend money against later payments is based upon the so-called "Three C's of Credit"—Character, Capacity, and Capital.

1. **Character** – how a person has handled past debt obligations.
2. **Capacity** – how much debt a borrower can comfortably handle.
3. **Capital** – current available assets of the borrower.

b. Seven Basic Types of Buyers (Subjective Analysis)

Seven basic types of buyers have been identified that you should recognize and deal with accordingly.

1. **The Selfish Buyer** wants a special deal—better than anyone else's.
2. **The Friendly Buyer** is optimistic, energetic, will give you his name right away, and is excited and enthusiastic about every property you show. It can, however, be difficult to pin this buyer down on any one property.
3. **The Worrier** is pessimistic and concerned about numerous problems. These buyers are afraid they won't like the neighbors, are concerned that prices will come down, etc. Such buyers need constant reassurance.
4. **The Shy Type** is often artistic or intellectual and may take a while to start talking. He or she is a good listener. Most particularly, don't get too personal.
5. **The Belligerent Type** must save face at all costs. These types need to win every argument. In fact, don't argue with these buyers at all—if you win the argument, you risk losing them. ▼

6. **The Detail-Minded Type** is often an engineer, lawyer, or accountant. These people usually expect to have their questions answered specifically. If you don't know an answer, don't approximate. Assure them you'll find out the answer and get back to them—then do it. Use lots of charts and graphs.

7. **The Highly Controlled Buyer** loves tradition, lives by a strict code of rules, will not deviate, and likes nothing new. Treat this type conservatively, and avoid getting personal. Assure them of the stability and respectability of the neighborhood, school districts, and your firm.

4. Planning the Showing

Observe the following three steps before showing properties:

1. Plan the most effective approach;

2. Plan the showing (i.e., in what order you will expose the features of each property); and

3. Plan which advantages to emphasize. "Sell the sizzle, not the steak" means selling the benefits, not the house. It's not uncommon to hear a high producer claim he or she "sold a buyer the swimming pool, and threw in the house to boot."

Often, prospects who are worn out from looking at so many properties appear to be incapable of making decisions. There is, in fact, a certain amount of inborn sales resistance in all of us. It's up to you to help them relax. Convince them that you really care for them, that you're concerned about their needs, and that you regard their concerns as important. Assure them that they're under no pressure and that "cold feet" are normal.

Avoid overwhelming your prospects by showing them too many properties at once, which can lead to sensory overload.

a. Planning the Approach (The Buyer Comment Sheet)

You should select three or four properties—rarely visit more at one time—to show a client. Visit each property first, make an appointment with the owners to show, and map out the most effective route. This means drawing a tour or downloading a map of the neighborhood. Mark parks, schools, convenient shopping, and points of interest. Generate the same amount of enthusiasm for the area (more house for the money) as the prospects had for the house they called about from the ad (see Buyer Comment Sheet, **Figure 5-5**).

The MLS auto alert system has space provided for recipients' comments that you as the broker are able to read! It will help you narrow down the clients' needs and likes.

Figure 5-5

Buyer Comment Sheet

Barbara Buyer   # 1
2760 E Hillside Dr,
List Price: **$ 898,000**   Poor (1)   Average (2)   Good (3)   Excellent (4)

Bedrooms: 5   Baths: 4.00   Showing Appeal: ☐   ☐   ☐   ☐
Sq. Feet: 3,879   Lot Size: 25155   Overall Condition: ☐   ☐   ☐   ☐

COMMENTS: _____

_____

_____

Elementary School: _____   Junior High: _____
High School: _____   College: _____

Barbara Buyer   # 2
1533 S Fairway Knolls Rd,
List Price: **$ 849,000**   Poor (1)   Average (2)   Good (3)   Excellent (4)

Bedrooms: 5   Baths: 3.75   Showing Appeal: ☐   ☐   ☐   ☐
Sq. Feet: 3,800   Lot Size: 18891   Overall Condition: ☐   ☐   ☐   ☐

COMMENTS: _____

_____

_____

Elementary School: _____   Junior High: _____
High School: _____   College: _____

Barbara Buyer   # 3
3013 E Hillside Dr,
List Price: **$ 699,888**   Poor (1)   Average (2)   Good (3)   Excellent (4)

Bedrooms: 4   Baths: 3.00   Showing Appeal: ☐   ☐   ☐   ☐
Sq. Feet: 2,844   Lot Size: 40218   Overall Condition: ☐   ☐   ☐   ☐

COMMENTS: _____

_____

_____

Elementary School: _____   Junior High: _____
High School: _____   College: _____

Information deemed to be reliable although not guaranteed.

---

b. Planning the Actual Showing

Know in advance what you want to emphasize about a property. If you're planning to save the best for last, map out the route accordingly. While some agents choose to drive into the driveway to give the prospects the feeling of "arriving home," others choose to pull up on the opposite side of the street to show them the "curb appeal." If the potential buyers like the looks of the house, it's appropriate for you to walk up to the front entry first and greet the owners. On the other hand, if a prospect declines to see the inside of a house based on the impression he or she gets from the exterior of the property, drive away, and use your mobile phone to call the owners and notify them that you will not be stopping by after all. Don't keep them waiting.

> *Spare the homeowner's feelings. If a buyer decides not to look inside a house based on its outside appearance, tell the seller that your clients have "chosen to go in another direction," and inform them you'll call when you have other potential buyers.*

5. The Showing

Once you've determined a client's needs and desires, you'll be better informed as to what features of a property you emphasize. Very few homes will completely fulfill a buyer's wish list of features, so it's important to draw attention to those elements that really do appeal to their tastes. (In Chapter 2, we discussed "staging" open houses; the same holds true here.) If the kitchen is dark or outdated, draw your client's attention back to the living room with the attractive fireplace. If it's winter, make sure to light a warm, inviting fire.

Find the most appealing room in the house to make your strongest pitch for the sale. Different buyers will have different tastes, so pay attention to the signals they send out. A couple with a child, for example, will no doubt consider a large den with built-in cabinets for storage more important than a formal living room. Sensitivity to your buyers' preferences reassures them that you're invested in their best interests and not just in trying to earn a commission.

It's imperative that you stay with the buyers while they tour the house, even if they ask for privacy. It's one thing to give them space and opportunity for private conversation, it's another to open the homeowner to thievery or invasion of privacy.

Never allow prospects access to personal or valuable property. Don't allow children to enter the property unless accompanied by both you and the parents. Insist that children stay with their parents—never leave them unattended.

Don't sell the "soft market," implying that a seller will accept less than the listed price. Avoid the temptation to take advantage of a seller's anxiety to sell. Sell the virtues of the property itself, not the virtues of the price, unless, of course, the price is such a bargain that it shouldn't be passed up. Keep in mind that a savvy buyer will know that if a property is very underpriced, it probably would have sold the moment the listing appeared.

Don't rush buyers. Give them as long as they need to inspect the property. Generally, the longer they stay, the greater their interest, particularly if they're "placing" their furniture in the room.

Assume that the prospects like the house. Ask them point blank if they do. If not, ask them what it is that they don't like. You can assure them that this is not, after all, your house, and that they can be candid with you, as you have other homes you can show them. On the other hand, if they say they like it, start to close!

Don't assume a property is a done deal until escrow closes! A buyer who was nervous after putting down a deposit can back out when he sees the property in an unflattering light, like a messy kitchen, during the final professional inspection. Ask homeowners to keep their place immaculate until move out day!

a. Feng Shui

We have been stressing throughout this book the importance of knowing your clients. As such, it's important to acknowledge that California has a large Asian population and is continuing to experience a strong influx from this growing cultural group. If you have clients from China, Korea, Vietnam, or Japan, it's likely you may encounter some who adhere to feng shui.

Feng Shui (pronounced "fung shway") means "wind and water," and its main purpose is to align an environment so as to live in harmony and balance with nature.

The proper orientation of a building on the property, its architectural design, and its interior layout are all influenced by a balance between the dark, female, and passive "yin" and the light, male, and active "yang." The ideal environment balances both yin and yang, which are expressed through five elements: wood, fire, earth, metal, and water.

There are many nuances to feng shui, but in terms of real estate, negatives and positives are often no different from any other "desirable" or "undesirable" features in a home. For example, a busy street, unless controlled by landscape, is a negative in any homebuyer's language. Furniture placement that prevents a door from opening or closing properly, or a table in the midst of a natural walkway is considered a negative factor, as it interrupts the "flow" of a house. In feng shui, the flow that's interrupted is called "ch'i."

Ch'i is the "breath," or "life force" of feng shui.

It is also important to remember that not all Asians practice feng shui, and to assume that they do may offend this growing group of clients, resulting in lost opportunities. Also, many non-Asians in the U.S. (particularly in California) are adhering to a reformed version of feng shui.

Demonstrating a tactful knowledge of feng shui (without a direct inquiry about your client's belief system) will make you appear more knowledgeable and show that you have given another community the respect of researching some of their needs and preferences. Be sensitive to your particular client and act accordingly. For a deeper understanding, you may want to attend some seminars and read books on this subject.

6. Overriding Objections

We've discussed overriding objections over the telephone in order to get a name and/or appointment. But you can expect to encounter many objections from buyers in day-to-day selling activities as well. Handle objections judiciously. You may represent the seller in a typical transaction, but you also have a position of trust with the buyer and the public. Overselling can be perilous, leading to problems with a reluctant buyer.

If you're holding an open house, your prospects will undoubtedly stop at other open houses. Give them extra business cards. Remind them to notify the open house agent that they are working with you.

7. The Close — A Natural Progression

CLOSING means getting the offer to buy. The close should never be a sudden transition, as if it were a separate and distinct entity apart from the entire selling process. If the rest of the presentation has been persuasive and complete (all the necessary points and arguments included), the close should take place calmly and naturally. Don't pressure the prospect into signing, or problems may arise later, even before escrow opens.

If you pressure clients who later back out of the deal your reputation may suffer. If a client can't afford a property show them one they can afford. If they are having second thoughts, gently help them over their concerns, but don't bulldoze them—you don't want a reputation of being a pushy salesperson who loses clients!

VI. The Sale

"A sale is made in the presentation—it's only lost in the close."

There are a number of closing questions you can ask to confirm that the buyers are "sold." "How do you want to take title?", for example. Your best ammunition, of course, are the prospects' past remarks. If they ask how soon they can move in, start writing the offer. Answering the question with a question can also be effective. "Will the sellers carry back a second?" can be answered with, "How much of a second would you like for the seller to take back?" Or state in a positive tone, as you begin to fill in the purchase offer, "Let's submit an offer right now, Mr. and Mrs. Buyer, to find out just how receptive the sellers are to helping finance the transaction."

Sometimes you need to be direct and actually ask your client to buy.

Some prospects, such as the shy or highly controlled types, won't buy unless asked. So ask them to buy! If they say no, sell them again, reviewing those things that were apparently not clear the first time. If they express concern that the home may not meet their needs, or what they really want is beyond their ability to pay, remind them that half a loaf of bread is better than none. In other words, "If you wait until you can afford a $400,000 house, you lose the benefits and pleasures of living in a $350,000 house in the meantime. Besides, this house will probably increase in value while you're living in it. Think of it as an investment that will eventually help you afford the house of your dreams."

A. CLOSING TECHNIQUES

How many times do you take "no" for an answer before accepting it as a final rejection? There is no absolute rule, but clearly, you should use as many different types of persuasion as you can muster. Always focus attention on the buyers' needs and incorporate them in the closing argument. For every argument your buyer has against buying a property, you need to have a better one in favor of buying.

Either convince the prospects to buy or the prospects convince you they will not.

There is no limit to ingenuity. The creative salesperson establishes a program of self-analysis and self-improvement. Every day, as an imaginative salesperson, you should try to learn new selling points, set up a work pattern for more efficiently taking care of current clients, and for uncovering new ones. You should also attend seminars and read books on listings, selling, and other real estate topics, so as to be constantly aware of new developments in this dynamic field.

B. SELLER RELOCATION

A Referral Fee is a commission earned by introducing your client to another broker.

After a house sells and closes escrow, some sellers may want to relocate to different areas where you don't do business. This is an opportunity for referral fees from brokers who sell to your clients. You need to contact two reputable brokers (whose names can be found in the CRS Roster) and send them a referral form for your client. The **CRS ROSTER** *is a list of Certified Residential Specialists (CRS) used for finding other professionals for referrals.* It is a National Association of REALTORS® subgroup designation that shows members have taken courses to earn the right to use the letters "CRS." If that broker earns a commission as a result of your referral, your referral fee is usually 20% to 30%, depending on the market.

VII. CHAPTER SUMMARY

For most buyers, buying a home is the most important financial decision they will ever make—and it can be the biggest asset over time as well. Most property owners move on an average of every six to eight years.

It's important to know where **specific school boundary lines** are drawn within a district—a slight miscalculation can result in a lost sale, or a lawsuit.

Get a **professional inspection** (as a condition of the contract) or a **waiver** on all real estate purchases. This is usually paid for by the buyer, with a copy going to the seller. The seller can make all of the repairs requested by the buyer, some of them, or none of them. Until the requested repairs are done, the offer can be rescinded, with the deposit returned to the buyers.

Functional obsolescence is the loss of value due to adverse factors WITHIN a property that affect the marketability of the property, like a single-car garage. **Economic** or **social obsolescence** is any loss of value due to conditions OUTSIDE of the property, and is considered "**incurable.**"

Some of the advantages of homeownership include possible **appreciation, tax benefits, equity buildup**, and **cash flow**. There is no **capital gains tax** ($250,000 of profits for singles and $500,000 of profits for married) if the house sold is a principal residence and the sellers have lived there for a minimum of two years during the last five years prior to sale.

When budgeting for a home, the buyers' housing payments **should not exceed 25% to 30% of their gross monthly income**. When personal debt is included with the house payment, the max should be no more than 33% to 38%. Try to get potential buyers **prequalified** whenever possible.

Selling is communicating, and the most effective way to communicate is through **direct contact**, or **face-to-face**. If that's not possible, the next best thing is by telephone. Listening is an important skill, both in person and on the phone. Keep track of all incoming calls with an incoming **call register** or **log book**. Use the phone to make appointments, and get that face-to-face contact.

Letters, the least effective form of communication, should be used to **precondition** a customer—prior to a phone call or meeting. When writing a letter, use the advertising technique of **AIDA—attention, interest, desire, and action**. Consider sending out postcards (with a photo) instead of letters, as they are less expensive and get read more often. Don't forget emails and auto alerts.

When asked about a listing on the phone, it's best to find out as much about the callers as possible. Find out what they are looking for, what they can afford, what school district they prefer, etc. Answer questions honestly, but strive to **get an appointment to show a property whenever possible**. Don't forget to inform a caller that your firm can look up information on other agents' listings—saving them the time and legwork. Using a **switch sheet** can steer a customer to other, similar properties.

An **office caravan** is a weekly outing where available salespeople preview all the newest brokerage listings and other listings. After caravaning, agents fill out an **agent comment sheet** describing and rating those properties.

Buyer's needs include four categories: The **need for trust, information, advice, and financing**.

Before buying a home, buyers must have **financial ability, desire, and intent to buy**.

Prequalifying your clients is coordinating your buyers' needs with their actual financial capacity. Lenders look for the **"Three C's" of credit: Character, Capacity, and Capital**.

Every salesperson should have a **sales kit**, including the listing, selling, and prospecting tools needed in real estate. A few of the items included in the kit should be a mobile phone, a notebook or handheld computer, market analysis software or forms, purchase contract forms, and more.

Don't overwhelm buyers by showing them too many properties at once. Help them to keep track of what they've seen with a **buyer comment sheet**. It's best to ask the owners not to be present during a showing.

Feng shui is just one way to make sure your clients see a home to its best advantage. Feng shui is the aligning of the environment so as to live in harmony and balance with nature. Many buyers of all nationalities adhere to these theories.

In the case of showing homes, **closing means getting the offer to buy**. There are many techniques used to close the deal, all of which involve finessing a client towards making that final decision to buy. Some techniques are more aggressive than others; it's up to you to determine the best route to take when nudging a client toward such a decision. This is true for overcoming hi sor her objections as well. Your integrity and professionalism during "the close" will determine whether you get the sale. The sale is not complete until escrow closes!

VIII. MATCHING VOCABULARY Fill in the blanks with the correct letter

A. Agent comment sheet
B. Buyer comment sheet
C. Closing the sale
D. Counseling/ Qualifying
E. Economic obsolescence
F. Floortime
G. Functional obsolescence
H. Feng shui
I. Incoming call register
J. Office caravan
K. Physical Depreciation
L. Referral fee
M. Switch sheet
N. Three C's of credit

1. _____ Any loss of value due to conditions outside of the property itself (external).

2. _____ Normal wear and tear as things need to be repaired or replaced.

3. _____ The loss of value due to adverse design factors within a structure that affect the marketability of the property.

4. _____ Time assigned to an agent to answer the company phone (new prospects are yours).

5. _____ This tool provides the salesperson with a series of questions to ask the caller, and furnishes a handy record of calls for follow-up now or later.

6. _____ A quick reference list of properties within a similar price range, school district, size, etc.

7. _____ A weekly outing whereby all available salespersons from one office preview all the newest brokerage listings as well as other brokerages' "listings."

8. _____ The process of reconciling a buyer's needs and desires with the reality of his or her financial capacity.

9. _____ Meaning "wind and water," the main purpose of this is to align an environment so as to live in harmony and balance with nature.

10. _____ A natural progresion culminating in getting an offer to buy.

11. _____ Character, Capacity, and Capital. Ways to evaluate someone's creditworthiness.

12. _____ After previewing available properties during a caravan, each agent is expected to fill out this form.

13. _____ A commission earned by introducing your client to another broker.

14. _____ Used when showing potential buyers properties to help them to keep track of what they've seen.

See Page 609 for Answers

IX. CHAPTER QUIZ

1. The loss of value due to conditions outside of the property is considered:

   a. functional obsolescence and curable.
   b. economic obsolescence and incurable.
   c. economic obsolescence and curable.
   d. none of the above.

2. The most effective communication usually occurs:

   a. by way of telephone calls.
   b. through letters.
   c. face-to-face.
   d. none of the above.

3. When selling an older home, it's important to remember that insurance claim disclosure must be made to the buyers of any major material repairs or insurance claims made within the last:

   a. three years.
   b. five years.
   c. ten years.
   d. fifteen years.

4. Which of the following would be considered a disadvantage of owning a home?

   a. Appreciation
   b. Upkeep and maintenance
   c. Equity buildup
   d. All of the above

5. The time assigned to a salesperson to answer the company telephones is referred to as:

   a. facetime.
   b. phonetime.
   c. floortime.
   d. downtime.

6. A quick reference list of "alternative listings" within a similar price range, school district, size, etc., is called a(n):

   a. switch sheet.
   b. cheat sheet.
   c. incoming call register.
   d. all of the above.

7. An office caravan consists of:

    a. a group of MLS cooperating brokers who visit each others' offices weekly.

    b. a weekly outing by office salespersons to preview new brokerage listings.

    c. a weekly visit to the car wash by all brokerage personnel.

    d. a brokerage that operates out of a mobile home rather than a traditional office.

8. The process of reconciling buyers' needs and desires with the reality of their financial capacity to buy may be called:

    a. qualifying buyers.

    b. counseling buyers.

    c. both a and b.

    d. neither a nor b.

9. Which of the following in NOT one of the three C's of credit?

    a. Character

    b. Capacity

    c. Capital

    d. Citizenship

10. The term "feng shui" literally means:

    a. for sale.

    b. air and earth.

    c. wind and water.

    d. none of the above.

ANSWERS: 1. b; 2. c; 3. b; 4. b; 5. c; 6. a; 7. b; 8. c; 9. d; 10. c

CHAPTER 6

The Purchase Offer: Filling Out the New Residential Purchase Contract

I. Overview of the Latest Purchase Agreement Contract

A. WHY PURCHASE AGREEMENT CONTRACTS ARE NECESSARY

Most transactions for the purchase and sale of real estate begin with a written offer purchase agreement contract between the buyer and seller.

In a real estate transaction, questions relating to financing, possession, the condition of title, liens or other interests in the property, and arrangements for conveying possession and title must be addressed.

The listing agent may request that all offers be presented on the latest CAR® Residential Purchase Agreement and Joint Escrow Instructions (RPA-CA) form—available online to REALTORS® by computer or mobile device at www.car.org.

B. MAJOR CHANGES IN THE PURCHASE AGREEMENT (RPA-CA Revised 11/14)

The latest CAR®, California Residential Purchase Agreement and Joint Escrow Instructions" (RPA-CA) form was released in November, 2014, and reflects the **latest "generational changes" essential to the offer and acceptance of a real estate sale.**

This landmark RPA-CA Revised 11/14 form requires agreement to many *specific items*, such as:

1. **Separating a loan contingency from appraisal contingency;**
2. **Filling-in boxes identifying a specific date or a number of days;**
3. **Buyers and sellers are the parties to this agreement, not brokers;**
4. **Deposits are sent electronically unless stated otherwise;**
5. **Specific time for escrow instructions to be signed and returned;**
6. **Expands personal property details included in the sale; and**
7. **Sellers now responsible to order and pay for HOA docs for buyer.**

CHAPTER 6

Increased clarity – more definite and certain terms are now required! The new form represents a "generational change."

This latest purchase agreement (**RPA-CA Revised 11/14**) has been significantly updated to include specific details that need to be addressed by the buyer and buyer's agent to make crystal clear the terms of the offer to the seller and seller's agent. The terms of the agreement are negotiated back and forth until all the parties (buyers and sellers) agree on the final terms.

In a typical purchase, buyers must make arrangements to borrow the money (from a bank or other lender). In this latest purchase agreement the time required to obtain the lender's approval is limited to a specific date or number of days.

This process, usually will involve: 1) an appraisal and inspection of the property, and 2) lender's approval of a specific loan and interest rate after reviewing the credit score of the borrowers. The buyers put down an initial deposit to keep the sellers obligated to sell during the specific time it takes them to arrange the financing as spelled out in the purchase agreement contract. The buyers don't want to borrow the money unless they get the exact (or better) financing terms they agreed to before they go ahead with the loan. This is called a **financing contingency**.

C. CONTINGENCY CLAUSES IN THE PURCHASE AGREEMENT

A *CONTINGENCY CLAUSE is a contract provision that requires a specific action to occur by a certain time in order for the contract to be considered enforceable.* If the party named to fulfill the requirements of the contingency clause is unable to do so, both parties are released from their obligations.

Real estate transactions are usually pretty complicated affairs. In addition, for most people, a large amount of their savings (money) is involved. Financing must be arranged, title searched, existing liens (such as the seller's mortgage or assessments for local improvements) must be paid off.

Additionally, there are often a number of other matters which must be handled prior to the time the buyer pays for the property and the seller delivers title and possession. During the time that both parties are performing their respective tasks, they both want to keep the other side obligated to perform. The new Purchase Agreement is meant to accomplish this!

II. Now More Detailed RPA-CA (Revised 11/14) Form

Writing the purchase agreement (offer) is a vital step in bringing the buyers and sellers together, and should be worded in simple and concise language.

The California Bureau of Real Estate (CalBRE) has often stated that the purchase agreement is the most important document in a real estate transaction; the broker's responsibilities in completing or supervising the purchase agreement contract accurately and unambiguously cannot be overemphasized.

There is no required contract to use for this purpose, but most agreements for the purchase of real estate in California use some variation of the purchase form, incorporating both the receipt for the consideration (deposit), and the terms of the offer. As mentioned

earlier, CAR's® **California Residential Purchase Agreement and Joint Escrow Instructions (RPA-CA Revised 11/14)** (see **Figure 6-1**) is the newest form available. This form is used in most simple transactions, including the sale of single-family, one- to four-unit residential dwellings.

A wise listing agent may request that all offers be presented on the latest CAR® RPA-CA form.

A. CHANGING THE PREPRINTED FORMS

The written or typed word supersedes (takes precedence over) the printed word if there is a contradiction.

Where there are inconsistencies between general and specific provisions, the specific provisions ordinarily clarify the meaning of the general provisions. The detailed blanks in this residential purchase agreement (contract) must be filled in correctly. What goes into them must express the understanding of the parties to the contract. You should strive for simplicity without leaving out essentials. It is essential that the terms be understood by all parties.

Use the form itself as a checklist that is complete in all important legal respects. Cross out printed sentences or paragraphs that are not applicable and have the changes dated and initialed by the impacted parties.

The buyer doesn't want to spend several hundred dollars on appraisal, credit report, and other financing-related fees, only to find out that the seller no longer wants to sell the house. On the other hand, the seller doesn't want to take the house off the market, and spend several hundred dollars in escrow fees and inspections, only to find out the buyer no longer wants to buy the house. It is, therefore, mutually advantageous that this enforceable purchase agreement contract to buy and sell the property be used. These purchase agreements are commonly known by a number of names in different states, such as "purchase and sales agreement," "earnest money agreement," "deposit receipt," "binder," and others. Among real estate professionals in California, the once widely used term "deposit receipt" has been replaced with the term "residential purchase contract" or "purchase agreement."

B. FORM: CALIFORNIA RESIDENTIAL PURCHASE AGREEMENT AND JOINT ESCROW INSTRUCTIONS (RPA-CA)

Figure 6-1

CALIFORNIA
ASSOCIATION
OF REALTORS®

**CALIFORNIA
RESIDENTIAL PURCHASE AGREEMENT
AND JOINT ESCROW INSTRUCTIONS**
For Use With Single Family Residential Property — Attached or Detached
(C.A.R. Form RPA-CA, Revised 11/14)

Date Prepared: June 14, 2020

1. **OFFER:**
   A. **THIS IS AN OFFER FROM** _Walter Buyer and Debbie Buyer_ ("Buyer").
   B. **THE REAL PROPERTY** to be acquired is _264 Beach Lane_ , situated
      in_ Costa Mesa _ (City), _Orange_ County, California,
      ____ (Zip Code), Assessor's Parcel No. ____ ("Property").
   C. **THE PURCHASE PRICE** offered is
      Eight Hundred Thousand Dollars $ _800,000.00_ .
   D. **CLOSE OF ESCROW** shall occur on ____ (date)(or _90_ **Days** After Acceptance).
   E. Buyer and Seller are referred to herein as the "Parties." Brokers are not Parties to this Agreement.
2. **AGENCY:**
   A. **DISCLOSURE:** The Parties each acknowledge receipt of a ☑"Disclosure Regarding Real Estate Agency Relationships" (C.A.R. Form AD).
   B. **CONFIRMATION:** The following agency relationships are hereby confirmed for this transaction:
      Listing Agent ____ _Sail Realty_ (Print Firm Name) is the agent of (check one):
      ☐ the Seller exclusively; or ☐ both the Buyer and Seller.
      Selling Agent ____ _Ramos Realty_ (Print Firm Name) (if not the same as the
      Listing Agent) is the agent of (check one): ☐ the Buyer exclusively; or ☐ the Seller exclusively; or ☐ both the Buyer and Seller.
   C. **POTENTIALLY COMPETING BUYERS AND SELLERS:** The Parties each acknowledge receipt of a ☑"Possible Representation of More than One Buyer or Seller - Disclosure and Consent" (C.A.R. Form PRBS).
3. **FINANCE TERMS:** Buyer represents that funds will be good when deposited with Escrow Holder.
   A. **INITIAL DEPOSIT:** Deposit shall be in the amount of ....$ _10,000.00_
      (1) Buyer Direct Deposit: Buyer shall deliver deposit directly to Escrow Holder by electronic funds
      transfer, ☐ cashier's check, ☐ personal check, ☐ other ____ within 3 business days
      after Acceptance (or ____);
      OR (2) ☑ Buyer Deposit with Agent: Buyer has given the deposit by personal check (or ____)
      to the agent submitting the offer (or to ____), made payable to
      ABC Escrow . The deposit shall be held uncashed until Acceptance and then deposited
      with Escrow Holder within 3 business days after Acceptance (or ____).
      Deposit checks given to agent shall be an original signed check and not a copy.
      (Note: Initial and increased deposits checks received by agent shall be recorded in Broker's trust fund log.)
   B. **INCREASED DEPOSIT:** Buyer shall deposit with Escrow Holder an increased deposit in the amount of ....$ ____
      within ____ **Days** After Acceptance (or ____).
      If the Parties agree to liquidated damages in this Agreement, they also agree to incorporate the increased
      deposit into the liquidated damages amount in a separate liquidated damages clause (C.A.R. Form RID)
      at the time the increased deposit is delivered to Escrow Holder.
   C. ☐ **ALL CASH OFFER:** No loan is needed to purchase the Property. Written verification of sufficient funds
      to close this transaction IS ATTACHED to this offer or ☐ Buyer shall, within **3 (or** ____ **) Days** After
      Acceptance, Deliver to Seller such verification.
   D. **LOAN(S):**
      (1) FIRST LOAN: in the amount of ....$ _640,000.00_
      This loan will be conventional financing or ☐ FHA, ☐ VA, ☐ Seller financing (C.A.R. Form SFA),
      ☐ assumed financing (C.A.R. Form AFA), ☐ Other ____. This loan shall be at a fixed
      rate not to exceed _8.0_ % or, ☐ an adjustable rate loan with initial rate not to exceed ____ %.
      Regardless of the type of loan, Buyer shall pay points not to exceed _2.0_ % of the loan amount.
      (2) ☐ **SECOND LOAN** in the amount of ....$ ____
      This loan will be conventional financing or ☐ Seller financing (C.A.R. Form SFA), ☐ assumed
      financing (C.A.R. Form AFA), ☐ Other ____. This loan shall be at a fixed rate not to
      exceed ____ % or, ☐ an adjustable rate loan with initial rate not to exceed ____ %. Regardless of
      the type of loan, Buyer shall pay points not to exceed ____ % of the loan amount.
      (3) FHA/VA: For any FHA or VA loan specified in 3D(1), Buyer has **17 (or** ____ **) Days** After Acceptance
      to Deliver to Seller written notice (C.A.R. Form FVA) of any lender-required repairs or costs that
      Buyer requests Seller to pay for or otherwise correct. Seller has no obligation to pay or satisfy lender
      requirements unless agreed in writing. A FHA/VA amendatory clause (C.A.R. Form FVAC) shall be a
      part of this transaction.
   E. **ADDITIONAL FINANCING TERMS:** ____
   F. **BALANCE OF DOWN PAYMENT OR PURCHASE PRICE** in the amount of....................................$ _150,000.00_
      to be deposited with Escrow Holder pursuant to Escrow Holder instructions.
   G. **PURCHASE PRICE (TOTAL):** ....$ _800,000.00_

Buyer's Initials (_WB_)(_DB_)   Seller's Initials (_TS_)(_RS_)

© 1991-2014, California Association of REALTORS®, Inc.
RPA-CA REVISED 11/14 (PAGE 1 OF 10) Print Date
CALIFORNIA RESIDENTIAL PURCHASE AGREEMENT (RPA-CA PAGE 1 OF 10)

When writing an offer for your client, do not suggest how to take title; this is best left to the buyer's attorney or an accountant. Have the check for the earnest money deposited in person or electronically with the escrow company. The buyers have 3 working days from acceptance to make the deposit.

Property Address: 264 Beach Lane, Costa Mesa, CA 92627   Date: June 14, 2020

H. **VERIFICATION OF DOWN PAYMENT AND CLOSING COSTS:** Buyer (or Buyer's lender or loan broker pursuant to paragraph 3J(1)) shall, within **3 (or ___) Days** After Acceptance, Deliver to Seller written verification of Buyer's down payment and closing costs. (☐ Verification attached.)

I. **APPRAISAL CONTINGENCY AND REMOVAL:** This Agreement is (or ☐ is NOT) contingent upon a written appraisal of the Property by a licensed or certified appraiser at no less than the purchase price. Buyer shall, as specified in paragraph 14B(3), in writing, remove the appraisal contingency or cancel this Agreement within **17 (or ___) Days** After Acceptance.

J. **LOAN TERMS:**
(1) LOAN APPLICATIONS: Within **3 (or ___) Days** After Acceptance, Buyer shall Deliver to Seller a letter from Buyer's lender or loan broker stating that, based on a review of Buyer's written application and credit report, Buyer is prequalified or preapproved for any NEW loan specified in paragraph 3D. If any loan specified in paragraph 3D is an adjustable rate loan, the prequalification or preapproval letter shall be based on the qualifying rate, not the initial loan rate. (☐ Letter attached.)
(2) LOAN CONTINGENCY: Buyer shall act diligently and in good faith to obtain the designated loan(s). Buyer's qualification for the loan(s) specified above **is a contingency** of this Agreement unless otherwise agreed in writing. If there is no appraisal contingency or the appraisal contingency has been waived or removed, then failure of the Property to appraise at the purchase price does not entitle Buyer to exercise the cancellation right pursuant to the loan contingency if Buyer is otherwise qualified for the specified loan. Buyer's contractual obligations regarding deposit, balance of down payment and closing costs **are not contingencies** of this Agreement.
(3) LOAN CONTINGENCY REMOVAL:
Within **21 (or ___) Days** After Acceptance, Buyer shall, as specified in paragraph 14, in writing, remove the loan contingency or cancel this Agreement. If there is an appraisal contingency, removal of the loan contingency shall not be deemed removal of the appraisal contingency.
(4) ☐ NO LOAN CONTINGENCY: Obtaining any loan specified above is NOT a contingency of this Agreement. If Buyer does not obtain the loan and as a result does not purchase the Property, Seller may be entitled to Buyer's deposit or other legal remedies.
(5) LENDER LIMITS ON BUYER CREDITS: Any credit to Buyer, from any source, for closing or other costs that is agreed to by the Parties ("Contractual Credit") shall be disclosed to Buyer's lender. If the total credit allowed by Buyer's lender ("Lender Allowable Credit") is less than the Contractual Credit, then (i) the Contractual Credit shall be reduced to the Lender Allowable Credit, and (ii) in the absence of a separate written agreement between the Parties, there shall be no automatic adjustment to the purchase price to make up for the difference between the Contractual Credit and the Lender Allowable Credit.

K. **BUYER STATED FINANCING:** Seller is relying on Buyer's representation of the type of financing specified (including but not limited to, as applicable, all cash, amount of down payment, or contingent or non contingent loan). Seller has agreed to a specific closing date, purchase price and to sell to Buyer in reliance on Buyer's covenant concerning financing. Buyer shall pursue the financing specified in this Agreement. Seller has no obligation to cooperate with Buyer's efforts to obtain any financing other than that specified in the Agreement and the availability of any such alternate financing does not excuse Buyer from the obligation to purchase the Property and close escrow as specified in this Agreement.

4. **SALE OF BUYER'S PROPERTY:**
A. This Agreement and Buyer's ability to obtain financing are NOT contingent upon the sale of any property owned by Buyer.
OR B. ☐ This Agreement and Buyer's ability to obtain financing are contingent upon the sale of property owned by Buyer as specified in the attached addendum (C.A.R. Form COP).

5. **ADDENDA AND ADVISORIES:**
A. **ADDENDA:**   ☐ Addendum # _____ (C.A.R. Form ADM)
☐ Back Up Offer Addendum (C.A.R. Form BUO)   ☐ Court Confirmation Addendum (C.A.R. Form CCA)
☐ Septic, Well and Property Monument Addendum (C.A.R. Form SWPI)
☐ Short Sale Addendum (C.A.R. Form SSA)   ☐ Other

B. **BUYER AND SELLER ADVISORIES:**   ☑ Buyer's Inspection Advisory (C.A.R. Form BIA)
☐ Probate Advisory (C.A.R. Form PAK)   ☑ Statewide Buyer and Seller Advisory (C.A.R. Form SBSA)
☐ Trust Advisory (C.A.R. Form TA)   ☐ REO Advisory (C.A.R. Form REO)
☐ Short Sale Information and Advisory (C.A.R. Form SSIA)   ☑ Other Purchase Agreement Addendum (C.A.R. Form PAA)

6. **OTHER TERMS:** _____
_____
_____

7. **ALLOCATION OF COSTS**
A. **INSPECTIONS, REPORTS AND CERTIFICATES:** Unless otherwise agreed in writing, this paragraph only determines who is to pay for the inspection, test, certificate or service ("Report") mentioned; it **does not determine who is to pay for any work** recommended or identified in the Report.
(1) ☐ Buyer ☐ Seller shall pay for a natural hazard zone disclosure report, including ☐ environmental and tax reports ☐ Other: _____ prepared by _____.
(2) ☐ Buyer ☑ Seller shall pay for the following Report   Wood Pest Report
prepared by   Bugs B Gone
(3) ☐ Buyer ☐ Seller shall pay for the following Report _____
prepared by _____

Buyer's Initials (*WB*)(*DB*)   Seller's Initials (*JS*)(*RJS*)

RPA-CA REVISED 11/14 (PAGE 2 OF 10) Print Date

Prior to writing the offer, the buyer's agent may also create a comparative market analysis for the buyer, similar to the seller's. This gives the buyers a better understanding of the property's value and he or she can then be in a better position to make a "reasonable" offer that can be accepted or countered by the seller. Brokers do not recommend prices.

Property Address: _____264 Beach Lane, Costa Mesa, CA 92627_____ Date: _June 14, 2020_

B. GOVERNMENT REQUIREMENTS AND RETROFIT:
(1) ☐ Buyer ☑ Seller shall pay for smoke alarm and carbon monoxide device installation and water heater bracing, if required by Law. Prior to Close Of Escrow ("COE"), Seller shall provide Buyer written statement(s) of compliance in accordance with state and local Law, unless Seller is exempt.
(2) (i)☐ Buyer ☐ Seller shall pay the cost of compliance with any other minimum mandatory government inspections and reports if required as a condition of closing escrow under any Law.
(ii)☐ Buyer ☐ Seller shall pay the cost of compliance with any other minimum mandatory government retrofit standards required as a condition of closing escrow under any Law, whether the work is required to be completed before or after COE.
(iii) Buyer shall be provided, within the time specified in paragraph 14A, a copy of any required government conducted or point-of-sale inspection report prepared pursuant to this Agreement or in anticipation of this sale of the Property.

C. ESCROW AND TITLE:
(1) (a) ☑ Buyer ☑ Seller shall pay escrow fee _50% / 50%_ .
(b) Escrow Holder shall be _ABC Escrow_ .
(c) The Parties shall, within 5 (or ___) Days After receipt, sign and return Escrow Holder's general provisions.
(2) (a) ☐ Buyer ☐ Seller shall pay for owner's title insurance policy specified in paragraph 13E _____ .
(b) Owner's title policy to be issued by _____
(Buyer shall pay for any title insurance policy insuring Buyer's **lender**, unless otherwise agreed in writing.)

D. OTHER COSTS:
(1) ☐ Buyer ☐ Seller shall pay County transfer tax or fee _____ .
(2) ☐ Buyer ☐ Seller shall pay City transfer tax or fee _____ .
(3) ☐ Buyer ☐ Seller shall pay Homeowners' Association ("HOA") transfer fee _____ .
(4) Seller shall pay HOA fees for preparing documents required to be delivered by Civil Code §4525.
(5) ☐ Buyer ☐ Seller shall pay HOA fees for preparing all documents other than those required by Civil Code §4525.
(6) ☐ Buyer ☐ Seller shall pay for any private transfer fee _____ .
(7) ☐ Buyer ☐ Seller shall pay for _____ .
(8) ☐ Buyer ☐ Seller shall pay for _____ .
(9) ☐ Buyer ☐ Seller shall pay for the cost, not to exceed $_____, of a standard (or ☐ upgraded) one-year home warranty plan, issued by _____ , with the following optional coverages: ☐Air Conditioner ☐Pool/Spa ☐Other: _____
Buyer is informed that home warranty plans have many optional coverages in addition to those listed above. Buyer is advised to investigate these coverages to determine those that may be suitable for Buyer.
OR ☐ Buyer waives the purchase of a home warranty plan. Nothing in this paragraph precludes Buyer's purchasing a home warranty plan during the term of this Agreement.

8. **ITEMS INCLUDED IN AND EXCLUDED FROM SALE:**
A. **NOTE TO BUYER AND SELLER:** Items listed as included or excluded in the MLS, flyers or marketing materials are **not** included in the purchase price or excluded from the sale unless specified in paragraph 8 B or C.
B. **ITEMS INCLUDED IN SALE:** Except as otherwise specified or disclosed,
(1) All EXISTING fixtures and fittings that are attached to the Property;
(2) EXISTING electrical, mechanical, lighting, plumbing and heating fixtures, ceiling fans, fireplace inserts, gas logs and grates, solar power systems, built-in appliances, window and door screens, awnings, shutters, window coverings, attached floor coverings, television antennas, satellite dishes, air coolers/conditioners, pool/spa equipment, garage door openers/remote controls, mailbox, in-ground landscaping, trees/shrubs, water features and fountains, water softeners, water purifiers, security systems/alarms and the following if checked: ☐ all stove(s), except_____ ; ☐ all refrigerator(s) except _____ ; ☐ all washer(s) and dryer(s), except _____ ;
(3) Existing integrated phone and home automation systems, including necessary components such as internet connected hardware or devices, control units (other than non-dedicated mobile devices, electronics and computers) and applicable software, permissions, passwords, codes and access information, are (☐ are NOT) included in the sale.
(4) **LEASED OR LIENED ITEMS AND SYSTEMS:** Seller shall, within the time specified in paragraph 14A, (i) disclose to Buyer if any item or system specified in paragraph 8B or otherwise included in the sale is leased, or not owned by Seller, or specifically subject to a lien or other encumbrance, and (ii) Deliver to Buyer all written materials (such as lease, warranty, etc.) concerning any such item. Buyer's ability to assume any such lease, or willingness to accept the Property subject to any such lien or encumbrance, is a contingency of this Agreement as specified in paragraph 14B.
(5) The following additional items:_____ .
(6) Seller represents that all items included in the purchase price, unless otherwise specified, (i) are owned by Seller and shall be transferred free and clear of liens and encumbrances, except the items and systems identified pursuant to 8B(4) and _____ , and (ii) are transferred without Seller warranty regardless of value.
C. **ITEMS EXCLUDED FROM SALE:** Unless otherwise specified, the following items are excluded from sale: (i) audio and video components (such as flat screen TVs, speakers and other items) if any such item is not itself attached to the Property, even if a bracket or other mechanism attached to the component or item is attached to the Property; (ii) furniture and other items secured to the Property for earthquake purposes; and (iii) _____
_____ . Brackets attached to walls, floors or ceilings for any such component, furniture or item shall remain with the Property (or ☐ will be removed and holes or other damage shall be repaired, but not painted).

Buyer's Initials (_*WB*_)(_*DB*_)   Seller's Initials (_*TS*_)(_*RJS*_)

RPA-CA REVISED 11/14 (PAGE 3 OF 10) Print Date

CALIFORNIA RESIDENTIAL PURCHASE AGREEMENT (RPA-CA PAGE 3 OF 10)

Property Address: _____ 264 Beach Lane, Costa Mesa, CA 92627 _____   Date: __ June 14, 2020 __

9. **CLOSING AND POSSESSION:**
   A. Buyer intends (or ☐ does not intend) to occupy the Property as Buyer's primary residence.
   B. **Seller-occupied or vacant property:** Possession shall be delivered to Buyer: (i) at 6 PM or (11:59 ☐ AM/☑ PM) on the date of Close Of Escrow; (ii) ☐ no later than ___ days after Close Of Escrow; or (iii) ☐ at ____ ☐ AM/☐ PM on _____.
   C. **Seller remaining in possession After Close Of Escrow:** If Seller has the right to remain in possession after Close Of Escrow, (i) the Parties are advised to sign a separate occupancy agreement such as ☐ C.A.R. Form SIP, for Seller continued occupancy of less than 30 days, ☐ C.A.R. Form RLAS for Seller continued occupancy of 30 days or more; and (ii) the Parties are advised to consult with their insurance and legal advisors for information about liability and damage or injury to persons and personal and real property; and (iii) Buyer is advised to consult with Buyer's lender about the impact of Seller's occupancy on Buyer's loan.
   D. **Tenant-occupied property: Property shall be vacant at least 5 (or ___) Days Prior to Close Of Escrow, unless otherwise** agreed in writing. **Note to Seller: If you are unable to deliver Property vacant in accordance with rent control and other applicable Law, you may be in breach of this Agreement.**
   OR ☐ Tenant to remain in possession (C.A.R. Form TIP).
   E. At Close Of Escrow: Seller assigns to Buyer any assignable warranty rights for items included in the sale; and Seller shall Deliver to Buyer available Copies of any such warranties. Brokers cannot and will not determine the assignability of any warranties.
   F. At Close Of Escrow, unless otherwise agreed in writing, Seller shall provide keys, passwords, codes and/or means to operate all locks, mailboxes, security systems, alarms, home automation systems and internet connected devices included in the purchase price, and garage door openers. If the Property is a condominium or located in a common interest subdivision, Buyer may be required to pay a deposit to the Homeowners' Association ("HOA") to obtain keys to accessible HOA facilities.

10. **STATUTORY AND OTHER DISCLOSURES (INCLUDING LEAD-BASED PAINT HAZARD DISCLOSURES) AND CANCELLATION RIGHTS:**
    A. **(1)** Seller shall, within the time specified in paragraph 14A, Deliver to Buyer: (i) if required by Law, a fully completed: Federal Lead-Based Paint Disclosures (C.A.R. Form FLD) and pamphlet ("Lead Disclosures"); and **(ii)** unless exempt, fully completed disclosures or notices required by sections 1102 et. seq. and 1103 et. seq. of the Civil Code ("Statutory Disclosures"). Statutory Disclosures include, but are not limited to, a Real Estate Transfer Disclosure Statement ("TDS"), Natural Hazard Disclosure Statement ("NHD"), notice or actual knowledge of release of illegal controlled substance, notice of special tax and/or assessments (or, if allowed, substantially equivalent notice regarding the Mello-Roos Community Facilities Act of 1982 and Improvement Bond Act of 1915) and, if Seller has actual knowledge, of industrial use and military ordnance location (C.A.R. Form SPQ or SSD).
    (2) Any Statutory Disclosure required by this paragraph is considered fully completed if Seller has answered all questions and completed and signed the seller section(s) and the Listing Agent, if any, has completed and signed the listing broker section(s), or, if applicable, an Agent Visual Inspection Disclosure (C.A.R. Form AVID). Nothing stated herein relieves a Buyer's Broker, if any, from the obligation to (i) conduct a reasonably competent and diligent visual inspection of the accessible areas of the Property and disclose, on Section IV of the TDS, or an AVID, material facts affecting the value or desirability of the Property that were or should have been revealed by such an inspection or (ii) complete any sections on all disclosures required to be completed by Buyer's Broker.
    (3) **Note to Buyer and Seller:** Waiver of Statutory and Lead Disclosures is prohibited by Law.
    (4) Seller, unless exempt from the obligation to provide TDS, shall, within the time specified in paragraph 14A, complete and provide Buyer with a Seller Property Questionnaire (C.A.R. Form SPQ) **OR** ☐ Supplemental Contractual and Statutory Disclosure (C.A.R. Form SSD).
    (5) Buyer shall, within the time specified in paragraph 14B(1), return Signed Copies of the Statutory, Lead and other disclosures to Seller.
    (6) In the event Seller or Listing Broker, prior to Close Of Escrow, becomes aware of adverse conditions materially affecting the Property, or any material inaccuracy in disclosures, information or representations previously provided to Buyer, Seller shall promptly provide a subsequent or amended disclosure or notice, in writing, covering those items. **However, a subsequent or amended disclosure shall not be required for conditions and material inaccuracies of which Buyer is otherwise aware, or which are disclosed in reports provided to or obtained by Buyer or ordered and paid for by Buyer.**
    (7) If any disclosure or notice specified in paragraph 10A(1), or subsequent or amended disclosure or notice is Delivered to Buyer after the offer is Signed, Buyer shall have the right to cancel this Agreement within **3 Days** After Delivery in person, or **5 Days** After Delivery by deposit in the mail, by giving written notice of cancellation to Seller or Seller's agent.
    B. **NATURAL AND ENVIRONMENTAL HAZARD DISCLOSURES AND OTHER BOOKLETS:** Within the time specified in paragraph 14A, Seller shall, if required by Law: **(i)** Deliver to Buyer earthquake guide(s) (and questionnaire), environmental hazards booklet, and home energy rating pamphlet; **(ii)** disclose if the Property is located in a Special Flood Hazard Area; Potential Flooding (Inundation) Area; Very High Fire Hazard Zone; State Fire Responsibility Area; Earthquake Fault Zone; and Seismic Hazard Zone; and **(iii)** disclose any other zone as required by Law and provide any other information required for those zones.
    C. **WITHHOLDING TAXES:** Within the time specified in paragraph 14A, to avoid required withholding, Seller shall Deliver to Buyer or qualified substitute, an affidavit sufficient to comply with federal (FIRPTA) and California withholding Law (C.A.R. Form AS or QS).
    D. **MEGAN'S LAW DATABASE DISCLOSURE:** Notice: Pursuant to Section 290.46 of the Penal Code, information about specified registered sex offenders is made available to the public via an Internet Web site maintained by the Department of Justice at www.meganslaw.ca.gov. Depending on an offender's criminal history, this information will include either the address at which the offender resides or the community of residence and ZIP Code in which he or she resides. (Neither Seller nor Brokers are required to check this website. If Buyer wants further information, Broker recommends that Buyer obtain information from this website during Buyer's inspection contingency period. Brokers do not have expertise in this area.)
    E. **NOTICE REGARDING GAS AND HAZARDOUS LIQUID TRANSMISSION PIPELINES:** This notice is being provided simply to inform you that information about the general location of gas and hazardous liquid transmission pipelines is available to the public via the National Pipeline Mapping System (NPMS) Internet Web site maintained by the United States Department of Transportation at http://www.npms.phmsa.dot.gov/. To seek further information about possible transmission pipelines near the Property, you may contact your local gas utility or other pipeline operators in the area. Contact information for pipeline operators is searchable by ZIP Code and county on the NPMS Internet Web site.

Buyer's Initials (__WB__)(__DB__)   Seller's Initials (__TS__)(__RJS__)

Property Address: _____ 264 Beach Lane, Costa Mesa, CA 92627 _____ Date: _June 14, 2020_

F. CONDOMINIUM/PLANNED DEVELOPMENT DISCLOSURES:
(1) SELLER HAS: 7 (or ___) Days After Acceptance to disclose to Buyer if the Property is a condominium, or is located in a planned development or other common interest subdivision (C.A.R. Form SPQ or SSD).
(2) If the Property is a condominium or is located in a planned development or other common interest subdivision, Seller has **3 (or ___) Days** After Acceptance to request from the HOA (C.A.R. Form HOA1): **(i)** Copies of any documents required by Law; **(ii)** disclosure of any pending or anticipated claim or litigation by or against the HOA; **(iii)** a statement containing the location and number of designated parking and storage spaces; **(iv)** Copies of the most recent 12 months of HOA minutes for regular and special meetings; and **(v)** the names and contact information of all HOAs governing the Property (collectively, "CI Disclosures"). Seller shall itemize and Deliver to Buyer all CI Disclosures received from the HOA and any CI Disclosures in Seller's possession. Buyer's approval of CI Disclosures is a contingency of this Agreement as specified in paragraph 14B(3). The Party specified in paragraph 7, as directed by escrow, shall deposit funds into escrow or direct to HOA or management company to pay for any of the above.

11. CONDITION OF PROPERTY: Unless otherwise agreed in writing: **(i)** the Property is sold (a) "AS-IS" in its PRESENT physical condition as of the date of Acceptance and (b) subject to Buyer's Investigation rights; **(ii)** the Property, including pool, spa, landscaping and grounds, is to be maintained in substantially the same condition as on the date of Acceptance; and **(iii)** all debris and personal property not included in the sale shall be removed by Close Of Escrow.
  A. Seller shall, within the time specified in paragraph 14A, DISCLOSE KNOWN MATERIAL FACTS AND DEFECTS affecting the Property, including known insurance claims within the past five years, and make any and all other disclosures required by law.
  B. Buyer has the right to conduct Buyer Investigations of the Property and, as specified in paragraph 14B, based upon information discovered in those investigations: (i) cancel this Agreement; or (ii) request that Seller make Repairs or take other action.
  C. **Buyer is strongly advised to conduct investigations of the entire Property in order to determine its present condition. Seller may not be aware of all defects affecting the Property or other factors that Buyer considers important. Property improvements may not be built according to code, in compliance with current Law, or have had permits issued.**

12. BUYER'S INVESTIGATION OF PROPERTY AND MATTERS AFFECTING PROPERTY:
  A. Buyer's acceptance of the condition of, and any other matter affecting the Property, is a contingency of this Agreement as specified in this paragraph and paragraph 14B. Within the time specified in paragraph 14B(1), Buyer shall have the right, at Buyer's expense unless otherwise agreed, to conduct inspections, investigations, tests, surveys and other studies ("Buyer Investigations"), including, but not limited to, the right to: **(i)** inspect for lead-based paint and other lead-based paint hazards; **(ii)** inspect for wood destroying pests and organisms. Any inspection for wood destroying pests and organisms shall be prepared by a registered Structural Pest Control company; shall cover the main building and attached structures; may cover detached structures; shall NOT include water tests of shower pans on upper level units unless the owners of property below the shower consent; shall NOT include roof coverings; and, if the Property is a unit in a condominium or other common interest subdivision, the inspection shall include only the separate interest and any exclusive-use areas being transferred, and shall NOT include common areas; and shall include a report ("Pest Control Report") showing the findings of the company which shall be separated into sections for evident infestation or infections (Section 1) and for conditions likely to lead to infestation or infection (Section 2); **(iii)** review the registered sex offender database; **(iv)** confirm the insurability of Buyer and the Property including the availability and cost of flood and fire insurance; **(v)** review and seek approval of leases that may need to be assumed by Buyer; and **(vi)** satisfy Buyer as to any matter specified in the attached Buyer's Inspection Advisory (C.A.R. Form BIA). Without Seller's prior written consent, Buyer shall neither make nor cause to be made: (i) invasive or destructive Buyer Investigations except to the extent required to prepare a Pest Control Report; or (ii) inspections by any governmental building or zoning inspector or government employee, unless required by Law.
  B. Seller shall make the Property available for all Buyer Investigations. Buyer shall (i) as specified in paragraph 14B, complete Buyer Investigations and either remove the contingency or cancel this Agreement, and (ii) give Seller, at no cost, complete Copies of all such Investigation reports obtained by Buyer, which obligation shall survive the termination of this Agreement.
  C. Seller shall have water, gas, electricity and all operable pilot lights on for Buyer's Investigations and through the date possession is made available to Buyer.
  D. **Buyer indemnity and seller protection for entry upon property:** Buyer shall: **(i)** keep the Property free and clear of liens; **(ii)** repair all damage arising from Buyer Investigations; and **(iii)** indemnify and hold Seller harmless from all resulting liability, claims, demands, damages and costs. Buyer shall carry, or Buyer shall require anyone acting on Buyer's behalf to carry, policies of liability, workers' compensation and other applicable insurance, defending and protecting Seller from liability for any injuries to persons or property occurring during any Buyer Investigations or work done on the Property at Buyer's direction prior to Close Of Escrow. Seller is advised that certain protections may be afforded Seller by recording a "Notice of Non-Responsibility" (C.A.R. Form NNR) for Buyer Investigations and work done on the Property at Buyer's direction. Buyer's obligations under this paragraph shall survive the termination of this Agreement.

13. TITLE AND VESTING:
  A. Within the time specified in paragraph 14, Buyer shall be provided a current preliminary title report ("Preliminary Report"). The Preliminary Report is only an offer by the title insurer to issue a policy of title insurance and may not contain every item affecting title. Buyer's review of the Preliminary Report and any other matters which may affect title are a contingency of this Agreement as specified in paragraph 14B. The company providing the Preliminary Report shall, prior to issuing a Preliminary Report, conduct a search of the General Index for all Sellers except banks or other institutional lenders selling properties they acquired through foreclosure (REOs), corporations, and government entities. Seller shall within 7 Days After Acceptance, give Escrow Holder a completed Statement of Information.
  B. Title is taken in its present condition subject to all encumbrances, easements, covenants, conditions, restrictions, rights and other matters, whether of record or not, as of the date of Acceptance except for: **(i)** monetary liens of record (which Seller is obligated to pay off) unless Buyer is assuming those obligations or taking the Property subject to those obligations; and **(ii)** those matters which Seller has agreed to remove in writing.
  C. Within the time specified in paragraph 14A, Seller has a duty to disclose to Buyer all matters known to Seller affecting title, whether of record or not.
  D. At Close Of Escrow, Buyer shall receive a grant deed conveying title (or, for stock cooperative or long-term lease, an assignment of stock certificate or of Seller's leasehold interest), including oil, mineral and water rights if currently owned by Seller. Title shall vest as designated in Buyer's supplemental escrow instructions. THE MANNER OF TAKING TITLE MAY HAVE SIGNIFICANT LEGAL AND TAX CONSEQUENCES. CONSULT AN APPROPRIATE PROFESSIONAL.

Buyer's Initials (_WB_)(_DB_)   Seller's Initials (_TS_)(_RJS_)

Property Address: _____264 Beach Lane, Costa Mesa, CA 92627_____ Date: June 14, 2020

    E. Buyer shall receive a CLTA/ALTA "Homeowner's Policy of Title Insurance", if applicable to the type of property and buyer. If not, Escrow Holder shall notify Buyer. A title company can provide information about the availability, coverage, and cost of other title policies and endorsements. If the Homeowner's Policy is not available, Buyer shall choose another policy, instruct Escrow Holder in writing and shall pay any increase in cost.

14. TIME PERIODS; REMOVAL OF CONTINGENCIES; CANCELLATION RIGHTS: The following time periods may only be extended, altered, modified or changed by mutual written agreement. Any removal of contingencies or cancellation under this paragraph by either Buyer or Seller must be exercised in good faith and in writing (C.A.R. Form CR or CC).

    A. SELLER HAS: 7 (or ___) Days After Acceptance to Deliver to Buyer all Reports, disclosures and information for which Seller is responsible under paragraphs 5, 6, 7, 8B(4), 10A, B, C, and F, 11A and 13A. If, by the time specified, Seller has not delivered any such item, Buyer after first Delivering to Seller a Notice to Seller to Perform (C.A.R. Form NSP) may cancel this Agreement.

    B. (1) BUYER HAS: 17 (or ___) Days After Acceptance, unless otherwise agreed in writing, to:

        (i) complete all Buyer Investigations; review all disclosures, reports, lease documents to be assumed by Buyer pursuant to paragraph 8B(4), and other applicable information, which Buyer receives from Seller; and approve all matters affecting the Property; and **(ii)** Deliver to Seller Signed Copies of Statutory and Lead Disclosures and other disclosures Delivered by Seller in accordance with paragraph 10A.

        (2) Within the time specified in paragraph 14B(1), Buyer may request that Seller make repairs or take any other action regarding the Property (C.A.R. Form RR). Seller has no obligation to agree to or respond to (C.A.R. Form RRRR) Buyer's requests.

        (3) By the end of the time specified in paragraph 14B(1) (or as otherwise specified in this Agreement), Buyer shall Deliver to Seller a removal of the applicable contingency or cancellation (C.A.R. Form CR or CC) of this Agreement. However, if any report, disclosure or information for which Seller is responsible is not Delivered within the time specified in paragraph 14A, then Buyer has **5 (or ___) Days** After Delivery of any such items, or the time specified in paragraph 14B(1), whichever is later, to Deliver to Seller a removal of the applicable contingency or cancellation of this Agreement.

        (4) Continuation of Contingency: Even after the end of the time specified in paragraph 14B(1) and before Seller cancels, if at all, pursuant to paragraph 14C, Buyer retains the right, in writing, to either (i) remove remaining contingencies, or (ii) cancel this Agreement based on a remaining contingency. Once Buyer's written removal of all contingencies is Delivered to Seller, Seller may not cancel this Agreement pursuant to paragraph 14C(1).

    C. SELLER RIGHT TO CANCEL:

        (1) Seller right to Cancel; Buyer Contingencies: If, by the time specified in this Agreement, Buyer does not Deliver to Seller a removal of the applicable contingency or cancellation of this Agreement, then Seller, after first Delivering to Buyer a Notice to Buyer to Perform (C.A.R. Form NBP), may cancel this Agreement. In such event, Seller shall authorize the return of Buyer's deposit, except for fees incurred by Buyer.

        (2) Seller right to Cancel; Buyer Contract Obligations: Seller, after first delivering to Buyer a NBP, may cancel this Agreement if, by the time specified in this Agreement, Buyer does not take the following action(s): **(i)** Deposit funds as required by paragraph 3A, or 3B or if the funds deposited pursuant to paragraph 3A or 3B are not good when deposited; **(ii)** Deliver a notice of FHA or VA costs or terms as required by paragraph 3D(3) (C.A.R. Form FVA); **(iii)** Deliver a letter as required by paragraph 3J(1); **(iv)** Deliver verification, or a satisfactory verification if Seller reasonably disapproves of the verification already provided, as required by paragraph 3C or 3H; **(v)** Return Statutory and Lead Disclosures as required by paragraph 10A(5); or **(vi)** Sign or initial a separate liquidated damages form for an increased deposit as required by paragraphs 3B and 21B; or **(vii)** Provide evidence of authority to sign in a representative capacity as specified in paragraph 19. In such event, Seller shall authorize the return of Buyer's deposit, except for fees incurred by Buyer.

    D. NOTICE TO BUYER OR SELLER TO PERFORM: The NBP or NSP shall: **(i)** be in writing; **(ii)** be signed by the applicable Buyer or Seller; and **(iii)** give the other Party at least **2 (or ___) Days** After Delivery (or until the time specified in the applicable paragraph, whichever occurs last) to take the applicable action. A NBP or NSP may not be Delivered any earlier than **2 Days** Prior to the expiration of the applicable time for the other Party to remove a contingency or cancel this Agreement or meet an obligation specified in paragraph 14.

    E. EFFECT OF BUYER'S REMOVAL OF CONTINGENCIES: If Buyer removes, in writing, any contingency or cancellation rights, unless otherwise specified in writing, Buyer shall conclusively be deemed to have: **(i)** completed all Buyer Investigations, and review of reports and other applicable information and disclosures pertaining to that contingency or cancellation right; **(ii)** elected to proceed with the transaction; and **(iii)** assumed all liability, responsibility and expense for Repairs or corrections pertaining to that contingency or cancellation right, or for the inability to obtain financing.

    F. CLOSE OF ESCROW: Before Buyer or Seller may cancel this Agreement for failure of the other Party to close escrow pursuant to this Agreement, Buyer or Seller must first Deliver to the other Party a demand to close escrow (C.A.R. Form DCE). The DCE shall: **(i)** be signed by the applicable Buyer or Seller; and **(ii)** give the other Party at least **3 (or ___) Days** After Delivery to close escrow. A DCE may not be Delivered any earlier than **3 Days** Prior to the scheduled close of escrow.

    G. EFFECT OF CANCELLATION ON DEPOSITS: If Buyer or Seller gives written notice of cancellation pursuant to rights duly exercised under the terms of this Agreement, the Parties agree to Sign mutual instructions to cancel the sale and escrow and release deposits, if any, to the party entitled to the funds, less fees and costs incurred by that party. Fees and costs may be payable to service providers and vendors for services and products provided during escrow. Except as specified below, **release of funds will require mutual Signed release instructions from the Parties, judicial decision or arbitration award.** If either Party fails to execute mutual instructions to cancel, one Party may make a written demand to Escrow Holder for the deposit. Escrow Holder, upon receipt, shall promptly deliver notice of the demand to the other Party. If, within 10 Days After Escrow Holder's notice, the other Party does not object to the demand, Escrow Holder shall disburse the deposit to the Party making the demand. If Escrow Holder complies with the preceding process, each Party shall be deemed to have released Escrow Holder from any and all claims or liability related to the disbursal of the deposit. Escrow Holder, at its discretion, may nonetheless require mutual cancellation instructions. **A Party may be subject to a civil penalty of up to $1,000 for refusal to sign cancellation instructions if no good faith dispute exists as to who is entitled to the deposited funds (Civil Code §1057.3).**

15. FINAL VERIFICATION OF CONDITION: Buyer shall have the right to make a final verification of the Property within 5 (or ☐ ___) **Days** Prior to Close Of Escrow, NOT AS A CONTINGENCY OF THE SALE, but solely to confirm: **(i)** the Property is maintained pursuant to paragraph 11; **(ii)** Repairs have been completed as agreed; and **(iii)** Seller has complied with Seller's other obligations under this Agreement (C.A.R. Form VP).

Buyer's Initials (___WB___)(___DB___)

Seller's Initials (___TS___)(___RJS___)

Property Address: _____264 Beach Lane, Costa Mesa, CA 92627_____ Date: _June 14, 2020_

16. **REPAIRS:** Repairs shall be completed prior to final verification of condition unless otherwise agreed in writing. Repairs to be performed at Seller's expense may be performed by Seller or through others, provided that the work complies with applicable Law, including governmental permit, inspection and approval requirements. Repairs shall be performed in a good, skillful manner with materials of quality and appearance comparable to existing materials. It is understood that exact restoration of appearance or cosmetic items following all Repairs may not be possible. Seller shall: **(i)** obtain invoices and paid receipts for Repairs performed by others; **(ii)** prepare a written statement indicating the Repairs performed by Seller and the date of such Repairs; and **(iii)** provide Copies of invoices and paid receipts and statements to Buyer prior to final verification of condition.

17. **PRORATIONS OF PROPERTY TAXES AND OTHER ITEMS:** Unless otherwise agreed in writing, the following items shall be PAID CURRENT and prorated between Buyer and Seller as of Close Of Escrow: real property taxes and assessments, interest, rents, HOA regular, special, and emergency dues and assessments imposed prior to Close Of Escrow, premiums on insurance assumed by Buyer, payments on bonds and assessments assumed by Buyer, and payments on Mello-Roos and other Special Assessment District bonds and assessments that are now a lien. The following items shall be assumed by Buyer WITHOUT CREDIT toward the purchase price: prorated payments on Mello-Roos and other Special Assessment District bonds and assessments and HOA special assessments that are now a lien but not yet due. Property will be reassessed upon change of ownership. Any supplemental tax bills shall be paid as follows: **(i)** for periods after Close Of Escrow, by Buyer; and **(ii)** for periods prior to Close Of Escrow, by Seller (see C.A.R. Form SPT or SBSA for further information). TAX BILLS ISSUED AFTER CLOSE OF ESCROW SHALL BE HANDLED DIRECTLY BETWEEN BUYER AND SELLER. Prorations shall be made based on a 30-day month.

18. **BROKERS:**
   A. **COMPENSATION:** Seller or Buyer, or both, as applicable, agree to pay compensation to Broker as specified in a separate written agreement between Broker and that Seller or Buyer. Compensation is payable upon Close Of Escrow, or if escrow does not close, as otherwise specified in the agreement between Broker and that Seller or Buyer.
   B. **SCOPE OF DUTY:** Buyer and Seller acknowledge and agree that Broker: **(i)** Does not decide what price Buyer should pay or Seller should accept; **(ii)** Does not guarantee the condition of the Property; **(iii)** Does not guarantee the performance, adequacy or completeness of inspections, services, products or repairs provided or made by Seller or others; **(iv)** Does not have an obligation to conduct an inspection of common areas or areas off the site of the Property; **(v)** Shall not be responsible for identifying defects on the Property, in common areas, or offsite unless such defects are visually observable by an inspection of reasonably accessible areas of the Property or are known to Broker; **(vi)** Shall not be responsible for inspecting public records or permits concerning the title or use of Property; **(vii)** Shall not be responsible for identifying the location of boundary lines or other items affecting title; **(viii)** Shall not be responsible for verifying square footage, representations of others or information contained in Investigation reports, Multiple Listing Service, advertisements, flyers or other promotional material; **(ix)** Shall not be responsible for determining the fair market value of the Property or any personal property included in the sale; **(x)** Shall not be responsible for providing legal or tax advice regarding any aspect of a transaction entered into by Buyer or Seller; and **(xi)** Shall not be responsible for providing other advice or information that exceeds the knowledge, education and experience required to perform real estate licensed activity. Buyer and Seller agree to seek legal, tax, insurance, title and other desired assistance from appropriate professionals.

19. **REPRESENTATIVE CAPACITY:** If one or more Parties is signing this Agreement in a representative capacity and not for him/herself as an individual then that Party shall so indicate in paragraph 31 or 32 and attach a Representative Capacity Signature Addendum (C.A.R. Form RCSA). Wherever the signature or initials of the representative identified in the RCSA appear on this Agreement or any related documents, it shall be deemed to be in a representative capacity for the entity described and not in an individual capacity, unless otherwise indicated. The Party acting in a representative capacity shall Deliver to the other Party and Escrow Holder, within 3 Days After Acceptance, evidence of authority to act in that capacity (such as but not limited to: applicable trust document, or portion thereof, letters testamentary, court order, power of attorney, resolution, or formation documents of the business entity).

20. **JOINT ESCROW INSTRUCTIONS TO ESCROW HOLDER:**
   A. **The following paragraphs, or applicable portions thereof, of this Agreement constitute the joint escrow instructions of Buyer and Seller to Escrow Holder,** which Escrow Holder is to use along with any related counter offers and addenda, and any additional mutual instructions to close the escrow: paragraphs 1, 3, 4B, 5A, 6, 7, 10C, 13, 14G, 17, 18A, 19, 20, 26, 29, 30, 31, 32 and paragraph D of the section titled Real Estate Brokers on page 10. If a Copy of the separate compensation agreement(s) provided for in paragraph 18A, or paragraph D of the section titled Real Estate Brokers on page 10 is deposited with Escrow Holder by Broker, Escrow Holder shall accept such agreement(s) and pay out from Buyer's or Seller's funds, or both, as applicable, the Broker's compensation provided for in such agreement(s). The terms and conditions of this Agreement not set forth in the specified paragraphs are additional matters for the information of Escrow Holder, but about which Escrow Holder need not be concerned. Buyer and Seller will receive Escrow Holder's general provisions, if any, directly from Escrow Holder and will execute such provisions within the time specified in paragraph 7C(1)(c). To the extent the general provisions are inconsistent or conflict with this Agreement, the general provisions will control as to the duties and obligations of Escrow Holder only. Buyer and Seller will execute additional instructions, documents and forms provided by Escrow Holder that are reasonably necessary to close the escrow and, as directed by Escrow Holder, within 3 (or ____) Days, shall pay to Escrow Holder or HOA or HOA management company or others any fee required by paragraphs 7, 10 or elsewhere in this Agreement.
   B. A Copy of this Agreement including any counter offer(s) and addenda shall be delivered to Escrow Holder within **3 Days After** Acceptance (or _____). Buyer and Seller authorize Escrow Holder to accept and rely on Copies and Signatures as defined in this Agreement as originals, to open escrow and for other purposes of escrow. The validity of this Agreement as between Buyer and Seller is not affected by whether or when Escrow Holder Signs this Agreement. Escrow Holder shall provide Seller's Statement of Information to Title company when received from Seller. If Seller delivers an affidavit to Escrow Holder to satisfy Seller's FIRPTA obligation under paragraph 10C, Escrow Holder shall deliver to Buyer a Qualified Substitute statement that complies with federal Law.
   C. Brokers are a party to the escrow for the sole purpose of compensation pursuant to paragraph 18A and paragraph D of the section titled Real Estate Brokers on page 10. Buyer and Seller irrevocably assign to Brokers compensation specified in paragraph 18A, and irrevocably instruct Escrow Holder to disburse those funds to Brokers at Close Of Escrow or pursuant to any other mutually executed cancellation agreement. Compensation instructions can be amended or revoked only with the written consent of Brokers. Buyer and Seller shall release and hold harmless Escrow Holder from any liability resulting from Escrow Holder's payment to Broker(s) of compensation pursuant to this Agreement.

Buyer's Initials (_WB_)(_DB_) Seller's Initials (_TS_)(_RJS_)

Property Address: _____264 Beach Lane, Costa Mesa, CA 92627_____ Date: _June 14, 2020_

D. Upon receipt, Escrow Holder shall provide Seller and Seller's Broker verification of Buyer's deposit of funds pursuant to paragraph 3A and 3B. Once Escrow Holder becomes aware of any of the following, Escrow Holder shall immediately notify all Brokers: (i) if Buyer's initial or any additional deposit or down payment is not made pursuant to this Agreement, or is not good at time of deposit with Escrow Holder; or (ii) if Buyer and Seller instruct Escrow Holder to cancel escrow.

E. A Copy of any amendment that affects any paragraph of this Agreement for which Escrow Holder is responsible shall be delivered to Escrow Holder within 3 Days after mutual execution of the amendment.

21. REMEDIES FOR BUYER'S BREACH OF CONTRACT:

A. **Any clause added by the Parties specifying a remedy (such as release or forfeiture of deposit or making a deposit non-refundable) for failure of Buyer to complete the purchase in violation of this Agreement shall be deemed invalid unless the clause independently satisfies the statutory liquidated damages requirements set forth in the Civil Code.**

B. **LIQUIDATED DAMAGES: If Buyer fails to complete this purchase because of Buyer's default, Seller shall retain, as liquidated damages, the deposit actually paid. If the Property is a dwelling with no more than four units, one of which Buyer intends to occupy, then the amount retained shall be no more than 3% of the purchase price. Any excess shall be returned to Buyer. Except as provided in paragraph 14G, release of funds will require mutual, Signed release instructions from both Buyer and Seller, judicial decision or arbitration award. AT TIME OF ANY INCREASED DEPOSIT BUYER AND SELLER SHALL SIGN A SEPARATE LIQUIDATED DAMAGES PROVISION INCORPORATING THE INCREASED DEPOSIT AS LIQUIDATED DAMAGES (C.A.R. FORM RID).**

Buyer's Initials _WB_ / _DB_   Seller's Initials _TS_ / _RJS_

22. DISPUTE RESOLUTION:

A. **MEDIATION:** The Parties agree to mediate any dispute or claim arising between them out of this Agreement, or any resulting transaction, before resorting to arbitration or court action through the C.A.R. Real Estate Mediation Center for Consumers (www.consumermediation.org) or through any other mediation provider or service mutually agreed to by the Parties. The Parties also agree to mediate any disputes or claims with Broker(s), who, in writing, agree to such mediation prior to, or within a reasonable time after, the dispute or claim is presented to the Broker. Mediation fees, if any, shall be divided equally among the Parties involved. If, for any dispute or claim to which this paragraph applies, any Party (i) commences an action without first attempting to resolve the matter through mediation, or (ii) before commencement of an action, refuses to mediate after a request has been made, then that Party shall not be entitled to recover attorney fees, even if they would otherwise be available to that Party in any such action. THIS MEDIATION PROVISION APPLIES WHETHER OR NOT THE ARBITRATION PROVISION IS INITIALED. Exclusions from this mediation agreement are specified in paragraph 22C.

B. **ARBITRATION OF DISPUTES:**
The Parties agree that any dispute or claim in Law or equity arising between them out of this Agreement or any resulting transaction, which is not settled through mediation, shall be decided by neutral, binding arbitration. The Parties also agree to arbitrate any disputes or claims with Broker(s), who, in writing, agree to such arbitration prior to, or within a reasonable time after, the dispute or claim is presented to the Broker. The arbitrator shall be a retired judge or justice, or an attorney with at least 5 years of residential real estate Law experience, unless the parties mutually agree to a different arbitrator. The Parties shall have the right to discovery in accordance with Code of Civil Procedure §1283.05. In all other respects, the arbitration shall be conducted in accordance with Title 9 of Part 3 of the Code of Civil Procedure. Judgment upon the award of the arbitrator(s) may be entered into any court having jurisdiction. Enforcement of this agreement to arbitrate shall be governed by the Federal Arbitration Act. Exclusions from this arbitration agreement are specified in paragraph 22C.
"NOTICE: BY INITIALING IN THE SPACE BELOW YOU ARE AGREEING TO HAVE ANY DISPUTE ARISING OUT OF THE MATTERS INCLUDED IN THE 'ARBITRATION OF DISPUTES' PROVISION DECIDED BY NEUTRAL ARBITRATION AS PROVIDED BY CALIFORNIA LAW AND YOU ARE GIVING UP ANY RIGHTS YOU MIGHT POSSESS TO HAVE THE DISPUTE LITIGATED IN A COURT OR JURY TRIAL. BY INITIALING IN THE SPACE BELOW YOU ARE GIVING UP YOUR JUDICIAL RIGHTS TO DISCOVERY AND APPEAL, UNLESS THOSE RIGHTS ARE SPECIFICALLY INCLUDED IN THE 'ARBITRATION OF DISPUTES' PROVISION. IF YOU REFUSE TO SUBMIT TO ARBITRATION AFTER AGREEING TO THIS PROVISION, YOU MAY BE COMPELLED TO ARBITRATE UNDER THE AUTHORITY OF THE CALIFORNIA CODE OF CIVIL PROCEDURE. YOUR AGREEMENT TO THIS ARBITRATION PROVISION IS VOLUNTARY."
"WE HAVE READ AND UNDERSTAND THE FOREGOING AND AGREE TO SUBMIT DISPUTES ARISING OUT OF THE MATTERS INCLUDED IN THE 'ARBITRATION OF DISPUTES' PROVISION TO NEUTRAL ARBITRATION."

Buyer's Initials _WB_ / _DB_   Seller's Initials _TS_ / _RJS_

C. **ADDITIONAL MEDIATION AND ARBITRATION TERMS:**
(1) **EXCLUSIONS:** The following matters are excluded from mediation and arbitration: (i) a judicial or non-judicial foreclosure or other action or proceeding to enforce a deed of trust, mortgage or installment land sale contract as defined in Civil Code §2985; (ii) an unlawful detainer action; and (iii) any matter that is within the jurisdiction of a probate, small claims or bankruptcy court.
(2) **PRESERVATION OF ACTIONS:** The following shall not constitute a waiver nor violation of the mediation and arbitration provisions: (i)The filing of a court action to enable the recording of a notice of pending action, for order of attachment, receivership, injunction, or other provisional remedies; or (ii) the filing of a mechanic's lien.
(3) **BROKERS:** Brokers shall not be obligated nor compelled to mediate or arbitrate unless they agree to do so in writing. Any Broker(s) participating in mediation or arbitration shall not be deemed a party to this Agreement.

Buyer's Initials (_WB_)(_RJS_)   Seller's Initials (_TS_)(_RJS_)

RPA-CA REVISED 11/14 (PAGE 8 of 10)   Print Date

CALIFORNIA RESIDENTIAL PURCHASE AGREEMENT (RPA-CA PAGE 8 OF 10)

Pay close attention to #22—mediation is generally mandatory, whereas arbitration is not.

Property Address: _____264 Beach Lane, Costa Mesa, CA 92627_____   Date: June 14, 2020

23. **SELECTION OF SERVICE PROVIDERS:** Brokers do not guarantee the performance of any vendors, service or product providers ("Providers"), whether referred by Broker or selected by Buyer, Seller or other person. Buyer and Seller may select ANY Providers of their own choosing.

24. **MULTIPLE LISTING SERVICE ("MLS"):** Brokers are authorized to report to the MLS a pending sale and, upon Close Of Escrow, the sales price and other terms of this transaction shall be provided to the MLS to be published and disseminated to persons and entities authorized to use the information on terms approved by the MLS.

25. **ATTORNEY FEES:** In any action, proceeding, or arbitration between Buyer and Seller arising out of this Agreement, the prevailing Buyer or Seller shall be entitled to reasonable attorney fees and costs from the non-prevailing Buyer or Seller, except as provided in paragraph 22A.

26. **ASSIGNMENT:** Buyer shall not assign all or any part of Buyer's interest in this Agreement without first having obtained the separate written consent of Seller to a specified assignee. Such consent shall not be unreasonably withheld. Any total or partial assignment shall not relieve Buyer of Buyer's obligations pursuant to this Agreement unless otherwise agreed in writing by Seller.

27. **EQUAL HOUSING OPPORTUNITY:** The Property is sold in compliance with federal, state and local anti-discrimination Laws.

28. **TERMS AND CONDITIONS OF OFFER:**
This is an offer to purchase the Property on the above terms and conditions. The liquidated damages paragraph or the arbitration of disputes paragraph is incorporated in this Agreement if initialed by all Parties or if incorporated by mutual agreement in a counter offer or addendum. If at least one but not all Parties initial, a counter offer is required until agreement is reached. Seller has the right to continue to offer the Property for sale and to accept any other offer at any time prior to notification of Acceptance. The Parties have read and acknowledge receipt of a Copy of the offer and agree to the confirmation of agency relationships. If this offer is accepted and Buyer subsequently defaults, Buyer may be responsible for payment of Brokers' compensation. This Agreement and any supplement, addendum or modification, including any Copy, may be Signed in two or more counterparts, all of which shall constitute one and the same writing.

29. **TIME OF ESSENCE; ENTIRE CONTRACT; CHANGES:** Time is of the essence. All understandings between the Parties are incorporated in this Agreement. Its terms are intended by the Parties as a final, complete and exclusive expression of their Agreement with respect to its subject matter, and may not be contradicted by evidence of any prior agreement or contemporaneous oral agreement. If any provision of this Agreement is held to be ineffective or invalid, the remaining provisions will nevertheless be given full force and effect. Except as otherwise specified, this Agreement shall be interpreted and disputes shall be resolved in accordance with the Laws of the State of California. **Neither this Agreement nor any provision in it may be extended, amended, modified, altered or changed, except in writing Signed by Buyer and Seller.**

30. **DEFINITIONS:** As used in this Agreement:
   A. **"Acceptance"** means the time the offer or final counter offer is accepted in writing by a Party and is delivered to and personally received by the other Party or that Party's authorized agent in accordance with the terms of this offer or a final counter offer.
   B. **"Agreement"** means this document and any incorporated addenda, counter offers and written terms Signed by all Parties collectively forming the binding agreement between the Parties. All terms and conditions of any addenda checked and Signed are incorporated into this Agreement.
   C. **"C.A.R. Form"** means the most current version of the specific form referenced or another comparable form agreed to by the parties.
   D. **"Close Of Escrow"**, including **"COE"**, means the date the grant deed, or other evidence of transfer of title, is recorded.
   E. **"Copy"** means copy by any means including photocopy, NCR, facsimile and electronic.
   F. **"Days"** means calendar days. However, after Acceptance, the last **Day** for performance of any act required by this Agreement (including Close Of Escrow) shall not include any Saturday, Sunday, or legal holiday and shall instead be the next Day.
   G. **"Days After"** means the specified number of calendar days after the occurrence of the event specified, not counting the calendar date on which the specified event occurs, and ending at 11:59 PM on the final day.
   H. **"Days Prior"** means the specified number of calendar days before the occurrence of the event specified, not counting the calendar date on which the specified event is scheduled to occur.
   I. **"Deliver"**, **"Delivered"** or **"Delivery"**, unless otherwise specified in writing, means and shall be effective upon: personal receipt by Buyer or Seller or the individual Real Estate Licensee for that principal as specified in the section titled Real Estate Brokers on page 10, regardless of the method used (i.e., messenger, mail, email, fax, other).
   J. **"Electronic Copy"** or **"Electronic Signature"** means, as applicable, an electronic copy or signature complying with California Law. Buyer and Seller agree that electronic means will not be used by either Party to modify or alter the content or integrity of this Agreement without the knowledge and consent of the other Party.
   K. **"Law"** means any law, code, statute, ordinance, regulation, rule or order, which is adopted by a controlling city, county, state or federal legislative, judicial or executive body or agency.
   L. **"Repairs"** means any repairs (including pest control), alterations, replacements, modifications or retrofitting of the Property provided for under this Agreement.
   M. **"Signed"** means either a handwritten or electronic signature on an original document, Copy or any counterpart.

31. **EXPIRATION OF OFFER:** This offer shall be deemed revoked and the deposit, if any, shall be returned to Buyer unless the offer is Signed by Seller and a Copy of the Signed offer is personally received by Buyer, or by _____Carmen Caro_____, who is authorized to receive it, by 5:00 PM on the third Day after this offer is signed by Buyer (or by ☐ _____ ☐AM/☐PM, on _____(date)).

☐ One or more Buyers is signing this Agreement in a representative capacity and not for him/herself as an individual. See attached Representative Capacity Signature Addendum (C.A.R. Form RCSA) for additional terms.

Date June 14, 2020   BUYER *Walter Buyer*_____

(Print name) Walter Buyer_____

Date June 14, 2020   BUYER *Debbie Buyer*_____

(Print name) Debbie Buyer_____

☐ Additional Signature Addendum attached (C.A.R. Form ASA).

RPA-CA REVISED 11/14 (PAGE 9 of 10)   Print Date   Seller's Initials (*TS*)(*RJS*)

CALIFORNIA RESIDENTIAL PURCHASE AGREEMENT   (RPA-CA PAGE 9 OF 10)

CHAPTER 6

Property Address: ___264 Beach Lane, Costa Mesa, CA 92627___   Date: __June 14, 2020__

32. ACCEPTANCE OF OFFER: Seller warrants that Seller is the owner of the Property, or has the authority to execute this Agreement. Seller accepts the above offer, agrees to sell the Property on the above terms and conditions. Seller has read and acknowledges receipt of a Copy of this Agreement, and authorizes Broker to Deliver a Signed Copy to Buyer.

☐ (If checked) SELLER'S ACCEPTANCE IS **SUBJECT TO ATTACHED COUNTER OFFER (C.A.R. Form SCO or SMCO) DATED:**
_____.

☐ One or more Sellers is signing this Agreement in a representative capacity and not for him/herself as an individual. See attached Representative Capacity Signature Addendum (C.A.R. Form RCSA) for additional terms.

Date _June 15, 2020_ SELLER _Tony Seller_____

(Print name) Tony Seller_____

Date _June 15, 2020_ SELLER _Ramona J. Seller_____

(Print name) Ramona J. Seller_____

☐ Additional Signature Addendum attached (C.A.R. Form ASA).

(_WB / DB_) (Do not initial if making a counter offer.) **CONFIRMATION OF ACCEPTANCE:** A Copy of Signed Acceptance was
(Initials) personally received by Buyer or Buyer's authorized agent on (date) ___June 15, 2020___ at _11:59_ ☐AM/☑PM. A binding Agreement is created when a Copy of Signed Acceptance is personally received by Buyer or Buyer's authorized agent whether or not confirmed in this document. Completion of this confirmation is not legally required in order to create a binding Agreement; it is solely intended to evidence the date that Confirmation of Acceptance has occurred.

REAL ESTATE BROKERS:
A. Real Estate Brokers are not parties to the Agreement between Buyer and Seller.
B. Agency relationships are confirmed as stated in paragraph 2.
C. If specified in paragraph 3A(2), Agent who submitted the offer for Buyer acknowledges receipt of deposit.
D. **COOPERATING BROKER COMPENSATION:** Listing Broker agrees to pay Cooperating Broker **(Selling Firm)** and Cooperating Broker agrees to accept, out of Listing Broker's proceeds in escrow, the amount specified in the MLS, provided Cooperating Broker is a Participant of the MLS in which the Property is offered for sale or a reciprocal MLS. If Listing Broker and Cooperating Broker are not both Participants of the MLS, or a reciprocal MLS, in which the Property is offered for sale, then compensation must be specified in a separate written agreement (C.A.R. Form CBC). Declaration of License and Tax (C.A.R. Form DLT) may be used to document that tax reporting will be required or that an exemption exists.

Real Estate Broker (Selling Firm) Ramos Realty_____ CalBRE Lic. # __00 000 000__
By _Joseph Ramos_____ Joseph Ramos CalBRE Lic. # __00 000 00__ Date _06/14/2020_
By _____ CalBRE Lic. # _____ Date _____
Address _777 Newport Blvd._ City _Newport Beach_ State _CA_ Zip _92663_
Telephone _(714) 647-0000_ Fax _(714) 647-0001_ E-mail _jr@ramosrealty.realtor_
Real Estate Broker (Listing Firm) Sail Realty_____ CalBRE Lic. # __00 000 000__
By _Carmen Caro_____ Carmen Caro CalBRE Lic. # __00 000 000__ Date _6/14/2020_
By _____ CalBRE Lic. # _____ Date _____
Address _227 Harbor Blvd._ City _Costa Mesa_ State _CA_ Zip _92627_
Telephone _(714) 626-2828_ Fax _(714) 626-2829_ E-mail _carmen@sailrealty.realtor_

ESCROW HOLDER ACKNOWLEDGMENT:
Escrow Holder acknowledges receipt of a Copy of this Agreement, (if checked, ☐ a deposit in the amount of $ _____),
counter offer numbers _____ ☐ Seller's Statement of Information and _____, and agrees to act as Escrow Holder subject to paragraph 20 of this Agreement, any supplemental escrow instructions and the terms of Escrow Holder's general provisions.

Escrow Holder is advised that the date of Confirmation of Acceptance of the Agreement as between Buyer and Seller is _____

Escrow Holder _____ Escrow # _____
By _____ Date _____
Address _____
Phone/Fax/E-mail _____
Escrow Holder has the following license number # _____
☐ Department of Business Oversight, ☐ Department of Insurance, ☐ Bureau of Real Estate.

PRESENTATION OF OFFER: (_____) Listing Broker presented this offer to Seller on _____ (date).
Broker or Designee Initials

REJECTION OF OFFER: (_____)(_____) No counter offer is being made. This offer was rejected by Seller on_____ (date).
Seller's Initials

©1991-2014, California Association of REALTORS®, Inc. United States copyright law (Title 17 U.S. Code) forbids the unauthorized distribution, display and reproduction of this form, or any portion thereof, by photocopy machine or any other means, including facsimile or computerized formats.
THIS FORM HAS BEEN APPROVED BY THE CALIFORNIA ASSOCIATION OF REALTORS® (C.A.R.). NO REPRESENTATION IS MADE AS TO THE LEGAL VALIDITY OR ACCURACY OF ANY PROVISION IN ANY SPECIFIC TRANSACTION. A REAL ESTATE BROKER IS THE PERSON QUALIFIED TO ADVISE ON REAL ESTATE TRANSACTIONS. IF YOU DESIRE LEGAL OR TAX ADVICE, CONSULT AN APPROPRIATE PROFESSIONAL.

Published and Distributed by:
REAL ESTATE BUSINESS SERVICES, INC.
a subsidiary of the CALIFORNIA ASSOCIATION OF REALTORS®
525 South Virgil Avenue, Los Angeles, California 90020

Reviewed by Broker or Designee ___JR___

RPA-CA REVISED 11/14 (PAGE 10 of 10)   Print Date

Buyer's Initials (_WB_)(_DB_)

CALIFORNIA RESIDENTIAL PURCHASE AGREEMENT   (RPA-CA PAGE 10 OF 10)

C. FILLING OUT THE FORM—A BREAKDOWN

The following is a step-by-step guide for filling out the purchase agreement contract.

CALIFORNIA ASSOCIATION OF REALTORS®	**CALIFORNIA** **RESIDENTIAL PURCHASE AGREEMENT** **AND JOINT ESCROW INSTRUCTIONS** For Use With Single Family Residential Property — Attached or Detached (C.A.R. Form RPA-CA, Revised 11/14)

START - PAGE 1 OF 10

TITLE

"Joint Escrow Instructions" – the form includes Buyer and Seller's instructions to escrow holder for one-to-four residential units.

Date Prepared: June 14, 2020

DATE

Do not use numbers ("1/2/20") to denote the date. Use month, day, and year to avoid confusion; i.e., "June 14, 2020."

Date – the date of preparation is usually the date the Buyer signs the offer. Note, however, that the key date is the **date that final acceptance by the Seller** is communicated back to the offeror. The date of acceptance is the date from which all the dates specified in the form are counted.

1. **OFFER:**
   A. THIS IS AN OFFER FROM ___Walter Buyer and Debbie Buyer___ ("Buyer").
   B. THE REAL PROPERTY to be acquired is ___264 Beach Lane___, situated in ___Costa Mesa___ (City), ___Orange___ County, California, ___ (Zip Code), Assessor's Parcel No. ___ ("Property").
   C. THE PURCHASE PRICE offered is ___ ___Eight Hundred Thousand___ Dollars $ ___800,000.00___.
   D. CLOSE OF ESCROW shall occur on ___ (date)(or ___90___ Days After Acceptance).
   E. Buyer and Seller are referred to herein as the "Parties." Brokers are not Parties to this Agreement.

1. OFFER (Buyer's Proposed Purchase Agreement)

A. Offer/Buyers – Identifies document as an offer from a named Buyer which may be accepted by the named Seller to create a binding contract.

B. Real Property to be Acquired – Describes property by common address, legal description, or assessor's parcel number.

C. Purchase Price – Price Buyer offers to pay. It does not include closing costs, insurance premiums, or any required funding fees.

D. Close of Escrow – May choose either of two dates: (1) specific date, or (2) a date a number of days after offer is accepted in writing.

E. Buyer and Seller are the "Parties" to the Agreement. Brokers are not Parties.

> 2. **AGENCY:**
>   A. **DISCLOSURE:** The Parties each acknowledge receipt of a ☑"Disclosure Regarding Real Estate Agency Relationships" (C.A.R. Form AD).
>   B. **CONFIRMATION:** The following agency relationships are hereby confirmed for this transaction:
>   Listing Agent _____ Sail Realty _____ (Print Firm Name) is the agent of (check one):
>   ☐ the Seller exclusively; or ☐ both the Buyer and Seller.
>   Selling Agent _____ Ramos Realty _____ (Print Firm Name) (if not the same as the
>   Listing Agent) is the agent of (check one): ☐ the Buyer exclusively; or ☐ the Seller exclusively; or ☐ both the Buyer and Seller.
>   C. **POTENTIALLY COMPETING BUYERS AND SELLERS:** The Parties each acknowledge receipt of a ☑"Possible Representation of More than One Buyer or Seller - Disclosure and Consent" (C.A.R. Form PRBS).

2. AGENCY

A. Disclosure – The Parties acknowledge in this paragraph prior receipt of the Disclosure Regarding Real Estate Agency Relationship form (CAR® AD). This form is required to be presented to:

(1) the Seller before taking a listing;

(2) the Buyer before signing a contract to purchase; and

(3) the Seller before presenting the offer (if the selling agent is not also the listing agent).

B. Confirmation – This confirmation of the agency relationship of listing and selling agents, which is required under Civil Code § 2079.17, needs to be signed concurrent with the execution of the Purchase Agreement.

If this paragraph on agency confirmation is not filled in at the time the Purchase Agreement is executed, then a written counter offer must include the statutory confirmation form attached to the counter offer.

Important Note: The selling broker, who wrote this offer, must sign and present a disclosure to the Seller before presenting this offer, even if the listing broker already gave the Seller a written disclosure.

C. Potentially Competing Buyers and Sellers – In this paragraph, the Parties each acknowledge receipt of a "Possible Representation of More than One Buyer or Seller - Disclosure and Consent" (C.A.R. Form PRBS).

> 3. **FINANCE TERMS:** Buyer represents that funds will be good when deposited with Escrow Holder.

3. FINANCE TERMS

Obtaining specified loans is a contingency of the agreement, unless it is an all cash offer, or it is specified that obtaining the loan is not a contingency. If that contingency fails, the Buyer need not perform and is not liable for breach of contract and, therefore, gets the deposit back, less any expenses already incurred.

Obtaining a deposit, down payment, closing costs, and the Buyer's promise that funds will be good are not contingencies. If any of these are not obtained, the contract may be considered breached, and the Seller is entitled to legal remedies or cancellation of the sale.

A. **INITIAL DEPOSIT:** Deposit shall be in the amount of ....$ _10,000.00_
    (1) Buyer Direct Deposit: Buyer shall deliver deposit directly to Escrow Holder by electronic funds transfer, ☐ cashier's check, ☐ personal check, ☐ other _____ within 3 business days after Acceptance (or _____);
    OR (2) ☑ Buyer Deposit with Agent: Buyer has given the deposit by personal check (or _____) to the agent submitting the offer (or to _____), made payable to ___ABC Escrow___. The deposit shall be held uncashed until Acceptance and then deposited with Escrow Holder within 3 business days after Acceptance (or _____).
    Deposit checks given to agent shall be an original signed check and not a copy.
    (Note: Initial and increased deposits checks received by agent shall be recorded in Broker's trust fund log.)
B. **INCREASED DEPOSIT:** Buyer shall deposit with Escrow Holder an increased deposit in the amount of ....$ _____
    within ____ **Days** After Acceptance (or _____).
    If the Parties agree to liquidated damages in this Agreement, they also agree to incorporate the increased deposit into the liquidated damages amount in a separate liquidated damages clause (C.A.R. Form RID) at the time the increased deposit is delivered to Escrow Holder.
C. ☐ **ALL CASH OFFER:** No loan is needed to purchase the Property. Written verification of sufficient funds to close this transaction IS ATTACHED to this offer or ☐ Buyer shall, within **3 (or _____) Days** After Acceptance, Deliver to Seller such verification.

A. Initial Deposit – The deposit is delivered by the Buyer directly to the Escrow Holder by electronic funds transfer, unless otherwise noted. The payee (usually an escrow company) is indicated on the blank line. The amount is written in numbers in the right hand column. Any deposit checks given to an agent shall be an original signed check and not a copy. The initial deposit check and any increased deposit checks received by an agent shall be recorded in the Broker's trust fund log.

Funds received must be delivered to the escrow holder within "three business days after acceptance of offer" according to the directions, unless instructed otherwise in writing. "Earnest money" deposit funds can now be delivered to the trust account, the seller, or the escrow holder directly, bypassing the broker.

B. Increased Deposit – A separate receipt for an increased deposit, at the time that it is delivered, is required in order for the increased deposit to be included in the amount of liquidated damages. *LIQUIDATED DAMAGES (Paragraph 21B) are the sum of money, agreed to in advance and stated in the contract, that will be paid by the buyer for not fulfilling a clause or condition in the contract.* If the Parties agree to liquidated damages, they also agree to incorporate the increased deposit into the liquidated damages amount in a separate liquidated damages clause (C.A.R. Form RID) at the time the increased deposit is delivered to the Escrow Holder. The Buyer might sign or initial the liquidated damages provision at the same time that it is delivered. **Write the amount in the column to the right.**

C. All Cash Offer – If this box is checked, no loan is needed to purchase the property.

D. **LOAN(S):**

(1) **FIRST LOAN:** in the amount of .... $ 640,000.00
This loan will be conventional financing or ☐ FHA, ☐ VA, ☐ Seller financing (C.A.R. Form SFA), ☐ assumed financing (C.A.R. Form AFA), ☐ Other _____. This loan shall be at a fixed rate not to exceed __8.0__ % or, ☐ an adjustable rate loan with initial rate not to exceed _____%. Regardless of the type of loan, Buyer shall pay points not to exceed __2.0__ % of the loan amount.

(2) ☐ **SECOND LOAN** in the amount of .... $ _____
This loan will be conventional financing or ☐ Seller financing (C.A.R. Form SFA), ☐ assumed financing (C.A.R. Form AFA), ☐ Other _____. This loan shall be at a fixed rate not to exceed _____% or, ☐ an adjustable rate loan with initial rate not to exceed _____%. Regardless of the type of loan, Buyer shall pay points not to exceed _____% of the loan amount.

(3) **FHA/VA:** For any FHA or VA loan specified in 3D(1), Buyer has **17 (or ___) Days** After Acceptance to Deliver to Seller written notice (C.A.R. Form FVA) of any lender-required repairs or costs that Buyer requests Seller to pay for or otherwise correct. Seller has no obligation to pay or satisfy lender requirements unless agreed in writing. A FHA/VA amendatory clause (C.A.R. Form FVAC) shall be a part of this transaction.

E. **ADDITIONAL FINANCING TERMS:** _____

D. Loan(s) – New loans can be either conventional or FHA/VA loans.

D(1) - First Loan - indicates type of financing. Sets forth terms specifically, not generally. If fixed rate and adjustable rate information are both filled in, Buyer is obligated to complete transaction with whichever of those two options is obtainable from the lender. Only fill in type of rate Buyer chooses.

D(2) - Second Loan - indicates type of financing for second loan. Paragraph requires Seller to pay points percentage, if he or she agrees to pay them. Seller also must pay: (a) other fees not allowed to be paid by the Buyer, up to a pre-agreed amount, inserted on blank line; and (b) lender required repairs, up to a pre-agreed amount, inserted on blank line. **Write the amount in the column to the right.**

It is prudent for the Seller to set a limit on the cost of repairs.

D(3) - FHA/VA - indicates that for FHA or VA loans the buyer has 17 days, unless otherwise specified in writing, after acceptance to deliver to the seller written notice of any lender-required repairs or costs the buyer requests to seller to pay for or repair. Also, an FHA/VA amendatory clause (C.A.R. Form FVAC) is required to be a part of the transaction.

E. Additional Financing Terms – This paragraph relates only to financing. Seller financing requires the CAR® Seller Financing Addendum and Disclosure (SFA) form (see Chapter 9). Check the appropriate block and attach the addendum to the agreement. **Write the amount in the column to the right.**

F. **BALANCE OF DOWN PAYMENT OR PURCHASE PRICE** in the amount of............................... $ 150,000.00
to be deposited with Escrow Holder pursuant to Escrow Holder instructions.

G. **PURCHASE PRICE (TOTAL):** .... $ 800,000.00

F. Balance of Down Payment or Purchase Price – The balance of purchase price will be deposited with escrow holder pursuant to the Escrow Holder's instructions. **Write the amount in the column to the right.**

G. Total Purchase Price – Add the amounts of the right hand columns in Sections 3A through F and **write in the column to the right**.

Should appraisal not match the purchase price, down payment and loan amount will be based on appraisal value.

Buyer's Initials (___*WB*___)(___*DB*___)   Seller's Initials (___*TS*___)(___*RJS*___)

© 1991-2014, California Association of REALTORS®, Inc.
RPA-CA REVISED 11/14 (PAGE 1 OF 10) Print Date

BUYER'S AND SELLER'S INITIALS/SELLING BROKER'S INITIALS

Pages one through seven of the Residential Purchase Agreement require the Buyer's and Seller's initials at the bottom of each page, which means the Buyers and Sellers have read the agreement, **but not necessarily accepted it** (all pages reviewed by Buyer's Broker).

Property Address: ___264 Beach Lane, Costa Mesa, CA 92627___   Date: ___June 14, 2020___

PROPERTY ADDRESS AND DATE

Pages one through eight of the Residential Purchase Agreement require the property address and the date to be filled in at the top of the page. This is very important as several offers could be coming through the fax machine or online zipForms® simultaneously.

H.   **VERIFICATION OF DOWN PAYMENT AND CLOSING COSTS:** Buyer (or Buyer's lender or loan broker pursuant to paragraph 3J(1)) shall, within **3 (or ___) Days** After Acceptance, Deliver to Seller written verification of Buyer's down payment and closing costs. (☐ Verification attached.)

I.   **APPRAISAL CONTINGENCY AND REMOVAL:** This Agreement is (or ☐ is NOT) contingent upon a written appraisal of the Property by a licensed or certified appraiser at no less than the purchase price. Buyer shall, as specified in paragraph 14B(3), in writing, remove the appraisal contingency or cancel this Agreement within **17 (or ___) Days** After Acceptance.

J.   **LOAN TERMS:**
   (1) LOAN APPLICATIONS: Within **3 (or ___) Days** After Acceptance, Buyer shall Deliver to Seller a letter from Buyer's lender or loan broker stating that, based on a review of Buyer's written application and credit report, Buyer is prequalified or preapproved for any NEW loan specified in paragraph 3D. If any loan specified in paragraph 3D is an adjustable rate loan, the prequalification or preapproval letter shall be based on the qualifying rate, not the initial loan rate. (☐ Letter attached.)
   (2) LOAN CONTINGENCY: Buyer shall act diligently and in good faith to obtain the designated loan(s). Buyer's qualification for the loan(s) specified above **is a contingency** of this Agreement unless otherwise agreed in writing. If there is no appraisal contingency or the appraisal contingency has been waived or removed, then failure of the Property to appraise at the purchase price does not entitle Buyer to exercise the cancellation right pursuant to the loan contingency if Buyer is otherwise qualified for the specified loan. Buyer's contractual obligations regarding deposit, balance of down payment and closing costs **are not contingencies** of this Agreement.
   (3) LOAN CONTINGENCY REMOVAL:
   Within **21 (or ___) Days** After Acceptance, Buyer shall, as specified in paragraph 14, in writing, remove the loan contingency or cancel this Agreement. If there is an appraisal contingency, removal of the loan contingency shall not be deemed removal of the appraisal contingency.
   (4) ☐ NO LOAN CONTINGENCY: Obtaining any loan specified above is NOT a contingency of this Agreement. If Buyer does not obtain the loan and as a result does not purchase the Property, Seller may be entitled to Buyer's deposit or other legal remedies.
   (5) LENDER LIMITS ON BUYER CREDITS: Any credit to Buyer, from any source, for closing or other costs that is agreed to by the Parties ("Contractual Credit") shall be disclosed to Buyer's lender. If the total credit allowed by Buyer's lender ("Lender Allowable Credit") is less than the Contractual Credit, then (i) the Contractual Credit shall be reduced to the Lender Allowable Credit, and (ii) in the absence of a separate written agreement between the Parties, there shall be no automatic adjustment to the purchase price to make up for the difference between the Contractual Credit and the Lender Allowable Credit.

H. Verification of Down Payment and Closing Costs – To avoid the possibility that the Buyer will be unable to obtain the required down payment and closing costs before the close of escrow, the Buyer may be required to verify the down payment and closing costs within **3 days after acceptance**, or a number of days inserted on the blank line. This is called "Proof of Funds."

I. Appraisal Contingency and Removal – Even if a lender is willing to lend the amount specified in Paragraph 3D(1), the Buyer is not obligated to purchase if the property appraises at less than the purchase price in Paragraph 3G. The **Buyer may check a box and opt out of this contingency.**

It's important to remember that if the Buyer is applying for an 80% loan and the appraisal does not come in at or above the specified purchase price, the Buyer will probably be "released from further obligation."

J. Loan Terms

J(1) - Loan Applications – If the Buyer does not provide the letter from a lender showing the Buyer is either prequalified or preapproved **within 3 days after acceptance**, or the number of days inserted on the blank line, the Seller may cancel the agreement. Most sellers will not consider an offer if the buyer is not at least pre-approved. If any loan specified in paragraph 3D is an adjustable rate loan, the prequalification or preapproval letter shall be based on the qualifying rate, not the initial loan rate.

J(2) - Loan Contingency – The Buyer must try to obtain the designated loans specified above. Obtaining the loan(s) is a contingency of this Agreement unless otherwise agreed in writing. If there is no appraisal contingency or the appraisal contingency has been waived or removed and the property fails to appraise at the purchase price, the Buyer may not exercise the cancellation right pursuant to the loan contingency if the Buyer is otherwise qualified for the specified loan. Deposit, balance of down payment, and closing costs are not considered contingencies of this agreement.

J(3) - Loan Contingency Removal – The financing contingency is effective until it is removed **within 21 days after acceptance**, or the number of days inserted on the blank line, or until the loan is actually funded (if that block is checked), although many sellers will not accept such a long contingency. If there is an appraisal contingency, it is not removed by this action.

J(4) - No Loan Contingency – The parties may agree to check the box in this paragraph to state that obtaining a loan is not a contingency. If so, the Buyer agrees to complete the transaction even if the lender does not fund the loan, and is in breach of the agreement if he does not complete it. **Must be checked to apply.**

J(5) - Lender Limits on Buyer Credits – Any credit to the Buyer from any source for closing or other costs agreed to by the Parties must be disclosed to the Buyer's lender.

> **K. BUYER STATED FINANCING:** Seller is relying on Buyer's representation of the type of financing specified (including but not limited to, as applicable, all cash, amount of down payment, or contingent or non contingent loan). Seller has agreed to a specific closing date, purchase price and to sell to Buyer in reliance on Buyer's covenant concerning financing. Buyer shall pursue the financing specified in this Agreement. Seller has no obligation to cooperate with Buyer's efforts to obtain any financing other than that specified in the Agreement and the availability of any such alternate financing does not excuse Buyer from the obligation to purchase the Property and close escrow as specified in this Agreement.

K. Buyer Stated Financing – Seller has relied on Buyer's representation as to the type of financing specified. However, if alternate financing is sought, the seller has no obligation to cooperate with such effort, and if that effort is unsuccessful, the buyer must pursue the financing method specified in this agreement. The buyer is not relieved of his/her obligation to purchase the property and close escrow.

> **4. SALE OF BUYER'S PROPERTY:**
> **A.** This Agreement and Buyer's ability to obtain financing are NOT contingent upon the sale of any property owned by Buyer.
> **OR B.** ☐ This Agreement and Buyer's ability to obtain financing are contingent upon the sale of property owned by Buyer as specified in the attached addendum (C.A.R. Form COP).

4. SALE OF BUYER'S PROPERTY

A. The sale of Buyer's property and the ability of the Buyer to obtain financing are generally not a contingency of the agreement, and therefore, will not be a loophole for the Buyer to get out of the contract.

B. If box is checked, the sale of the Buyer's property and the ability to obtain financing are a contingency, and a separate addendum, the **Contingency for Sale or Purchase of Other Property (COP)** (see Chapter 7, Figure 7-3), must be attached to the agreement.

> **5. ADDENDA AND ADVISORIES:**
> **A. ADDENDA:**   ☐ Addendum # _____ (C.A.R. Form ADM)
> ☐ Back Up Offer Addendum (C.A.R. Form BUO)   ☐ Court Confirmation Addendum (C.A.R. Form CCA)
> ☐ Septic, Well and Property Monument Addendum (C.A.R. Form SWPI)
> ☐ Short Sale Addendum (C.A.R. Form SSA)   ☐ Other
>
> **B. BUYER AND SELLER ADVISORIES:**   ☑ Buyer's Inspection Advisory (C.A.R. Form BIA)
> ☐ Probate Advisory (C.A.R. Form PAK)   ☑ Statewide Buyer and Seller Advisory (C.A.R. Form SBSA)
> ☐ Trust Advisory (C.A.R. Form TA)   ☐ REO Advisory (C.A.R. Form REO)
> ☐ Short Sale Information and Advisory (C.A.R. Form SSIA)   ☑ Other Purchase Agreement Addendum (C.A.R. Form PAA)
> **6. OTHER TERMS:** _____
> _____
> _____
> _____

5. ADDENDA AND ADVISORIES ; 6. OTHER TERMS

Additional provisions to this agreement must be in writing, and should be set forth here or on written attachments. Two additional terms, the Buyer's Inspection Advisory

(CAR® form BIA) and the Statewide Buyer and Seller Advisory (CAR® form SBSA), may be checked to supplement the agreement.

---

7. ALLOCATION OF COSTS

A. INSPECTIONS, REPORTS AND CERTIFICATES: Unless otherwise agreed in writing, this paragraph only determines who is to pay for the inspection, test, certificate or service ("Report") mentioned; it does not determine who is to pay for any work recommended or identified in the Report.

(1) ☐ Buyer ☐ Seller shall pay for a natural hazard zone disclosure report, including ☐ environmental and tax reports ☐ Other: _____ prepared by _____ .

(2) ☐ Buyer ☑ Seller shall pay for the following Report ___Wood Pest Report___ prepared by ___Bugs B Gone___ .

(3) ☐ Buyer ☐ Seller shall pay for the following Report _____ prepared by _____ .

---

7. ALLOCATION OF COSTS

Termite clearance is not mandated by law—it's usually a lender's requirement. Who pays for the inspection (termite report) is negotiable.

Unless otherwise agreed to in writing, this paragraph only determines who is to pay for inspection, test, certificate, or service "Report."

A. Inspections, Reports, and Certificates

A(1) – The Parties identify who wil pay for a natural hazard zone disclosure report and which company is to prepare the report.

A(2) and A(3) – These sections identify who will pay for other reports, such as wood destroying pests and sewage system inspection and who will prepare those reports.

B. GOVERNMENT REQUIREMENTS AND RETROFIT:

(1) ☐ Buyer ☑ Seller shall pay for smoke alarm and carbon monoxide device installation and water heater bracing, if required by Law. Prior to Close Of Escrow ("COE"), Seller shall provide Buyer written statement(s) of compliance in accordance with state and local Law, unless Seller is exempt.

(2) (i) ☐ Buyer ☐ Seller shall pay the cost of compliance with any other minimum mandatory government inspections and reports if required as a condition of closing escrow under any Law.

(ii) ☐ Buyer ☐ Seller shall pay the cost of compliance with any other minimum mandatory government retrofit standards required as a condition of closing escrow under any Law, whether the work is required to be completed before or after COE.

(iii) Buyer shall be provided, within the time specified in paragraph 14A, a copy of any required government conducted or point-of-sale inspection report prepared pursuant to this Agreement or in anticipation of this sale of the Property.

START - PAGE 3 OF 10

B. Government Requirements and Retrofit

B(1) - B(2) – The Parties may negotiate who has to pay for compliance with smoke detector and carbon monoxide installation, water heater bracing, and any other retrofits required by any governmental agency. **Seller must deliver a statement of compliance with such requirements to the Buyer, unless the Seller is exempt**. It is wise to protect the seller by inserting the term "Seller to approve cost."

C. **ESCROW AND TITLE:**
   (1) (a) ☑ Buyer ☑ Seller shall pay escrow fee _50% / 50%_____.
      (b) Escrow Holder shall be _____ABC Escrow_____.
      (c) The Parties shall, within **5** (or ___) **Days** After receipt, sign and return Escrow Holder's general provisions.
   (2) (a) ☐ Buyer ☐ Seller shall pay for **owner's** title insurance policy specified in paragraph 13E _____.
      (b) Owner's title policy to be issued by _____.
      (Buyer shall pay for any title insurance policy insuring Buyer's **lender**, unless otherwise agreed in writing.)

C. Escrow and Title

C(1) - C(2) – The Parties decide who is to pay for the title policy and escrow fee—which includes the "bare" escrow fee only—and who will be the provider. **Seller, however, must pay entire escrow fee for VA transactions**. Within 5 days after receipt, or by an agreed to date, the Parties shall sign and return the Escrow Holder's general provisions.

D. **OTHER COSTS:**
   (1) ☐ Buyer ☐ Seller shall pay County transfer tax or fee _____.
   (2) ☐ Buyer ☐ Seller shall pay City transfer tax or fee _____.
   (3) ☐ Buyer ☐ Seller shall pay Homeowners' Association ("HOA") transfer fee _____.
   (4) Seller shall pay HOA fees for preparing documents required to be delivered by Civil Code §4525.
   (5) ☐ Buyer ☐ Seller shall pay HOA fees for preparing all documents other than those required by Civil Code §4525.
   (6) ☐ Buyer ☐ Seller shall pay for any private transfer fee _____.
   (7) ☐ Buyer ☐ Seller shall pay for _____.
   (8) ☐ Buyer ☐ Seller shall pay for _____.
   (9) ☐ Buyer ☐ Seller shall pay for the cost, not to exceed $ _____, of a standard (or ☐ upgraded) one-year home warranty plan, issued by _____, with the following optional coverages: ☐ Air Conditioner ☐ Pool/Spa ☐ Other: _____.
      Buyer is informed that home warranty plans have many optional coverages in addition to those listed above. Buyer is advised to investigate these coverages to determine those that may be suitable for Buyer.
   OR ☐ Buyer waives the purchase of a home warranty plan. Nothing in this paragraph precludes Buyer's purchasing a home warranty plan during the term of this Agreement.

D. Other Costs

The parties decide who will pay the fees for the enumerated costs, and any other cost items. The Buyer also has the option of waiving the purchase of a home warranty plan.

Some home warranties carry additional insurance covering Seller's liabilities in case of lawsuits.

8. **ITEMS INCLUDED IN AND EXCLUDED FROM SALE:**
   A. **NOTE TO BUYER AND SELLER:** Items listed as included or excluded in the MLS, flyers or marketing materials are **not** included in the purchase price or excluded from the sale unless specified in paragraph 8 B or C.
   B. **ITEMS INCLUDED IN SALE:** Except as otherwise specified or disclosed,
      (1) All EXISTING fixtures and fittings that are attached to the Property;
      (2) EXISTING electrical, mechanical, lighting, plumbing and heating fixtures, ceiling fans, fireplace inserts, gas logs and grates, solar power systems, built-in appliances, window and door screens, awnings, shutters, window coverings, attached floor coverings, television antennas, satellite dishes, air coolers/conditioners, pool/spa equipment, garage door openers/remote controls, mailbox, in-ground landscaping, trees/shrubs, water features and fountains, water softeners, water purifiers, security systems/alarms and the following if checked: ☐ all stove(s), except _____; ☐ all refrigerator(s) except _____; ☐ all washer(s) and dryer(s), except _____.
      (3) Existing integrated phone and home automation systems, including necessary components such as internet connected hardware or devices, control units (other than non-dedicated mobile devices, electronics and computers) and applicable software, permissions, passwords, codes and access information, are (☐ are NOT) included in the sale.
      (4) **LEASED OR LIENED ITEMS AND SYSTEMS:** Seller shall, within the time specified in paragraph 14A, (i) disclose to Buyer if any item or system specified in paragraph 8B or otherwise included in the sale is leased, or not owned by Seller, or specifically subject to a lien or other encumbrance, and (ii) Deliver to Buyer all written materials (such as lease, warranty, etc.) concerning any such item. Buyer's ability to assume any such lease, or willingness to accept the Property subject to any such lien or encumbrance, is a contingency of this Agreement as specified in paragraph 14B.
      (5) The following additional items:_____.
      (6) Seller represents that all items included in the purchase price, unless otherwise specified, (i) are owned by Seller and **shall** be transferred free and clear of liens and encumbrances, except the items and systems identified pursuant to 8B(4) and _____ and (ii) are transferred without Seller warranty regardless of value.
   C. **ITEMS EXCLUDED FROM SALE:** Unless otherwise specified, the following items are excluded from sale: (i) audio and video components (such as flat screen TVs, speakers and other items) if any such item is not itself attached to the Property, even if a bracket or other mechanism attached to the component or item is attached to the Property; (ii) furniture and other items secured to the Property for earthquake purposes; and (iii) _____. Brackets attached to walls, floors or ceilings for any such component, furniture or item shall remain with the Property (or ☐ will be removed and holes or other damage shall be repaired, but not painted).

8. ITEMS INCLUDED IN AND EXCLUDED FROM SALE

A. The contract alone determines what is or is not included in the sale of the property.

B. The sale includes all existing attached fixtures and fittings. Certain items are listed, like an integrated phone and home automation system, and others may be specified. All items are free of liens, and without warranty.

C. The Seller and the Buyer may specify items excluded from the sale.

9. **CLOSING AND POSSESSION:**
   A. Buyer intends (or ☐ does not intend) to occupy the Property as Buyer's primary residence.
   B. **Seller-occupied or vacant property:** Possession shall be delivered to Buyer: (i) at 6 PM or (11:59 ☐ AM/☑ PM) on the date of Close Of Escrow; (ii) ☐ no later than ___ days after Close Of Escrow; or (iii) ☐ at ____ ☐ AM/☐ PM on _____.
   C. **Seller remaining in possession After Close Of Escrow:** If Seller has the right to remain in possession after Close Of Escrow, (i) the Parties are advised to sign a separate occupancy agreement such as ☐ C.A.R. Form SIP, for Seller continued occupancy of less than 30 days, ☐ C.A.R. Form RLAS for Seller continued occupancy of 30 days or more; and (ii) the Parties are advised to consult with their insurance and legal advisors for information about liability and damage or injury to persons and personal and real property; and (iii) Buyer is advised to consult with Buyer's lender about the impact of Seller's occupancy on Buyer's loan.
   D. **Tenant-occupied property:** Property shall be vacant at least 5 (or ___) Days Prior to Close Of Escrow, unless otherwise agreed in writing. **Note to Seller: If you are unable to deliver Property vacant in accordance with rent control and other applicable Law, you may be in breach of this Agreement.**
   OR ☐ Tenant to remain in possession (C.A.R. Form TIP).
   E. At Close Of Escrow: Seller assigns to Buyer any assignable warranty rights for items included in the sale; and Seller shall Deliver to Buyer available Copies of any such warranties. Brokers cannot and will not determine the assignability of any warranties.
   F. At Close Of Escrow, unless otherwise agreed in writing, Seller shall provide keys, passwords, codes and/or means to operate all locks, mailboxes, security systems, alarms, home automation systems and internet connected devices included in the purchase price, and garage door openers. If the Property is a condominium or located in a common interest subdivision, Buyer may be required to pay a deposit to the Homeowners' Association ("HOA") to obtain keys to accessible HOA facilities.

START - PAGE 4 OF 10

9. CLOSING AND POSSESSION

A. Buyer Occupancy – Whether the Buyer intends to occupy the property is important to matters such as liquidated damages, loan qualification, rate, and terms. Box should be checked if Buyer does not intend to occupy the property.

"CE + 3" means the Buyer will take possession 3 days after the close of escrow.

B. Seller-Occupied or Vacant Property – Occupancy is to be delivered to the Buyer at the time specified in the purchase agreement between the Buyer and Seller, or some other specified date. If the Buyer moves in before the close of escrow, the parties should enter into a written agreement to document that separate legal relationship, and consult with their insurance and legal advisors respecting insurance and risk of loss if property is damaged during that period. Applicable addendums include: "Residential Lease Agreement After Sale" or "Interim Occupancy Agreement" (CAR® Forms RLAS or IOA), or "Purchase Agreement Addendum" (if for less than 30 days, CAR® Forms PAA, paragraph 2, "Seller to Remain in Possession after Close of Escrow"). This should be avoided if possible.

C. Seller Remaining in Possession After Close of Escrow – If the Seller has the right to remain in possession After Close of Escrow, the Parties are advised to sign a separate occupancy agreement.

D. Tenant-Occupied Property – Seller is responsible to deliver the property vacant for a t least 5 days prior to Close of Escrow, unless otherwise agreed, so that the Buyer can inspect the property. If not possible or practicable, the Buyer and Seller may check the following options: **Tenant to Remain in Possession** (Use CAR® Form TIP).

It's important to remember that a tenant with a valid lease may remain in possession after the sale. "Security deposits are to be transferred to the new owner if the tenants remain in possession."

E. Warranties – Warranties of third parties are automatically assigned by the contract on close of escrow. Seller provides Buyer with the warranty documentation.

F. Keys – Seller delivers, at time of possession, all keys and means of opening all locks and all passwords, codes, and/or means to operate all locks, mailboxes, security systems, alarms, home automation systems and Internet connected devices included in the purchase price, and garage door openers.

10. STATUTORY AND OTHER DISCLOSURES (INCLUDING LEAD-BASED PAINT HAZARD DISCLOSURES) AND CANCELLATION RIGHTS:

A. (1) Seller shall, within the time specified in paragraph 14A, Deliver to Buyer: (i) if required by Law, a fully completed: Federal Lead-Based Paint Disclosures (C.A.R. Form FLD) and pamphlet ("Lead Disclosures"); and (ii) unless exempt, fully completed disclosures or notices required by sections 1102 et. seq. and 1103 et. seq. of the Civil Code ("Statutory Disclosures"). Statutory Disclosures include, but are not limited to, a Real Estate Transfer Disclosure Statement ("TDS"), Natural Hazard Disclosure Statement ("NHD"), notice or actual knowledge of release of illegal controlled substance, notice of special tax and/or assessments (or, if allowed, substantially equivalent notice regarding the Mello-Roos Community Facilities Act of 1982 and Improvement Bond Act of 1915) and, if Seller has actual knowledge, of industrial use and military ordnance location (C.A.R. Form SPQ or SSD).

(2) Any Statutory Disclosure required by this paragraph is considered fully completed if Seller has answered all questions and completed and signed the seller section(s) and the Listing Agent, if any, has completed and signed the listing broker section(s), or, if applicable, an Agent Visual Inspection Disclosure (C.A.R. Form AVID). Nothing stated herein relieves a Buyer's Broker, if any, from the obligation to (i) conduct a reasonably competent and diligent visual inspection of the accessible areas of the Property and disclose, on Section IV of the TDS, or an AVID, material facts affecting the value or desirability of the Property that were or should have been revealed by such an inspection or (ii) complete any sections on all disclosures required to be completed by Buyer's Broker.

(3) **Note to Buyer and Seller:** Waiver of Statutory and Lead Disclosures is prohibited by Law.

(4) Seller, unless exempt from the obligation to provide TDS, shall, within the time specified in paragraph 14A, complete and provide Buyer with a Seller Property Questionnaire (C.A.R. Form SPQ) **OR ☐** Supplemental Contractual and Statutory Disclosure (C.A.R. Form SSD).

(5) Buyer shall, within the time specified in paragraph 14B(1), return Signed Copies of the Statutory, Lead and other disclosures to Seller.

(6) In the event Seller or Listing Broker, prior to Close Of Escrow, becomes aware of adverse conditions materially affecting the Property, or any material inaccuracy in disclosures, information or representations previously provided to Buyer, Seller shall promptly provide a subsequent or amended disclosure or notice, in writing, covering those items. **However, a subsequent or amended disclosure shall not be required for conditions and material inaccuracies of which Buyer is otherwise aware, or which are disclosed in reports provided to or obtained by Buyer or ordered and paid for by Buyer.**

(7) If any disclosure or notice specified in paragraph 10A(1), or subsequent or amended disclosure or notice is Delivered to Buyer after the offer is Signed, Buyer shall have the right to cancel this Agreement within **3 Days** After Delivery in person, or **5 Days** After Delivery by deposit in the mail, by giving written notice of cancellation to Seller or Seller's agent.

B. **NATURAL AND ENVIRONMENTAL HAZARD DISCLOSURES AND OTHER BOOKLETS:** Within the time specified in paragraph 14A, Seller shall, if required by Law: (i) Deliver to Buyer earthquake guide(s) (and questionnaire), environmental hazards booklet, and home energy rating pamphlet; (ii) disclose if the Property is located in a Special Flood Hazard Area; Potential Flooding (Inundation) Area; Very High Fire Hazard Zone; State Fire Responsibility Area; Earthquake Fault Zone; and Seismic Hazard Zone; and (iii) disclose any other zone as required by Law and provide any other information required for those zones.

C. **WITHHOLDING TAXES:** Within the time specified in paragraph 14A, to avoid required withholding, Seller shall Deliver to Buyer or qualified substitute, an affidavit sufficient to comply with federal (FIRPTA) and California withholding Law (C.A.R. Form AS or QS).

D. **MEGAN'S LAW DATABASE DISCLOSURE:** Notice: Pursuant to Section 290.46 of the Penal Code, information about specified registered sex offenders is made available to the public via an Internet Web site maintained by the Department of Justice at www.meganslaw.ca.gov. Depending on an offender's criminal history, this information will include either the address at which the offender resides or the community of residence and ZIP Code in which he or she resides. (Neither Seller nor Brokers are required to check this website. If Buyer wants further information, Broker recommends that Buyer obtain information from this website during Buyer's inspection contingency period. Brokers do not have expertise in this area.)

E. **NOTICE REGARDING GAS AND HAZARDOUS LIQUID TRANSMISSION PIPELINES:** This notice is being provided simply to inform you that information about the general location of gas and hazardous liquid transmission pipelines is available to the public via the National Pipeline Mapping System (NPMS) Internet Web site maintained by the United States Department of Transportation at http://www.npms.phmsa.dot.gov/. To seek further information about possible transmission pipelines near the Property, you may contact your local gas utility or other pipeline operators in the area. Contact information for pipeline operators is searchable by ZIP Code and county on the NPMS Internet Web site.

10. STATUTORY AND OTHER DISCLOSURES (INCLUDING LEAD-BASED PAINT HAZARD DISCLOSURES) AND CANCELLATION RIGHTS

A(1) – This paragraph summarizes the Statutory Disclosure requirements for Seller to deliver two mandated forms: **(i)** the **Transfer Disclosure Statement (TDS)**, and **(ii)** a **Natural Hazard Disclosure Statement (NHD)**. It also summarizes the requirement to obtain a disclosure notice from the taxing authorities if the property is in a **Mello-Roos District, or subject to an assessment under the Improvement Bond Act of 1915.**

If the Seller has actual knowledge, he or she must disclose to the Buyer if: (a) there has been a release of illegal substances on the property; (b) if the property is in or affected by an industrial use zone (manufacturing, commercial, or airport use), or located within one mile of a former military ordnance location. Because of the amount of complexity of this requirement, most agents use a 3rd party provider ($75-$150) with the capacity of disclosing natural hazards, which is usually paid for by the Seller.

The Seller must also provide the Buyer with a "Lead-Based Paint Disclosure" as an attachment to the contract if the residential property was constructed before 1978.

Also, "local option" disclosures are required in some areas, and must be provided on the statutory format under Civil Code §1102. Those local option disclosures trigger a 3-5 day rescission period.

A(2) – Any Statutory Disclosure required by this paragraph is considered fully completed if Seller has answered all questions and completed and signed the Seller section(s) and the Listing Agent, if any, has completed and signed the Listing Broker section(s).

A(3) – Statutory and lead disclosures by law cannot be waived by either the Buyer or the Seller.

A(4) – The Seller, unless exempt from the obligation to provide a Transfer Disclosure Statement (TDS), shall, within the time specified in paragraph 14A, complete and provide the Buyer with a Seller Property Questionnaire (C.A.R. Form SPQ) or a Supplemental Contractual and Statutory Disclosure (C.A.R. Form SSD).

A(5) – By the terms of the contract, the Buyer must return the signed statutory, lead, and other disclosures to the Seller within the time specified in **Paragraph 14B(1)**.

A(6) – The Seller must give the Buyer an amended written disclosure if the Seller or Listing Broker become aware of any adverse material condition before the close of escrow.

A(7) – The Buyer has a right of cancellation **within 3 days of personal delivery** of the Transfer Disclosure Statement, Natural Hazard Disclosure Statement, and Lead-Based Disclosure or amended disclosure, or **5 days after mailing**, if given to the Buyer after acceptance of the contract. **Therefore, it's important to have all disclosures acknowledged as promptly as possible**. If given before acceptance, there is no cancellation period.

B. Natural and Environmental Hazard Disclosures and Other Booklets – The Seller must provide to the Buyer the natural hazard disclosures within the time specified in Paragraph 14A. The Natural Hazard Disclosure Statement (NHD) is required to be used to make six natural hazard zone disclosures:

1. **Special Flood Hazard Area** (designated by the Federal Emergency Management Agency [FEMA]; flood insurance usually required);

2. **Potential Flooding (Inundation) Area** (subject to flooding if dam fails);

3. **Very High Fire Hazard Zone** (subject to high fire risks, which may require maintaining firebreaks, clearing brush, etc.);

4. **State Fire Responsibility Area** (Seller must inform Buyer that the state has no responsibility to provide fire protection services to any building unless an agreement is reached with local fire fighting agency);

5. **Earthquake Fault Zone** (Seller must complete questionnaire page of *The Homeowner's Guide to Earthquake Safety* booklet and give it to the Buyer, but no additional information need be given); and

6. **Seismic Hazard Zone**

However, both the Seller and the Broker must disclose known structural defects and earthquake hazards on the property.

If the Seller and Broker deliver a copy of the *Environmental Hazard Booklet* (which discusses environmental hazards such as asbestos, formaldehyde, hazardous waste, household hazardous waste, lead, mold, and radon), they need not provide additional information, unless they have actual knowledge about the presence of those items on the property.

Neither the Transfer Disclosure Statement nor the Natural Hazard Disclosure Statement are warranties or part of the contract.

C. Withholding Taxes – The two tax withholding laws that affect the transfer of all real property are:

(1) Buyer is responsible under Federal law for withholding 10% of the Seller's gross selling price if the Seller is a "foreign person" as defined by the Foreign Investment in Real Property Tax Act (FIRPTA). Buyer and escrow are responsible for the amount of the tax.

(2) 3.33% of the gross selling price must be withheld under California law, on all non-personal residences, if the Seller's last known address is outside of California or if the Seller's proceeds are being paid to a financial intermediary. The Buyer is responsible for withholding the funds if he or she is notified by the escrow holder of the requirement to withhold. If not notified, the escrow holder is liable for the actual amount of the tax due.

D. Megan's Law Database Disclosure – Statute requires the Seller to inform the Buyer that information is available regarding the location of registered sexual offenders from law enforcement officials. Information regarding specified registered sex offenders is available at **www.meganslaw.ca.gov**.

Most Forms and Disclosures listed in this purchase contract can be found in Chapter 7 of this textbook.

E. Notice Regarding Gas and Hazardous Liquid Transmission Pipelines – This notice informs the parties that information about gas and hazardous liquid transmission pipelines that may be in the area can be obtained via the National Pipeline Mapping System (NPMS) or from local gas utility pipeline operators.

F. CONDOMINIUM/PLANNED DEVELOPMENT DISCLOSURES:

(1) **SELLER HAS: 7 (or ___) Days** After Acceptance to disclose to Buyer if the Property is a condominium, or is located in a planned development or other common interest subdivision (C.A.R. Form SPQ or SSD).

(2) If the Property is a condominium or is located in a planned development or other common interest subdivision, Seller has **3 (or ___) Days** After Acceptance to request from the HOA (C.A.R. Form HOA1): (i) Copies of any documents required by Law; (ii) disclosure of any pending or anticipated claim or litigation by or against the HOA; (iii) a statement containing the location and number of designated parking and storage spaces; (iv) Copies of the most recent 12 months of HOA minutes for regular and special meetings; and (v) the names and contact information of all HOAs governing the Property (collectively, "CI Disclosures"). Seller shall itemize and Deliver to Buyer all CI Disclosures received from the HOA and any CI Disclosures in Seller's possession. Buyer's approval of CI Disclosures is a contingency of this Agreement as specified in paragraph 14B(3). The Party specified in paragraph 7, as directed by escrow, shall deposit funds into escrow or direct to HOA or management company to pay for any of the above.

F. Condominium/Planned Development Disclosures

F(1) – This paragraph informs the Buyer, within a specified number of days after acceptance, if the property is part of a development where property is shared in common with other owners and is subject to certain common rules.

F(2) – Seller must, within a specified number of days after acceptance, request from the Homeowner's Association (HOA) and provide to the Buyer certain contractually specified documents.

---

11. CONDITION OF PROPERTY: Unless otherwise agreed in writing: (i) the Property is sold (a) "AS-IS" in its PRESENT physical condition as of the date of Acceptance and (b) subject to Buyer's Investigation rights; (ii) the Property, including pool, spa, landscaping and grounds, is to be maintained in substantially the same condition as on the date of Acceptance; and (iii) all debris and personal property not included in the sale shall be removed by Close Of Escrow.

A. Seller shall, within the time specified in paragraph 14A, DISCLOSE KNOWN MATERIAL FACTS AND DEFECTS affecting the Property, including known insurance claims within the past five years, and make any and all other disclosures required by law.

B. Buyer has the right to conduct Buyer Investigations of the Property and, as specified in paragraph 14B, based upon information discovered in those investigations: (i) cancel this Agreement; or (ii) request that Seller make Repairs or take other action.

C. **Buyer is strongly advised to conduct investigations of the entire Property in order to determine its present condition. Seller may not be aware of all defects affecting the Property or other factors that Buyer considers important. Property improvements may not be built according to code, in compliance with current Law, or have had permits issued.**

---

11. CONDITION OF PROPERTY

The property is to be transferred "AS-IS" in its present physical condition as of the date of the acceptance of the offer.

A. The Seller must also disclose known adverse material facts, including known insurance claims affecting the property, within the time specified in Paragraph 14A, which is usually the past five years.

B. The Buyer has the right to conduct Buyer investigations of the property and (as specified in paragraph 14B), based on the results, either cancel the agreement or request actions, including making repairs.

C. The Buyer is advised to conduct his or her own investigation of the property for any possible defects because the property is sold without any warranties.

After an inspection of the property, preferably by a professional, the Buyer, under Paragraph 14 of the agreement, may either: (1) cancel the agreement, or (2) request the Seller to make repairs or take other action.

---

12. BUYER'S INVESTIGATION OF PROPERTY AND MATTERS AFFECTING PROPERTY:

A. Buyer's acceptance of the condition of, and any other matter affecting the Property, is a contingency of this Agreement as specified in this paragraph and paragraph 14B. Within the time specified in paragraph 14B(1), Buyer shall have the right, at Buyer's expense unless otherwise agreed, to conduct inspections, investigations, tests, surveys and other studies ("Buyer Investigations"), including, but not limited to, the right to: (i) inspect for lead-based paint and other lead-based paint hazards; (ii) inspect for wood destroying pests and organisms. Any inspection for wood destroying pests and organisms shall be prepared by a registered Structural Pest Control company; shall cover the main building and attached structures; may cover detached structures; shall NOT include water tests of shower pans on upper level units unless the owners of property below the shower consent; shall NOT include roof coverings; and, if the Property is a unit in a condominium or other common interest subdivision, the inspection shall include only the separate interest and any exclusive-use areas being transferred, and shall NOT include common areas; and shall include a report ("Pest Control Report") showing the findings of the company which shall be separated into sections for evident infestation or infections (Section 1) and for conditions likely to lead to infestation or infection (Section 2); (iii) review the registered sex offender database; (iv) confirm the insurability of Buyer and the Property including the availability and cost of flood and fire insurance; (v) review and seek approval of leases that may need to be assumed by Buyer; and (vi) satisfy Buyer as to any matter specified in the attached Buyer's Inspection Advisory (C.A.R. Form BIA). Without Seller's prior written consent, Buyer shall neither make nor cause to be made: (i) invasive or destructive Buyer Investigations except to the extent required to prepare a Pest Control Report; or (ii) inspections by any governmental building or zoning inspector or government employee, unless required by Law.

B. Seller shall make the Property available for all Buyer Investigations. Buyer shall (i) as specified in paragraph 14B, complete Buyer Investigations and either remove the contingency or cancel this Agreement, and (ii) give Seller, at no cost, complete Copies of all such Investigation reports obtained by Buyer, which obligation shall survive the termination of this Agreement.

C. Seller shall have water, gas, electricity and all operable pilot lights on for Buyer's Investigations and through the date possession is made available to Buyer.

D. Buyer indemnity and seller protection for entry upon property: Buyer shall: (i) keep the Property free and clear of liens; (ii) repair all damage arising from Buyer Investigations; and (iii) indemnify and hold Seller harmless from all resulting liability, claims, demands, damages and costs. Buyer shall carry, or Buyer shall require anyone acting on Buyer's behalf to carry, policies of liability, workers' compensation and other applicable insurance, defending and protecting Seller from liability for any injuries to persons or property occurring during any Buyer Investigations or work done on the Property at Buyer's direction prior to Close Of Escrow. Seller is advised that certain protections may be afforded Seller by recording a "Notice of Non-Responsibility" (C.A.R. Form NNR) for Buyer Investigations and work done on the Property at Buyer's direction. Buyer's obligations under this paragraph shall survive the termination of this Agreement.

---

12. BUYER'S INVESTIGATION OF PROPERTY AND MATTERS AFFECTING PROPERTY

A. The Buyer's acceptance of the condition of the property or other matters affecting the property is a contingency in the agreement. Under Paragraph 14B(1), the Buyer, at his or her own expense unless otherwise agreed, has a stated period of time in which to conduct an investigation of the property, including the specified types of investigations.

B. The Buyer, after completing the investigation, shall remove the contingency or cancel the agreement within the time specified in Paragraph 14B. The Buyer will also provide the Seller with copies of any investigation reports at no cost.

C. Seller will have water, gas, electricity, and all operable pilot lights on for the Buyer's investigations.

D. The Buyer must assure the Seller that the Seller will not be harmed as a result of the Buyer's investigations. Assurances include the Buyer will: (1) keep property free and clear of liens; (2) repair all damage arising from his or her investigations; and (3) indemnify and hold the Seller harmless for any damage or claims.

Seller may protect himself or herself by, among other things, recording a **"Notice of Non-Responsibility."**

---

13. TITLE AND VESTING:

    A. Within the time specified in paragraph 14, Buyer shall be provided a current preliminary title report ("Preliminary Report"). The Preliminary Report is only an offer by the title insurer to issue a policy of title insurance and may not contain every item affecting title. Buyer's review of the Preliminary Report and any other matters which may affect title are a contingency of this Agreement as specified in paragraph 14B. The company providing the Preliminary Report shall, prior to issuing a Preliminary Report, conduct a search of the General Index for all Sellers except banks or other institutional lenders selling properties they acquired through foreclosure (REOs), corporations, and government entities. Seller shall within 7 Days After Acceptance, give Escrow Holder a completed Statement of Information.

    B. Title is taken in its present condition subject to all encumbrances, easements, covenants, conditions, restrictions, rights and other matters, whether of record or not, as of the date of Acceptance except for: (**i**) monetary liens of record (which Seller is obligated to pay off) unless Buyer is assuming those obligations or taking the Property subject to those obligations; and (**ii**) those matters which Seller has agreed to remove in writing.

    C. Within the time specified in paragraph 14A, Seller has a duty to disclose to Buyer all matters known to Seller affecting title, whether of record or not.

    D. At Close Of Escrow, Buyer shall receive a grant deed conveying title (or, for stock cooperative or long-term lease, an assignment of stock certificate or of Seller's leasehold interest), including oil, mineral and water rights if currently owned by Seller. Title shall vest as designated in Buyer's supplemental escrow instructions. THE MANNER OF TAKING TITLE MAY HAVE SIGNIFICANT LEGAL AND TAX CONSEQUENCES. CONSULT AN APPROPRIATE PROFESSIONAL.

---

13. TITLE AND VESTING (Ownership Interest Insured)

A. The Buyer has the amount of time specified in Paragraph 14B to review the preliminary title report and notify the Seller of any corrective action.

B. The Buyer takes title in its present condition subject to all liens and encumbrances as of the date of acceptance, whether of record or not, except: (1) monetary lien of record (which Seller is obligated to pay off) unless assumed by the Buyer or taken by the Buyer subject to them, and (2) matters to which the Seller has agreed to remove.

C. Seller must disclose to Buyer all matters affecting title, whether of record or not, that are known to Seller.

D. Buyers shall decide how title is to be held and so inform escrow.

As an agent, you should never give legal advice on how to "take title" (ownership interest). For more information on the methods of taking title (vesting), see Chapter 10.

    E. Buyer shall receive a CLTA/ALTA "Homeowner's Policy of Title Insurance", if applicable to the type of property and buyer. If not, Escrow Holder shall notify Buyer. A title company can provide information about the availability, coverage, and cost of other title policies and endorsements. If the Homeowner's Policy is not available, Buyer shall choose another policy, instruct Escrow Holder in writing and shall pay any increase in cost.

E. This paragraph provides that a Buyer will receive a CLTA/ALTA HOMEOWNER'S POLICY OF TITLE INSURANCE, if applicable to the type of property and Buyer. If not, Escrow Holder shall notify Buyer.

---

14. TIME PERIODS; REMOVAL OF CONTINGENCIES; CANCELLATION RIGHTS: The following time periods may only be extended, altered, modified or changed by mutual written agreement. Any removal of contingencies or cancellation under this paragraph by either Buyer or Seller must be exercised in good faith and in writing (C.A.R. Form CR or CC).

 A. **SELLER HAS: 7 (or ___) Days** After Acceptance to Deliver to Buyer all Reports, disclosures and information for which Seller is responsible under paragraphs 5, 6, 7, 8B(4), 10A, B, C, and F, 11A and 13A. If, by the time specified, Seller has not delivered any such item, Buyer after first Delivering to Seller a Notice to Seller to Perform (C.A.R. Form NSP) may cancel this Agreement.

 B. **(1) BUYER HAS: 17 (or ___) Days** After Acceptance, unless otherwise agreed in writing, to:

   (i) complete all Buyer Investigations; review all disclosures, reports, lease documents to be assumed by Buyer pursuant to paragraph 8B(4), and other applicable information, which Buyer receives from Seller; and approve all matters affecting the Property; and **(ii)** Deliver to Seller Signed Copies of Statutory and Lead Disclosures and other disclosures Delivered by Seller in accordance with paragraph 10A.

   (2) Within the time specified in paragraph 14B(1), Buyer may request that Seller make repairs or take any other action regarding the Property (C.A.R. Form RR). Seller has no obligation to agree to or respond to (C.A.R. Form RRRR) Buyer's requests.

   (3) By the end of the time specified in paragraph 14B(1) (or as otherwise specified in this Agreement), Buyer shall Deliver to Seller a removal of the applicable contingency or cancellation (C.A.R. Form CR or CC) of this Agreement. However, if any report, disclosure or information for which Seller is responsible is not Delivered within the time specified in paragraph 14A, then Buyer has **5 (or ___) Days** After Delivery of any such items, or the time specified in paragraph 14B(1), whichever is later, to Deliver to Seller a removal of the applicable contingency or cancellation of this Agreement.

   (4) Continuation of Contingency: Even after the end of the time specified in paragraph 14B(1) and before Seller cancels, if at all, pursuant to paragraph 14C, Buyer retains the right, in writing, to either (i) remove remaining contingencies, or (ii) cancel this Agreement based on a remaining contingency. Once Buyer's written removal of all contingencies is Delivered to Seller, Seller may not cancel this Agreement pursuant to paragraph 14C(1).

 C. **SELLER RIGHT TO CANCEL:**

   (1) Seller right to Cancel; Buyer Contingencies: If, by the time specified in this Agreement, Buyer does not Deliver to Seller a removal of the applicable contingency or cancellation of this Agreement, then Seller, after first Delivering to Buyer a Notice to Buyer to Perform (C.A.R. Form NBP), may cancel this Agreement. In such event, Seller shall authorize the return of Buyer's deposit, except for fees incurred by Buyer.

   (2) Seller right to Cancel; Buyer Contract Obligations: Seller, after first delivering to Buyer a NBP, may cancel this Agreement if, by the time specified in this Agreement, Buyer does not take the following action(s): **(i)** Deposit funds as required by paragraph 3A, or 3B or if the funds deposited pursuant to paragraph 3A or 3B are not good when deposited; **(ii)** Deliver a notice of FHA or VA costs or terms as required by paragraph 3D(3) (C.A.R. Form FVA); **(iii)** Deliver a letter as required by paragraph 3J(1); **(iv)** Deliver verification, or a satisfactory verification if Seller reasonably disapproves of the verification already provided, as required by paragraph 3C or 3H; **(v)** Return Statutory and Lead Disclosures as required by paragraph 10A(5); or **(vi)** Sign or initial a separate liquidated damages form for an increased deposit as required by paragraphs 3B and 21B; or **(vii)** Provide evidence of authority to sign in a representative capacity as specified in paragraph 19. In such event, Seller shall authorize the return of Buyer's deposit, except for fees incurred by Buyer.

---

14. TIME PERIODS; REMOVAL OF CONTINGENCIES; CANCELLATION RIGHTS

The time period for each contingency, which runs from the date of acceptance of the agreement, is specified in the applicable paragraph and set forth for both the Seller and Buyer.

A. Seller Time Periods – The Seller must deliver within **7 days, or the specified number of days,** all reports and disclosures for which he or she is responsible under Paragraphs: 5A and B (Addenda and Advisories), 7 (Allocation of Costs), 10A, B, C, and F (Seller's Statutory Disclosures), 11A (Condition of Property), and 13 (Title and Vesting).

B. Buyer Time Periods – The Buyer must, **within 17 days, or the specified number of days:**

 (1) complete all investigations and review all disclosures, reports, and lease documents to be assumed by the Buyer, and return copies of signed statutory disclosures.

(2) request Seller to make repairs, but the Seller may opt not to make them.

(3) in writing, either remove the contingency or cancel the agreement. However, if the Seller does not deliver mandated disclosures which are a condition to closing, the Buyer has 5 days after receipt of such notice in writing, to either remove the contingency or cancel the agreement.

(4) **Continuation of Contingency** – Buyer retains the right to make requests of Seller, remove contingencies, or cancel agreement until Seller exercises cancellation rights—even after expiration of time periods provided in Paragraph 14B(1).

C. Seller Right to Cancel

(1) **Seller Right to Cancel; Buyer Contingencies** – After first giving the Buyer a Notice to Buyer to Perform (C.A.R. Form NBP), the Seller may cancel the agreement and return the deposit (except for fees incurred by the Buyer) if the Buyer does not remove the contingencies or cancel the agreement within the time period specified in Paragraph 14B.

(2) **Seller Right to Cancel; Buyer Contract Obligations** – After giving the Buyer a Notice to Buyer to Perform, Seller may cancel the agreement and return the Buyer's deposit if, by the time specified in the Agreement, the Buyer does not take the following actions:

(i) Buyer fails to deposit required funds as required by 3A or 3B or if the deposited funds not good when deposited as required by 3A or 3B;

(ii) Buyer fails to deliver a notice of FHA or VA costs or terms as required by 3D(3) (C.A.R.Form FVA);

(iii) Buyer fails to deliver a letter as required by 3J(1);

(iv) Buyer fails to deliver verification as required by 3C or 3H or Seller reasonably disapproves of the verification provided by 3C or 3H;

(v) Buyer fails to return Statutory and Lead Disclosures as required by 10A(5);

(vi) Buyer fails to sign or initial a separate liquidated damage form for an increased deposit as required by 3B and 21B. **Liquidated damage may be increased by an additional deposit not to exceed 3% of purchase price.**

(vii) Buyer does not provide evidence of authority to sign in a representative capacity as specified in paragraph 19.

D. **NOTICE TO BUYER OR SELLER TO PERFORM:** The NBP or NSP shall: (i) be in writing; (ii) be signed by the applicable Buyer or Seller; and (iii) give the other Party at least **2 (or ___) Days After Delivery** (or until the time specified in the applicable paragraph, whichever occurs last) to take the applicable action. A NBP or NSP may not be Delivered any earlier than **2 Days** Prior to the expiration of the applicable time for the other Party to remove a contingency or cancel this Agreement or meet an obligation specified in paragraph 14.

E. **EFFECT OF BUYER'S REMOVAL OF CONTINGENCIES:** If Buyer removes, in writing, any contingency or cancellation rights, unless otherwise specified in writing, Buyer shall conclusively be deemed to have: (i) completed all Buyer Investigations, and review of reports and other applicable information and disclosures pertaining to that contingency or cancellation right; (ii) elected to proceed with the transaction; and (iii) assumed all liability, responsibility and expense for Repairs or corrections pertaining to that contingency or cancellation right, or for the inability to obtain financing.

F. **CLOSE OF ESCROW:** Before Buyer or Seller may cancel this Agreement for failure of the other Party to close escrow pursuant to this Agreement, Buyer or Seller must first Deliver to the other Party a demand to close escrow (C.A.R. Form DCE). The DCE shall: (i) be signed by the applicable Buyer or Seller; and (ii) give the other Party at least **3 (or ___) Days** After Delivery to close escrow. A DCE may not be Delivered any earlier than **3 Days** Prior to the scheduled close of escrow.

D. Notice to Buyer or Seller to Perform – The Seller's written and signed Notice to Buyer to Perform may be given after 2 days, or a time specified, and no earlier than 2 days before the applicable time for the Buyer to remove a contingency or cancel the agreement.

E. Effect of Buyer's Removal of Contingencies – If Buyers remove, in writing, any contingency or cancellation rights, Buyers will conclusively be deemed to have: (i) completed all that needed to be done pertaining to the contingency or cancellation; (ii) elected to proceed with the transaction; and (iii) assumed all responsibility for completing the transaction, such as relinquishing their deposit.

F. Close of Escrow – Before Seller or Buyer may cancel this Agreement for failure of the other party to close escrow pursuant to this agreement, Seller or Buyer must first give the other a demand to close escrow.

> **G.   EFFECT OF CANCELLATION ON DEPOSITS:** If Buyer or Seller gives written notice of cancellation pursuant to rights duly exercised under the terms of this Agreement, the Parties agree to Sign mutual instructions to cancel the sale and escrow and release deposits, if any, to the party entitled to the funds, less fees and costs incurred by that party. Fees and costs may be payable to service providers and vendors for services and products provided during escrow. Except as specified below, **release of funds will require mutual Signed release instructions from** the Parties, **judicial decision or arbitration award.** If either Party fails to execute mutual instructions to cancel, one Party may make a written demand to Escrow Holder for the deposit. Escrow Holder, upon receipt, shall promptly deliver notice of the demand to the other Party. If, within 10 Days After Escrow Holder's notice, the other Party does not object to the demand, Escrow Holder shall disburse the deposit to the Party making the demand. If Escrow Holder complies with the preceding process, each Party shall be deemed to have released Escrow Holder from any and all claims or liability related to the disbursal of the deposit. Escrow Holder, at its discretion, may nonetheless require mutual cancellation instructions. **A Party may be subject to a civil penalty of up to $1,000 for refusal to sign cancellation instructions if no good faith dispute exists as to who is entitled to the deposited funds (Civil Code §1057.3).**

G. Effect of Cancellation on Deposits – If the agreement is cancelled, the Buyer and Seller agree that the Buyer's deposit, less costs and fees, shall be returned to the party entitled to the funds. A notice of cancellation signed by the Buyer and the Seller will be provided to the escrow holder to release the deposit (it's never automatic). There are certain procedures to follow if either party fails to execute the mutual instructions to cancel.

> **15. FINAL VERIFICATION OF CONDITION:** Buyer shall have the right to make a final verification of the Property within 5 (or ☐ ___) **Days** Prior to Close Of Escrow, NOT AS A CONTINGENCY OF THE SALE, but solely to confirm: **(i)** the Property is maintained pursuant to paragraph 11; **(ii)** Repairs have been completed as agreed; and **(iii)** Seller has complied with Seller's other obligations under this Agreement (C.A.R. Form VP).

15. FINAL VERIFICATION OF CONDITION

This paragraph authorizes a "final walk-through" for the Buyer, within a specified number of days before close of escrow, to verify that the condition of the property is as agreed and that Seller has complied with repair duties and other obligations. This is not a time to further investigate the physical condition of the property.

> *A buyer may back out of a deal if, during the final verification, he or she gets "cold feet" by seeing the home in unflattering, messy, or ill-repair condition. Convince your sellers to maintain the utmost appearance of their home!*

> **16. REPAIRS:** Repairs shall be completed prior to final verification of condition unless otherwise agreed in writing. Repairs to be performed at Seller's expense may be performed by Seller or through others, provided that the work complies with applicable Law, including governmental permit, inspection and approval requirements. Repairs shall be performed in a good, skillful manner with materials of quality and appearance comparable to existing materials. It is understood that exact restoration of appearance or cosmetic items following all Repairs may not be possible. Seller shall: **(i)** obtain invoices and paid receipts for Repairs performed by others; **(ii)** prepare a written statement indicating the Repairs performed by Seller and the date of such Repairs; and **(iii)** provide Copies of invoices and paid receipts and statements to Buyer prior to final verification of condition.

16. REPAIRS

Repairs, if any, must be done with permits and in compliance with building codes and completed before the Buyer's final verification of condition of the property. Seller must obtain invoices and paid receipts for repairs, and prepare a written statement of performed repairs and dates for the Buyer.

> **17. PRORATIONS OF PROPERTY TAXES AND OTHER ITEMS:** Unless otherwise agreed in writing, the following items shall be PAID CURRENT and prorated between Buyer and Seller as of Close Of Escrow: real property taxes and assessments, interest, rents, HOA regular, special, and emergency dues and assessments imposed prior to Close Of Escrow, premiums on insurance assumed by Buyer, payments on bonds and assessments assumed by Buyer, and payments on Mello-Roos and other Special Assessment District bonds and assessments that are now a lien. The following items shall be assumed by Buyer WITHOUT CREDIT toward the purchase price: prorated payments on Mello-Roos and other Special Assessment District bonds and assessments and HOA special assessments that are now a lien but not yet due. Property will be reassessed upon change of ownership. Any supplemental tax bills shall be paid as follows: **(i)** for periods after Close Of Escrow, by Buyer; and **(ii)** for periods prior to Close Of Escrow, by Seller (see C.A.R. Form SPT or SBSA for further information). TAX BILLS ISSUED AFTER CLOSE OF ESCROW SHALL BE HANDLED DIRECTLY BETWEEN BUYER AND SELLER. Prorations shall be made based on a 30-day month.

17. PRORATIONS OF PROPERTY TAXES AND OTHER ITEMS

Prorated items shall be paid current by the Seller and assumed by the Buyer as of the close of escrow. The Mello-Roos and other Special Assessments District Bonds and assessments and Homeowner's Association (HOA) special assessments not yet due, but a lien, do not constitute a credit toward the purchase price.

> **18. BROKERS:**
>   **A. COMPENSATION:** Seller or Buyer, or both, as applicable, agree to pay compensation to Broker as specified in a separate written agreement between Broker and that Seller or Buyer. Compensation is payable upon Close Of Escrow, or if escrow does not close, as otherwise specified in the agreement between Broker and that Seller or Buyer.
>   **B. SCOPE OF DUTY:** Buyer and Seller acknowledge and agree that Broker: **(i)** Does not decide what price Buyer should pay or Seller should accept; **(ii)** Does not guarantee the condition of the Property; **(iii)** Does not guarantee the performance, adequacy or completeness of inspections, services, products or repairs provided or made by Seller or others; **(iv)** Does not have an obligation to conduct an inspection of common areas or areas off the site of the Property; **(v)** Shall not be responsible for identifying defects on the Property, in common areas, or offsite unless such defects are visually observable by an inspection of reasonably accessible areas of the Property or are known to Broker; **(vi)** Shall not be responsible for inspecting public records or permits concerning the title or use of Property; **(vii)** Shall not be responsible for identifying the location of boundary lines or other items affecting title; **(viii)** Shall not be responsible for verifying square footage, representations of others or information contained in Investigation reports, Multiple Listing Service, advertisements, flyers or other promotional material; **(ix)** Shall not be responsible for determining the fair market value of the Property or any personal property included in the sale; **(x)** Shall not be responsible for providing legal or tax advice regarding any aspect of a transaction entered into by Buyer or Seller; and **(xi)** Shall not be responsible for providing other advice or information that exceeds the knowledge, education and experience required to perform real estate licensed activity. Buyer and Seller agree to seek legal, tax, insurance, title and other desired assistance from appropriate professionals.

18. BROKERS

A. Compensation – The Seller or Buyer agrees to pay the broker compensation specified in a separate, written agreement. Most brokers do not get paid until escrow closes. If escrow doesn't close, the Broker is paid the compensation specified in the separate, written agreement.

B. Scope of Duty – The Buyer and Seller agree that the Broker: (i) Does not decide the sale price; (ii) Does not guarantee the condition of the property; (iii) Does not quarantee the adequacy or completeness of inspections; (iv) Does not have an obligation to inspect the common areas of the property; (v) Shall not be responsible for idendifying defects on the property or in common areas; (vi) Shall not be responsible for inspecting public records or permits concerning the title of the property; (vii) Shall not be responsible for identifying boundary lines; (viii) Shall not be responsible for identifying square footage; (ix) Shall not be responsible for determining the fair market value of the property or any personal property; (x) Shall not be responsible for providing any legal or tax advice; (xi) Shall not be responsible for providing any other information that exceeds his or her knowledge, education or experience.

---

19. **REPRESENTATIVE CAPACITY:** If one or more Parties is signing this Agreement in a representative capacity and not for him/herself as an individual then that Party shall so indicate in paragraph 31 or 32 and attach a Representative Capacity Signature Addendum (C.A.R. Form RCSA). Wherever the signature or initials of the representative identified in the RCSA appear on this Agreement or any related documents, it shall be deemed to be in a representative capacity for the entity described and not in an individual capacity, unless otherwise indicated. The Party acting in a representative capacity shall Deliver to the other Party and Escrow Holder, within 3 Days After Acceptance, evidence of authority to act in that capacity (such as but not limited to: applicable trust document, or portion thereof, letters testamentary, court order, power of attorney, resolution, or formation documents of the business entity).

---

19. REPRESENTATIVE CAPACITY

If one or more of the Parties signing the Agreement is acting in a representative capacity and not as an individual, then that Party shall indicate this in paragraph 31 and 32 and attach a Representative Capacity Signature Addendum (C.A.R. Form RCSA).

---

20. **JOINT ESCROW INSTRUCTIONS TO ESCROW HOLDER:**
   A. **The following paragraphs, or applicable portions thereof, of this Agreement constitute the joint escrow instructions of Buyer and Seller to Escrow Holder,** which Escrow Holder is to use along with any related counter offers and addenda, and any additional mutual instructions to close the escrow: paragraphs 1, 3, 4B, 5A, 6, 7, 10C, 13, 14G, 17, 18A, 19, 20, 26, 29, 30, 31, 32 and paragraph D of the section titled Real Estate Brokers on page 10. If a Copy of the separate compensation agreement(s) provided for in paragraph 18A, or paragraph D of the section titled Real Estate Brokers on page 10 is deposited with Escrow Holder by Broker, Escrow Holder shall accept such agreement(s) and pay out from Buyer's or Seller's funds, or both, as applicable, the Broker's compensation provided for in such agreement(s). The terms and conditions of this Agreement not set forth in the specified paragraphs are additional matters for the information of Escrow Holder, but about which Escrow Holder need not be concerned. Buyer and Seller will receive Escrow Holder's general provisions, if any, directly from Escrow Holder and will execute such provisions within the time specified in paragraph 7C(1)(c). To the extent the general provisions are inconsistent or conflict with this Agreement, the general provisions will control as to the duties and obligations of Escrow Holder only. Buyer and Seller will execute additional instructions, documents and forms provided by Escrow Holder that are reasonably necessary to close the escrow and, as directed by Escrow Holder, within 3 (or ___) Days, shall pay to Escrow Holder or HOA or HOA management company or others any fee required by paragraphs 7, 10 or elsewhere in this Agreement.

20. JOINT ESCROW INSTRUCTIONS TO ESCROW HOLDER

A. This paragraph specifies **which portions of the purchase agreement constitute instructions from the Buyer and Seller to the escrow holder**. The escrow holder will disburse broker's compensation under separate compensation agreements provided for in Paragraph 18A or Paragraph D in the Real Estate Broker section of the agreement (page 10 of the Purchase Offer Contract).

B. A Copy of this Agreement including any counter offer(s) and addenda shall be delivered to Escrow Holder within **3 Days After** Acceptance (or _____). Buyer and Seller authorize Escrow Holder to accept and rely on Copies and Signatures as defined in this Agreement as originals, to open escrow and for other purposes of escrow. The validity of this Agreement as between Buyer and Seller is not affected by whether or when Escrow Holder Signs this Agreement. Escrow Holder shall provide Seller's Statement of Information to Title company when received from Seller. If Seller delivers an affidavit to Escrow Holder to satisfy Seller's FIRPTA obligation under paragraph 10C, Escrow Holder shall deliver to Buyer a Qualified Substitute statement that complies with federal Law.

C. Brokers are a party to the escrow for the sole purpose of compensation pursuant to paragraph 18A and paragraph D of the section titled Real Estate Brokers on page 10. Buyer and Seller irrevocably assign to Brokers compensation specified in paragraph 18A, and irrevocably instruct Escrow Holder to disburse those funds to Brokers at Close Of Escrow or pursuant to any other mutually executed cancellation agreement. Compensation instructions can be amended or revoked only with the written consent of Brokers. Buyer and Seller shall release and hold harmless Escrow Holder from any liability resulting from Escrow Holder's payment to Broker(s) of compensation pursuant to this Agreement.

B. The parties agree to deliver the agreement and any counter offers to escrow within 3 business days after acceptance, unless otherwise specified. The agreement is valid whether or when the escrow holder signs the agreement.

C. Brokers are parties to the agreement solely for compensation purposes. The Buyer and Seller agree to irrevocably assign the compensation that is provided in the agreement to the brokers and irrevocably instruct the escrow holder to disburse those funds at the close of escrow, or under a mutually executed cancellation agreement.

D. Upon receipt, Escrow Holder shall provide Seller and Seller's Broker verification of Buyer's deposit of funds pursuant to paragraph 3A and 3B. Once Escrow Holder becomes aware of any of the following, Escrow Holder shall immediately notify all Brokers: **(i)** if Buyer's initial or any additional deposit or down payment is not made pursuant to this Agreement, or is not good at time of deposit with Escrow Holder; or **(ii)** if Buyer and Seller instruct Escrow Holder to cancel escrow.

E. A Copy of any amendment that affects any paragraph of this Agreement for which Escrow Holder is responsible shall be delivered to Escrow Holder within 3 Days after mutual execution of the amendment.

D. Upon receipt, Escrow Holder shall provide Seller and Seller's Broker verification of Buyer's deposit of funds pursuant to paragraph 3A and 3B.

E. The Buyer and Seller agree to provide the escrow holder with a copy of any written amendment affecting any paragraph of the agreement that is also an escrow instruction within 3 days after it is executed.

21. REMEDIES FOR BUYER'S BREACH OF CONTRACT:

    A. Any clause added by the Parties specifying a remedy (such as release or forfeiture of deposit or making a deposit non-refundable) for failure of Buyer to complete the purchase in violation of this Agreement shall be deemed invalid unless the clause independently satisfies the statutory liquidated damages requirements set forth in the Civil Code.

    B. **LIQUIDATED DAMAGES:** If Buyer fails to complete this purchase because of Buyer's default, Seller shall retain, as liquidated damages, the deposit actually paid. If the Property is a dwelling with no more than four units, one of which Buyer intends to occupy, then the amount retained shall be no more than 3% of the purchase price. Any excess shall be returned to Buyer. Except as provided in paragraph 14G, release of funds will require mutual, Signed release instructions from both Buyer and Seller, judicial decision or arbitration award. **AT TIME OF ANY INCREASED DEPOSIT BUYER AND SELLER SHALL SIGN A SEPARATE LIQUIDATED DAMAGES PROVISION INCORPORATING THE INCREASED DEPOSIT AS LIQUIDATED DAMAGES (C.A.R. FORM RID).**

Buyer's Initials _WB_ / _DB_   Seller's Initials _TS_ / _RJS_

21. REMEDIES FOR BUYER'S BREACH OF CONTRACT

A. Any clause added by the Parties specifying a remedy for the failure of the Buyer to complete the purchase in violation of the Agreement is invalid unless the clause independently satisfies the statutory liquidated damages requirements set forth in the Civil Code.

B. Liquidated Damages – This paragraph provides the amount of money that the Buyer agrees to pay the Seller if the Buyer breaches the agreement. It limits the amount to which the Seller is entitled. The remedy is the amount of the deposit, up to 3% of the purchase price, if the property is a one- to four-unit dwelling, one of which was to be occupied by the Buyer. If not, the liquidated damages are for a reasonable amount of the deposit. **Buyers and Sellers must initial this section where indicated in order for this clause to apply.**

22. DISPUTE RESOLUTION:

    A. **MEDIATION:** The Parties agree to mediate any dispute or claim arising between them out of this Agreement, or any resulting transaction, before resorting to arbitration or court action through the C.A.R. Real Estate Mediation Center for Consumers (www.consumermediation.org) or through any other mediation provider or service mutually agreed to by the Parties. The Parties also agree to mediate any disputes or claims with Broker(s), who, in writing, agree to such mediation prior to, or within a reasonable time after, the dispute or claim is presented to the Broker. Mediation fees, if any, shall be divided equally among the Parties involved. If, for any dispute or claim to which this paragraph applies, any Party (i) commences an action without first attempting to resolve the matter through mediation, or (ii) before commencement of an action, refuses to mediate after a request has been made, then that Party shall not be entitled to recover attorney fees, even if they would otherwise be available to that Party in any such action. THIS MEDIATION PROVISION APPLIES WHETHER OR NOT THE ARBITRATION PROVISION IS INITIALED. Exclusions from this mediation agreement are specified in paragraph 22C.

    B. **ARBITRATION OF DISPUTES:**
The Parties agree that any dispute or claim in Law or equity arising between them out of this Agreement or any resulting transaction, which is not settled through mediation, shall be decided by neutral, binding arbitration. The Parties also agree to arbitrate any disputes or claims with Broker(s), who, in writing, agree to such arbitration prior to, or within a reasonable time after, the dispute or claim is presented to the Broker. The arbitrator shall be a retired judge or justice, or an attorney with at least 5 years of residential real estate Law experience, unless the parties mutually agree to a different arbitrator. The Parties shall have the right to discovery in accordance with Code of Civil Procedure §1283.05. In all other respects, the arbitration shall be conducted in accordance with Title 9 of Part 3 of the Code of Civil Procedure. Judgment upon the award of the arbitrator(s) may be entered into any court having jurisdiction. Enforcement of this agreement to arbitrate shall be governed by the Federal Arbitration Act. Exclusions from this arbitration agreement are specified in paragraph 22C.

▼

"NOTICE: BY INITIALING IN THE SPACE BELOW YOU ARE AGREEING TO HAVE ANY DISPUTE ARISING OUT OF THE MATTERS INCLUDED IN THE 'ARBITRATION OF DISPUTES' PROVISION DECIDED BY NEUTRAL ARBITRATION AS PROVIDED BY CALIFORNIA LAW AND YOU ARE GIVING UP ANY RIGHTS YOU MIGHT POSSESS TO HAVE THE DISPUTE LITIGATED IN A COURT OR JURY TRIAL. BY INITIALING IN THE SPACE BELOW YOU ARE GIVING UP YOUR JUDICIAL RIGHTS TO DISCOVERY AND APPEAL, UNLESS THOSE RIGHTS ARE SPECIFICALLY INCLUDED IN THE 'ARBITRATION OF DISPUTES' PROVISION. IF YOU REFUSE TO SUBMIT TO ARBITRATION AFTER AGREEING TO THIS PROVISION, YOU MAY BE COMPELLED TO ARBITRATE UNDER THE AUTHORITY OF THE CALIFORNIA CODE OF CIVIL PROCEDURE. YOUR AGREEMENT TO THIS ARBITRATION PROVISION IS VOLUNTARY."

"WE HAVE READ AND UNDERSTAND THE FOREGOING AND AGREE TO SUBMIT DISPUTES ARISING OUT OF THE MATTERS INCLUDED IN THE 'ARBITRATION OF DISPUTES' PROVISION TO NEUTRAL ARBITRATION."

Buyer's Initials ___*WB*_ / _*DB*___  Seller's Initials ___*TS*_ / _*RJS*___

22. DISPUTE RESOLUTION

A. Mediation – Under this dispute resolution provision, the Buyer and Seller agree to mediation by a neutral mediator to attempt to resolve any disputes.

Mediation is required whether the parties (buyers, sellers, or brokers) agree to arbitrate or not! If a party does not seek mediation before filing a lawsuit, that party shall not be entitled to recover attorney's fees, even if that party is the prevailing party in the lawsuit.

B. Arbitration of Disputes – This paragraph must be initialed by both the Buyer and Seller to be included in the agreement. By initialing this contract provision, the Parties agree in advance to arbitrate disputes arising out of their agreement. Arbitration of Disputes sets forth the terms of the arbitration agreement, including the lack of right to discovery. Although the mediation is non-binding, the arbitration will result in a binding decision made by a neutral arbitrator, with no appeal rights.

Mediation is not binding, but arbitration is a binding decision with no right to appeal.

C. ADDITIONAL MEDIATION AND ARBITRATION TERMS:
(1) EXCLUSIONS: The following matters are excluded from mediation and arbitration: (i) a judicial or non-judicial foreclosure or other action or proceeding to enforce a deed of trust, mortgage or installment land sale contract as defined in Civil Code §2985; (ii) an unlawful detainer action; and (iii) any matter that is within the jurisdiction of a probate, small claims or bankruptcy court.
(2) PRESERVATION OF ACTIONS: The following shall not constitute a waiver nor violation of the mediation and arbitration provisions: (i)The filing of a court action to enable the recording of a notice of pending action, for order of attachment, receivership, injunction, or other provisional remedies; or (ii) the filing of a mechanic's lien.
(3) BROKERS: Brokers shall not be obligated nor compelled to mediate or arbitrate unless they agree to do so in writing. Any Broker(s) participating in mediation or arbitration shall not be deemed a party to this Agreement.

C. Additional Mediation and Arbitration Terms

(1) Exclusions – sets forth the matters which are excluded from mediation and arbitration.

(2) Preservation of Actions – The filing of a court action to enable the recording of a notice of pending action or the filing of a mechanic's lien do not constitute a waiver nor violation of the mediation and arbitration provisions.

(3) Brokers – sets forth the agreement of the Buyer and Seller to mediate and arbitrate claims involving the broker(s), if they agree within a reasonable time after the claim is made. It's important for all parties to be aware that they are giving up their rights to appeal and other rights.

The Broker should never advise either the Seller or the Buyer whether to initial the arbitration provision in Paragraph 22B. Never give legal or tax advice.

> **23. SELECTION OF SERVICE PROVIDERS:** Brokers do not guarantee the performance of any vendors, service or product providers ("Providers"), whether referred by Broker or selected by Buyer, Seller or other person. Buyer and Seller may select ANY Providers of their own choosing.

23. SELECTION OF SERVICE PROVIDERS

START - PAGE 9 OF 10

Service providers may be selected by the Seller and the Buyer, but the Broker does not guarantee their performance.

> **24. MULTIPLE LISTING SERVICE ("MLS"):** Brokers are authorized to report to the MLS a pending sale and, upon Close Of Escrow, the sales price and other terms of this transaction shall be provided to the MLS to be published and disseminated to persons and entities authorized to use the information on terms approved by the MLS.

24. MULTIPLE LISTING SERVICE (MLS)

The parties authorized to report the price, terms, and financing to authorized persons and entities.

> **25. ATTORNEY FEES:** In any action, proceeding, or arbitration between Buyer and Seller arising out of this Agreement, the prevailing Buyer or Seller shall be entitled to reasonable attorney fees and costs from the non-prevailing Buyer or Seller, except as provided in paragraph 22A.

25. ATTORNEY FEES

This paragraph relates to disputes between only the Buyer and the Seller. Under this paragraph, the prevailing party is entitled to attorney's fees from the non-prevailing party in any arbitration or court action. But if a party initiates an arbitration or court action without first attempting to mediate the dispute under Paragraph 22A, that party is not entitled to attorney's fees even if he or she is the prevailing party. **This is very important and should stand out!**

> **26. ASSIGNMENT:** Buyer shall not assign all or any part of Buyer's interest in this Agreement without first having obtained the separate written consent of Seller to a specified assignee. Such consent shall not be unreasonably withheld. Any total or partial assignment shall not relieve Buyer of Buyer's obligations pursuant to this Agreement unless otherwise agreed in writing by Seller.

26. ASSIGNMENT

The Buyer shall not assign all or any part of the Buyer's interest in the Agreement without having obtained the separate written consent of the Seller to a specified assignee.

---

27. EQUAL HOUSING OPPORTUNITY: The Property is sold in compliance with federal, state and local anti-discrimination Laws.

---

27. EQUAL HOUSING OPPORTUNITY

It is illegal to discriminate on the basis of race, color, religion, sex, handicap, familial status, or national origin under both Federal and California law.

---

28. TERMS AND CONDITIONS OF OFFER:
This is an offer to purchase the Property on the above terms and conditions. The liquidated damages paragraph or the arbitration of disputes paragraph is incorporated in this Agreement if initialed by all Parties or if incorporated by mutual agreement in a counter offer or addendum. If at least one but not all Parties initial, a counter offer is required until agreement is reached. Seller has the right to continue to offer the Property for sale and to accept any other offer at any time prior to notification of Acceptance. The Parties have read and acknowledge receipt of a Copy of the offer and agree to the confirmation of agency relationships. If this offer is accepted and Buyer subsequently defaults, Buyer may be responsible for payment of Brokers' compensation. This Agreement and any supplement, addendum or modification, including any Copy, may be Signed in two or more counterparts, all of which shall constitute one and the same writing.

---

28. TERMS AND CONDITIONS OF OFFER

This paragraph provides that the agreement is an offer to purchase property on the terms and conditions set forth in the agreement.

The terms of paragraphs with spaces for initials by both Parties are incorporated into the agreement only if initialed by all Parties. If all Parties have not initialed those paragraphs, a counter offer is required because a Party has not accepted the offer exactly as written.

Remember: To be enforceable, a contract must be accepted by all parties in its entirety.

---

29. TIME OF ESSENCE; ENTIRE CONTRACT; CHANGES: Time is of the essence. All understandings between the Parties are incorporated in this Agreement. Its terms are intended by the Parties as a final, complete and exclusive expression of their Agreement with respect to its subject matter, and may not be contradicted by evidence of any prior agreement or contemporaneous oral agreement. If any provision of this Agreement is held to be ineffective or invalid, the remaining provisions will nevertheless be given full force and effect. Except as otherwise specified, this Agreement shall be interpreted and disputes shall be resolved in accordance with the Laws of the State of California. **Neither this Agreement nor any provision in it may be extended, amended, modified, altered or changed, except in writing Signed by Buyer and Seller.**

---

29. TIME OF ESSENCE; ENTIRE CONTRACT; CHANGES

The Buyer and Seller agree that any act must take place on the time and date stated in the agreement. Any changes to the agreement must be in writing. Evidence of any prior oral agreements may not be used to contradict the written terms of this agreement.

This agreement incorporates all prior oral and written agreements.

30. **DEFINITIONS:** As used in this Agreement:
   A. **"Acceptance"** means the time the offer or final counter offer is accepted in writing by a Party and is delivered to and personally received by the other Party or that Party's authorized agent in accordance with the terms of this offer or a final counter offer.
   B. **"Agreement"** means this document and any incorporated addenda, counter offers and written terms Signed by all Parties collectively forming the binding agreement between the Parties. All terms and conditions of any addenda checked and Signed are incorporated into this Agreement.
   C. **"C.A.R. Form"** means the most current version of the specific form referenced or another comparable form agreed to by the parties.
   D. **"Close Of Escrow"**, including **"COE"**, means the date the grant deed, or other evidence of transfer of title, is recorded.
   E. **"Copy"** means copy by any means including photocopy, NCR, facsimile and electronic.
   F. **"Days"** means calendar days. However, after Acceptance, the last Day for performance of any act required by this Agreement (including Close Of Escrow) shall not include any Saturday, Sunday, or legal holiday and shall instead be the next Day.
   G. **"Days After"** means the specified number of calendar days after the occurrence of the event specified, not counting the calendar date on which the specified event occurs, and ending at 11:59 PM on the final day.
   H. **"Days Prior"** means the specified number of calendar days before the occurrence of the event specified, not counting the calendar date on which the specified event is scheduled to occur.
   I. **"Deliver"**, **"Delivered"** or **"Delivery"**, unless otherwise specified in writing, means and shall be effective upon: personal receipt by Buyer or Seller or the individual Real Estate Licensee for that principal as specified in the section titled Real Estate Brokers on page 10, regardless of the method used (i.e., messenger, mail, email, fax, other).
   J. **"Electronic Copy"** or **"Electronic Signature"** means, as applicable, an electronic copy or signature complying with California Law. Buyer and Seller agree that electronic means will not be used by either Party to modify or alter the content or integrity of this Agreement without the knowledge and consent of the other Party.
   K. **"Law"** means any law, code, statute, ordinance, regulation, rule or order, which is adopted by a controlling city, county, state or federal legislative, judicial or executive body or agency.
   L. **"Repairs"** means any repairs (including pest control), alterations, replacements, modifications or retrofitting of the Property provided for under this Agreement.
   M. **"Signed"** means either a handwritten or electronic signature on an original document, Copy or any counterpart.

30. DEFINITIONS

This paragraph defines certain terms for the purpose of the Agreement. For purposes of calendaring time periods, the definitions of "Days," "Days after," and "Days prior" should be reviewed.

31. **EXPIRATION OF OFFER:** This offer shall be deemed revoked and the deposit, if any, shall be returned to Buyer unless the offer is Signed by Seller and a Copy of the Signed offer is personally received by Buyer, or by _____Carmen Caro_____, who is authorized to receive it, by 5:00 PM on the third Day after this offer is signed by Buyer (or by ☐ _____ ☐AM/☐PM, on _____(date)).
☐ One or more Buyers is signing this Agreement in a representative capacity and not for him/herself as an individual. See attached Representative Capacity Signature Addendum (C.A.R. Form RCSA) for additional terms.

Date June 14, 2020   BUYER *Walter Buyer*
(Print name) Walter Buyer

Date June 14, 2020   BUYER *Debbie Buyer*
(Print name) Debbie Buyer

☐ Additional Signature Addendum attached (C.A.R. Form ASA).

31. EXPIRATION OF OFFER

This provision specifies who is authorized to receive the Seller's acceptance on behalf of the Buyer, and how long the offer will remain open. It specifies that the Buyer (or authorized person) must personally receive the acceptance by a certain time and date.

32. ACCEPTANCE OF OFFER: Seller warrants that Seller is the owner of the Property, or has the authority to execute this Agreement. Seller accepts the above offer, agrees to sell the Property on the above terms and conditions. Seller has read and acknowledges receipt of a Copy of this Agreement, and authorizes Broker to Deliver a Signed Copy to Buyer.

☐ (If checked) SELLER'S ACCEPTANCE IS **SUBJECT TO ATTACHED COUNTER OFFER (C.A.R. Form SCO or SMCO) DATED:**
_____

☐   One or more Sellers is signing this Agreement in a representative capacity and not for him/herself as an individual. See attached Representative Capacity Signature Addendum (C.A.R. Form RCSA) for additional terms.

Date June 15, 2020   SELLER *Tony Seller*_____

(Print name) Tony Seller_____

Date June 15, 2020   SELLER *Ramona J. Seller*_____

(Print name) Ramona J. Seller_____

☐   Additional Signature Addendum attached (C.A.R. Form ASA).

(*WB* / *DB*)   (Do not initial if making a counter offer.) **CONFIRMATION OF ACCEPTANCE:** A Copy of Signed Acceptance was
(Initials)   personally received by Buyer or Buyer's authorized agent on (date) ___June 15, 2020___ at __11:59__
☐AM/☑PM. **A binding Agreement is created when a Copy of Signed Acceptance is personally received by Buyer or Buyer's authorized agent whether or not confirmed in this document. Completion of this confirmation is not legally required in order to create a binding Agreement; it is solely intended to evidence the date that Confirmation of Acceptance has occurred.**

32. ACCEPTANCE OF OFFER

The Seller warrants that he or she has authority to sell the property, agrees to the confirmation of agency relationships set forth in Paragraph 2B, and authorizes the Broker to deliver the signed contract to the Buyer to create a valid acceptance.

Seller's Signature Section – The Seller acknowledges the following by signing the agreement:

(1) Acceptance of the exact terms and conditions of the offer.
(2) Agreement to sell the property.
(3) Agreement with the agency confirmation.

Confirmation of Acceptance – A contract is formed when the Seller's acceptance is personally received by the Buyer or the Buyer's authorized agent. This paragraph provides written evidence of the date of acceptance.

REAL ESTATE BROKERS:
A.   Real Estate Brokers are not parties to the Agreement between Buyer and Seller.
B.   Agency relationships are confirmed as stated in paragraph 2.
C.   If specified in paragraph 3A(2), Agent who submitted the offer for Buyer acknowledges receipt of deposit.
D.   **COOPERATING BROKER COMPENSATION:** Listing Broker agrees to pay Cooperating Broker **(Selling Firm)** and Cooperating Broker agrees to accept, out of Listing Broker's proceeds in escrow, the amount specified in the MLS, provided Cooperating Broker is a Participant of the MLS in which the Property is offered for sale or a reciprocal MLS. If Listing Broker and Cooperating Broker are not both Participants of the MLS, or a reciprocal MLS, in which the Property is offered for sale, then compensation must be specified in a separate written agreement (C.A.R. Form CBC). Declaration of License and Tax (C.A.R. Form DLT) may be used to document that tax reporting will be required or that an exemption exists.

Real Estate Broker (Selling Firm) Ramos Realty   CalBRE Lic. # 00 000 000
By *Joseph Ramos*   Joseph Ramos CalBRE Lic. # 00 000 00   Date 06/14/2020
By_____   CalBRE Lic. #_____   Date_____
Address 777 Newport Blvd.   City Newport Beach   State CA   Zip 92663
Telephone (714) 647-0000   Fax (714) 647-0001   E-mail jr@ramosrealty.realtor
Real Estate Broker (Listing Firm) Sail Realty   CalBRE Lic. # 00 000 000
By *Carmen Caro*   Carmen Caro CalBRE Lic. # 00 000 000   Date 6/14/2020
By_____   CalBRE Lic. #_____   Date_____
Address   227 Harbor Blvd.   City Costa Mesa   State CA   Zip 92627
Telephone (714) 626-2828   Fax (714) 626-2829   E-mail carmen@sailrealty.realtor

REAL ESTATE BROKERS (Signature Section)

In this paragraph the Listing and Selling Brokers acknowledge that:

A. The Brokers are not parties to the agreement.

B. The agency relationships stated in Paragraph 2 are confirmed.

C. The Buyer's agent's receipt of the deposit if he/she is designated in Paragraph 3A(2).

D. Listing Broker's agreement to pay cooperating broker compensation.

ESCROW HOLDER ACKNOWLEDGMENT:

Escrow Holder acknowledges receipt of a Copy of this Agreement, (if checked, ☐ a deposit in the amount of $ _____),

counter offer numbers _____ ☐ Seller's Statement of Information and _____

_____ , and agrees to act as Escrow Holder subject to paragraph 20 of this Agreement, any supplemental escrow instructions and the terms of Escrow Holder's general provisions.

Escrow Holder is advised that the date of Confirmation of Acceptance of the Agreement as between Buyer and Seller is _____

Escrow Holder _____ Escrow # _____
By _____ Date _____
Address _____
Phone/Fax/E-mail _____
Escrow Holder has the following license number # _____
☐ Department of Business Oversight, ☐ Department of Insurance, ☐ Bureau of Real Estate.

PRESENTATION OF OFFER: (_____) Listing Broker presented this offer to Seller on _____ (date).
Broker or Designee Initials

REJECTION OF OFFER: (_____)(_____) No counter offer is being made. This offer was rejected by Seller on _____ (date).
Seller's Initials

ESCROW HOLDER ACKNOWLEDGEMENT

The Escrow Holder acknowledges receipt of the contract and agrees to act as escrow holder.

PRESENTATION OF OFFER

Listing Broker presents offer to Seller.

REJECTION OF OFFER

Seller rejects offer with no counter offer.

> *It's important for the sellers and brokers to initial/sign the "Rejection of Offer" to eliminate any concerns regarding the offer not having been presented.*

III. CHAPTER SUMMARY

A **contingency** is a condition which calls for anything to be a requirement before the performance or completion of something else. The usual contingencies are financial qualifications or rate, appraisal amounts, inspections and requirements that are required to be completed by certain times. If a contingency is not satisfied or not met, the purchase contract agreement can be terminated. In any case, if the parties are willing, the contract may be renegotiated.

Most transactions for the purchase and sale of real estate in California involve the sellers and buyers entering into a **legal contractual arrangement**. Commonly referred to as the **Purchase Agreement** or the **Purchase Contract**, the most frequently used contract is the CAR® form **California Residential Purchase Agreement and Joint Escrow Instructions**. Intended to be a legally binding contract (not just a preliminary agreement), it's imperative that it is filled out accurately, read carefully, and signed by all parties.

Written or typed-in instructions supersede (take precedence over) the preprinted terms of the form. Specific provisions ordinarily qualify the meaning of general provisions, should inconsistencies arise.

When filling out the form, **write out dates** rather than using numbers. Strive for simplicity in language, as both buyer and seller must clearly understand the terms of the contract.

The specific amount of **Liquidated Damages** might be agreed to (in advance) and stated in the Residential Purchase Agreement contract, determining how much money will be paid for not fulfilling a clause or condition in the contract (breach of contract).

Seller financing, **secondary financing**, and/or **assumption** require an **addendum** that must be attached to the agreement.

If the **appraisal or appraisals** don't come in at or above the specified purchase price, a buyer applying for an 80% loan is usually released from further obligation. Sellers/buyers may choose to renegotiate the selling price.

It's possible that a tenant with a **valid lease** may remain in possession after the sale of a property.

To avoid a **buyer's right to cancel**, all **disclosures** must be **acknowledged** as promptly as possible within the agreed upon time frame.

Mediation of disputes is required whether the parties (buyers, sellers, or brokers) agree to arbitrate or not! **Mediation** is an attempt by the parties to agree to resolve the dispute informally with a third person mediator, who assists them, but does not make a binding decision.

If the parties do agree to arbitrate, they give up the right to a jury trial, discovery, and appeal, unless those rights are specifically included in the agreement. **Arbitration** is an attempt by the parties to resolve the dispute with a neutral judge or attorney, who makes a binding decision.

Agents must never offer advice concerning how title should be taken or price to be offered.

IV. MATCHING VOCABULARY Fill in the blanks with the correct letter

A. Allocation of termite costs
B. CE + 3
C. Cancellation rights (Buyer and Seller)
D. Initial deposit
E. Joint escrow instructions
F. Lead-based paint notice
G. Liquidated damages
H. Offer

I. Policy of title insurance
J. Purchase agreement (residential)
K. Seller-fianancing addendum
L. Statutory disclosures
M. Three business days after offer acceptance
N. Title and vesting
O. Written or typed word

1. _____ The sum of money, agreed to in advance and stated in the contract, that will be paid if a clause or condition in the contract is breached.

2. _____ The policy issued after the title insurance company conducts its title search.

3. _____ Takes precedence over all other preprinted instructions on a real estate document.

4. _____ This part of the form combines the Buyer's and Seller's instructions and sends them to the escrow holder for purchase of 1- to 4-residential units.

5. _____ Amount of time in which funds must be delivered as an initial escrow deposit.

6. _____ Earnest money deposit—usually a check given with the offer.

7. _____ Party who agrees to pay for inspections and reports.

8. _____ Buyer will take possession three days after the close of escrow.

9. _____ If the residential property was constructed before 1978, the seller must provide the Buyer with this notice.

10. _____ Buyer's or Seller's right to cancel the agreement if certain contigencies or time period requirements are not met.

11. _____ A written proposal to purchase real property for a specified sum.

12. _____ The written contract signed by both the Buyer and Seller of real property.

13. _____ Requires Seller to deliver these two mandated forms: 1) Transfer Disclosure Statement (TDS) and 2) Natural Hazard Disclosure Statement (NHD).

14. _____ The legal means of documenting the type of ownership interest in real property.

15. _____ In this type of agreement, the Seller helps to finance the purchase by giving the Buyer a trust deed loan on the property.

See Page 610 for Answers

V. CHAPTER QUIZ

1. In a typical residential real estate transaction, what types of questions must be addressed?

   a. Financing
   b. Possession
   c. Condition of title
   d. All of the above

2. In California, who customarily conducts the title search, prepares preliminary reports, and issues policies of title insurance?

   a. Title insurance company
   b. Escrow company
   c. Real estate agent
   d. None of the above

3. The California Residential Purchase Agreement and Joint Escrow Instructions is also commonly referred to as the:

   a. purchase agreement.
   b. purchase contract.
   c. listing agreement.
   d. both a and b.

4. When interpreting the completed purchase agreement contract:

   a. the handwritten word takes precedence over the preprinted words.
   b. the preprinted words take precedence over the written words.
   c. a lawyer must fill in the written words to be legal.
   d. none of the above.

5. When there are inconsistencies between general provisions and specific provisions:

   a. the general provisions ordinarily qualify the meaning of the specific provisions.
   b. the broker could lose his or her license.
   c. specific provisions will be ignored.
   d. the specific provisions ordinarily qualify the meaning of the general provisions.

6. When filling out the date at the top of the purchase agreement contract, it's important to:

   a. use digits, like 02/04/20.
   b. use words and full dates, like February 2, 2020.
   c. postdate the form to cover any oversights.
   d. none of the above.

7. The sum of money, agreed to in advance and stated in the purchase agreement contract, that will be paid for not fulfilling a clause or condition in the contract, is called:

   a. solid damages.

   b. soft damages.

   c. liquidated damages.

   d. none of the above.

8. If a buyer applies for an 80% loan and the appraisal does not come at or above the specified purchase price:

   a. the buyer will still have to go through with the purchase.

   b. the buyer "may" be released from obligation or renegotiate price.

   c. the seller must get a new appraisal.

   d. none of the above.

9. In the closing and occupancy section of the purchase agreement contract, the words "CE+3" mean:

   a. the buyer will take possession 3 days after the close of escrow.

   b. the seller will make a counter offer 3 days after the creation of escrow.

   c. the buyer will take possession 2 days from closing of escrow.

   d. none of the above.

10. Which of the following is true concerning wood-destroying pest inspection?

   a. Termite clearance is not mandated by law, it's usually a lender's requirement.

   b. Who pays for the inspection is negotiable.

   c. Section one refers to actual termite inspection and section two, to conditions that may allow for termite inspection.

   d. All of the above.

ANSWERS: 1. d; 2. a; 3. d; 4. a; 5. d; 6. b; 7. c; 8. b; 9. a; 10. d

IT'S ALL

5 times faster *than previous versions*
and **mobile responsive.**

Special

»Obeo
Property
Website

CLARUS ▲ CONNECT®

We Personally Take Care of
All Your Social Media Needs

With Clarus Connect™ Concierge Service our team of social marketing
experts will create and manage your social media, so you can focus on
your real estate business.

What Concierge Service will do for you:

Kick-Off Call -
In a 30 minute call
your Concierge will:
- Provide an overview
- Understand and learn your
  business
- Plan your first campaign
- Discuss next steps

Account Set Up -
Over the next week,
your Concierge will:
- Create or optimize your
  social media profiles
- Upload and add your contacts
  and business information

Launch Call -
It's time to launch!
Your Concierge will:
- Get your feedback and approval

Ongoing Management
We don't stop! After launch,
your Concierge will continue to:
- Regularly post engaging content
- Advise on growing fans and followers
- Track and learn for success
- Run Facebook Ads
  (Optional, additional fees apply)
- Call or email your Concierge at
  any time

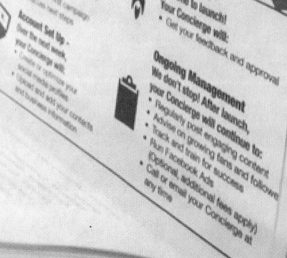

3 Things You Can
Do Today for Results

Additional Forms for the Purchase Agreement: More Required Forms and Disclosures

I. Forms Supplied to the Buyer

Congratulations! Your buyer and seller have agreed on the price and terms of the property and the Purchase Agreement contract has been completed, accepted by the parties, and communicated back to the buyer. Still, you do not yet have a binding transaction until all the seller's disclosures have been approved by the buyer! Even then, a legally binding contract is not completed until all contingencies have been removed (like getting financing, buyer is unconditionally qualified, physical inspections, and requested repairs complied with).

To have a binding transaction: 1) All seller disclosures must be approved by the buyer and 2) All contigencies must be removed.

A. LIST OF FORMS

The following is a list of most CAR® forms you will supply your buyer. Some will not apply:

1. Commission Agreement (CA) (**Figure 7-1**)

2. California Residential Purchase Agreement and Joint Escrow Instructions (RPA-CA) (See Chapter 6, **Figure 6-1**)

3. Estimated Buyer Costs (EBC) (**Figure 7-2**)

4. Contingency for Sale or Purchase of Other Property (COP) (**Figure 7-3**)

5. Real Estate Transfer Disclosure Statement (TDS) (**Figure 7-4**) (Seller and Agents must fill in)

6. Buyer's Inspection Advisory (BIA-A) (**Figure 7-5**)

7. Buyer's Inspection Waiver (BIW) (**Figure 7-6**)

CHAPTER 7

8. Wood Destroying Pest Inspection and Allocation of Cost Addendum
   (WPA) (**Figure 7-7**)

9. Counter Offer (CO) (**Figure 7-8**)

10. Listing Kit (See Chapter 4, page 108)

Buyers are to approve all the seller's disclosures as quickly as possible to insure a binding contract.

11. Buyer's Affidavit (AB) (FIRPTA Compliance) (**Figure 7-9**)

12. Request for Repair (RR) (**Figure 7-10**)

13. Receipt for Reports (RFR) (**Figure 7-11**)

14. Contingency Removal (CR) (**Figure 7-12**)

15. Notice to Seller to Perform (NSP) (**Figure 7-13**)

16. Notice to Buyer to Perform (NBP) (**Figure 7-14**)

17. Verification of Property Condition (VP) (**Figure 7-15**)

18. Carbon Monoxide Detector Notice (CMD) (**Figure 7-16**)

19. Statewide Buyer and Seller Advisory (SBSA) (**Figure 7-17**)

20. Home Warranty Waiver (See Chapter 4, **Figure 4-6**)

Figure 7-1

CALIFORNIA
ASSOCIATION
OF REALTORS®

COMMISSION AGREEMENT
(C.A.R. Form CA, Revised 11/12)

1. COMPENSATION: Notice: The amount or rate of real estate commissions is not fixed by law. They are set by each broker individually and may be negotiable between the Seller/Buyer/Landlord/Tenant/Optionor/Optionee ("Principal") and Broker.

_____ ("Principal"),
agrees to pay to _____ , ("Broker(s)"),
as compensation for services, irrespective of agency relationships, the sum of either ☐ _____ percent of the transaction price, or
☐ _____
Dollars ($ _____), for property situated in the City of _____*Marina del Rey*_____ , County of
_____ , California, described as _____*123 Sail Avenue*_____
Compensation is payable if Principal accepts an offer on the above described property no later than _____ (date) as follows: **(i)** On recordation of the deed or other evidence of title or, if a lease, on execution of the lease, or if an option, on execution of the option agreement; or **(ii)** If completion of the transaction is prevented by default of Principal, then upon such default; or **(iii)** If completion of the transaction is prevented by a party to the transaction other than Principal, then only if and when Principal collects damages by suit, settlement, or otherwise, and then in an amount equal to the lesser of one-half of the damages recovered, or the above compensation, after first deducting title and escrow expenses and the expenses of collection, if any. Broker may cooperate with other brokers, and divide with other brokers such compensation in any manner acceptable to Broker. Principal hereby irrevocably assigns to Broker the above compensation from Principal's funds and proceeds in escrow.

2. ATTORNEY FEES: In any action, proceeding, or arbitration between Principal and Broker(s) arising out of this Agreement, the prevailing party shall be entitled to reasonable attorney fees and costs.

3. DISPUTE RESOLUTION:

A. **MEDIATION:** Principal and Broker agree to mediate any dispute or claim arising between them out of this Agreement, or any resulting transaction, before resorting to arbitration or court action. Mediation fees, if any, shall be divided equally among the parties involved. If, for any dispute or claim to which this paragraph applies, any party (i) commences an action without first attempting to resolve the matter through mediation, or (ii) before commencement of an action, refuses to mediate after a request has been made, then that party shall not be entitled to recover attorney fees, even if they would otherwise be available to that party in any such action. THIS MEDIATION PROVISION APPLIES WHETHER OR NOT THE ARBITRATION PROVISION IS INITIALED. **Exclusions from this mediation agreement are specified in paragraph 3C.**

B. **ARBITRATION OF DISPUTES:**
Principal and Broker agree that any dispute or claim in Law or equity arising between them out of this Agreement or any resulting transaction, which is not settled through mediation, shall be decided by neutral, binding arbitration. The arbitrator shall be a retired judge or justice, or an attorney with at least 5 years of residential real estate Law experience, unless the parties mutually agree to a different arbitrator. The parties shall have the right to discovery in accordance with Code of Civil Procedure §1283.05. In all other respects, the arbitration shall be conducted in accordance with Title 9 of Part 3 of the Code of Civil Procedure. Judgment upon the award of the arbitrator(s) may be entered into any court having jurisdiction. Enforcement of this agreement to arbitrate shall be governed by the Federal Arbitration Act. Exclusions from this arbitration agreement are specified in paragraph 3C.
"NOTICE: BY INITIALING IN THE SPACE BELOW YOU ARE AGREEING TO HAVE ANY DISPUTE ARISING OUT OF THE MATTERS INCLUDED IN THE 'ARBITRATION OF DISPUTES' PROVISION DECIDED BY NEUTRAL ARBITRATION AS PROVIDED BY CALIFORNIA LAW AND YOU ARE GIVING UP ANY RIGHTS YOU MIGHT POSSESS TO HAVE THE DISPUTE LITIGATED IN A COURT OR JURY TRIAL. BY INITIALING IN THE SPACE BELOW YOU ARE GIVING UP YOUR JUDICIAL RIGHTS TO DISCOVERY AND APPEAL, UNLESS THOSE RIGHTS ARE SPECIFICALLY INCLUDED IN THE 'ARBITRATION OF DISPUTES' PROVISION. IF YOU REFUSE TO SUBMIT TO ARBITRATION AFTER AGREEING TO THIS PROVISION, YOU MAY BE COMPELLED TO ARBITRATE UNDER THE AUTHORITY OF THE CALIFORNIA CODE OF CIVIL PROCEDURE. YOUR AGREEMENT TO THIS ARBITRATION PROVISION IS VOLUNTARY."
"WE HAVE READ AND UNDERSTAND THE FOREGOING AND AGREE TO SUBMIT DISPUTES ARISING OUT OF THE MATTERS INCLUDED IN THE 'ARBITRATION OF DISPUTES' PROVISION TO NEUTRAL ARBITRATION."

Principal's Initials _____ / _____   Broker's Initials _____ / _____

C. **ADDITIONAL MEDIATION AND ARBITRATION TERMS:** The following matters shall be excluded from mediation and arbitration: (i) a judicial or non-judicial foreclosure or other action or proceeding to enforce a deed of trust, mortgage or installment land sale contract as defined in Civil Code §2985; (ii) an unlawful detainer action; (iii) the filing or enforcement of a mechanic's lien; and (iv) any matter that is within the jurisdiction of a probate, small claims or bankruptcy court. The filing of a court action to enable the recording of a notice of pending action, for order of attachment, receivership, injunction, or other provisional remedies, shall not constitute a waiver or violation of the mediation and arbitration provisions.

4. OTHER TERMS AND CONDITIONS: _____

Principal has read and acknowledges receipt of a copy of this Agreement.
Principal _____   Principal _____

_____   _____
(Print name)   (Print name)
Address _____   Address _____

_____   _____
Date _____ Phone/Fax/Email _____   Date _____ Phone/Fax/Email _____
Real Estate Broker agrees to the foregoing:
Broker _____   By _____ Date _____
BRE Lic. # _____

The copyright laws of the United States (Title 17 U.S. Code) forbid the unauthorized reproduction of this form by any means, including facsimile or computerized formats. Copyright © 1986-2012, CALIFORNIA ASSOCIATION OF REALTORS® Inc. All Rights Reserved
THIS FORM HAS BEEN APPROVED BY THE CALIFORNIA ASSOCIATION OF REALTORS® (C.A.R.). NO REPRESENTATION IS MADE AS TO THE LEGAL VALIDITY OR ADEQUACY OF ANY PROVISION IN ANY SPECIFIC TRANSACTION. A REAL ESTATE BROKER IS THE PERSON QUALIFIED TO ADVISE ON REAL ESTATE TRANSACTIONS. IF YOU DESIRE LEGAL OR TAX ADVICE, CONSULT AN APPROPRIATE PROFESSIONAL.
This form is available for use by the entire real estate industry. It is not intended to identify the user as a REALTOR®. REALTOR® is a registered collective membership mark which may be used only by members of the NATIONAL ASSOCIATION OF REALTORS® who subscribe to its Code of Ethics.

Published and Distributed by:
REAL ESTATE BUSINESS SERVICES, INC.
a subsidiary of the California Association of REALTORS®
525 South Virgil Avenue, Los Angeles, California 90020
CA REVISED 11/12 (PAGE 1 OF 1)

Reviewed by _____ Date _____

COMMISSION AGREEMENT (CA PAGE 1 OF 1)

Agent: WALT HUBER	Phone:	Fax:	Prepared using zipForm® software
Broker: WALT HUBER REALTOR			

Figure 7-2

ESTIMATED BUYER COSTS
(C.A.R. Form EBC, Revised 4/06)

CALIFORNIA ASSOCIATION OF REALTORS®

BUYER: _____ DATE: _____

PROPERTY ADDRESS: 123 Sail Avenue, Marina del Rey CA 90292

PROJECTED CLOSING DATE: _____ PROJECTED PURCHASE PRICE: $ _____

New First Loan: $_____ Rate:_____% ☐ Fixed or ☐ Adjustable ☐ Interest Only Term:_____years

New Second Loan: $_____ Rate:_____% ☐ Fixed or ☐ Adjustable ☐ Interest Only Term:_____years

Current Annual Property Taxes: $_____ Rate:_____% If Rented, Current Monthly Rent $_____

FINANCING CHARGES		**ESTIMATED CREDITS**	
New First Loan Origination Fee/Points _____% $_____		Prorated Property Taxes # Days_____ $_____	
Secondary Financing Orig. Fee/Points _____% $_____		Prorated Rents # Days_____ $_____	
Prepaid Interest (First Loan) # Days_____ $_____		Tenant Security Deposits $_____	
Prepaid Interest (Secondary Financing) # Days_____ $_____		Credit from Seller $_____	
Impounds: - Property Taxes # Months_____ $_____		Other _____ $_____	
- Insurance # Months_____ $_____		**Total Estimated Credits** $_____	
Processing/Underwriting Fees $_____		**ESTIMATED CASH NEEDED TO CLOSE**	
Document Preparation Fees $_____		Purchase Price $_____	
Appraisal Fees $_____		LESS Total Loans -_____	
Funding Fees $_____		Down Payment =_____	
Other Lender Fees (Tax Service, Flood Certificates, etc.) $_____		PLUS Total Estimated Expenses +_____	

ESCROW AND TITLE CHARGES

LESS Total Estimated Credits -_____

Escrow Fee ☐ including any Sub-Escrow Fee $_____ LESS Initial Deposits -_____

Owner's Title Insurance Policy $_____ **Est. Cash Needed to Close Escrow** $_____

Lender's Title Insurance Policy $_____

Document Preparation, Recording, Notary & other Fees $_____

OTHER EXPENSES & PRORATIONS

ESTIMATED MONTHLY PAYMENTS	
Prorated Property Taxes # Days_____ $_____	New First Loan* $_____
Homeowners Dues _____ # Days_____ $_____	Secondary Financing* $_____
Transfer Tax (if charged to Buyer) Rate per $1,000 $_____ $_____	New Property Taxes $_____
Buyer Brokerage Fee $_____	Insurance (ex. flood & earthquake) $_____
Annual Insurance Premium (excluding flood & earthquake) $_____	Mortgage Insurance $_____
Home Warranty Program $_____	Homeowners Dues $_____
Wood-Destroying Pest Inspection $_____	Mello Roos $_____
Other Physical Inspection Fees _____ $_____	Other $_____
HOA Transfer and/or Move-In Fees $_____	**Total Estimated Payment** $_____
Other _____ $_____	
_____ $_____	

* Buyer is aware that with regard to adjustable rate loans, the monthly payments may increase at various times over the life of the loan. Buyer should confirm directly with lenders all terms and conditions of said loans.

TOTAL ESTIMATED EXPENSES $_____

This estimate, based upon the above proposed purchase price, type of financing and projected closing date, has been prepared to assist Buyer in computing costs. Amounts will vary depending upon differences between actual and estimated repairs that may occur in the transaction, assessments, liens, impound accounts, charges by lenders, escrow companies, title insurers and other service providers and other items. Not all liens may yet have been identified. Neither Broker nor Agent guarantee these figures represent the actual, or only, amounts and charges.
By signing below Buyer acknowledges that Buyer has read, understands and received a copy of this Estimated Buyer's Costs.

Buyer _____ Date_____

Buyer _____ Date_____

Real Estate Broker (Firm) _____ DRE Lic. # _____

By (Agent) _____ DRE Lic. # _____ Date_____

Address _____ City _____ State____ Zip _____

Telephone _____ Fax _____ E-mail _____

The copyright laws of the United States (Title 17 U.S. Code) forbid the unauthorized reproduction of this form, or any portion thereof, by photocopy machine or any other means, including facsimile or computerized formats. Copyright © 1988-2006, CALIFORNIA ASSOCIATION OF REALTORS®, INC. ALL RIGHTS RESERVED.
THIS FORM HAS BEEN APPROVED BY THE CALIFORNIA ASSOCIATION OF REALTORS® (C.A.R.). NO REPRESENTATION IS MADE AS TO THE LEGAL VALIDITY OR ADEQUACY OF ANY PROVISION IN ANY SPECIFIC TRANSACTION. A REAL ESTATE BROKER IS THE PERSON QUALIFIED TO ADVISE ON REAL ESTATE TRANSACTIONS. IF YOU DESIRE LEGAL OR TAX ADVICE, CONSULT AN APPROPRIATE PROFESSIONAL.
This form is available for use by the entire real estate industry. It is not intended to identify the user as a REALTOR®. REALTOR® is a registered collective membership mark which may be used only by members of the NATIONAL ASSOCIATION OF REALTORS® who subscribe to its Code of Ethics.

Published and Distributed by:
REAL ESTATE BUSINESS SERVICES, INC.
a subsidiary of the California Association of REALTORS®
525 South Virgil Avenue, Los Angeles, California 90020

Reviewed by _____ Date _____

EQUAL HOUSING OPPORTUNITY

EBC REVISED 4/06 (PAGE 1 OF 1) **ESTIMATED BUYER COSTS (EBC PAGE 1 OF 1)**

Agent: WALT HUBER Phone: Fax: Prepared using zipForm® software
Broker: WALT HUBER REALTOR

The buyer needs to know the total costs of this purchase, including the monthly payments, before making the offer. This is an estimate you calculate working with the lender and various affiliates involved in the transaction, such as homeowner's insurance companies, home inspection providers, etc.

Figure 7-3

CALIFORNIA ASSOCIATION OF REALTORS®

CONTINGENCY FOR SALE OR PURCHASE OF OTHER PROPERTY
(C.A.R. Form COP, Revised 11/12)

This is an addendum to the ☐ California Residential Purchase Agreement, ☐ Counter Offer, ☐ Other _____
("Agreement"), dated _____
on property known as _____ 123 Sail Avenue, Marina del Rey, _____ ("Seller's Property"),
between _____ ("Buyer")
and _____ ("Seller").

A. ☐ **(If checked) SALE OF BUYER'S PROPERTY:**
1. **(a)** The Agreement is contingent on the close of escrow of Buyer's property, described as: _____
("Buyer's Property").
   (b) If Buyer's Property does not close escrow by the earliest of: **(i)** the scheduled close of escrow of Seller's Property; **(ii)** the date specified in paragraph A3; or **(iii)** Other ☐ _____ , then either Seller, after first giving Buyer a Notice to Buyer to Perform (C.A.R. Form NBP), or Buyer may cancel the Agreement in writing.
2. ☐ (If checked) Buyer's Property is **not** now in escrow and (check boxes as applicable):
   (a) ☐ is not yet listed for sale.
   (b) ☐ is listed for sale with _____ company and is offered for sale in the _____ MLS, # _____ .
   (c) Buyer shall, within **17 (or** ☐ _____ **) Days** After Acceptance, provide Seller with Copies of the contract, escrow instructions and all related documents ("Escrow Evidence") for the sale of Buyer's Property showing that Buyer's Property has entered escrow.
3. ☐ (If checked) Buyer's Property **is in escrow** with _____
   escrow holder, (escrow # _____) scheduled to close escrow on _____ (date).
   Buyer shall, within **5 Days** After Acceptance, deliver to Seller Escrow Evidence that Buyer's Property is in escrow.
4. If Buyer fails to provide to Seller Escrow Evidence within the time specified in A2(c) or A3, Seller, after first giving Buyer a Notice to Buyer to Perform, may cancel the Agreement in writing.
5. If Buyer's Property is in or enters escrow, Buyer shall give Seller written notice if either party to that escrow gives notice to the other of intent to cancel. If such notice is given **prior** to Buyer's removal of the contingency for sale of Buyer's Property, either Buyer or Seller may cancel the Agreement in writing. However, if such notice is given **after** Buyer has removed the contingency for sale of Buyer's Property only Seller shall have the option to cancel the Agreement under this paragraph, which cancellation must be in writing.
6. After Acceptance, Seller shall have the right to continue to offer Seller's Property for sale for Back-up Offers. If Seller accepts a written back-up offer:
   (a) Immediate Right to Notify Buyer to Remove Sale of Property Contingency: Seller shall have the right to immediately give written notice to Buyer to, in writing: **(i)** remove this contingency; **(ii)** remove the loan contingency, if any; **(iii)** provide verification of sufficient funds to close escrow without the sale of Buyer's Property; and **(iv)** comply with the following additional requirement(s): _____
   If Buyer fails to complete these actions within **3 (or** ☐ _____ **) Days** after receipt of such notice, Seller may then immediately cancel the Agreement in writing.
   OR (b) ☐ (If checked) **Delayed Right to Notify Buyer:** Seller shall not invoke the notice provisions in paragraph A6(a): **(i)** within the first **17 (or** ☐ _____ **) Days** After Acceptance, or **(ii)** (if checked) ☐ during the term of the Agreement.

B. ☐ (If checked) **SELLER'S PURCHASE OR REPLACEMENT PROPERTY:**
1. The Agreement is contingent on Seller entering a contract to acquire replacement property.
2. Seller shall, within **17 (or** ☐ _____ **) Days** After Acceptance, remove this contingency or cancel the Agreement. If Seller does not remove this contingency in writing within that time, Buyer, after giving Seller a Notice to Seller to Perform (C.A.R. Form NSP), may cancel the Agreement in writing.
3. **(a)** Time periods in the Agreement for inspections, contingencies, covenants and other obligations shall begin: **(i)** as specified in the Agreement; **(ii)** (if checked) ☐ the day after Seller delivers to Buyer a written notice removing this contingency; or **(iii)** (if checked) ☐ Other _____
   (b) Buyer and Seller agree that Seller may, by providing Buyer written notice at the time Seller removes this contingency, extend the Close Of Escrow date for a maximum of _____ additional Days or until ☐ _____ (date).
4. Even after the expiration of the time specified in B2, Seller retains, until Buyer cancels pursuant to B2, the right to remove in writing this contingency or cancel the Agreement. Once Buyer receives Seller's written removal of this contingency, Buyer may not cancel pursuant to B2.

By signing below, Buyer and Seller each acknowledge that they have read, understand, accept and have received a copy of this Addendum.

Date _____   Date _____
Buyer _____   Seller _____

Buyer _____   Seller _____

The copyright laws of the United States (TITLE 17 U.S. Code) forbid the unauthorized reproduction of this form by any means, including facsimile or computerized formats.
Copyright © 2008-2012, CALIFORNIA ASSOCIATION OF REALTORS® Inc. All Rights Reserved.
THIS FORM HAS BEEN APPROVED BY THE CALIFORNIA ASSOCIATION OF REALTORS® (C.A.R.). NO REPRESENTATION IS MADE AS TO THE LEGAL VALIDITY OR ADEQUACY OF ANY PROVISION IN ANY SPECIFIC TRANSACTION. A REAL ESTATE BROKER IS THE PERSON QUALIFIED TO ADVISE ON REAL ESTATE TRANSACTIONS. IF YOU DESIRE LEGAL OR TAX ADVICE, CONSULT AN APPROPRIATE PROFESSIONAL.
This form is available for use by the entire real estate industry. It is not intended to identify the user as a REALTOR®. REALTOR® is a registered collective membership mark which may be used only by members of the NATIONAL ASSOCIATION OF REALTORS® who subscribe to its Code of Ethics.

Published and Distributed by:
REAL ESTATE BUSINESS SERVICES, INC.
a subsidiary of the California Association of REALTORS®
525 South Virgil Avenue, Los Angeles, California 90020

Reviewed by _____ Date _____

COP 11/12 (PAGE 1 OF 1)   **CONTINGENCY FOR SALE OR PURCHASE OF OTHER PROPERTY (COP PAGE 1 OF 1)**

Agent: WALT HUBER   Phone: Fax: Prepared using zipForm® software
Broker: WALT HUBER REALTOR

All contingencies, including the sale of the buyer's property or the seller's purchase of a replacement property, should be noted in the appropriate sections of this form and become part of the Purchase Agreement, or any counter offer. Become familiar with this form as it contains several options on how to remove this contingency and the remedy, if the prescribed time constriction is not adhered to. Please note 6(a) additional instructions if appropriate.

B. REAL ESTATE TRANSFER DISCLOSURE STATEMENT (TDS) (Seller Must Provide This Form)

The law requires sellers of residential property of from one-to-four units (which includes triplexes) to provide prospective buyers with a Real Estate Transfer Disclosure Statement. (The TDS is the basis of many court cases.)

The **REAL ESTATE TRANSFER DISCLOSURE STATEMENT (TDS)** *identifies items of value attached to the structure or land and states whether these items are operational* (see **Figure 7-4**). It also asks the seller to identify any structural or material defects. This form provides an opportunity for the seller to completely disclose problems of any kind that might adversely affect the value or the desirability of the property. The obligation to prepare and deliver the Transfer Disclosure Statement to the prospective buyer is imposed upon **the seller and the seller's broker** (see Civil Code Section 1102.6 for exemptions).

A buyer has two years to sue an agent for failure to make proper disclosures in the Transfer Disclosure Statement. Make sure the seller and you disclose.

The following sequence of events may help explain how the four parties **(seller, seller's agent, buyer, and buyer's agent) fill in and sign the Transfer Disclosure Statement form:**

1. The Transfer Disclosure Statement form should be filled out and signed completely by the seller at the time of listing the property. Since the seller is the one most familiar with the property, he or she must be encouraged to be forthright and honest about all known defects.

2. The seller's agent makes a visual, diligent inspection of the property, fills out the appropriate section of the Transfer Disclosure Statement, and signs at the same time the seller lists the property for sale. (Never leave this section empty!)

The entire Real Estate Transfer Disclosure Statement needs to be completed by the seller who is legally responsible for identifying any structural or material defects.

3. The buyer, after making a written offer, should receive a copy of the Transfer Disclosure Statement and sign that he or she has received it.

4. The buyer's agent must also visually inspect the property, fill out the appropriate section of the statement, and sign it. **(Should not be empty!)**

5. If the buyer fails to receive the Transfer Disclosure Statement form prior to signing the contractual offer (purchase agreement), he or she has the right to cancel, after receipt of the Transfer Disclosure Statement, for any reason (three days if delivered by hand or five days if mailed). A written notice of termination must be delivered to the seller or to the seller's broker.

A "TDS" is required for an "as is" sale of a single-family residence by a private person.

Figure 7-4

CALIFORNIA ASSOCIATION OF REALTORS®

REAL ESTATE TRANSFER DISCLOSURE STATEMENT
(CALIFORNIA CIVIL CODE §1102, ET SEQ.)
(C.A.R. Form TDS, Revised 4/14)

THIS DISCLOSURE STATEMENT CONCERNS THE REAL PROPERTY SITUATED IN THE CITY OF
_____ , COUNTY OF _____ *Los Angeles* _____ , STATE OF CALIFORNIA,
DESCRIBED AS _____ *123 Sail Avenue, , 90292* _____ .
THIS STATEMENT IS A DISCLOSURE OF THE CONDITION OF THE ABOVE DESCRIBED PROPERTY IN
COMPLIANCE WITH SECTION 1102 OF THE CIVIL CODE AS OF (date) _____ . IT IS NOT A
WARRANTY OF ANY KIND BY THE SELLER(S) OR ANY AGENT(S) REPRESENTING ANY PRINCIPAL(S) IN THIS
TRANSACTION, AND IS NOT A SUBSTITUTE FOR ANY INSPECTIONS OR WARRANTIES THE PRINCIPAL(S) MAY
WISH TO OBTAIN.

I. COORDINATION WITH OTHER DISCLOSURE FORMS

This Real Estate Transfer Disclosure Statement is made pursuant to Section 1102 of the Civil Code. Other statutes require disclosures, depending upon the details of the particular real estate transaction (for example: special study zone and purchase-money liens on residential property).

Substituted Disclosures: The following disclosures and other disclosures required by law, including the Natural Hazard Disclosure Report/Statement that may include airport annoyances, earthquake, fire, flood, or special assessment information, have or will be made in connection with this real estate transfer, and are intended to satisfy the disclosure obligations on this form, where the subject matter is the same:

☐ Inspection reports completed pursuant to the contract of sale or receipt for deposit.
☐ Additional inspection reports or disclosures: _____
_____

II. SELLER'S INFORMATION

The Seller discloses the following information with the knowledge that even though this is not a warranty, prospective Buyers may rely on this information in deciding whether and on what terms to purchase the subject property. Seller hereby authorizes any agent(s) representing any principal(s) in this transaction to provide a copy of this statement to any person or entity in connection with any actual or anticipated sale of the property.

THE FOLLOWING ARE REPRESENTATIONS MADE BY THE SELLER(S) AND ARE NOT THE REPRESENTATIONS OF THE
AGENT(S), IF ANY. THIS INFORMATION IS A DISCLOSURE AND IS NOT INTENDED TO BE PART OF ANY CONTRACT BETWEEN
THE BUYER AND SELLER.

Seller ☐ is ☐ is not occupying the property.

A. The subject property has the items checked below: *

☐ Range	☐ Wall/Window Air Conditioning	☐ Pool:
☐ Oven	☐ Sprinklers	☐ Child Resistant Barrier
☐ Microwave	☐ Public Sewer System	☐ Pool/Spa Heater:
☐ Dishwasher	☐ Septic Tank	☐ Gas ☐ Solar ☐ Electric
☐ Trash Compactor	☐ Sump Pump	☐ Water Heater:
☐ Garbage Disposal	☐ Water Softener	☐ Gas ☐ Solar ☐ Electric
☐ Washer/Dryer Hookups	☐ Patio/Decking	☐ Water Supply:
☐ Rain Gutters	☐ Built-in Barbecue	☐ City ☐ Well
☐ Burglar Alarms	☐ Gazebo	☐ Private Utility or
☐ Carbon Monoxide Device(s)	☐ Security Gate(s)	Other _____
☐ Smoke Detector(s)	☐ Garage:	☐ Gas Supply:
☐ Fire Alarm	☐ Attached ☐ Not Attached	☐ Utility ☐ Bottled (Tank)
☐ TV Antenna	☐ Carport	☐ Window Screens
☐ Satellite Dish	☐ Automatic Garage Door Opener(s)	☐ Window Security Bars
☐ Intercom	☐ Number Remote Controls _____	☐ Quick Release Mechanism on
☐ Central Heating	☐ Sauna	Bedroom Windows
☐ Central Air Conditioning	☐ Hot Tub/Spa:	☐ Water-Conserving Plumbing Fixtures
☐ Evaporator Cooler(s)	☐ Locking Safety Cover	

Exhaust Fan(s) in _____ 220 Volt Wiring in _____ Fireplace(s) in _____
☐ Gas Starter _____ ☐ Roof(s): Type: _____ Age: _____ (approx.)
☐ Other: _____

Are there, to the best of your (Seller's) knowledge, any of the above that are not in operating condition? ☐ Yes ☐ No. If yes, then describe. (Attach additional sheets if necessary): _____

(*see note on page 2)
Buyer's Initials (_____) (_____)   Seller's Initials (_____) (_____)

©1991 - 2014, California Association of REALTORS®, Inc.

TDS REVISED 4/14 (PAGE 1 OF 3)   Reviewed by _____ Date _____

EQUAL HOUSING OPPORTUNITY

REAL ESTATE TRANSFER DISCLOSURE STATEMENT (TDS PAGE 1 OF 3)

Agent: WALT HUBER   Phone: Fax: Prepared using zipForm® software
Broker: WALT HUBER REALTOR,

Property Address: *123 Sail Avenue* _____ Date: _____

B. Are you (Seller) aware of any significant defects/malfunctions in any of the following? ☐ Yes ☐ No. If yes, check appropriate space(s) below.

☐ Interior Walls ☐ Ceilings ☐ Floors ☐ Exterior Walls ☐ Insulation ☐ Roof(s) ☐ Windows ☐ Doors ☐ Foundation ☐ Slab(s) ☐ Driveways ☐ Sidewalks ☐ Walls/Fences ☐ Electrical Systems ☐ Plumbing/Sewers/Septics ☐ Other Structural Components (Describe: _____
_____)

If any of the above is checked, explain. (Attach additional sheets if necessary.): _____
_____
_____

*Installation of a listed appliance, device, or amenity is not a precondition of sale or transfer of the dwelling. The carbon monoxide device, garage door opener, or child-resistant pool barrier may not be in compliance with the safety standards relating to, respectively, carbon monoxide device standards of Chapter 8 (commencing with Section 13260) of Part 2 of Division 12 of, automatic reversing device standards of Chapter 12.5 (commencing with Section 19890) of Part 3 of Division 13 of, or the pool safety standards of Article 2.5 (commencing with Section 115920) of Chapter 5 of Part 10 of Division 104 of, the Health and Safety Code. Window security bars may not have quick-release mechanisms in compliance with the 1995 edition of the California Building Standards Code. Section 1101.4 of the Civil Code requires all single-family residences built on or before January 1, 1994, to be equipped with water-conserving plumbing fixtures after January 1, 2017. Additionally, on and after January 1, 2014, a single-family residence built on or before January 1, 1994, that is altered or improved is required to be equipped with water-conserving plumbing fixtures as a condition of final approval. Fixtures in this dwelling may not comply with section 1101.4 of the Civil Code.

C. Are you (Seller) aware of any the following:

1. Substances, materials, or products which may be an environmental hazard such as, but not limited to, asbestos, formaldehyde, radon gas, lead-based paint, mold, fuel or chemical storage tanks, and contaminated soil or water on the subject property . . . . ☐ Yes ☐ No
2. Features of the property shared in common with adjoining landowners, such as walls, fences, and driveways, whose use or responsibility for maintenance may have an effect on the subject property . . . . ☐ Yes ☐ No
3. Any encroachments, easements or similar matters that may affect your interest in the subject property . . . . ☐ Yes ☐ No
4. Room additions, structural modifications, or other alterations or repairs made without necessary permits. . . . . . . ☐ Yes ☐ No
5. Room additions, structural modifications, or other alterations or repairs not in compliance with building codes. . . . ☐ Yes ☐ No
6. Fill (compacted or otherwise) on the property or any portion thereof . . . . ☐ Yes ☐ No
7. Any settling from any cause, or slippage, sliding, or other soil problems . . . . ☐ Yes ☐ No
8. Flooding, drainage or grading problems . . . . ☐ Yes ☐ No
9. Major damage to the property or any of the structures from fire, earthquake, floods, or landslides . . . . ☐ Yes ☐ No
10. Any zoning violations, nonconforming uses, violations of "setback" requirements . . . . ☐ Yes ☐ No
11. Neighborhood noise problems or other nuisances . . . . ☐ Yes ☐ No
12. CC&R's or other deed restrictions or obligations . . . . ☐ Yes ☐ No
13. Homeowners' Association which has any authority over the subject property . . . . ☐ Yes ☐ No
14. Any "common area" (facilities such as pools, tennis courts, walkways, or other areas co-owned in undivided interest with others) . . . . ☐ Yes ☐ No
15. Any notices of abatement or citations against the property . . . . ☐ Yes ☐ No
16. Any lawsuits by or against the Seller threatening to or affecting this real property, claims for damages by the Seller pursuant to Section 910 or 914 threatening to or affecting this real property, claims for breach of warranty pursuant to Section 900 threatening to or affecting this real property, or claims for breach of an enhanced protection agreement pursuant to Section 903 threatening to or affecting this real property, including any lawsuits or claims for damages pursuant to Section 910 or 914 alleging a defect or deficiency in this real property or "common areas" (facilities such as pools, tennis courts, walkways, or other areas co-owned in undivided interest with others) . . . . ☐ Yes ☐ No

If the answer to any of these is yes, explain. (Attach additional sheets if necessary.): _____
_____
_____
_____

D.1. The Seller certifies that the property, as of the close of escrow, will be in compliance with Section 13113.8 of the Health and Safety Code by having operable smoke detector(s) which are approved, listed, and installed in accordance with the State Fire Marshal's regulations and applicable local standards.
2. The Seller certifies that the property, as of the close of escrow, will be in compliance with Section 19211 of the Health and Safety Code by having the water heater tank(s) braced, anchored, or strapped in place in accordance with applicable law.

Buyer's Initials (_____) (_____)   Seller's Initials (_____) (_____)   ⬄ EQUAL HOUSING OPPORTUNITY

TDS REVISED 4/14 (PAGE 2 OF 3) | Reviewed by _____ Date _____ |

REAL ESTATE TRANSFER DISCLOSURE STATEMENT (TDS PAGE 2 OF 3)   Untitled

Property Address: *123 Sail Avenue* _____ Date: _____

Seller certifies that the information herein is true and correct to the best of the Seller's knowledge as of the date signed by the Seller.

Seller _____ Date _____

Seller _____ Date _____

III. AGENT'S INSPECTION DISCLOSURE
(To be completed only if the Seller is represented by an agent in this transaction.)

THE UNDERSIGNED, BASED ON THE ABOVE INQUIRY OF THE SELLER(S) AS TO THE CONDITION OF THE PROPERTY AND BASED ON A REASONABLY COMPETENT AND DILIGENT VISUAL INSPECTION OF THE ACCESSIBLE AREAS OF THE PROPERTY IN CONJUNCTION WITH THAT INQUIRY, STATES THE FOLLOWING:

☐ See attached Agent Visual Inspection Disclosure (AVID Form)
☐ Agent notes no items for disclosure.
☐ Agent notes the following items: _____
_____
_____
_____

Agent (Broker Representing Seller) _____ By _____ Date _____
                                        (Please Print)   (Associate Licensee or Broker Signature)

IV. AGENT'S INSPECTION DISCLOSURE
(To be completed only if the agent who has obtained the offer is other than the agent above.)

THE UNDERSIGNED, BASED ON A REASONABLY COMPETENT AND DILIGENT VISUAL INSPECTION OF THE ACCESSIBLE AREAS OF THE PROPERTY, STATES THE FOLLOWING:

☐ See attached Agent Visual Inspection Disclosure (AVID Form)
☐ Agent notes no items for disclosure.
☐ Agent notes the following items: _____
_____
_____
_____

Agent (Broker Obtaining the Offer) _____ By _____ Date _____
                                        (Please Print)   (Associate Licensee or Broker Signature)

V. BUYER(S) AND SELLER(S) MAY WISH TO OBTAIN PROFESSIONAL ADVICE AND/OR INSPECTIONS OF THE PROPERTY AND TO PROVIDE FOR APPROPRIATE PROVISIONS IN A CONTRACT BETWEEN BUYER AND SELLER(S) WITH RESPECT TO ANY ADVICE/INSPECTIONS/DEFECTS.

I/WE ACKNOWLEDGE RECEIPT OF A COPY OF THIS STATEMENT.

Seller _____ Date _____   Buyer _____ Date _____

Seller _____ Date _____   Buyer _____ Date _____

Agent (Broker Representing Seller) _____ By _____ Date _____
                                    (Please Print)   (Associate Licensee or Broker Signature)

Agent (Broker Obtaining the Offer) _____ By _____ Date _____
                                    (Please Print)   (Associate Licensee or Broker Signature)

SECTION 1102.3 OF THE CIVIL CODE PROVIDES A BUYER WITH THE RIGHT TO RESCIND A PURCHASE CONTRACT FOR AT LEAST THREE DAYS AFTER THE DELIVERY OF THIS DISCLOSURE IF DELIVERY OCCURS AFTER THE SIGNING OF AN OFFER TO PURCHASE. IF YOU WISH TO RESCIND THE CONTRACT, YOU MUST ACT WITHIN THE PRESCRIBED PERIOD.

A REAL ESTATE BROKER IS QUALIFIED TO ADVISE ON REAL ESTATE. IF YOU DESIRE LEGAL ADVICE, CONSULT YOUR ATTORNEY.

©1991 - 2014, California Association of REALTORS®, Inc. THIS FORM HAS BEEN APPROVED BY THE CALIFORNIA ASSOCIATION OF REALTORS® (C.A.R.). NO REPRESENTATION IS MADE AS TO THE LEGAL VALIDITY OR ACCURACY OF ANY PROVISION IN ANY SPECIFIC TRANSACTION. A REAL ESTATE BROKER IS THE PERSON QUALIFIED TO ADVISE ON REAL ESTATE TRANSACTIONS. IF YOU DESIRE LEGAL OR TAX ADVICE, CONSULT AN APPROPRIATE PROFESSIONAL.

Published and Distributed by:
REAL ESTATE BUSINESS SERVICES, INC.
a subsidiary of the California Association of REALTORS®
525 South Virgil Avenue, Los Angeles, California 90020

Reviewed by _____ Date _____

TDS REVISED 4/14 (PAGE 3 OF 3)

REAL ESTATE TRANSFER DISCLOSURE STATEMENT (TDS PAGE 3 OF 3)   Untitled

Figure 7-5

CALIFORNIA
ASSOCIATION
OF REALTORS®

BUYER'S INSPECTION ADVISORY
(C.A.R. Form BIA-A, Revised 10/02)

Property Address: _264 Beach Lane, Costa Mesa   CA   92627_ ("Property").

A. IMPORTANCE OF PROPERTY INVESTIGATION: The physical condition of the land and improvements being purchased is not guaranteed by either Seller or Brokers. For this reason, you should conduct thorough investigations of the Property personally and with professionals who should provide written reports of their investigations. A general physical inspection typically does not cover all aspects of the Property nor items affecting the Property that are not physically located on the Property. If the professionals recommend further investigations, including a recommendation by a pest control operator to inspect inaccessible areas of the Property, you should contact qualified experts to conduct such additional investigations.

B. BUYER RIGHTS AND DUTIES: You have an affirmative duty to exercise reasonable care to protect yourself, including discovery of the legal, practical and technical implications of disclosed facts, and the investigation and verification of information and facts that you know or that are within your diligent attention and observation. The purchase agreement gives you the right to investigate the Property. If you exercise this right, and you should, you must do so in accordance with the terms of that agreement. This is the best way for you to protect yourself. It is extremely important for you to read all written reports provided by professionals and to discuss the results of inspections with the professional who conducted the inspection. You have the right to request that Seller make repairs, corrections or take other action based upon items discovered in your investigations or disclosed by Seller. If Seller is unwilling or unable to satisfy your requests, or you do not want to purchase the Property in its disclosed and discovered condition, you have the right to cancel the agreement if you act within specific time periods. If you do not cancel the agreement in a timely and proper manner, you may be in breach of contract.

C. SELLER RIGHTS AND DUTIES: Seller is required to disclose to you material facts known to him/her that affect the value or desirability of the Property. However, Seller may not be aware of some Property defects or conditions. Seller does not have an obligation to inspect the Property for your benefit nor is Seller obligated to repair, correct or otherwise cure known defects that are disclosed to you or previously unknown defects that are discovered by you or your inspectors during escrow. The purchase agreement obligates Seller to make the Property available to you for investigations.

D. BROKER OBLIGATIONS: Brokers do not have expertise in all areas and therefore cannot advise you on many items, such as soil stability, geologic or environmental conditions, hazardous or illegal controlled substances, structural conditions of the foundation or other improvements, or the condition of the roof, plumbing, heating, air conditioning, electrical, sewer, septic, waste disposal, or other system. The only way to accurately determine the condition of the Property is through an inspection by an appropriate professional selected by you. If Broker gives you referrals to such professionals, Broker does not guarantee their performance. You may select any professional of your choosing. In sales involving residential dwellings with no more than four units, Brokers have a duty to make a diligent visual inspection of the accessible areas of the Property and to disclose the results of that inspection. However, as some Property defects or conditions may not be discoverable from a visual inspection, it is possible Brokers are not aware of them. If you have entered into a written agreement with a Broker, the specific terms of that agreement will determine the nature and extent of that Broker's duty to you. **YOU ARE STRONGLY ADVISED TO INVESTIGATE THE CONDITION AND SUITABILITY OF ALL ASPECTS OF THE PROPERTY. IF YOU DO NOT DO SO, YOU ARE ACTING AGAINST THE ADVICE OF BROKERS.**

E. YOU ARE ADVISED TO CONDUCT INVESTIGATIONS OF THE ENTIRE PROPERTY, INCLUDING, BUT NOT LIMITED TO THE FOLLOWING:
1. **GENERAL CONDITION OF THE PROPERTY, ITS SYSTEMS AND COMPONENTS:** Foundation, roof, plumbing, heating, air conditioning, electrical, mechanical, security, pool/spa, other structural and non-structural systems and components, fixtures, built-in appliances, any personal property included in the sale, and energy efficiency of the Property. (Structural engineers are best suited to determine possible design or construction defects, and whether improvements are structurally sound.)
2. **SQUARE FOOTAGE, AGE, BOUNDARIES:** Square footage, room dimensions, lot size, age of improvements and boundaries. Any numerical statements regarding these items are APPROXIMATIONS ONLY and have not been verified by Seller and cannot be verified by Brokers. Fences, hedges, walls, retaining walls and other natural or constructed barriers or markers do not necessarily identify true Property boundaries. (Professionals such as appraisers, architects, surveyors and civil engineers are best suited to determine square footage, dimensions and boundaries of the Property.)
3. **WOOD DESTROYING PESTS:** Presence of, or conditions likely to lead to the presence of wood destroying pests and organisms and other infestation or infection. Inspection reports covering these items can be separated into two sections: Section 1 identifies areas where infestation or infection is evident. Section 2 identifies areas where there are conditions likely to lead to infestation or infection. A registered structural pest control company is best suited to perform these inspections.
4. **SOIL STABILITY:** Existence of fill or compacted soil, expansive or contracting soil, susceptibility to slippage, settling or movement, and the adequacy of drainage. (Geotechnical engineers are best suited to determine such conditions, causes and remedies.)

The copyright laws of the United States (Title 17 U.S. Code) forbid the unauthorized reproduction of this form, or any portion thereof, by photocopy machine or any other means, including facsimile or computerized formats.
Copyright © 1991-2004, CALIFORNIA ASSOCIATION OF REALTORS®, INC. ALL RIGHTS RESERVED.

Buyer's Initials (_____) (_____)
Seller's Initials (_____) (_____)

| Reviewed by _____ Date _____ |

EQUAL HOUSING
OPPORTUNITY

BIA-A REVISED 10/02 (PAGE 1 OF 2)

BUYER'S INSPECTION ADVISORY (BIA-A PAGE 1 OF 2)

Agent: WALT HUBER	Phone:	Fax:	Prepared using zipForm® software
Broker: WALT HUBER REALTOR			

Along with the Purchase Agreement, the buyer is required to read and approve this two-page broker's recommendations on the values of obtaining and paying for qualified inspections from the appropriate professionals prior to finalizing the transaction. You must provide the seller with a signed copy of the Buyer's Inspection Advisory, have it signed and initialed by seller, and return a copy to the selling agent.

Property Address: _264 Beach Lane, Costa Mesa CA 92627_ Date: _June 14, 20xx_

5. **ROOF:** Present condition, age, leaks, and remaining useful life. (Roofing contractors are best suited to determine these conditions.)
6. **POOL/SPA:** Cracks, leaks or operational problems. (Pool contractors are best suited to determine these conditions.)
7. **WASTE DISPOSAL:** Type, size, adequacy, capacity and condition of sewer and septic systems and components, connection to sewer, and applicable fees.
8. **WATER AND UTILITES; WELL SYSTEMS AND COMPONENTS:** Water and utility availability, use restrictions and costs. Water quality, adequacy, condition, and performance of well systems and components.
9. **ENVIRONMENTAL HAZARDS:** Potential environmental hazards, including, but not limited to, asbestos, lead-based paint and other lead contamination, radon, methane, other gases, fuel oil or chemical storage tanks, contaminated soil or water, hazardous waste, waste disposal sites, electromagnetic fields, nuclear sources, and other substances, materials, products, or conditions (including mold (airborne, toxic or otherwise), fungus or similar contaminants). (For more information on these items, you may consult an appropriate professional or read the booklets "Environmental Hazards: A Guide for Homeowners, Buyers, Landlords and Tenants," "Protect Your Family From Lead in Your Home" or both.)
10. **EARTHQUAKES AND FLOODING:** Susceptibility of the Property to earthquake/seismic hazards and propensity of the Property to flood. (A Geologist or Geotechnical Engineer is best suited to provide information on these conditions.)
11. **FIRE, HAZARD AND OTHER INSURANCE:** The availability and cost of necessary or desired insurance may vary. The location of the Property in a seismic, flood or fire hazard zone, and other conditions, such as the age of the Property and the claims history of the Property and Buyer, may affect the availability and need for certain types of insurance. Buyer should explore insurance options early as this information may affect other decisions, including the removal of loan and inspection contingencies. (An insurance agent is best suited to provide information on these conditions.)
12. **BUILDING PERMITS, ZONING AND GOVERNMENTAL REQUIREMENTS:** Permits, inspections, certificates, zoning, other governmental limitations, restrictions, and requirements affecting the current or future use of the Property, its development or size. (Such information is available from appropriate governmental agencies and private information providers. Brokers are not qualified to review or interpret any such information.)
13. **RENTAL PROPERTY RESTRICTIONS:** Some cities and counties impose restrictions that limit the amount of rent that can be charged, the maximum number of occupants; and the right of a landlord to terminate a tenancy. Deadbolt or other locks and security systems for doors and windows, including window bars, should be examined to determine whether they satisfy legal requirements. (Government agencies can provide information about these restrictions and other requirements.)
14. **SECURITY AND SAFETY:** State and local Law may require the installation of barriers, access alarms, self-latching mechanisms and/or other measures to decrease the risk to children and other persons of existing swimming pools and hot tubs, as well as various fire safety and other measures concerning other features of the Property. Compliance requirements differ from city to city and county to county. Unless specifically agreed, the Property may not be in compliance with these requirements. (Local government agencies can provide information about these restrictions and other requirements.)
15. **NEIGHBORHOOD, AREA, SUBDIVISION CONDITIONS; PERSONAL FACTORS:** Neighborhood or area conditions, including schools, proximity and adequacy of law enforcement, crime statistics, the proximity of registered felons or offenders, fire protection, other government services, availability, adequacy and cost of any speed-wired, wireless internet connections or other telecommunications or other technology services and installations, proximity to commercial, industrial or agricultural activities, existing and proposed transportation, construction and development that may affect noise, view, or traffic, airport noise, noise or odor from any source, wild and domestic animals, other nuisances, hazards, or circumstances, protected species, wetland properties, botanical diseases, historic or other governmentally protected sites or improvements, cemeteries, facilities and condition of common areas of common interest subdivisions, and possible lack of compliance with any governing documents or Homeowners' Association requirements, conditions and influences of significance to certain cultures and/or religions, and personal needs, requirements and preferences of Buyer.

Buyer and Seller acknowledge and agree that Broker: **(i)** Does not decide what price Buyer should pay or Seller should accept; **(ii)** Does not guarantee the condition of the Property; **(iii)** Does not guarantee the performance, adequacy or completeness of inspections, services, products or repairs provided or made by Seller or others; **(iv)** Does not have an obligation to conduct an inspection of common areas or areas off the site of the Property; **(v)** Shall not be responsible for identifying defects on the Property, in common areas or offsite unless such defects are visually observable by an inspection of reasonably accessible areas of the Property or are known to Broker; **(vi)** Shall not be responsible for inspecting public records or permits concerning the title or use of Property; **(vii)** Shall not be responsible for identifying the location of boundary lines or other items affecting title; **(viii)** Shall not be responsible for verifying square footage, representations of others or information contained in Investigation reports, Multiple Listing Service, advertisements, flyers or other promotional material; **(ix)** Shall not be responsible for providing legal or tax advice regarding any aspect of a transaction entered into by Buyer or Seller; and **(x)** Shall not be responsible for providing other advice or information that exceeds the knowledge, education and experience required to perform real estate licensed activity. Buyer and Seller agree to seek legal, tax, insurance, title and other desired assistance from appropriate professionals.

By signing below, Buyer and Seller each acknowledge that they have read, understand, accept and have received a Copy of this Advisory. Buyer is encouraged to read it carefully.

	_06/14/20xx_			_06/14/20xx_
Buyer Signature	Date		Buyer Signature	Date
Walter Buyer			_Debbie Buyer_	
	_6/15/20xx_			_06/15/20xx_
Seller Signature	Date		Seller Signature	Date
Tony Seller			_Ramona J. Seller_	

THIS FORM HAS BEEN APPROVED BY THE CALIFORNIA ASSOCIATION OF REALTORS® (C.A.R.). NO REPRESENTATION IS MADE AS TO THE LEGAL VALIDITY OR ADEQUACY OF ANY PROVISION IN ANY SPECIFIC TRANSACTION. A REAL ESTATE BROKER IS THE PERSON QUALIFIED TO ADVISE ON REAL ESTATE TRANSACTIONS. IF YOU DESIRE LEGAL OR TAX ADVICE, CONSULT AN APPROPRIATE PROFESSIONAL.
This form is available for use by the entire real estate industry. It is not intended to identify the user as a REALTOR®. REALTOR® is a registered collective membership mark which may be used only by members of the NATIONAL ASSOCIATION OF REALTORS® who subscribe to its Code of Ethics.

Published and Distributed by:
REAL ESTATE BUSINESS SERVICES, INC.
a subsidiary of the California Association of REALTORS®
525 South Virgil Avenue, Los Angeles, California 90020

| Reviewed by _____ Date _____ |

BIA-A REVISED 10/02 (PAGE 2 OF 2)

BUYER'S INSPECTION ADVISORY (BIA-A PAGE 2 OF 2)

Cal Principles -

Figure 7-6

CALIFORNIA ASSOCIATION OF REALTORS®

BUYER'S INSPECTION WAIVER
(C.A.R. Form BIW, 4/08)

Property Address: _123 Sail Avenue, Marina del Rey, CA 90292_ ("Property").

A. IMPORTANCE OF PROPERTY INVESTIGATION: Unless otherwise specified in the purchase agreement used, the physical condition of the land and any improvements being purchased is not guaranteed by either Seller or Brokers. For this reason, **(i)** you should conduct thorough inspections, investigations, tests, surveys and other studies (Investigations) of the Property personally and with professionals of your own choosing who should provide written reports/disclosures of their findings and recommendations, and **(ii)** you should not rely solely on reports/disclosures provided by Seller or others. A general physical (home) inspection typically does not cover all aspects of the Property nor items affecting the Property that are not physically located on the Property. If any professional recommends additional Investigations, including a recommendation by a pest control operator to inspect inaccessible areas of the Property, you should contact qualified experts to conduct such additional Investigations.

B. BUYER RIGHTS AND DUTIES: You have an affirmative duty to exercise reasonable care to protect yourself, including discovery of the legal, practical and technical implications of disclosed facts, and to investigate and verify information and facts that you know or that are within your diligent attention and observation. If the purchase agreement gives you the right to investigate the Property the best way to protect yourself is to exercise this right. However, you must do so in accordance with the terms of, and time specified in, that agreement. It is extremely important for you to read all written reports/disclosures provided by professionals and to discuss the results of Investigations with the professionals who conducted the Investigations.

C. WAIVERS:
1. **HOME INSPECTION WAIVER:** Broker recommends that Buyer obtain a home inspection, **even if Seller or Broker has provided Buyer with a copy of a home inspection report/disclosures obtained by Seller or a previous buyer. IF YOU DO NOT DO SO, YOU ARE ACTING AGAINST THE ADVICE OF BROKERS.**
(_____)(_____) Buyer has decided not to obtain a general home inspection at this time. Unless Buyer makes a subsequent election in writing during Buyer's investigation period, if any, Buyer waives the right to obtain a general home inspection.

2. **WOOD DESTROYING PEST INSPECTION WAIVER:** Broker recommends that Buyer obtain an inspection for wood destroying pests and organisms (whether paid for by Buyer or Seller). **IF YOU DO NOT DO SO, YOU ARE ACTING AGAINST THE ADVICE OF BROKERS.**
(_____)(_____) Buyer has decided not to obtain an inspection for wood destroying pests and organisms at this time. Unless Buyer makes a subsequent election in writing during Buyer's investigation period, if any, Buyer waives the right to obtain an inspection for wood destroying pests and organisms.

3. **OTHER:** Broker recommends that Buyer obtain an inspection for the following items: _____
_____
IF YOU DO NOT DO SO, YOU ARE ACTING AGAINST THE ADVICE OF BROKERS.
(_____)(_____) Buyer has decided not to obtain the inspection(s) noted above at this time. Unless Buyer makes a subsequent election in writing during Buyer's investigation period, if any, Buyer waives the right to obtain such inspection(s).

4. **ADDITIONAL WAIVERS:** Buyer has received a:
☐ General Home Inspection Report/Disclosure, prepared by _____ dated _____,
☐ Wood Destroying Pest and Organism Report/Disclosure, prepared by _____ dated _____,
☐ Other _____ Report/Disclosure, prepared by _____ dated _____,
That report/disclosure recommends that Buyer obtain additional Investigations, Broker recommends that Buyer obtain those additional Investigations. **IF YOU DO NOT DO SO, YOU ARE ACTING AGAINST THE ADVICE OF BROKERS.**
(_____)(_____) Buyer has decided not to obtain any of the additional inspections or reports/disclosures at this time and, unless Buyer makes a subsequent election in writing during Buyer's investigation period, if any, Buyer waives the right to obtain such additional inspections or reports/disclosures.

Buyer represents and agrees that Buyer has independently considered the above, and all other investigation options, has read all written reports/disclosures provided by professionals and discussed the results with the professional who conducted the Investigation. Buyer further agrees that unless Buyer makes a subsequent election in writing during Buyer's Investigation period, if any, Buyer waives the right to conduct the Investigation(s) above.

Buyer _____ Date _____

Buyer _____ Date _____

The copyright laws of the United States (Title 17 U.S. Code) forbid the unauthorized reproduction of this form, or any portion thereof, by photocopy machine or any other means, including facsimile or computerized formats. Copyright © 2006-2008, CALIFORNIA ASSOCIATION OF REALTORS®, INC. ALL RIGHTS RESERVED.
THIS FORM HAS BEEN APPROVED BY THE CALIFORNIA ASSOCIATION OF REALTORS® (C.A.R.). NO REPRESENTATION IS MADE AS TO THE LEGAL VALIDITY OR ADEQUACY OF ANY PROVISION IN ANY SPECIFIC TRANSACTION. A REAL ESTATE BROKER IS THE PERSON QUALIFIED TO ADVISE ON REAL ESTATE TRANSACTIONS. IF YOU DESIRE LEGAL OR TAX ADVICE, CONSULT AN APPROPRIATE PROFESSIONAL.
This form is available for use by the entire real estate industry. It is not intended to identify the user as a REALTOR®. REALTOR® is a registered collective membership mark which may be used only by members of the NATIONAL ASSOCIATION OF REALTORS® who subscribe to its Code of Ethics.

Published and Distributed by:
REAL ESTATE BUSINESS SERVICES, INC.
a subsidiary of the CALIFORNIA ASSOCIATION OF REALTORS®
525 South Virgil Avenue, Los Angeles, California 90020

Reviewed by _____ Date _____

BIW 4/08 (PAGE 1 OF 1)   **BUYER'S INSPECTION WAIVER (BIW PAGE 1 OF 1)**

Agent: WALT HUBER   Phone: Fax: Prepared using zipForm® software
Broker: WALT HUBER REALTOR

Should the buyer choose not to get a physical inspection, this addendum can be added to the original purchase contract.

Figure 7-7

CALIFORNIA ASSOCIATION OF REALTORS®

WOOD DESTROYING PEST INSPECTION AND ALLOCATION OF COST ADDENDUM
(C.A.R. Form WPA, Revised 11/12)

This is an addendum to the ☐ California Residential Purchase Agreement or ☐ Other _____
_____ ("Agreement"), dated _____ ,
on property known as *123 Sail Avenue, Marina del Rey,* _____
_____ ("Property"),
between _____ ("Buyer"),
and _____ ("Seller").

1. Unless otherwise specified, the Agreement permits the Buyer to inspect the property and investigate its condition. One of the inspections the Buyer may obtain is for wood destroying pests and organisms "Wood Pest Report". Whether obtained and paid for by Buyer or Seller, Buyer's review and approval of a Wood Pest Report would generally be covered by the inspection contingency of the Agreement. Before Buyer removes or waives the inspection contingency, or other contingency specifically related to a Wood Pest Report, Buyer may cancel the Agreement if dissatisfied with the condition described in the Wood Pest Report, even if this Wood Pest Addendum is not made part of the Agreement.

2. **A.** The Wood Pest Report shall be paid for and prepared as specified in the Agreement, or if checked, ☐ Buyer ☐ Seller shall pay for a Wood Pest Report prepared by _____ , a registered Structural Pest Control company.

   B. The Wood Pest Report shall cover the main building and attached structures and, if checked: ☐ detached garages and carports, ☐ detached decks, ☐ the following other structures on the Property: _____
   _____ . The Wood Pest Report shall not include roof coverings. If the Property is a unit in a condominium or other common interest subdivision, the Wood Pest Report shall include only the separate interest and any exclusive-use areas being transferred, and shall not include common areas. Water tests of shower pans on upper level units may not be performed unless the owners of property below the shower consent.

   C. The Wood Pest Report shall be separated into sections for evident infestation or infection (Section 1) and for conditions likely to lead to infestation or infection (Section 2).
   (1) (Section 1) ☐ Buyer ☐ Seller shall pay for work recommended to correct "Section 1" conditions described in the Wood Pest Report and the cost of inspection, entry and closing of those inaccessible areas where active infestation or infection is discovered.
   (2) (Section 2) ☐ Buyer ☐ Seller shall pay for work recommended to correct "Section 2" conditions described in the Wood Pest Report if requested by Buyer.

   D. If the Wood Pest Report identifies inaccessible areas, and Buyer requests inspection of those inaccessible areas, the person identified in C1 shall pay for the cost of entry, inspection and closing of only those inaccessible areas where Section 1 conditions are discovered and Buyer shall pay for the cost of entry, inspection and closing of all other inaccessible areas.

   E. Seller shall Deliver to Buyer, prior to Close Of Escrow, with a written pest control certification ("Certification") showing that no infestation or infection is found or that required corrective work is completed. If paragraph 2A does not refer to a specific registered Structural Pest Control company and Seller obtains more than one Wood Pest Report pursuant to this Addendum, Seller may choose which Wood Pest Report to use as the basis of the Certification provided that Seller Delivers to Buyer all Wood Pest Reports obtained by Seller before Buyer removes any contingency for Wood Pest inspection.

By signing below, the undersigned acknowledge that each has read, understands and has received a copy of this Addendum.

Date _____   Date _____

Buyer _____   Seller _____

Buyer _____   Seller _____

The copyright laws of the United States (Title 17 U.S. Code) forbid the unauthorized reproduction of this form, or any portion thereof, by photocopy machine or any other means, including facsimile or computerized formats. Copyright © 2012, CALIFORNIA ASSOCIATION OF REALTORS®, INC. ALL RIGHTS RESERVED.
THIS FORM HAS BEEN APPROVED BY THE CALIFORNIA ASSOCIATION OF REALTORS® (C.A.R.). NO REPRESENTATION IS MADE AS TO THE LEGAL VALIDITY OR ADEQUACY OF ANY PROVISION IN ANY SPECIFIC TRANSACTION. A REAL ESTATE BROKER IS THE PERSON QUALIFIED TO ADVISE ON REAL ESTATE TRANSACTIONS. IF YOU DESIRE LEGAL OR TAX ADVICE, CONSULT AN APPROPRIATE PROFESSIONAL.
This form is available for use by the entire real estate industry. It is not intended to identify the user as a REALTOR®. REALTOR® is a registered collective membership mark which may be used only by members of the NATIONAL ASSOCIATION OF REALTORS® who subscribe to its Code of Ethics.

Published and Distributed by:
REAL ESTATE BUSINESS SERVICES, INC.
a subsidiary of the California Association of REALTORS®
525 South Virgil Avenue, Los Angeles, California 90020

Reviewed by _____ Date _____

EQUAL HOUSING OPPORTUNITY

WPA REVISED 11/12 (PAGE 1 OF 1)
WOOD DESTROYING PEST INSPECTION AND ALLOCATION OF COST ADDENDUM (WPA PAGE 1 OF 1)

Agent: WALT HUBER	Phone:	Fax:	Prepared using zipForm® software
Broker: WALT HUBER REALTOR			

It is customary for the Seller to pay for Section 2C-1 (active infestation), but Section 2C-2 is often paid by the Buyer. Some brokers will recommend that the Buyer not check that box, but leave it blank. If the Buyer checks the box, the lender may require that this condition be met as part of the contract. The Buyer may decide to have the recommended work done and pay for it now, not have it done at all, or have it done later.

Figure 7-8

SAMPLE

CALIFORNIA ASSOCIATION OF REALTORS®

COUNTER OFFER No. _____
For use by Seller or Buyer. May not be used for multiple counter offer.
(C.A.R. Form CO, Revised 11/13)

Date _____

This is a counter offer to the: ☐ California Residential Purchase Agreement, ☐ Counter Offer No. _____ , or ☐ Other _____ ("Offer"),
dated _____ , on property known as **264 Beach Lane**
Costa Mesa, CA   92627 ("Property"),
between **Walter Buyer, Debbie Buyer** ("Buyer") and
Tony Seller, Ramona J. Seller ("Seller").

1. **TERMS:** The terms and conditions of the above referenced document are accepted subject to the following:
   A. **Paragraphs in the Offer that require initials by all parties, but are not initialed by all parties, are excluded from the final agreement unless specifically referenced for inclusion in paragraph 1C of this or another Counter Offer or an addendum.**
   B. **Unless otherwise agreed in writing, down payment and loan amount(s) will be adjusted in the same proportion as in the original Offer.**
   C. **OTHER TERMS:** _____
   _____
   _____
   _____
   _____
   _____
   _____
   _____
   _____

   D. The following attached addenda are incorporated into this Counter Offer: ☐ Addendum No. _____
   ☐ _____

2. **EXPIRATION:** This Counter Offer shall be deemed revoked and the deposits, if any, shall be returned:
   A. Unless by 5:00pm on the third Day After the date it is signed in paragraph 3 (if more than one signature then, the last signature date)(or by
   _____ ☐ AM ☐ PM on _____ (date) (i) it is signed in paragraph 4, by the Buyer or Seller to
   whom it is sent and (ii) a copy of the signed Counter Offer is personally received by the person making it or _____ ,
   who is authorized to receive it.
   OR B. If the Buyer or Seller who made the Counter Offer withdraws it in writing (CAR Form WOO) anytime prior to Acceptance.

3. **OFFER: BUYER OR SELLER MAKES THIS COUNTER OFFER ON THE TERMS ABOVE AND ACKNOWLEDGES RECEIPT OF A COPY.**
   ☐ Buyer ☐ Seller _____ Date _____
   ☐ Buyer ☐ Seller _____ Date _____

4. **ACCEPTANCE: I/WE** accept the above Counter Offer (If checked ☐ **SUBJECT TO THE ATTACHED COUNTER OFFER**) and acknowledge
   receipt of a Copy.
   ☐ Buyer ☐ Seller _____ Date _____ Time _____ ☐ AM ☐ PM
   ☐ Buyer ☐ Seller _____ Date _____ Time _____ ☐ AM ☐ PM

CONFIRMATION OF ACCEPTANCE:

(_____ / _____) (Initials) **Confirmation of Acceptance:** A Copy of Signed Acceptance was personally received by the maker of the
Counter Offer, or that person's authorized agent as specified in paragraph 2A on (date) _____ at _____ ☐ AM ☐ PM.
A binding Agreement is created when a Copy of Signed Acceptance is personally received by the maker of the Counter Offer, or that person's
authorized agent whether or not confirmed in this document.

© 2008-2013, California Association of REALTORS®, Inc. United States copyright law (Title 17 U.S. Code) forbids the unauthorized distribution, display and reproduction of this
form, or any portion thereof, by photocopy machine or any other means, including facsimile or computerized formats.

THIS FORM HAS BEEN APPROVED BY THE CALIFORNIA ASSOCIATION OF REALTORS® (C.A.R.). NO REPRESENTATION IS MADE AS TO THE LEGAL VALIDITY OR
ACCURACY OF ANY PROVISION IN ANY SPECIFIC TRANSACTION. A REAL ESTATE BROKER IS THE PERSON QUALIFIED TO ADVISE ON REAL ESTATE
TRANSACTIONS. IF YOU DESIRE LEGAL OR TAX ADVICE, CONSULT AN APPROPRIATE PROFESSIONAL.

This form is made available to real estate professionals through an agreement with or purchase from the California Association of REALTORS®. It is not intended to identify the
user as a REALTOR®.

Published and Distributed by:
REAL ESTATE BUSINESS SERVICES, INC.
a subsidiary of the California Association of REALTORS®
525 South Virgil Avenue, Los Angeles, California 90020

Reviewed by _____ Date _____

CO REVISED 11/13 (PAGE 1 OF 1)

COUNTER OFFER (CO PAGE 1 OF 1)

Agent: **WALT HUBER**   Phone: Fax: Prepared using zipForm® software
Broker: **WALT HUBER REALTOR**

Counter Offers have changed. Multiple counters are now separately used. It is important to remember that it is only to be used when there are actually multiple counters and not an encouragement for overbidding. When the counter offer is accepted by the offeree, the listing agent usually faxes the counters and the original Purchase Agreement, as well as Cooperating Broker Compensation Agreement and Escrow Instruction (CBC), to the selected escrow company. The escrow company prepares the escrow instructions that are to represent the intention of the parties based on the original contract and all counters. The earnest money deposit is delivered to the escrow company by the buyer's agent within three days from acceptance. It is from the acceptance date that all time contingencies begin, as well as the escrow period. You and the other agent receive a receipt for this deposit from the escrow company as proof of timely deposit. When the CalBRE audits a real estate company, this is usually the first document that is attached.

Figure 7-9

BUYER'S AFFIDAVIT
That Buyer is acquiring property for use as a residence
and that sales price does not exceed $300,000.
(FOREIGN INVESTMENT IN REAL PROPERTY TAX ACT)

1. I am the transferee (buyer) of real property located at *123 Sail Avenue,*

2. The sales price (total of all consideration in the sale) does not exceed $300,000.

3. I am acquiring the real property for use as a residence. I have definite plans that I or a member of my family will reside in it for at least 50 percent of the number of days it will be in use during each of the first two 12 month periods following the transfer of the property to me. I understand that the members of my family that are included in the last sentence are my brothers, sisters, ancestors, descendents, or spouse.

4. I am making this affidavit in order to establish an exemption from withholding a portion of the sales price of the property under Internal Revenue Code §1445.

5. I understand that if the information in this affidavit is not correct, I may be liable to the Internal Revenue Service for up to 10 percent of the sales price of the property, plus interest and penalties.

Under penalties of perjury, I declare that the statements above are true, correct and complete.

Date _____   Signature _____

Typed or Printed Name _____

Date _____   Signature _____

Typed or Printed Name _____

IMPORTANT NOTICE: An affidavit should be signed by each individual transferee to whom it applies. Before you sign, any questions relating to the legal sufficiency of this form, or to whether it applies to a particular transaction, or to the definition of any of the terms used, should be referred to an attorney, certified public accountant, other professional tax advisor, or the Internal Revenue Service.

THIS FORM HAS BEEN APPROVED BY THE CALIFORNIA ASSOCIATION OF REALTORS® (C.A.R.). NO REPRESENTATION IS MADE AS TO THE LEGAL VALIDITY OR ADEQUACY OF ANY PROVISION IN ANY SPECIFIC TRANSACTION. A REAL ESTATE BROKER IS THE PERSON QUALIFIED TO ADVISE ON REAL ESTATE TRANSACTIONS. IF YOU DESIRE LEGAL OR TAX ADVICE, CONSULT AN APPROPRIATE PROFESSIONAL.

This form is available for use by the entire real estate industry. It is not intended to identify the user as a REALTOR®. REALTOR® is a registered collective membership mark which may be used only by members of the NATIONAL ASSOCIATION OF REALTORS® who subscribe to its Code of Ethics.

The copyright laws of the United States (Title 17 U.S. Code) forbid the unauthorized reproduction of this form by any means, including facsimile or computerized formats.
Copyright© 1988-1997, CALIFORNIA ASSOCIATION OF REALTORS®

Published and Distributed by:
REAL ESTATE BUSINESS SERVICES, INC.
a subsidiary of the California Association of REALTORS®
525 South Virgil Avenue, Los Angeles, California 90020

OFFICE USE ONLY
Reviewed by Broker
or Designee _____
Date _____

FORM AB-11 REVISED 2/91

Agent: **WALT HUBER**   Phone: Fax: Prepared using zipForm® software
Broker: **WALT HUBER REALTOR**

This should be signed by the buyer when appropriate; it involves the Foreign Investment in Real Property Tax Act (FIRPTA). There are exemptions from the withholding portion of the sales price of the property being purchased, such as the price being no more than $300,000, and that the property will be the buyer's principal residence. If the buyer has any questions about this form, refer him or her to an attorney, certified public accountant, other professional tax advisor, or the Internal Revenue Service.

Figure 7-10

CALIFORNIA
ASSOCIATION
OF REALTORS®

REQUEST for REPAIR No. _____
(Or Other Corrective Action)
(C.A.R. Form RR, Revised 11/13)

In accordance with the terms and conditions of the: ☐ California Residential Purchase Agreement or ☐ Other _____
_____ ("Agreement"), dated _____ ,
on property known as _____ *123 Sail Avenue, Marina del Rey,*
("Property"), between _____ ("Buyer"),
and _____ ("Seller").

1. BUYER REQUEST:

    A. **(i)** ☐ Buyer requests that Seller, prior to final verification of condition, repair or take the other specified action for each item listed below, or if checked, ☐ on the attached list dated _____ :

_____
_____
_____
_____
_____
_____
_____

      (ii) ☐ Buyer requests that Seller credit Buyer $ _____ at Close of Escrow.
_____

    B. A copy of the following inspection or other report is attached.
      ☐ _____ ☐ _____
      ☐ _____ ☐ _____

Buyer _____ Date _____

Buyer _____ Date _____

2. SELLER RESPONSE TO BUYER REQUEST:

    A. If Buyer agrees to **(a)** remove in writing the following contingency(ies) _____

      ☐ or those contingencies identified on the attached Contingency Removal form (C.A.R. Form CR No. _____), or ☐ none and **(b)** release Seller and Brokers from any loss, liability, expense, claim or cause of action regarding the disclosed condition of the Property (Release), (Check all that apply)
      (i) ☐ Seller agrees to all of Buyer's requests in 1A above.
      (ii) ☐ Seller agrees to all of Buyer's requests in 1A above, except: _____
_____
_____

      (iii) ☐ Seller agrees, at Close of Escrow, to credit Buyer $ _____
OR B. ☐ Seller does not agree to any of Buyer's requests.
OR C. ☐ Other: _____

Seller _____ Date _____

Seller _____ Date _____

3. BUYER REPLY TO SELLER RESPONSE:

    A. ☐ Buyer accepts Seller's response, withdraws all requests for items and credits that Seller has not agreed to, and both removes the contingency(ies) identified or the attached C.A.R.Form CR and agrees to the Release identified in 2A above.
    B. ☐ Buyer withdraws the request in 1A above, and makes a new request as specified in the attached Request for Repair No. _____ .

Buyer _____ Date _____

Buyer _____ Date _____

The copyright laws of the United States (TITLE 17 U.S. Code) forbid the unauthorized reproduction of this form by any means, including facsimile or computerized formats.
Copyright © 2001-2013, CALIFORNIA ASSOCIATION OF REALTORS®
THIS FORM HAS BEEN APPROVED BY THE CALIFORNIA ASSOCIATION OF REALTORS® (C.A.R.). NO REPRESENTATION IS MADE AS TO THE LEGAL VALIDITY OR ADEQUACY OF ANY PROVISION IN ANY SPECIFIC TRANSACTION. A REAL ESTATE BROKER IS THE PERSON QUALIFIED TO ADVISE ON REAL ESTATE TRANSACTIONS. IF YOU DESIRE LEGAL OR TAX ADVICE, CONSULT AN APPROPRIATE PROFESSIONAL.
This form is available for use by the entire real estate industry. It is not intended to identify the user as a REALTOR®. REALTOR® is a registered collective membership mark which may be used only by members of the NATIONAL ASSOCIATION OF REALTORS® who subscribe to its Code of Ethics.

Published and Distributed by:
REAL ESTATE BUSINESS SERVICES, INC.
a subsidiary of the CALIFORNIA ASSOCIATION OF REALTORS®
525 South Virgil Avenue, Los Angeles, California 90020

Reviewed by _____ Date _____

RR REVISED 11/13 (PAGE 1 OF 1)   **REQUEST FOR REPAIR (RR PAGE 1 OF 1)**

Agent: WALT HUBER	Phone:	Fax:	Prepared using zipForm® software
Broker: WALT HUBER REALTOR			

Figure 7-11

CALIFORNIA
ASSOCIATION
OF REALTORS®

RECEIPT FOR REPORTS No. _____

(C.A.R. Form RFR, 4/10)

In accordance with the terms and conditions of the: ☐ California Residential Purchase Agreement or ☐ Other _____
_____ ("Agreement"), dated _____ on property known

as _____123 Sail Avenue, Marina del Rey CA 90292_____ ("Property"),

between _____ ("Buyer")

and _____ ("Seller").

Buyer acknowledges receipt of the following written report(s), document(s), inspection report(s) or disclosure(s) ("Reports") checked below. Brokers have not verified such Reports and make no representation regarding their adequacy, completeness, or the performance of the person preparing such inspections or Reports.

NOTE: Pre-printed paragraph numbers are for reference only and refer to the specified paragraph in the California Residential Purchase Agreement (C.A.R. Form RPA-CA).

<u>Report</u>	<u>Prepared By</u>	<u>Dated</u>
A. ☐ Wood Destroying Pest Inspection (Paragraph 4A)	_____	_____
B. ☐ Domestic Well Test (Paragraph 4A)	_____	_____
C. ☐ Septic/Private Sewage Inspection (Paragraph 4A)	_____	_____
D. ☐ Government Inspection or Report (Paragraph 4B)	_____	_____
E. ☐ Other Inspection or Report (Paragraph 4 ____)	_____	_____
F. ☐ Condominium/Planned Development (HOA or OA)	_____	_____
Disclosures (Paragraph 7B)	_____	_____
G. ☐ Home Inspection Report (Paragraph 10)	_____	_____
H. ☐ Title: Preliminary Report (Paragraph 12)	_____	_____
I. ☐ _____	_____	_____
J. ☐ _____	_____	_____
K. ☐ _____	_____	_____

L. ☐ The following Reports obtained by or prepared for Seller prior to Acceptance. **These Reports should not be considered as a substitute for obtaining your own inspections and Reports covering the same items and any other matter affecting the value and desirability of the property.**

☐ _____ _____ _____
☐ _____ _____ _____
☐ _____ _____ _____
☐ _____ _____ _____

_____   _____
Buyer   Date

_____   _____
Buyer   Date

The copyright laws of the United States (Title 17 U.S. Code) forbid the unauthorized reproduction of this form, or any portion thereof, by photocopy machine or any other means, including facsimile or computerized formats. Copyright © 2001-2010, CALIFORNIA ASSOCIATION OF REALTORS®, INC. ALL RIGHTS RESERVED.
THIS FORM HAS BEEN APPROVED BY THE CALIFORNIA ASSOCIATION OF REALTORS® (C.A.R.). NO REPRESENTATION IS MADE AS TO THE LEGAL VALIDITY OR ADEQUACY OF ANY PROVISION IN ANY SPECIFIC TRANSACTION. A REAL ESTATE BROKER IS THE PERSON QUALIFIED TO ADVISE ON REAL ESTATE TRANSACTIONS. IF YOU DESIRE LEGAL OR TAX ADVICE, CONSULT AN APPROPRIATE PROFESSIONAL.
This form is available for use by the entire real estate industry. It is not intended to identify the user as a REALTOR®. REALTOR® is a registered collective membership mark which may be used only by members of the NATIONAL ASSOCIATION OF REALTORS® who subscribe to its Code of Ethics.

Published and Distributed by:
REAL ESTATE BUSINESS SERVICES, INC.
a subsidiary of the California Association of REALTORS®
525 South Virgil Avenue, Los Angeles, California 90020

Reviewed by _____ Date _____

EQUAL HOUSING OPPORTUNITY

RFR 4/10 (PAGE 1 OF 1)

RECEIPT FOR REPORTS (RFR PAGE 1 OF 1)

Agent: WALT HUBER	Phone:	Fax:	Prepared using zipForm® software
Broker: WALT HUBER REALTOR			

Figure 7-12

CALIFORNIA
ASSOCIATION
OF REALTORS®

CONTINGENCY REMOVAL No. _____
(C.A.R. Form Revised CR, 11/13)

In accordance with the terms and conditions of the: ☐ California Residential Purchase Agreement (C.A.R. Form RPA-CA), or ☐ Residential Income Property Purchase Agreement (C.A.R. Form RIPA), or ☐ Commercial Property Purchase Agreement (C.A.R. Form CPA), or ☐ Vacant Land Purchase Agreement (C.A.R. Form VLPA) or ☐ Other _____ _____ ("Agreement"), dated _____ , on property known as _____123 Sail Avenue, Marina del Rey,_____ ("Property"), between _____ ("Buyer") and _____ ("Seller").

BUYER REMOVAL OF BUYER CONTINGENCIES: Buyer removes those contingencies specified below. With respect to any contingency and cancellation right that Buyer removes, unless otherwise specified in a separate written agreement between Buyer and Seller (such as C.A.R Form RR), as applicable, Buyer shall conclusively be deemed to have: **(i)** completed all Buyer Investigations and review of reports and other applicable information and disclosures; **(ii)** elected to proceed with the transaction; and **(iii)** assumed all liability, responsibility and expense, **if any,** for Repairs, corrections, or for the inability to obtain financing.

   A. **ONLY the following individually checked Buyer contingencies are removed:**
   1. ☐ Loan (Paragraph 3H) (NOTE: Removing the loan contingency also removes the appraisal contingency unless the appraisal contingency is separately selected in the Agreement.)
   2. ☐ Appraisal (Paragraph 3I)
   3. ☐ Reports/Disclosures (Paragraphs 4 and 6)
   4. ☐ Condominium/Planned Development (HOA or OA) Disclosures (Paragraph 7B)
   5. ☐ Buyer's Investigation, including insurability (Paragraph 10)
   6. ☐ Title: Preliminary Report (Paragraph 12)
   7. ☐ Sale of Buyer's Property (Paragraph 13)
   8. ☐ _____
   9. ☐ _____
   10. ☐ _____

OR B. ☐ **ALL Buyer contingencies are removed, EXCEPT:** ☐ Loan Contingency (Paragraph 3H); ☐ Appraisal Contingency (Paragraph 3I); (NOTE: Unless separately selected in the Agreement, the appraisal contingency is removed when the loan contingency is removed); ☐ Contingency for the Sale of Buyer's Property (C.A.R. Form COP) (Paragraph 13); ☐ Condominium/Planned Development (HOA) Disclosures (Paragraph 7B);
   ☐ Other _____
   C. ☐ **BUYER HEREBY REMOVES ANY AND ALL BUYER CONTINGENCIES.**

NOTE: Paragraph numbers refer to the California Residential Purchase Agreement (C.A.R. Form RPA-CA). Applicable paragraph numbers for each contingency or contractual action in other C.A.R. contracts are found in Contract Paragraph Matrix (C.A.R. Form CPM).

Once all contingencies are removed, whether or not Buyer has satisfied him/herself regarding all contingencies or received any information relating to those contingencies, Buyer may not be entitled to a return of Buyer's deposit if Buyer does not close escrow. This could happen even if, for example, Buyer does not approve of some aspect of the Property or lender does not approve Buyer's loan.

Buyer _____ **Date** _____

Buyer _____ **Date** _____

SELLER REMOVAL OF SELLER CONTINGENCIES: Seller hereby removes the following Seller contingencies: ☐ Contingency for Seller's purchase of replacement property (C.A.R. Form COP); ☐ Other _____ _____

Seller _____ **Date** _____

Seller _____ **Date** _____

(____/____) (Initials) **CONFIRMATION OF RECEIPT:** A copy of this signed Contingency Removal was personally received by ☐ Buyer ☐ Seller or authorized agent on _____ (date), at _____ ☐ AM/ ☐ PM.

The copyright laws of the United States (Title 17 U.S. Code) forbid the unauthorized reproduction of this form by any means, including facsimile or computerized formats. Copyright ©2003-2013, CALIFORNIA ASSOCIATION OF REALTORS®, Inc. All Rights Reserved.
THIS FORM HAS BEEN APPROVED BY THE CALIFORNIA ASSOCIATION OF REALTORS® (C.A.R.). NO REPRESENTATION IS MADE AS TO THE LEGAL VALIDITY OR ADEQUACY OF ANY PROVISION IN ANY SPECIFIC TRANSACTION. A REAL ESTATE BROKER IS THE PERSON QUALIFIED TO ADVISE ON REAL ESTATE TRANSACTIONS. IF YOU DESIRE LEGAL OR TAX ADVICE, CONSULT AN APPROPRIATE PROFESSIONAL.
This form is available for use by the entire real estate industry. It is not intended to identify the user as a REALTOR®. REALTOR® is a registered collective membership mark which may be used only by members of the NATIONAL ASSOCIATION OF REALTORS® who subscribe to its Code of Ethics.

Published and Distributed by:
REAL ESTATE BUSINESS SERVICES, INC.
a subsidiary of the California Association of REALTORS®
525 South Virgil Avenue, Los Angeles, California 90020

Reviewed by _____ Date _____

EQUAL HOUSING OPPORTUNITY

CR REVISED 11/13 (PAGE 1 OF 1)   **CONTINGENCY REMOVAL (CR PAGE 1 OF 1)**

Agent: WALT HUBER	Phone:	Fax:	Prepared using zipForm® software
Broker: WALT HUBER REALTOR			

Figure 7-13

CALIFORNIA
ASSOCIATION
OF REALTORS®

NOTICE TO SELLER TO PERFORM
No. _____
(C.A.R. Form NSP, Revised 04/10)

In accordance with the terms and conditions of the ☐ California Residential Purchase Agreement (C.A.R. Form RPA) or ☐ Residential Income Property Purchase Agreement (C.A.R. Form RIPA), or ☐ Commercial Property Purchase Agreement (C.A.R. Form CPA), or ☐ Vacant Land Purchase Agreement (C.A.R. Form VLPA), or ☐ Other _____ _____ ("Agreement"), dated _____ , on property known as _____123 Sail Avenue, Marina del Rey CA 90292_____ ("Property"),
between _____ ("Buyer"),
and _____ ("Seller").

Buyer hereby gives Seller notice that Buyer has not yet received from Seller the items checked below. If Seller does not provide Buyer with these items, Buyer may be entitled to cancel the Agreement or delay removing an applicable contingency:

<u>Contractual Action</u>

A. ☐ Delivery of Wood Destroying Pest Inspection (Paragraph 4A)
B. ☐ Delivery of the following Inspection or Report (Paragraph 4 _____): _____
   _____
C. ☐ Delivery of Lead Disclosures (Paragraph 6A)
D. ☐ Delivery of the following Statutory Disclosures (Paragraph 6A): _____
   _____
E. ☐ Delivery of the following Booklets/guides (Paragraph 6B): _____
   _____
F. ☐ Disclosure of Property in Condominium/Planned Development (Paragraph 7A)
G. ☐ Delivery of Condominium/Planned Development (HOA or OA) Disclosures (Paragraph 7B)
H. ☐ Disclosure of Known Property Insurance Claims (Paragraph 9A)
I. ☐ Delivery of Preliminary Title Report (Paragraph 12A)
J. ☐ Approval of verification of down payment and closing costs (Paragraph 14C(2))
K. ☐ Approval of verification of cash (Paragraph 14C(2))
L. ☐ Removal of contingency for Seller's Purchase of Replacement Property (C.A.R. Form COP, Paragraph B)
M. ☐ Other Disclosures and Deliveries: _____
   _____
N. ☐ _____
O. ☐ _____
P. ☐ _____

NOTE: Paragraph numbers refer to the California Residential Purchase Agreement (C.A.R. Form RPA-CA). Applicable paragraph numbers for each contingency or contractual action in other C.A.R. contracts are found in Contract Paragraph Matrix (C.A.R. Form CPM).

SELLER: If you do not take the specified contractual action indicated above, Buyer may cancel the Agreement.

Buyer _____ Date _____

Buyer _____ Date _____

(_____ / _____) (Initials) **CONFIRMATION OF RECEIPT:** A Copy of this Signed Notice to Seller to Perform was personally received by Seller or authorized agent on _____ (date), at _____ ☐ AM ☐ PM.

The copyright laws of the United States (Title 17 U.S. Code) forbid the unauthorized reproduction of this form by any means, including facsimile or computerized formats. Copyright © 2010, CALIFORNIA ASSOCIATION OF REALTORS®, INC. All Rights Reserved.
THIS FORM HAS BEEN APPROVED BY THE CALIFORNIA ASSOCIATION OF REALTORS® (C.A.R.). NO REPRESENTATION IS MADE AS TO THE LEGAL VALIDITY OR ADEQUACY OF ANY PROVISION IN ANY SPECIFIC TRANSACTION. A REAL ESTATE BROKER IS THE PERSON QUALIFIED TO ADVISE ON REAL ESTATE TRANSACTIONS. IF YOU DESIRE LEGAL OR TAX ADVICE, CONSULT AN APPROPRIATE PROFESSIONAL.
This form is available for use by the entire real estate industry. It is not intended to identify the user as a REALTOR®. REALTOR® is a registered collective membership mark which may be used only by members of the NATIONAL ASSOCIATION OF REALTORS® who subscribe to its Code of Ethics.

Published and Distributed by:
REAL ESTATE BUSINESS SERVICES, INC.
a subsidiary of the California Association of REALTORS®
525 South Virgil Avenue, Los Angeles, California 90020

Reviewed by _____ Date _____

EQUAL HOUSING OPPORTUNITY

NSP REVISED 04/10 (PAGE 1 OF 1)
NOTICE TO SELLER TO PERFORM (NSP PAGE 1 OF 1)

Agent: WALT HUBER	Phone:	Fax:	Prepared using zipForm® software
Broker: WALT HUBER REALTOR			

If the seller is not able or not willing to perform the terms and conditions agreed upon in the original Purchase Agreement, the buyer's agent forwards this form to the listing agent, advising that the buyer may cancel the transaction if this request is not complied within a timely fashion.

Figure 7-14

CALIFORNIA
ASSOCIATION
OF REALTORS®

NOTICE TO BUYER TO PERFORM
No. _____
(C.A.R. Form NBP, Revised 04/10)

In accordance with the terms and conditions of the: ☐ California Residential Purchase Agreement (C.A.R. Form RPA) or ☐ Residential Income Property Purchase Agreement (C.A.R. Form RIPA), or ☐ Commercial Property Purchase Agreement (C.A.R. Form CPA), or ☐ Vacant Land Purchase Agreement (C.A.R. Form VLPA), or ☐ Other _____
_____ ("Agreement"), dated _____ ,
on property known as _____ 123 Sail Avenue, Marina del Rey CA 90292 _____ ("Property"),
between _____ ("Buyer"),
and _____ ("Seller").

SELLER hereby gives Buyer notice to remove the following contingencies and take the specified contractual action:

I. Contingency

☐ **ALL CONTINGENCIES**

A. ☐ Loan (Paragraph 3H)
B. ☐ Appraisal (Paragraph 3I)
C. ☐ Disclosures/Reports (Paragraphs 4 and 6)
D. ☐ Condominium/Planned Development Disclosures (HOA or OA) (Paragraph 7B)
E. ☐ Buyer Investigation, including insurability (Paragraph 10)
F. ☐ Title: Preliminary Report (Paragraph 12)
G. ☐ Sale of Buyer's Property (Paragraph 13)
H. ☐ _____
I. ☐ _____
J. ☐ _____

II. Contractual Action

L. ☐ Initial Deposit (Paragraph 3A)
M. ☐ Increased Deposit (Paragraph 3B)
N. ☐ Form FVA (Paragraph 3C)
O. ☐ Loan Application Letter (Paragraph 3H)
P. ☐ Down Payment Verification (Paragraph 3G)
Q. ☐ All Cash Verification (Paragraph 3J)
R. ☐ Return of Statutory Disclosures (Paragraph 6A(2))
S. ☐ Return of Lead Disclosures (Paragraph 6A(2))
T. ☐ Receipt for Increased Deposit (Paragraph 25)
U. ☐ Escrow Evidence, Sale of Buyer's Property (C.A.R. Form COP, Paragraph A2 or A3)
V. ☐ _____
W. ☐ _____
X. ☐ _____

NOTE: Paragraph numbers refer to the California Residential Purchase Agreement (C.A.R. Form RPA-CA). Applicable paragraph numbers for each contingency or contractual action in other C.A.R. contracts are found in Contract Paragraph Matrix (C.A.R. Form CPM).

BUYER: If you do not remove the contingency(ies) (C.A.R. Forms RR and CR) or take the contractual actions specified above within 2 (or ☐ _____) Days After Delivery (but no less than the time specified in the Agreement) of this Notice to Buyer to Perform, Seller may cancel the Agreement.

_____   _____
Seller   Date

_____   _____
Seller   Date

(_____ / _____) (Initials) **CONFIRMATION OF RECEIPT:** A Copy of this Signed Notice to Buyer to Perform was personally received by Buyer or authorized agent on _____ (date), at _____ ☐ AM ☐ PM.

The copyright laws of the United States (Title 17 U.S. Code) forbid the unauthorized reproduction of this form by any means, including facsimile or computerized formats. Copyright © 2002-2010, CALIFORNIA ASSOCIATION OF REALTORS®
THIS FORM HAS BEEN APPROVED BY THE CALIFORNIA ASSOCIATION OF REALTORS® (C.A.R.). NO REPRESENTATION IS MADE AS TO THE LEGAL VALIDITY OR ADEQUACY OF ANY PROVISION IN ANY SPECIFIC TRANSACTION. A REAL ESTATE BROKER IS THE PERSON QUALIFIED TO ADVISE ON REAL ESTATE TRANSACTIONS. IF YOU DESIRE LEGAL OR TAX ADVICE, CONSULT AN APPROPRIATE PROFESSIONAL.
This form is available for use by the entire real estate industry. It is not intended to identify the user as a REALTOR®. REALTOR® is a registered collective membership mark which may be used only by members of the NATIONAL ASSOCIATION OF REALTORS® who subscribe to its Code of Ethics.

Published and Distributed by:
REAL ESTATE BUSINESS SERVICES, INC.
a subsidiary of the California Association of REALTORS®
525 South Virgil Avenue, Los Angeles, California 90020

Reviewed by _____ Date _____

NBP REVISED 04/10 (PAGE 1 OF 1)

NOTICE TO BUYER TO PERFORM (NBP PAGE 1 OF 1)

Agent: WALT HUBER	Phone:	Fax:	Prepared using zipForm® software
Broker: WALT HUBER REALTOR			

This form is more specific than the Notice to Seller to Perform (NSP), as it gives the right to the seller to cancel the escrow within 24 hours if the buyer does not take the contractual actions specified within and remove the contingencies. It is important to remember that this time must not be less than the time specified in the Purchase Agreement or any pertinent counter offer.

Figure 7-15

CALIFORNIA
ASSOCIATION
OF REALTORS®

VERIFICATION OF PROPERTY CONDITION
(BUYER FINAL INSPECTION)
(C.A.R. Form VP, Revised 4/07)

Property Address _____ *123 Sail Avenue, Marina del Rey CA 90292*

The purpose of this inspection is to satisfy Buyer regarding the condition of the Property. Buyer and Seller understand and agree that unless otherwise agreed in the prior contractual agreement between Buyer and Seller: (i) a final inspection is not a contingency of the purchase and sale, and (ii) the inspection or waiver is not intended in any way to alter the contractual obligations of Seller regarding the condition of Property to be delivered to Buyer at possession date. The inspection or waiver is not based upon any statement or representation by Broker(s), Associate-Licensee(s) or brokerage employees. The undersigned agree to hold Broker(s), Associate licensees and brokerage employees harmless from any liability, claims, demands, damages or costs arising out of the contractual obligations of Buyer and Seller concerning the condition of Property.

1. Buyer acknowledges that: (1) Property is in substantially the same condition as on the date of acceptance of the offer to purchase/sell; and (2) Seller has completed any repairs, alterations, replacements or modifications as agreed to by Buyer and Seller with the following exceptions:

_____

The evaluation of the condition of the Property, including any items listed above, is based upon a personal inspection by Buyer and/or tests, surveys, inspections, or other studies performed by inspector(s) selected by Buyer.

OR (if checked):
2. Broker recommends that Buyer conduct a final inspection. If Buyer does not do so, Buyer is acting against the advice of the Broker.
☐ Buyer waives the right to conduct a final inspection.

Receipt of a copy is hereby acknowledged.

Date _____ Buyer _____

Date _____ Buyer _____

Date _____ Seller _____

Date _____ Seller _____

The copyright laws of the United States (Title 17 U.S. Code) forbid the unauthorized reproduction of this form, or any portion thereof, by photocopy machine or any other means, including facsimile or computerized formats. Copyright © 1986-2007, CALIFORNIA ASSOCIATION OF REALTORS®, INC. ALL RIGHTS RESERVED.

THIS FORM HAS BEEN APPROVED BY THE CALIFORNIA ASSOCIATION OF REALTORS® (C.A.R.). NO REPRESENTATION IS MADE AS TO THE LEGAL VALIDITY OR ADEQUACY OF ANY PROVISION IN ANY SPECIFIC TRANSACTION. A REAL ESTATE BROKER IS THE PERSON QUALIFIED TO ADVISE ON REAL ESTATE TRANSACTIONS. IF YOU DESIRE LEGAL OR TAX ADVICE, CONSULT AN APPROPRIATE PROFESSIONAL.

This form is available for use by the entire real estate industry. It is not intended to identify the user as a REALTOR®. REALTOR® is a registered collective membership mark which may be used only by members of the NATIONAL ASSOCIATION OF REALTORS® who subscribe to its Code of Ethics.

Published and Distributed by:
REAL ESTATE BUSINESS SERVICES, INC.
a subsidiary of the CALIFORNIA ASSOCIATION OF REALTORS®
525 South Virgil Avenue, Los Angeles, California 90020

Reviewed by _____ Date_____

VP REVISED 4/07 (PAGE 1 OF 1)   **VERIFICATION OF PROPERTY CONDITION (VP PAGE 1 OF 1)**

Agent: WALT HUBER   Phone: Fax: Prepared using zipForm® software
Broker: WALT HUBER REALTOR

This is used as a final walk-through, a few days prior to closing the sale, confirming that the property is basically in the same condition as when the offer was made and that the agreed upon repairs and/or alterations have been satisfactorily performed. Remember, this is not the time to test switches and check for leaks—your buyer has already had the physical inspections. If the buyer declines to have a final inspection, it must be so noted on this form and signed by the buyer.

C. CARBON MONOXIDE AND RADON TESTING

1. Carbon Monoxide

Senate Bill 183 enacted the **Carbon Monoxide Poisoning Prevention Act** of 2010. This bill requires owners of dwellings intended for human occupancy to install carbon monoxide (CO) devices in existing dwelling units having a fossil fuel burning heater or appliance, fireplace, or attached garage (see **Figure 7-16**).

It is critical to ensure that all fuel burning devices are properly ventilated and receive regular inspections. Fireplaces need to be kept free of debris, and chimneys and flues should be maintained. Ovens, along with gas or charcoal barbecue grills, should never be used for heating. SB 183 also mandates that CO devices shall be certified by the Office of the State Fire Marshal.

Symptoms of carbon monoxide poisoning are headache, dizziness, chest pain, nausea, and vomiting. In severe cases, people can become increasingly irritable, agitated, and confused, eventually becoming lethargic and lapsing into unconsciousness. If you suspect carbon monoxide poisoning, call 911 and get the victim to fresh air immediately.

It is advisable to check your carbon monoxide detector's batteries regularly.

2. Radon

The U.S. Surgeon General has stated that indoor radon gas is the second-leading cause of lung cancer in the United States and breathing it over prolonged periods can present a significant health risk to families.

While California may have, on average, a small percentage of houses expected to have elevated radon, it has a huge population. Also, there are areas of potentially high radon levels located in densely populated areas of the state. As a result, some urban areas may have a large number of houses with elevated radon levels.

Radon does not have to stop a real estate transaction. Radon levels can be reduced to acceptable levels with relatively simple systems.

The important thing is to have the house tested prior to buying or tested after you move in. If you don't have radon, that's great—it didn't cost you much to find out and you don't have to worry about it. If you do have radon, you will know and you can address the problem, knowing that you have eliminated at least one substantial hazard.

Radon measurements for real estate transactions must be conducted by certified radon testers. For more information about radon and real estate see the EPA booklet "Home Buyer's and Seller's Guide to Radon."

Figure 7-16

CALIFORNIA
ASSOCIATION
OF REALTORS®

CARBON MONOXIDE DETECTOR NOTICE
(C.A.R. Form CMD, 4/12)

Property Address: _123 Sail Avenue, Marina del Rey, CA 90292_

1. INSTALLATION OF CARBON MONOXIDE DETECTORS:

    A. Requirements: California law (Health and Safety Code sections 13260 to 13263 and 17296 to 17296.2) requires that as of July 1, 2011, all existing single-family dwellings have carbon monoxide detectors installed and that all other types of dwelling units intended for human occupancy have carbon monoxide detectors installed on or before January 1, 2013. The January 1, 2013 requirement applies to a duplex, lodging house, dormitory, hotel, condominium, time-share and apartment, among others.

    B. Exceptions: The law does not apply to a dwelling unit which does not have any of the following: a fossil fuel burning heater or appliance, a fireplace, or an attached garage. The law does not apply to dwelling units owned or leased by the State of California, the Regents of the University of California or local government agencies. Aside from these three owner types, there are **no other owner exemptions** from the installation requirement; it applies to all owners of dwellings, be they individual banks, corporations, or other entities. There is no exemption for REO properties.

2. DISCLOSURE OF CARBON MONOXIDE DETECTORS: The Health and Safety Code does not require a disclosure regarding the existence of carbon monoxide detectors in a dwelling. However, a seller of residential 1-4 property who is required to complete a Real Estate Transfer Disclosure Statement, (C.A.R. Form TDS) or a Manufactured Home and Mobilehome Transfer Disclosure Statement (C.A.R. Form MHTDS) must use section II A of that form to disclose whether or not the dwelling unit has a carbon monoxide detector.

3. COMPLIANCE WITH INSTALLATION REQUIREMENT: State building code requires at a minimum, placement of carbon monoxide detectors in applicable properties outside of each sleeping area, and on each floor in a multi-level dwelling but additional or different requirements may apply depending on local building standards and manufacturer instructions. An owner who fails to install a carbon monoxide detector when required by law and continues to fail to install the detector after being given notice by a governmental agency could be liable for a fine of up to $200 for each violation. A transfer of a property where a seller, as an owner, has not installed carbon monoxide detectors, when required to do so by law, will not be invalidated, but the seller/owner could be subject to damages of up to $100, plus court costs and attorney fees. Buyer and Seller are each advised to consult with their own home inspector, contractor or building department to determine the exact location for installation of carbon monoxide detectors. Buyer is advised to consult with a professional of Buyer's choosing to determine whether the property has carbon monoxide detector(s) installed as required by law, and if not to discuss with their counsel the potential consequences.

4. LOCAL REQUIREMENTS: Some localities maintain their own retrofit or point of sale requirements which may include the requirement that a carbon monoxide detector be installed prior to a transfer of property. Therefore, it is important to check the local city or county building and safety departments regarding point of sale or retrofit requirements when transferring property.

The undersigned hereby acknowledge(s) receipt of a copy of this Carbon Monoxide Detector Notice.

Seller _____ _____ **Date** _____
       (Signature)   (Print Name)

Seller _____ _____ **Date** _____
       (Signature)   (Print Name)

Buyer _____ _____ **Date** _____
       (Signature)   (Print Name)

Buyer _____ _____ **Date** _____
       (Signature)   (Print Name)

The copyright laws of the United States (Title 17 U.S. Code) forbid the unauthorized reproduction of this form, or any portion thereof, by photocopy machine or any other means, including facsimile or computerized formats. Copyright © 2012 CALIFORNIA ASSOCIATION OF REALTORS®, INC. ALL RIGHTS RESERVED.
THIS FORM HAS BEEN APPROVED BY THE CALIFORNIA ASSOCIATION OF REALTORS® (C.A.R.). NO REPRESENTATION IS MADE AS TO THE LEGAL VALIDITY OR ADEQUACY OF ANY PROVISION IN ANY SPECIFIC TRANSACTION. A REAL ESTATE BROKER IS THE PERSON QUALIFIED TO ADVISE ON REAL ESTATE TRANSACTIONS. IF YOU DESIRE LEGAL OR TAX ADVICE, CONSULT AN APPROPRIATE PROFESSIONAL.
This form is available for use by the entire real estate industry. It is not intended to identify the user as a REALTOR®. REALTOR® is a registered collective membership mark which may be used only by members of the NATIONAL ASSOCIATION OF REALTORS® who subscribe to its Code of Ethics.

Published and Distributed by:
REAL ESTATE BUSINESS SERVICES, INC.
a subsidiary of the California Association of REALTORS®
525 South Virgil Avenue, Los Angeles, California 90020

Reviewed by _____ Date _____

EQUAL HOUSING OPPORTUNITY

CMD 4/12 (PAGE 1 OF 1)

CARBON MONOXIDE DETECTOR NOTICE (CMD PAGE 1 OF 1)

Agent: WALT HUBER	Phone:	Fax:	Prepared using zipForm® software
Broker: WALT HUBER REALTOR			

The Carbon Monoxide Poisoning Prevention Act requires carbon monoxide detectors to be installed in every "dwelling unit intended for human occupancy."

II. Statewide Buyer and Seller Advisory (SBSA)

The bold first words of each section allows you to select what you want to read.

The CAR© *STATEWIDE BUYER AND SELLER ADVISORY (SBSA) form (Figure 7-17) advises both buyer and seller of various factors that may affect the decision to buy, different types of inspections that can be obtained, and questions to ask about or research and information to be disclosed.* The Buyer is advised in each particular section to contact appropriate professionals for concerns. This form is designed to work in conjunction with local disclosure addenda. This form is not mandated by statute or contract.

Recent additions to the SBSA include information on: Smoking Restrictions (28), Underground Pipelines and Utilities (29), Marijuana and Methamphetamine Labs (30), Title Insurance After Foreclosure (31), and Death on Property (51).

This updated form acknowledges the growing concern among real estate consumers about living near a natural gas transmission pipeline. A Pacific Gas and Electric (PG&E) pipeline exploded in a residential neighborhood on the San Francisco Peninsula, killing eight people and destroying 38 homes and damaging 61 others. In the aftermath, the utility formally took the extraordinary act of notifying millions of California residents that they reside within 2,000 feet of a PG&E gas transmission pipeline. The State of California also enacted five new laws to strengthen transmission pipeline safety. However, newly mandated testing of existing pipelines continues to expose potentially dangerous leaks in old buried pipelines.

The SBSA explains to the consumer that underground pipelines transporting natural gas, liquid fuel, and other potentially hazardous materials exist throughout California. The form also directs the consumer to hazard disclosure companies and other public sources that can provide detailed information as to the location of existing pipelines with respect to a specific property.

The SBSA defines what the buyer and seller can expect, and explains their mutual and exclusive rights and duties. Sellers will see it at the time of the listing, and buyers may review it before making an offer.

When signed by all parties, the SBSA helps protect brokers by suggesting buyers seek professional advice and that brokers have no expertise in these matters.

Figure 7-17

CALIFORNIA
ASSOCIATION
OF REALTORS®

STATEWIDE BUYER AND SELLER ADVISORY
(This Form Does Not Replace Local Condition Disclosures.
Additional Addenda May Be Attached to This Advisory. See Paragraph 51)
(C.A.R. Form SBSA, Revised 11/13)

Property Address *123 Sail Avenue Marina del Rey,* _____ Date _____

BUYER RIGHTS AND DUTIES:
- The physical condition of the land and improvements being purchased are not guaranteed by Seller or Brokers.
- You should conduct thorough investigations of the Property both personally and with appropriate professionals.
- If professionals recommend further inspections, you should contact qualified experts to conduct such inspections.
- You should retain your own professional even if Seller or Broker has provided you with existing reports.
- You should read all written reports given to you and discuss those reports with the persons who prepared them.
- You have the right to request that the Seller make repairs or corrections or take other actions based on inspections or disclosures, but the Seller is not obligated to make any such repairs, corrections or other requested actions.
- If the Seller is unwilling or unable to satisfy your requests, and you act within certain time periods, you may have the right to cancel the Agreement (the Purchase Agreement and any Counter Offer and Addenda together are the "Agreement"). If you cancel outside of these periods, you may be in breach of the Agreement and your deposit might be at risk.
- The terms of the purchase agreement and any counter offers and addenda establish your rights and responsibilities.

YOU ARE STRONGLY ADVISED TO INVESTIGATE THE CONDITION AND SUITABILITY OF ALL ASPECTS OF THE PROPERTY. IF YOU DO NOT DO SO, YOU ARE ACTING AGAINST THE ADVICE OF BROKERS.

SELLER RIGHTS AND DUTIES:
- You have a duty to disclose material facts known to you that affect the value or desirability of the Property.
- You are obligated to make the Property available to the Buyer and have utilities on for inspections as allowed by the Agreement.
- This form is not a substitute for completing a Real Estate Transfer Disclosure Statement, if required, and any other property-specific questionnaires or disclosures.
- The terms of the Agreement establish your rights and responsibilities.

BROKER RIGHTS AND DUTIES:
- Brokers do not have expertise in all areas and matters affecting the Property or your evaluation of it.
- For most sales of residential properties with no more than four units, Brokers have a duty to make a reasonably competent and diligent visual inspection of the accessible areas of the Property and disclose to you material facts or defects that the inspection reveals.
- Many defects and conditions may not be discoverable by a Broker's visual inspection.
- If Brokers give a referral to another professional, Brokers do not guarantee that person's performance. You may select any professional of your own choosing.
- Any written agreement between a Broker and either Buyer or Seller or both establishes the rights and responsibilities of those parties.

1. INSPECTIONS: Buyer and Seller are advised that Buyer has the right to obtain various inspections of the Property under most residential purchase agreements. Buyer is advised to have the Property inspected by a professional property inspection service within Buyer's inspection contingency period. A licensed building contractor or other professional may perform these services. The inspector generally does not look behind walls or under carpets, or take equipment apart. Certain items on the Property, such as chimneys and spark arresters, plumbing, heating, air conditioning, electrical wiring, pool and spa, septic system, well, roof, foundation and structural items may need to be inspected by another professional, such as a chimney sweep, plumber, electrician, pool and spa service, septic or well company or roofer. A general physical inspection typically will not test for mold, wood destroying pests, lead-based paint, radon, asbestos and other environmental hazards, geologic conditions, age, remaining useful life or water-tightness of roof, cracks, leaks or operational problems associated with a pool or spa or connection of the Property to a sewer system. If Buyer wants further information on any aspect of the Property, Broker recommends that Buyer have a discussion with the professional property inspector and that Buyer hire an appropriate professional for the area of concern to Buyer. Brokers do not have expertise in these areas. Brokers do not verify the results of any such inspection or guarantee the performance of any such inspector or service. Any election by Buyer to waive the right to a physical inspection of the Property or to rely on somebody other than an appropriate professional is against the advice of Brokers. Not all inspectors are licensed and licenses are not available for all types of inspection activities.

Buyer's Initials (_____)

The copyright laws of the United States (Title 17 U.S. Code) forbid the unauthorized reproduction of this form, or any portion thereof, by photocopy machine or any other means, including facsimile or computerized formats. Copyright © 2004-2013, CALIFORNIA ASSOCIATION OF REALTORS®, INC. ALL RIGHTS RESERVED.

SBSA REVISED 11/13 (PAGE 1 OF 12)

Seller's Initials (_____) (_____)

Reviewed by _____ Date _____

EQUAL HOUSING
OPPORTUNITY

STATEWIDE BUYER AND SELLER ADVISORY (SBSA PAGE 1 OF 12)

Agent: WALT HUBER	Phone:	Fax:	Prepared using zipForm® software
Broker: WALT HUBER REALTOR			

Property Address: *123 Sail Avenue*
Marina del Rey, _____ Date: _____

2. SQUARE FOOTAGE, LOT SIZE, BOUNDARIES AND SURVEYS: Buyer and Seller are advised that only an appraiser or land surveyor, as applicable, can reliably confirm square footage, lot size, Property corners and exact boundaries of the Property. Representations regarding these items that are made in a Multiple Listing Service, advertisements, and from property tax assessor records are often approximations, or based upon inaccurate or incomplete records. Fences, hedges, walls or other barriers may not represent actual boundary lines. Unless otherwise specified by Broker in writing, Brokers have not verified any such boundary lines or any representations made by Seller or others. Brokers do not have expertise in this area. Standard title insurance does not insure the boundaries of the Property. If Buyer wants information about the exact square footage, lot size or location of Property corners or boundaries, Broker recommends that Buyer hire an appraiser or licensed surveyor to investigate these matters or to prepare a survey of the property during Buyer's inspection contingency period.

3. SOIL AND GEOLOGIC CONDITIONS: Buyer and Seller are advised that real estate in California is subject to settling, slippage, contraction, expansion erosion, subsidence, earthquakes and other land movement. The Property may be constructed on fill or improperly compacted soil and may have inadequate drainage capability. Any of these matters can cause structural problems to improvements on the Property. Civil or geo-technical engineers are best suited to evaluate soil stability, grading, drainage and other soil conditions. Additionally, the Property may contain known or unknown mines, mills, caves or wells. Brokers do not have expertise in this area. If Buyer wants further information, Broker recommends that Buyer hire an appropriate professional. Not all inspectors are licensed and licenses are not available for all types of inspections.

4. GEOLOGIC HAZARDS: Buyer and Seller are advised that California has experienced earthquakes in the past, and there is always a potential of future earthquakes. Damage caused by an earthquake may not be discoverable by a visual inspection of Buyer(s) or Broker(s). Inspection by a licensed, qualified professional is strongly recommended to determine the structural integrity and safety of all structures and improvements on the Property. If the Property is a condominium, or located in a planned unit development or in a common interest subdivision, Buyer is advised to contact the homeowners association about earthquake repairs and retrofit work and the possibility of an increased or special assessment to defray the costs of earthquake repairs or retrofit work. Buyer is encouraged to obtain and read the booklet entitled, "The Homeowner's Guide to Earthquake Safety." In most cases a questionnaire within the booklet must be completed by Seller and the entire booklet given to the Buyer if the Property was built prior to 1960. If the Property was built before 1975, and contains structures constructed of masonry or precast (tilt up) concrete walls, with wood frame floors or roof, or if the building has unreinforced masonry walls, then Seller must provide Buyer a pamphlet entitled "The Commercial Property Owner's Guide to Earthquake Safety." Many areas have a wide range of geologic problems and numerous studies have been made of these conditions. Some of this information is available for public review at city and county planning departments. Buyer is encouraged to review the public maps and reports and/or obtain a geologist's inspection report. Brokers do not have expertise in this area. Buyer may be able to obtain earthquake insurance to protect their interest in the Property. Sellers who agree to provide financing should also consider requiring Buyers to obtain such insurance naming Seller(s) as insured lien holder(s).

5. ENVIRONMENTAL HAZARDS: Buyer and Seller are advised that the presence of certain kinds of organisms, toxins and contaminants, including, but not limited to, mold (airborne, toxic or otherwise), fungi, mildew, lead-based paint and other lead contamination, asbestos, formaldehyde, radon, pcb's, methane, other gases, fuel oil or chemical storage tanks, contaminated soil or water, hazardous waste, waste disposal sites, electromagnetic fields, nuclear sources, urea formaldehyde, or other materials may adversely affect the Property and the health of individuals who live on or work at the property as well as pets. If Buyer wants further information, Buyer is advised and Broker(s) recommends, that Buyer have the Property inspected for the existence of such conditions and organisms, and conditions that may lead to their formation. Not all inspectors are licensed and licenses are not available for all types of inspection activities. Buyer is also advised to consult with appropriate experts regarding this topic during Buyer's inspection contingency period. Brokers do not have expertise in this area. Broker recommends that Buyer and Seller read the booklets titled, "Residential Environmental Hazards: A Guide for Homeowners, Homebuyers, Landlords and Tenants," and "Protect Your Family From Lead In Your Home."

6. EPA's LEAD-BASED PAINT RENOVATION, REPAIR AND PAINTING RULE: The new rule requires that contractors and maintenance professionals working in pre-1978 housing, child care facilities, and schools with lead-based paint be certified; that their employees be trained; and that they follow protective work practice standards. The rule applies to renovation, repair, or painting activities affecting more than six square feet of lead-based paint in a room or more than 20 square feet of lead-based paint on the exterior. Enforcement of the rule begins October 1, 2010. See the EPA website at www.epa.gov/lead for more information. Buyer and Seller are advised to consult an appropriate professional.

Buyer's Initials (_____) (_____)

Copyright © 2004-2013, CALIFORNIA ASSOCIATION OF REALTORS®, INC.

SBSA REVISED 11/13 (PAGE 2 OF 12)

Seller's Initials (_____) (_____)

| Reviewed by _____ Date _____ |

STATEWIDE BUYER AND SELLER ADVISORY (SBSA PAGE 2 OF 12)

Untitled

Property Address: *123 Sail Avenue*
Marina del Rey,   Date: _____

7. FORMALDEHYDE: Formaldehyde is a substance known to the State of California to cause cancer. Exposure to formaldehyde may be caused by materials used in the construction of homes. The United States Environmental Protection Agency, the California Air Resources Board, and other agencies have measured the presence of formaldehyde in the indoor air of select homes in California. Levels of formaldehyde that present a significant cancer risk have been measured in most homes that were tested. Formaldehyde is present in the air because it is emitted by a variety of building materials and home products used in construction. The materials include carpeting, pressed wood products, insulation, plastics, and glues. Most homes that have been tested elsewhere do contain formaldehyde, although the concentrations vary from home to home with no obvious explanation for the differences. One of the problems is that many suppliers of building materials and home products do not provide information on chemical ingredients to builders. Buyers may have further questions about these issues. Buyer is advised to consult with appropriate experts regarding this topic during Buyer's investigation period. Brokers do not have expertise in this area. Broker(s) recommend that Buyer and Seller read the booklet titled "Residential Environmental Hazards: A Guide for Homeowners, Homebuyers, Landlords and Tenants."

8. MOLD: Buyer and Seller are advised that the presence of certain kinds of mold, fungi, mildew and other organisms, sometimes referred to as "toxic mold" (collectively "Mold"), may adversely affect the Property and the health of individuals who live on or work at the Property as well as pets. Mold does not affect all people the same way, and may not affect some people at all. Mold may be caused by water leaks or other sources of moisture such as, but not limited to, flooding, and leaks in windows, pipes and roof. Seller is advised to disclose the existence of any such conditions of which he or she is aware. Buyer should carefully review all of Seller's disclosures for any indication that any of these conditions exist. It is, however, possible that Mold may be hidden and that Seller is completely unaware of its existence. In addition, Mold is often undetectable from a visual inspection, a professional general property inspection and even a structural pest control inspection. Brokers do not have expertise in this area. If Buyer wants further information, Broker recommends that Buyer have the Property tested for Mold by an environmental hygienist or other appropriate professional during Buyer's inspection contingency period. Not all inspectors are licensed and licenses are not available for all types of inspection activities.

9. WATER INTRUSION: Buyer and Seller are advised that many homes suffer from water intrusion or leakage. The causes of water intrusion are varied, and can include defective construction, faulty grading, deterioration of building materials and absence of waterproof barriers. Water intrusion can cause serious damage to the Property. This damage can consist of wood rot, mold, mildew and even damage to the structural integrity of the Property. The cost of repairing and remediating water intrusion damage and its causes can be very significant. The existence and cause of water intrusion is often difficult to detect. Because you, your Broker or a general home inspector cannot visually observe any effects of water intrusion, Buyer and Seller should not assume that such intrusion does not exist. Broker recommends that Buyer have the Property inspected for water intrusion by an appropriate professional. Brokers do not have expertise in this area.

10. SEPTIC SYSTEMS: Buyer and Seller are advised that a property may be served by one or more septic systems even though adjoining properties are connected to a sewer line. Buyer and Seller are also advised that some septic tanks and systems may have been abandoned or have leaked into ground water sources. Buyer is advised to contact the appropriate government agency to verify that the Property is connected to a sewer or served by a septic system. If the Property is served by a septic system, it may consist of a septic tank, cesspool, pits, leach lines or a combination of such mechanisms ("collectively, System"). No representation or warranty is made by Seller or Broker concerning the condition, operability, size, capacity or future expansion of a System, nor whether a System is adequate for use by the intended occupants of the Property. A change in the number of occupants or the quantity, composition or methods of depositing waste may affect the efficiency of the System. In addition, the amount of rainfall and ground water table may also affect the efficiency of the System. Many factors including, but not limited to, natural forces, age, deterioration of materials and the load imposed on a System can cause the System to fail at any time. Broker recommends that Buyer obtain an independent evaluation of any System by a qualified sanitation professional during Buyer's inspection contingency period. Brokers do not have expertise in this area. Buyer should consult with their sanitation professional to determine if their report includes the tank only, or other additional components of the System such as pits and leach fields. Not all inspectors are licensed and licenses are not available for all types of inspection activities. In some cases, Buyer's lender as well as local government agencies may require System inspection. System-related maintenance costs may include, but not be limited to, locating, pumping or providing outlets to ground level. Brokers are unable to advise Buyer or Seller regarding System-related issues or associated costs, which may be significant. If Buyer and Seller agree to obtain a System inspection, Buyer and Seller are cautioned that the inspection cost may include, but not be limited to, the costs of locating, pumping or providing outlets to ground level.

Buyer's Initials (_____) (_____)

Copyright © 2004-2013, CALIFORNIA ASSOCIATION OF REALTORS®, INC.

SBSA REVISED 11/13 (PAGE 3 OF 12)

Seller's Initials (_____) (_____)

Reviewed by _____ Date _____

EQUAL HOUSING OPPORTUNITY

STATEWIDE BUYER AND SELLER ADVISORY (SBSA PAGE 3 OF 12)

Untitled

Property Address: **123 Sail Avenue**
Marina del Rey, _____ Date: _____

11. WELL AND WATER SYSTEM(S): Buyer and Seller are advised that the Property may be served by one or more water wells, springs, or private community or public water systems. Any of these private or public water systems may contain bacteria, chemicals, minerals and metals, such as chromium. Well(s) may have been abandoned on the Property. Buyer is advised to have both the quality and the quantity of water evaluated, and to obtain an analysis of the quality of any domestic and agricultural water in use, or to be used at the Property, from whatever source. Water quality tests can include not only tests for bacteria, such as coliform, but also tests for organic and inorganic chemicals, metals, mineral content and gross alpha testing for radioactivity. Broker recommends that Buyer consult with a licensed, qualified well and pump company and local government agency to determine whether any well/spring or water system will adequately serve Buyer's intended use and that Buyer have a well consultant perform an extended well output test for this purpose. Water well or spring capacity, quantity output and quality may change at any time. There are no guarantees as to the future water quality, quantity or duration of any well or spring. If Buyer wants further information, Broker(s) recommend that Buyer obtain an inspection of the condition, age, adequacy and performance of all components of the well/spring and any water system during Buyer's inspection contingency period. Brokers do not have expertise in this area.

12. WOOD DESTROYING PESTS: Buyer and Seller are advised that the presence of, or conditions likely to lead to the presence of infestation or infection of wood destroying pests and organisms may adversely affect the Property. Inspection reports covering these items can be separated into two sections: Section 1 identifies areas where infestation or infection is evident. Section 2 identifies areas where there are conditions likely to lead to infestation or infection. Brokers do not have expertise in this area. If Buyer wants further information, Buyer is advised and Broker recommends that Buyer have the Property inspected for the existence of such conditions and organisms, and conditions that may lead to their formation, by a registered structural pest control company during Buyer's inspection contingency period.

13. EASEMENTS, ACCESS AND ENCROACHMENTS: Buyer and Seller are advised that confirming the exact location of easements, shared or private driveways or roadways, and encroachments on or to the Property may be possible only by conducting a survey. There may be unrecorded easements, access rights, encroachments and other agreements affecting the Property that may not be disclosed by a survey. Representations regarding these items that are made in a Multiple Listing Service or advertisements, or plotted by a title company are often approximations, or based upon inaccurate or incomplete records. Unless otherwise specified by Broker in writing, Brokers have not verified any such matters or any representations made by Seller(s) or others. If Buyer wants further information, Buyer is advised and Broker(s) recommend that Buyer hire a licensed surveyor during Buyer's inspection contingency period. Brokers do not have expertise in this area.

14. EARTHQUAKE FAULT ZONES AND SEISMIC HAZARD ZONES: Buyer and Seller are advised that California Public Resources Code Sections 2622 and 2696 require the delineation and mapping of "Earthquake Fault Zones" along known active faults and "Seismic Hazard Zones" in California. Affected cities and counties must regulate certain development projects within these zones. Construction or development on affected properties may be subject to the findings of a geological report prepared by a registered California geologist. Generally, Seller must disclose if the Property is in such a zone and can use a research company to aid in the process. If Buyer wants further information, Broker recommends that, during Buyer's inspection contingency period, Buyer make independent inquiries with such research companies or with appropriate government agencies concerning the use and improvement of the Property. Brokers do not have expertise in this area. Buyer is advised that there is a potential for earthquakes and seismic hazards even outside designated zones.

15. FIRE HAZARDS: Buyer and Seller are advised that fires annually cause the destruction of thousands of homes. Due to varied climate and topography, certain areas have higher risks of fires than others. Certain types of materials used in home construction create a greater risk of fire than others. If the Property is located within a State Fire Responsibility Area or a Very High Fire Hazard Zone, generally Seller must disclose that fact to Buyer under California Public Resources Code Section 4136 and California Government Code Sections 51178 and 51183.5, and may use a research company to aid in the process. Owners of property may be assessed a fire prevention fee of up to $150.00 per structure on each parcel in such zones. The fee may be adjusted annually commencing July 1, 2013. If Buyer wants further information, Broker recommends that, during Buyer's inspection contingency period, Buyer contact the local fire department and Buyer's insurance agent regarding the risk of fire. Brokers do not have expertise in this area. Buyer is advised that there is a potential for fires even outside designated zones.

16. FLOOD HAZARDS: Buyer and Seller are advised that if the Property is located within a Special Flood Hazard Area, as designated by the Federal Emergency Management Agency (FEMA), or an area of Potential Flooding pursuant to California Government Code Section 8589.3, generally Seller must disclose this fact to Buyer and may use a research company to aid in the process. The National Flood Insurance Program was established to identify all flood plain areas and establish

Buyer's Initials (_____) (_____)
Copyright © 2004-2013, CALIFORNIA ASSOCIATION OF REALTORS®, INC.
SBSA REVISED 11/13 (PAGE 4 OF 12)

Seller's Initials (_____) (_____)

| Reviewed by _____ Date _____ |

STATEWIDE BUYER AND SELLER ADVISORY (SBSA PAGE 4 OF 12)

EQUAL HOUSING OPPORTUNITY

Untitled

Property Address: *123 Sail Avenue*
Marina del Rey, _____ Date: _____

flood-risk zones within those areas. The program mandates flood insurance for properties within high-risk zones if loans are obtained from a federally-regulated financial institution or are insured by any agency of the United States Government. The extent of coverage and costs may vary. If Buyer wants further information, Broker(s) recommend that Buyer consult his or her lender and/or insurance agent during Buyer's inspection contingency period. Brokers do not have expertise in this area. Buyer is advised that there is a potential for flooding even outside designated zones.

17. ZONE MAPS MAY CHANGE: Maps that designate, among other things, Earthquake Fault Zones, Seismic Hazard Zones, State Fire Responsibility Areas, Very High Fire Hazard Zones, Special Flood Hazard Areas, and Potential Flooding Areas are occasionally redrawn by the applicable Government Agency. Properties that are currently designated in a specified zone or area could be removed and properties that are not now designated in a specified zone or area could be placed in one or more such zones or areas in the future. A property owner may dispute a FEMA flood hazard location by submitting an application to FEMA.

18. BUILDING PERMITS, ZONING AND CODE COMPLIANCE: Buyer and Seller are advised that any structure on the Property, including the original structure and any addition, modification, remodel or improvement may have been built without permits, not according to building codes, or in violation of zoning laws. Further, even if such structure was built according to the then-existing code or zoning requirement, it may not be in compliance with current building standards or local zoning. It is also possible that local law may not permit structures that now exist to be rebuilt in the event of damage or destruction. Buyer is advised to check with appropriate government agencies or third party professionals to verify permits and legal requirements and the effect of such requirements on current and future use of the Property, its development and size. If Buyer wants further information, Broker(s) recommend that Buyer discuss the issue with an appropriate professional during Buyer's inspection contingency period. Brokers do not have expertise in this area.

19. VIEWS: Buyer and Seller are advised that present views from the Property may be affected by future development or growth of trees and vegetation on adjacent properties and any other property within the line of sight of the Property. Brokers make no representation regarding the preservation of existing views. If Buyer wants further information, Broker(s) recommend that Buyer review covenants, conditions and restrictions, if any, and contact neighboring property owners, government agencies and homeowner associations, if any, during Buyer's inspection contingency period. Brokers do not have expertise in this area.

20. FUTURE REPAIRS, REPLACEMENTS AND REMODELS: Buyer and Seller are advised that replacement or repairs of certain systems or rebuilding or remodeling of all or a portion of the Property may trigger requirements that homeowners comply with laws and regulations that either come into effect after Close of Escrow or are not required to be complied with until the replacement, repair, rebuild or remodel has occurred. Permit or code requirements or building standards may change after Close of Escrow, resulting in increasing costs to repair existing features. In particular, changes to state and federal energy efficiency regulations impact the installation, replacement and some repairs of heating and air conditioning units (HVAC). Federal regulations now require manufacturers of HVAC units to produce only units meeting a new higher Seasonal Energy Efficiency Rating (SEER). This will likely impact repairs and replacements of existing HVAC units. State regulations now require that when installing or replacing HVAC units, with some exceptions, duct work must be tested for leaks. Duct work leaking more than 15 percent must be repaired to reduce leaks. The average existing duct work typically leaks 30 percent. More information is available at the California Energy Commission's website http://www.energy.ca.gov/title24/changeout. Home warranty policies may not cover such inspections or repairs. If Buyer wants further information, Broker recommends that Buyer discuss the issue with an appropriate professional during Buyer's inspection contingency period. Brokers do not have expertise in this area.

21. GOLF COURSE DISCLOSURES: Buyer and Seller are advised that if the Property is located adjacent to or near a golf course the following may apply: **(i)** Stray golf balls – Any residence near a golf course may be affected by errant golf balls, resulting in personal injury or destruction to property. Golfers may attempt to trespass on adjacent property to retrieve golf balls even though the project restrictions may expressly prohibit such retrieval. **(ii)** Noise and lighting – The noise of lawn mowers, irrigation systems and utility vehicles may create disturbances to homeowners. Maintenance operations may occur in the early morning hours. Residents living near the clubhouse may be affected by extra lighting, noise, and traffic. **(iii)** Pesticides and fertilizer use – A golf course may be heavily fertilized, as well as subjected to other chemicals during certain periods of the year. **(iv)** Irrigation system – Golf course sprinkler systems may cause water overspray upon adjacent property and structures. Also the irrigation system of a golf course may use reclaimed and retreated wastewater. **(v)** Golf carts – Certain lots may be affected more than others by the use of golf carts. Lots adjacent to a tee or putting green may be subject to noise disturbances and loss of privacy. **(vi)** Access to golf course from residences – It is likely that most residences will not have direct access from their lots to the golf course. The project restrictions may disclaim any right of access or other easements from a resident's lot onto the golf course. **(vii)** View obstruction – Residents living near a golf course may have their views over the golf course impacted by maturing trees and landscaping or by changes to the course's configuration. **(viii)** Water restrictions - As some municipalities face water shortages, the continued availability of water to the golf course may be restricted or otherwise reduced by the local water agency. If Buyer wants further information, Broker(s) recommend that Buyer contact the local water agency regarding this matter.

Buyer's Initials (_____) (_____)

Seller's Initials (_____) (_____)

Copyright © 2004-2013, CALIFORNIA ASSOCIATION OF REALTORS®, INC.
SBSA REVISED 11/13 (PAGE 5 OF 12)

| Reviewed by _____ Date _____ |

EQUAL HOUSING OPPORTUNITY

STATEWIDE BUYER AND SELLER ADVISORY (SBSA PAGE 5 OF 12)

Untitled

Property Address: *123 Sail Avenue*
Marina del Rey, _____ Date: _____

22. SCHOOLS: Buyer and Seller are advised that children living in the Property may not, for numerous reasons, be permitted to attend the school nearest the Property. Various factors including, but not limited to, open enrollment policies, busing, overcrowding and class size reductions may affect which public school serves the Property. School district boundaries are subject to change. Buyer is advised to verify whether the Property is now, and at the Close of Escrow will be, in the school district Buyer understands it to be in and whether residing in the Property entitles a person to attend any specific school in which that Buyer is interested. Broker(s) recommend that Buyer contact the local school or school district for additional information during Buyer's inspection contingency period. Brokers do not have expertise in this area.

23. NEIGHBORHOOD NOISE SOURCES: Buyer and Seller are advised that even if the Property is not in an identified airport noise influence area, the Property may still be subject to noise and air disturbances resulting from airplanes and other aircraft, commercial or military or both, flying overhead. Other common sources of noise include nearby commercial districts, schools, traffic on streets, highways and freeways, trains and general neighborhood noise from people, dogs and other animals. Noise levels and types of noise that bother one person may be acceptable to others. Buyer is advised to satisfy him/herself with regard to any sources of and amounts of noise at different times of day and night. Brokers do not have expertise in this area.

24. PETS AND ANIMALS: Buyer and Seller are advised that the current or previous owner(s) may have had domesticated or other pets and animals at the Property. Odors from animal urine or other contamination may be dormant for long periods of time and then become active because of heat, humidity or other factors and might not be eliminated by cleaning or replacing carpets or other cleaning methods. Pet urine and feces can also damage hardwood floors and other floor coverings. Additionally, an animal may have had fleas, ticks and other pests that remain on the Property after the animal has been removed. If Buyer wants further information, Broker(s) recommend that Buyer discuss the issue with an appropriate professional during Buyer's inspection contingency period. Brokers do not have expertise in this area.

25. SWIMMING POOL, SECURITY AND SAFETY: Buyer and Seller are advised that state and local Law may require the installation of barriers, anti-entrapment grates, access alarms, self-latching mechanisms and/or other measures to decrease the risk to children and other persons of existing swimming pools and hot tubs, as well as various fire safety and other measures concerning other features of the Property. Compliance requirements differ from city to city and county to county. Unless specifically agreed, the Property may not be in compliance with these requirements. Brokers do not have expertise in this area. If Buyer wants further information, Broker(s) recommend that Buyer contact local government agencies about these restrictions and other requirements.

26. RETROFIT, BUILDING REQUIREMENTS, AND POINT OF SALE REQUIREMENTS: Buyer and Seller are advised that state and local Law may require (i) the installation of operable smoke detectors, (ii) bracing or strapping of water heaters, and (iii) upon sale completion of a corresponding written statement of compliance that is delivered to Buyer. Although not a point of sale or retrofit obligation, state law may require the property to have operable carbon monoxide detection devices. Additionally, some city and county governments may impose additional retrofit standards at time of sale including, but not limited to, installing low-flow toilets and showerheads, gas shut-off valves, and tempered glass. Brokers do not have expertise in this area. Broker(s) recommend that Buyer and Seller consult with the appropriate government agencies, inspectors, and other professionals to determine the retrofit standards for the Property, the extent to which the Property complies with such standards, and the costs, if any, of compliance.

27. WATER SHORTAGES AND CONSERVATION: Buyer and Seller are advised that the Property may be located in an area that could experience water shortages. The policies of local water districts and the city or county in which the Property is located can result in the occurrence of any or all of the following: (i) limitations on the amount of water available to the Property, (ii) restrictions on the use of water, and (iii) an increasingly graduated cost per unit of water use, including, but not limited to, penalties for excess usage. For further information, Broker recommends that Buyer contact the supplier of water to the Property regarding the supplier's current or anticipated policies on water usage and to determine the extent to which those policies may affect Buyer's intended use of the Property. If the Property is serviced by a private well, Buyer is advised that drought conditions and/or a low water table may make it necessary to arrange, through a private supplier, for delivery of water to the Property. Buyers should contact water truck companies for the costs involved. Brokers do not have expertise in this area.

28. NEIGHBORHOOD, AREA, PERSONAL FACTORS, HIGH SPEED RAILS, AND SMOKING RESTRICTIONS: Buyer and Seller are advised that the following may affect the Property or Buyer's intended use of it: neighborhood or area conditions, including schools, proximity and adequacy of law enforcement, crime, fire protection, other government services, availability, adequacy and cost of any speed-wired, wireless internet connections or other telecommunications or other technology services and installations, proximity to medical marijuana growing or distribution locations, cell phone towers, manufacturing, commercial, industrial, airport or agricultural activities or military ordnance locations, existing and proposed transportation, construction, and development, any other source that may affect noise, view, traffic, or odor, wild and domestic animals, susceptibility to tsunami and adequacy of tsunami warnings, other nuisances, hazards, or circumstances, protected species, wetland properties, botanical diseases, historic or other governmentally-protected sites

Buyer's Initials (_____) (_____)   Seller's Initials (_____) (_____)

Copyright © 2004-2013, CALIFORNIA ASSOCIATION OF REALTORS®, INC.
SBSA REVISED 11/13 (PAGE 6 OF 12)

Reviewed by _____ Date _____

STATEWIDE BUYER AND SELLER ADVISORY (SBSA PAGE 6 OF 12)

Untitled

Property Address: *123 Sail Avenue*
Marina del Rey, _____ Date: _____

or improvements, cemeteries, conditions and influences of significance to certain cultures and/or religions, and personal needs, requirements and preferences of Buyer. California is potentially moving toward high speed rail service between Northern and Southern California. This rail line could have an impact on the Property if it is located nearby. More information on the timing of the project and routes is available from the California High-Speed Rail Authority at http://cahighspeedrail.ca.gov. The State of California has long-standing no smoking laws in place restricting smoking in most business and some public spaces. Local jurisdictions may enact laws that are more restrictive than state law. Many California cities have enacted restrictions on smoking in parks, public sidewalks, beaches and shopping areas. Some jurisdictions have restrictions entirely banning smoking inside privately owned apartments and condominiums as well as in the common areas of such structures, or limiting smoking to certain designated areas. If Buyer wants further information, Broker(s) recommend that Buyer contact local government agencies about these restrictions.

29. UNDERGROUND PIPELINES AND UTILITIES: Throughout California underground pipelines transport natural gas, liquid fuel and other potentially hazardous materials. These pipelines may or may not provide utility services to the Property. Information about the location of some of the pipelines may be available from a company that also provides disclosures of natural and other hazards or from other sources of public maps or records. Proximity to underground pipelines, in and of itself, does not affirmatively establish the risk or safety of the property. If Buyer wants further information about these underground pipelines and utilities, Buyer is advised to consult with appropriate experts during Buyer's investigation contingency period. Brokers do not have expertise in this area.

30. MARIJUANA AND METHAMPHETAMINE LABS: Buyer and Seller are advised that California law permits individual patients to cultivate, possess and use marijuana for medical purposes. Furthermore, California law permits primary caregivers, lawfully organized cooperatives, and collectives to cultivate, distribute and possess marijuana for medicinal purposes. California's medical marijuana law is in direct conflict with federal law which recognizes no lawful use for marijuana and has no exemptions for medical use. Federal criminal penalties, some of which mandate prison time, remain in effect for the possession, cultivation and distribution of marijuana. Buyer and Seller are strongly advised to seek legal counsel as to the legal risks and issues surrounding owning or purchasing a property where medical or any other marijuana activity is taking place. Marijuana storage, cultivation and processing carry the risk of causing mold, fungus or moisture damage to a property, additionally, some properties where marijuana has been cultivated have had alterations to the structure or the electrical system which may not have been done to code or with permits and may affect the safety of the structure or the safe operation of the electrical system. Buyer is strongly advised to retain an environmental hygienist contractor and other appropriate professionals to inspect a property where medical or any other marijuana activity has taken place. Broker recommends that Buyer and Seller involved with a property where there is medical marijuana activity or where it may take place review the California Attorney General's Guidelines for the "Security and Non-Diversion of Marijuana Grown for Medical Use" (http://ag.ca.gov/cms_attachments/press/pdfs/n1601_medicalmarijuanaguidelines.pdf) and the U.S. Department of Justice memo regarding marijuana prosecutions at http://www.justice.gov.opa/documents/medical-marijuana.pdf. Brokers do not have expertise in this area. While no state law permits the private production of methamphetamine, some properties have been the site of an illegal methamphetamine laboratory. State law imposes an obligation to notify occupants, a ban on occupying the property and clean up requirements when authorities identify a property as being contaminated by methamphetamine. Buyer is advised that a property where methamphetamine has been produced may pose a very serious health risk to occupants. Buyer is strongly advised to retain an environmental hygienist contractor or other appropriate professionals to inspect the property if methamphetamine production is suspected to have taken place. Brokers do not have expertise in this area.

31. INSURANCE AND TITLE INSURANCE AFTER FORECLOSURE: Buyer and Seller are advised that Buyer may have difficulty obtaining insurance regarding the Property if there has been a prior insurance claim affecting the Property or made by Buyer but unrelated to the Property. Seller is required by C.A.R. Form RPA to disclose known insurance claims made during the past five years (C.A.R. Form SPQ or SSD). Sellers may not be aware of claims prior to their ownership. If Buyer wants further information, Broker(s) recommend that, during Buyer's inspection contingency period, Buyer conduct his or her own investigation for past claims. Buyer may need to obtain Seller's consent in order to have access to certain investigation reports. If the Property is a condominium, or is located in a planned unit development or other common interest subdivision, Buyer and Seller are advised to determine if the individual unit is covered by the Homeowner Association Insurance. Broker(s) recommend that Buyer consult Buyer's insurance agents during Buyer's inspection contingency period to determine the need, availability and possibility of securing any and all forms of other insurance or coverage or any conditions imposed by insurer as a requirement of issuing insurance. If Buyer does any repairs to the property during the escrow period or Buyer takes possession prior to Close of Escrow or Seller remains in possession after Close of Escrow, whether for a limited or extended period of time, Broker(s) recommend that Buyer and Seller each consult with their own insurance agent regarding insurance or coverage that could protect them in the transaction (including but not limited to: personal property, flood, earthquake, umbrella and renter's). Buyer and Seller are advised that traditional title insurance generally protects Buyer's title acquired through the sale of the property. While all title insurance policies, as do all insurance policies, contain some exclusions, some title insurance policies contain exclusions for any liability arising from a previous foreclosure. This can occur when a short sale has occurred but the lender mistakenly has also proceeded with a foreclosure. Buyer is strongly advised to consult with a title insurer to satisfy themselves that the policy to be provided adequately protects their title to the property against other possible claimants. Brokers do not have expertise in this area.

Buyer's Initials (_____) (_____)   Seller's Initials (_____) (_____)

Copyright © 2004-2013, CALIFORNIA ASSOCIATION OF REALTORS®, INC.
SBSA REVISED 11/13 (PAGE 7 OF 12)

Reviewed by _____ Date _____

STATEWIDE BUYER AND SELLER ADVISORY (SBSA PAGE 7 OF 12)   Untitled

Property Address: 123 Sail Avenue
Marina del Rey, _____ Date: _____

32. CALIFORNIA FAIR PLAN: Buyer and Seller are advised that insurance for certain hillside, oceanfront and brush properties may be available only from the California Fair Plan. This may increase the cost of insurance for such properties and coverage may be limited. Broker(s) recommend that Buyer consult with Buyer's own insurance agent during Buyer's inspection contingency period regarding the availability of coverage under the California Fair Plan and the length of time it may take for processing of a California Fair Plan application. Brokers do not have expertise in this area.

33. HISTORICAL DESIGNATION, COASTAL COMMISSION, ARCHITECTURAL, LANDSCAPE, AGRICULTURAL OR OPEN SPACE AND OTHER RESTRICTIONS ON BUILDINGS OR IMPROVEMENTS: Buyer and Seller are advised that the Property may be: **(i)** designated as a historical landmark, **(ii)** protected by a historical conservancy, **(iii)** subject to an architectural or landscaping review process, **(iv)** within the jurisdiction of the California Coastal Commission or other government agency, or **(v)** subject to a contract preserving use of all or part of the Property for agriculture or open space. If the Property is so designated or within the jurisdiction of any such, or similar, government agency, then there may be restrictions on Buyer's ability to develop, remove or trim trees or other landscaping, remodel, make improvements to and build on or rebuild the Property. Broker(s) recommend that Buyer satisfy him/herself during Buyer's inspection contingency period if any of these issues are of concern to Buyer. Brokers do not have expertise in this area.

34. 1915 IMPROVEMENT BOND MELLO-ROOS COMMUNITY DISTRICT, AND OTHER ASSESSMENT DISTRICTS: Buyer and Seller are advised that the Property may be subject to an improvement bond assessment under the Improvement Bond Act of 1915, a levy of a special tax pursuant to a Mello-Roos Community Facilities district, and/or a contractual assessment as provided in Section 5898.24 of the Streets And Highways Code or other assessment districts. Seller is generally required to make a good faith effort to obtain a disclosure notice from any local agency collecting such taxes and deliver such notice to Buyers. Brokers do not have expertise in this area.

35. HOMEOWNER ASSOCIATIONS AND COVENANTS, CONDITIONS AND RESTRICTIONS ("CC&Rs"); CHARGING STATIONS: Buyer and Seller are advised that if the Property is a condominium, or located in a planned unit development, or in a common interest subdivision, there are typically restrictions on use of the Property and rules that must be followed. Restrictions and rules are commonly found in Declarations and other governing documents. Further there is likely to be a homeowner association (HOA) that has the authority to affect the Property and its use. Whether or not there is a HOA, the Property may still be subject to CC&Rs restricting use of the Property. The HOA typically has the authority to enforce the rules of the association, assess monetary payments (both regular monthly dues and special assessments) to provide for the upkeep and maintenance of the common areas, and enforce the rules and assessment obligations. If you fail to abide by the rules or pay monies owed to the HOA, the HOA may put a lien against your Property. Additionally, if an electric vehicle charging station is installed in a common area or an exclusive use common area, each Seller whose parking space is on or near that charging station must disclose its existence and that the Buyer will have the responsibilities set forth in California Civil Code §1353.9. The law requires the Seller to provide the Buyer with the CC&Rs and other governing documents, as well as a copy of the HOA's current financial statement and operating budget, among other documents. Buyer is advised to carefully review all HOA documents provided by Seller and the CC&Rs, if any, and satisfy him/herself regarding the use and restrictions of the Property, the amount of monthly dues and/or assessments, the adequacy of reserves, current and past insurance coverage and claims, and the possibility of any legal action that may be taken by or against the HOA. The HOA may not have insurance or may not cover personal property belonging to the owner of the unit in the condominium, common interest or planned unit development. See paragraph 31 for further information regarding insurance. See C.A.R.'s Common Interest Development Basic Information Guide on ePUBS® in zipForm®6 for further information. Brokers do not have expertise in this area.

36. LEGAL ACTION: Buyer and Seller are advised that if Seller or a previous owner was involved in a legal action (litigation or arbitration) affecting the Property, Buyer should obtain and review public and other available records regarding the legal action to determine: (i) whether the legal action or any resolution of it affects Buyer and the Property, (ii) if any rights against any parties involved in the legal action survive the legal action or have been terminated or waived as a result of the legal action, whether or not involving the same issue as in the legal action, and (iii) if any recommendations or requirements resulting from the legal action have been fulfilled and, if so, that Buyer is satisfied with any such action. Buyer should seek legal advice regarding these matters.

37. COMMUNITY ENHANCEMENT AND PRIVATE TRANSFER FEES: Buyer and Seller are advised that some areas or communities may have enhancement fees or user-type fees, or private transfer taxes and fees, over and above any stated fees. The Federal Housing Finance Agency has issued a rule that prohibits Fannie Mae and Freddie Mac from purchasing loans made on properties with private transfer fees if those fees were established on or after February 8, 2011. See title 12 Code of Federal Regulations Section 1228 for more information and exceptions. Private transfer fees: (i) may last for a fixed period of time or in perpetuity, (ii) are typically calculated as a percentage of the sales price, and (iii) may have private parties, charitable organizations or interest-based groups as their recipients who may use the funds for social issues unrelated to the property. Brokers do not have expertise in this area.

38. GENERAL RECALL/DEFECTIVE PRODUCT/CLASS ACTION INFORMATION: Buyer and Seller are advised that government entities and manufacturers may at any time issue recall notices and/or warnings about products that may be present in the Property, and that these notices or warnings can change. The following nonexclusive, non-exhaustive list contains examples of

Buyer's Initials (_____) (_____)   Seller's Initials (_____) (_____)

Copyright © 2004-2013, CALIFORNIA ASSOCIATION OF REALTORS®, INC.

SBSA REVISED 11/13 (PAGE 8 OF 12)

Reviewed by _____ Date _____

STATEWIDE BUYER AND SELLER ADVISORY (SBSA PAGE 8 OF 12)

Untitled

Property Address: **123 Sail Avenue**
Marina del Rey, _____ Date: _____

recalled/defective products/class action information: horizontal furnaces, Whirlpool Microwave Hood Combination; RE-Con Building products roof tiles; Central Sprinkler Company Fire Sprinklers; Robert Shaw Water Heater Gas Control Valves; Trex Decking; water heaters; aluminum wiring; galvanized, abs, polybutylene and copper pipe; and dry wall manufactured in China. There is no single, all-inclusive source of information on product recalls, defective products or class actions; however, the U.S. Consumer Product Safety Commission (CPSC) maintains a website that contains useful information. If Buyer wants further information regarding the items listed above, Broker(s) recommend that Buyer review the CPSC website at http://www.cpsc.gov during Buyer's inspection contingency period. Another source affiliated with the CPSC is Saferproducts.gov which allows a Buyer to search by product type or product name. Buyers may also search using the various search engines on the Internet for the specified product or products in question. Brokers recommend that Buyers satisfy themselves regarding recalled or defective products. Brokers do not have expertise in this area and Brokers will not determine if any aspect of the Property is subject to a recall or is affected by a class action lawsuit.

39. RENTAL PROPERTY RESTRICTIONS: Buyer and Seller are advised that some cities and counties impose restrictions that limit the rent that can be charged to a tenant, the maximum number of tenants who can occupy the property and the right of a landlord to terminate a tenancy and the costs to do so. If Buyer wants further information, Broker(s) recommend that Buyer investigate the issue with an appropriate government authority during Buyer's inspection contingency period. Brokers do not have expertise in this area.

40. LAND LEASE: Buyer and Seller are advised that certain developments are built on leased land. This means that: (i) Buyer does not own the land, (ii) the right to occupy the land will terminate at some point in time, (iii) the cost to lease the land may increase at some point in the future, and (iv) Buyer may not be able to obtain title insurance or may have to obtain a different type of title insurance. If Buyer wants further information, Broker recommends that Buyer discuss the issue with an attorney or other appropriate professional. Brokers do not have expertise in this area.

41. HOME WARRANTY: Buyer and Seller are advised that Buyer and Seller can purchase home warranty plans covering certain standard systems of the Property both before and after Close of Escrow. Seller can obtain coverage for the Property during the listing period. For an additional premium, an upgraded policy providing additional coverage for air conditioning, pool and spa and other features can be purchased. Home warranties do not cover every aspect of the Property and may not cover inspections or upgrades for repairs required by state or federal laws or pre-existing conditions. Broker(s) recommend that Buyer review the policy for details. Brokers do not have expertise in this area.

42. INTERNET ADVERTISING; INTERNET BLOGS; SOCIAL MEDIA: Buyer and Seller are advised that Broker may employ a service to provide a "virtual tour" or Internet marketing of the Property, permitting potential buyers to view the Property over the Internet. Neither the service provider nor Brokers have control over who will obtain access to such services or what action such persons might take. Additionally, some Internet sites and other social media provide formats for comments or opinions of value of properties that are for sale. Information on the Property, or its owner, neighborhood, or any homeowner association having governance over the Property may be found on the internet on individual or commercial web sites, blogs, Facebook pages, or other social media. Any such information may be accurate, speculative, truthful or lies. Broker will not investigate any such sites, blogs, social media or other internet sites or the representations contained therein. Buyer is advised to make an independent search of electronic media and online sources prior to removing any investigation contingency. Buyer and Seller are advised that Brokers have no control over how long the information concerning the Property will be available on the Internet or through social media. Brokers do not have expertise in this area.

43. ESCROW FUNDS: Buyer and Seller are advised that California Insurance Code Section 12413.1 provides that escrow companies cannot disburse funds unless there are sufficient "good funds" to cover the disbursement. "Good funds" are defined as cash, wire transfers and cashiers' or certified checks drawn on California depositories. Escrow companies vary in their own definitions of "good funds." Broker(s) recommend that Buyer and Seller ask the escrow company regarding its treatment of "good funds." All samples and out-of-state checks are subject to waiting periods and do not constitute "good funds" until the money is physically transferred to and received by the escrow holder. Brokers do not have expertise in this area.

44. NOTICE OF YOUR "SUPPLEMENTAL" PROPERTY TAX BILL: Buyer and Seller are advised that pursuant to Civil Code § 1102.6(c), Seller, or his or her agent is required to provide the following "Notice of Your 'Supplemental' Property Tax Bill" to the Buyer:

"California property tax law requires the Assessor to revalue real property at the time the ownership of property changes. Because of this law, you may receive one or two supplemental tax bills, depending on when your loan closes.

The supplemental tax bills are not mailed to your lender. If you have arranged for your property tax responsibility payments to be paid through an impound account, the supplemental tax bills will not be paid by your lender. It is your responsibility to pay these supplemental bills directly to the Tax Collector. If you have any questions concerning this matter, please call your Tax Collector's Office."

Although the notice refers to loan closing as a trigger, it is actually the change of ownership which triggers this reassessment of property taxes. Therefore, the Property can be reassessed even if there is no loan involved in the purchase of the Property. The Purchase Agreement may allocate supplemental tax bills received after the Close of Escrow

Buyer's Initials (_____) (_____)   Seller's Initials (_____) (_____)

Copyright © 2004-2013, CALIFORNIA ASSOCIATION OF REALTORS®, INC.

SBSA REVISED 11/13 (PAGE 9 OF 12)

Reviewed by _____ Date _____

STATEWIDE BUYER AND SELLER ADVISORY (SBSA PAGE 9 OF 12)

EQUAL HOUSING OPPORTUNITY

Untitled

Property Address: *123 Sail Avenue*
Marina del Rey, _____ Date: _____

to the Buyer. If Buyer wants further information concerning these matters, Broker(s) recommend that Buyer discuss the issue with the County Assessor or Tax Collector or their own tax or legal advisor. Brokers do not have expertise in this area.

45. NON CONFIDENTIALITY OF OFFERS: Buyer is advised that Seller or Listing Agent may disclose the existence, terms, or conditions of Buyer's offer, unless all parties and their agent have signed a written confidentiality agreement (such as C.A.R. Form CND). Whether any such information is actually disclosed depends on many factors, such as current market conditions, the prevailing practice in the real estate community, the Listing Agent's marketing strategy and the instructions of the Seller.

46. FIRPTA/CALIFORNIA WITHHOLDING: Buyer and Seller are advised that: (i) Internal Revenue Code Section 1445 requires a Buyer to withhold and to remit to the Internal Revenue Service 10% of the purchase price of the property if the Seller is a non-resident alien, unless an express exemption applies. Seller may avoid withholding by providing Buyer a statement of non-foreign status. The statement must be signed by Seller under penalty of perjury and must include Seller's tax identification number. Buyer can also avoid having to withhold Federal taxes from Seller's Proceeds if the property price is $300,000 or less, and the Buyer signs an affidavit stating Buyer intends to occupy the property as a principal residence. (ii) California Revenue and Taxation Code Section 18662 requires that a Buyer withhold and remit to the California Franchise Tax Board 3 1/3% of the purchase price of the property unless the Seller signs an affidavit that the property was the Seller's (or the decedent's, if a trust or probate sale) principal residence or that the sales price is $100,000 or less or another express exemption applies. Exemptions from withholding also apply to legal entities such as corporations, LLCs, and partnerships. Brokers cannot give tax or legal advice. Broker recommends that Buyer and Seller seek advice from a CPA, attorney or taxing authority. Brokers do not have expertise in this area.

47. LIQUIDATED DAMAGES: Buyer and Seller are advised that a liquidated damages clause is a provision Buyer and Seller can use to agree in advance to the amount of damages that a seller will receive if a buyer breaches the Agreement. The clause usually provides that a seller will retain a buyer's initial deposit paid if a buyer breaches the agreement, and generally must be separately initialed by both parties and meet other statutory requirements to be enforceable. For any additional deposits to be covered by the liquidated damages clause, there generally must be another separately signed or initialed agreement (see C.A.R. Form RID). However, if the Property contains from 1 to 4 units, one of which a buyer intends to occupy, California Civil Code Section 1675 limits the amount of the deposit subject to liquidated damages to 3% of the purchase price. Even though both parties have agreed to a liquidated damages clause, an escrow company will usually require either a judge's or arbitrator's decision or instructions signed by both parties in order to release a buyer's deposit to a seller. Buyers and Sellers must decide on their own, or with the advice of legal counsel, whether to agree to a liquidated damages clause. Brokers do not have expertise in this area.

48. MEDIATION: Buyer and Seller are advised that mediation is a process by which the parties hire a neutral person to facilitate discussion and negotiation between the parties with the goal of helping them reach a settlement of their dispute. The parties generally share in the cost of this confidential, non-binding negotiation. If no agreement is reached, either party can pursue further legal action. Under C.A.R. Form RPA-CA: (i) the parties must mediate any dispute arising out of their agreement (with a few limited exceptions, such as matters within the jurisdiction of a small claims court) before they resort to arbitration or court, and (ii) if a party proceeds to arbitration or court without having first attempted to mediate the dispute, that party risks losing the right to recover attorney fees and costs even if he or she prevails.

49. ARBITRATION: Buyer and Seller are advised that arbitration is a process by which the disputing parties hire a neutral person to render a binding decision. Generally, arbitration is faster and less expensive than resolving disputes by litigating in court. The rules are usually less formal than in court, and it is a private process not a matter of public record. By agreeing to arbitration, the parties give up the right to a jury trial and to appeal the arbitrator's decision. Arbitration decisions have been upheld even when arbitrators have made a mistake as to the law or the facts. If the parties agree to arbitration, then after first attempting to settle the dispute through mediation, any dispute arising out of their agreement (with a few limited exceptions) must be submitted to binding arbitration. Buyer and Seller must weigh the benefits of a potentially quicker and less expensive arbitration against giving up the right to a jury trial and the right to appeal. Brokers cannot give legal advice regarding these matters. Buyers and Sellers must decide on their own, or with the advice of legal counsel, whether to agree to arbitration. Brokers do not have expertise in this area.

Buyer's Initials (_____) (_____)   Seller's Initials (_____) (_____)

Copyright © 2004-2013, CALIFORNIA ASSOCIATION OF REALTORS®, INC.
SBSA REVISED 11/13 (PAGE 10 OF 12)

| Reviewed by _____ Date _____ |

STATEWIDE BUYER AND SELLER ADVISORY (SBSA PAGE 10 OF 12)   Untitled

Property Address: *123 Sail Avenue Marina del Rey,* _____ Date: _____

50. MEGAN'S LAW DATABASE DISCLOSURE: Notice: Pursuant to Section 290.46 of the Penal Code, information about specific registered sex offenders is made available to the public via an Internet Web site maintained by the Department of Justice at www.meganslaw.ca.gov. Depending on an offender's criminal history, this information will include either the address at which the offender resides or the community of residence and ZIP Code in which he or she resides. (Neither Seller nor Brokers are required to check this website. If Buyer wants further information, Broker recommends that Buyer obtain information from this website during Buyer's inspection contingency period. Brokers do not have expertise in this area.)

51. DEATH ON THE PROPERTY: California Civil Code Section 1710.2 protects a seller from: (i) failing to disclose a death on the property that occurred more than 3 years before a buyer has made an offer on a property; and (ii) failing to disclose if an occupant of a property was afflicted with HIV/AIDS, regardless of whether a death occurred or if so, when. Section 1710.2 does not protect a seller from making a misrepresentation in response to a direct inquiry. If the Buyer has any concerns about whether a death occurred on the Property or the manner, location, details or timing of a death, the buyer should direct any specific questions to the Seller in writing.

52. LOCAL ADDENDA (IF CHECKED):
The following local disclosures or addenda are attached:

A. ☐ _____
B. ☐ _____
C. ☐ _____
D. ☐ _____

Buyer and Seller acknowledge and agree that Brokers: **(i)** do not decide what price Buyer should pay or Seller should accept; **(ii)** do not guarantee the condition of the Property; **(iii)** do not guarantee the performance, adequacy or completeness of inspections, services, products or repairs provided or made by Seller or others; **(iv)** do not have any obligation to conduct an inspection of common areas or areas off the site of the Property **(v)** shall not be responsible for identifying defects on the Property, in common areas, or offsite unless such defects are visually observable by an inspection of reasonably accessible areas of the Property or are known to Brokers; **(vi)** shall not be responsible for inspecting public records or permits concerning the title or use of Property; **(vii)** shall not be responsible for identifying the location of boundary lines or other items affecting title; **(viii)** shall not be responsible for verifying square footage, representations of others or information contained in investigation reports, Multiple Listing Service, advertisements, flyers or other promotional material; **(ix)** shall not be responsible for providing legal or tax advice regarding any aspect of a transaction entered into by Buyer or Seller; and **(x)** shall not be responsible for providing other advice or information that exceeds the knowledge, education and experience required to perform real estate licensed activity. Buyer and Seller agree to seek legal, tax, insurance, title and other desired assistance from appropriate professionals.

Buyer and Seller are encouraged to read this Advisory carefully. By signing below, Buyer and Seller acknowledge that each has read, understands and received a copy of this Advisory.

BUYER _____ Date _____

BUYER _____ Date _____

(Address) _____

SELLER _____ Date _____

SELLER _____ Date _____

(Address) _____

Buyer's Initials (_____) (_____)

Copyright © 2004-2013, CALIFORNIA ASSOCIATION OF REALTORS®, INC.

SBSA REVISED 11/13 (PAGE 11 OF 12)

Seller's Initials (_____) (_____)

Reviewed by _____ Date _____

STATEWIDE BUYER AND SELLER ADVISORY (SBSA PAGE 11 OF 12)

Untitled

Property Address: _123 Sail Avenue_
Marina del Rey, _____ Date: _____

Real Estate Broker (Selling Firm) _____ Cal BRE Lic. # _____

By _____ Cal BRE Lic. # _____ Date _____

Address _____ City _____ State ___ Zip _____

Telephone _____ Fax _____ Email _____

Real Estate Broker (Listing Firm) _____ Cal BRE Lic. # _____

By _____ Cal BRE Lic. # _____ Date _____

Address _____ City _____ State ___ Zip _____

Telephone _____ Fax _____ Email _____

THIS FORM HAS BEEN APPROVED BY THE CALIFORNIA ASSOCIATION OF REALTORS® (C.A.R.). NO REPRESENTATION IS MADE AS TO THE LEGAL VALIDITY OR ADEQUACY OF ANY PROVISION IN ANY SPECIFIC TRANSACTION. A REAL ESTATE BROKER IS THE PERSON QUALIFIED TO ADVISE ON REAL ESTATE TRANSACTIONS. IF YOU DESIRE LEGAL OR TAX ADVICE, CONSULT AN APPROPRIATE PROFESSIONAL.

This form is available for use by the entire real estate industry. It is not intended to identify the user as a REALTOR®. REALTOR® is a registered collective membership mark which may be used only by members of the NATIONAL ASSOCIATION OF REALTORS® who subscribe to its Code of Ethics.

Published and Distributed by:
REAL ESTATE BUSINESS SERVICES, INC.
a subsidiary of the California Association of REALTORS®
525 South Virgil Avenue, Los Angeles, California 90020

Reviewed by _____ Date _____

SBSA REVISED 11/13 (PAGE 12 OF 12)

STATEWIDE BUYER AND SELLER ADVISORY (SBSA PAGE 12 OF 12)   Untitled

III. CAR® Summary Disclosure Chart

The CAR *SUMMARY DISCLOSURE CHART* is designed to provide REALTORS® and their clients with an easy-to-use reference guide for determining the applicability of the state and federal laws to real estate transactions most commonly handled by real estate licensees.

The CAR "Summary Disclosure Chart" is an easy-to-use reference guide that can be downloaded by REALTORS® from the CAR® website at www.car.org.

The Real Estate Disclosure Summary Chart provides a disclosure "trigger" as well as a brief summary of the disclosure requirement, but does not cover all disclosures required by law. Some of the disclosures addressed in this chart, though generally applicable to a particular type of transaction, may be subject to exceptions which, unless otherwise noted, are not addressed in this publication. More detailed information regarding disclosure and other legal topics is available to CAR® members at CAR® Online.

 www.car.org
California Association of REALTORS®

The Disclosure Regarding Real Estate Agency Relationship form (see Chapter 3) is signed by both the agent and seller (or buyer), explaining what agency relationship is being offered, before any contract is written.

Disclosures on the "Real Estate Disclosure Summary Chart" include the following items:

Advisability of Title Insurance

Agency Disclosure

Agency Confirmation

Airport in Vicinity

Area of Potential Flooding

Broker's Statutory Duty to Inspect Property

Carbon Monoxide Detector Disclosure & Compliance

Commercial Property Owner's Guide to Earthquake Safety

Death (in last 3 years)

Earthquake Fault Zone

Farm or Ranch Proximity

FHA/HUD Inspection Notice

Federal Withholding (FIRPTA) and California Withholding Tax

Flood Disaster Insurance Requirements

Home Energy Rating System (HERS) Booklet

Homeowner's Guide to Earthquake Safety Booklet and *Residential Earthquake Hazards Report*

Industrial Use Zone Location

Lead-Based Paint Pamphlet and Form

Material Facts

A few days prior to closing, listing and selling agents should contact the escrow officer and request an Estimate of Closing Costs Statement for their individual clients. This avoids many errors in fees to be paid and there are no unhappy surprises on closing day. Remind your buyer to have an official or approved bank check for the remainder of the down payment and closing costs.

Remind the sellers that any payments (such as mortgage payments and taxes) that are due near the closing date should be made through escrow with verified funds. Otherwise, the escrow company will withhold a sufficient amount from the seller's proceeds to cover more than the estimated costs of these items. Also, remind the sellers that their bank will probably put a hold for a few days on their closing check when it is deposited. The seller should cancel the home insurance policy, unless it is being transferred to the buyer; escrow officers usually do not do this. You, as a salesperson, must provide the buyer with the names and telephone numbers of all utility companies.

Note: When escrow closes, if the seller is receiving proceeds in excess of $250,000 (the amount insured by FDIC), escrow should be instructed to cut more than one check so that none of them is greater than the insured amount.

IV. CHAPTER SUMMARY

Once the buyer and seller have agreed on a price and terms and the Purchase Agreement Contract has been completed, you need to supply your buyer with an additional set of forms as needed.

The **Commission Agreement** form sets out the amout of compensation to paid to the broker(s) for the sale of a property. Stated is the fact that the amount or rate of real estate commissions is not fixed by law, rather they are set by each broker individually and are negotiable.

The buyer needs to know the total costs of purchasing a property. Working with the lender and various affiliates involved, you can calculate these costs on the form entitled **Estimated Buyer's Costs**.

All contingencies about the sale of the buyer's property or the seller's purchase of a replacement property are noted in the **Contingency For Sale or Purchase of Other Property** form. There are several options for removing this contingency and remedies for noncompliance with time restrictions.

The **Buyer's Inspection Advisory** must be read and accepted by the buyer. It recommends obtaining and paying for qualified inspections before finalizing the transaction. The seller receives a copy signed by the buyer, signs it, and returns a copy to the selling agent. If the buyer gets a physical inspection performed, he or she is not entitled to rely on the broker's statement about the property.

If the buyers decline to have a professional inspection, it would be wise to have them sign a waiver attesting to this. CAR® provides the **Buyer's Inspection Waiver** form to specifically waive this option.

The **Wood Destroying Pest Inspection and Allocation of Cost Addendum** is an agreement between seller and buyer covering who will pay for required repairs (Section 1) and recommended repairs (Section 2). Often, the seller pays for work recommended under Section 1 and the buyer pays for repairs recommended under for Section 2. You should guide your clients to be sure all buildings on the site are included, such as detached garages, covered patios, decking, cabanas, etc.

When an offer is not accepted in its entirety, counter offers are made back and forth between the buyer and seller using a **Counter Offer** form. Escrow instructions are drawn up based on the intention of the parties as reflected in the original contract or any following accepted counter offers. As such, if more than two counter offers are made, it's best to start over with a new purchase offer to eliminate confusion.

The **Foreign Investment in Real Property Tax Act (FIRPTA)** requires a buyer to sign a **Buyer's Affidavit** if the property is to be used as a principal residence and the price does not exceed $300,000.

Based on various inspections, the **Request for Repair** is a buyer's wish list of repairs he or she would like the seller to make. The seller then indicates whether he or she agrees to make all of the repairs, some of the repairs, or none of the repairs. Based on the seller's response, the buyer either agrees to remove contingencies and follow through on the sale or opts to cancel the escrow. If escrow is cancelled, the buyer gets the deposit back, possibly minus incurred expenses, and the seller can put the property back on the market. (The buyer may write in contingencies other than repairs that he or she wants the seller to address in this form.) Both buyer and seller sign.

The **Transfer Disclosure Statement (TDS)** law requires the seller to identify any structural or material defects. This form mandates that the seller completely disclose problems of any kind that might adversely affect the value or the desirability of the property. The obligation to prepare and deliver the Transfer Disclosure Statement to the prospective buyer is imposed upon the seller and the seller's broker.

A **counter offer** is the rejection of the original offer and is a new offer detailing the new terms and conditions.

The **Receipt for Reports** and **Contingency Removal** forms are signed by the buyer to acknowledge which reports and disclosures he or she received, and whether those contingencies are removed. If the buyer has not received the appropriate reports and disclosures from the seller, or other terms and conditions agreed upon in the purchase contract have not been met by the seller, the buyer's agent forwards a **Notice to Seller to Perform** to the seller's agent. This notice gives the seller the right to cancel escrow within 24 hours (unless otherwise specified in the offer or counter offer). Buyer signs the form to indicate receipt.

A few days prior to closing the sale, the buyer makes a final **walk-through** of the property. He or she fills out a **Verification of Property Condition** confirming that the property is in basically the same condition as when the offer was made, and that the agreed-upon repairs or alterations have been satisfactorily performed. If the buyer declines a final inspection, it must be noted on the form and signed by the buyer.

The **Carbon Monoxide Poisoning Prevention Act** requires carbon monoxide detectors to be installed in every dwelling unit intended for human occupancy. The **Carbon Monoxide Detector Notice** is used for this purpose.

The CAR© **Statewide Buyer and Seller Advisory (SBSA)** form advises both buyer and seller of various factors that may affect the decision to buy, different types of inspections that can be obtained, questions to ask about or research, and information to be disclosed.

V. MATCHING VOCABULARY Fill in the blanks with the correct letter

A. Buyer
B. Buyer's Inspection Advisory
C. Commission agreement
D. Contingency removal
E. Counter offer
F. Estimate of buyer costs
G. Real Estate Transfer Disclosure Statement (TDS)

H. Seller
I. Statewide Buyer and Seller Advisory (SBSA)
J. Two years
K. Verification of property condition
L. Wood Destroying Pest Inspection and Allocation of Cost Addendum

1. _____ This form sets the amount or rate of real estate commissions which are negotiable between the seller and broker.

2. _____ This form lets the buyers know, before making an offer, the approximate total costs of the purchase, including monthly payments.

3. _____ This statement identifies items of value attached to the structure or land and states whether these items are operational.

4. _____ How long does a buyer have to sue an agent for failure to make proper disclosures in the Transfer Disclosure Statement.

5. _____ Who is NOT legally required to fill out and complete the Transfer Disclosure Statement.

6. _____ Who customarily pays for an active infestation of wood destroying pests on the property?

7. _____ As offers are rejected and new offers made, this form details the exact terms of the newest offer.

8. _____ This CAR® form educates and illuminates over 50 disclosures that both buyers and sellers should be made aware of.

9. _____ Buyer is advised to conduct an investigation of the entire property.

10. _____ Section 2C-1 of this report denotes active insect infestation, elimination of which is usually paid by the seller.

11. _____ Buyer can choose to remove certain terms and conditions of the purchase using this form.

12. _____ Buyer's final inspection of the property to determine if the property is in substantially the same condition as on the date of acceptance.

See Page 610 for Answers

VI. CHAPTER QUIZ

1. Which of the following seller's listing forms does the buyer NOT receive a copy of?

   a. Residential Listing Agreement
   b. Estimated Seller's Proceeds
   c. Both "a" and "b" are for seller's eyes only
   d. The buyer gets a copy of all listing documents

2. "FIRPTA" refers to:

   a. Fiduciary Information for Real Property Agency.
   b. Federal Inspection of Real Property Act.
   c. Foreign Interest in Real Property Acquisitions.
   d. Foreign Investment in Real Property Tax Act.

3. When making an offer contingent on the sale of the buyer's home:

   a. the buyer and agent need not inform the seller of this contingency.
   b. the buyer is still obligated to consummate the sale, regardless of whether his or her house sells.
   c. the buyer is offering to trade properties with the seller in a 1031 exchange.
   d. always use the Contingency for Sale or Purchase of Other Property (COP) form, and make this an amendment to the Purchase Agreement.

4. Which of the following is TRUE concerning a selling agent's commission?

   a. The selling agent can ask for any acceptable commission split prior to close of escrow.
   b. The selling agent must abide by the commission details placed on the MLS by the listing agent.
   c. The selling agent can renegotiate his or her percentage of the commission with the seller regardless of the MLS information.
   d. All of the above.

5. After the physical inspection, the buyer requests the seller to repair the defects noted in the report. Which of the following is correct?

   a. The seller must comply and do all the work.
   b. The seller is responsible for making the repairs, but the buyer has to pay for them.
   c. The seller may do some, all, or none of the repairs.
   d. None of the above are correct.

6. With regard to contingencies, the buyer must deliver designated documents to the seller within five days. If the buyer fails to do so, the seller:

   a. may send the buyer a Notice to Buyer to Perform.
   b. may cancel the Agreement in writing.
   c. cannot cancel, even if the buyer does not remove the contingencies.
   d. both a and b are correct.

7. The home warranty:

   a. is always paid by the seller.

   b. is always paid by the buyer.

   c. can be paid by anybody.

   d. is not a valuable option.

8. The Agency Relationship Disclosure:

   a. can be signed at any time prior to close of escrow.

   b. is a requirement for the seller only.

   c. is a requirement for buyer only.

   d. is a requirement for both parties prior to entering into any real estate contract.

9. Wood Destroying Pest Inspection and Allocation of Cost Addendum (WPA):

   a. states whether the seller or the buyer will be responsible for the costs of the required work.

   b. states that inspection and repairs are usually paid by the agents.

   c. states that the seller always pays for Section 1 and Section 2.

   d. is not applicable in California.

10. When doing the final walk-through:

   a. the buyer and seller sign the Verification of Property Condition, after noting that the requested repairs have been performed and the property is in the same condition as when the offer was made.

   b. the buyer checks for the first time for leaks, electrical outlets and switches, and checks all the windows.

   c. the seller must be accompanied by his or her attorney.

   d. all of the above.

ANSWERS: *1. c; 2. d; 3. d; 4. b; 5. c; 6. d; 7. c; 8. d; 9. a; 10. a*

For Sale
310-424-5512
BermanKandel.com
FOR INSTANT PRICE, PICS & INFO
TEXT: MLS99664
85377

CHAPTER 8

Online Search, Alerts, and Beyond: Constantly Evolving Technology

The Online Growth of Our Real Estate Industry

Most brokerages have established a sizeable online presence to meet changing customer practices. This allows customers to be informed about current home prices and the home-buying process by doing a lot of "searches" online.

I. Homebuyers: Taking the Search Online

Most homebuyers say they use the Internet "search" as part of their home research. The Internet has not rendered real estate agents obsolete, but has increased business.

The vast majority of buyers say they would still use a real estate agent for information in their hunt for a future home.

More and more buyers are using the Internet first, rather than agents. Even homebuyers using agents still use the Internet to enhance their home search.

Online real estate research sites have not put real estate agents out of business, but they have taken viewers away from the old traditional sources of information.

In the past, homebuyers relied heavily on newspapers and newsstand real estate magazines to get their home search started.

Today, fewer prospective buyers utilize newspaper ads and fewer yet use the home books and magazines available outside local stores.

A. ONLINE HOME SEARCHES

Most agents meet with prospective homebuyers after the buyers have done extensive research online.

CHAPTER 8

Many homebuyers view a home "walkthrough" online, which is a good reason to create "virtual tours" online. A third of the home searchers found a real estate agent as a result of an online home search and about a fifth at least drove by a home they saw online.

The brick and mortar real estate offices are still thriving. *BRICK AND MORTAR refers to businesses that have physical (rather than virtual or online) presences—in other words, stores (built of physical material such as bricks and mortar) that you can drive to and enter physically to see, touch, and purchase merchandise.* This is unlike the travel industry, where more and more consumers are taking the entire booking process into their own hands. Online real estate-related services are only the beginning for potential buyers who usually want a skilled agent to help them through the disclosure, buying, and closing process.

The Internet has supplemented homebuyers' search options dramatically. The majority of homebuyers are still using real estate agents, but they're utilizing online search resources to conduct initial research and look for homes first, often for several months, before contacting an agent.

B. BROKERS AND SALESPEOPLE - GOING ONLINE

Most real estate agents have responded well to the increasing demand for increased online brokerage presence, which included getting more involved with evolving technology.

Most California agents say they are using a smartphone with Internet, text, and email in order to better stay in touch with customers.

The majority of the people in the U.S. have smartphones and utilize some form of social media.

II. The Three Most Popular Real Estate Brokerage Websites

Over 85% of real estate transactions start online these days. It is more important than ever to assure that "your" real estate business is getting the exposure it needs on the Internet.

Real Estate websites attract over 60 million visitors each month in the U.S.

Here are the three Most Popular Real Estate Sites as ranked by viewers.

A. REALTOR.COM® (Owned by Murdoch - News Corp.)

Homes for sale on realtor.com® span thousands of cities and towns across the U.S. and Canada. Real estate listings represent over 800 multiple listing services so you get the most accurate and reliable information possible. To find condos, townhomes, single-family homes or land, the user can simply use the property search function.

MLS data is updated every 15 minutes, making it the most accurate online real estate search engine or search service.

www.realtor.com

B. ZILLOW®

Zillow has data on over 100 million homes across the United States, not just those homes currently for sale (they include past sales figures as well). In addition to giving value estimates of homes, Zillow offers several features, including value changes of each home in a given time frame (such as one, five, or 10 years), aerial views of homes, and prices of comparable homes in the area. Where it can access appropriate public data, it also provides basic information on a given home, such as square footage and the number of bedrooms and bathrooms.

Zillow teamed with Microsoft to offer "bird's eye view," a feature in Microsoft Virtual Earth, that shows (in certain areas) clearer aerial photographs taken from airplanes rather than conventional satellite imagery.

Zillow has expanded its services to include the rental market.

Unfortunately, Zillow doesn't have x-ray vision and can't tell the viewer about the quality of one home over another. Because they use arithmatical values, or "Automated Valuation Models (AVMs)," there is no way to accurately price a home that has granite countertops and custom cabinets over formica and plywood. With the expertise of an agent, a buyer can judge the true value of a home.

 www.zillow.com

C. TRULIA® (Owned By Zillow)

Trulia is an online residential real estate site for homebuyers, sellers, renters, and real estate professionals. It lists properties for sale and rent as well as neighborhood information and community insights. The company is headquartered in downtown San Francisco. Trulia was purchased by Zillow but may continue to use its original name.

Trulia provides several paid advertising products for real estate agents. These include Trulia Pro, Local Ads, and Mobile Ads. Trulia Pro provides featured listings which appear higher in search results. Local Ads allow real estate agents to "lock up" their local area on the website by purchasing all available spots in a ZIP code or city. Agents can also advertise via Trulia's Mobile Ads apps. As with Local Ads, agents can select the "ZIP codes or cities" where their ads will be shown.

 www.trulia.com

D. MULTIPLE LISTING SERVICES (Members Only)

MLS data is updated every 15 minutes, making it the most accurate online real estate search engine or search service.

Although the most accurate, an MLS is also the most exclusionary. You must be a member of a particular multiple listing service, which may require you also be a member of local, state, or national association of REALTORS®. Multiple Listing Services charge their members fees, but are well worth it as they give many more details than other websites that only reveal a fraction of the information on the MLS listing. Other real estate search engines are fed limited information from the original MLS website.

III. Aggregation of MLS Real Estate Information

MLS AGGREGATION means the collection of large amounts of seller information from several Multiple Listing Services (MLSs) to post digital listing data and photos online. The aggregation allows the data from neighborhood MLSs to be collected and put onto one site for easier comparison.

Most agents these days plan to list homes not just in the local newspaper and real estate magazines, but also online. Many agents own or control their own websites (a good idea because it may follow you everywhere you might want to move.)

MLS sites are always important, because they spread listing and sales information which is usually then aggregated by popular home search sites like Zillow® and Realtor.com.

Over one million real estate agents are on the cutting edge of technology.

Real estate professionals state they must commonly use social media and networking: 1) to build relationships, 2) for increased visibilty/exposure and marketing, 3) for free advertising, and 4) to promote listings.

IV. Ownership of Your Real Estate Website

In a landmark case, the 9th U.S. Circuit Court of Appeals has stated that domain names, despite their virtual nature, should be treated exactly as a "plot of land" would be.

This was a huge victory for all domain name registrants (our registered websites).

This ruling means that traditional property protections can now be legally applied to domain names (website names). Further, the ruling firmly establishes that domain names are valuable properties and shows that old-fashioned property laws also apply to the registration of your web addresses.

Website domain name holders should be aware of their legal rights and take steps to protect them.

Just as your home or other property is considered to be an investment, so are your rights to a domain name. In the event of your death your domain rights will become part of your estate. If you were to get a divorce, it may be left up to the courts to decide who gets to keep the domain name, and whether one party will need to pay the other party for half of the value of the name.

Since your domain name is your piece of cyber real estate, it should be valued in the same fashion as your home or other property, using the same tried and true principles.

Domain names are now officially considered cyber real estate—like walthuber.REALTOR.

V. Real Estate Agents are Still Needed!

The general public realizes that when they purchase a home or are looking for other brokerage services, they need to find an agent to trust and should take the advice of a seasoned professional.

Thanks to the ease and accessibility of online searches, many service-oriented middlemen, such as travel agents and soft-good retailers, have been rendered obsolete. Expedia and Priceline have deeply impacted the travel industry, while Amazon.com is outpacing retail sales. Real Estate brokers and agents, however, have not been as adversely affected as these other industries. This could be due to the fact that home values vary by location, local economic conditions, size, recent sales, etc. These differences are best demonstrated through unbiased, publicly available data, usually acquired from MLS listings, then crunched and presented on free websites like Realtor.com and Zillow.com.

Real estate agents are still with us. Their professional learning and licensing make them irreplaceable when filling out contracts, disclosures, and forms.

According to the National Association of REALTORS®, agents are as widely used as ever. It's the same on the seller side, where only nine percent of sellers sold a home without an agent.

There are a few reasons why agents are still around. **The post-crash real estate world is more complex** — Tighter lending standards, as well as the prevalence of foreclosures, have made the average transaction harder to navigate without expert help. Getting financing, negotiating, filling out many "disclosure forms," for example, probably should not be done by your clients on your own. There's always something coming down the pike that makes the process more complicated.

The **Internet improves productivity** — Buyers can find the homes they want through online research; as an agent, you have to spend less time touring them around. Often, you can then just come in and help with closing and pick up the same commission.

To adapt and add value, brokerages have scaled back on their office space —thanks to the Internet, more agents now work from home, rather than private cubicles.

Most people don't trust cheap brokerages — Buying a home is a big decision, and people don't tend to want to take a risk on a cut-rate agent or brokerage, which is why there hasn't been much undercutting or negotiation of commissions. This is the biggest asset they've ever owned, so if you can make people believe you'll handle the negotiation, paperwork, and disclosure process correctly, people are willing to pay for it.

VI. Marketing & Advertising Basics

The "Marketing Concept" for real estate agents, as with all marketing, is that success begins and continues with your clients. An ongoing relationship with your clients is the foundation to becoming a successful business.

A. MARKETING

REAL ESTATE MARKETING is the entire process of communicating the benefit of your real estate service to your customers (buyers, sellers, tenants and landlords).

TARGET MARKETING (NICHE) is the ability to select and cultivate a subgroup of people to whom you directly promote your services in a way strategically designed to satisfy their specific needs and preferences (see section XIV). The people in your target market are collectively referred to as your SPHERE OF INFLUENCE.

The key to marketing is understanding your selected client's needs and requirements so you may satisfy their specific preferences.

The very word "service" involves a personal interaction. You, as an independent contractor, need to provide great service, usually via face-to-face interaction. A marketing campaign that builds continuing personal relationships is essential to your success. Your customer needs to know that you will cater your services to fit their special needs.

Let customers know you. A good business relationship is built on trust.

Self promotion, both paid (advertising) and unpaid (publicity and public relations), encourages and persuades your buyer or seller to ask you to solve their real estate needs.

A successful service business is developed by using your name or a brand identity to "differentiate you" from your competitors.

A BRAND is a name, your name, term, logo, or design that identifies you and your particular service, that differentiates you from your competitors.

B. ADVERTISING AND PUBLICITY (Online and Print)

ADVERTISING is paid promotion used to encourage—and involves a method used to identify—your service to help persuade your buyer or seller to talk to you and discuss how you can help them solve their real estate desires.

PUBLICITY is giving out information about a broker, brokerage, or salesperson using websites, social medias, blogs, news media, and even newspapers articles. Giving and servicing local nonprofit events is also a good way to meet "movers and shakers" in your neighborhood.

PUBLIC RELATIONS (PR) is unpaid communication and relationships with various public audiences

VII. REALTORS® (Educated Professionals)

A. REALTOR® FORMAL EDUCATION BACKGROUND

1. High school graduate: 9%
2. Some college: 30%
3. Associate degree: 11%

4. Bachelor's degree: 30%
5. Graduate degree and above: 13%
6. Some graduate school: 8%

> **Did you know: Real estate professionals, by and large, are a very educated lot (many having multiple degrees). This education has allowed them to flourish in a business where it is important (actually mandated) to continue their education. As such, it is important that you don't rest on your educational laurels, but continue to learn about and utilize new technologies affecting the industry. As your clients become a younger demographic, you'll need to keep up with their knowledge base, including the use of computer technology!**

VIII. "Homebuyer" Advertising Statistics

The six advertising sources listed below are eye opening! These important facts about what sources work, and the percentage of buyers that use them, are shaping our advertising behavior.

Some of the important information sources (leads) used in a home search:

1. Internet: 90%
2. Real estate agent: 87%
3. Yard sign: 53%
4. Open house: 45%
5. Newspaper ad: 27%
6. Home book or magazine: 18%

These are the new methods and sources of information that buyers typically use to obtain information about their upcoming home purchases. With these insights, we all have been adjusting to how we react to and use our smartphones, tablets, mini-iPads, and notebook or office/home computers.

What buyers respond to in today's market is far different from what the public responded to just a decade ago. Internet search engines, websites, social media, email, and texting have forever changed the way the real estate industry operates.

Use this information when determining how to spend your advertising budget.

IX. Real Estate Online Search (90% of People)

90% of buyers search online before contacting an agent.

A. HOW HOMEBUYERS USE THE INTERNET

According to Google, the average homebuyer performs eleven searches before action is taken.

Buyers use search engines and general websites to make searches on homes. Through utilizing apps such as Google Maps online, they can see the exact location and view the street and surrounding areas to the prospected homes. A *MOBILE APPLICATION is a software application that runs in a smartphone, tablet, or other portable device.* Mobile Applications (wireless apps) are constantly expanding to make browsing on the go easier for users.

Close to one million people yearly use YouTube searches for "buying a home" and "finding a real estate agent."

X. Owners: Get Loans, Refinance With Lenders Online

Current owners can get loans, compare interest rates, points and fees with Online lenders. See Chapter 9 when prequalifying and getting qualified for a new home purchase loan.

A. HOME LOAN PRODUCTS

1. Mortgage Refinance Loans
2. Home Equity Loans
3. FHA Loans
4. VA Loans
5. Reverse Mortgage Loans
6. Mortgage Rates

B. DIRECT-TO-LENDER LOANS ONLINE

Need home financing? Choosing a home mortgage loan can feel like getting dressed in the dark—you manage to get clothing on your body, but it might not be the most appropriate ensemble. LendingTree® helps you clearly see differences between mortgage lenders and products and choose the right one for you—whether you're a first-time homebuyer or a seasoned veteran.

Corporations and their websites are in constant flux; the authors and publisher of this book are not endorsing any particular corporation, website, or product.

1. LendingTree Loans

a. The LendingTree® Mortgage Loan Process

Here's how the LendingTree home loan process works:

1. Complete the simple, secure online mortgage loan request
2. Receive up to five home loan offers from lenders
3. Compare mortgage interest rates and terms
4. Choose the offer that best fits your needs

LendingTree requires no personal information, no commitment, and offers several personalized quotes in seconds. It compares offers, but doesn't give loans.

 **www.lendingtree.com**

2. Quicken Loans®

Quicken Loans® is the largest online retail mortgage lender and the second largest overall retail lender in the United States. The company consists of Quicken Loans, One Reverse Mortgage, and Title Source, a mortgage settlement service provider.

LeBron James has Come Home to Cleveland

"I'm Coming Home" is the song adopted by Clevelanders for LeBron James's return to his hometown and home team. Owner of the Cavaliers and Quicken Loans Arena, Dan Gilbert, has been instrumental in the buying of homes through Quicken Loans, the leading provider of direct-consumer home loans on the Internet. He is also part owner of the giant Intuit, which owns Quicken Loans, as well as Quickbooks and Quicken Online accounting systems. Real estate lending and technology has its perks—just ask Dan Gilbert next time he's hangin' with LeBron. — Walt Huber

---

Quicken Loans **www.quickenloans.com**
Engineered to **Amaze**

3. GreenLight Loans®

Greenlight Financial Services is a mortgage lender that is HUD and FHA approved. Loans obtained through Greenlight are backed with a low rate and fee guarantee. Greenlight can also refinance current loans at lower interest rates to help you save money on your monthly mortgage payments.

 **www.greenlightloans.com**

XI. The Internet Real Estate Office (Traditional to Tech)

A. TRADITIONAL OFFICE METHODS

Let's face it, some clients, particularly older potential listing clients, may not be tech-savvy and may be intimidated by the newest technology.

It is your job to walk them through the process in the simplest of terms and use your visual tools to show them that you have the capability of listing their property with numerous websites. Combined with a well-formulated marketing plan—which you have under your control—your client need not know more than just how to send an email.

> *For the uninitiated, for example, clients who don't have access to the Internet, you need to assure them that you will keep them abreast of the latest developments in the sale of their home—whether that means a phone call or a visit to their home or your office. Don't assume everyone has even a rudimentary basic knowledge of computers and the Internet.*

1. Listing Presentation (Getting Sellers to List Their Homes)

When approaching a potential listing client, you can take a photo of their property and input it into your computer **Listing Presentation** so you have a visual to show them. Even if they don't know how you did it, they will be impressed that you were able to include their property into a listing presentation on the spot.

You never know how much of a computer background a client may have. Be prepared with a good old-fashioned folder that includes a **Comparative Market Analysis (CMA)** with currently sold properties printed on paper! Additionally, you'll want to include your personal bio and any paper versions of what you may be showing them on your mobile device. That way you can leave it behind with the client when you leave and they are not intimidated about trying to contact you via the Internet.

2. Online Real Estate Forms/Contracts are Mobile

The California Association of REALTORS® has made forms, contracts, and addendums available to not only your desktop or laptop, but also to your mobile devices, often for a fee.

zipForm® Plus is your free C.A.R. member benefit that lets you manage all your real estate transactions online. This essential real estate application helps you maximize workflow efficiency while reducing risk. zipForm® 6 Standard is offered as a free member benefit for users who prefer the desktop version (no Internet required to use forms).

As a C.A.R. member, you have free access to C.A.R.'s real estate forms and transaction management platform zipForm®. This secure and easy-to-use software is designed to increase your professional productivity and help complete contracts mor eefficiently.

B. TECHNOLOGICAL ADVANCES ARE FAST MOVING

Once you've established that the clients need not have computer science degrees, you can lead them down a more sophisticated path, allowing them to see the inner workings and tremendous potential of the different technological applications you have.

For example, among others, Realtor.com has an *APP (or web application)* called **Keynote for Listing Presentations** that allows you to download information to your iTunes or iCloud account that can replace the more standard power-point presentation. It is up to you how sophisticated you make the presentation, including charts, personal bio info, photos of your brokerages current listings, names and access to numerous different websites and destinations. Explain how you share information with the local MLS and mention any other tools you use to market yourself and your properties.

You can store your presentation on your mobile device so you need not access the Internet to show your files to the client. This is because you never know whether that client will have access to the Internet.

That said, if you don't have unlimited **Data** on your mobile tablet, for example, you may only have access to the web through wi-fi. Even if the client has a wi-fi connection, you don't want to have to ask for their wi-fi name and password.

Why not set up a personal HOTSPOT to be used with your smartphone so you bring a wi-fi connection wherever you go?

Ever been stuck in a situation where you need to get a device online but there's no nearby Wi-Fi? Your problem can be easily solved using Personal Hotspot. PERSONAL HOTSPOT (TETHERING) is a feature that lets smartphone users share their wireless data connection with other nearby devices via Wi-Fi, Bluetooth, or USB. In this scenario, your smartphone acts like a wireless router for the other devices, transmitting and receiving data for them. Setting up a personal hotspot usually requires a small fee from your phone company, but it's well worth it when showing clients listings or getting them to fill out forms, contracts or sign up for alert notifications.

C. LISTING SYNDICATIONS

A *LISTING SYNDICATION is the process of getting a listing's information displayed on numerous other websites around the Internet.* The MLS syndicates (shares) new listing information with several other sites like Realtor.com, Zillow, and Trulia. Furthermore, a local newspaper, like the *Los Angeles Times*, may be automatically notified of the new listing and allow non-licensees to browse the websites looking for properties.

There are secondary sites that may still be free, but require the broker to sign up with an account before the MLS will share listing information with them.

As part of your marketing plan, you should show your clients how sharing MLS information with a listing syndication will further expand the distribution of their information.

D. ALERT NOTIFICATIONS - LISTING SYNDICATIONS

1. Alert Notifications (Auto Email Alerts)

When you encounter potential buyers, you should get them to help you fill out an MLS "wish list" for their dream property! They will be notified if such a house listing appears in the next month or so. The choices they can make for what they are looking for are endless. You can fill out the number of bedrooms and bathrooms, the square footage, the neighborhood down to the particular block, the price, and amenities such as swimming pool or Jacuzzi.

The difference between helping a buyer and helping a seller is that buyers want to know what listings have not been sold. The sellers, on the other hand, want to know what homes have already sold (CMA).

Once the information has been processed, you have the option of clicking on the print icon, the email icon, or the automated alert icon. We are currently speaking of the automated alert icon. Once you have selected that option, you can decide if you want the MLS to notify your client, just you, or both you and/ or client when an appropriate property comes up for sale that fits the criteria you have entered. You then have the option of deciding how often to send out these alerts: daily, morning, afternoon, weekly, monthly, etc. Every client has different preferences—all of which go into a local database kept through the local MLS office, referred to as your personal MLS portal. **Figure 8-1** is an example of an email sent to a client explaining how to access their personalized page on the MLS Portal.

Don't let the computer do all the work for you. When you see a potential buyer has commented on or viewed a property, follow up with a phone call or text and an offer to show them property in person!

2. Open Houses (Excellent Places to Find Clients)

When holding an open house, you can use a number of different downloadable Apps and programs to help you keep track of potential buyers and sellers as well as create a "contact list."

Create a digital contact list instead of a paper "Guest Book."

a. Open House Apps (New Trend)

Once you've been assured the buyer is NOT interested in the house you're showing (you don't want to short change your current homeowner), you can ask visitors to sign in on your tablet or iPad, which is easier to read than a smartphone.

Your tablet is like a sign in sheet, but much more helpful in that you can ask potential buyers to fill out their "wish list of important features"—asking them for the details of the perfect home. You and your clients will get notified by "Email Alerts" (notifications) when such a property has just been listed with your MLS.

Figure 8-1

Welcome to The "MLS Portal"

All messages I send to you containing MLS® listing information - those I send you manually as well as those I set our system to send you automatically - will contain a link to your personalized page on the MLS Portal.

You can access your MLS Portal with your favorite web browser, where you'll be able to view the MLS® listing information I've prepared for you in several different formats. For your convenience, you'll be able to sort these listings and categorize them. You'll be able to see all associated photographs. And you'll be able to see them pinned on a map, a high-level aerial photograph or a low-level "Bird's Eye" photograph.

I hope you enjoy working with your MLS Portal and I will be happy to receive your feedback. In the meantime, please click on the link below to begin your MLS Portal experience.

Click the following link to view ALL property listings
http://www.mrmlsmatrix.com/DAE.asp?ID=0-2296334363-10

Arlette Lyons, CRS, GRI
2820 E. Garvey Avenue South
West Covina, CA 91791
So. of #10 Freeway, East of Citrus
Office: (626) 331-0141 - Fax: 626-331-9772
Mobile: (626) 825-0023
License No. 00414792

Note: The Web link above will expire 30 days after the date of this email.
Please review our Privacy Policy.
Delivered by CRMLS, 180 Via Verde, Suite 200, San Dimas, CA 91773 | 909.859.2040
Click this link if you wish to Unsubscribe:
http://www.mrmlsmatrix.com/UAE.asp?ID=0-2296334363-00&Eml=bGlsbHl3aXRlQGFvbC5jb20%3d

Auto email alerts, which have been programmed to the clients' specifications with your help, are the latest way we help our clients find the home of their dreams first.

Auto email alerts show you and notify your clients of the new listings that have just come on the market for sale that meet their requirements. This is the best new way your clients can get the most up-to-date information as soon as possible. You can indicate the frequency of alerts—daily, weekly, even hourly.

b. Add a Property Address "Domain Name (URL)" to Your Yard Sign

Why not "assign" a domain name (i.e, ".com") to each of your just listed properties?

In this day of web searches, most real estate brokers pay for a hosting service to buy a domain name for each property they have listed. For example, "1234 W. Covina St.com or .net," depending on what's available. The hosting company owns the domain name, and you essentially lease it from them monthly for a small fee, like $12 a month until the house is sold or your employment contract with the listing has expired.

Add a hanger—1234 W. Covina Blvd.com—to brokerage "for sale" yard signs!

c. Hire a Company to Do All Your Address Domain Hosting

These companies maintain the website with all the pertinent information from the MLS listing and may charge extra for more elaborate information, such as walk-through videos. The company may also make money by charging you for yard sign riders that you slip on the top of or hang from your brokerage sign with the website address for information about that property.

Often potential buyers are hesitant to speak to an agent for fear of getting caught in an endless web which they may feel borders on harassment. A website with the home information and the broker's contact information is often preferable to those who wish to remain anonymous or are really just curious and not shopping.

Keep in mind that, for a fee, many of these domain providers can and will provide you, the broker, with a list of the people who viewed the website—if not for you to contact back, at least to give you an idea of how much interest has been generated in the property.

Professor Huber also adds a "walthuber.REALTOR" hanger to his yard signs!

Apps and programs like Open House Pro and numerous others can be used as a guest sign-in sheet and at the same time captures the guests contact information and needs. The agents can reach their Multiple Listing Service at that time and show their open house guests other listings matching their requirements.

XII. Social Media Possibilites

Don't let the word "social" fool you. Social media sites are booming advertising opportunities for real estate professionals. As their income increases from paying advertising customers, the number of methods you can utilize to promote your company's image increases.

Social media is the most effective way to practice inbound marketing. **Nielsen studies have found that social networks occupy the bulk of consumers' online time.** Internet users spend three times as much time on Facebook as on any other site. They also spend far more time on other social networks such as Twitter and LinkedIn than they do on the rest of the Internet. Social media is too important to be ignored.

Social media users are not just talking with their friends; they are making decisions about how to spend their money. Recent research has shown that 55% of consumers use social media as a source of information and 75% use social media as part of their purchasing process.

For real estate agents, in addition to the 90% of housing searches that begin online, 20% of positive reviews now come from social media. This is a major marketing opportunity!

A. SOCIAL NETWORKING - A MORE SOPHISTICATED ADVERTISING PLATFORM

There's nothing wrong with using the traditional advertising methods to get the attention of both buyers and sellers, however, social networking sites are quickly becoming an indispensable avenue of marketing revenue and the real estate business can take advantage of the speed with which clients can access their properties and benefit from brand recognition that the Internet and social media sites can offer.

Don't let new technology Intimidate you. Spend a little time searching the following sites to familiarize yourself with them. Do a Google search on how to use social media sites to your brokerage's advantage. You'll find that some sites make it as easy for beginners.

1. Facebook

Facebook is by far the most often visited social networking site on the Internet, with over 700 million people worldwide connecting separately with friends and businesses contacts.

While many readers are familiar with the "friends" aspect of Facebook, it's important to know that the advertising potential created by the mega-popular is wide open. The revenue coming in for mobile ads, motivates Facebook to help you create business ads in addition your personal posts.

Some of the benefits of having an ad on Facebook is that the company has tools to help measure your ads' performance, as well as target a very specific audience that you are trying to reach.

a. Use Facebook to Reach Your Target Market

You can create specific advertisements (ads) for current and new customers based on their:

1. **Location:** Target customers in specific counties, cities or zip codes
2. **Age & Gender:** Select the age range and economic group of the people who will find your ad relevant. Clients with children will be interested in school districts for example.

3 **Interests:** Reach audiences based on their listed interests. For example, if your customers are in the market for an artist's loft in the downtown area, you can target people who like "downtown living" or "artist's lofts" as well as people who are in the broad category Property for Sale (Downtown).

4. **Connections:** Decide which Facebook users with which to share your ads. For example, people who have liked your Page or joined your target group or Facebook Event.

It's best to start out with one particular social media and become proficient with that site. Spreading yourself too thin over too many sites may diminish the quality of the advertising method you're using. Better to be master of one than novice of several.

> **Keep a separate list of "friends" from "business connections" as you don't necessarily want to cross-contaminate the two. When a viewer clicks on your ad you want it to link to your business website and not your vacation pictures from Hawaii—unless, of course, you're trying to sell that property in Oahu!**

2. Twitter

Twitter uses "tweets" (or short messages of 140 of characters or less) that can be 'retweeted' over and over again. So if you're advertising a new listing and one of your followers reads it, he or she can "retweet" it to someone they know looking for a specific type of house. Your followers become built-in promoters of your business and your listings.

Twitter also allows you to track your account, and for a fee will "amplify" your Tweet so that it reaches a larger more targeted audience. You can get real-time updates on your campaigns and quickly make improvements to drive even greater results or for example, relay that a home has just been sold so followers don't get their hopes up about a particular property, but also see how successful you are at selling!

a. Twitter Target Marketing

Like many social networking sites with an eye on the financial windfall of advertising, Twitter allows you to target an audience. To get your account in front of the right audience who are more likely to become followers and improve your "brand recognition," you can target by:

1. Interests
2. Keywords
3. @usernames
4. Geography
5. Gender

The brevity (shortness) of Tweets is often desirable from followers who don't want to wade through long messages. A picture paints a thousand words, so posting a picture of a home you've listed is a terrific way to get that home seen online. Make sure you use your words to indicate how to contact you or your brokerage and include a link to the more detailed page!

3. Pinterest

Pinterest is a virtual bulletin board. You can "pin" images or videos from all over the net to different boards under your profile. The number of pins and boards that you can have are unlimited. Each pin has a description and links directly to the website you got the image or video from.

Once you share a pin, your followers can like it and re-pin it to one of their boards, which goes to all of their friends and family on the site. That can mean a lot of visibility in a small amount of time.

You know the real estate business has taken notice of Pinterest by virtue of the fact that NAR has its own Pinterest page at http://pinterest.com/realtors.

For advertising purposes your brokerage can pay for Promoted Pins which appear in category and search results on Pinterest.com and its mobile apps.

You want to link your Pinterest page to all your other social media pages. It's a form of "image management." Not only does your Pinterest page reflect your personality (depending on the elements you choose to post, like interesting suggestions on drought resistant plants) but it can direct your "pinners" to more business-oriented sites where they can view your webpage or your list of homes for sale.

a. List of Potential Subjects You Can "Pin" to Get Attention

1. **Home Listings -** Of course you have to have a board for all of the homes you have for sale. Take pictures that will really grab your followers' attention, like a scenic view, dream master bathroom, or unique architecture.

2. **Neighborhood Information -** Another fun idea is to have a board reserved for each of the main neighbors you sell homes in.

3. **Additional Information -** This site allows you to build an identity your clients can relate to—be creative.

When you go to "pin" something you will have to fill in three fields: Description, Link, and Board.

1. **Description -** When writing your description, compose something catchy and creative. It is also important to include keywords and hash tags so that your pin can be easily found by Pinterest's search feature.

2. **Link -** This is where the image will take the user when it is clicked.

3. **Board -** You will be given a drop down menu of all of the boards you have created. Simply choose the one that is the best fit for what you are pinning.

4. LinkedIn

With more than 187 million members across 200 countries, Linkedin has changed the way real estate professionals do business. Initially viewed as an online resume, Linkedin is now thought to be the "online social site for business professionals to connect, network and engage."

Linked in gives you the ability to "link" to your website, blog or any other website you choose.

a. Tips to a Successful LinkedIn Real Estate Profile

1. Include all relevant skills and training you've earned throughout your career.

2. Let your unique personality and abilities to shine through. While this is a professional network, you do want to inject character into your profile. This will create differentiation from the other real estate professionals in your area.

3. Update your professional headline, which acts as your short bio. To be found when peers or potential clients search for "real estate" or "Realtor®" within your area, use words related to your industry, niche and area.

4. Optimize your Linkedin profile with keywords specific to your expertise and location. For example, if you specialize in short sales in Glendale, CA, your keywords would be "Short Sale Specialist, Glendale, California." These are searchable terms that allow people to quickly find you in your local area.

5. Customize your profile URL (website) with your name (first and last) making it easier to locate and market your profile. For branding and marketing purposes, you will want to customize this link and create your unique LinkedIn destination.

B. REAL ESTATE SPECIFIC SITES

Although not really "social media" sites, real estate search engines are are often linked to and influenced by social media sites. For example, when searching under Realtor.com, you may encounter an agent's name and their links to specific social media sites!

As mentioned earlier, the most popular real estate websites for searches include:

1. Realtor.com®
2. Zillow.com® and Trulia.com®
3. Multiple Listing Service (Not open to public)

Obviously, there are many more sites on the web, but certain sites float to the top when it comes to active searches. Many of them are also hooked into the syndication cycle of local MLSs so they get the latest listing information the quickest.

Remember: It's important to take down any ad or post once a property has sold, as potential clients will soon become frustrated if every time they inquire about one of your properties that is already sold.

Plus the MLS gives you 24 to 48 hours to remove a listing from their records once the listing is closed or expired. But if you are personally putting ads out there, it's your responsibility to make sure they too are taken down immediately upon close of escrow!

C. YOUR BROKERAGE WEBSITES

Your brokerage needs to maintain a presence on the Internet, making it easy to find and contact you. Listings must be updated constantly as well as sold items listed to show clients your success rate. Be sure to make your phone number prominent on the first page of the website, so clients don't have to search for a way to contact you by phone. After all, you are trying to get to meet them personally as well as over the Web.

D. QUICK RESPONSE (QR) CODES

A *QUICK RESPONSE (QR) CODE is a type of barcode that consists of black modules (square dots) arranged in a square grid on a white background, which can be read by an imaging device (such as a camera) and processed until the image can be appropriately interpreted.* The required data are then extracted from patterns present in both horizontal and vertical components of the image. This technology may be a little sophisticated for a traditionalist, but students and active smartphone users are more than aware of QR codes. These boxes are everywhere, including on yard signs. You can point your smartphone at the QR and retrieve all the information that is attached to that insignia.

If it's too complicated for you to wrap your head around, hire someone to help you. QR codes are now appearing on Broker's For Sale Signs, on their business cards, and any other advertising technique they use!

XIII. Six Steps to Successful Real Estate Marketing on the Internet

STEP 1: OWN YOUR WEBSITE DOMAIN NAME OR SUFFIX .REALTOR

As a real estate agent, you are more than likely an independent contractor (Business Owner), and your career is built upon marketing and making a name for yourself. In addition to using your broker's website, you should own an independent website in your own name that can go with you if you change brokers. While it's great for you as a career agent to have the support of a company or franchise, most of your business and repeat business is because of you, and not just the company.

Develop your own website that people will visit and return to frequently. Make it fresh, relevant, and full of local interest. Have clients sign up for your newsletter so you know they've requested your information and you're not just spamming them. Make sure your viewers have a way of opting out of receiving your emails—your consideration may even keep them on the list!

Also, consider compiling useful information about local schools, restaurants, sights of interest, churches, and clubs. Combine this with a visual tour of the scenic points of interest in your area. This information may also contribute to real estate values!

People are always looking for local information online, and you can help them—which may actually result in new sales. People will remember your brand name, hopefully for life!

When the Hsi Lai Buddhist Temple opened in Hacienda Heights, the Chinese immigrant community rushed to buy in the area, increasing housing prices dramatically. This particular point of interest also related to increased real estate values!

STEP 2: INCREASE YOUR INTERNET PRESENCE

Keep track of how and where your listings and services are currently being marketed on the Internet, and then decide what you can do to improve your current position.

You can maximize your current exposure, with Trulia.com®, for example, by paying an extra fee to move YOUR listings to the top of the list for matching searches.

Take digital pictures at every listing appointment. Submit the maximum number of pictures your listing services will allow. Virtual video tours add a dynamic feel to your presentations and websites, allowing potential sellers to see how their house looks to a buyer and vice versa.

Use email to drive visitors to your site. Create an email distribution list of your sphere of influence. Whenever you add a new feature to your website such as an article about recent changes in the tax laws, send out an announcement by email and include a direct link to the new page. ▼

STEP 3: INTEGRATE TRADITIONAL WITH INTERNET MARKETING TECHNIQUES

Creating a successful Internet marketing strategy requires the integration of conventional, proven, and successful marketing strategies (old school) with the marketing opportunities available on the Internet (new school).

If you look at all the companies on the Internet today, they are spending millions of dollars to market and brand their websites. Be your ambassador; direct everyone you know to your website! Your website address should be on all your conventional marketing pieces, even your sign riders.

Keep abreast of all new developments in marketing techniques, like the Quick Response (QR) code (see page 281) that allows consumers to click on an app and get information about a property or your business instantly.

STEP 4: USE THE WEB FOR YOUR LISTING PRESENTATION

Include the following in your listing presentation:
1. Copies of past ads, brokerage information, personal bio, and recent Comparative Market Analysis (CMA).
2. Use a template or create your own method of keeping track of all Internet traffic.
3. You can create a listing presentation on site that will include photos of a potential seller's home to show them how quickly you can put their property on the market.

Web applications for open houses also capture information about your potential clients by finding out what type of properties they are looking for. It allows you to get their email and contact information so you can send them instant alerts when a new listing that fits their needs arises.

STEP 5: KEEP UP WITH THE TIMES

Loan sites, rate watch sites, agent matching sites—dozens of helpful opportunities and services are coming online. Not all of the new sites promise success, but it can cost your business if you are unaware of the changing real estate landscape on the Internet. One of the best ways to stay on top of the evolving landscape is to visit real estate news sites and subscribe to email alerts.

NAR.org, CAR.org, and Inman.com have up-to-date websites and newsletters that may prove very reliable.

STEP 6: KEEP IT PERSONAL AS WELL

The Internet is fantastic for marketing, but you must follow up with personal attention and interest. Potential clients want to know they are more than just an anonymous email or Facebook address.

When you find a customer has been notified by an "instant alert" system that one or more emails have been sent to your client with links to homes for sale, be sure and give them a phone call to ask for feedback. Better yet, offer to show them the house in person at their earliest convenience. Don't wait for them to call you when they get around to it—unless they've specifically asked not to be contacted. Watch the alert systems to see what comments your clients are posting about the homes they are seeing and contact them when a particularly appropriate house comes up for sale.

XIV. Niche Marketing Opportunites

Use the Internet to your advantage to market to "niche" groups. Different social media sites can give you feedback regarding your specific target market.

NICHE MARKETING (Market Segmentation) is the division of a total market into smaller focused, manageable, and specialized subsets to experience increased marketing to a specific group. Niche specialization allows an agent to spend less money for in-depth and effective advertising. Face-to-face promotion encourages an agent to establish personal relationships that directly bring listings and sales.

It seems counterintuitive, but specializing by narrowing your client base is valuable and cost effective. Concentration of marketing allows a reduction in advertising expenses. It increases consumer awareness considerably.

Developing a smaller core business helps establish a constant and consistent commission flow from repeat clientele. Why not have several "niche" markets in which you specialize? You may decide to develop several niche markets that may work for your geographic area.

Here are some ideas for establishing different types of real estate niches that may give you some models for developing a submarket that may work for you.

A. DIVORCING COUPLES

Become proficient in the emotional art of working with couples early in the divorce cycle, hopefully before they start making assumptions about their home's value. As your experience grows with parting partnerships, so will your commissions. Establish a working relationship with several divorce attorneys.

B. ONE- TO FOUR-UNIT ZONING

Most cities and counties have one- to four-unit zoning for very small apartment complexes. One- to four-unit zoning ordinances are usually located between larger apartment complexes and single-family zoning. Networking by social media or just walking and talking to people in the neighborhood will help bring you a list of all 1- to 4-units' owners in that zone. These owners may own a single-family house, duplex, tri-plex, or a 4-unit apartment.

Fannie Mae and other types of government backed residential 1- to 4-unit loans use the same lending requirements as one would have with a single-family home. One of the 1- to 4-units must be owner occupied, just as a borrower is required to be owner occupied to have lower interest rates and fees on a single-family home.

This is why most loan applications are for single-family homes or 1- to 4-units that are owner occupied.

C. MILITARY-RELATED SERVICES

Communities near a military facility have a built-in market for buyers, sellers and renters. Apartment owners and sellers usually experience a greater turnover, so there should be more opportunities for more fees and commissions.

D. LAND EXPERT

Builders and developers are constantly interested in available land for development of apartments, condos, strip malls, malls and even larger projects. Buyer's interest depends on current interest rates, types of financing that are available, tax incentives and of course the most important, supply and demand. If you desire this to be your niche market, promote yourself with builders and developers

E. LARGE CONDOMINIUM COMPLEXS

It may be a good practice to create an Internet "domain name" that includes the name of a specific condo complex as it is one of your target markets. Because an agent consistently posts subjects of interest to the current condo owners, they will think of your name and website when they want to sell. Buyers will find your site when searching the Internet for information about the condo complex. Some agents own a unit in the complex, which means you will have lots of face-to-face time while chatting with your neighbors.

F. LUXURY PROPERTIES

In the face of economic uncertainty and potentially higher taxes in China and other Pacific Rim countries, for example, wealthy individuals are drawn to California's year-round sunshine and prices that are still relatively low when compared with other global capitals. Using the Internet, you can reach a world-wide audience who may be looking to "park" their multi-millions on American soil. California has some of the most exclusive and expensive neighborhoods in the country, so it's a good place to specialize in upscale properties. From the beachfront of Malibu to San Francisco, there is a certain client who is looking for a statement property to reflect their lifestyle and tastes.

G. URBAN LIVING SPECIALIST

Many large cities are experiencing a surge in "downtown" living, whether it's new construction or renovated warehouses turned into artist lofts, specializing in this

particular area has its rewards. With the revitalization of once derelict neighborhoods your clientele will want specifics as to what neighborhoods are "hot" and which perhaps should be avoided. You can supply them with tips for urban living, like the challenges of grocery shopping in a high-rise jungle. The appeal of walking from home to work and then out to dinner or other nightlife is drawing more and more people back to the inner-city and hopefully to your real estate brokerage.

Warning Regarding "ONLINE" Rental Schemes
Wayne S. Bell, Real Estate Commissioner
California Bureau of Real Estate

The California Bureau of Real Estate ("CalBRE") issued warnings to prospective renters about (i) imposter landlords and (ii) scams perpetrated by or in connection with Prepaid Rental Listing Services (PRLS).

Consumer Alert – Beware of Imposter Landlords and Consumer Fraud Alert and Warning – Prepaid Rental Listing Services (PRLS). There are almost endless varieties of real estate and rental fraud.

CalBRE has received reports and been made aware of online rental scams (often using such Internet sites such as Zillow, Trulia, and Craigslist, and we want to warn the public about some of the most common ones.

Common Scams

In most cases, the fraud involves a scammer who:

1. Duplicates or "hijacks" an actual listing of a property that is for rent.
2. Creates a fake or fictitious listing for a rental property.
3. Offers for rent a real, but unavailable, property.
4. Rents a property that is in foreclosure and which will soon be sold, or that has been fully foreclosed (or is in pre-foreclosure).

In the cases mentioned above, the perpetrators do not own the properties (although they oft-times pretend to be the owners) and they are not authorized or licensed to rent the properties.

In most of these cases, the scammers collect money (usually via wire transfer) from the victims for deposits, fees and rents, and in a number of the cases obtain enough personal information, such as social security, driver license and bank account numbers, to steal the identities of the "renter" victims.

The perpetrators engage in these crimes (via the Internet) either because they have found success with such scams and continue to find victims who send money and/or who provide personally identifying information that can be used by the scammers to commit additional crimes.

▼

The anonymity and widespread availability of the Internet means an online rental scam can be started and operated from anywhere in the United States or in other countries.

"Red" Flags

While none of the "red" flags below is definitive proof of fraud, the following are warning signs of a possible scam:

1. The advertised rental rates are low (many times very low) compared to other rentals in the area. Always remember the time-tested adage that if something seems too good to be true, it probably is.

2. The purported landlord or agent requests that the advance payment of rents and deposits (and possibly other fees) be made via cash or wire transfer (such as Western Union), and/or asks for personal information such as social security number, bank account information, and driver license number. It is important to note that payments made by cash or wire transfer provide little—and usually no—recourse, especially since the scammer to whom the funds are wired usually disappears and cannot be found. While credit card payments are not accepted by many landlords or property rental agents, prospective renters should—to provide an amount of self-protection—ask to pay for rents, deposits and fees by credit card.

3. The supposed owner or rental agent is either out of the country or in another state, or is in a hurry to leave California, and states that the rental property cannot be shown or toured.

4. The prospective landlord or property agent is NOT willing to meet in person, and/or applies pressure to complete the rental transaction as soon as possible.

Ways that Prospective Renters Can Protect Themselves

Prospective renters should be wary and should conduct their own due diligence, and investigate the person with whom they are dealing or negotiating, as well as the property itself. Potential renters should:

1. Confirm or verify the identity of the supposed landlord or property agent. To see who owns the property, contact a licensed California real estate agent, the county recorder's office in the county where the property is located, and/or a title company. Talk with neighbors about the property and ask who owns it, and ask a lot of questions about the rental history of the property. If dealing with a property manager or leasing agent (who does not live at the property), look them up on the CalBRE website (www.calbre.ca.gov) to see if they are licensed. If they are, check to see if they are disciplined or

▼

otherwise restricted in the real estate practice that they can do. Also, check the person out on Google or other search engines, and through the Better Business Bureau.

2. Confirm that the property is not in foreclosure or pre-foreclosure. This is especially true when renting a house. The mortgage loan should be in good standing and not in default.

3. Do not rent a property without viewing and touring it in person.

4. Do not pay or transfer any money without reviewing all rental documents, and getting copies of all writings pertaining to the property.

5. Demand to meet and then actually meet the supposed owner or property manager in person, and ask many questions about the property and the neighborhood.

6. Work with an experienced, competent, and licensed California real estate broker, or salesperson working under the supervision of a broker.

7. Take photographs of the property.

8. Do not pay anything in cash or wire transfer money.

9. Do research on what comparable properties rent for.

The essential point here is that prospective renters, in order to protect their interests and not become a scammer's next victim, must remain skeptical, proceed cautiously, do their own investigation of the property and individuals involved with the rental(s), and be aware of and look for revealing signs of fraud.

XV. Marketing Demographics

A. BABY BOOMERS (Old School)

The "Life Cycle of Real Estate Purchasing" reveals statistics than help determine how to cater to a particular group (old school vs. new school).

DEMOGRAPHICS *is the study and prediction of things people do as they age; it is the ultimate tool for understanding population trends.* We can generally predict the average age that people make certain types of decisions based on their age and the number of people that are in that age group. For instance the baby boomers (1946-1964) are retiring in such large numbers that one can predict real estate trends in the future.

The U. S. Census Bureau, Bureau of Labor Statistics has published data that allows us to forecast "The Life Cycle of Real Estate Purchasing" if you analyze the data.

The following list illustrates by "Average Peak Age" that people will:

1. Rent Apartments – age 26 or 27
2. Purchase a Starter House – age 31 or 32

3. Trade-Up to a Larger Houses – age 41, 42 or 43
4. Begin Staying or Buying Into Resorts – age 60
5. Start Buying Vacation or Retirement Homes – age 65
6. Purchase an Interest in a Nursing Home – age 84

These statistics are simply stated, but they make sense and give us data that can help plan our careers, investments and future home purchases. Remember, real estate markets are diverse, controlled by the economic and demographic conditions of that region and all economic circumstances are "local."

If marketing starter homes, emails and social media may be the way to go. However, if you're trying to sell a second/vacation home, you may want to send out more postcards and direct mail. Keep in mind the technology level of the audience to whom you are trying to appeal.

B. MILLENNIALS (Tech Savvy)

Tech-savvy Millennials (born 1982-2004), will create the next house buying wave.

The **MILLENNIALS**, *who were born between 1982 and 2004*, are such a large segment of our population their sheer numbers will cause the USA to experience the "Next Housing Buying Wave" that will cause real estate prices to increase.

Demographic studies show that the millennials, who are the children of the baby boomers, just started to buy real estate in larger numbers and will continue through 2031. That demand will lead to an increase in real estate prices due to a limited supply, which in turn will lead to an increase in supply. If prices go up, builders will increase the supply.

The "Millennials" are so large that they will eventually make up 50% of the work force.

They have grown up with digital technology and as such are expected to reinvent the Internet. As a result the "tech side" of real estate brokerages is expected to grow and change in unimaginable ways.

Fortunately, real estate professionals are expected to continue their education throughout their careers, and it would be wise to focus some of that study on the changes being made in the technology areas of the field. While there will always be a need for the face-to-face interaction between agent and client, that personal element of the relationship has already been altered by buyers accessing the Internet for months before even choosing an agent. And the speed with which transactions has changed dramatically over the last few years. This is just the tip of the iceberg. Fortunately, organizations like CAR® and NAR® offer educational seminars or online "webinars" to help members learn new techniques as they emerge.

Know your clientele! When conducting real estate business to a younger-skewed target audience, like the millennials, don't be surprised if they expect to be tweeted or texted instead of phoned directly.

XVI. CHAPTER SUMMARY

The majority of homebuyers begin their search for a home on the Internet. **Zillow.com®, Trulia.com®, and Realtor.com®** are the most popular sites. Local Multiple Listing Services share their aggregation of listing information with other online real estate services called Web Syndication in order to reach the most buyers possible.

It's important to own your own **domain name (registered website)** as the courts have determined they are the same as property rights. The Internet is just the beginning of the buying process, as brokers are necessary to complete transactions due to their expertise and experience. Your success may depend on using advertising, particularly online, to your advantage. The more free publicity you get, the more your brand name is recognized by consumers.

Initially, information on refinancing and home equity loan products are more frequently being sought online. This includes refinancing, home equity FHA, VA, Reverse Mortgage, and mortgage rates.

Traditional methods are still valuable in the selling and marketing of real estate, like preparing a comparative market analysis for a client. However, technological advances are growing at a rapid pace and it's important to keep up with both old school and new school techniques. One of the most convenient tech applications is **auto email alert notifications**, whereby a client is emailed when a property comes up for sale that fits his or her requirements. The agent as well as the client is notified of the listing, allowing for you, as the agent, to follow through with an offer to show the property as soon as possible.

Another smartphone or tablet App that is proving helpful in creating relationships with new clients is the **"open house" app**, where a client at an open house fills out an online form for your MLS and elects when to be notified when his or her dream house is listed with the MLS. Yet another smartphone app that is popular is the **Quick Response (QR) Code**, which is a type of barcode that allows clients to just scan an icon on an advertisement (be it a flyer or a for sale sign) that gives them all the pertinent MLS listing information on a particular property.

It's important to keep a high online profile with social networking sites like Facebook, Twitter, LinkedIn, and Instagram. Even if you upload information via "the cloud," it's recommended that you keep paper copies as well. It's a way to back up your material and also allows less sophisticated clients to see transactions they might not understand online.

There are six basic steps to successful Internet marketing, including:

1. own your own domain name,
2. increase your Internet presence,
3. integrate traditional with modern marketing techniques,
4. use the Internet for marketing presentations,
5. include information of interest when contacting clients, and
6. keep abreast of newest technology

If you choose to effectively specialize in smaller groups (**niche marketing**), some of the avenues to explore include:

1. divorcing couples,
2. one- to four-unit zoning,
3. military related services,
4. land expertise,
5. huge condo complexes,
6. luxury properties, and
7. urban living specialist

Finally, be aware of potential Internet scams, particularly with rental properties. Do your homework.

XVII. MATCHING VOCABULARY Fill in the blanks with the correct letter

A. Advertising
B. Brand
C. CAR.org
D. Facebook
E. MLS auto email alerts notification (online)

F. Niche marketing
G. "Online" rental schemes
H. Smartphones
I. Over 90%
J. Portal
K. Publicity

L. Quick Response (QR) Codes
M. Realtor.com®
N. Search (Online)
O. Trulia.com®
P. Zillow.com®

1. _____ The division of a total market into smaller focused (manageable and specialized subsets) to experience an increase in marketing efficiency and lower costs.

2. _____ A type of barcode that consists of black modules (square dots) arranged in a square grid on a white background, which can be read by an imaging device (such as a camera) and processed until the image can be appropriately interpreted.

3. _____ The most often visited social networking site on the Internet.

4. _____ A name, your name, term, logo, or design that identifies you and your particular service that differentiates you from your competitors.

5. _____ Paid promotion to encourage the identifying of your service to help persuade your buyers or sellers to talk to you and discuss how you can help them solve their real estate desires.

6. _____ A form of unpaid placement of information that promotes a broker, brokerage, or salesperson.

7. _____ Most homebuyers now use this function on their smartphone, tablet, or computer before contacting a REALTOR®.

8. _____ One of the top three real estate search engines in the country, this site has data on over 100 million homes across the United States, featuring homes currently for sale, giving value estimates of homes, aerial views of homes, and prices of comparable homes in the area.

9. _____ The popular real estate website for residential homebuyers, sellers, renters, and real estate professionals that lists properties for sale or rent and offers community insights, according to ZIP codes or cities, and encourages advertising for real estate agents to "lock up" their local area on this website. No other agents may advertise on that zip code through this website.

10. _____ Homes for sale on this site span thousands of cities and towns across the U.S. and Canada. Real estate listings represent over 800 MLSs so you get the most accurate and reliable information possible. To find condos, townhomes, single-family homes or land, the user can simply use the property search function. Data is controlled by NAR.

11. _____ The REALTOR® trade group that represents California and supplies zipForms to assist in filling out most contracts and disclosures.

12. _____ 50% of the people in the U.S. use this mobile device.

13. _____ What percentage of people in the U.S. shopping for homes search online?

14. _____ A machine-to-person communication that notifies you and/or your client when a property that meets your client's specifications is posted on the MLS.

15. _____ The commissioner of real estate has advised agents and the consumers to be aware of these tricks used by individuals to rent properties they do not own or manage.

16. _____ A website specifically designed to bring information together in a uniform way.

See Page 610 for Answers

XVIII. CHAPTER QUIZ

1. MLS Aggregation refers to which of the following?

   a. Seller information
   b. Property data information
   c. Property photos
   d. All of the above

2. In most "ONLINE" rental scheme cases, the fraud involves a scammer who:

   a. duplicates or "hijacks" an actual listing of a property that is for rent.
   b. creates a fake or fictitious listing for a rental property.
   c. offers for rent a real but unavailable property.
   d. all of the above.

3. What age group is commonly referred to as the "Millennials"?

   a. 1946-1964
   b. 1960-1975
   c. 1970-1980
   d. 1982-2004

4. Which of the following real estate websites has the most information about a property listing and is available only to dues-paying members?

   a. LinkedIn
   b. Facebook
   c. Multiple Listing Service (MLS)
   d. None of the above

5. Online mortgage home lenders specialize in most loans, except:

   a. motorcycle loans.
   b. home equity loans.
   c. reverse mortgage loans.
   d. FHA loans and VA loans.

6. The <u>first</u> step for a successful independent contractor real estate agent, who wants to market on the Internet for life, is to:

  a. own or control your own domain.
  b. make the most out of your Internet presence.
  c. help buyers find information on the web
  d. create an Internet marketing presence as part of your "listing presentation."

7. Most buyers check out what service before contacting an agent?

  a. Billboards and signs
  b. Newspaper classifieds
  c. Search online
  d. Magazines

8. Social media sites that can be used to encourage people to purchase a specific property include all of the following, except:

  a. bre.ca.gov.
  b. Facebook.com.
  c. Twitter.com.
  d. LinkedIn.com & Instagram.com.

9. Which of the following is not a good example of niche marketing or market segmentation?

  a. Divorcing couples
  b. Military related services
  c. The city of San Francisco
  d. A huge condominium complex

10. Renters should conduct their own due diligence and do which of the following to help identify the person and property they are thinking of renting from?

  a. Take cell phone photos of the property.
  b. Tour the property in person.
  c. Don't pay with cash or wire transfer.
  d. All of the above.

ANSWERS: 1. d; 2. d; 3. d; 4. c; 5. c; 6. a; 7. c; 8. a; 9. c; 10. d

BOLETO PERDIDO

GRACIAS PAGA

BANCO POPULAR PAGA TAR

MORTGAGE SERVICING

2 HORAS GRATIS

POR SU PAT

Finance: Understanding the Finance Process

I. Nature of Financing

A. INTRODUCTION TO THE FINANCING PROCESS

Financing is the key to most real estate transactions.

The buying and selling of real estate would grind to a halt without trust deed and mortgage funds. You, as a real estate professional, can play a big part in your clients obtaining their mortgages. Although you will have a lender qualify your buyers and provide them with a "pre-approval letter" prior to showing them properties, it's important for you to familiarize yourself with the various types of loans presently available.

1. California Calls Trust Deeds "Mortgages"

Although mortgages are rarely used in California, the term "mortgage" is so ingrained in the tradition of lending that often trust deeds and other loans are referred to as "mortgages." **However, adjustable rate mortgages and fixed rate mortgages are usually deeds of trust in California**.

This chapter reinforces Real Estate Principles' information. We will use the general words "mortgage" and "deed of trust" interchangeably. But remember, "mortgagee" or "mortgagor" refer only to mortgages. "Trustee," "trustor," and "beneficiary" refer only to trust deeds.

a. Parties to a Trust Deed

In a trust deed there are three parties. The ***TRUSTOR*** *is usually the party that is borrowing the money.* This is usually the buyer, but may also be the owner if the property is being refinanced. The ***BENEFICIARY*** *is the lender who is lending money for the purchase of real property.* Home lenders in California are usually savings banks, but may also be commercial banks and mortgage companies

CHAPTER OUTLINE

(mortgage bankers). The **TRUSTEE** *is the third, disinterested party (usually a corporation) who holds naked legal title to the property, but only in so far as the trustee may have to sell the property for the beneficiary, should the trustor default.* This is normally a title insurance company. **Figure 9-1** illustrates this three-party relationship.

Figure 9-1

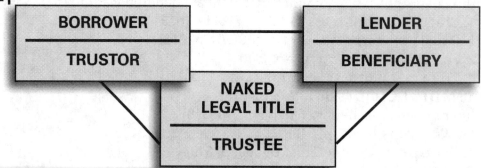

B. THE COST OF BORROWING MONEY

1. Interest Rates

INTEREST is the charge for borrowing money. In real estate, we use simple interest, not compound interest. Interest can be thought of as a rental charge for the use of money.

The "Nominal Interest Rate" is the rate stated in the note. The "Effective Interest Rate" is the rate the borrower is actually paying (including interest, points, and loan fees).

2. Origination Fees

A *LOAN ORIGINATION FEE is a charge based on the loan amount and is collected as compensation by the lender for processing the loan.* On FHA-insured and VA-guaranteed loans, buyers may be charged only one percent. This restriction, however, does not apply to conventional loans.

3. Points

Discounts (or points) paid to lenders are, in effect, prepaid interest.

They are used by lenders to adjust the effective interest rate so that it is equal to, or nearly equal to, the *PREVAILING MARKET RATE (the interest rate charged on conventional loans).* The discounts (points) are sometimes absorbed by the sellers, depending on the terms of the loan and the market conditions.

The charge for making a loan at most institutions is usually called a loan fee, service charge, commitment fee, or points. These charges vary considerably. Whether called points, discounts, loan brokerage fees, or new loan fees, they're all the same.

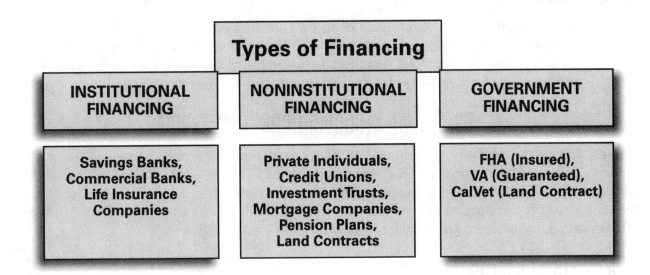

Points are used in over half the home sales in California. It pays to shop around.

How are points figured? One point is one percent of the new loan amount. For example, if the current market is "5 points," it means that the cost for a $100,000 loan is 5 percent x $100,000, or $5,000.

Points are figured on the amount of the new loan, not the selling price of the property.

4. Annual Percentage Rate (APR)

The ***ANNUAL PERCENTAGE RATE (APR)*** *represents the relationship between the total of the finance charges (interest rate, points, and the loan fees) and the total amount financed, expressed as a percentage.* It is the actual cost of borrowing money. It must be computed to the nearest one-eighth of one percent and the APR must be printed on the loan form more conspicuously than the rest of the printed material.

When shopping for a loan, advise your buyers to look at the APR rather than just the advertised interest rate.

5. Prepayment Penalties

A ***PREPAYMENT PENALTY*** *is a charge to the borrower for paying off all or part of a loan balance before the due date.*

A prepayment penalty is only enforceable during the first five years of a one-to-four unit home loan.

6. Impound Accounts (Reserves Held by Lenders)

IMPOUND ACCOUNTS *are prepaid items consisting of property taxes, hazard insurance, and mortgage insurance reserves.* Some programs require a buyer to invest a down payment and establish an impound account, while others may

require only an impound account to be paid in cash by the buyer. The account is often referred to as a "trust fund" or "trust account" and, once established, it is maintained by being included in the regular monthly loan payments and disbursed when taxes and insurance are paid.

II. Institutional (Conventional) Financing

These loans are not backed—guaranteed or insured—by any government agency. The three primary sources of such conventional loans are referred to as *INSTITUTIONAL LENDERS*, namely, *savings banks, commercial banks, and life insurance companies*. These three institutional giants account for approximately 80 percent of all home loans nationwide. Many of them rely on mortgage bankers and mortgage loan brokers to initiate loans.

A. MORTGAGE BANKERS

MORTGAGE BANKING companies are direct lenders that underwrite for usually hundreds of investors, such as Bank of America, Chase Bank, and so on. They actually fund the loan themselves under one of their investor's guidelines and then sell the loan to that investor, who then often sells the loan to FNMA or FHMLC to be securitized. Many of these mortgage backed securities are presently being purchased by the Federal Reserve in an effort to stimulate the economy and support the housing industry by keeping mortgage rates lower.

1. Mortgage Bankers vs. Mortgage Brokers

Mortgage companies can be both. Mortgage bankers lend their own money. They can either keep the loan in their portfolio or sell the loan to another lender. *MORTGAGE BROKERS shop for a lender for the borrowers and earn a fee by putting lender and borrower together.*

B. SAVINGS BANKS

Savings Banks are one source for conventional real estate loans, since their operational charters normally restrict them to investments connected with real estate financing. Conversely, commercial banks and life insurance companies may have varied investments and frequently withdraw from the normal real estate investment market as interest rates change.

Certain circumstances permit up to 95 percent financing, but, as a rule, savings banks are restricted to originating loans in an amount equal to 80 percent of the sale price or appraisal value, whichever is less. A 10 percent second loan (on top of the first loan) may be permitted when the buyer makes a 10 percent down payment. Buyers with only 10 percent down will probably be required to purchase Private Mortgage Insurance (PMI).

Loans on well-located properties to borrowers with good income and credit are referred to as PRIME LOANS and will carry an interest rate from at least 2 percent to 7 percent above the rate of interest the lending association pays to its depositors. The interest charged on a prime loan is apt to be in the 4 percent to 6 percent range. Any change

---

Priorities of Institutional Lenders

SAVINGS BANKS (Residential Lenders)	COMMERCIAL BANKS (General Purpose Lenders)	LIFE INSURANCE COMPANIES (Big Money Lenders)
1. Single-family homes and condos	1. Business and auto loans	1. Large shopping centers and office buildings
2. Apartment buildings	2. Conventional home loans	2. Hotels and industrial properties
3. Home improvement loans	3. Government-backed FHA and VA home loans	3. FHA and VA home loans through mortgage companies (Government-backed loans)
4. Manufactured homes	4. Credit cards	
	5. Construction loans	

from this rule is determined by the element of risk involved with the property and the buyer.

Both savings and lender interest rates are generally determined by market conditions, but are greatly influenced by the actions of the Federal Reserve Board (www.federalreserve.gov) and the Federal Housing Finance Board (www.fhfb.gov).

Savings banks often allow the buyer to put as little as a 10 percent cash down payment on a property, if the seller or someone else will carry 10 percent of the purchase price on a note and second deed of trust on the property. The savings bank will then provide an 80 percent loan on the purchase price.

Banking regulators consider you to be a *SUBPRIME BORROWER if you have a FICO score of 650 or lower, two (or more) 30-day late payments in the past 12 months, or one 60-day late payment in the past 24 months, a foreclosure or charge-off in the past 24 months, any bankruptcy in the last 60 months (FHA - 24 months), qualifying debt-to-income ratios of 50 percent or higher, or "limited ability to cover family living expenses each month."* The Dodd-Frank Act mandated that borrowers must meet stricter ability-to-pay requirements.

1. Qualified Mortgages

The Dodd-Frank Act provides that *QUALIFIED MORTGAGES are entitled to a presumption that the creditor making the loan satisfies the ability-to-repay requirements.*

The gist of one of the main rules is simple: Lenders will be required to ensure that borrowers have the ability to repay their mortgages. In return, lenders will be protected from borrower lawsuits so long as they issue "safe" mortgages that follow "qualified mortgage guidelines."

C. COMMERCIAL BANKS

Commercial banks are usually more selective about both properties and buyers than savings banks when making loans.

Commercial banks may make their own appraisals and, by law, may not generally exceed loans over 80 percent of appraised value. At the present time, conventional bank loans are normally limited to a period of 30 years.

The Federal Reserve (our nation's central bank) Board plays an important role in the loan policies of national banks, that is, banks that are members of the Federal Reserve System. When the Federal Reserve Board raises or lowers the Fed funds or the Discount Rate, or the required ratio of loans to deposits, the consumer/borrower is directly affected.

D. LIFE INSURANCE COMPANIES

Generally considered the third most important source of conventional real estate loans, lending policies of life insurance companies are governed by the laws of the state in which the company is chartered, the laws of the state in which the loan is originated, as well as the policies of management and the availability of loan funds.

Life insurance companies are generally NOT interested in "originating" individual single-family residential real estate loans but will make conservative 25 year loans.

Insurance companies are heavily involved in the secondary market (after the loan is made), buying vast quantities of already existing home loans from banks and other institutional lenders.

The secondary mortgage (trust deed) market provides an opportunity for financial institutions to buy and sell first mortgages (trust deeds) for a profit from one another.

E. PRIVATE MORTGAGE INSURANCE (PMI) (Provide a Valuable Service)

Private mortgage insurance companies insure conventional loans that have less than 20 percent down. These private insurers are similar to the Federal Housing Administration (FHA) in that they insure the lender against loss in the event of foreclosure. However, rather than insuring the lender for the full amount of the loan, the private insurers generally cover only the top 10 to 20 percent of the loan and leave the lender exposed for approximately 80 to 90 percent of the loan.

The cost of private mortgage insurance varies with the type of contract coverage the lender requires.

The PMI commonly used for 90 percent loans costs the buyer (in addition to the interest rate already being paid) between .39 percent and .71 percent (depending on the credit score) of the original loan amount for the first year premium for fixed rate loans. The annual premium for ARMs can be as high as .89 percent. PMI payments may be deductible for income tax purposes. Check with your tax consultant for current PMI deductibility laws.

Private mortgage insurance allows institutional lenders (savings banks, commercial banks, and insurance companies) to make loans above the usual 75 to 80 percent of the sale's price.

1. Credit Requirements

Credit requirements for the 90 and 95 percent, privately insured loan plans vary from institution to institution. In general, however, the verified income, employment, and credit analysis of the borrower must be favorable in relation to family obligations. **The borrower's total mortgage payments generally should not exceed 25 to 30 percent of gross income (3.5 to 1 ratio); total obligations (debts) to income should not exceed 33 percent (3 to 1 ratio).** A co-borrower's income will be considered, given an adequate employment history. Part-time jobs, overtime, bonuses, and other income sources must be substantiated by W-2 statements to be accepted as stable income. Because of the high price of housing in California, there is a trend toward more liberal ratios in qualifying buyers.

A high net worth, insurance, and guaranteed retirement income indicate the ability to continue making payments in spite of illness, unemployment, or retirement. Paying habits indicate an individual's stability and probability of performance on the contract. When the borrower is self-employed, recent financial statements and income tax reports for previous years are necessary to substantiate income.

F. FIXED RATE MORTGAGES

A FIXED RATE MORTGAGE is a loan for which the payments are usually the same each month for the life of the loan. The equal monthly payment includes both the principal and the interest.

G. ADJUSTABLE RATE MORTGAGES (ARMs)

The *variable rate mortgage is more popularly referred to as an ADJUSTABLE RATE MORTGAGE, or ARM.* About 100 different types of ARMs are used in California, with no standardized ARM. Before recommending an ARM to a client, you should ask the following questions of the lender:

1. What is the initial interest rate, and how long will it be used?
2. What causes the interest rate to change? (The index to which the rate is tied may be six-month Treasury bill rates, lender's cost of funds, and so on.)

3. How often can the interest rate change?

4. How much can the rate change? (This is usually no more than 2% in any one year.)

5. Is there a ceiling, or cap, on the total adjustment rate? (A 5 percent interest rate cap is the most common.)

6. Can the payments be changed? (Rate increases are normally accompanied by payment increases, within given limits. Lenders do try to keep a reasonable ratio between a borrower's income and the monthly payments.)

As a licensee, you owe the duty of full disclosure in any loan arrangement, especially in cases which may involve an increase in rates, payments, or both. Be sure that the lender is trustworthy.

After all, borrowers may lose their homes if surprise increases occur and they are unable to meet the heavier obligation. (See **Figure 9-2** to see how ARMs work.)

H. SPECIAL PURPOSE LOANS

1. Graduated Payment Mortgage (GPM) (For First-Time Buyers)

With a *GRADUATED PAYMENT MORTGAGE (GPM), the rate and term are fixed, but monthly payments are smaller at the beginning of the term and increase over time.*

The GPM is just one instrument that addresses the problem of borrowers who cannot afford housing with their current income. With a GPM, a family is expected to raise its average income over the term of the loan.

The instrument has drawbacks for both lender and borrower. In the early years, the low monthly payments are not sufficient to cover interest owed, so the loan balance actually increases for the first few years. This results in negative amortization. Since, under most conditions, the increase in property value is greater than the increase in principal, the buyer retains a positive equity, but the risk to the lender increases.

NEGATIVE AMORTIZATION occurs when monthly installment payments are insufficient to pay the interest accruing on the principal balance, so that the unpaid interest must be added to the principal due. Your borrower may choose, whenever possible, to make larger monthly payments to possibly reduce the unpaid balance.

Negatively amortizing loans are not approved under the "Qualified Mortgage" definition and therefore are generally not being approved for residential property loans.

2. Biweekly Mortgage (26 Payments)

A *BIWEEKLY MORTGAGE (trust deed) is a fixed interest rate loan for which the payments are made every two weeks, but each payment is one-half the amount of a regular monthly payment.* Since there are 52 weeks in a year, the borrower pays a total of 26 payments.

3. 15-Year Fixed and Adjustable Rate Loans

Fifteen-year fixed-rate loans are gaining in popularity because, for a slight increase in the monthly payment, the loan can be paid off in only 15 years, usually at a lower interest rate than 30-year loans.

Figure 9-2   # How ARMs Work

THE INDEX

The **INDEX** *is the starting interest rate used as the indicator so that changes from it can be calculated.* If the index rises 1%, the ARM interest rate you pay goes up 1%. The index must be: 1) beyond the control of the lender, and 2) available and verifiable by the public. Examples of indexes used are the Cost of Living Index, the 11th District Cost of Funds Index, the One Year T-Bill, and the London Interbank Offered Rate (LIBOR).

THE ADJUSTABLE INTERVAL

The **ADJUSTABLE INTERVAL** *is the frequency with which interest rates are reset.* This period can be monthly, quarterly, every six months, or even once a year. If the index has risen .3% by the end of the interval period, the interest rate you pay goes up .3%.

THE CAP (On Interest Rate)

The **CAP** *is a percentage interest rate ceiling or restriction on the: 1) periodic (adjustable) interval, and/or 2) lifetime change in interest rates or payments.* An adjustable interval cap limits the percentage of change upward to, or downward to, for example, 1/2% every quarter. The lifetime cap is often around a maximum of 5% above or below the initial agreed-to contract rate.

THE MARGIN

The **MARGIN** *is the spread between the index interest rate and the initial contract rate from which the lender will make a profit and cover its costs.* It is the amount of profit for the lender, agreed to in advance. If the index rate is 4% and the margin is 3%, then the current interest rate paid by the borrower is 7%. Even if the index rate moves up to 5%, the margin will always remain at 3% and the new interest rate will be 8%. Some adjustables have **teaser rates** that are even below the starting rate to entice the borrower into the transaction. The borrower is qualified based on the teaser rate, which only lasts for a short period of time and then goes up to the agreed upon rate.

ADVANTAGES OF ARMS

The main advantage of an ARM is a lower initial monthly payment which generally results from a lower initial interest rate than can be found with a fixed rate loan because the lender is protected if interest rates rise over the loan period. This makes an ARM more affordable, thus more people can qualify for it. Generally there are no prepayment penalties, and an assumption is usually permitted if the new buyer meets credit standards. ARMs benefit first-time buyers and short-term investors who just want a lower interest rate, because interest rates are initially lower.

© 2015 ETC., Inc.

4. Reverse Mortgage Loans (Seniors Who Need Income)

With **REVERSE MORTGAGE LOANS**, *the borrower can receive monthly installments or can receive a lump sum (other plans are often available). The loan is usually due and payable if the borrower discontinues occupying the property.* As the borrower ages, many, if not most, end up having to go into a care facility. At that time the home may have to be sold at any price and under any terms, regardless of the market conditions, to pay off the reverse mortgage. Reverse mortgages are very expensive!

III. The Secondary Mortgage Market

Savings banks, commercial banks, life insurance companies, and others can easily resell their first trust deed loans if they conform to secondary market loan standards.

A. SECONDARY MORTGAGE (TRUST DEED) MARKET

Lenders in the secondary market are concerned with the "liquidity and marketability" of loans.

The **SECONDARY MORTGAGE (TRUST DEED) MARKET** *provides an opportunity for financial institutions to buy and sell first mortgages (trust deeds) to and from other financial institutions.* California traditionally has a growing real estate market that will pay higher interest rates than other parts of the country. Therefore, California's financial institutions will make trust deed loans and sell them to other institutions for a profit. The secondary mortgage market enables lenders to keep an adequate supply of money for new loans.

The secondary mortgage (trust deed) market is the market where lenders buy and sell mortgages. When lenders need cash, they can often sell their first trust deeds hopefully for a profit.

1. Federal National Mortgage Association (Fannie Mae)

Fannie Mae is the nation's largest investor in residential mortgages.

The **FEDERAL NATIONAL MORTGAGE ASSOCIATION (FNMA)**, *also known as "Fannie Mae," dominates the secondary mortgage market.* Originally it bought and sold only FHA and VA loans.

FNMA is currently under conservatorship by the Federal Housing Finance Agency (FHFA).

www.fanniemae.com
Fannie Mae

2. Government National Mortgage Association (Ginnie Mae)

The *GOVERNMENT NATIONAL MORTGAGE ASSOCIATION, or "Ginnie Mae," was created with the passage of the **Housing and Urban Development Act (1968)**.* It is a wholly owned government corporation, which in effect, replaced FNMA when FNMA became privately owned.

GNMA operates under the Department of Housing and Urban Development (HUD).

At the time of its creation, GNMA was given the responsibility for managing and eventually liquidating the remaining FNMA mortgages. Another function of GNMA is that of "special assistance"—GNMA assists the financing (does not loan money) of urban renewal and housing projects by providing below-market rates to low-income families.

www.ginniemae.gov
Ginnie Mae

3. Federal Home Loan Mortgage Corporation (Freddie Mac)

The *FEDERAL HOME LOAN MORTGAGE CORPORATION (FHLMC), which is also known as "Freddie Mac," was created through the **Emergency Home Finance Act (1970)**.* Initially, FHLMC was a nonprofit, federally chartered institution, which was controlled by the Federal Home Loan Bank System. FHLMC basically operates in a manner that is similar to FNMA.

FHLMC is currently under conservatorship by the Federal Housing Finance Agency (FHFA).

www.freddiemac.com
Freddie Mac

B. FINAL WORD ON CONVENTIONAL LOANS (Risk — Loans Without Government Backing)

Since conventional loans are loans made without government backing or guarantees, they are riskier. Even if conventional loans have lower loan-to-value (LTV) ratios, which make them safer, government-backed loans are the safest because the government will then pay off if there is a foreclosure. Fannie Mae and Freddie Mac currently have maximum loan limits. *If the requested loan amount is higher than the Fannie Mae and Freddie Mac loan limit, it is called a **JUMBO LOAN**.*

IV. Government Financing (Government-Backed Loans)

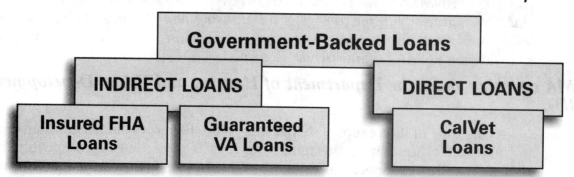

The three primary sources of government financing are the Federal Housing Administration (FHA), the Veterans Administration (VA), and the California Department of Veterans Affairs (CalVet).

Only the California Department of Veteran's Affairs is a direct lender of funds; the FHA and VA being insurers or guarantors of loans otherwise made by approved institutional lenders.

A. FEDERAL HOUSING ADMINISTRATION (FHA)

The primary purpose of FHA Section 203b is to encourage and assist people to become homeowners.

FHA is not a lender; it merely insures lenders against loss after an approved loan is processed in accordance with FHA regulations. In the event of foreclosures, FHA reimburses the lender for the loan balance. In order to reduce the possibilities of a foreclosure, the buyer's income and credit history must measure up to certain standards.

Points or discount points may be paid by either the buyer or the seller under either FHA or VA financing.

1. Purchaser Requirements

The FHA requires the purchaser to have some financial interest in the (one-to-four unit) property on which a loan is to be insured.

Cash investment requirements vary in each of the numerous programs offered, depending on price and buyer's qualifications. For example, some FHA programs require the buyer to invest a down payment and establish an impound account, while others may require only an impound account to be paid in cash.

The borrower must meet standard FHA credit qualifications. He or she is eligible for approximately 97 percent financing and may finance the up-front mortgage insurance premium into the mortgage.

MORTGAGE INSURANCE is a policy that protects lenders against losses that result from defaults on home mortgages. FHA requirements include mortgage

A practical way to qualify buyers for the highest appropriate FHA loan is to use a ratio of 35% of total housing expenses to net effective income. However, make sure that, when added to other fixed obligations, the ratio does not exceed 50%. Your buyers enter dangerous territory if, after installment payments are deducted from gross monthly income, their net effective income is dropped below three times their monthly house payments.

insurance primarily for borrowers making a down payment of less than 20 percent. FHA mortgage insurance premiums (MIPs) are significantly higher than Private Mortgage Insurance (PMI) on conventional loans due to the minimal down payment requirements for FHA insured loans.

From the standpoint of income, FHA may consider the applicant's base salary plus all of the usual overtime and bonuses verified by the employer. A VA school allotment or any other verified income may be included. Net income from rental properties may also be considered when substantiated by tax returns.

2. Loan Discount Fee

Buyers are allowed to pay part or all of the loan discount fee or points. Buyers may also be charged a 1 percent loan origination fee. The discount fee is not collected; it is withheld by the lender to equalize the yield. For example, a mortgage broker collects the 1 percent loan origination fee for processing the loan, but the lender, for whom the broker is a correspondent, withholds the discount fee from the seller's proceeds when funds are placed in escrow.

3. Calculating the Maximum Loan

The maximum insurable FHA loan amounts vary, depending on the median priced home in a particular area, including basic areas, high-cost areas, and ceiling limits set for Hawaii and Alaska.

4. FHA Section 245 – Graduated Payment Mortgage (GPM)

FHA has several graduated payment plans to choose from, providing lower payments in earlier years.

The outstanding principal amount due on a Graduated Payment Mortgage increases during the initial years as unpaid interest is added to the principal balance and negative amortization is created.

Homebuyers may choose the GPM plan that suits their needs. The five plans vary the rate at which the monthly payments increase, from approximately 2 to 7.5 percent per year, depending on interest rate fluctuations. Borrowers also have the option of choosing the number of years (either five or ten) over which the payments increase before levelling off for the remainder of the loan. Larger than usual down payments are required to prevent the total amount of the loan from exceeding the statutory loan-to-value ratios. Down payments required for GPMs

vary in proportion to interest rates on the loans. In all other ways, the GPM is subject to the rules governing ordinary HUD-insured home loans.

www.hud.gov
U.S. Department of Housing and Urban Delelopment (HUD)

The greater the rate of increase or the longer the period of increase, the lower the mortgage payments in early years. Remember that these types of loans are used when the buyer cannot qualify with other programs.

B. DEPARTMENT OF VETERANS AFFAIRS (VA) (www. benefits.va.gov/homeloans)

A "VA Loan" is not a loan, but rather a guarantee to an approved lender.

In 1944, the Servicemen's Readjustment Act was passed. It contained a great many special benefits for the returning veterans of World War II to help them adjust to civilian life. The Veterans Home Loan Guaranty program was initiated within the framework of the Readjustment Act. Since that time, additional laws and regulations have created changes in the loan guaranty program.

Federal funds are not used, except in isolated areas where private lenders are not available. However, the Department of Veterans Affairs guarantees 25% of the loan limit. Most loans are between $417,000 and $1,000,000.

1. Certificate of Reasonable Value (CRV)

A *CERTIFICATE OF REASONABLE VALUE (CRV) is an appraisal of the property a veteran wishes to buy*. The Department of Veterans Affairs appoints accredited "fee" appraisers to submit appraisal reports, from which a Certificate of Reasonable Value (CRV) is issued. A CRV is effective for six months and specifies the maximum amount to be loaned on the property in connection with the loan guaranty.

2. Secondary Financing

There can be secondary (junior) financing on the subject property to help obtain the new loan if the terms of the second, lower priority loan, run concurrently with the first trust deed.

Borrowers in such cases must be able to qualify for both the first and second loans. Once the loan has been established, junior financing may also be utilized if the veteran should resell the home, or borrow on it for any reason. Secondary financing is discussed in more detail later in the chapter.

3. Eligibility and Entitlement

Any eligible veteran may obtain a VA loan on the purchase of residential property from one-to-four units, provided he or she is going to occupy one of the units. All applicants will need to obtain a Certificate of Eligibility from the VA. Veterans will need a copy of their DD214 (Discharge paper). Active duty personnel will need a Statement of Service form filled out by their unit personnel officer. The COE can be obtained online or by mail. Most lenders can get one in minutes while processing the loan preapproval.

4. Reinstatement of Veterans Loan Entitlement

Eligibility for another VA loan under the same entitlement is restored for the veteran when the loan has been paid off.

If the veteran has not fully used the entitlement, he or she is eligible for the difference between the maximum entitlement and the amount already used.

C. CALIFORNIA DEPARTMENT OF VETERANS AFFAIRS (CalVet) (www.calvet.ca.gov)

Along with other benefits to qualified wartime veterans, California provides a special assistance program for farm and home purchases. Laws pertaining to the program are governed by the Military and Veterans' Code. Loan funds are obtained from bond issues.

The California Department of Veterans Affairs administers the program. Operating budgets must be approved by the legislature.

Operating costs of the program, plus retirement of the bonds and interest thereon, are reflected in the interest rates charged on CalVet loans. The state has never been forced to repay any portion of a bond issue, as the program is self-sustaining.

Interest rates vary on a fluctuating or "floating" basis. Amortization periods fluctuate between 25 and 40 years. Whenever the interest rate is increased, the increased interest merely extends the amortization period for outstanding loans and does not increase the original loan interest and principal payments paid each month.

When a farm or a home and the veteran are approved for a CalVet loan, the property is purchased by the state and, in turn, is resold to the veteran on an agreement of sale. In reality, this is a **sales contract** popularly referred to as a **land contract of sale**. Title to the property remains with the state until the loan is paid in full.

With the exception of establishing a loan trust account to cover property taxes on the property, the costs of obtaining a new CalVet loan are practically nil. There are no discount points, and loan origination fees are low. Usually the interest rate is the lowest.

All qualified veterans are eligible for the CalVet program. The same person could be eligible for a VA, FHA, and CalVet loan.

1. Insurance Requirements

A low-cost group term life insurance policy on the veteran is paid for by the veteran, along with regular monthly loan payments. In case the veteran should die, the loan balance is paid off through the life insurance policy. A fire and extended coverage insurance policy is also purchased by the state and paid for by the veteran as a part of regular monthly payments.

2. Maximum Loans

CalVet's maximum loan amount for most counties is dependent upon varying loan features, such as the loan program or property type. CalVet offers a loan amount that exceeds conventional conforming loan amount limits. The veteran must pay to the seller, as a down payment, the difference between the sales price and the CalVet loan.

V. Qualifying the Borrower

The borrower-purchaser must be able to qualify, based on the risks involved.

Before your client meets with a lender, you can make a "ballpark" assessment of his or her purchasing budget by using the following formula: Gross monthy income times 43% minus any fixed debt payments, such as credit cards, loan payments, etc.

A. THE LOAN APPLICATION (Uniform Residential Loan Application)

In the purchase of a home, all prospective lenders ask for a completed application that contains personal and financial data, such as that shown in **Figure 9-3**. Among the items are employment history of the borrowers, other income, bank references, legal actions, current and past creditors, and a summary of assets and liabilities.

1. Credit Scoring (Access to Credit Profile)

CREDIT SCORING gives lenders a fast, objective measurement of your ability to repay a loan or make timely credit payments. It is based solely on information in consumer credit reports maintained at one of the credit reporting agencies. Factors comprising a credit score include:

1. Payment History - What is your track record?
2. Amounts Owed - How much is too much?
3. Length of Credit History - How established is yours?
4. New Credit - Are you taking on more debt?
5. Types of Credit Use - Is it a "healthy" mix?

*The most widely used credit bureau scores are developed by Fair, Isaac, and Company. These are known as **FICO SCORES**.* If a credit agency refuses to provide a copy of a credit report to an applicant who is denied credit because of a credit problem, the applicant can:

1. file civil action against the credit agency;
2. negotiate a settlement, and/or
3. require the credit agency to pay all legal fees.

Figure 9-3

Uniform Residential Loan Application

This application is designed to be completed by the applicant(s) with the Lender's assistance. Applicants should complete this form as "Borrower" or "Co-Borrower," as applicable. Co-Borrower information must also be provided (and the appropriate box checked) when ☐ the income or assets of a person other than the Borrower (including the Borrower's spouse) will be used as a basis for loan qualification or ☐ the income or assets of the Borrower's spouse or other person who has community property or similar rights pursuant to applicable state law will not be used as a basis for loan qualification, but his or her liabilities must be considered because the spouse or other person who has community property or similar rights and the Borrower resides in a community property state, the security property is located in a community property state, or the Borrower is relying on other property located in a community property state as a basis for repayment of the loan.

If this is an application for joint credit, Borrower and Co-Borrower each agree that we intend to apply for joint credit (sign below):

Borrower _____ Co-Borrower _____

I. TYPE OF MORTGAGE AND TERMS OF LOAN

Mortgage Applied for:	☐ VA ☐ USDA/Rural Housing Service ☐ FHA ☐ Conventional ☐ Other (explain):	Agency Case Number	Lender Case Number

Amount $	Interest Rate %	No. of Months	Amortization Type:	☐ Fixed Rate ☐ Other (explain): ☐ GPM ☐ ARM (type):

II. PROPERTY INFORMATION AND PURPOSE OF LOAN

Subject Property Address (street, city, state & ZIP)	No. of Units
Legal Description of Subject Property (attach description if necessary)	Year Built

Purpose of Loan ☐ Purchase ☐ Refinance ☐ Construction ☐ Construction-Permanent ☐ Other (explain):

Property will be: ☐ Primary Residence ☐ Secondary Residence ☐ Investment

Complete this line if construction or construction-permanent loan.

Year Lot Acquired	Original Cost $	Amount Existing Liens $	(a) Present Value of Lot $	(b) Cost of Improvements $	Total (a + b) $

Complete this line if this is a refinance loan.

Year Acquired	Original Cost $	Amount Existing Liens $	Purpose of Refinance	Describe Improvements	☐ made ☐ to be made

Title will be held in what Name(s)	Manner in which Title will be held	Estate will be held in: ☐ Fee Simple ☐ Leasehold (show expiration date)

Source of Down Payment, Settlement Charges, and/or Subordinate Financing (explain)

Uniform Residential Loan Application
Freddie Mac Form 65   7/05 (rev.6/09)   Page 1 of 8   Fannie Mae Form 1003   7/05 (rev.6/09)

III. BORROWER INFORMATION

Borrower		Co-Borrower	
Borrower's Name (include Jr. or Sr. if applicable)		Co-Borrower's Name (include Jr. or Sr. if applicable)	

Social Security Number	Home Phone (incl. Area code)	DOB (mm/dd/yyyy)	Yrs. School	Social Security Number	Home Phone (incl. Area code)	DOB (mm/dd/yyyy)	Yrs. School

☐ Married ☐ Separated ☐ Unmarried (include single, divorced, widowed)	Dependents (not listed by Co-Borrower) no. ages	☐ Married ☐ Separated ☐ Unmarried (include single, divorced, widowed)	Dependents (not listed by Borrower) no. ages

Present Address (street, city, state, ZIP) ☐ Own ☐ Rent ___No. Yrs.	Present Address (street, city, state, ZIP) ☐ Own ☐ Rent ___No. Yrs.

Mailing Address, if different from Present Address	Mailing Address, if different from Present Address

If residing at present address for less than two years, complete the following:

Former Address (street, city, state, ZIP) ☐ Own ☐ Rent ___No. Yrs.	Former Address (street, city, state, ZIP) ☐ Own ☐ Rent ___No. Yrs.

IV. EMPLOYMENT INFORMATION

Borrower		Co-Borrower	
Name & Address of Employer ☐ Self Employed	Yrs. on this job	Name & Address of Employer ☐ Self Employed	Yrs. on this job
	Yrs. employed in this line of work/profession		Yrs. employed in this line of work/profession
Position/Title/Type of Business	Business Phone (incl. area code)	Position/Title/Type of Business	Business Phone (incl. area code)

If employed in current position for less than two years or if currently employed in more than one position, complete the following:

Name & Address of Employer ☐ Self Employed	Dates (from - to)	Name & Address of Employer ☐ Self Employed	Dates (from - to)
	Monthly Income $		Monthly Income $
Position/Title/Type of Business	Business Phone (incl. area code)	Position/Title/Type of Business	Business Phone (incl. area code)

Name & Address of Employer ☐ Self Employed	Dates (from - to)	Name & Address of Employer ☐ Self Employed	Dates (from - to)
	Monthly Income $		Monthly Income $
Position/Title/Type of Business	Business Phone (incl. area code)	Position/Title/Type of Business	Business Phone (incl. area code)

Uniform Residential Loan Application
Freddie Mac Form 65   7/05 (rev.6/09)   Page 2 of 8   Fannie Mae Form 1003   7/05 (rev.6/09)

V. MONTHLY INCOME AND COMBINED HOUSING EXPENSE INFORMATION

Gross Monthly Income	Borrower	Co-Borrower	Total	Combined Monthly Housing Expense	Present	Proposed
Base Empl. Income*	$	$	$	Rent	$	
Overtime				First Mortgage (P&I)		$
Bonuses				Other Financing (P&I)		
Commissions				Hazard Insurance		
Dividends/Interest				Real Estate Taxes		
Net Rental Income				Mortgage Insurance		
Other (before completing, see the notice in "describe other income," below)				Homeowner Assn. Dues		
				Other:		
Total	$	$	$	Total	$	$

* Self Employed Borrower(s) may be required to provide additional documentation such as tax returns and financial statements.

Describe Other Income   Notice: Alimony, child support, or separate maintenance income need not be revealed if the Borrower (B) or Co-Borrower (C) does not choose to have it considered for repaying this loan.

B/C		Monthly Amount
		$

VI. ASSETS AND LIABILITIES

This Statement and any applicable supporting schedules may be completed jointly by both married and unmarried Co-Borrowers if their assets and liabilities are sufficiently joined so that the Statement can be meaningfully and fairly presented on a combined basis; otherwise, separate Statements and Schedules are required. If the Co-Borrower section was completed about a non-applicant spouse or other person, this Statement and supporting schedules must be completed about that spouse or other person also.

Completed ☐ Jointly ☐ Not Jointly

ASSETS Description	Cash or Market Value	Liabilities and Pledged Assets. List the creditor's name, address, and account number for all outstanding debts, including automobile loans, revolving charge accounts, real estate loans, alimony, child support, stock pledges, etc. Use continuation sheet, if necessary. Indicate by (*) those liabilities, which will be satisfied upon sale of real estate owned or upon refinancing of the subject property.
Cash deposit toward purchase held by:	$	LIABILITIES	Monthly Payment & Months Left to Pay	Unpaid Balance
List checking and savings accounts below		Name and address of Company	$ Payment/Months	$
Name and address of Bank, S&L, or Credit Union				
		Acct. no.		
Acct. no.	$	Name and address of Company	$ Payment/Months	$

Uniform Residential Loan Application
Freddie Mac Form 65   7/05 (rev.6/09)   Page 3 of 8   Fannie Mae Form 1003   7/05 (rev.6/09)

VI. ASSETS AND LIABILITIES (cont'd)

Name and address of Bank, S&L, or Credit Union		Acct. no.		
Acct. no.	$	Name and address of Company	$ Payment/Months	$
Name and address of Bank, S&L, or Credit Union				
		Acct. no.		
Acct. no.	$	Name and address of Company	$ Payment/Months	$
Name and address of Bank, S&L, or Credit Union				
		Acct. no.		
Acct. no.	$	Name and address of Company	$ Payment/Months	$
Stocks & Bonds (Company name/number & description)	$			
		Acct. no.		
Life insurance net cash value	$	Name and address of Company	$ Payment/Months	$
Face amount: $				
Subtotal Liquid Assets	$	Acct. no.		
Real estate owned (enter market value from schedule of real estate owned)	$	Alimony/Child Support/Separate Maintenance Payments Owed to:	$	$
Vested interest in retirement fund	$			
Net worth of business(es) owned (attach financial statement)	$	Job-Related Expense (child care, union dues, etc.)	$	
Automobiles owned (make and year)	$			
Other Assets (itemize)	$			
		Total Monthly Payments	$	
Total Assets a.	$	Net Worth (a minus b)	$	Total Liabilities b. $

Uniform Residential Loan Application
Freddie Mac Form 65   7/05 (rev.6/09)   Page 4 of 8   Fannie Mae Form 1003   7/05 (rev.6/09)

315

Top-Left Quadrant

Schedule of Real Estate Owned (If additional properties are owned, use continuation sheet.)

Property Address (enter S if sold, PS if pending sale or R if rental being held for income)	Type of Property	Present Market Value	Amount of Mortgages & Liens	Gross Rental Income	Mortgage Payments	Insurance, Maintenance, Taxes & Misc.	Net Rental Income
		$	$	$	$	$	$
Totals		$	$	$	$	$	$

List any additional names under which credit has previously been received and indicate appropriate creditor name(s) and account number(s):

Alternate Name	Creditor Name	Account Number

VII. DETAILS OF TRANSACTION / VIII. DECLARATIONS

	VII. DETAILS OF TRANSACTION		VIII. DECLARATIONS	Borrower		Co-Borrower	
			If you answer "Yes" to any questions a through i, please use continuation sheet for explanation.	Yes	No	Yes	No
a.	Purchase price	$					
b.	Alterations, improvements, repairs		a. Are there any outstanding judgments against you?	☐	☐	☐	☐
c.	Land (if acquired separately)		b. Have you been declared bankrupt within the past 7 years?	☐	☐	☐	☐
d.	Refinance (incl. debts to be paid off)		c. Have you had property foreclosed upon or given title or deed in lieu thereof in the last 7 years?	☐	☐	☐	☐
e.	Estimated prepaid items		d. Are you a party to a lawsuit?	☐	☐	☐	☐
f.	Estimated closing costs		e. Have you directly or indirectly been obligated on any loan which resulted in foreclosure, transfer of title in lieu of foreclosure, or judgment?	☐	☐	☐	☐
g.	PMI, MIP, Funding Fee		(This would include such loans as home mortgage loans, SBA loans, home improvement loans, educational loans, manufactured (mobile) home loans, any mortgage, financial obligation, bond, or loan guarantee. If "Yes," provide details, including date, name, and address of Lender, FHA or VA case number, if any, and reasons for the action.)				
h.	Discount (if Borrower will pay)		f. Are you presently delinquent or in default on any Federal debt or any other loan, mortgage, financial obligation, bond, or loan guarantee?	☐	☐	☐	☐
			If "Yes," give details as described in the preceding question.				
i.	Total costs (add items a through h)		g. Are you obligated to pay alimony, child support, or separate maintenance?	☐	☐	☐	☐
j.	Subordinate financing		h. Is any part of the down payment borrowed?	☐	☐	☐	☐

Top-Right Quadrant

VII. DETAILS OF TRANSACTION (cont'd) / VIII. DECLARATIONS (cont'd)

	VII. DETAILS OF TRANSACTION (cont'd)		VIII. DECLARATIONS (cont'd)				
k.	Borrower's closing costs paid by Seller		i. Are you a co-maker or endorser on a note?	☐	☐	☐	☐
l.	Other Credits (explain)						
			j. Are you a U.S. citizen?	☐	☐	☐	☐
			k. Are you a permanent resident alien?	☐	☐	☐	☐
m.	Loan amount (exclude PMI, MIP, Funding Fee financed)		l. Do you intend to occupy the property as your primary residence?	☐	☐	☐	☐
			If "Yes," complete question m below.				
n.	PMI, MIP, Funding Fee financed		m. Have you had an ownership interest in a property in the last three years?	☐	☐	☐	☐
o.	Loan amount (add m & n)		(1) What type of property did you own–principal residence (PR), second home (SH), or investment property (IP)?	......	......	......	......
p.	Cash from/to Borrower (subtract j, k, l & o from i)		(2) How did you hold title to the home– by yourself (S), jointly with your spouse or jointly with another person (O)?	......	......	......	......

ACKNOWLEDGEMENT AND AGREEMENT

Each of the undersigned specifically represents to Lender and to Lender's actual or potential agents, brokers, processors, attorneys, insurers, servicers, successors and assigns and agrees and acknowledges that: (1) the information provided in this application is true and correct as of the date set forth opposite my signature and that any intentional or negligent misrepresentation of this information contained in this application may result in civil liability, including monetary damages, to any person who may suffer any loss due to reliance upon any misrepresentation that I have made on this application, and/or in criminal penalties including, but not limited to, fine or imprisonment or both under the provisions of Title 18, United States Code, Sec. 1001, et seq.; (2) the loan requested pursuant to this application (the "Loan") will be secured by a mortgage or deed of trust on the property described in this application; (3) the property will not be used for any illegal or prohibited purpose or use; (4) all statements made in this application are made for the purpose of obtaining a residential mortgage loan; (5) the property will be occupied as indicated in this application; (6) the Lender, its servicers, successors or assigns may retain the original and/or an electronic record of this application, whether or not the Loan is approved; (7) the Lender and its agents, brokers, insurers, servicers, successors, and assigns may continuously rely on the information contained in the application, and I am obligated to amend and/or supplement the information provided in this application if any of the material facts that I have represented should change prior to closing of the Loan; (8) in the event that my payments on the Loan become delinquent, the Lender, its servicers, successors or assigns may, in addition to any other rights and remedies that it may have relating to such delinquency, report my name and account information to one or more consumer reporting agencies; (9) ownership of the Loan and/or administration of the Loan account may be transferred with such notice as may be required by law; (10) neither Lender nor its agents, brokers, insurers, servicers, successors or assigns has made any representation or warranty, express or implied, to me regarding the property or the condition or value of the property; and (11) my transmission of this application as an "electronic record" containing my "electronic signature," as those terms are defined in applicable federal and/or state laws (excluding audio and video recordings), or my facsimile transmission of this application containing a facsimile of my signature, shall be as effective, enforceable and valid as if a paper version of this application were delivered containing my original written signature.

Acknowledgement. Each of the undersigned hereby acknowledges that any owner of the Loan, its servicers, successors and assigns, may verify or reverify any information contained in this application or obtain any information or data relating to the Loan, for any legitimate business purpose through any source, including a source named in this application or a consumer reporting agency.

Borrower's Signature	Date	Co-Borrower's Signature	Date
X		X	

X. INFORMATION FOR GOVERNMENT MONITORING PURPOSES

Bottom-Left Quadrant

The following information is requested by the Federal Government for certain types of loans related to a dwelling in order to monitor the lender's compliance with equal credit opportunity, fair housing and home mortgage disclosure laws. You are not required to furnish this information, but are encouraged to do so. The law provides that a lender may not discriminate either on the basis of this information, or on whether you choose to furnish it. If you furnish the information, please provide both ethnicity and race. For race, you may check more than one designation. If you do not furnish ethnicity, race, or sex, under Federal regulations, this lender is required to note the information on the basis of visual observation and surname if you have made this application in person. If you do not wish to furnish the information, please check the box below. (Lender must review the above material to assure that the disclosures satisfy all requirements to which the lender is subject under applicable state law for the particular type of loan applied for.)

BORROWER
☐ I do not wish to furnish this information
Ethnicity: ☐ Hispanic or Latino
☐ Not Hispanic or Latino
Race: ☐ American Indian or Alaska Native
☐ Asian
☐ Black or African American
☐ Native Hawaiian or Other Pacific Islander
☐ White
Sex: ☐ Female ☐ Male

CO-BORROWER
☐ I do not wish to furnish this information
Ethnicity: ☐ Hispanic or Latino
☐ Not Hispanic or Latino
Race: ☐ American Indian or Alaska Native
☐ Asian
☐ Black or African American
☐ Native Hawaiian or Other Pacific Islander
☐ White
Sex: ☐ Female ☐ Male

To be Completed by Loan Originator
This information was provided:
☐ In a face-to-face interview
☐ In a telephone interview
☐ By the applicant and submitted by fax or mail
☐ By the applicant and submitted via e-mail or the Internet

Loan Originator's Signature		Date

Loan Originator's Name (print or type)	Loan Originator Identifier	Loan Originator's Phone Number (including area code)

Loan Origination Company's Name	Loan Origination Company Identifier	Loan Origination Company's Address

---

Bottom-Right Quadrant

CONTINUATION SHEET/RESIDENTIAL LOAN APPLICATION

Use this continuation sheet if you need more space to complete the Residential Loan Application. Mark **B** for Borrower or **C** for Co-Borrower.	Borrower:	Agency Case Number:
	Co-Borrower:	Lender Case Number:

I/We fully understand that it is a Federal crime punishable by fine or imprisonment, or both, to knowingly make any false statements concerning any of the above facts as applicable under the provisions of Title 18, United States Code, Section 1001, et seq.

Borrower's Signature	Date	Co-Borrower's Signature	Date
X		X	

See **Figure 9-4** for a more complete description of credit scoring, which is often difficult to explain.

Figure 9-4

Credit Scoring

A credit score is a three-digit number assigned to consumers based on credit history that is used by lenders to determine the level of risk they may be taking if they lend to someone. The system awards points based on information in the credit report, and compared to others with similar profiles, lenders can use this information to predict how likely someone is to repay a loan and make payments on time, and therefore decide whether or not to make a loan and at what interest rate.

Credit scores are often referred to as *FICO SCORES, due to the fact that Fair, Isaac, and Company was the first company to develop a mathematical credit scoring model based on selected criteria in a credit report.* The following are the systems now used:

Experian – Experian/Fair Isaac system
TransUnion – Empirica system
Equifax – Beacon system

FICO scores, which still dominate the industry, range from 300 to 850. Any score under 650 is considered high risk, and subject to higher interest rates, and anything over 720 qualifies for the best interest rate.

Loan applicants are entitled to know the specific credit scores and the "reason codes" used in determining their scores. Reason codes may include too high a debt-to-credit limit ratio, late payments, or too short a credit history.

In addition to a consumer's right to receive a free credit report from each of the three national credit reporting agencies once a year, by law, credit reporting agencies are required to correct inaccurate information in a timely manner, and are subject to legal recourse if inaccurate information continues to be reported once they are made aware of mistakes.

www.experian.com/consumer/index.html
Experian
www.transunion.com
TransUnion
www.equifax.com
Equifax

SUBPRIME LOANS are generally made to borrowers with less than excellent credit scores. Due to higher risk, they are generally charged higher interest rates, points, fees, and prepayment penalties. These are rarely used anymore!

2. Equal Credit Opportunity Act (ECOA)

This law requires that financial institutions and other persons engaged in the extension of credit make that credit equally available to all creditworthy customers without regard to sex, marital status, race, color, religion, national origin, or age.

Lenders may ask but not require information regarding the applicant's sex, marital status, race, color, religion, national origin, or age.

3. Fair Credit Reporting Act

The *FAIR CREDIT REPORTING ACT allows loan applicants who have data collected on them to see their files.* Incorrect information may be gathered because of faulty reporting, or a revenging party may furnish half-truths and even outright lies. The law states that the credit bureau must quickly correct mistakes found in its records.

4. Truth in Lending Act

The *TRUTH IN LENDING ACT ("Regulation Z") lets borrowers and customers know the cost of credit so that they can compare costs with those of other credit sources and thereby avoid the uninformed use of credit.* It requires disclosure of fees charged for arranging the loan, prepaid interest amount, buyer's escrow fee, application fee, mortgage inspection fee, VA funding fee, prepaid mortgage insurance premiums on FHA loans, finder's fees, costs of termite inspection, tax service fee, disclosure statement fee, origination or closing fee, loan discount fee and points paid by the seller, and any other costs that increase the effective interest rate. Through the use of tables available at any Federal Reserve Board office, these finance costs, when added to the total interest charged, show the effective yield, or **annual percentage rate (APR)**. Of course, if there are no charges connected with the granting of a loan, the APR equals the stated or nominal rate.

VI. Noninstitutional Financing

There are many sources of private, noninstitutional financing. *NONINSTITUTIONAL FINANCING is financing by parties who are not governed or controlled by federal and state agencies in the stringent manner in which the savings banks, commercial banks, and life insurance companies are.* A list of such noninstitutional lenders includes pension funds, credit unions, mortgage companies, real estate investment trusts (REITs), private and public syndications, and individuals. For a complete treatment of these and other forms of financing, consult *Real Estate Finance*, 9th edition, by Walt Huber and Walt Zozula (see order form in back of book).

A. JUNIOR LOANS (Secondary Financing)

JUNIOR LOANS (also referred to as "secondary financing") are secured by a second trust deed or mortgage, and any other loans on a property that come after the first, or prime, security.

A junior loan is best illustrated by an example. When the owner sells a property for $300,000, with a down payment of $30,000, representing 10 percent of the selling price, the buyers will be short of the purchase price if they are unable to obtain financing for $270,000, or 90 percent of the purchase price. In practice, most conventional loans are made for 80 percent of the selling price or appraised value, whichever is lower. It can be seen, then, that the buyer will be deficient by $30,000. Solution? The seller "carries back" the 10 percent balance of the price as a purchase money second trust deed loan. Thus, the seller carries back a loan, "the paper," as it is called, for the difference between the first loan plus down payment and the selling price. Some lenders will carry the first and second trust deeds.

The seller "carrying back" is a junior mortgage (trust deed) holder. See Figure 9-5 for the Seller Financing Addendum and Disclosure (SFA), which details the first and second trust deed information.

1. Alienation Clause

Frequently, a trust deed contains an **ALIENATION CLAUSE**, *which states that, should the property be subsequently sold (or default occur), the entire note becomes due and payable.* ARMs are usually fully assumable.

2. Discounting Second Trust Deeds

Many purchase money trust deeds are written under terms that call for one percent of the loan balance as a monthly payment, which may include interest of 10 percent or more per annum, all due and payable at the end of five years. Because of the need for cash and because of the relatively low yield in relation to the risk, sellers very often do not want to keep the second trust loan for the full term. Brokers are frequently called upon to sell such notes, almost always at a discount.

A trust deed note is "discounted" when it sells for less than the principal amount or less than the unpaid balance.

3. Balloon Payments

Secondary financing usually involves **BALLOON PAYMENTS** *(any payment that is twice as high as the regular payment); that is, junior trust deed loans that are not self-amortizing will require a large payment to pay off the remainder of the loan.*

B. ALL-INCLUSIVE TRUST DEED (AITD)

The all-inclusive trust deed (AITD) is a purchase money encumbrance that includes, yet is subject to, the existing loans. The installments received by the seller from the buyer are used first to pay the underlying liens, the balance going to the sellers as recovery of their remaining equity. Also referred to as a **wraparound deed of trust**, overriding, overlapping, or hold harmless, the AITD is especially useful in tight money markets.

A sales contract financed through an AITD should include the following statement:

BUYER AND SELLER ARE AWARE THAT THE UNDERLYING NOTES SECURED BY TRUST DEEDS MAY CONTAIN A "DUE-ON-SALE" CLAUSE WHICH MAY GIVE THE LENDER THE ELECTION TO CALL THE LOAN DUE UPON RECORDATION OF THE DEED AND A.I.T.D. BUYER AND SELLER ARE ADVISED TO SEEK LEGAL COUNSEL TO EXPLAIN THEIR RIGHTS AND/OR LIABILITIES IN SUCH EVENT.

C. CONTRACT OF SALE (Land Contract)

The "contract of sale," also referred to as a "land contract," is sometimes used in real estate transactions, but it is not always advisable to do so. Be sure the sellers obtain legal counsel.

A land contract is generally employed when a buyer invests little or no cash in the purchase. In a **LAND CONTRACT**, *the seller, as owner of record, retains legal title to the property until a certain point in time, which is generally after the buyer has paid a substantial amount of cash toward the seller's equity, if not all of it.* Meanwhile, the buyer obtains what is referred to as "equitable title," that is, a buildup of ownership in increments, through payments on the principal indebtedness, in addition to appreciation arising outside the principal reduction itself.

A land contract is like a car loan—you may be driving the car, but you don't own the title until it's paid off.

When the agreed amount is paid, the seller transfers legal title to the buyer, who might, in turn, assume the existing loan. Until that time, however, the principal payments, interest on the unpaid balance of the contract, and the monthly tax and insurance payments might be paid to the seller, who, in turn, makes the monthly payments on the underlying trust deed. This, of course, is the seller's assurance that the loan payments are kept current. On the other hand, the buyer has no assurance that the seller is making the existing loan payments.

To overcome the problems of the simple two-party (vendor-vendee) land contract, the parties may agree to a three-party instrument in which the rights of the parties are insured by a policy of title insurance. (See Stewart Title Insurance.)

www.stewart.com/title-insurance

In the typical insured transaction, a title company is designated as trustee "with power of sale" in the same way as trustees are vested in the normal trust deed.

The contract should be drawn by a real estate attorney to assure a complete agreement, with no details omitted. Repossession of the property often requires court action; if the court rules that both parties be restored to their original positions, the repercussions could be disastrous.

D. ALL-CASH TRANSACTIONS

An all cash transaction is less complicated than a traditional loan situation. If you're representing the buyer you should use due diligence to be sure the purchase price is legitimately within market value. As a broker advising a client, you should be sure that all the proper forms, inspections, and appraisals are done correctly—you are the only one protecting your buyers because there's no lender protecting their interests. In recent years, given the global economic uncertainties, all cash transactions have become more common, not only with domestic investor/flippers, but also with foreign nationals seeking the safe haven of United States real estate.

VII. Loan Takeovers

A. "ASSUMPTION" vs. "SUBJECT TO"

A *LOAN ASSUMPTION occurs when a buyer pays a seller for part or all of the equity in a property and assumes the responsibility for payment of the existing loans.* From then on, the buyer makes the necessary payments until the existing loans are paid in full or until another disposition of the loans is made. *EQUITY is the difference between market value and existing loans against the property.*

When allowing a buyer to assume the seller's existing loan(s), it is imperative that the seller obtain an unconditional release from the lender. Otherwise, if the buyer defaults, the seller would still be obligated to pay.

Taking title *SUBJECT TO a prior loan constitutes an agreement to take over and make the loan payments or lose the property.* The original party, however, remains liable for the debt should the second party default. This method of purchasing is normally more desirable, from the standpoint of saving buyer's and seller's expenses, provided the buyer has sufficient funds to complete the transaction.

Taking title "subject to" can trigger the "alienation (due on sale) clause," which is in most trust deeds securing a fixed-rate loan.

1. FHA Loan Assumption

In most situations, FHA loans may be assumed.

2. VA Loan Assumption

The Veterans Administration (VA) holds the original maker of the loan responsible for any losses resulting from foreclosure on a GI loan. However, liability may be eliminated from the original veteran by obtaining a release from the VA and transferring responsibility for the loan to the buyer.

3. CalVet Loan Assumption

A CalVet loan may be assumed by another qualified California veteran at the prevailing interest rate. Non-vets may not assume a CalVet loan.

In all instances, prior approval must be obtained from the California Department of Veterans Affairs.

4. Conventional Loan Assumption

Conventional fixed loans are usually not assumable.

A lender's approval of the buyer is always required the before allowing the buyer to assume the loan. A conventional lender may require a favorable credit report and a higher-than-normal assumption fee and may also have the option of increasing the interest rate to a new owner. Therefore, it is advisable to determine in advance of a sale what the lender's requirements are going to be with respect to the loan assumption.

When interest rates are low, it sometimes does not make economic sense to assume an existing loan.

However, there may be other considerations besides interest rates that make assuming a loan desirable. For instance, the loan qualifying requirements may be more liberal compared to obtaining a new loan or the time factor may be important, etc.

5. Seller Carryback Assumption

Buyers frequently do not have sufficient cash to pay the difference between the purchase price and the existing loan and, for one reason or another, prefer not to refinance with a new loan.

Circumstances may make it more beneficial for the seller not to receive all the equity in cash because of adverse income tax consequences. If the seller has no immediate need for all the cash, he or she could carry a part of the equity on a second deed of trust and receive a greater yield than a savings account would provide. When the seller carries back a note and trust deed for part or all of the purchase price, the CAR® form Seller Financing Addendum and Disclosure (SFA) should be used (see **Figure 9-5**).

VIII. Loan Brokerage

Being a broker or salesperson, as part of most real estate transactions, you may help your buyer fill out a loan application for a financial institution or arrange financing for your buyer. In either case, there are certain restrictions that apply to a real estate licensee acting as a loan broker in buying, selling, or exchanging loans. Most of these loans are in the form of a trust deed since it is the usual financing instrument in California.

California law allows real estate licensees (with NMLS endorsement) who negotiate mortgage loans to receive compensation for their services (as arrangers, managers of loans, middlemen, or intermediaries).

They must obtain an MLO license endorsement from CalBRE.

Figure 9-5

CALIFORNIA ASSOCIATION OF REALTORS®

SELLER FINANCING ADDENDUM AND DISCLOSURE
(SEE IMPORTANT DISCLOSURE ON PAGE 4)
(California Civil Code §§2956-2967)
(C.A.R. Form SFA, Revised 11/13)

This is an addendum to the ☐ Residential Purchase Agreement, ☐ Counter Offer, or ☐ Other _____, ("Agreement"), dated _____,
On property known as _____ *264 Beach Lane, Costa Mesa, CA   92627* _____ ("Property"),
between _____ *Walter Buyer, Debbie Buyer* _____ ("Buyer"),
and _____ *Tony Seller, Ramona J. Seller* _____ ("Seller").
Seller agrees to extend credit to Buyer as follows:

1. **PRINCIPAL; INTEREST; PAYMENT; MATURITY TERMS:** ☐ Principal amount $ _____, interest at _____ % per annum, payable at approximately $ _____ per ☐ month, ☐ year, or ☐ other _____, remaining principal balance due in _____ years.

2. **LOAN APPLICATION; CREDIT REPORT:** Within **5 (or** ☐ _____**) Days** After Acceptance: **(a)** Buyer shall provide Seller a completed loan application on a form acceptable to Seller (such as a FNMA/FHLMC Uniform Residential Loan Application for residential one to four unit properties); and **(b)** Buyer authorizes Seller and/or Agent to obtain, at Buyer's expense, a copy of Buyer's credit report. Buyer shall provide any supporting documentation reasonably requested by Seller. Seller, after first giving Buyer a Notice to Buyer to Perform, may cancel this Agreement in writing and authorize return of Buyer's deposit if Buyer fails to provide such documents within that time, or if Seller disapproves any above item within **5 (or** ☐ _____**) Days** After receipt of each item.

3. **CREDIT DOCUMENTS:** This extension of credit by Seller will be evidenced by: ☐ Note and deed of trust; ☐ All-inclusive note and deed of trust; ☐ Installment land sale contract; ☐ Lease/option (when parties intend transfer of equitable title); OR ☐ Other (specify) _____

THE FOLLOWING TERMS APPLY ONLY IF CHECKED. SELLER IS ADVISED TO READ ALL TERMS, EVEN THOSE NOT CHECKED, TO UNDERSTAND WHAT IS OR IS NOT INCLUDED, AND, IF NOT INCLUDED, THE CONSEQUENCES THEREOF.

4. ☐ **LATE CHARGE:** If any payment is not made within _____ Days After it is due, a late charge of either $ _____, or _____ % of the installment due, may be charged to Buyer. **NOTE:** On single family residences that Buyer intends to occupy, California Civil Code §2954.4(a) limits the late charge to no more than 6% of the total installment payment due and requires a grace period of no less than 10 days.

5. ☐ **BALLOON PAYMENT:** The extension of credit will provide for a balloon payment, in the amount of $ _____, plus any accrued interest, which is due on _____ (date).

6. ☐ **PREPAYMENT:** If all or part of this extension of credit is paid early, Seller may charge a prepayment penalty as follows (if applicable): _____. Caution: California Civil Code §2954.9 contains limitations on prepayment penalties for residential one to four unit properties.

7. ☐ **DUE ON SALE:** If any interest in the Property is sold or otherwise transferred, Seller has the option to require immediate payment of the entire unpaid principal balance, plus any accrued interest.

8.* ☐ **REQUEST FOR COPY OF NOTICE OF DEFAULT:** A request for a copy of Notice of Default as defined in California Civil Code §2924b will be recorded. If not, Seller is advised to consider recording a Request for Notice of Default.

9.* ☐ **REQUEST FOR NOTICE OF DELINQUENCY:** A request for Notice of Delinquency, as defined in California Civil Code §2924e, to be signed and paid for by Buyer, will be made to senior leinholders. If not, Seller is advised to consider making a Request for Notice of Delinquency. Seller is advised to check with senior leinholders to verify whether they will honor this request.

10.* ☐ **TAX SERVICE:**
   A. If property taxes on the Property become delinquent, tax service will be arranged to report to Seller. **If not,** Seller is advised to consider retaining a tax service, or to otherwise determine that property taxes are paid.
   B. ☐ Buyer, ☐ Seller, shall be responsible for the initial and continued retention of, and payment for, such tax service.

11. ☐ **TITLE INSURANCE:** Title insurance coverage will be provided to **both** Seller and Buyer, insuring their respective interests in the Property. **If not,** Buyer and Seller are advised to consider securing such title insurance coverage.

12. ☐ **HAZARD INSURANCE:**
   A. The parties' escrow holder or insurance carrier will be directed to include a loss payee endorsement, adding Seller to the Property insurance policy. **If not,** Seller is advised to secure such an endorsement, or acquire a separate insurance policy.
   B. Property insurance **does not** include earthquake or flood insurance coverage, unless checked:
   ☐ Earthquake insurance will be obtained; ☐ Flood insurance will be obtained.

13. ☐ **PROCEEDS TO BUYER:** Buyer will receive cash proceeds at the close of the sale transaction. The amount received will be approximately $ _____, from _____ (indicate source of proceeds). Buyer represents that the purpose of such disbursement is as follows: _____

14. ☐ **NEGATIVE AMORTIZATION; DEFERRED INTEREST:** Negative amortization results when Buyer's periodic payments are less than the amount of interest earned on the obligation. Deferred interest also results when the obligation does not require periodic payments for a period of time. In either case, interest is not payable as it accrues. This accrued interest will have to be paid by Buyer at a later time, and may result in Buyer owing more on the obligation than at its origination. The credit being extended to Buyer by Seller will provide for negative amortization or deferred interest as indicated below. (Check A, B, or C. CHECK ONE ONLY.)
   ☐ **A.** All negative amortization or deferred interest shall be added to the principal _____ (e.g., annually, monthly, etc.), and thereafter shall bear interest at the rate specified in the credit documents (compound interest);
   OR ☐ **B.** All deferred interest shall be due and payable, along with principal, at maturity;
   OR ☐ **C.** Other _____.

*(For Paragraphs 8-10) In order to receive timely and continued notification, Seller is advised to record appropriate notices and/or to notify appropriate parties of any change in Seller's address.

Buyer's Initials (_____) (_____)   Seller's Initials (_____) (_____)

The copyright laws of the United States (Title 17 U.S. Code) forbid the unauthorized reproduction of this form, or any portion thereof, by photocopy machine or any other means, including facsimile or computerized formats. Copyright© 1997-2013, CALIFORNIA ASSOCIATION OF REALTORS®, INC. ALL RIGHTS RESERVED.

SFA REVISED 11/13 (PAGE 1 OF 3)

Reviewed by _____ Date _____   **EQUAL HOUSING OPPORTUNITY**

SELLER FINANCING ADDENDUM AND DISCLOSURE (SFA PAGE 1 OF 4)

Agent: WALT HUBER	Phone:	Fax:	Prepared using zipForm® software
Broker: WALT HUBER REALTOR			

Property Address: *264 Beach Lane, Costa Mesa, CA 92627* Date: _____

15. ☐ **ALL-INCLUSIVE DEED OF TRUST; INSTALLMENT LAND SALE CONTRACT:** This transaction involves the use of an all-inclusive (or wraparound) deed of trust or an installment land sale contract. That deed of trust or contract shall provide as follows:
A. In the event of an acceleration of any senior encumbrance, the party responsible for payment, or for legal defense is: ☐ Buyer ☐ Seller ; OR ☐ **Is not** specified in the credit or security documents.
B. In the event of the prepayment of a senior encumbrance, the responsibilities and rights of Buyer and Seller regarding refinancing, prepayment penalties, and any prepayment discounts are: _____ ; OR ☐ **Are not** specified in the documents evidencing credit.
C. Buyer will make periodic payments to _____ (Seller, collection agent, or any neutral third party), who will be responsible for disbursing payments to the payee(s) on the senior encumbrance(s) and to Seller.
NOTE: The Parties are advised to designate a neutral third party for these purposes.

16. ☐ **TAX IDENTIFICATION NUMBERS:** Buyer and Seller shall each provide to each other their Social Security Numbers or Taxpayer Identification Numbers.
17. ☐ **OTHER CREDIT TERMS:** _____
18. ☐ **RECORDING:** The documents evidencing credit (paragraph 3) will be recorded with the county recorder where the Property is located. **If not,** Buyer and Seller are advised that their respective interests in the Property may be jeopardized by intervening liens, judgments, encumbrances, or subsequent transfers.
19. ☐ **JUNIOR FINANCING:** There will be additional financing, secured by the Property, junior to this Seller financing. Explain: _____

20. **SENIOR LOANS AND ENCUMBRANCES:** The following information is provided on loans and/or encumbrances that will be **senior** to Seller financing. **NOTE:** The following are estimates, unless otherwise marked with an asterisk (*). If checked: ☐ A separate sheet with information on additional senior loans/encumbrances is attached.

	1st	2nd
A. Original Balance	$	$
B. Current Balance	$	$
C. Periodic Payment (e.g. $100/month):	$	$ /
Including Impounds of:	$	$ /
D. Interest Rate (per annum)	%	%
E. Fixed or Variable Rate:		
If Variable Rate: Lifetime Cap (Ceiling)		
Indicator (Underlying Index)		
Margins		
F. Maturity Date		
G. Amount of Balloon Payment	$	$
H. Date Balloon Payment Due		
I. Potential for Negative Amortization? (Yes, No, or Unknown)		
J. Due on Sale? (Yes, No, or Unknown)		
K. Pre-payment penalty? (Yes, No, or Unknown)		
L. Are payments current? (Yes, No, or Unknown)		

21. **BUYER'S CREDITWORTHINESS:** (CHECK EITHER A OR B. Do not check both.) In addition to the loan application, credit report and other information requested under paragraph 2:
A. ☐ No other disclosure concerning Buyer's creditworthiness has been made to Seller;
OR B. ☐ The following representations concerning Buyer's creditworthiness are made by Buyer(s) to Seller:

Borrower	Co-Borrower
1. Occupation	1. Occupation
2. Employer	2. Employer
3. Length of Employment	3. Length of Employment
4. Monthly Gross Income	4. Monthly Gross Income
5. Other	5. Other

22. **ADDED, DELETED OR SUBSTITUTED BUYERS:** The addition, deletion or substitution of any person or entity under this Agreement or to title prior to close of escrow shall require Seller's written consent. Seller may grant or withhold consent in Seller's sole discretion. Any additional or substituted person or entity shall, if requested by Seller, submit to Seller the same documentation as required for the original named Buyer. Seller and/or Brokers may obtain a credit report, at Buyer's expense, on any such person or entity.

Buyer's Initials (_____)(_____)   Seller's Initials (_____)(_____)

Copyright© 1997-2013, CALIFORNIA ASSOCIATION OF REALTORS®, INC.

SFA REVISED 11/13 (PAGE 2 OF 4)

Reviewed by _____ Date _____

SELLER FINANCING ADDENDUM AND DISCLOSURE (SFA PAGE 2 OF 4)

CA RPA

Property Address: _264 Beach Lane, Costa Mesa, CA 92627_ _____ Date: _____

23. CAUTION:

A. If the Seller financing requires a balloon payment, Seller shall give Buyer written notice, according to the terms of Civil Code §2966, at least 90 and not more than 150 days before the balloon payment is due if the transaction is for the purchase of a dwelling for not more than four families.

B. If **any** obligation secured by the Property calls for a balloon payment, Seller and Buyer are aware that refinancing of the balloon payment at maturity may be difficult or impossible, depending on conditions in the conventional mortgage marketplace at that time. There are no assurances that new financing or a loan extension will be available when the balloon prepayment, or any prepayment, is due.

C. If **any** of the existing or proposed loans or extensions of credit would require refinancing as a result of a lack of full amortization, such refinancing might be difficult or impossible in the conventional mortgage marketplace.

D. In the event of default by Buyer: (1) Seller may have to reinstate and/or make monthly payments on any and all senior encumbrances (including real property taxes) in order to protect Seller's secured interest; (2) Seller's rights are generally limited to foreclosure on the Property, pursuant to California Code of Civil Procedure §580b; and (3) the Property may lack sufficient equity to protect Seller's interests if the Property decreases in value.

If this three-page Addendum and Disclosure is used in a transaction for the purchase of a dwelling for not more than four families, it shall be prepared by an Arranger of Credit as defined in California Civil Code §2957(a). (The Arranger of Credit is usually the agent who obtained the offer.)

Arranger of Credit - (Print Firm Name) _____ By _____ Date _____

Address _____ City _____ State _____ Zip _____

Phone _____ Fax _____

> BUYER AND SELLER ACKNOWLEDGE AND AGREE THAT BROKERS: (A) WILL NOT PROVIDE LEGAL OR TAX ADVICE; (B) WILL NOT PROVIDE OTHER ADVICE OR INFORMATION THAT EXCEEDS THE KNOWLEDGE, EDUCATION AND EXPERIENCE REQUIRED TO OBTAIN A REAL ESTATE LICENSE; OR (C) HAVE NOT AND WILL NOT VERIFY ANY INFORMATION PROVIDED BY EITHER BUYER OR SELLER. BUYER AND SELLER AGREE THAT THEY WILL SEEK LEGAL, TAX AND OTHER DESIRED ASSISTANCE FROM APPROPRIATE PROFESSIONALS. BUYER AND SELLER ACKNOWLEDGE THAT THE INFORMATION EACH HAS PROVIDED TO THE ARRANGER OF CREDIT FOR INCLUSION IN THIS DISCLOSURE FORM IS ACCURATE. BUYER AND SELLER FURTHER ACKNOWLEDGE THAT EACH HAS RECEIVED A COMPLETED COPY OF THIS DISCLOSURE FORM.

Buyer _____ _Walter Buyer_ Date _____
(signature)

Address _100 Boat Avenue_ City _Marina del Rey_ State _CA_ Zip _90292_

Phone _____ Fax _____ E-mail _____

Buyer _____ _Debbie Buyer_ Date _____
(signature)

Address _____ City _____ State _____ Zip _____

Phone _____ Fax _____ E-mail _____

Seller _____ _Tony Seller_ Date _____
(signature)

Address _264 Beach Lane_ City _Costa Mesa_ State _CA_ Zip _92627_

Phone _____ Fax _____ E-mail _____

Seller _____ _Ramona J. Seller_ Date _____
(signature)

Address _____ City _____ State _____ Zip _____

Phone _____ Fax _____ E-mail _____

THIS FORM HAS BEEN APPROVED BY THE CALIFORNIA ASSOCIATION OF REALTORS® (C.A.R.). NO REPRESENTATION IS MADE AS TO THE LEGAL VALIDITY OR ADEQUACY OF ANY PROVISION IN ANY SPECIFIC TRANSACTION. A REAL ESTATE BROKER IS THE PERSON QUALIFIED TO ADVISE ON REAL ESTATE TRANSACTIONS. IF YOU DESIRE LEGAL OR TAX ADVICE, CONSULT AN APPROPRIATE PROFESSIONAL.

This form is available for use by the entire real estate industry. It is not intended to identify the user as a REALTOR®. REALTOR® is a registered collective membership mark which may be used only by members of the NATIONAL ASSOCIATION OF REALTORS® who subscribe to its Code of Ethics.

Published and Distributed by:
REAL ESTATE BUSINESS SERVICES, INC.
a subsidiary of the California Association of REALTORS®
525 South Virgil Avenue, Los Angeles, California 90020

Reviewed by _____ Date _____

SFA REVISED 11/13 (PAGE 3 OF 4)

SELLER FINANCING ADDENDUM AND DISCLOSURE (SFA PAGE 3 OF 4)

CA RPA

Property Address: *264 Beach Lane, Costa Mesa, CA 92627*   Date: _____

IMPORTANT SELLER FINANCING DISCLOSURE - PLEASE READ CAREFULLY

The Dodd-Frank Wall Street Reform and Consumer Protection Act (Dodd-Frank) has made significant and important changes affecting seller financing on residential properties. Effective January 10, 2014, sellers who finance the purchase of residential property containing 1-4 units may be considered "loan originators" required to comply with certain Truth In Lending Act ("TILA") requirements. Even under Dodd-Frank however, the following two exemptions exist:

1. The seller finances only **ONE** property in any 12 month period and:
   a. The seller is a natural person, a trust or an estate, and
   b. The seller did not construct the property, and
   c. The financing has a fixed rate or does not adjust for the first 5 years, and
   d. The financing does not result in negative amortization.

    OR

2. The seller finances no more than **THREE** properties in any 12 month period and:
   a. The seller is a natural person or organization (corporation, LLC, partnership, trust, estate, association, etc.), and
   b. The seller did not construct the property, and
   c. The loan is fully amortized, i.e., no balloon payment, and
   d. The financing has a fixed rate or does not adjust for the first 5 years, and
   e. The borrower has the reasonable ability to repay the loan.

Sellers who finance the purchase of residential property containing 1-4 units meeting either of the two exemptions are not subject to the TILA requirements above may continue to, and are required by California Law to, use the Seller Financing Addendum.

Sellers who finance the purchase of residential property containing 1-4 units who do not meet either of the two tests above should still complete the Seller Finance Addendum and speak to a lawyer about other TILA disclosures that may be required.

Sellers who finance the purchase of residential property containing 5 or more units, vacant land, or commercial properties are not subject to the TILA disclosures nor are they required to use the Seller Financing Addendum.

A seller who originates a single extension of credit through a mortgage broker and additionally meets the definition of a "high-cost" mortgage under Dodd-Frank may be subject to the Truth in Lending Act's requirement to verify the borrower's ability to repay.

Buyer's Initials (_____) (_____)   Seller's Initials (_____) (_____)

Copyright ©1997-2013, CALIFORNIA ASSOCIATION OF REALTORS®, INC.
SFA REVISED 11/13 (PAGE 4 OF 4)

Reviewed by _____ Date _____

SELLER FINANCING ADDENDUM AND DISCLOSURE (SFA PAGE 4 OF 4)   CA RPA

A. SAFE MORTGAGE LICENSING ACT

Title V – The *SECURE AND FAIR ENFORCEMENT MORTGAGE LICENSING ACT (SAFE ACT) of the Housing and Economic Recovery Act of 2008 enhances consumer protection and reduces fraud in mortgage loan transactions.* It requires all 50 states and 5 territories to put into place a system for licensing mortgage loan originators that meets the minimum requirements of the SAFE Act.

The Conference of State Bank Supervisors (CSBS) and the American Association of Residential Mortgage Regulators (AARMR) have created, and will maintain, the Nationwide Mortgage Licensing System and Registry (NMLS&R) to streamline the licensing process with oversight by HUD. In addition to state requirements, NMLS&R will contain a single license record for each mortgage loan lender, broker, brand, and mortgage loan originator which can be used to apply for, amend, and renew a license in any participating jurisdiction.

All CalBRE licensees who conduct residential Mortgage Loan Originator (MLO) activities, as outlined in the SAFE Act, must meet separate requirements to qualify for a MLO endorsement (see **www.leginfo.ca.gov**).

1. What Does the SAFE Act Require?

The SAFE Act mandates that each person performing business activities that fit the definition of a mortgage loan originator meet certain minimum pre-licensing and continuing education requirements in order to be licensed as a loan originator in any state. In addition to existing state requirements, each person must also take and pass a test consisting of 125 questions. This test is in addition to the CalBRE real estate salesperson or broker examination.

In California, the SAFE Act requires 20 hours of additional pre-licensing education, after which eight hours of continuing education is required annually.

Each mortgage loan originator applicant is required to provide a set of fingerprints directly to NMLS&R in order to obtain criminal background histories through the FBI. The applicant also must authorize NMLS&R to obtain an independent credit report from a consumer reporting agency. The SAFE Act also mandates mortgage call reports, reporting of enforcement actions, and certain public access to licensing information. When registering with NMLS&R, each person is issued a **unique identifier**. This unique identifier does not replace the real estate license identification number, but allows information to be shared among states in the event of complaints and/or disciplinary actions.

The California Bureau of Real Estate (CalBRE) will add an "endorsement" to a real estate licensee's broker or salesperson license for those persons engaging in mortgage loan activities. Each mortgage loan originator will hold a California real estate license plus the "endorsement." The endorsement will be renewed annually while the real estate license will remain on a four-year renewal cycle. The **Department of Business Oversight (DBO)** has also implemented a licensing

system that is compliant with SAFE for all mortgage loan originators under the **California Finance Lenders Licensing Law (CFL)** and **California Residential Mortgage Loan Act** (Mortgage Bankers).

The CalBRE has been working with CSBS and AARMR on a number of issues that would affect current and future licensees, such as pre-licensing education, testing, and continuing education requirements. There is continuously more information, provided as it emerges, in future *Real Estate Bulletins* and on the CalBRE website. Additionally, information on the SAFE Act and NMLS&R can be obtained at **www.csbs.org/srr/Pages/default.aspx** and at **http://mortgage. nationwidelicensingsystem.org/Pages/default.aspx**.

B. MORTGAGE LOAN DISCLOSURE STATEMENT

As a real estate licensee negotiating a loan for a prospective borrower, you (or the lender) must present to the prospective borrower a completed loan disclosure statement. This statement must be given to the borrower prior to his or her signing the loan documents. It is usually referred to as the Mortgage Loan Disclosure Statement.

A *MORTGAGE LOAN DISCLOSURE STATEMENT (MS) is a form that completely and clearly states all the information and charges connected with a particular loan*. It must be kept on file for three years (see **Figure 9-7**).

C. BUSINESS AND PROFESSIONS CODE (Commissions and Other Requirements)
1. Article 7 - Loan Broker Laws (Smaller Hard Money Loans)

Brokers negotiating trust deed loans are subject to certain limitations regarding commissions and expenses and must meet other requirements set out by the Real Estate Commissioner (see **Figure 9-6**). Legislation also requires that brokers provide both the borrower and the lender, on property for first trust deed loans under $30,000 and seconds under $20,000, with copies of the appraisal report. Anyone performing these services, whether soliciting borrowers or lenders in home loans secured by real property, must have a real estate license. This restriction applies even if no advance fee is paid. If the collateral is a 1-4 unit residential property and is or will be owner occupied as a principle residence, then the broker must also have a Nationwide Mortgage

Figure 9-6 **Loan Broker Commission Limits**

	Loans for Less Than 2 Years	Loans for 2 Years and Less Than 3 Years	Loans for 3 Years and Over	Transactions That are Exempt
First Trust Deeds	5%	5%	10%	**Loans of $30,000 and over**
Junior Trust Deeds	5%	10%	15%	**Loans of $20,000 and over**

Figure 9-7

CALIFORNIA
ASSOCIATION
OF REALTORS®

MORTGAGE LOAN DISCLOSURE STATEMENT
(BORROWER)
(As required by the Business and Professions Code §10241
and Title 10, California Administrative Code, §2840)
(C.A.R. Form MS, Revised 08/08)

_____
(Name of Broker/Arranger of Credit)

_____
(Business Address of Broker)

I. SUMMARY OF LOAN TERMS
  A. PRINCIPAL AMOUNT . . . . $ _____
  B. ESTIMATED DEDUCTIONS FROM PRINCIPAL AMOUNT
    1. Costs and Expenses (See Paragraph III-A) . . . . $ _____
    2. Broker Commission/Origination Fee (See Paragraph III-B) . . . . $ _____
    3. Lender Origination Fee/Discounts (See Paragraph III-B) . . . . $ _____
    4. Additional compensation will/may be received from lender not deducted from loan proceeds.
      ☐ YES $ _____ (if known) or ☐ NO
    5. Amount to be Paid on Authorization of Borrower (See Paragraph III-C) . . . . . . $ _____
  C. ESTIMATED CASH PAYABLE TO BORROWER (A less B) . . . . $ _____

II. GENERAL INFORMATION ABOUT LOAN
  A. PROPOSED LOAN INFORMATION
    1. Proposed loan term   ☐ Years   ☐ Months

☐ FIXED RATE LOAN	☐ ADJUSTABLE RATE LOAN (EXAMPLE 6-MONTH ARM; 1-YEAR ARM)
Fixed rate loan _____ % payable at $ _____ month	Proposed interest rate _____ % Fully indexed rate _____ % Proposed monthly payment: $ _____ Maximum interest rate _____ % Interest rate can increase _____ % each _____ months Maximum loan payment can be $ _____ after _____ months
☐ INITIAL FIXED RATE LOAN (EXAMPLE 2/28; 3/1; 5/1)	☐ INITIAL ADJUSTABLE RATE LOAN (EXAMPLE LOW ENTRY RATE ARM)
Proposed initial fixed interest rate _____ % Initial fixed interest rate in effect for _____ months Proposed initial monthly payment: $ _____ Adjustable interest rate of _____ % will begin after fixed rate period ends Monthly payment can increase to $ _____ after fixed rate period ends Fully indexed rate _____ % Maximum interest rate _____ % Interest rate can increase _____ % each _____ months Maximum loan payment can be $ _____ after _____ months	Proposed initial adjustable interest rate _____ % Initial fixed interest rate in effect for _____ months Proposed initial monthly payment: $ _____ Fully indexed rate _____ % Maximum interest rate _____ % Interest rate can increase _____ % each _____ months Monthly payment can increase to $ _____ after initial adjustable rate period ends Maximum loan payment can be $ _____ after _____ months

    2. This loan is based on limited or no documentation of your income and/or assets and may have a higher interest rate, or more points or fees than other products requiring documentation: ☐ No ☐ Yes.
    3. The loan is subject to a balloon payment: ☐ No ☐ Yes. If Yes, the following paragraph applies and a final balloon payment of $ _____ will be due on _____ [estimated date (month/day/year)].

    NOTICE TO BORROWER: IF YOU DO NOT HAVE THE FUNDS TO PAY THE BALLOON PAYMENT WHEN IT COMES DUE, YOU MAY HAVE TO OBTAIN A NEW LOAN AGAINST YOUR PROPERTY TO MAKE THE BALLOON PAYMENT. IN THAT CASE, YOU MAY AGAIN HAVE TO PAY COMMISSIONS, FEES AND EXPENSES FOR THE ARRANGING OF THE NEW LOAN. IN ADDITION, IF YOU ARE UNABLE TO MAKE THE MONTHLY PAYMENTS OR THE BALLOON PAYMENT, YOU MAY LOSE THE PROPERTY AND ALL OF YOUR EQUITY THROUGH FORECLOSURE. KEEP THIS IN MIND IN DECIDING UPON THE AMOUNT AND TERMS OF THIS LOAN.

  B. This loan will be evidenced by a promissory note and secured by a deed of trust on property identified as (street address or legal description):
    123 Sail Avenue , _____

The copyright laws of the United States (Title 17 U.S. Code) forbid the unauthorized reproduction of this form by any means, including facsimile or computerized formats. Copyright © 1991 - 2008, CALIFORNIA ASSOCIATION OF REALTORS® Inc. All Rights Reserved.

MS REVISED 08/08 (PAGE 1 OF 3)

Buyer's Initials (_____)(_____)
Seller's Initials (_____)(_____)

Reviewed by _____ Date_____

EQUAL HOUSING OPPORTUNITY

MORTGAGE LOAN DISCLOSURE STATEMENT (MS PAGE 1 OF 3)

Agent: WALT HUBER	Phone:	Fax:	Prepared using zipForm® software
Broker: WALT HUBER REALTOR			

C. 1. Liens presently against this property (do not include loan being applied for):

Nature of Lien	Priority	Lienholder's Name	Amount Owing
_____	_____	_____	_____
_____	_____	_____	_____
_____	_____	_____	_____

2. Liens that will remain against this property after the loan being applied for is made or arranged (include loan being applied for):

Nature of Lien	Priority	Lienholder's Name	Amount Owing
_____	_____	_____	_____
_____	_____	_____	_____
_____	_____	_____	_____

NOTICE TO BORROWER: Be sure that you state the amount of all liens as accurately as possible. If you contract with the broker to arrange this loan, but it cannot be arranged because you did not state these liens correctly, you may be liable to pay commissions, fees and expenses even though you do not obtain the loan.

D. Prepayments: The proposed loan has the following prepayment provisions:

☐ No prepayment penalty (you will not be charged a penalty to pay off or refinance the loan before maturity)

☐ You will have to pay a prepayment penalty if the loan is paid off or refinanced in the first _____ years. The prepayment penalty could be as much as $ _____ . Any prepayment of principal in excess of 20% of the
   ☐ original loan balance or
   ☐ unpaid balance
for the first _____ years will include a penalty not to exceed _____ months interest at the note interest rate but not more than the interest you would be charged if the loan were paid to maturity.

☐ Other - you will have to pay a prepayment penalty if the loan is paid off or refinanced in the first _____ years as follows: _____
_____
_____

E. Taxes and Insurance:

☐ There will be an impound (escrow) account which will collect approximately $ _____ a month in addition to your principal and interest payments for the payment of ☐ county property taxes** ☐ hazard insurance ☐ mortgage insurance ☐ flood insurance ☐ other _____ .

☐ If there is no impound (escrow) account or if your escrow (impound) account does not include one or more of the payments described above, you will have to plan for the payment of ☐ county property taxes** ☐ hazard insurance of approximately $ _____ per year.

**In a purchase transaction, county property taxes are calculated based on the sales price of the property and may require the payment of an additional (supplemental) tax bill from the county tax authority by your lender (if escrowed) or you (if not escrowed).

F. Late Charges: ☐ YES, see loan documents or ☐ NO

G. The purchase of credit life and/or credit disability insurance by a borrower is not required as a condition of making this loan.

III. DEDUCTIONS FROM LOAN PROCEEDS

A. Estimated Maximum Costs and Expenses of Arranging the Loan to be Paid Out of Loan Principal:

	PAYABLE TO	
	Broker	Others
1. Appraisal fee	_____	_____
2. Escrow fee	_____	_____
3. Title insurance policy	_____	_____
4. Notary fees	_____	_____
5. Recording fees	_____	_____
6. Credit investigation fees	_____	_____
7. Other costs and expenses:		
_____	_____	_____
_____	_____	_____
Total Costs and Expenses	$ _____	_____
B. Compensation	$ _____	
1. Brokerage Commission/Origination Fee ...	$ _____	

Buyer's Initials (_____)(_____)
Seller's Initials (_____)(_____)

Copyright © 1991 - 2008, CALIFORNIA ASSOCIATION OF REALTORS® Inc.

MS REVISED 08/08 (PAGE 2 OF 3)

Reviewed by _____ Date _____

MORTGAGE LOAN DISCLOSURE STATEMENT (MS PAGE 2 OF 3)

Untitled

2. Lender Origination Fee/Discounts .... $ _____

C. Estimated Payment to be Made out of Loan Principal on Authorization of Borrower

	PAYABLE TO	
	Broker	Others
1. Fire or other hazard insurance premiums	_____	_____
2. Credit life or disability insurance premiums (See Paragraph II-G)	_____	_____
3. Beneficiary statement fees	_____	_____
4. Reconveyance and similar fees	_____	_____
5. Discharge of existing liens against property:		
_____	_____	_____
_____	_____	_____
6. Other:		
_____	_____	_____
_____	_____	_____

Total to be Paid on Authorization of Borrower .... $ _____

Article 7 Compliance: If this loan is secured by a first deed of trust on dwellings in a principal amount of less than $30,000 or secured by a junior lien on dwellings in a principal amount of less than $20,000, the undersigned licensee certifies that the loan will be made in compliance with Article 7 of Chapter 3 of the Real Estate Law.

This loan **may / will / will not** (delete two) be made wholly or in part from broker-controlled funds as defined in Section 10241(j) of the Business and Professions Code.

IV. NOTICES TO BORROWER:

1. This disclosure statement may be used if the Broker is acting as an agent in arranging the loan by a third person or if the loan will be made with funds owned or controlled by the broker. If the Broker indicates in the Article 7 Compliance immediately above, that the loan "may" be made out of Broker-controlled funds, the Broker must notify the borrower prior to the close of escrow if the funds to be received by the Borrower are in fact Broker-controlled funds.

2. THIS IS NOT A LOAN COMMITMENT. Do not sign this statement until you have read and understood all of the information in it. All parts of this form must be completed before you sign. Borrower hereby acknowledges the receipt of a copy of this statement.

_____ _____ _____ _____
Name of Broker License Number Broker Representative License Number

_____
Broker's Address

OR

_____ _____ _____ _____
Signature of Broker Date Signature of Representative Date

_____ _____ _____ _____
Borrower Date Borrower Date

The Department of Real Estate License Information phone number is 916-227-0931, or check license status at www.dre.ca.gov.

THIS FORM HAS BEEN APPROVED BY THE CALIFORNIA ASSOCIATION OF REALTORS® (C.A.R.). NO REPRESENTATION IS MADE AS TO THE LEGAL VALIDITY OR ADEQUACY OF ANY PROVISION IN ANY SPECIFIC TRANSACTION. A REAL ESTATE BROKER IS THE PERSON QUALIFIED TO ADVISE ON REAL ESTATE TRANSACTIONS. IF YOU DESIRE LEGAL OR TAX ADVICE, CONSULT AN APPROPRIATE PROFESSIONAL.

This form is available for use by the entire real estate industry. It is not intended to identify the user as a REALTOR®. REALTOR® is a registered collective membership mark which may be used only by members of the NATIONAL ASSOCIATION OF REALTORS® who subscribe to its Code of Ethics.

Published and Distributed by:
REAL ESTATE BUSINESS SERVICES, INC.
a subsidiary of the California Association of REALTORS®
525 South Virgil Avenue, Los Angeles, California 90020

Reviewed by _____ Date_____

MS REVISED 08/08 (PAGE 3 OF 3)

MORTGAGE LOAN DISCLOSURE STATEMENT (MS PAGE 3 OF 3)

Untitled

Licensing System and Registry (NMLS&R) endorsement to his/her real estate license (refer back to section A).

Loans on owner-occupied homes negotiated by brokers for a term of six years or less may not have a balloon payment. For loans on non-owner occupied properties of less than three years, balloon payments are not allowed. Neither of these restrictions apply to transactions where the seller extends credit to the buyer. When such transactions have balloon payments, the seller is obligated to notify the buyer 60 to 150 days before the balloon payment is due. Also, the broker is obligated to inform the buyer regarding the likelihood of obtaining new financing.

D. USURY LIMITATIONS

USURY is *charging more than the legally allowed percentage of interest.* In California, the maximum interest rate charged for various loans is set by law. Anyone charging more than the designated rate is committing usury and is breaking the law. In determining whether an interest charge is usurious or not, all loan fees and points are added to the interest rate. Prepayment penalties are not included in the usury law test.

The constitutional usury rate in California is ten percent, or five percent above the discount rate charged by the Federal Reserve Bank of San Francisco, whichever is higher. This limit only applies to lenders who are not exempt from the law. Nearly every conventional source of real estate financing, however, has been exempted from the usury limit. Banks, savings banks, and other institutional lenders are all exempt. Sellers carrying back a purchase money trust deed as part of their equity in a real estate sale are exempt. **Any transaction made through a licensed broker is also exempt from usury laws**. The problem arises when a private individual lends money to another private individual. Check with an attorney first.

www.frbsf.org
Federal Reserve Bank of San Francisco, 12th District
www.fdic.gov
Federal Deposit Insurance Corporation (FDIC)

IX. Loan Defaults and REO Advisory

When the owners can no longer afford to pay for a loan on a property, they usually sell the property or the loan goes into default. *Property which is in the possession of a lender as a result of foreclosure or forfeiture is known as **REAL ESTATE OWNED (REO)** property.* REO properties are usually in poor shape in terms of repairs and maintenance.

Figure 9-8 is the REO Advisory (Listing) form that is recommended for properties being sold by a lender after acquiring them by foreclosure or receiving a "deed in lieu of foreclosure." This form advises both the buyer and seller of their remaining obligation in a REO sale.

If the current owner is not able to sell the property in cooperation with a *SHORT SALE* *(where a lender accepts less than what is owed in the loan),* then the loan on the property may or may not go into foreclosure (see Short Sale Addendum [SSA] **Figure 9-9**). Once a property is an REO, the bank or lender will usually try to get rid of the property by either selling it

Figure 9-8

CALIFORNIA
ASSOCIATION
OF REALTORS®

REO ADVISORY
For Properties Being Sold by a Lender After Foreclosure
(C.A.R. Form REO, Revised 4/11)

Property Address: _____123 Sail Avenue_____
_____Marina del Rey, CA 90292_____ ("Property").

The Seller of the Property is a lender who has acquired title to the Property either by foreclosure or through a deed given in lieu of foreclosure. Many obligations imposed upon sellers, particularly sellers of real property containing one-to-four dwelling units, may not be applicable to the sale of the Property. However, even though Seller is exempt from many obligations, Seller must still comply with many others. Further, even though a Seller may be exempt from certain obligations, a real estate broker's obligations may still apply. This Advisory is intended to inform Buyer and Seller of their rights and obligations independent of those established by the contract between them.

EXEMPTIONS:

1. **TDS, NHD, Mello-Roos, Improvement Bond Act, Supplemental Property Taxes, Private Transfer Fee:** Seller is <u>exempt</u> from providing Buyer with the Real Estate Transfer Disclosure Statement (TDS), Natural Hazard Disclosure Statement (NHD), a Mello-Roos district lien disclosure, an Improvement Bond Act of 1915 notice, a Supplemental Property Tax notice, and a Notice of Private Transfer Fee pursuant to California Civil Code §§ 1102 et seq.

2. **Earthquake Guides:** Seller is <u>exempt</u> from providing either a Homeowner's or Commercial Property Owner's Guide to Earthquake Safety.

REQUIREMENTS:

1. **Disclosures:** Seller is <u>not exempt</u> from common law and statutory duties concerning fraud and deceit, even though the specific TDS Form is not required to be completed. Seller remains obligated to disclose known material facts affecting the value and desirability of the Property.

2. **Hazard Zones:** Seller is <u>not exempt</u> from applicable statutory obligations to disclose earthquake fault zones, seismic hazard zones, state fire responsibility areas, very high fire hazard severity zones, special flood hazard areas and flood hazard zones pursuant to the Public Resources Code, Government Code and United States Code, even though, pursuant to the Civil Code, the specific NHD Form is not required to be completed.

3. **Smoke Detectors:** The sale is <u>not exempt</u> from the State requirements that, for <u>single family residences</u>, operable smoke detectors be in place and that a written statement of compliance be provided to Buyer. It is negotiable between Buyer and Seller who is to pay for the cost of compliance.

4. **Water Heaters:** The sale is <u>not exempt</u> from the State requirement that water heaters be properly anchored, braced or strapped and that Seller provide a written statement of compliance to Buyer. It is negotiable between Buyer and Seller who is to pay for the cost of compliance.

5. **Lead-based Paint:** The Seller is <u>not exempt</u> from the federal obligation to: **(i)** disclose known lead-based paint and lead-based paint hazards; **(ii)** provide Buyer with copies of reports or studies covering lead-based paint and hazards on the Property; **(iii)** provide Buyer with the pamphlet "Protect Your Family From Lead In Your Home"; and **(iv)** give Buyer a 10-day opportunity to inspect for lead-based paint and hazards, if the Property contains residential dwelling units and was constructed prior to 1978.

6. **Carbon Monoxide Devices:** The sale is <u>not exempt</u> from the State requirements that on or before July 1, 2011, for all existing single family dwelling units, and on or before January 1, 2013, for all other existing dwelling units, the owner must install a carbon monoxide device approved and listed by the State Fire Marshall in the dwelling unit if the dwelling unit has a fossil fuel burning heater or appliance, fireplace, or an attached garage.

7. **Tax Withholding:** The sale is <u>not exempt</u> from providing information pertaining to the withholding obligation under either the federal "FIRPTA" or the California withholding requirements upon the sale of real property. However, an REO Seller which is a corporation or limited liability company, formed within the United States, and qualified either with the Secretary of State to do business in California or with a permanent place of business in California, will be exempt from withholding under both federal and California law.

Buyer's Initials (_____)(_____)   Seller's Initials (_____)(_____)

The copyright laws of the United States (Title 17 U.S. Code) forbid the unauthorized reproduction of this form, or any portion thereof, by photocopy machine or any other means, including facsimile or computerized formats. Copyright © 2008-2011, CALIFORNIA ASSOCIATION OF REALTORS®, INC. ALL RIGHTS RESERVED.

REO REVISED 4/11 (PAGE 1 OF 2)

Reviewed by _____ Date _____

REO ADVISORY (REO PAGE 1 OF 2)

Agent: WALT HUBER   Phone: Prepared using zipForm® software
Broker:

Property Address: _____ **123 Sail Avenue**
Marina del Rey, CA 90292 _____ Date: _____

8. **Megan's Law Database Disclosure:** The sale is <u>not exempt</u> from the requirement that residential sales contracts contain the following notice regarding the availability of information about registered sex offenders. "Notice: Pursuant to Section 290.46 of the Penal Code, information about specified registered sex offenders is made available to the public via an Internet Web site maintained by the Department of Justice at www.meganslaw.ca.gov. Depending on an offender's criminal history, this information will include either the address at which the offender resides or the community of residence and ZIP Code in which he or she resides." (Neither Seller nor Brokers are required to check this website. If Buyer wants further information, Broker recommends that Buyer obtain information from this website during Buyer's inspection contingency period. Brokers do not have expertise in this area.)

9. **Brokers:**
   A. Inspection: The sale is <u>not exempt</u> from the Broker's obligation to conduct a reasonably competent and diligent visual inspection of the accessible areas of the Property and disclose to Buyer material facts revealed by such an inspection in the sale of residential property containing one-to-four dwelling units. Brokers may do so on C.A.R. Form AVID.
   B. Agency: The sale is <u>not exempt</u> from the obligation to provide agency relationship disclosure and confirmation forms in the sale of residential property containing one-to-four dwelling units.

OTHER CONSIDERATIONS:

1. **Selection of Title and Escrow:** California Civil Code section 1103.22 prohibits Seller from requiring, directly or indirectly, a Buyer to purchase title insurance or escrow services from a particular title insurer or escrow agent in connection with the sale of residential property improved with four or fewer dwellings. The Buyer may agree to use the title or escrow provider recommended by Seller if the Buyer has been informed of the right to make an independent selection of the applicable service. This law is in effect until January 1, 2015. Federal law, 12 U.S.C. Section 2608, prohibits Seller from requiring, directly or indirectly, that the Buyer purchase title insurance from any particular title company as a condition of selling residential property improved with four or fewer dwellings if the purchase will be made with a federally-related mortgage loan. Seller and Buyer understand that Brokers do not require Buyer to purchase title or escrow services from any particular provider. Any communications from Seller that Broker may deliver to Buyer or Buyer's agent concerning the selection of title or escrow services should not be construed as Broker's endorsement or recommendation of, or request for Buyer to use, any particular title or escrow provider.

2. **Local Law:** Local law may impose obligations on the transfer of real property (such as the installation of low flow toilets or shower heads, emergency gas shut-off valves or installation of smoke detectors). Local law should be consulted to determine if sales of Lender-owned property are exempt from such requirements.

3. **Amendments to Contract:** Seller-prepared addenda, amendments, or counter-offers or a Seller-prepared contract, may conflict with, contradict or be inconsistent with terms in Buyer's offer. Brokers cannot advise Buyer or Seller: **(i)** which specific terms in any offer may be affected; **(ii)** whether the terms in any such Seller-prepared documents are permissible under California Law; or **(iii)** in the event of a discrepancy between the Seller-prepared documents and any other Agreement between Buyer and Seller, which document or which terms may supersede the other. Buyer is advised to seek legal counsel to discuss the applicability and interpretation of any Seller-prepared documents prior to signing any such documents.

4. **Rental Property:** If the Property was occupied by a tenant at the time the lender acquired the Property and the tenant had a bona fide arm's length rental agreement at a fair market rate, the tenant may be entitled to the balance of their lease term, or at least a 90-day notice for termination of a month-to-month tenancy. In addition, certain rent control jurisdictions have asserted that the tenant has rights under rent control after a foreclosure. Moreover, the tenant may be entitled to the return of their security deposit even if the security deposit was not given to the lender after the foreclosure sale or to the buyer of the REO Property.

By signing below, the undersigned acknowledge that each has read, understands and has received a copy of this REO Advisory.

Buyer _____ Date _____

Buyer _____ Date _____

Seller _____ Date _____

Seller _____ Date _____

THIS FORM HAS BEEN APPROVED BY THE CALIFORNIA ASSOCIATION OF REALTORS® (C.A.R.). NO REPRESENTATION IS MADE AS TO THE LEGAL VALIDITY OR ADEQUACY OF ANY PROVISION IN ANY SPECIFIC TRANSACTION. A REAL ESTATE BROKER IS THE PERSON QUALIFIED TO ADVISE ON REAL ESTATE TRANSACTIONS. IF YOU DESIRE LEGAL OR TAX ADVICE, CONSULT AN APPROPRIATE PROFESSIONAL.

This form is available for use by the entire real estate industry. It is not intended to identify the user as a REALTOR®. REALTOR® is a registered collective membership mark which may be used only by members of the NATIONAL ASSOCIATION OF REALTORS® who subscribe to its Code of Ethics.

Published and Distributed by:
REAL ESTATE BUSINESS SERVICES, INC.
a subsidiary of the California Association of REALTORS®
525 South Virgil Avenue, Los Angeles, California 90020

Reviewed by _____ Date _____

REO REVISED 4/11 (PAGE 2 OF 2)   REO ADVISORY (REO PAGE 2 OF 2)   Untitled

Figure 9-9

CALIFORNIA
ASSOCIATION
OF REALTORS®

SHORT SALE ADDENDUM
(C.A.R. Form SSA, Revised 4/12)

This is an addendum to the ☐ California Residential Purchase Agreement, ☐ Counter Offer, ☐ Other _____
("Agreement"), dated _____ ,
on property known as _____ *123 Sail Avenue, Marina del Rey, CA 90292* _____
("Property"), between _____
("Buyer") and _____
("Seller").

1. **SHORT SALE APPROVAL:**

   A. This Agreement is contingent upon Seller's receipt of and delivery to Buyer of written consent ("Short Sale Lenders' Consent") to the Agreement from all existing secured lenders and lienholders ("Short Sale Lenders"), by 5:00 P.M. no later than **45 (or ☐ _____)** Days After Acceptance (or ☐ on_____ (date) ("Short Sale Contingency Date"). If Buyer or Seller cancels this Agreement prior to the Short Sale Contingency Date, that party may be in breach of the Agreement unless the cancellation is made pursuant to some other paragraph in this addendum or in the Agreement, whether or not time periods in the Agreement have commenced.

   B. Short Sale Lenders' Consent means that all Short Sale Lenders shall collectively agree to reduce their respective loan balances by an amount sufficient to permit the proceeds from the sale of the Property to pay the existing balances on loans secured by the Property, real property taxes, brokerage commissions, closing costs, and other monetary obligations the Agreement requires Seller to pay at Close Of Escrow (including, but not limited to, escrow charges, title charges, documentary transfer taxes, prorations, retrofit costs, Homeowners Association Fees and Repairs) without requiring Seller to place any funds into escrow or have any continuing obligation to Short Sale Lenders.

   C. **(i)** Seller shall Deliver to Buyer a copy of Short Sale Lenders' Consent or term sheet(s) within 3 (or ☐ _____) Days After receipt by Seller. **(ii)** Seller's presentation to Buyer of Short Sale Lender's Consent satisfying 1B removes the contingency in 1A.

   D. If by the Short Sale Contingency Date, **(i)** Seller has not received Short Sale Lenders' Consent satisfying 1B, Seller may in writing cancel this Agreement, or **(ii)** Buyer has not received a copy of Short Sale Lenders' Consent satisfying 1B, Buyer may cancel this Agreement in writing. In either case, Buyer shall be entitled to return of any remaining deposit delivered to escrow.

   E. Seller shall reasonably cooperate with existing Short Sale Lenders in the short sale process, but neither Seller nor Buyer is obligated to change the terms of their Agreement to satisfy Short Sale Lenders' consent or term sheet(s).

   F. If Short Sale Lenders' written consent or term sheet(s) provided to Seller require changes to the Agreement in order to satisfy the terms of 1B, **(i)** neither Buyer nor Seller shall be obligated to continue negotiations to satisfy any of the requirements of the term sheet(s) **(ii)** either party may in writing cancel this Agreement and **(iii)** Seller is advised to seek legal, accounting and tax advice before agreeing to any such changes. If the Agreement is cancelled pursuant to this paragraph, Buyer shall be entitled to return of any remaining deposit delivered to escrow.

2. **TIME PERIODS.** Time periods in the Agreement for inspections, contingencies, covenants, and other obligations:
   (i) shall begin the Day After Seller delivers to Buyer Short Sale Lenders' Consent satisfying 1B. However, time periods for providing pre-approval/pre-qualification letters and verification of down payment and closing costs shall nonetheless begin as otherwise specified in the Agreement;
   or **(ii)** (if checked) ☐ shall begin as specified in the Agreement.

Buyer's Initials (_____) (_____)   Seller's Initials (_____) (_____)

The copyright laws of the United States (TITLE 17 U.S. Code) forbid the unauthorized reproduction of this form by any means, including facsimile or computerized formats. Copyright © 2007-2012, CALIFORNIA ASSOCIATION OF REALTORS®. ALL RIGHTS RESERVED.
THIS FORM HAS BEEN APPROVED BY THE CALIFORNIA ASSOCIATION OF REALTORS® (C.A.R.). NO REPRESENTATION IS MADE AS TO THE LEGAL VALIDITY OR ADEQUACY OF ANY PROVISION IN ANY SPECIFIC TRANSACTION. A REAL ESTATE BROKER IS THE PERSON QUALIFIED TO ADVISE ON REAL ESTATE TRANSACTIONS. IF YOU DESIRE LEGAL OR TAX ADVICE, CONSULT AN APPROPRIATE PROFESSIONAL.
This form is available for use by the entire real estate industry. It is not intended to identify the user as a REALTOR®. REALTOR® is a registered collective membership mark which may be used only by members of the NATIONAL ASSOCIATION OF REALTORS® who subscribe to its Code of Ethics.

Published and Distributed by:
REAL ESTATE BUSINESS SERVICES, INC.
a subsidiary of the California Association OF REALTORS®
525 South Virgil Avenue, Los Angeles, California 90020

Reviewed by _____ Date _____

SSA REVISED 4/12 (PAGE 1 OF 2)   **SHORT SALE ADDENDUM (SSA PAGE 1 OF 2)**

Agent: WALT HUBER	Phone:	Fax:	Prepared using zipForm® software
Broker: WALT HUBER REALTOR			

Property Address: *123 Sail Avenue Marina del Rey, CA 90292* _____ Date: _____

3. **BUYER'S DEPOSIT CHECK.** Buyer's deposit check shall be delivered to escrow within: **(i)** 3 business Days After Seller delivers to Buyer Short Sale Lenders' Consent satisfying 1B, or **(ii)** (if checked) ☐ as specified in the Agreement.

4. **NO ASSURANCE OF LENDER APPROVAL.** Buyer and Seller understand that Short Sale Lenders: **(i)** are not obligated to give consent to a short sale; **(ii)** may require Seller to forward any other offer received; and **(iii)** may give consent to other offers. Additionally, Short Sale Lenders may require that, in order to obtain their approval for a short sale, some terms of the Agreement, such as the Close of Escrow, be amended or that Seller sign a personal note or some other obligation for all or a portion of the amount of the secured debt reduction. Buyer and Seller do not have to agree to any of Short Sale Lenders' proposed terms. Buyer, Seller and Brokers do not have control over whether Short Sale Lenders will consent to a short sale, or control over any act, omission, or decision by any Short Sale Lender in the short sale process.

5. **BUYER AND SELLER COSTS.** Buyer and Seller acknowledge that each of them may incur costs in connection with rights or obligations under the Agreement. These costs may include, but are not limited to, payments for loan applications, inspections, appraisals, and other reports. Such costs will be the sole responsibility of the party incurring them if Short Sale Lenders do not consent to the transaction or either party cancels the transaction pursuant to the Agreement.

6. **OTHER OFFERS.** Unless otherwise agreed in writing, after Buyer's offer has been accepted by Seller, **(i)** Seller has the right to continue to market the Property for back-up offers; **(ii)** Seller has the right to accept back-up offers (C.A.R. Form PAA, Paragraph 1), and subject to Short Sale Lender(s) requirements present to Short Sale Lender(s) any accepted back-up offers that are received; and **(iii)** Seller shall notify buyer when any accepted back-up offers, are presented to Short Sale Lender(s).

7. **CREDIT, LEGAL AND TAX ADVICE.** Seller is informed that a short sale may have credit or legal consequences and may result in taxable income to Seller. **Seller is advised to seek advice from an attorney, certified public accountant or other expert regarding such potential consequences of a short sale.**

By signing below, Buyer and Seller each acknowledge that they have read, understand, accept and have received a copy of this Short Sale Addendum.

Date _____ Date _____

Buyer _____ Seller _____

Buyer _____ Seller _____

THIS FORM HAS BEEN APPROVED BY THE CALIFORNIA ASSOCIATION OF REALTORS® (C.A.R.). NO REPRESENTATION IS MADE AS TO THE LEGAL VALIDITY OR ADEQUACY OF ANY PROVISION IN ANY SPECIFIC TRANSACTION. A REAL ESTATE BROKER IS THE PERSON QUALIFIED TO ADVISE ON REAL ESTATE TRANSACTIONS. IF YOU DESIRE LEGAL OR TAX ADVICE, CONSULT AN APPROPRIATE PROFESSIONAL.

This form is available for use by the entire real estate industry. It is not intended to identify the user as a REALTOR®. REALTOR® is a registered collective membership mark which may be used only by members of the NATIONAL ASSOCIATION OF REALTORS® who subscribe to its Code of Ethics.

Published and Distributed by:
REAL ESTATE BUSINESS SERVICES, INC.
a subsidiary of the California Association of REALTORS®
525 South Virgil Avenue, Los Angeles, California 90020

Reviewed by _____ Date _____

SSA REVISED 4/12 (PAGE 2 OF 2)   **SHORT SALE ADDENDUM (SSA PAGE 2 OF 2)**

directly themselves or through an established broker. Many larger banks have REO asset management departments that can accept bids and offers, oversee property management, and handle sales. The majority of REO properties that are on the open market are listed in MLS by a local broker.

When a short sale occurs, the amount of forgiven debt, known as "mortgage relief," may be considerd taxable income to the borrower.

The REO Advisory (Listing) form is recommended. Although sellers of REO properties (1- to 4-units) are exempt from many obligations, including Transfer Disclosure Statement obligations, the seller is obligated to disclose known material facts affecting the value and desirability of the property. In addition, the broker is not exempted from his or her obligation to conduct a reasonably competent and diligent visual inspection and disclose to the buyer material facts discovered in such an inspection. Also, the broker is not exempt from agency relationship disclosure requirements.

X. CHAPTER SUMMARY

In California, the commonly used term **"mortgage"** usually refers to a **trust deed**. The parties to a trust deed include the **trustor** (borrower), **beneficiary** (lender), and **trustee** (disinterested third party who holds naked legal title).

The **cost of borrowing money** includes **interest rates**, **origination fees**, and **points**, which are included in the **annual percentage rate (APR)**, as well as prepayment penalties and impound accounts.

Institutional (or **conventional loans**) are not backed by any government agency. Institutional lenders include **savings banks**, **commercial banks**, and **insurance companies**. **Mortgage bankers** are direct lenders that underwrite for larger investors and often act as **correspondents** for those loans. Life insurance companies are usually the most selective about the properties and borrowers to whom they will lend money, but also offer the best rates. **Private mortgage insurance (PMI)** insures these conventional loans when they have less than 20 percent down.

The loan payments on a **fixed-rate mortgage** are the same each month for the life of the loan, and the loan is payed off at the end of the term, making it **"fully amortized."** With an **adjustable rate mortgage (or ARM)**, the interest rates are variable. With a **graduated payment mortgage (GPM)**, the rate and term are fixed, but monthly payments are smaller at the beginning of the term and increase over time. This may result in **negative amortization**, and borrowers need to know in advance of this possibility.

The **secondary mortgage market** is where lenders buy and sell mortgages (trust deeds). The **FNMA (Fannie Mae)**, **GNMA (Ginnie Mae)**, and **FHLMC (Freddie Mac)** are all involved in the secondary mortgage market.

The three primary sources of **government-backed financing** are the **Federal Housing Administration (FHA)**, the **Department of Veterans Affairs (VA)**, and the **California**

Department of Veterans Affairs (CalVet). Only the CalVet is a direct lender of funds; the FHA insured and VA guaranteed loans are made by approved institutional lenders.

A **certificate of reasonable value (CRV)** is the appraisal necessary for a veteran to buy a property. Operating expenses of the CalVet program come from the sale of **general obligation bonds**, with the state guaranteeing the repayment of the bonds from the general fund.

A **credit score** gives lenders a good idea of a borrower's ability and willingness to repay a loan and make timely credit payments. A **FICO score** is used most often (developed by Fair, Isaac, and Company).

The **Equal Credit Opportunity Act** protects against discrimination in lending practices. The **Fair Credit Reporting Act** allows not only loan applicants but all consumers to see their files, and the **Truth in Lending Act** (also known as **Regulation Z**) lets borrowers know the true cost of credit (what their APR will be).

Noninstitutional financing is by parties who are not as strictly governed or controlled by federal and state agencies. Some of these parties include pension funds, public syndications, and individuals. **Junior loans** (secondary financing) are secured by a **second deed of trust**, meaning they are secondary to any first or primary trust deeds.

An **acceleration clause** states that the loan is due and payable if the property is sold or something else occurs. A **balloon payment** is a large payment due at the end of the loan term in order to pay off the balance of the loan.

With a **land contract**, sometimes known as a **contract of sale**, the seller retains the legal title to the property until the buyer has paid off the loan (like a car loan).

A **loan assumption** occurs when a buyer pays a seller for part or all of the equity in a property and assumes the responsibility for payment of the existing loan(s).

Equity is the difference between market value and existing liens against the property. Taking title **"subject to"** a prior loan substitutes an agreement to take over and make the loan payments, or lose the property. The seller remains liable in case of default or foreclosure.

CalBRE allows licensees with an MLO endorsement to negotiate **mortgage loans**, and receive compensation for their services as managers, arrangers of loans, middlemen, or intermediaries. A **mortgage loan disclosure statement** must be given to the borrower and kept on file for three years for the Real Estate Commissioner's inspection. If dealing with 1- to 4-unit owner-occupied residential property, real estate licensees must also have a Mortgage Loan Originator (MLO) endorsement to their license.

Usury is the illegal charging of too much interest on a loan.

The **Secure and Fair Enforcement Mortgage Licensing Act (SAFE Act)** of the Housing and Economic Recovery Act of 2008 enhances consumer protection and attempts to reduce fraud in mortgage loan transactions. It requires all 50 states and 5 territories to put into place a system for licensing mortgage loan originators that meets the minimum requirements of the SAFE Act.

When the bank or other lender repossesses a property at a foreclosure sale, it is listed on their accounting books as a non-performing asset and goes to their **Real Estate Owned (REO)** department. REO properties are often in poor shape in terms of repairs and maintenance.

If the current owner is not able to sell the property in cooperation with a **short sale**, where a lender accepts less than what is owed in the loan using a **Short Sale Addendum (SSA)**, then the loan on the property may or may not go into foreclosure.

XI. MATCHING VOCABULARY Fill in the blanks with the correct letter

A. Acceleration clause
B. Adjustable rate mortgage
C. Beneficiary
D. Credit scoring (FICO)
E. Fannie Mae
F. Fixed rate mortgage
G. Graduated payment mortgage
H. Impound account
I. Institutional lenders
J. Interest
K. Loan origination fee
L. Mortgage banker
M. Mortgage loan broker
N. Mortgages
O. Negative amortization
P. Prepayment penalty
Q. Prevailing market rate
R. Prime loan
S. Private mortgage insurance
T. Reverse annuity loan
U. Short sale
V. Trustee
W. Trustor
X. Truth in Lending Act (Reg Z)
Y. Usury

1. _____ In California, based on lending tradition, trust deeds and other loans are commonly referred to as:
2. _____ The party borrowing the money.
3. _____ The lender who is lending money for the purchase of real property.
4. _____ The third, disinterested party who holds naked legal title to the property.
5. _____ The charge for borrowing money.
6. _____ This fee is based on the loan amount and is collected as compensation for processing the loan and setting it up on the books.
7. _____ The rate charged on conventional loans.
8. _____ A charge to the borrower for paying off all or part of a loan balance before the due date.
9. _____ Reserves to cover property taxes, insurance, and/or MIP.
10. _____ Savings banks, commercial banks, and life insurance companies.
11. _____ Direct lenders that underwrite for usually hundreds of investors.
12. _____ These brokers shop for a lender for the borrowers and earn a fee by putting lender and borrower together.
13. _____ What a loan on well-located properties to borrowers with good income and credit is called.

14. _____ This type of insurance allows institutional lenders to make loans above the usual 75 to 80 percent of the sale's price.

15. _____ A loan for which the payments are usually the same each month for the life of the loan.

16. _____ A variable rate mortgage.

17. _____ With this type of special purpose loan, the rate and term are fixed, but monthly payments are smaller at the beginning of the term and increase over time.

18. _____ This occurs when monthly installment payments are insufficient to pay the interest accruing on the principal balance, so that the unpaid interest must be added to the principal due.

19. _____ This type of loan for senior citizens, is a loan where the lender pays the borrower a fixed monthly payment based on the value of the property.

20. _____ The Federal National Mortgage Association dominates the secondary mortgage market.

21. _____ This gives lenders a fast, objective measurement for your ability to repay a loan or make timely credit payments.

22. _____ This act lets borrowers and customer's know the cost of credit so that they can compare costs with those of other credit sources and thereby avoid the uninformed use of credit.

23. _____ In a trust deed, this clause makes the entire note due and payable, should the property be sold or default occur.

24. _____ Charging more than the legally allowed percentage of interest.

25. _____ When a lender accepts less than what is owed in the loan.

See Page 610 for Answers

XII. CHAPTER QUIZ

1. Which of the following is NOT a party to a trust deed?

   a. Beneficiary
   b. Executor
   c. Trustor
   d. Trustee

2. Loans that are neither insured nor guaranteed by an agency of the government are termed:

   a. prime loans.
   b. fixed interest loans.
   c. institutional loans.
   d. none of the above.

3. In addition to the amount financed, the annual percentage rate (APR) includes:

   a. interest rates.
   b. points.
   c. loan fees.
   d. all of the above.

4. Which institutional lender is heavily involved in the secondary market?

   a. Savings banks
   b. Commercial banks
   c. Life insurance companies
   d. None of the above

5. Which type of loan is repayed in equal monthly payments for the life of the loan?

   a. Fixed rate
   b. Adjustable rate
   c. Graduated payment
   d. None of the above

6. A drawback of the graduated payment mortgage is its:

   a. negative amortization.
   b. positive amortization.
   c. fluctuating interest rate.
   d. none of the above.

7. When allowing a buyer to assume the seller's existing loan(s), the seller should:

   a. demand an increase in the purchase price.
   b. pay for any cost to the buyer.
   c. get a full release from the lender(s).
   d. all of the above.

8. Taking title "subject to" existing loans:

   a. can trigger an alienation (due on sale) clause.
   b. relieves the seller of any further responsibility for the loans.
   c. is illegal in California.
   d. none of the above.

9. The SAFE Act requires:

   a. all real estate licensees to be tested for communicable diseases.
   b. all real estate licensees to be psychologically evaluated annually.
   c. all real estate licensees performing duties as MLOs to have a CalBRE endorsement to their license.
   d. all trust funds to be kept in an office safe until deposited in a bank.

10. The SAFE Act is administered by the:

   a. SPCA.
   b. DOJ.
   c. CDC.
   d. NMLS&R.

ANSWERS: 1. b; 2. d; 3. d; 4. c; 5. a; 6. a; 7. c; 8. a; 9. c; 10. d

I. The Escrow Procedure

An escrow is the processing, by a neutral party, of the paperwork and money involved in a sale or other real estate transaction. The purpose of an escrow is to assure that the appropriate parties perform all the terms of the contract.

An **ESCROW** is created when a new written agreement instructs a neutral third party to hold funds and proceed only when all the agreed to conditions have been performed. This information is usually taken from the CAR® California Residential Purchase Agreement and Joint Escrow Instructions. In California, an escrow is usually a requirement for the sale of a home or any other real estate. Although it is not always required by law, it is an indispensable process by which an independent third party handles the legal paperwork of a real estate sale. An escrow is not only an effective tool for handling normal real estate transactions, like sales or refinancing, but it is also an effective tool for handling the sale of trust deeds, completing exchanges, as well as completing the transfer of liquor licenses, businesses, securities, and court-required transfers. The legally required and recommended uses of an escrow are illustrated in **Figure 10-1**.

Figure 10-1

Highly Recommended	Required by Law
1. Sales of Real Property	1. Liquor License Transfers
2. Loans	2. Security Sales (Impound Accounts)
3. Exchanges	3. Court Ordered Transfers (Probate Sales)

© 2015 ETC., Inc.

A. REQUIREMENTS FOR A VALID ESCROW

The Escrow Act is found in the Financial Code.

The three requirements for a valid escrow are:

1. Signed escrow instructions (found in the Joint Escrow section of the residential purchase agreement), forming a binding contract between two or more parties—usually a buyer and seller.

2. A neutral party, which is the escrow company, acting as a dual agent of the buyer and seller.

3. Conditional delivery of funds and documents, after all the conditions in the escrow are met.

When escrow closes, dual agency (representing both parties, usually buyers and sellers, at once) changes to separate agency (handling each party's separate paperwork requirements).

An escrow is usually initiated with the CAR® California Residential Purchase Agreement and Joint Escrow Instructions, or (rarely) through oral instructions. It is important to have agreed upon written instructions drawn by the escrow company. Since this may be a new experience for most people, the escrow agent will, when necessary, explain each step to a buyer or seller. A helpful escrow officer can point out possible problems, and suggest alternatives, **but cannot give legal advice**.

B. ESCROW HOLDER

An escrow holder can be: 1) a corporation, 2) an attorney, or 3) a real estate broker acting as a real estate agent in the transaction.

A **NEUTRAL DEPOSITORY** *is an escrow business that accepts payments and funds as a licensed escrow holder. An **ESCROW OFFICER, HOLDER, or AGENT**, though not licensed by the state, is an employee of a licensed escrow company who acts as the agent.* Escrow law is found in the California Financial Code. An independent escrow corporation must be licensed by the Department of Business Oversight (DBO) to handle escrows. Corporations that are exempt from the escrow law, but can handle escrows, include banks, savings banks, and title insurance companies, because they are under the supervision of their respective authorizing agencies.

In Northern California, the majority of escrows are handled by escrow departments of title insurance companies, which are governed by the Insurance Commissioner. In Southern California, many escrows are handled by independent escrow companies which, by law, must be incorporated and are governed by the Commissioner of Corporations.

There are two other types of escrow holders: Attorneys who perform escrow duties as a part of their practice, and real estate brokers who handle their own escrows (must be the broker in the transaction). Regardless of the type of escrow

company, the functions of an escrow may be summarized in four broad categories (see **Figure 10-2**).

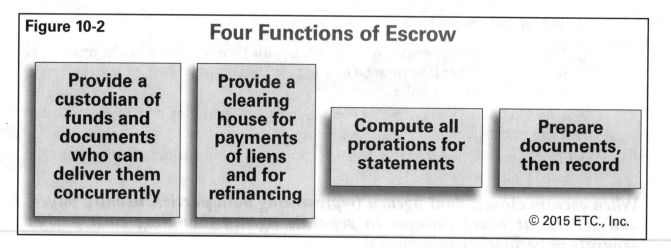

Figure 10-2

Four Functions of Escrow

| Provide a custodian of funds and documents who can deliver them concurrently | Provide a clearing house for payments of liens and for refinancing | Compute all prorations for statements | Prepare documents, then record |

© 2015 ETC., Inc.

The complete sequence of events in an escrow is:

1. Preliminary title search and report
2. Lender's demand (amount owed, pay-off statement)
3. Request for new loan documents
4. Completion of conditions and depositing of funds
5. Adjustments and prorations
6. Transfer of existing fire policies, or creation of new ones
7. Recording and issuing of title policy
8. Disbursement of funds
9. Escrow closing statements sent to each party

After these steps have been completed and all other escrow conditions have been met, the closing of an escrow is usually routine (see **Figure 10-3**).

The escrow agent is authorized to call for a buyer's documents and funds.

C. REAL ESTATE BROKERS CAN CONDUCT ESCROWS

A broker can handle escrows for a fee only if the broker is acting as a real estate agent or principal in that transaction.

As a licensed broker, you can handle an escrow for a fee only if you are acting as a broker in that real estate transaction. This right is personal to the broker, and the broker shall not delegate any duties other than escrow duties normally performed under the direct supervision of the broker.

All written escrow instructions executed by a buyer or seller must contain a statement, in not less than 10-point type, that includes the licensee's name and the fact that he or she is licensed by the California Bureau of Real Estate (CalBRE).

California Customs (North vs. South) for Escrow Services and Title Insurance

When are signed escrow instructions delivered?

Customarily, in Southern California, the (bilateral) escrow instructions are signed by both the buyer and seller just after the **start of escrow**.

Customarily, in Northern California, the (unilateral) escrow instructions are given to the escrow officer just before the **close of escrow**.

Who performs the escrow services?

Escrow services in Southern California are traditionally performed by **independent escrow companies** (corporations) or **financial institutions**.

Escrow services in Northern California are traditionally performed by **title insurance companies**.

Who pays the escrow fees?

Escrow service fees in Southern California are usually **split 50-50 between the buyer and the seller**.

Escrow service fees in Northern California are usually **paid for by the buyer**.

Who traditionally pays title insurance fees?

Customarily, in Southern California, the **seller pays for the California Land Title Association (CLTA) policy (standard policy)**.

Customarily, in Northern California, the **buyer pays for the California Land Title Association (CLTA) policy (standard policy)**.

In both the North and the South, the **buyers pay for any coverage above the California Standard Title Insurance (CLTA) policy** that protects the lender's interest.

© 2015 ETC., Inc.

II. How Escrows Work

The basis for the escrow instructions is the CAR® Califorina Residential Purchase Agreement and Joint Escrow Instructions. Of course, its terms can be modified by mutual agreement.

A. FAX PURCHASE AGREEMENT TO ESCROW

The last page of the CAR® California Residential Purchase Agreement and Joint Escrow Instructions contains an acknowledgement for receipt of the completed agreement (see **Figure 10-4**). Escrow companies often write a disclaimer regarding any discrepancies between the Purchase Agreement and the escrow instructions, stating that it's not their intention to supersede the original terms of the Purchase Agreement. To avoid any discrepancies, always double check for mistakes and file addendums for changes.

Figure 10-4

ESCROW HOLDER ACKNOWLEDGMENT:
Escrow Holder acknowledges receipt of a Copy of this Agreement, (if checked, ☐ a deposit in the amount of $_____), counter offer number _____ ☐ Seller's Statement of Information and _____ _____ , and agrees to act as Escrow Holder subject to paragraph 24 of this Agreement, any supplemental escrow instructions and the terms of Escrow Holder's general provisions.
Escrow Holder is advised that the date of Confirmation of Acceptance of the Agreement as between Buyer and Seller is _____
Escrow Holder _____ Escrow # _____
By _____ Date _____
Address _____
Phone/Fax/E-mail _____
Escrow Holder is licensed by the California Department of ☐ Corporations, ☐ Insurance, ☐ Real Estate. License # _____

Once the California Residential Purchase Agreement and Joint Escrow Instructions form has been filled out and executed properly, you will fax or deliver it to the escrow company for their signature, acknowledging a receipt. Always ask for a receipt when delivering the earnest money deposit to escrow. The funds must be delivered to escrow within 3 days of the offer's acceptance.

B. FOLLOW-THROUGH CHECKLIST

Follow-through services are the responsibility of both the listing and selling agents. These services include ordering a structural pest control report, getting loan applications to the borrower and arranging all necessary financing, ordering the preliminary title report, followed by the ultimate issuance of the title insurance policy, securing property insurance, getting the various documents in order, and all other things necessary to carry out the terms of the purchase and sale agreement. Although a large part of these services are performed by others, it's your job to assist the escrow company and keep a record of progress to see that the sale is properly consummated.

As a conscientious agent, you won't simply put the contract in the lap of the escrow company and hope that "everything will be taken care of." Your follow-up is so important that if you do not continue your service through escrow, you may find yourself confronted with many problems, and even a falling-out of the escrow. Too often the salesperson who does not follow through on the escrow winds up losing the sale. You can end up with disgruntled buyers and sellers on your hands, or even worse, a lawsuit.

Always follow up on your escrows—it's much better for you to call the escrow officer and check the status of the process than to hope the officer calls you.

To keep track of the escrow process, you'll want to use an agent/broker escrow checklist (see **Figure 10-5**). Servicing includes tasks before and during escrow, and post-escrow activities as well. You should check everything on your progress chart as thoroughly as possible to assure a smooth and consummated transaction.

After the escrow has closed and the buyers have moved in, you can visit them to determine what else can be done—introduce them to their new neighbors or show them the nearby shopping facilities. This is bound to earn goodwill—and referrals!

It's a good idea to drop your former buyers an occasional note—reminding them to follow through on updating insurance and filing for a homeowner exemption as soon as possible, for example—or simply telling them you like what they've done with the landscaping, paint job, etc.

C. OPENING ESCROW

When opening escrow, always double-check the spelling of names and addresses. This helps keep the loan documents and deed from being drawn incorrectly.

You can call the escrow company with instructions, and then fax or email the Purchase Agreement. As a broker, your instructions should set forth clear communications as to who will open escrow and where, the date escrow is opened, length of escrow, terms of the loans being sought, contingencies that may have been incorporated into the purchase agreement, commissions (not shown on the buyers' copy), termite report instructions, personal property that may be included, legal description, earnest money deposit, and any other information that went into the contract.

If it's available, provide escrow with the property profile (obtained from the title company) when you open escrow.

After typing the escrow instructions, the escrow holder sends them to the buyers' and sellers' agents with copies for their clients. At the time of mailing, the escrow officer encloses the grant deed and a statement of information for the seller. Included with the buyers' papers is a statement of information for them to complete as well.

Figure 10-5

Escrow Checklist

Contracts & Disclosures	Form Abreviation	Seller	Buyer	Broker Initials
Agency - Seller and Buyer (both should be in file)	AD			
Listing / Termite and Title Clauses stated on 2nd page & Sellers Advisory	RLA & SA			
Transfer Disclosure (Do not qualiify problems)	TDS			
FRPTA/Fed Calif. Law (Seller/Buyer)	QS & AS			
Smoke Detector/Water Heater **(Mostly included in the TDS)**		/	/	/
Carbon Monoxide Detector	CMD			
Horizontale Defective Furnaces (if applicable)				
Lead base Paint Disclosure (housing blt. Prior to 1978)	FLD			
Res. Earthquake Booklet and receipt of same		/	/	/
Zone Disclosures appropriatley signed : Nat. Hazard, Mold, Database, Airport, ect. (3rd Party)				
Supplemental Statutory Contractual Disclosure	SSD			
Statewide Buyer & Seller Advisory	SBSA			
Seller Property Questionaire	SPQ			
Agent Visual Inspection Disclosure- Both Agents	AVID			
Sellers/Buyers Estimate Costs	ESP/EBC			
Prequalification Letter & Copy of Check				
Res. Purchase Agreement (All pages initialed including buyer's agency & advisory)	RPA-CA, AD &BIA			
Counters to Purchase Agreement & Muliple Offer (item	CO			
Compensation to cooperating broker	CCB			
Escrow Ints. & Prelim **(Read Both Carefully)**				
Appraisal (odered and appointment made); Provide comps				
Physical Inspection or Waiver (Do not Meddle)				
Termite Inspection **signed by buyers** and clearance report				
Allocation of Termite costs	WPA			
Exchange of forms between brokers				
Request for Repairs from Buyers/Response from seller	RRI			
Removal of Contingencies or Cancellation	CR			
Home Warranty/ Waiver (Watch the amount to be paid by seller) Keep whole application/waiver in file (do not detach)				
Walk through or prior to close of escrow/ waiver	VP			
Remove Lock box and have sign taken down				
Report Sale to Association (otherwise you will be fined by the Association)				
Contact Neighbors/ Introduce new owners/ Follow up				
Probate Advisory				
REO Advisory	REO			
Short Sale Addendum	SSA			
Short Sale Information and Advisory	SSIA			
Trust Sale	TAL			
ALWAYS USE LATEST FORMS				

Revised 3/25/2014

© 2015 ETC., Inc.

D. ESCROW RULES

Once the escrow instructions have been drawn from the original purchase contract (deposit receipt) and signed by each party, neither party may change the escrow instructions without the written agreement of the other. (All time frames commence from the time the contract became binding; usually the purchase contract has a provision for escrow to acknowledge receipt of this document.) The escrow is complete when: 1) all conditions of the escrow have been met, 2) all conditions of the parties have been met, and 3) the parties have received an accounting of the procedure. If both parties mutually agree to change the instructions in writing, the change can be put into effect at any time. However, if a dispute should arise, the escrow company will not proceed until both parties come to terms. If the parties cannot agree to terms, an escrow company will bring an **interpleader action (court action)** to determine where the money or consideration goes. **Figure 10-6** illustrates the three ways in which an escrow can be terminated.

Figure 10-6

If the seller wants to rescind an escrow, the seller cannot do so without the consent of the buyer.

E. WHO SELECTS THE ESCROW COMPANY?

A real estate licensee is prohibited by law from receiving any "kickback" for solicitation of escrow business.

Selection of an escrow company and an escrow officer are part of the negotiation between buyer and seller. Like any other item in a real estate transaction, it is part of the negotiated agreement. Either one of the parties may suggest the escrow company, which should be explained when completing the purchase contract. As a salesperson, you may certainly suggest a preferred escrow company for both the buyer and seller. If the buyer and seller each desire a different escrow company, then you must work for a mutual agreement before there can be an offer and acceptance of the sale.

Death does not cancel an escrow; it is binding on the heirs (estate) because of the prior, agreed-to contract.

It is imperative that you, the salesperson, disclose in writing any shared interest that you or your broker has with the selected escrow company. This disclosure must be made either at the time of listing or whenever the escrow company is selected. Disciplinary action will be taken against any salesperson or broker who, in bad faith and against the wishes of the buyer and seller, attempts to force the use of a particular escrow company. Furthermore, a real estate licensee is prohibited by law from receiving any "kickback" for solicitation of escrow business.

F. ESCROW INSTRUCTIONS

ESCROW INSTRUCTIONS are formal instructions drawn from the information contained in the original agreement, usually the signed purchase contract (California Residential Purchase Agreement and Joint Escrow Instructions). When these instructions are drawn and signed, they become an enforceable contract binding on all parties.

Since the escrow instructions supplement the original contract, both are interpreted together whenever possible. Escrow companies often use a disclaimer stating that it's not their intention to supersede the original intent of the Purchase Agreement.

All parties to the escrow should read the escrow instructions very carefully, and sign them only after every detail is absolutely correct and the terms meet with their approval.

G. FINANCING IS AN IMPORTANT ASPECT OF THE ESCROW

Most escrows for the sale of a home include obtaining a new loan and the payoff or assumption of an old loan. As an agent/broker, you can be helpful to the buyer obtaining new financing by providing the necessary loan documentation to the escrow company in a timely manner. Keeping the buyer and seller informed about the progress of the financing and escrow helps to maintain good client-agent communication and trust.

The *PAYOFF DEMAND STATEMENT is a formal demand statement from the lender that details the amounts owed, as calculated by the lender, for the purpose of **paying off the loan in full**.* The failure to obtain a payoff or beneficiary statement in a timely manner could hold up the escrow. A payoff demand statement is different from a beneficiary's statement. A *BENEFICIARY'S (LENDER'S) STATEMENT is a statement by a lender, under a deed of trust, that provides information, such as the unpaid balance, monthly payment, and interest rate.* The lender may charge a fee for furnishing the payoff or beneficiary statement, except when the loan is insured by the FHA or guaranteed by the VA.

During escrow, if a buyer receives loan approval and requests to move into the property before escrow closes, he or she must obtain written permission from the seller, as well as a "hold harmless" clause. Note: An interim occupancy agreement should be executed.

H. ESCROW EXAMPLE

To help illustrate the closing statements used in a simple escrow, let's assume the following facts:

Figure 10-7 illustrates the seller's escrow statement, and **Figure 10-8** illustrates the buyer's statement. These statements include many other miscellaneous costs that are a usual part of the escrow.

An Escrow Example

BUYER	**Bob Buyer and Bonnie Buyer**	
SELLER	**Sam Seller and Suzie Seller**	
SALES PRICE		**$395,000**
1ST TRUST DEED		**$316,000**
DOWN PAYMENT		**$89,000**
BROKER	**Real Estate Excellence Realtors**	**$21,725**
EXISTING LIENS		
1) 1ST TRUST DEED		**$248,500**
2) STREET ASSESSMENT BOND		**$1,300**
CLTA TITLE POLICY PAID BY SELLER		**$1,285**
Date of Closing is June 1, 2020		

© 2015 ETC., Inc.

I. CLOSING DATE IS THE DATE OF RECORDATION

Closing is the process of signing, transfering of documents, and distribution of funds. When time is not specified, the escrow will close by mutual consent or within a reasonable period.

The **CLOSING DATE** *is usually the date that the documents are recorded.* Escrow usually approximates the closing date, but the actual date is when all the conditions of the escrow have been completed, the buyer's remaining money (cashier's checks) is received, and when all the documents are recorded. Most escrows are for handling the paperwork of property sale and loan financing, but escrows can be for almost any purpose.

At the close of escrow, if a seller decides not to pay the commission, the broker/ agent can file civil action in court.

Note: In closing statements, the buyer's and seller's totals are different. However, each closing statement must balance within itself. In the buyer's closing statement, the purchase price is generally a debit item.

Figure 10-7

HUBIE ESCROW, Inc.
1500 N. Verdugo Rd.
Glendale CA 91208
Tel: (818) 555-1212
Fax: (818) 555-1213

SELLER FINAL SETTLEMENT STATEMENT

PROPERTY: 135 Shady Lane   **CLOSING DATE:** 06/01/20
           La Crescenta CA 91201   **ESCROW NO.:**   1-10533
SELLER: Sam Seller and Suzie Seller

	DEBITS	CREDITS
FINANCIAL		
Total Consideration	$	$ 395,000.00
PRORATIONS AND ADJUSTMENTS		
Taxes at $1875.00/6 mo. From 06/01/20 To 07/01/20		312.50
PAYOFF CHARGES TO ABC MORTGAGE		
Principal Balance	248,500.00	
Interest on Principal Balance at 6.00% from 05/01/20 to 06/01/20	1,242.50	
Forwarding fee	50.00	
Reconveyance fee	60.00	
OTHER DISBURSEMENTS		
Pest Control, Inc. for Termite Report/Work	1,000.00	
Home Warranty, Inc. for Home Protection Policy	450.00	
COMMISSION		
Listing Broker: Real Estate Excellence Realtors	21,725.00	
TITLE CHARGES TO GOLDEN STATE TITLE		
Title Policy Premium	1,285.00	
Sub Escrow Fee	75.00 *	
Documentary Transfer Tax	434.50	
Recording Reconveyance	7.00	
Street Assessment Bond	1,300.00	
ESCROW CHARGES TO HUBIE ESCROW, INC.		
Escrow Fee	1,040.00	
Processing Demands	50.00	
Drawing Documents Fee	85.00	
NET PROCEEDS	117,998.50	
TOTALS	395,312.50	395,312.50

SAVE FOR INCOME TAX PURPOSES
 * A Sub Escrow Fee is usually only charged to the Seller or Buyer, not both.

Figure 10-8

HUBIE ESCROW, Inc.
1500 N. Verdugo Rd.
Glendale CA 91208
Tel: (818) 555-1212
Fax: (818) 555-1213

BUYER FINAL SETTLEMENT STATEMENT

PROPERTY: 135 Shady Lane
La Crescenta CA 91201
BUYER: Bob Buyer and Bonnie Buyer

CLOSING DATE: 06/01/20
ESCROW NO.: 1-10533

	DEBITS	CREDITS
FINANCIAL		
Total Consideration	$ 395,000.00	$
Cash Deposit Bob Buyer		5,000.00
Cash Deposit Bob Buyer		84,000.00
New 1st Trust Deed		316,000.00
PRORATIONS AND ADJUSTMENTS		
Taxes at $1875.00/6 mo. From 06/01/20 To 07/01/20	312.50	
OTHER DISBURSEMENTS		
Lucky Insurance, Inc. for Casualty Insurance	837.00	
Exquisite Property Inspections For property inspection	500.00	
TITLE CHARGES TO GOLDEN STATE TITLE		
Title Policy Premium	390.50	
Sub Escrow Fee	75.00 *	
Recording Grant Deed	10.00	
Recording Trust Deed	20.00	
Title Endorsement Fee(s)	100.00	
ESCROW CHARGES TO HUBIE ESCROW, INC.		
Escrow Fee	1,040.00	
Express Mail fee	24.00	
Loan Tie In Fee	125.00	
Notary Fee	60.00	
NEW FIRST TRUST DEED TO MEGA BUCKS SAVINGS BANK		
Loan Fees	4,545.00	
Credit Report	22.50	
Appraisal	500.00	
Tax Service	89.00	
Document Fee	250.00	
Interest at 4.00% from 05/31/20 to 06/01/20	35.11	
REFUND	1,064.39	
TOTALS	405,000/00	405,000.00

SAVE FOR INCOME TAX PURPOSES

* A Sub Escrow Fee is usually only charged to the Seller or Buyer, not both.

III. Proration

Property taxes, interest, fire insurance premiums, and rents are are often prorated, but not title insurance fees or nonrecurring fees.

PRORATION *is the process of proportionately dividing expenses or income to the precise date that escrow closes, or any other date previously agreed upon.* It enables the buyer and seller to pay or receive their proportionate share of expenses or income. Items that are commonly prorated include:

1. property taxes,
2. fire insurance premiums,
3. interest, and
4. rents.

A. 30 DAYS IS THE BASIS FOR PRORATION

All escrow companies use 30 days as a base month. For example, if an escrow closes on the 10th day of the month, all prepaid rents for that month would constitute 9/30 of the rent left for the seller, and 21/30 of the rent would go to the buyer. If the rent is $2,000, the seller's portion would be 9/30 of $2,000, or $600, and the buyer's portion would be 21/30 of $2,000, or $1,400. (Rents belong to the buyer as of the closing date.)

The two important dates associated with proration are: (1) date escrow closes, and (2) the date item is paid.

The date used in calculating proration is usually assumed to be the date of closing, but any date may be used if agreed upon by all parties. This is the case when the possession date differs from the closing date.

Property tax prorations are based on the amount the seller is paying. Escrow uses the old assessed valuation when prorating.

Taxes are prorated either from July 1, which marks the beginning of the county fiscal year, or January 1, the middle of the fiscal year. If the property taxes on a home, amounting to $2,400 per year, have been paid up to July 1, what is the proration if escrow is to be closed on June 1? In this case, the buyer would reimburse the seller for one month's taxes (or $2,400 divided by twelve months, equaling $200 per month). The seller would then be credited for the $200 in property taxes that he or she had already paid in advance.

Escrow Company Reports Information to the I.R.S.

All real estate transactions must be reported to the Internal Revenue Service. This is done by the escrow company or whomever handles the closing. A 1099 Form is required for any sale or exchange.

Escrow reports real estate transactions to the I.R.S. using the seller's social security number.

IV. Termites and Other Problems

A. STRUCTURAL PEST CONTROL CERTIFICATION REPORT (Report and Clearance) (www.pestboard.ca.gov)

A Structural Pest Control Certification Report is usually a condition of the escrow.

Pest control inspection reports are not required by law in California, but many lenders will require this report. A **STRUCTURAL PEST CONTROL CERTIFICATION REPORT** *is a written report given by a licensed pest control company, identifying any wood-destroying pests or conditions likely to cause pest infestation.* The report states the condition and correction cost of any pest, dry rot, excessive moisture, earth-wood contacts, or fungus damage in accessible areas of a structure. Who pays for the (1) pest control inspection report and/or (2) any required or recommended repair work is up to the buyer and seller, although they are usually paid for by the seller subject to certain dollar limits. Sometimes there may be a local custom that dictates who will pay.

Under the Business and Professions Code, any person, whether or not a party to a real property transaction, has a right to request and, upon payment of the required fee, to obtain directly from the Structural Pest Control Board in Sacramento, a certified copy of all inspection reports and completion notices filed during the preceding two years. As a real estate agent, you have a duty to disclose structural defects and wood-destroying organisms, if you know of any. This requirement is also written into the Commissioner's Regulations under Section 2903, which requires agents' full disclosure to buyers and sellers of any knowledge or information they may have concerning any infestations or structural defects caused by termites or other wood-destroying organisms. If there is more than one inspection, the buyer must approve, in writing, all inspections and agree to the selected trades people.

The best time for a seller to have a termite report issued is before putting the home on the market, keeping in mind that any replaced wood is usually not painted by the termite company.

California law requires that the buyer must receive a copy of the pest control certificate, and sign off on it, before the close of escrow.

B. BROKER MAINTAINS PEST CONTROL DOCUMENTATION

The Civil Code requires that the broker shall deliver a copy of the Structural Pest Control Certification Report and Notice of Work Completed to the buyer if such a report is a condition of the purchase agreement or is a requirement imposed as a condition of financing. If more than one broker is acting as an agent in the transaction, the broker who obtained the offer (selling broker) made by the buyer, shall deliver the required documents to the buyer, who needs to sign acknowledging their receipt.

V. Fire Insurance

When one party agrees to indemnify another for loss in return for periodic premium payments, it is called "insurance."

A. FIRE INSURANCE . . . A MUST!

Fire insurance is very inexpensive compared to the possible dollar loss due to fire, and all property owners should have this financial protection. A lending institution will require coverage for the amount of its loan. However, it is in the owner's best interest to carry sufficient fire insurance to replace the structure if it is totally destroyed. It is only necessary to insure the current replacement value of the dwelling, since the land itself cannot be destroyed by fire.

The *CALIFORNIA STANDARD FORM FIRE INSURANCE POLICY insures the dwelling against (1) fire and (2) lightning.* If your clients desire, they may procure an *EXTENDED COVERAGE ENDORSEMENT that will insure them against the additional perils of windstorm, explosion, hail, aircraft, smoke, riot, and vehicles not attributed to a strike or civil commotion.* Other types of endorsements may insure against vandalism, malicious mischief, floods, and other damage. Coverage depends on your buyer's needs and the perils common to that area.

B. FIRE INSURANCE PRORATION

When purchasing property, a buyer usually obtains a new policy. **If the seller/owner has filed an insurance claim during the previous five years, he or she must disclose this to the buyer in writing.** This may cause some hardship to the new owner/buyer in obtaining his or her own insurance. Cancellation of the seller's insurance must be initiated by the seller after close of escrow, with any unused premium to be short rated and reimbursed to the seller. It is always the buyer's choice to select his or her own house insurance.

Condo insurance is chosen by the homeowners' association.

> **Recommend to your clients who are buying insurance that they review the policy carefully to determine if they have the correct type of coverage and are carrying an adequate amount of insurance, particularly when their property value has increased.**

VI. Title Insurance

A. CHAIN OF TITLE (Recorded Public History)

Abstract of title: A written summary of a property's documents that evidences title.

If one person sells a property to another person, a *recorded public history of a specific property, called the CHAIN OF TITLE*, is compiled. These public records include files at the county recorder's office, various tax agencies, federal court clerk, and the Secretary of State. *All such information about people and their real property is stored in computers (within a grantor-grantee index) and is referred to as a TITLE PLANT.*

A title insurance company is primarily concerned with a search of the public records, which includes the Federal Lands Office, the County Clerk's Office, the County Recorder's Office, and other sources. This search reveals what is called the "chain of title."

B. TITLE INSURANCE (Has Four Functions)

Title insurance companies are regulated by the California Insurance Commissioner. Fee schedules must be available to the general public upon request. To guarantee solvency, each title insurance company must set aside reserves.

Because many things outside the public records can affect the marketability of the property, title insurance functions to protect the insured.

TITLE INSURANCE also insures a lender (and property owner for an additional fee) against losses that result from imperfections in title. Title insurance companies examine the records documenting chain of title, review any risks that might not be found in the public records, interpret legality, help the seller correct any defects, and insure marketable title to the property. Title insurance is only paid once, unlike auto or fire insurance, which must be paid annually. **Figure 10-9** emphasizes the four most important functions of title insurance.

C. PRELIMINARY TITLE REPORT (Ordered First)

The first step in a title search is the ordering of the preliminary title report by the escrow officer. *After the buyer or borrower completes a STATEMENT OF INFORMATION, a title search can begin* (see **Figure 10-10**). A *PRELIMINARY TITLE REPORT is a report showing the condition of title before a sale or loan transaction.* After completion of the transaction, a title insurance policy is issued.

Figure 10-9

© 2015 ETC., Inc.

State law requires that buyers acknowledge receipt of the preliminary title report.

The preliminary title report consists of the following items:

1. The name of the owner and a description of the property.

2. A list of any outstanding taxes, bonds, or other assessments.

3. The identity of any covenants, conditions, or restrictions.

4. Any recorded liens or other encumbrances that must be eliminated before any loan is made.

A "preliminary title report" gives the current status of items from the county records that affect the property's title.

VII. Types of Title Insurance Policies

All title insurance policies in California cover policyholders as of the date of the policy.

A. CALIFORNIA LAND TITLE ASSOCIATION (CLTA) (Standard Coverage Policy)

In California, the standard title insurance policy is the CLTA. The *CALIFORNIA LAND TITLE ASSOCIATION (CLTA) policy is the basic title insurance policy.* It may be issued to insure a lender only, or an owner only, or it may insure both the lender and the owner (a joint-protection standard coverage policy). This standard policy insures the lender only, unless the owner requests and pays for owner coverage. For more detailed information regarding CLTA policies, go to **www.clta.org**.

CLTA is the acronym for the state trade association, California Land Title Association®.

Besides insuring against all items of record, the CLTA policy offers protection against many off-record risks. Some of these off-record risks include forgeries, acts of minors and incompetents, acts of an agent whose authority has terminated, invalid deed delivery, unrecorded federal estate tax liens, undisclosed rights of husband

Figure 10-10

Complete, Sign and Return

NORTH AMERICAN TITLE COMPANY

STATEMENT OF INFORMATION

Order No. 5278

To expedite the completion of your escrow, please fill out and return this form at your earliest convenience. This information is for confidential use by North American Title Company in searching the land records in connection with the order number shown above. Further explanation of the need for this information is printed on the reverse side of this form.

Please Print all information

PERSONAL IDENTIFICATION

Name

_____
FIRST NAME   FULL MIDDLE NAME—IF NONE, INDICATE   LAST NAME

Year of Birth _____ Birthplace _____ Social Security No. _____

Full name of Wife / Husband _____
     FIRST NAME   FULL MIDDLE NAME—IF NONE, INDICATE   LAST NAME

Year of Birth _____ Birthplace _____ Social Security No. _____

We were married on _____ at _____
     DATE   CITY AND STATE

Wife's maiden name _____

RESIDENCES DURING PAST 10 YEARS

NUMBER AND STREET	CITY	FROM (DATE)	TO (DATE)
NUMBER AND STREET	CITY	FROM (DATE)	TO (DATE)
NUMBER AND STREET	CITY	FROM (DATE)	TO (DATE)

(If more space is needed, use reverse side of form)

OCCUPATIONS DURING PAST 10 YEARS

Husband's

OCCUPATION	FIRM NAME	STREET AND CITY	FROM (DATE) TO (DATE)
OCCUPATION	FIRM NAME	STREET AND CITY	FROM (DATE) TO (DATE)
OCCUPATION	FIRM NAME	STREET AND CITY	FROM (DATE) TO (DATE)

Wife's

OCCUPATION	FIRM NAME	STREET AND CITY	FROM (DATE) TO (DATE)
OCCUPATION	FIRM NAME	STREET AND CITY	FROM (DATE) TO (DATE)

(If more space is needed, use reverse side of form)

FORMER MARRIAGE(S), IF ANY

If no former marriages, write "None" _____ Otherwise, please complete the following:

Name of former wife _____

Deceased ☐   Divorced ☐   When _____ Where _____

Name of former husband _____

Deceased ☐   Divorced ☐   When _____ Where _____

(If more space is needed, use reverse side of form)

Buyer intends to reside on the property in this transaction   Yes ☐   No ☐

THIS PORTION IS TO BE COMPLETED BY THE SELLER

The Street Address of the property in this transaction is _____
     (LEAVE BLANK IF NONE)

The land is unimproved ☐ or improved with a structure of the following type;

IMPROVEMENTS: ☐ SINGLE RESIDENCE OR 1-4 FAMILY   ☐ MULTIPLE RESIDENCE   ☐ COMMERCIAL

OCCUPIED BY: ☐ OWNER   ☐ LESSEE   ☐ TENANTS

ANY PORTION OF NEW LOAN FUNDS TO BE USED FOR CONSTRUCTION

IMPROVEMENTS, REMODELING OR REPAIRS TO THIS PROPERTY HAVE BEEN MADE WITHIN THE PAST SIX MONTHS   ☐ YES   ☐ NO

IF YES, HAVE ALL COSTS FOR LABOR AND MATERIALS ARISING IN CONNECTION THEREWITH BEEN PAID IN FULL?   ☐ YES   ☐ NO

The undersigned declare, under penalty of perjury, that the foregoing is true and correct.

DATE _____

HOME PHONE _____   BUSINESS PHONE _____

(IF MARRIED, BOTH HUSBAND AND WIFE SHOULD SIGN)

and/or wife when the chain of title states "unmarried," and the expenses (including attorneys' fees) incurred in defending title.

The "standard" and most common title insurance policy in California is the CLTA policy (no survey). The CLTA policy protects against:

1) someone else who owns a recorded interest in your title;
2) a document not properly signed;
3) forgery, fraud, duress, incompetency;
4) defective delivery of a document;
5) unmarketability of title;
6) restrictive covenants; and
7) lack of a right of access to and from the land.

It is very important to note those items NOT included in the standard policy. The items NOT included are:

1. Easements, encumbrances, and liens that are not shown by the public record.
2. Rights or claims of persons in physical possession of the land.
3. Unrecorded claims not shown by the public record that could be ascertained by physical inspection or correct survey.
4. Mining claims, reservations in patents, water rights, and government actions, such as zoning ordinances.

Standard title insurance (CLTA) does NOT insure against undisclosed liens placed on a property by a grantor (although it is warranted in a grant deed). NO title insurance policy covers everything.

B. AMERICAN LAND TITLE ASSOCIATION (ALTA)
(Extended Coverage Policy — Survey Included) (www.alta.org)

Most lenders require more protection than provided for by the standard coverage (CLTA) policy. They require the extended coverage (ALTA) policy.

The *AMERICAN LAND TITLE ASSOCIATION (ALTA) policy is an extended coverage policy that insures against many exclusions in the standard coverage (CLTA) policy.* The ALTA policy (which includes a competent survey or physical inspection) is usually required by California lenders and by out-of-state lenders who are not able to make a personal physical inspection of the property.

An extended ALTA title insurance policy is a lender's policy. It protects only the lender. If an owner wants this kind of protection, he or she should request the extended ALTA Owner's Policy.

Purchasers should note that there are still certain exceptions to the CLTA standard policy and even to the ALTA extended policy. There is no insurance coverage for the following:

1. Defects known to the insured at the time the policy was issued, but not designated in writing.
2. Government regulations regarding occupancy and use (zoning).

No title insurance protects against governmental regulations (zoning changes) or defects known to the insured.

There are three different kinds of standard coverage title insurance: 1) an owner's policy; 2) a lender's policy; and 3) a joint protection policy. A smart agent makes sure the buyer and lender get the kind they want and understand the kind they have!

C. ALTA-R (One- to Four-Residential Units)

The *ALTA-R POLICY is recommended by title companies for one-to-four unit owner-occupied residential dwellings*. It doesn't include a survey because the property lines are already established by a recorded subdivision map. Since the title company does not have to do a survey, it gives the buyer more coverage for the same price. The CAR® residential purchase agreement includes the ALTA-R as the preferred residential title policy choice.

D. WHO PAYS TITLE INSURANCE FEES?

Title insurance fees are a part of the escrow closing costs. Title insurance companies are required to publish rate schedules and charge according to the published rates. Who assumes payment of the fees, however, varies depending upon the area in which one lives.

In Southern California, it is customary for the seller to pay the title fees, whereas in Northern California it is usually the buyer who assumes the cost. Because there is no law determining who must pay, it should be stated in the purchase agreement to prevent any misunderstanding. This, however, covers only the standard CLTA policy. The additional cost of the ALTA extended policy is usually charged to the party purchasing the property (the buyer/borrower).

E. TITLE INSURANCE DISCLOSURE

In any escrow transaction for the purchase or exchange of real property where a title insurance policy will not be issued to the buyer (or exchanger), the buyer (or exchanger) must sign and acknowledge a disclosure statement stating that it may be advisable to obtain title insurance.

VIII. Real Estate Settlement Procedures Act (RESPA)

RESPA allows borrowers to shop for settlement services. The law covers first loans on one-to-four unit residential dwellings.

The **Real Estate Settlement Procedures Act (RESPA)** *is a law for the sale or transfer of one-to-four residential units requiring: 1) specific procedures and 2) forms for settlements (closing costs) involving most home loans from financial institutions with federally insured deposits, including FHA and VA loans.*

This law, although amended several times, states that the closing settlement cost of a real estate transaction must be made known to the borrower on or before the settlement date, although, at the buyer's request, it must be provided one business day before escrow closes. Before this law was passed, buyers were unaware of the exact amount needed until the actual escrow closing day. Sometimes the buyers were surprised to find that more money than expected was needed to complete the procedure. The current law alleviates this problem.

RESPA disclosure requirements are for federally related lenders. This means almost all lenders.

Other provisions required by the Real Estate Settlement Procedures Act include the following:

1. At the time of loan application, or within three business days, the lender must give a good faith estimate of the total closing charges to the borrower.

2. At the same time, the lender must furnish the buyer with an information booklet.

3. The escrow agent must give a uniform settlement statement to the borrower, the seller, and the lender. The settlement statement must be furnished by the time of settlement, except when the borrower waives it, or in areas where the HUD (Department of Housing and Urban Development) permits a later date for supplying it.

The settlement statement must be delivered on or before the date of settlement, at no charge. The buyer can request it one business day before closing.

4. Individuals are prohibited from receiving kickbacks and unearned fees. Payments to cooperating brokerages and referral agreements between brokers are exempt.

5. No seller may require a buyer to purchase title insurance from any particular company as a condition of sale.

There are penalties for "kickbacks" and unearned fees. The seller may request a specific title insurer, but only the buyer can require a specific insurance company.

Vesting Chart - Methods of Holding Title

	Tenancy in Common	Joint Tenancy	Community Property	Community Property w/Right of Survivorship
Parties	Any number of persons (rarely husband and wife).	Any number of persons (can be husband and wife).	Husband and wife, Husband and Husband, or Wife and Wife.	Husband and wife, Husband and Husband, or Wife and Wife.
Division	Ownership can be divided into any number of interests equal or unequal.	Ownership interests must be equal and cannot be divided.	Ownership interests are equal.	Ownership interests are equal.
Title	Each co-owner can have a separate legal title to the individual's undivided interest in the whole property.	There is only one title for the whole property.	Title in "community," similar to title of being in partnership.	Title in "community," similar to title of being in partnership.
Possession	Equal right of possession.	Equal right of possession.	Equal right of possession.	Equal right of possession.
Conveyance	Each co-owner's interest may be conveyed separately by its owner.	Conveyance by one co-owner w/o others breaks joint tenancy—owners become tenants in common.	Both co-owners must join in conveyance of real property. Separate interests cannot be conveyed.	Both co-owners must join in conveyance of real property. Separate interests cannot be conveyed.
Purchaser's Status	Purchaser becomes a tenant in common with other co-owners.	Purchaser becomes a tenant in common with other co-owners.	Purchaser can only acquire whole title of community, not part of it.	Purchaser can only acquire whole title of community, not part of it.
Death	Upon co-owners death, interest passes by will to the devisees or heirs. No survivorship right.	Upon co-owner's death, his/her interest ends & cannot be willed. Survivor(s) owns property by survivorship.	Upon co-owner's death, it goes to survivor in severalty (by will to devisee, or by succession to survivor).	Upon co-owner's death, it goes to survivor in severalty.
Successor's Status	Devisees or heirs become tenants in common.	Last survivor owns property in severalty.	If passing by will, tenancy in common between devisee and survivor results.	Each survivor owns property in severalty.
Creditor's Rights	Co-owner's interest may be sold on execution sale to satisfy a creditor, who may become a tenant in common.	Co-owner's interest may be sold on execution sale to satisfy a creditor. Joint tenancy is broken. Creditor may become a tenant in common.	Co-owner's interest cannot be seized and sold separately. The whole property may be sold to satisfy debts of either spouse.	Co-owner's interest cannot be seized and sold separately. The whole property may be sold to satisfy debts of either spouse.
Presumtion	Favored in doubtful cases except husband and wife (community property).	Must be expressly stated and properly formed. Not favored.	Strong presumption that property acquired by spouses is community.	Strong presumption that property acquired by spouses is community.

IX. California Escrow Association

The California Escrow Association has developed a statewide program to promote professional service and educational opportunities for its members. Many community colleges have also adopted certificate courses for escrow personnel and real estate brokers to provide a better understanding of the highly technical escrow field (see **www.ceaescrow.org**).

X. CHAPTER SUMMARY

An **escrow** is created when a written agreement (usually from a **Purchase Contract**) instructs a **neutral third party** to hold funds and proceed only when all the agreed to conditions have been completed. An escrow is strongly recommended in connection with real estate sales, loan agreements, or exchanges made in California. Escrows are required for liquor license transfers, security sales, and court ordered transfers (**probate sales**).

A **valid escrow** requires: 1) signed escrow instructions (a written escrow contract) between the buying and selling parties; 2) a neutral escrow company acting as a dual agent for the buyer and the seller; and 3) conditional delivery of funds until the escrow conditions are completed.

An **escrow holder** can be a corporation, an attorney, or a real estate broker acting as a real estate agent in the transaction. An escrow officer, holder, or agent, though not licensed by the state, must be an employee of a **licensed escrow company** acting as agent. The duties of an escrow company include conditional delivery of funds until escrow conditions are met, confidentiality of escrow instructions, and acting as a deposit holder until funds are disbursed when escrow closes.

A real estate broker can handle escrow for a fee, but only if the broker acts as a real estate agent in that transaction, or if the broker is a principal (buyer or seller).

The escrow is complete when: 1) all escrow conditions of the parties have been met; and 2) the parties have received an accounting of the procedure. Escrows can be **terminated** in three ways: by **completion**, **mutual agreement**, or court action **interpleader**.

Amendments changing escrow instructions must be signed by both parties. The seller cannot rescind escrow without consent of the buyer, but the salesperson may recommend an escrow company. **Selection of an escrow company and officer is negotiated between buyer and seller**. It is illegal for a real estate licensee to receive a **kickback** for solicitation of escrow business.

Escrow instructions for the sale of a house are formal instructions drawn from the information contained in the **purchase contract**. They are usually interpreted together, but if a conflict arises, the latest signed document will usually prevail. Most escrows for home sales include getting a new loan and the payoff or assumption of an old one.

The **payoff demand statement** details the lender's calculations of the amounts owed for the purpose of paying off the loan in full. If a loan is to be assumed, a **beneficiary's (lender's) statement** under a deed of trust provides information, such as the unpaid balance, monthly payment, interest rate, and assumption fees.

Closing escrow is the process of signing various documents, transfer of documents, recordation of deed and trust deeds, and distribution of funds. The **closing date** is usually the date that the documents are recorded.

Proration is the process of dividing expenses or income proportionately, between buyer and seller, to the precise date that escrow closes, or an agreed upon date. Items commonly prorated include: **property taxes, fire insurance premiums, interest,** and **rents.** All escrow companies use **30 days as a "base month."** The two important dates in determining proration amounts are the dates escrow closes and when the item is paid.

A **Structural Pest Control Report** (termite report) is usually a condition of the escrow. This report is given by a licensed pest control company to identify any wood-destroying pests or conditions likely to cause pest infestation. It also states the conditions and correction costs of any pest, dry rot, excessive moisture, earth-wood contacts, or fungus damage in accessible areas of a structure. Payment for the report is negotiated between parties, but is usually made by the seller, as indicated in the allocation of costs signed by both parties. **Required repairs** are usually paid for by the seller (subject to certain dollar limits), then a notice of work completed is obtained. **Recommended repairs** are negotiated between the parties.

Most lenders require a pest control inspection before making a loan. Every VA and FHA loan requires one. A copy of the pest control report and **notice of work completed** must be delivered to the buyer if it's a condition of the purchase agreement or financing.

Lending institutions require fire coverage for the amount of its loan. A **California Standard Form Fire Insurance Policy** insures the dwelling **only against fire and lightning.** An **Extended Coverage Endorsement** insures against windstorms, explosions, hail, aircraft, smoke, riot, and vehicles not attributed to a strike or civil commotion. Buyers might be able to **assume** existing fire insurance policies or obtain new ones. (NOTE: If the seller has a non-smoking policy but the buyer smokes, the buyer would not be able to assume that poicy.) When assuming fire insurance policies, the premium amount will be prorated in escrow.

Chain of title is the recorded public history of a specific property. Information about people and their real property is stored in computers in a grantor-grantee index and referred to as a **title plant. Title insurance companies** examine chain of title records, review any risks not found in public records, seek legal interpretation of deeds or other real estate documents, help the seller correct any defects, and insure marketable title to the property.

A **preliminary title report** is the first step in a title search. It shows the condition of title before a sale or loan transaction.

Title insurance policies in California include the **California Land Title Association (CLTA) Policy**, the more comprehensive **American Land Title Association (ALTA)** Policy, or the **ALTA-R Policy**.

The **CLTA policy** is the most common and basic title insurance policy. The standard CLTA policy insures only the lender, unless the owner pays for "owner" coverage. It protects against lack of capacity of a party in a the chain of title, deeds not properly delivered, and forgery.

The **ALTA policy** is an extended coverage policy that insures against many exclusions in the standard coverage (CLTA) policy. The ALTA policy (which includes a competent survey or physical inspection) is usually required by California lenders and out of state lenders unable to make personal inspections of the property. Neither ALTA or CLTA covers undisclosed title defects known to the insured at the time of policy issuance or **zoning changes**.

The **ALTA-R policy** is recommended by title companies for one-to-four unit owner-occupied residential dwellings. It offers more coverage at the same price because no survey is necessary.

Payment for the CLTA policy insurance fees is negotiable, but the purchase agreement must state who pays the insurance fees to prevent any misunderstanding. In Southern California, the seller customarily pays for the CLTA policy. In Northern California, the buyer customarily pays for the CLTA policy. The difference between a CLTA policy and an ALTA policy is 'always' paid by the buyer in either part of the state.

Escrow service fees are usually split 50-50 in Southern California. The buyer usually pays in Northern California.

The **Real Estate Settlement Procedures Act (RESPA)** involves most federally insured home loans. It is a Federal law relating to the sale or transfer of one-to-four residential units requiring specific procedures and forms for settlement closing costs. All settlement closing costs must be disclosed to the borrower one business day before escrow closes.

XI. MATCHING VOCABULARY Fill in the blanks with the correct letter

A. 30 days
B. ALTA
C. Beneficiary's statement
D. Chain of title
E. Civil action
F. CLTA
G. Closing date
H. Escrow

I. Escrow instructions
J. Escrow officer
K. Insurance
L. Neutral depository
M. Payoff demand statement
N. Preliminary title report
O. Proration

P. RESPA
Q. Statement of information
R. Structural pest control certification report
S. Title insurance

1. _____ The processing, by a neutral party, of the paperwork and money involved in a sale or other real estate transaction.

2. _____ An escrow business conducted by a licensed escrow holder who accepts documents and funds while representing each party equally.

3. _____ An employee of a licensed escrow company who acts as the agent.

4. _____ A formal demand statement from the lender that details the amounts owed, as calculated by the lender, for the purpose of paying off the loan in full.

5. _____ The date that the documents are recorded.

6. _____ Formal instructions drawn from the information contained in the original agreement, usually the signed purchase contract.

7. _____ The process of proportionately dividing expenses or income to the precise date that escrow closes, or any other date previously agreed upon.

8. _____ A written report given by a licensed pest control company, identifying any wood-destroying pests or conditions likely to cause pest infestation.

9. _____ A recorded public history of a specific property.

10. _____ This policy insures a lender and/or property oner against losses that result from imperfections in title.

11. _____ A report showing the condition of the title before a sale or loan transaction.

12. _____ The basic title insurance policy.

13. _____ This federal law covers first loans on 1-to-4 unit residential dwellings and allows borrowers to shop for settlement services.

14. _____ A statement by a lender, under a deed of trust, that provides information, such as the unpaid balance, monthly payment, and interest rate, necessary if the loan is to be assumed.

15. _____ At the close of escrow, if a seller decides not to pay the commission, the broker/agent can file this in court.

16. _____ For proration, all escrow companies use this number of days as a base month.

17. _____ To begin a title search, the borrower first completes this form.

18. _____ When one company agrees to indemnify another for loss in return for periodic premium payments, it is called:

19. _____ An extended coverage policy that insures against many exclusions in the standard coverage policy.

See Page 610 for Answers

XII. CHAPTER QUIZ

1. The processing of paperwork and money involved in a sale or other real estate transaction is called:

   a. property transfer.
   b. acknowledgment.
   c. escrow.
   d. none of the above.

2. Which of the following is a requirement of a valid escrow?

   a. Signed instructions
   b. Neutral third party
   c. Conditional delivery
   d. All of the above

3. Of the following, which would be the last function in an escrow sequence of events?

   a. Recording and issuing of title policy
   b. Request of new loan documents
   c. Adjustments and prorations
   d. None of the above

4. In California, an independent escrow company:

   a. must be a corporation.
   b. is governed by the Department of Business Oversight.
   c. both a and b.
   d. none of the above.

5. The best way that escrow instructions can be changed, once they have been drawn and signed by each party, is by:

   a. the escrow officer.
   b. mutual consent of the parties.
   c. the listing broker.
   d. operation of law.

6. Escrow information is usually taken from the:

   a. California Residential Purchase Agreement and Joint Escrow Instructions.
   b. title policy.
   c. Transfer Disclosure Statement.
   d. all of the above.

7. When calculating prorations, how many days are in the standard base period?

   a. 31 days
   b. 30 days
   c. 28 days
   d. Depends on the month being prorated

8. What title policy would cover most of the exclusions of a standard policy?

   a. ALTA
   b. MLTA
   c. CLTA
   d. All of the above

9. Escrow companies are selected by:

   a. the broker.
   b. the buyer and seller.
   c. the seller only.
   d. the agent only.

10. Which of the following is an annual recurring charge?

   a. County recording fees
   b. Title insurance fees
   c. Escrow fees
   d. Property tax fees

ANSWERS: 1. c; 2. d; 3. a; 4. c; 5. b; 6. a; 7. b; 8. a; 9. b; 10. d

CHAPTER 11

Taxation: Real Estate-Related Taxes

Taxes are an important aspect of all real estate transactions. Property owners are taxed annually on the property they own. In addition, there are other state and federal taxes that must be paid in order to buy, sell, or give away real property. **Figure 11-1** illustrates the five taxes with which every taxpayer, investor, and salesperson should be familiar. The amount of tax and who must pay the tax are often major factors to consider in the transfer of real estate. Although tax considerations are important, as an investor, that aspect of any purchase should not be the only consideration, as tax laws can change.

Figure 11-1

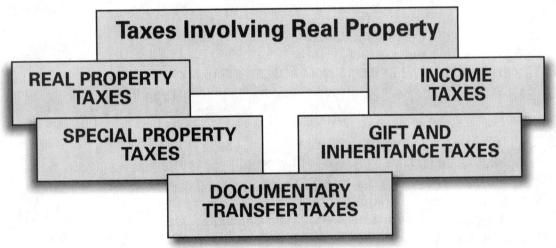

Taxes Involving Real Property

REAL PROPERTY TAXES

INCOME TAXES

SPECIAL PROPERTY TAXES

GIFT AND INHERITANCE TAXES

DOCUMENTARY TRANSFER TAXES

I. Real Property Taxes

A city or county receives most of its operating revenue from the assessment and collection of real property taxes. *REAL PROPERTY TAXES are determined according to the value of the real property, and are paid annually or semi-annually.* These taxes are called ad valorem taxes. An *AD VALOREM TAX is a tax that is charged in proportion to the value of the property.*

CHAPTER OUTLINE

Property taxes are based on the concept that taxes should be assessed in accordance with a person's ability to pay. In the case of real estate, the higher the value of the property, the higher the property taxes.

The *COUNTY ASSESSOR is the county officer who has the responsibility of determining the assessed valuation of land, improvements, and personal property used in business.* The county assessor determines the value of both county and city properties, except in a few cities that use their own assessors.

http://assessor.lacounty.gov
L. A. County Assessor

In general, all real property, except that owned by the government, and some tangible personal property except inventory used in a business, is subject to property tax assessment in California. **Intangible personal property, such as goodwill of a business opportunity, as well as tangible property, such as household furnishings and personal effects of individuals, are not assessed or taxed.**

The *COUNTY TAX COLLECTOR is the county officer who collects the real property taxes.* He or she only collects taxes; the county tax collector has nothing to do with determining how much tax is levied. If the real property taxes are not paid, the county tax collector will eventually require that the property be sold at a tax sale.

www.boe.ca.gov/proptaxes/assessors.htm
List of Assessors

A. PROPOSITION 13

"Prop 13" (Jarvis-Gann Initiative) sent shock waves through the nation by rolling back the California property tax to 1 percent of the owner's value, making it the lowest rate in the country.

PROPOSITION 13 limits the amount of taxes to a maximum of 1 percent of the March 1, 1975, market value of the property plus the cumulative increase of 2 percent in market value each year thereafter. Voted indebtedness may increase this rate beyond 1 percent from

area-to-area with voter approval. Improvements made after March 1, 1975, are added to the value in the year they are made. If ownership has changed after March 1, 1975, the tax is limited to 1 percent of the market value plus the 2 percent cumulative increase each succeeding year. Any state-allowed exemptions are deducted after figuring the basic tax (see **Figure 11-2**).

A "rough" estimate of property tax is approximately 1.25 percent of the sales price. (1 percent of sales price + .25 percent for other voter-approved indebtedness.) Annual property tax increase is limited to 2 percent.

Property tax assessment is subject to an adjustment in the event that a purchase, new construction, or a change in ownership has taken place after the 1975 lien date. If the property has undergone such a change, it is subject to a new assessor's appraisal. If the new value is higher, the tax will be increased. If the new value is lower, the tax will be decreased. Due to rising property values, Prop 13 can be a burden for new buyers, especially when similar properties in the neighborhood, which haven't changed ownership in several years, are taxed considerably lower.

NEW CONSTRUCTION means any addition or improvement to land, including alterations of existing improvements if the alterations result in conversion to another use or an extension of the economic life of the improvement. An example of a *TAXABLE ALTERATION would be anything that increases the usefulness of the structure, such as the addition of a bedroom or bathroom.*

Construction, reconstruction, or alteration performed for the purpose of routine or normal maintenance and repair would not trigger Proposition 13. Thus, interior or exterior painting, replacement of roof coverings, or the addition of aluminum siding would not cause an adjustment in the assessed value. An example of an alteration that does not result in an increased usefulness of existing facilities is the modernization of a kitchen.

Escrow agents fill out property tax information forms to help the county recorder facilitate the distribution of the forms, but they are not statutorily required to prepare the form or file it. Hence, as a real estate agent, you need to be aware of your responsibility to draw your clientele's attention to the statement and assure compliance.

1. Transfers Can Trigger Reassessment (Under Prop 13)

As stated above, Prop 13 determines property tax rates when a property "changes" ownership. What constitutes a change, for purposes of establishing a new valuation, is not always easy to define.

Be very careful when changing anything concerning the title. Changing from Joint Tenancy to Community Property With Rights of Survivorship may trigger tax increase if not clearly indicated that it is not a conveyance of property.

Figure 11-2

Proposition 13

That Article XII A is added to the Constitution to read:

Section 1.

(a) The maximum amount of any ad valorem tax on real property shall not exceed one percent (1%)* of the full cash value of such property. The one percent (1%)* tax to be collected by the counties and apportioned according to law to the districts within the counties.

(b) The limitation provided for in subdivision (a) shall not apply to ad valorem taxes or special assessments to pay the interest and redemption charges on any indebtedness approved by the voters prior to the time this section becomes effective.

Section 2.

(a) The full cash value means the county assessors valuation of real property as shown on the 1975-76 tax bill under "full cash value," or thereafter, the appraised value of real property when purchased, newly constructed, or a change in ownership has occurred after the 1975 assessment. All real property not already assessed up to the 1975-76 tax levels may be reassessed to reflect that valuation.

(b) The fair market value base may reflect, from year to year, the inflationary rate, not to exceed two percent (2%) for any given year or reduction as shown in the consumer price index or comparable data for the area under taxing jurisdiction.

Section 3.

From and after the effective date of this article, any changes in state taxes enacted for the purpose of increasing revenues collected pursuant thereto whether by increased rates or changes in methods of computation must be imposed by an Act passed by not less than two-thirds of all members elected to each of the two houses of the Legislature, except that no new ad valorem taxes on real property, or sales or transaction taxes on the sales of real property may be imposed.

Section 4.

Cities, counties, and special districts, by a two-thirds vote of the qualified electors of such district, may impose special taxes on such district, except ad valorem taxes on real property or a transaction tax or sales tax on the sale of real property within such city, county, or special district.

Section 5.

This article shall take effect for the tax year beginning on July 1 following the passage of this Amendment, except Section 3 which shall become effective upon the passage of this article.

Section 6.

If any section, part, clause, or phrase hereof is for any reason held to be invalid or unconstitutional, the remaining sections shall not be affected but will remain in full force and effect.

* Voted indebtedness may increase this rate beyond 1% from local area to area, with voter approval.

Figure 10-3

Chapter 11

2. Propositions Altering Prop 13 (Propositions 58/60/90)

Californians have voted for several changes to alter Proposition 13.

Under the following conditions (based on Propositions 60 and 90), homeowners may be permitted to transfer their current Proposition 13 tax base with them when they buy a new home:

1. Homeowners over the age of 55, and
2. Home purchased within two years of original sale, and
3. Replacement home of equal or lesser value, and
4. New home must be in the same county, or another participating county (check first). As long as the purchased property is located in a county that participates in Proposition 90, it is not necessary for the relinquished property to be in a Propositions 60/90 county.

Proposition 58 allows real property transfers from one spouse to another or to children without property tax reassessment. Because tax laws change, call a tax advisor regarding possible forgiveness of property tax increases when alterations are made in real estate ownership.

Propositions 60 and 90 allow "empty-nesters" to purchase new homes (one at a time) while holding onto their low tax base, thus freeing up larger multiple bedroom homes for younger families.

ASSESSED VALUATION is set at 100 percent of the property's selling price or fair market value, whichever is higher, plus a 2 percent increase for every year the property has been owned, but only as far back as March 1, 1975. The tax rate is set at 1 percent of fair market value (or selling price, whichever is higher) plus any voter-approved indebtedness. Properties that are transferred and new construction are subject to a new appraisal based upon the current market value or selling price, whichever is higher. Existing properties are given a new assessment each year as of January 1. New construction and transfers are assessed immediately upon the first day of the next month. See **Figures 11-3 and 11-4** for an example of a property tax bill.

B. PROPERTY TAXES BECOME A SPECIFIC LIEN

Property taxes are, in effect, liens against that specific property. Business personal property taxes also become liens against that specific real property on the same tax bill. For example, the furniture in furnished apartments is taxed as business personal property and is usually included on the property tax bill.

Property taxes for the following fiscal year become a lien against the real property on January 1 of the current year. Officially, the first installment for half of the taxes becomes due on November 1, and is delinquent after 5 P.M. on December 10. The second installment is due on February 1, and is delinquent if not paid by 5 P.M. on April 10. If either December 10 or April 10 falls on a Saturday, Sunday, or legal holiday, the delinquency date is extended to the close of the next business day.

Figure 11-3

2014	ANNUAL PROPERTY TAX BILL	2014

CITIES, COUNTY, SCHOOLS AND ALL OTHER TAXING AGENCIES IN LOS ANGELES COUNTY

SECURED PROPERTY TAX FOR FISCAL YEAR JULY 1, 2014 TO JUNE 30, 2015

MARK J. SALADINO, TREASURER AND TAX COLLECTOR

FOR ASSISTANCE CALL 1(213) 974-2111 OR 1(888) 807-2111, ON THE WEB AT lacountypropertytax.com

ASSESSOR'S ID. NO.   CK

DETAIL OF TAXES DUE FOR   **4225 011 081 14 000   04**

PROPERTY IDENTIFICATION
ASSESSOR'S ID.NO.: 4225 011 081 14 000
OWNER OF RECORD AS OF JANUARY 1, 2014
SAME AS BELOW

MAILING ADDRESS

Wolfgang Hubie
100 Internet Highway
Culver City, CA 90230

AGENCY	AGENCY PHONE NO.	RATE	AMOUNT
GENERAL TAX LEVY			
ALL AGENCIES		1.000000	$ 2,587.07
VOTED INDEBTEDNESS			
CITY-LOS ANGELES		.028096	$ 72.69
METRO WATER DIST		.003500	9.05
COMMNTY COLLEGE		.040174	103.93
UNIFIED SCHOOLS		.146881	379.99
DIRECT ASSESSMENTS			
LA STORMWATER	(213) 485-2422		$ 8.04
COUNTY PARK DIST	(213) 738-2983		15.38
LACITY PARK DIST	(213) 847-4722		14.30
TRAUMA/EMERG SRV	(866) 587-2862		66.65
FLOOD CONTROL	(626) 458-5165		10.09
LA WEST MOSQ AB	(310) 915-7370		11.83

ELECTRONIC FUND TRANSFER (EFT) NUMBER

ID#:19 4225 011 081 9 YEAR:14 SEQUENCE:000 4
PIN: FIV036

For **American Express, Mastercard and Visa** payments call 1(888) 473-0835
and have available the EFT number listed above. Service fees will be charged.
SPECIAL INFORMATION

PROPERTY LOCATION AND/OR PROPERTY DESCRIPTION
100 Internet Highway   Culver City
*TR=P M 72-26-27 CONDOMINIUM*UNITS
1 AND A

TOTAL TAXES DUE   **$3,279.02**
FIRST INSTALLMENT TAXES   DUE NOV. 1, 2014   **$1,639.52**
SECOND INSTALLMENT TAXES DUE FEB. 1, 2015   **$1,639.50**

VALUATION INFORMATION

ROLL YEAR 14-15	CURRENT ASSESSED VALUE	TAXABLE VALUE
LAND	152,080	152,080
IMPROVEMENTS	113,627	113,627

ASSESSOR'S REGIONAL OFFICE
REGION #07 INDEX: TRA:00067
WEST DISTRICT OFFICE
6120 BRISTOL PARKWAY
CULVER CITY CA 90230
(310)665-5300

ACCT. NO.:   PRINT NO.: 457515 BILL ID.:

TOTAL		265,707
LESS EXEMPTION:	HOME	7,000
NET TAXABLE VALUE		258,707

ANY RETURNED PAYMENT MAY BE SUBJECT TO A FEE UP TO $50.00.

Figure 11-4

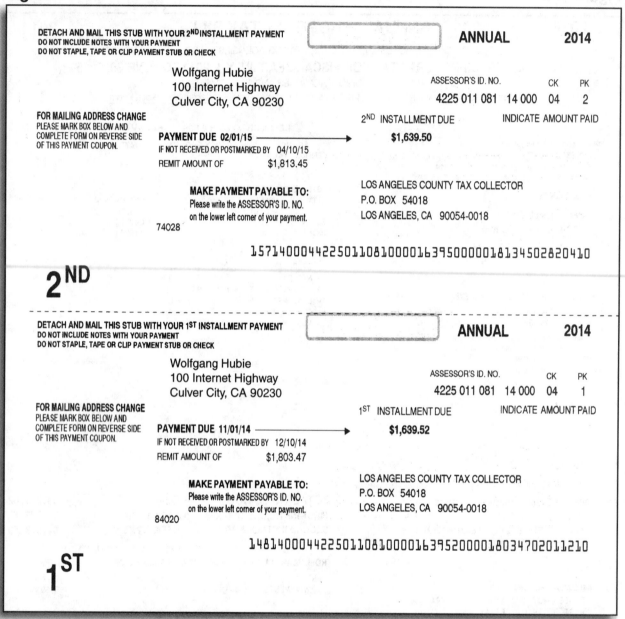

DETACH AND MAIL THIS STUB WITH YOUR 2ND INSTALLMENT PAYMENT
DO NOT INCLUDE NOTES WITH YOUR PAYMENT
DO NOT STAPLE, TAPE OR CLIP PAYMENT STUB OR CHECK

ANNUAL   2014

Wolfgang Hubie
100 Internet Highway
Culver City, CA 90230

ASSESSOR'S ID. NO.   CK   PK

4225 011 081   14 000   04   2

2ND INSTALLMENT DUE   INDICATE AMOUNT PAID

FOR MAILING ADDRESS CHANGE
PLEASE MARK BOX BELOW AND
COMPLETE FORM ON REVERSE SIDE
OF THIS PAYMENT COUPON.

PAYMENT DUE 02/01/15 ——————→ $1,639.50

IF NOT RECEIVED OR POSTMARKED BY 04/10/15

REMIT AMOUNT OF $1,813.45

MAKE PAYMENT PAYABLE TO:
Please write the ASSESSOR'S ID. NO.
on the lower left corner of your payment.
74028

LOS ANGELES COUNTY TAX COLLECTOR
P.O. BOX 54018
LOS ANGELES, CA   90054-0018

1571400044225011081000016395000001813450282041

2ND

DETACH AND MAIL THIS STUB WITH YOUR 1ST INSTALLMENT PAYMENT
DO NOT INCLUDE NOTES WITH YOUR PAYMENT
DO NOT STAPLE, TAPE OR CLIP PAYMENT STUB OR CHECK

ANNUAL   2014

Wolfgang Hubie
100 Internet Highway
Culver City, CA 90230

ASSESSOR'S ID. NO.   CK   PK

4225 011 081   14 000   04   1

1ST INSTALLMENT DUE   INDICATE AMOUNT PAID

FOR MAILING ADDRESS CHANGE
PLEASE MARK BOX BELOW AND
COMPLETE FORM ON REVERSE SIDE
OF THIS PAYMENT COUPON.

PAYMENT DUE 11/01/14 ——————→ $1,639.52

IF NOT RECEIVED OR POSTMARKED BY 12/10/14

REMIT AMOUNT OF $1,803.47

MAKE PAYMENT PAYABLE TO:
Please write the ASSESSOR'S ID. NO.
on the lower left corner of your payment.
84020

LOS ANGELES COUNTY TAX COLLECTOR
P.O. BOX 54018
LOS ANGELES, CA   90054-0018

1481400044225011081000016395200001803470201121

1ST

C. PROPERTY TAX TIME TABLE

The city or county fiscal year starts on July 1 and ends on June 30. All revenues and expenditures are planned for this period of time. **Figure 11-5** illustrates all the important dates that are associated with property taxes. Assessable property is evaluated by the assessor on January 1 for the upcoming year in the name of the property's legal owner on that date. Most cities allow the county assessor to evaluate the property in both the county and the incorporated parts of the county (which are the cities). In a few rare cases, as stated earlier, cities may use their own assessors. County assessors complete their assessment rolls by July 1, the beginning of the government (fiscal) year.

Figure 11-5

Property Tax Time Table

January 1	July 1	November 1	February 1
Property tax becomes a lien on real property	Fiscal year starts	1st installment is due November 1, and delinquent after December 10 at 5 P.M.	2nd installment is due February 1, and delinquent after April 10 at 5 P.M.

Important tax dates can be remembered "**No Darn Fooling Around**" as follows:

N November 1 (first installment due)
D December 10 (first installment is delinquent)
F February 1 (second installment due)
A April 10 (second installment is delinquent)

The government fiscal tax year is July 1 through June 30.

D. PROPERTY TAX PRORATION PROBLEM

Proration question: Who owes how much to whom?

Problem: If the seller of the subject property has paid both the 1st and 2nd installments of the property taxes for a total annual bill of $2,760, what is the proration of property taxes for both the seller and buyer if the buyer takes possession on May 1?

Remember: Escrow prorates property taxes using old (seller's) assessed value (tax bill).

Solution: The first step is to determine the amount of taxes per month. The annual tax bill of $2,760 is divided by 12 months to determine that the monthly tax is $230. Since the seller paid the property taxes through the month of June (the end of the fiscal tax year, which is July 1 through June 30), and the buyer took possession on May 1, two months of paid property taxes are owed the seller. The buyer would owe the seller for two months (May and June) that were already paid by the seller. This amount would be $460 (2 x $230).

When a property is sold, the buyer will receive one new property tax bill, but it may be followed by other updated property tax bills referred to as supplemental property tax bills (see **Figure 11-6**).

E. HOMEOWNER'S PROPERTY TAX EXEMPTION

The homeowner's property tax exemption is $7,000 of assessed valuation.

The *HOMEOWNER'S PROPERTY TAX EXEMPTION is a deduction on the property tax bill of the first $7,000 of assessed value of an owner-occupied property.*

Figure 11-6

SUPPLEMENTAL PROPERTY TAX BILLS

The law requires reassessment of property immediately after it changes ownership or after new construction is completed. While the amount of the supplemental assessment is still determined in accordance with Proposition 13, the actual effect is to "speed up" reassessment of property.

The Office of Assessor enters the new property value onto the assessment roll as of the first of the month following the month in which the property changes ownership, or new construction is completed.

Depending upon the date your client purchased property or the date construction is completed, he or she will receive one or more supplemental tax bills in addition to his or her regular tax bill. Taxes on the supplemental tax roll become a lien against the real property on the date of change in ownership or the date new construction is completed.

A homeowner's exemption on a home does the following:

1. All personal property of the homeowner is exempt from property taxes.
2. A resident owner receives a $7,000 homeowner's exemption in assessed value if the property is the principal residence on the 1st of March.

Advise your buyers to file immediately for homeowner exemption.

The time to file for the homeowner's exemption is from January 1 to February 15 in order to receive the full exemption. Once the exemption is filed, it remains on the property until the homeowner terminates it. If the exemption is terminated, a new claim form must be obtained from, and filed with, the assessor to regain eligibility.

Qualifying owner-occupied residential property receives a $7,000 homeowner's exemption. For example, an assessed value of $500,000 minus the homeowner's exemption of $7,000 is $493,000. (Prop 13 tax rate is 1% of the $7,000 exemption, so your buyer's tax savings, in reality, is only $70 per year.)

F. DISABLED AND SENIOR CITIZEN'S PROPERTY TAX POSTPONEMENT

Seniors who are 62 years of age or older and have a household income of $24,000 or less may qualify for this tax postponement assistance program. This program offers them the option of having the state pay all or part of the taxes on their homes. In return, a lien is placed on the property for the amount that the state has to pay. This specific lien becomes payable when the taxpayer moves or dies. In effect, the homeowner is relieved of his or her tax burden in exchange for a lien on his or her home to be paid upon death. California has extended this program to include persons under the age of 62 who are legally disabled. **Further information is available from the State Controller at www.sco.ca.gov.**

G. VETERAN'S EXEMPTION

Any California resident who served in the military during a time of war is entitled to an annual $4,000 property tax exemption against the assessed value of one property. This exemption also applies to the widow, widowed mother, or pensioned father of a deceased veteran. Disabled California veterans who qualify can have an exemption from property taxation on that part of the full value of the residence that does not exceed $100,000, as adjusted for the relevant assessment year.

A veteran cannot have a veteran's exemption and a homeowner's property tax exemption on the same property.

H. TAX EXEMPT PROPERTY

In California there are some properties that are partially or totally tax exempt. All real property that is owned by the federal, state, county, or city government is automatically tax exempt. This is a huge benefit to the federal government (and detriment to the state), as the federal government owns 45% of California land. Eastern states benefit because only about 10 percent of their land is owned by the federal government. **A lessee with possessory interest in oil and gas rights on government owned property is not exempt from property taxes.**

Since California has so many national and state parks, the majority of land in this state is tax exempt.

Any property that is used exclusively by non-profit organizations for religious, charitable, medical, or educational purposes is also tax exempt. In addition, 50 percent of all growing crops, young orchard trees, immature timber, and young grapevines are tax exempt.

Property of non-profit organizations used for religious, charitable, medical, or educational purposes is tax exempt.

II. Special Assessment Tax

A *SPECIAL ASSESSMENT TAX is levied by a city council or a county board of supervisors, often with the voters' approval, for the cost of specific local improvements such as streets, sewers, irrigation, or drainage.* **Assessments differ from property taxes in that property taxes finance the general functions of government and go into the general fund, whereas a special assessment is levied once (usually) by the city, county, or "improvement district" for a particular work or improvement.**

The *official body that levies a special assessment is called a SPECIAL ASSESSMENT DISTRICT BOARD*. According to state law, any self-governing area, such as a city or county, may establish a special assessment district for the purpose of levying a special assessment.

As a rule, a district issues its own bonds to finance particular improvements, such as water distribution systems, parking facilities, street lighting, and many other types of

developments. To repay the funds borrowed through the bonds issued, these districts have the power to assess all lands included in the district. Such loans constitute liens on the land until paid. These liens can be foreclosed by sale similar to a tax sale and have priority over private property interests.

A. IMPROVEMENT BOND ACT OF 1915

The *IMPROVEMENT BOND ACT OF 1915 finances street and highway improvements through an assessment to property owners based upon the frontage of the property facing the improved street.* Through the issuance of municipal bonds, it allows property owners up to 30 years to pay off their portion of the improvement assessment. As the broker, you and the seller must give the buyer a disclosure notice of assessment amount and the amount applicable to the property.

B. MELLO-ROOS COMMUNITY FACILITIES ACT

The Mello-Roos Community Facilities Act is another type of improvement bond. **Figure 11-7** explains Mello-Roos in detail.

III. Documentary Transfer Tax

Documentary transfer taxes are paid only on the new amount of money (cash down plus new financing), not on any assumed financing.

The *DOCUMENTARY TRANSFER TAX is a tax that is applied to the consideration paid or money borrowed when transferring real property, except for any remaining loans or liens on the property.* This tax is computed at the rate of 55 cents for each $500 of consideration (or fraction thereof). If the consideration is in even thousands, it could be computed at $1.10 per $1,000. The consideration is any amount of cash payment plus any new loans. However, this tax does not apply to any liens or encumbrances that remain on the property as part of the transfer. If a house were sold for $230,000 and a buyer assumed the old loan of $30,000, the documentary transfer tax would be $220.

$$\frac{\$200,000}{\$500} \times \$.55 = \$220$$

The documentary transfer tax is handled as part of the escrow. According to state law, the county is allowed to charge this tax. However, a city within a county can charge that county for one-half of this tax. Therefore, in most cities, the county collects the documentary transfer tax and gives half of it to the city. Based on the information found at the county recorder's office, the documentary transfer tax can be used, in many cases, to determine a close approximation of the previous sale price of a property. Simply divide 55 cents into the amount of the documentary transfer tax and multiply by $500. If any loans have been assumed by the new owner, also add that amount to arrive at the total prior sale price of the property.

Figure 11-7

Mello-Roos Liens
DISCLOSURE REQUIRED

As an agent, if you fail to disclose a Mello-Roos lien, the buyer has a three-day right of rescission, and it may result in disciplinary action against you.

MELLO-ROOS LIENS *are municipal bonds issued to fund streets, sewers, and other infrastructure needs before a housing development is built.* This financial device allows developers to raise money to complete off-site improvements in a house or condo subdivision. The developer is usually responsible for making payments on the bond until the home is sold. The homeowner then becomes responsible for payment via a special tax.

The Mello-Roos Community Facilities Act is a way that a city or governmental district can skirt the property tax limitations of Proposition 13. The city can include the cost and maintenance of infrastructure items in the property tax bill as a special tax, which is allowed to go above the limits of Proposition 13.

This has been a boon for developers who need help financing their projects and for municipalities anxious to upgrade new developments under the restrictions of Proposition 13. The downside is that, if something goes wrong with the economy or the project, the municipality may have to foreclose on the developer.

The primary responsibility for disclosure of any Mello-Roos bonds lies with the seller.

A broker must disclose to property buyers that a project is subject to a Mello-Roos special tax levy. If the agent fails to provide this disclosure, he or she is subject to discipline by the Real Estate Commissioner. A disclosure notice of the amount assessed and the amount of special tax applicable to the property is required on the sale or lease (for more than five years) of property subject to this lien. Failure to give notice before signing the sales contract permits the buyer or tenant a three-day right of rescission, after receipt of the notice.

Warning: Whereas property taxes are totally deductible from state and federal income taxes, Mello-Roos taxes may only be partially deductible depending upon whether they are for maintenance or improvements. Consult with your C.P.A. before claiming such a deduction.

IV. Gift and Estate Taxes

For federal purposes, the transfer of property by a gift or inheritance is taxed. Exemptions may reduce the taxes and sometimes eliminate them. **Figure 11-8** illustrates the federal taxes encountered by transferring property as a gift or by inheritance.

Figure 11-8

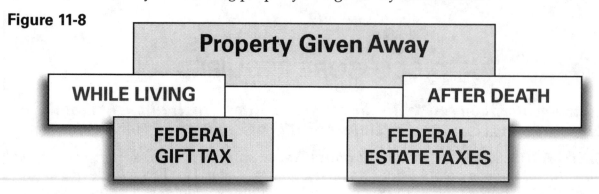

A. FEDERAL GIFT TAXES

Both a husband and wife may give away $5.34 million each over a lifetime (2014 rate) without paying any gift tax. Of course, you need to stay current with new laws.

Frequently, as an individual family matures, the value of the real property owned by the family increases, and the owning family may consider bestowing it as a gift.

When a family gives property, whether real or personal, to another individual, there may be federal gift taxes that must be paid. If the value of the property is higher than an exempt amount, the donor is responsible for a gift tax. A **DONOR** *is the person or persons giving the property as a gift. Generally, people give their property away to relatives on a systematic basis so that taxes are avoided.* The **DONEE** *is the person or persons who receive the property as a gift.* The federal gift tax law also provides for a $14,000 annual exemption per donee.

B. FEDERAL ESTATE TAX

A **FEDERAL ESTATE TAX RETURN** *must be filed for the estate of every U.S. citizen or resident whose gross estate, plus adjusted taxable gifts and specific exemption, is more than $5,340,000.* The highest federal marginal estate and gift tax rate is 40 percent. Ironically, the estate has paid income taxes on most of it before. Again, you must stay current with new limits.

C. NO STATE GIFT AND INHERITANCE TAXES

In 1982, California repealed both the state gift and inheritance taxes.

V. Federal and State Income Taxes

The annual Federal Income Tax Form 1040 and the California State Income Tax Form 540 are bookkeeping or accounting summaries of the prior year's financial facts. These facts are a history and cannot be altered at the time of filing the income tax return.

www.irs.ustreas.gov
Internal Revenue Service (IRS)
www.ftb.ca.gov
Franchise Tax Board (FTB)

Californians have to pay both federal and state income taxes (see **Figure 11-9**). That's right! California residents pay both income taxes, which ranks us among the most taxed people in the United States. It is no wonder that Californians are very interested in understanding the effects of income taxes on both their personal residence and income-producing properties.

Figure 11-9   **CALIFORNIA vs. FEDERAL INCOME TAX**

California's income tax system differs from federal tax law in many ways. Unfortunately, this means that many of your federal deductions may be limited or disallowed in California. But the Golden State does have some of its own deductions and many credits that may benefit you.

California deductions & credits taken directly on tax amount owed.

1. State does not tax Social Security benefits or Railroad benefits.
2. State does not tax it's own lottery earnings. So California residents, make sure to buy your winning ticket in our home state.
3. Part of your annual vehicle registration fee may be deducted on your California income tax.

The state taxes at a maximum of 13.3 percent, but tends to be more restrictive on deductions. State taxes paid are themselves deductible from the federal return.

Tax credits are deducted directly from your tax due, which can sometimes make them more valuable than deductions.

1. **Renters Credit** (Powerful because it is subtracted from actual taxes owed: A $60 credit for single renters if income is less than $34,412 and $120 if married/register partner if joint income is less than $68,824.
2. **Exemption credit for all:** A credit of $98 each for yourself, your spouse, and your dependents. If you are blind or over 65 you can claim an extra $98 credit.
3. **Dependent Parent:** For married/RDP taxpayers filing separately who also have a dependent parent.
4. **Adoption:** Cost 50% Credit.
5. **Joint Custody Credit:** May deduct 30% of their tax liability up to $387.

Because of the complexity and vast scope of income taxation, we can offer here only a basic primer on some income tax aspects of real estate. You cannot be expected to become an expert in taxation, but you should have a working acquaintance with some basics. After all, you will often be consulted when a prospect or client wants guidance in the purchase, sale, exchange, or transfer of real property, and with investment decisions. As a real estate professional, you need to recognize opportunities and drawbacks with respect to clients' holdings and understand that tax liabilities differ according to the specific transaction. You should also know when to call a C.P.A. or attorney, and to advise your client to consult with either or both when significant tax and legal implications are involved. Property tax laws change frequently. For example, the recent community property laws changed to include a spouse's right to survivorship, allowing a surviving spouse to maintain previous tax basis without being penalized for inheriting the deceased spouse's portions of the properties.

> *Never give legal or tax advice to your clients. Always refer them to professionals. This applies to this text as well—don't rely on this information as legal or tax advice, but as a general guide only.*

We will discuss only the most basic concepts of reducing the income tax bite for the average citizen. A basic knowledge of the requirements necessary to take advantage of federal and state income tax incentives is helpful. Arranging the purchase of real estate in a manner that reduces your personal income taxes is the purpose of tax planning. This may allow you to reduce the income taxes you pay, or at least postpone such taxes.

Tax shelters reduce the amount of income taxes paid. Advise your clients to start tax planning for their future income tax returns now.

Figure 11-10 shows the five main areas of the federal and state income tax laws that are incentives to owning real estate. Each area will be explained only to give the general concepts or ideas behind the laws. To obtain the exact meaning and clauses of the law, an owner or investor should seek the help of a Certified Public Accountant for advice on accounting, or an attorney who is familiar with tax problems. Remember, these are only generalizations, and our income tax laws are more complex than the basic concepts presented here.

Figure 11-10

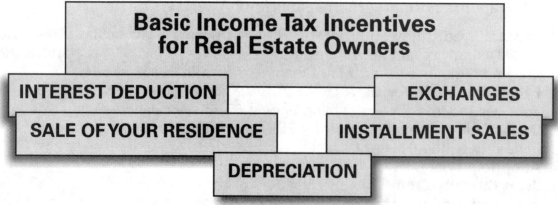

Basic Income Tax Incentives for Real Estate Owners

INTEREST DEDUCTION

EXCHANGES

SALE OF YOUR RESIDENCE

INSTALLMENT SALES

DEPRECIATION

VI. Taxes on Personal Residence

Homeowners can deduct these items from their income taxes based on their personal residence:

1. Mortgage Interest on Loan (Trust Deeds)
2. Property Taxes
3. Prepayment Penalties
4. Sale of a Residence (capital gains or losses)

A. DEDUCTION OF INTEREST

Deduction of interest on your client's home loan from his or her income taxes is one of the major tax advantages of owning real estate.

Buying a first and second home provides the average family with the biggest buffer against income taxes that they are likely to enjoy. Federal tax laws provide incentives to those who purchase a first and even a second home. When buying these homes your clients may finance up to $1 million ($1,000,000) with all the interest paid out during the year fully tax deductible. An additional deduction is available on the interest from home equity loans, taken for any purpose, even buying a second home, of up to $100,000 in principal. The $1,000,000 and $100,000 debit limit is a total applied against both first and second homes together or one owner-occupied home taken separately.

B. DEDUCTION OF PROPERTY TAXES

Property taxes on your first and second homes are deductible from your income taxes. This can make us feel a little better about paying local property taxes.

C. DEDUCTION OF PREPAYMENT PENALTIES

Prepayment penalties are also deductible from your clients' income taxes. If they pay off, or drastically reduce, their home loan balance, there may be a prepayment penalty.

Interest, property taxes, and prepayment penalties paid on a personal residence can be deducted from income taxes.

D. SALE OF A RESIDENCE

This capital gains exclusion is by far your client's best tax benefit of home ownership.

When selling a personal residence, the seller can exclude up to $250,000 ($500,000 if married) of any capital gain. This can be used only once every two years.

Federal income tax laws allow a taxpayer to exclude up to $250,000 of gain for each individual ($500,000 if married and on the title). This benefit may only be used once every two years for a residence.

While the law allows this deduction once every two years, **your client must reside in the home for two out of the last five years to qualify**. In other words, if he or she lives in the home for a year, then rents it out for three years, he or she would have to move back in for another year in order to take advantage of this tax break. Any personal residence acquired from a 1031 exchange has a holding time of five years.

Your clients can deduct a loss on sale of a personal residence if they have turned it into income producing property by renting it.

The only way to deduct a loss on the sale of a personal residence is to turn that property into income producing property first by renting it for an approved length of time. Then, any loss based on its sale is deductible because it is income producing property, not a personal residence.

VII. Taxes for Income Producing Properties

Investors of income producing properties can annually deduct these items from their income taxes:

1. Mortgage Interest on Loans (no maximum)
2. Property Taxes
3. Prepayment Penalties
4. Operating Expenses
5. Depreciation of Improvements

In addition to deducting mortgage interest (no maximum), property taxes, and prepayment penalties, income property owners can deduct operating expenses and depreciation. Owners cannot deduct losses due to vacancies.

A. DEPRECIATION OF BUSINESS PROPERTY (Federal and State)

DEPRECIATION FOR TAX PURPOSES is a yearly tax deduction for wear and tear on improved investment property that is deducted from the taxpayer's income on his or her income tax form. This deduction applies only to investment property or property used in a business, not on a taxpayer's personal residence. Apartment buildings, commercial buildings, and any building improvements to investment property can be depreciated. The land itself cannot be depreciated.

Only the buildings and other improvements on income, trade, or business property can be depreciated, not the land.

One can only depreciate property that is improved. Since land cannot usually be depreciated, only the improvements can be depreciated. Currently, the straight-line method is the accepted way to depreciate buildings and other improvements.

Residential property (homes and apartments) depreciation schedule:
  Minimum 27.5 years (Straight-line)

Commercial improvements depreciation schedule:
  Minimum 39 years (Straight-line)

The amount of depreciation must be spread uniformly over the useful life of the building (or improvements), with the same amount deducted each year (straight-line depreciation). Since most buildings in these inflationary times actually increase in value, depreciation is usually just a technique for postponing income taxes until the property is sold.

> **Example:** If you own a cabin in the desert that rent to vacationers that you bought for $100,000 and the land value is $25,000, this leaves improvements of $75,000. Divide this $75,000 by 28 years, giving you a depreciation of $2,678.57 for each year of the 28 years.

Remember: A property owner can deduct depreciation on income, trade, or business real property, not on a personal residence.

B. ADVANTAGES OF "SALE-LEASEBACK" (New Buyer Gets to Depreciate the Value of the Building)

If the owner of a business sells his or her building for cash, and then leases it back, the seller becomes a lessee and the buyer the lessor.

The advantage to the seller: all lease payments can be deducted from income taxes and he or she receives cash for the building.

The advantage to the buyer: he or she can use the purchase price as the new basis for depreciation and establish a new depreciation schedule.

Your seller, now a renter, deducts 100 percent of future rents paid. The new owner can depreciate new cost of buildings (even if they have been depreciated previously).

VIII. Sale of Real Property

A. CAPITAL ASSETS (Gains and Losses)

In real estate, a capital asset includes a personal residence (including a second home) and any other real estate, because they are long-term investments. When your client sells a primary residence (Note: it cannot be "other real estate"), there will probably be a capital gain. If that capital gain is not more than $250,000 for a single taxpayer or $500,000 for married taxpayers, there is a special capital gains tax exclusion whereby NO tax may be due. *CAPITAL GAINS are taxed at a lower rate than is ordinary income,* but *CAPITAL LOSSES can be deducted from capital gains.*

B. CALIFORNIANS PAY BOTH STATE AND FEDERAL INCOME TAXES

All gains for Individual income tax are as high as 13.3 percent in California.

Currently, the United States places a high tax burden on capital gains income. The current federal top marginal tax rate on long-term capital gains in the United States is 23.8 percent (20 percent top rate plus 3.8 percent tax to fund the Affordable Care Act).

Our state has the highest top marginal "Capital Gains" tax rate (Federal and California State together is a whopping 33 percent).

The Federal Capital Gains marginal rate is (20 percent top rate plus 3.8 percent tax to fund the Affordable Care Act, i.e., ObamaCare) and California's Capital Gains marginal rate of 13.3 percent adds up to a total of 33 percent.

If you want to relocate, consider the nine states with no personal income tax or Capital Gains Taxes (Alaska, Florida, Nevada, New Hampshire, South Dakota, Tennessee, Texas, Washington, and Wyoming). This tells us why so many businesses and wealthy entrepreneurs are leaving California for a tax-friendlier state.

C. FEDERAL INCOME TAX RATES

As the old saying goes, "Nothing in life is certain, except death and taxes." One other certainty is the constant change in federal tax rates. Income tax rates are progressive. *PROGRESSIVE TAXES are taxes where the rates (percentage paid) increase as the amount to be taxed increases.* So as you make more money, not only does the amount increase, but the rate at which income is taxed also increases. The end effect is that higher income families (the exact ones who usually own businesses and can expand job opportunities) pay most of the income taxes.

The *MARGINAL TAX RATE is the rate that the next dollar earned puts you into.*
REGRESSIVE TAXES use the same rate no matter how much is earned. Sales tax is an example of a regressive tax. The rate is the same, so in effect the poor pay a higher percent of their income.

Income tax rates are progressive. Sales tax rates are regressive.

D. ALTERNATIVE MINIMUM TAX (AMT) (Must Calculate Taxes Twice)

The *ALTERNATIVE MINIMUM TAX (AMT) requires taxpayers who make above a certain amount of gross income to figure their taxes twice.* First, they have to calculate their tax liability, using the actual itemized deductions method. They then have to refigure it, by limiting their itemized deductions and using the Alternative Minimum Tax rate, paying whichever is higher. Consult your tax preparer for more details.

E. ACCOUNTING FOR THE SALE OF REAL ESTATE (Investment/Commercial)

The method of determining a profit or loss on the sale of real property is spelled out by the Internal Revenue Service. Steps 1 and 2 must be completed before determining the profit or loss on a sale (Step 3).

"Adjusted cost basis" is the base cost, plus capital improvements, minus depreciation and sale expenses. As a broker, your commission is an expense of the sale.

(1) Cost Basis (Purchase price)	$500,000
+ Improvements	200,000
	$700,000
- Depreciation (tax records)	30,200
= Adjusted Cost Basis	$669,800
(2) Sale price	$1,000,000
- Sale Expenses	32,500
= Adjusted Sale Price	$967,500
(3) Adjusted Sale Price	$967,500
- Adjusted Cost Basis	669,800
= Capital Gain	$297,700

IX. Installment Sales and Exchanges

A. INSTALLMENT SALES OF REAL ESTATE

An *INSTALLMENT SALE is the sale of real estate in which the payments for the property extend over more than one calendar year*. Installment sales are used to spread a gain over two or more calendar years so that the entire gain is not taxed all in the first year. Our income tax system has progressive rates, which means that the higher the income, the higher the income tax rate for that year. If a person can spread a gain over more than one calendar year, the same income may be taxed at a lower rate.

By doing this, your seller avoids the disadvantages of paying for his or her entire gain in one year and, thereby, has a substantial savings on his or her income taxes. This method is usually used when selling large tracts of land held for a period of time or large buildings owned by one individual.

Installment sales are used because a gain is only taxed in the year that it is received. Spreading the gain over several years may drop you into a lower tax bracket (marginal tax rate).

B. EXCHANGES TAX-DEFERRED (Federal and State) (Section 1031 of the IRS Code)
1. Simultaneous 1031 Exchanges (Clients' Investment Properties)

Appreciated real estate investment property, when sold, creates a capital gain. The capital gain is usually taxed by the state up to 13.3%, plus federal income taxes up to 39.6%, in the year sold.

A simple explanation of *EXCHANGING is the trading of one property for another.*

Exchanging may allow your client to save a lot on income taxes now, yet obtain the same desired result as selling a property and buying a new investment property later.

Under Internal Revenue Service (IRS) Section 1031, property held for productive use in a trade or business is exchanged for like-kind property. Some of the reasons your clients may want to exchange property include the following:

1. Difficulty refinancing to improve property.
2. Trade a highly appreciated property for a property that generates a good cash flow income.
3. Trade non-productive land for a property that generates cash flow income.
4. Exchange to change lifestyle (less management worries).
5. Trade many properties for one big property.

1031 Exchanges can be complex. It is advisable to talk to a professional middleman or facilitator in the exchange of a property.

a. Like-Kind Property

A **LIKE-KIND PROPERTY** *is any real property held for investment that can be exchanged for other investment property under IRS Section 1031.* They include:

1. apartments and residential rentals;
2. commercial property;
3. industrial property; and
4. farms or land.

In a 1031 Exchange where an out-of-state property is involved, the owner must file a new form every year for tax purposes, as the California Franchise Tax Board (FTB) is concerned about collecting its appropriate taxes.

2. Starker Delayed Exchange

The Starker Court Case was the first court decision to allow a delayed exchange (up to 180 days). Simultaneous exchanges were common until Starker Delayed Exchanges came into existence.

A "delayed exchange" takes place (one day up to 180 days) in between the initial sale of the (relinquished) property and subsequent acquisitions of the new (replacement) property.

3. Reverse 1031 Exchanges

Another version of a 1031 exchange is the "Reverse" exchange.

A "reverse exchange" takes place (one day up to 180 days) in between the initial purchase of the new (replacement) property and subsequent sale of the old (relinquished) properties.

4. Accounting for Exchanges

An exchange may be a straight trade (tax-free) or one party may receive cash in addition to the property (partially tax-free). An exchange can be income tax free, partially taxed, or fully taxed, depending on the cash received and amount of mortgage loan relief in each particular exchange. Exchanges are too detailed to fully explain here, but it is a way of deferring, or possibly eliminating, income taxes on the transfer of real estate.

To defer all current taxes, a party in an exchange needs to receive a more valuable building with a larger loan on it than the current property, and to pay compensation to the other party for any difference in the equities. *Any net cash or net mortgage relief that a participant in an exchange might receive, in addition to the actual property, is known as **BOOT***. All boot is taxable to the extent of the gain in this partially tax-free exchange.

"Boot" is cash or debt relief where the receiver has recognized gain. If there is no boot in an exchange, the old basis is the new basis.

Exchanges are popular among apartment owners and commercial property investors. This is because these owners are usually in high-income tax brackets, and exchanging enables them to move up to a more valuable property without paying taxes on the gain. People in higher income tax brackets often keep their money invested in real estate, and they find exchanges to be a way of selling and buying simultaneously.

In 1031 exchanges, California property owners who live out of state must file a new form every year with the California Franchise Tax Board.

X. Dealer Property

DEALER PROPERTY is the inventory of properties held primarily for sale to customers. Hence, it is frequently called "inventory property," as it is held as the dealer's stock in trade like the merchandise on the shelves of a retail store. What constitutes dealer property is often the subject of much controversy; profits on the sale of such property are taxed as ordinary income (highest tax rate), and losses are treated as ordinary losses. During the holding period, the dealer is entitled to deductions for all expenses incurred on the property, except for depreciation allowances, unless the property also produces income or is held for such purposes.

Unlike investment, income, or business property, dealer property does not qualify for a tax-deferred exchange.

To be classified as a dealer, a number of factors are applied. Among these factors are: 1) frequency of sales; 2) dollar volume; 3) extent to which the property represents the taxpayer's major source of income; 4) listing and selling activities; 5) maintenance of a sales office; 6) reinvestment of sales proceeds into more real estate; 7) evidence that the property was purchased for immediate resale; 8) real estate license status; 9) subdivision activity; and 10) amount of income generated from the property.

Brokers have to be careful or they may be classified as "dealers," which has few tax advantages.

The taxpayer's entire background in real estate is evaluated before a property sale is labeled a "dealer sale of inventory." Each case is judged on the facts. Real estate licensees, subdividers, developers, and builders are naturally suspect, but the fact that they are more knowledgeable in real estate matters does not conclusively place them in the dealer category. Indeed, they may be considered investors in some transactions and dealers in others. Each sale should be explained in terms of economic justification or overriding consideration, and not judged solely on the fact of its quick turnover.

XI. We Are Now Tax Collectors (Federal and State Income Tax Laws)

A. FEDERAL TAX COLLECTION REQUIREMENTS AND EXEMPTIONS (If a Foreigner)

If your client is buying property from foreign investors (sellers), your buyer is required to set aside 10 percent of the purchase price for the Internal Revenue Service. This 10 percent withholding is kept by the IRS to ensure that property capital gains taxes are paid on the transaction. Both the buyer and broker/escrow company share liability.

If this amount is not withheld, you, as the broker/escrow company, may be liable for the full amount of the tax not paid.

This law holds brokers responsible to check the citizenship of all sellers and see to it that the buyer retains either a 10 percent deposit, an affidavit from the seller stating that he or she is not a foreigner, or a waiver from the IRS. Residential property, purchased for under $300,000 and to be used as the buyer's residence, is exempted from this withholding.

The key points for licensees to remember are these:

1. **Inquire** into the citizenship or nonforeign status of all sellers of **residential** properties priced at **$300,000 or more**, even if a foreigner holds only partial or syndicate interest.

2. **Require a statement of nonforeign status** as part of the listing agreement.

3. Do not discriminate. Require this information of all sellers in transactions of $300,000 or more, even if someone does not appear to be an alien.

The CAR® Seller's Affidavit of Nonforeign Status and/or California Withholding Exemption (AS) (see Chapter 4, Figure 4-2) is a form for the seller to sign swearing that he or she is not a nonresident alien. If the seller completes the lower portion of this sworn statement, the buyer and broker may no longer be liable for any portions of unpaid taxes.

A Buyer's Affidavit form is available from CAR®. This form states that the sales price is less than $300,000 and that the property will be used as a residence. It is signed by the buyer under penalty of perjury. If these two considerations can be met, the buyer is immediately exempted from the withholding requirement. If neither of these forms can truthfully be completed, then the broker should see to it that 10 percent of the sales price is withheld in escrow, or that the proper waiver is obtained from the IRS. The escrow officer will help you with this matter.

B. STATE TAX COLLECTION REQUIREMENTS AND EXEMPTIONS (If a Foreigner or Resident of Another State)

If your client is buying property from foreign or out-of-state investors, or non-owner occupied properties, he or she may be required to set aside 3.3 percent of the sales price for the Franchise Tax Board. If this amount is not withheld, you, as the broker, and the buyer may be liable for the full amount of income taxes not paid. Escrow usually handles this, but the buyer and broker are responsible.

The exemptions from the buyer withholding 3.3 percent of the sales price for the Franchise Tax Board are:

1. Sales price is $100,000 or less.

2. Property is seller's principal residence, under certain conditions.

3. Seller signs California Residency Declaration.

4. Seller receives a waiver – Franchise Tax Board Form 593-C.

These laws put the burden on the buyer, not the seller. Escrow officers will help with these requirements. Buyer and broker must retain the documentation for five years.

XII. Other Taxes Paid by Brokers

A. BUSINESS LICENSE TAXES (City Taxes)

*A city may levy a tax against real estate brokerage firms, which is based upon the gross receipts, through a **BUSINESS LICENSE TAX**. In most areas of California, this annual city business license tax is a nominal amount that usually starts at about $100. Other city taxes may also include employee payroll taxes.*

A city tax on a real estate brokerage firm's gross receipts is called a business license tax.

A. OTHER CALIFORNIA TAXES

1. **State Sales Tax:** California's state-only sales tax is 6.50 percent. There is a statewide county tax of 1%, and therefore, the lowest rate anywhere in California is 7.5%. Rates will be higher in cities and counties with special taxing districts— between 1.0 percent and 3.5 percent.

2. **Gasoline Tax:** 68.18 cents/gallon (Includes all taxes).

3. **Diesel Fuel Tax:** 74.94 cents/gallon (Includes all taxes).

4. **Cigarette Tax:** 87 cents/$2.00 ballot measure.

5. **Internet purchases sale taxes for Californians:** Online business must collect sales tax on Internet sales within California from customers if mail order businesses are an out-of-state seller and have a California physical presence, such as a(n) warehouse, store, or office or sales representative.

XIII. CHAPTER SUMMARY

Real property taxes are determined by the value of the real property (**ad valorem**), and the property is reassessed each time a property is sold at 1% of its selling price. The **County Assessor** assesses property, the **County Tax Collector** collects taxes. **Proposition 13** limits the amount of taxes to 1% of the market value of the property plus a cumulative increase of 2% in assessed value each year thereafter, called **assessed valuation**.

Property taxes due (or even not yet due and payable) are liens against that specific property. Important **tax dates** include **November 1** (first installment), **December 10** (first installment is delinquent), **February 1** (second installment) and **April 10** (second installment is delinquent), or remember: No Darn Fooling Around (NDFA).

The **homeowner's property tax exemption** is $7,000 of assessed valuation. California has no exemption for low-income families. It does have senior citizen and disabled person postponements, as well as veterans' and nonprofit organizations' tax exemptions.

Local improvement taxes for off-site improvements, like streets, sewers, irrigation, etc., are called **special assessment taxes**. Additional taxes may be incurred, including: **documentary transfer taxes, Mello-Roos liens** (construction bonds for which disclosure is required), **federal gift taxes**, and **federal estate taxes**.

Interest, property taxes, and prepayment penalties paid on a personal residence can be deducted from income taxes. Federal income tax laws allow a taxpayer to exclude up to $250,000 of gain for each individual ($500,000 if married and on title). When you sell your home (capital asset), a capital gain or loss may result. **Capital gains** are taxed at a lower rate (up to 13.3 percent) than ordinary income tax rates.

A loss on a sale of a personal residence can also be deducted if it is turned into **income producing property** by renting it. Income property owners can deduct **mortgage interest**, **property taxes**, and **prepayment penalties**, as well as **operating expenses** and **depreciation**, but not losses due to vacancies. If a business owner sells a building for cash, then leases it back (a **sale-leaseback**), the seller becomes the lessee and the buyer the lessor, and the seller can deduct 100% of future rents paid.

Federal taxes are **progressive**, meaning the percentage paid increases as the amount to be taxed increases, which is the opposite of sales taxes, which are **regressive**.

In addition to depreciation, two major tax benefits of owning income producing property are **installment sales** (gain is "only taxed" in the year it is received) and **1031 tax-deferred exchanges** (a means of deferring or eliminating income taxes on property transfers). Cash or debt relief gained in a tax deferred exchange is known as **boot**.

Persons buying property from **foreign investors** are required to set aside 10% of the purchase price for the IRS to insure the property capital gains taxes are paid on the transaction. An additional 3.3% of the sales price for the Franchise Tax Board may also have to be withheld. In both cases, the burden is on the buyer and broker, not the seller. Brokers may also have to pay a **business license tax**, which is a city tax based on gross receipts.

XIV. MATCHING VOCABULARY Fill in the blanks with the correct letter

A. $1 million dollars
B. Ad valorem tax
C. April 10
D. A tax shelter
E. Boot
F. County assessor
G. County tax collector
H. December 10

I. Depreciation
J. Documentary transfer tax
K. Donor
L. February 1
M. Homeowner's Property tax exemption
N. Like-kind property

O. Mello-Roos
P. New construction
Q. November 1
R. Progressive taxes
S. Proposition 13
T. Real property taxes
U. Special assessment tax
V. Taxable alteration

1. _____ These taxes are determined according to the value of the real property owned, and are paid annually or semi-annually.
2. _____ A tax that is charged in proportion to the value of the property.
3. _____ The county officer who has the responsibility of determining the assessed valuation of land, improvements, and personal property used in business.
4. _____ The county officer who collects the real property taxes.
5. _____ This law limits the amount of property taxes to a maximum of 1 percent of the March 1, 1975, market value of the property plus the cumulative increase of 2 percent in market value each year thereafter.
6. _____ Any addition or improvement to land, including alterations of existing improvements if the alterations result in conversion to another use or an extension of the economic life of the improvement.
7. _____ Anything that increases the usefulness of the structure, such as the addition of a bedroom or bathroom.
8. _____ A tax deduction on the property tax bill that allows the owner to get a tax break by reducing the assessed value for tax computation purposes by $7,000.
9. _____ The first installment of property tax is due:
10. _____ The first installment of property tax is delinquent:
11. _____ The second installment of property tax is due:
12. _____ The second installment of property tax is delinquent:
13. _____ This tax is levied by a city council or a county board of supervisors often, with the voters' approval, for the cost of specific local improvements such as streets, sewers, irrigation, or drainage.
14. _____ Municipal bonds issued to fund streets, sewers, and other infrastructure needs before a housing development is built.

15. _____ This documentary tax is applied to the consideration paid or money borrowed when transferring property, except for any remaining loans or liens on the property.

16. _____ What a person is called who gives real property as a gift.

17. _____ Over a lifetime, a husband and wife may give away how much money without paying any gift tax?

18. _____ This type of deduction can reduce the amount of income taxes paid.

19. _____ Taxes where the marginal income rates increase as the amount to be taxed increases.

20. _____ A yearly tax deduction for wear and tear on improved investment real property that is deducted from the taxpayer's income on his or her income tax form.

21. _____ Any real property held for investment that can be exchanged for other investment property under IRS Section 1031.

22. _____ Any net cash or net mortgage relief that a participant in an exchange might receive, in addition to the actual property.

See Page 610 for Answers

XV. CHAPTER QUIZ

1. The first installment on property taxes would be considered delinquent after 5:00 P.M. on:

　a. July 10.
　b. April 10.
　c. December 10.
　d. March 10.

2. The second installment on property taxes becomes due on:

　a. June 30.
　b. February 1.
　c. March 1.
　d. November 1.

3. Of the following, which one is a progressive tax?

　a. Gas Tax
　b. Income Tax
　c. Sales Tax
　d. All of the above

4. A tax that is charged in proportion to the value of the property is referred to as a(n):

　a. progressive tax.
　b. progression tax.
　c. ad valorem tax.
　d. excise tax.

5. Proposition 13 set the maximum amount property taxes can increase each year at:

a. 1 percent.
b. 2 percent.
c. 5 percent.
d. 10 percent.

6. How much gain (profit) can one person (who lived in his or her house for two of the last five years) exclude from income taxes on the sale of that home?

a. $100,000
b. $200,000
c. $250,000
d. $500,000

7. Which of the following is TRUE concerning long term capital gains?

a. Capital gains are taxed at a lower rate than ordinary income tax rates.
b. Captial gains are taxed at a higher rate than ordinary income tax rates.
c. Captial gains are taxed at the same rate as ordinary income tax rates.
d. Capital gains are not taxed.

8. The documentary transfer tax is how much per $1,000 of new loans and considerations?

a. 6 percent
b. $1.10
c. $.55
d. None of the above

9. Another word for cash or debt relief is:

a. boot.
b. shoe.
c. pocket money.
d. none of the above.

10. The person who receives a gift is called a:

a. trustor.
b. donee.
c. donor.
d. none of the above.

ANSWERS: 1. c; 2. b; 3. b; 4. c; 5. b; 6. c; 7. a; 8. b; 9. a; 10. b

REAL ESTATE
INVESTMENTS
IN THE CENTER
OF

ME
XI
CO

GR

The
Real Esta
La Revista de Bienes
B

MÉXICO

Incluye: Ciudad de México, Cancún, Celaya, Cuernavaca, y Valle

Se Publica cada 4 Semanas

NOTE: THE

30 Y

CUSTOM

FULL

e

Raíce

Investing and Other Broker-Related Fields

This chapter covers real property investments as well as other broker-related fields and businesses. From the investment perspective it explains why people invest in income-producing real estate, including the numerous benefits derived from maintaining an income cash flow from real estate. It covers the financing of income properties. The appraisal techniques for residential income-producing properties is emphasized, as this will allow you to better advise your clients as to how to invest in and maintain these rentable properties. As a broker you are not limited to just listing and selling properties but have opportunities to sell businesses, manage properties, run escrow operations and, with the proper CalBRE licensing MLO endorsement requirements, become a loan broker, which is covered by the SAFE Act.

I. Why Invest in Real Estate?

People invest in property for a variety of reasons: to meet their personal goals and objectives, to give them a means to meet their other financial retirement commitments, and to make money.

A. OBJECTIVES

Investors may be seeking additional income through well-chosen properties to act as an income tax shelter to help reduce the bite on otherwise taxable income and appreciation. Other considerations may be prestige, personal enjoyment in the properties or activities, and the creation of an estate. You need to help your investor decide which of these, or which combination, is important in order to select the income producing property most likely to accomplish those objectives.

The number one objective for investing in real estate is to make money.

B. CAPACITY

The investor in real estate needs to have the financial ability to handle carrying the costs of the investment—such as cash down payment, debt service (loan payments), and taxes—and still retain a cash reserve for emergencies.

The costs of the monthly operating expenses continue to escalate.

CHAPTER OUTLINE

C. SOUNDNESS

After deciding on objectives and analyzing your financial investor's capacity to carry a given amount of debt, the economic health of the property's neighborhood must be considered. This includes the economic trends of the surrounding area, growth trends in the community, zoning (both current and planned), and income projections.

The investment should be sound from an economic point of view, that is, investors ought to look beyond projected figures. Projected figures should reflect financial reality. Paper figures could include market and economic analysis. The market for the property should be properly and objectively analyzed. There should be a real need for the revenue services (rents, sales, and fees) the property is expected to produce. All too often, only income tax consequences are presented to the buyer, without regard to the basic financial soundness of the venture. It's important to remember that the income tax treatment of income property may change over the years.

II. Benefits of Investing

Income properties are generally high-priced real estate. As such, you can expect larger commissions than you would earn selling single-unit properties.

Whether investment factors are beneficial or not depends on the degree to which they meet or exceed your investor's specific objectives. In the following discussions, you'll discover how financially rewarding real estate investing can be over a period of time and become aware of some cautionary factors as well.

A. TAX SHELTER (Ways to Reduce Taxable Income)

Your clients in high income tax brackets may benefit from tax planning to conserve part of their income through wise planning, selection, and operation of an income producing property. Depreciation expenses on real and personal property may reduce a portion of the taxable cash flow generated from the operation of the property. The amount of your investor's income subject to ordinary income tax rates can be reduced through proper deductions for operating expenses from the rental income generated from the investment property. Many highly taxed investors seek ways to reduce a large amount of their income subject to property taxation. They may also reduce their income tax liability on their regular (job) income from wages or salary.

B. OTHER TAX BENEFITS

As demonstrated in Chapter 11, capital gains can be mainly deferred through one of several selling methods: 1) a tax-free exchange, 2) a deferred sale, or 3) an installment sale. As a side benefit, the proceeds from a profitable sale could be reinvested into another profitable venture.

C. APPRECIATION POTENTIAL

While population increase, land does not!

Growth through **APPRECIATION** (*selling a property for more than it's worth*) is a function of supply and demand, economic conditions, influx of population, inflation, and scarcity. The amount of land is fixed in relation to the demand. This tends to drive prices upward over a given period of time. One trait of real estate, especially urban property, is the ability to determine its growth potential, within reasonable limits.

D. HEDGE AGAINST INFLATION

California's real estate usually rebounds from cycles and continues to appreciate in value over the long run.

Real estate tends to beat the fluctuations of the purchasing power of the U.S. Dollar.

During inflationary periods, the cost of everything rises, including real estate. However, real estate historically outpaces inflation, although during a recession, housing prices may dip.

E. INCOME

"Cash flow" (either positive or negative) is the difference between the income generated from an income property and the expenses associated with it, including property taxes, mortgage payments, and operating expenses.

Many investors purchase property with the objective of providing a cash annuity for themselves. How much this monthly cash income will be is dependent upon many variables, the most important of which are the size of the investment and the amount of leverage (debt) and interest rate involved. For example, a well-managed apartment house containing, say, 30 units, will provide the investor with a very high monthly cash income, while a smaller expensive property encumbered with a large trust deed loan will net little, if any, cash flow. Properly structured, the property could well provide the investor with an independent (or supplemental) source of retirement funds.

F. INTERIM USE

INTERIM USE *means a property temporarily generates rents for other than its future zoned use.* Real property ownership offers the purchaser of a ranch, farm, or other investment the opportunity to use the property to make some income while waiting for appreciation of value to take place. This future increase in value may come from a zoning change, increase in demand, and/or inflation. In a big city, vacant land might be used for some interim use, like a parking lot or a golf driving range, until it is slated for development.

G. STABILITY

Many types of real estate, particularly commercial and industrial properties, enjoy long-term leases with top corporations, producing a dependable, stable investment for as long as twenty years or more. In the case of apartments, strong neighborhood patterns can produce the same kind of effect as long-term leases, based upon such things as favorable zoning and community planning, shopping conveniences, and transportation routes.

Growth trends can often be charted in such a way that educated investors can see the benefits of owning. Demographic trends require careful analysis and the assistance of well-informed brokers.

H. CONTROL AND USE

As a real estate professional, you have the opportunity to assist your investors to thoroughly study the environment and economic background of their investments before buying. This is achieved by analyzing them for income tax benefits, inflation hedge, financing opportunities, income and cash flow appreciation, and stability. All of these can be changed from time-to-time to serve the goal of improving the investment. Rezoning of a property, for example, can enhance its highest and best use, which could increase its value. A new demand pattern from lessees can increase rents. That improves gross income and the value of the income property.

I. REFINANCING (To Buy More Property)

Let's take the case of one of your clients who has an investment property with a large equity. If your owner decides to refinance the property in order to purchase more income property, three things can be accomplished. First, the cash proceeds from refinancing are currently tax-free. Second, the interest paid on the new debt is fully tax deductible. Third, your investor is acquiring another investment property, adding to his or her worth, and you have gained another commission.

J. AMENITIES

Other benefits to the investor include pride of ownership, security, status, achievement, estate building, and the opportunity to improve profits.

Non-liquidity is the only downside to owning real estate. It takes time to sell real estate and turn it into cash.

III. Financing Income Properties

One of the outstanding advantages of income-producing real estate is the financing and refinancing opportunities available to the investor. The type of leverage he or she is seeking may be available through a variety of lenders.

A. SOURCES OF FINANCING

Miscellaneous sources of funds needed for the purchase of investment properties include: syndicates and trusts (to be discussed in a separate section), real estate bonds and debentures, bank-administered pension trust funds, sellers under purchase money transactions and land contracts, and a variety of others to a lesser degree. Real estate syndicates and REITs (real estate investment trusts) have proved to be useful devices for higher-income investors as well as small investors who pool their resources to develop and operate residential income and commercial properties. Seller carryback purchase money trust deeds and contracts of sales are, perhaps, the most important sources of financing for raw land and many special purpose projects.

During tight money periods in particular, sellers frequently become the only source of financing for raw land and special purpose projects, wherein the seller effectively operates as a bank, actually supplying the financing, which the buyer agrees to replace when, and if, outside financing can be secured.

Of the three large institutional lending sources available for residential property, at least two are also active, to varying degrees, in financing investment properties. As such, a summary of these lending sources bears repeating here.

SAVINGS BANKS specialize in housing loans, particularly for single-family dwellings up to four units. However, increasingly, they are expanding into the large apartment unit's market. They are not active in special purpose properties, such as individual and commercial buildings.

COMMERCIAL BANKS are very active in the urban mortgage market. Banks are short-term lenders, so an investor who is seeking a high-leverage position or low payments over a long period will find the commercial bank inadequate.

Commercial banks make the majority of their funds available for high-interest, short-term loans, like credit cards, automobile, and construction loans.

LIFE INSURANCE COMPANIES, along with their correspondents, show a different pattern of lending than the other institutions. They invest in large commercial projects, like shopping malls, and serve markets far away from their home offices.

IV. Your Role in the Investment Process

What follows is a discussion of selling investment real property. Naturally, different salespeople have different approaches to selling. The following suggestions are, in the authors' opinions, the best approach to marketing.

A. APARTMENT PROSPECTING AND MARKETING

Sources of prospects for listing and buying investment properties include many of the same as those for residential properties. While it may be true that the sale of a home appeals more to your prospect's emotions, and that the sale of investments relies more on an economic accounting and rational approach, similarities do exist. It was pointed out previously that the reasons for investing include providing supplemental income or building an estate. Why not approach the sellers of a home with the idea

that they replace their home with a four-plex, occupy one of the units, and rent out the other three? This could well be the start of a happy, long-term broker/client relationship as the client increases his or her investments.

Suppose that you were the listing agent on a ten-unit apartment house. You would advertise in the newspapers, by direct mailing to your prospect list, through the multiple listing services and their outsources, like Realtor.com®, so that other brokers will become aware of the new offering.

Don't overlook the current tenants as potential buyers.

After all, tenants very likely are satisfied with the property, location, and so on, or they would not be living there. Many tenants with no children and a working spouse will have more money saved than single occupants. These tenants may consequently need more shelter from income taxes and are, in many ways, logical candidates for purchasing the property. It might be noted that commercial property tenants are even more likely prospects than residential tenants. You should consider sending a letter to the tenants informing them of the sale.

1. Getting the Listing

Listing an apartment house is like listing a house. You meet the owners, ask searching questions, come prepared with valuation data, and create opportunities for the sellers by showing them how the proceeds can be reinvested.

In buying income-producing property, greater emphasis is placed on financial benefits than on sentimental attachments.

When gathering information, you'll also need to get detailed facts about the property, such as:

1. needed repairs,
2. condition of units,
3. quality of tenants,
4. rent schedules,
5. lease terms,
6. vacancy factors, and
7. evaluation of income and expenses.

Showing the owners how they can improve their estate or income through selling and buying or exchanging for more profitable property, will help you secure a saleable listing. Point out, for example, how the owners' objectives are no longer being met if their property has been **FULLY DEPRECIATED**, *which menas that the property has already been charged with the maximum amount of depreciation allowed by the IRS for accounting purposes,* or has a low **BOOK VALUE**, *meaning the value of the property is low according to its balance sheet account balance.* This might promote a listing at a price that will sell.

The owner of a fully depreciated property is an excellent listing prospect!

B. INVESTMENT PLANNING AND COUNSELING

As a broker who expects to build up a following in the field of real estate investments, you will need to do more than the typical agent. To pick up repeat business, you will have to earn the respect and confidence of your clients. This can come only with a thorough understanding of your client's total financial and family picture. A confidential file should be maintained for each of your clients. By integrating all of the data and information about the client, you're in a better position to render superior service.

Investment planning may be thought of as the integration of a number of steps, starting with a thorough analysis of your client's investment requirements.

At some point, conferring with your client's attorney, accountant, or business advisor may be advisable.

Researching and selecting properties to meet the financial objectives of your client is the second step. A decision to buy a particular property is then made, and you negotiate its acquisition, followed by title search and escrow. Management of the property is next—to safeguard the investment, to minimize expenses, and to maximize profits. Along every step of the way, you must be aware of change—offering suggestions and making recommendations as the circumstances warrant.

V. Residential Income Properties

The factors to be considered before your client purchases an apartment house, and the advantages and disadvantages of such a purchase, are about the same as in any income producing real estate investment. In this section, analysis, valuation, management, and the rental market will be explained in detail.

A. PROPERTY ANALYSIS (Appraisal)

The preparation of a comprehensive income and expense analysis on a given apartment project is a complicated and difficult process. The income and expense analysis should be focused on the future operating income of the building.

Because most apartments are held for long-term investment, the third year, the seventh year, and the tenth year can all be as important to the investor as the first year.

To understand the analysis of an income-producing property, an Income Property—Residential Statement is shown in **Figure 12-1**. A four-unit apartment house listed at $468,000 is illustrated, along with all the pertinent data. You should study the form in order to understand the financial details of the rental property.

PRICE is the listing price; the proposed sale price. LOANS include all first and junior trust deeds that comprise the financing (loans) for the purchaser. DOWN PAYMENT is the amount the buyer is to pay towards the purchase price. SCHEDULED INCOME is that gross income that the property would generate if there were no vacancies.

Figure 12-1 Income Property - Residential Statement

PRESENTED BY CBA Realtors
6515 Van Nuys Blvd.
Van Nuys, CA 91411
Tele: 818-786-2663

IMPROVEMENT 4 unit apartment building
ADDRESS 12548 Compton Ave.
CITY Compton
(3) BLOCKS N (S) OF Broadview Blvd.
(1) BLOCKS E (W) OF Watts Ave.
SALES REPRESENTATIVE L. Galivez
TELEPHONE 818-781-5937
SHOWING INSTRUCTIONS Call Mr. F. Topik
OWNER (MANAGER) TENANT
TELEPHONE 818-769-2929 _____ KEY _____

(Picture of property or business card may be placed in above space)

SPECIAL FEATURES

GENERAL INFORMATION

LOT SIZE 90 x 150 ____ ZONE R-3 ___ AGE 11 __ CONST La & Stucco ___ ELEVATOR No __ STYLE English Tudor
LEGAL Lot 14, Tract 16829 _____ PARKING 10 stalls ___ STORIES 2 ___ SEWER Y ___ HEAT F/A __ AIR COND Y

EXISTING INFORMATION NO YEARS   **INVESTMENT INFORMATION BASED ON**

FIRST LOAN 225,000 PYMT 2,124 INT 9 ORIG 25 TO GO 14   FIRST LOAN 300,000 PAYMENT 3,000 INT 11 NO YRS 5
LENDER Housing Savings Bank LOCKED IN YES __ NO X   LENDER Seller
SECOND LOAN 24,000 PYMT 360 INT 9 DUE 2010 ACCEL NO   SECOND LOAN_____ PAYMENT____ INT___ DUE___
LENDER Private party   LENDER
OTHER LOANS None PYMT ____ INT ___ DUE ____ ACCEL____   SELLER WILL CARRY Above PAYMENT____ INT__ DUE___

SCHEDULED INCOME

#	DESC	RENT
1	3 bd - 2 ba	$ 1,590
2	2 bd - 1.5 ba	$ 1,410
3	2 bd - 1.5 ba	$ 1,410
4	3 bd - 2 ba	$ 1,590

TOTAL SCHEDULED MONTHLY INCOME $ 4,730

Above information is from sources believed reliable but not guaranteed.

© 2015 ETC., Inc.

PROJECTED OPERATING EXPENSES:

Taxes	$ 5,850
Insurance F&L	$ 3,600
License & Fees	$ 195
Utilities	
Water	$ 1,050
Electricity	$ 2,487
Gas	$ 1,440
Management	$ 3,600
	$
Trash	$ 1,440
Gardener	$ 1,080
Maintenance (Est.) ___%$	7,200
Other	$
TOTAL	$ 27,942

ASSESSED VALUE

	Amount	Percent
Land	$ 93,600	20 %
Improvement	$ 369,720	79 %
Pers Prop	$ 4,680	1 %
TOTAL	$ 468,000	100%

PROJECTED INVESTMENT INFORMATION:

Price	$ 468,000
Loan (1)	$ 300,000
Down Payment	$ 168,000
Scheduled Income	$ 72,000
Vacancy Factor (Est.) 2 %	$ 1,440
Gross Operating Income	$ 70,560
Projected Operating Expenses	$ 27,942
Net Operating Income (Est.)	$ 42,618
Loan Payments	$ 36,000
Gross Spendable (Est.)	$ 6,618
Furniture Reserve (Est.)	$ 750
Carpet Reserve (Est.)	$ 600
Adj. Gross Spendable (Est.)	$ 5,268
Paid on Principal	$ 3,048
Projected Total Return	$ 8,316
Earns 9.11	% on Sale Price
Spendable at 3.13	% on Down Payment
Earns 4.95	% on Down Payment
Purchase Price is 6.5	Times Gross

The steps listed below are arranged in the order you will need to follow to complete a property analysis.

1. Potential Gross Income

POTENTIAL GROSS INCOME is the total income that the property is capable of producing at full occupancy, without any deductions for expenses. For example, if the rental rate for a two-bedroom unit is $1,410 per month, an apartment with ten two-bedroom units would have a potential gross income of $14,100 per month (10 x $1,410).

VACANCY FACTOR is an allowance for vacancies and uncollectible rents. Few, if any, properties will maintain a fully occupied building year after year. The amount of allowance will vary from one apartment building to another, depending on the location, rent schedule, amenities, management, and other factors. Ordinarily, a five percent minimum vacancy should be shown even if there are no present or recent vacancies. An exception might be for rental homes or very small apartment buildings in well-located areas, where high occupancy can be demonstrated on a continuous basis.

Vacancies can be calculated in one of three ways: 1) actual current vacancy as shown by the records; 2) an average percentage of historical vacancies for the subject property; or 3) by checking out vacancies for comparable properties in the area. This last method can be accomplished by determining the number of idle electric meters, periodic post office surveys, statistical data revealed by institutional lenders and some governmental agencies, and personal interviews with apartment house owners, landlords, and tenants.

As a professional, you should counsel with your apartment investors to estimate at least a five percent vacancy factor, even if it is currently lower. No vacancies could mean the the rents are too low!

2. Effective Gross Income

EFFECTIVE GROSS INCOME is the scheduled gross income adjusted (subtracting) for vacancy. It represents the amount of money the owner will receive from rent collections before deductions for expenses and debts. *OPERATING EXPENSES include fixed and variable expenses, as detailed in the bottom half of the Income Property Statement.* You can remember the largest of these expenditures, which are found in every statement, by an acronym **MITUM**. *The initials stand for Maintenance, Insurance (not interest), Taxes (not trust deed), Utilities, and Management (not mortgage).* These are items which are operational in nature, and are encountered whether the property is fully financed or free and clear. Therefore, loan payments are not included, nor are depreciation allowances or provision for income taxes.

Operating expenses do not include loan payments, depreciation allowances, or income tax provisions, which are not considerations in the Net Operating Income (NOI).

3. Net Operating Income

NET OPERATING INCOME (NOI) is the form of income that is most often used in direct capitalization. Operating expenses are subtracted from effective gross income. Net operating income is a more reliable indicator of value than potential or effective gross income because it represents the amount of income (after all net operating expenses) that is available as a return to the investor. Properties with similar gross incomes may have widely different net operating incomes due to differences in operating expenses.

Example: Two properties each have effective gross incomes of $900,000 per year. Property A has annual operating expenses of $540,000 per year, while Property B has annual operating expenses of $720,000. In this case, Property A has twice as much net operating income as Property B, even though their effective gross incomes are the same.

Property A: $900,000 - $540,000 = $360,000 NOI

Property B: $900,000 - $720,000 = $180,000 NOI   © 2015 ETC., Inc.

To determine net operating income (NOI), all the operating expenses for the property are subtracted from the effective gross income. Payments on principal and interest are not deducted. Depreciation is not a cash expense and is not deducted.

OPERATING EXPENSES are any ongoing expenses that are necessary to maintain the flow of income from the property. For appraisal purposes, operating expenses fall into three categories:

1. fixed expenses,
2. variable expenses, and
3. reserves for replacement.

*FIXED EXPENSES are operating expenses that **do not** vary depending on the occupancy of the property.* They must be paid regardless of whether the property is leased or vacant. The most common examples of fixed expenses are property taxes and hazard insurance premiums. In California, an apartment complex with 16 or mor eunits requires an **onsite property manager**.

*VARIABLE EXPENSES are operating expenses that **do** vary depending on occupancy.* They may include a variety of expenses, such as utility costs, property management fees, cleaning and maintenance expenses, and leasing commissions.

RESERVES FOR REPLACEMENT are funds that are set aside for replacing short-lived components of the property. A SHORT-LIVED COMPONENT is an item that has a life span that is less than the expected life of the building, such as roofing or mechanical equipment. Normally, the amount of the reserves is calculated by dividing the replacement cost of the item by its remaining useful life in years.

Example: The cost to replace the roofing on a building is $24,000. If the existing roof has a remaining useful life of 10 years, the annual amount to be set aside for replacement would be $2,400.

$24,000 ÷ 10 years = $2,400

Note that some items that are often listed as expenses for accounting or tax purposes are not included as operating expenses when calculating net operating income. The most notable of these are mortgage principal and interest, depreciation (book depreciation), and income taxes.

4. Times Gross (Estimation)

Real estate agents often refer to the gross income multiplier as the "times gross." *TIMES GROSS is simply the proposed selling price divided by the scheduled gross income, with the multiple used as a ballpark figure to weigh the prospective value of the investment.*

Example: The subject property has potential gross income of $108,000 per year. The appraiser has determined that the annual potential gross income multiplier for this type of property is "11." The value of the property, therefore, is estimated to be:

$1,188,000 ($108,000 x 11)

Multipliers are most often used to convert gross income to value. The use of gross income multipliers is limited almost exclusively to appraisers of single-family and small multi-family residences.

While times gross is a useful tool to screen out properties, it measures only the quantity of income and, therefore, should be considered along with other tests to determine its value as an acceptable investment. All too often, however, brokers misuse it by ignoring other factors that measure the quality and durability of the income, like the age of the property.

Investors are looking for a low (or at least reasonable) times gross of eight or less. The higher the gross multiplier, the higher the price.

5. Capitalization of Net Income

There are a number of techniques that are employed in the determination of capitalization. However, all have a simple common denominator. *The net operating income is divided by the selling price to determine the appropriate CAPITALIZATION RATE (CAP RATE).* As a simple example of its application, the worksheet in Figure 12-1 shows the breakdown of a property listed at $468,000 whose net operating income (N.O.I.) is $42,618. This represents a 9.1 percent capitalization rate, or yield, arrived at as follows:

$$\frac{\text{Net Operating Income}}{\text{Sales Price}} = \frac{\$42,618}{\$468,000} = 9.1\% \text{ Capitalization Rate}$$

Stated differently, if four-unit apartment buildings of this grade and quality attract investors only if they offer a 9.1 percent rate of return, the cap rate or yield is 9.1 percent. Thus, if records reveal that a certain income-producing property is producing a net operating income of $42,618, and the prospective purchaser wants at least a 9.1 percent return on his or her total investment, he or she will not pay more than $468,000. The capitalized value as indicated by the net income, computed as follows:

$$\frac{\text{Net Operating Income}}{\text{Cap Rate}} = \frac{\$42,618}{9.1\%} = \$468,000 \textbf{ Selling Price}$$

Simple substitution of other numbers for those shown in the denominator will reveal larger or smaller amounts of value, assuming the purchaser requires at least a 9.1 percent return. For instance, if the annual net operating income was $91,000, the capitalized value ($91,000 ÷ 9.1%) would indicate the value of $1 million. In contrast, if the income after allowance for all operating expenses was, say, only $18,200, then the investor could afford to pay only as much as $200,000 ($18,200 ÷ 9.1%) and still get a return of 9.1 percent.

While it's important to know how cap rates are determined, in actual practice, most agents will just make a phone call to a friendly appraiser and ask what the estimated cap rate is for such an investment.

B. CHARACTERISTICS OF THE RENTAL MARKET
1. Income Characteristics

The success of an apartment project depends to a considerable extent upon the income characteristics of families attracted to the area. The changing distribution of income should be analyzed with an eye toward future possibilities for increasing rent in the project or future necessities to decrease rent.

2. Rent-to-Income Relationships

In California, it is generally held that across the income range a family can, or will, pay about 25 to 38 percent of its income for shelter.

This varies, however, from a lower income range to a higher income range, and this variance could be a critical matter in determining future rents.

3. Current Rental Ranges

In this part of the study, an attempt is made to analyze competition in a particular study area. The percentage of families prepared to pay a certain amount of money for shelter is a theoretical one, while the number of families actually paying certain rates for certain types of facilities is a matter of practical experience and must be investigated. The theoretical ability to pay is balanced against practical ability to pay, related specifically to services (utilities and parking) and facilities (number of bedrooms, number of baths, furnishings, etc.).

4. Current Vacancy Rates

Vacancy rate data is quite reliable in most areas of California and is of maximum importance in determining the amount of new space an area can absorb monthly.

Vacancy by type of facility is more significant than the overall vacancy rate in the area and should be analyzed carefully.

5. Rent Control

Communities and municipalities that impose rent control or rent stabilization adversely impact the potential earnings of a project. Rent control looms large as an important negative consideration in the maximization of rents and, therefore, capitalized values.

Rent control diminishes an investor's income potential. As such, it discourages new construction, thereby driving up the cost of available apartments.

6. Desirable Distribution of Units by Type and Price Class

With any project, it's important to determine the amount of emphasis to place on single units versus other units. Additional consideration must be given to the requirements for furnishing each unit and demands for amenities by size of unit. The square footage involved in each type of unit is also important and must be considered in light of the kind of tenant to whom your investor wants to appeal. For example, units that are appealing to families with children or high-income tenants will require more space than units designed for singles or marrieds without children.

VI. Syndication (Purchase Group)

Syndications are based on complex legal concepts, so advise your clients to seek advice from an attorney.

Another area open to you, as a licensee, is the marketing and financing of real estate through syndication. Opportunities for syndication abound because of increasing demand for a shrinking supply of land, population influx, relatively small outlays required of investors, and the solution which the syndication vehicle provides to the problem of tight money.

A. DEFINITION

A **SYNDICATION** *is an association of two or more people who combine their financial resources for the purpose of achieving one or more investment objectives.* It is the process whereby investment capital is pooled or combined for the purpose of acquiring real estate, which ordinarily could not be bought by individuals alone. The rights, responsibilities, benefits, and obligations of the syndicator or promoter toward the

investment group, and the investors toward each other, are governed by the legal form of business organization adopted by the participants.

B. BROKERAGE OPPORTUNITIES

Creating a real estate syndication can be creative, challenging, and profitable for the enterprising broker. The market for group investing is likely to continue growing and is bound to seriously challenge other investment media for the dollars of the typical investor.

The many benefits available to you as the organizer/promoter of a syndicate include the commissions earned from the sale of the property to the investment group, management fees, a percentage of ownership in exchange for organizational and promotional skills, resale commissions, opportunities for creation of new syndications, and options to acquire one or more interests through right of first refusal provisions. If you are a syndicator who is a licensed contractor, there is the additional opportunity to develop a site through a separate entity and earn the usual contractor's profit, which is customarily a percentage of the cost of development.

Aside from all of the monetary rewards, there is also the satisfaction derived from developing your creative skills and from making it possible for the small investor, by joining a group of investors, to reap the benefits of real estate ownership without the liabilities and problems associated with sole ownership.

As a broker/syndicator, it's possible to make more money in different ways than in any other single real estate endeavor. By taking the initiative to bring together a group of investors, you may expect to earn the following:

1. Commission from purchase of large property: 3% - 6%
2. Management fees on rents collected: 5% - 8%
3. Percentage of ownership for creating syndicate: 10% - 20%
4. Commission on resale of syndicated property: 3% - 6%

C. FORMS OF LEGAL ORGANIZATION

Syndications may assume a number of different legal forms of business organizations, depending upon the specific objectives of the individual participants.

A **LIMITED PARTNERSHIP (most preferred)** *consists of two or more persons who have joined together for their mutual investment benefit to share profits and losses.* It consists of at least one general partner, plus up to 35 limited partners.

A **GENERAL PARTNERSHIP (not recommended)** *is defined as an "association of two or more persons doing business as co-owners for profit."*

A **CORPORATION** *is legally defined as "an artificial being, intangible, invisible, and existing only in contemplation of law."*

Under prescribed conditions, where there are fewer than eleven stockholders and where no more than 20 percent of the corporate income is derived from rents, interest, and dividends, the investors may elect to have their corporation taxed as a **SUBCHAPTER S CORPORATION.** *This is the small business corporation which is taxed like the partnership forms, thus avoiding being taxed twice (corporation and personal).*

1. Real Estate Investment Trust (REIT)

A *REAL ESTATE INVESTMENT TRUST (REIT) is a type of real estate investment company that sells ownership shares.* Ownership in such investments is evidenced by "shares of equity." Because of very stringent tests that must be met to qualify for the trust's favored tax status, this form of organization is rarely used in the typical syndication. It is commonly used to raise mortgage funds. *When the main function of the trust is lending money, it is referred to as a REAL ESTATE MORTGAGE TRUST (REMT). Another form of trust actually purchases property, and is referred to as a REAL ESTATE EQUITY TRUST (REET). If it is used for investments in both mortgages and real property, it would be labeled a HYBRID TRUST.* The requirements that must be met to establish this form of unincorporated trust or association relate to the number of shareholders allowed, management, receipt and distribution of income, tax consequences, transferability of interests, sources of revenue, and other factors.

The principal benefit from the REIT form of ownership is that the qualified trust itself pays no income taxes if at least 90% of the income is distributed to the owners/participants.

Since at least 90 percent of its income must be distributed to the participants annually (subject to some exemption), the income tax is imposed on the individual recipients to the extent of the distributions.

VII. Small Business Opportunities

California licensees are allowed to sell businesses. For example, you may specialize in selling restaurants. As a broker, you may also wish to engage in a variety of activities that complement your basic real estate brokerage operation. Not only can each activity supplement income from real estate sales, but they can also provide you with additional sources of prospects. In all circumstances, the client's best interest must be of the highest priority.

A client may purchase a security interest, such as a trust deed note, through the same broker whom he or she considers a financial adviser. Notary services are a convenience for your daily operations and can provide an additional source of income and prospects. Exchanging and broker specialization are other activities, for which no specialized license is required.

You should be aware of the value of informing all your clients about other services offered by your company, such as property management.

VIII. Details of Selling a Business

The Real Estate Law defines a *BUSINESS OPPORTUNITY as the sale of a business. Since this transaction consists of the sale of personal property, the rules and laws governing the transfer of chattels (personal property) apply.* Examples of this kind of business opportunity are drug stores, service stations, cocktail bars, restaurants, auto parts stores, garages, photo stores,

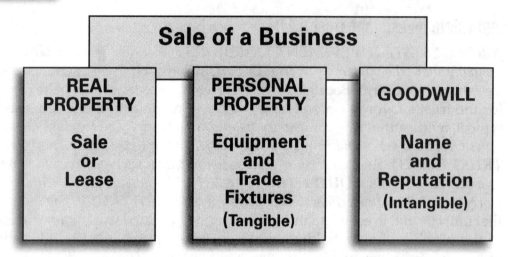

beauty shops, dress shops, liquor stores, and others. The principal assets that are transferred in these sales are stock-in-trade or inventory, fixtures, equipment, and *GOODWILL, defined as the value of a company's brand name, solid customer base, good customer relations, good employee relations, and any patents or proprietary technology.* Real property is seldom sold in the transaction; instead, the existing lease, or leasehold interest, is normally transferred to the purchaser.

A. LISTING AGREEMENT

In the first step, an agency relationship is created by securing a listing "of the business," just as in a real estate sale.

B. UNIFORM COMMERCIAL CODE (UCC)

The *UNIFORM COMMERCIAL CODE (UCC) is a body of law adopted throughout the United States that standardizes a number of practices in the selling of inventory commonly found in commerce and business.*

Article 6 covers the subject of **Bulk Transfers**. It stipulates that whenever there is a sale or transfer in bulk of inventory, and not in the ordinary course of the transferor's business, certain requirements must be met in order to protect creditors of the business being transferred.

In real estate talk, the expression "bulk transfer" means the same thing as a business opportunity—an extraordinary sale of more than half of a seller's merchandise, inventory, and equipment.

Most entrepreneurs, who wish to grow in their businesses, borrow money for working capital to purchase inventory, to buy or lease equipment, and so on. The creditors who have played a part in the growth of the business must be protected when the owner transfers the business to another. The requirements imposed under Article 6 of the UCC mitigate against such fraudulent practices of avoiding paying off existing creditors.

Whenever a bulk sale or transfer is made, the transferee must give public notice to the transferor's creditors by recording a Notice to Creditors of Bulk Sale at least twelve business days before the bulk transfer is consummated.

Moreover, the "Notice to Creditors" must be delivered to the county tax collector before the transfer is to be consummated. This procedure must be followed in the office of the county recorder in which the property is located. At least twelve days before the bulk transfer, the notice of its intended sale must be published, at least once, in a newspaper of general circulation in the judicial district in which the property is located.

Accurate completion of the **Notice to Creditors of Bulk Sale** form assures that the specific requirements of the UCC are met.

Noncompliance with the notice requirements renders the transfer fraudulent and void against those creditors of the transferor whose claims are based on credit transactions prior to the bulk transfer. With compliance, on the other hand, the creditors' recourse is against sellers only, not against the business or buyers.

C. SECURITY AGREEMENT AND FINANCING STATEMENT

Under **Article 9** of the Uniform Commercial Code, titled "Secured Transactions; Sales of Accounts, Contract Rights, and Chattel Paper," a filing system is established as additional protection for creditors and for purchasers. It regulates security transactions in personal property, replacing a variety of previously used security instruments (conditional sales contracts, chattel mortgages, trust receipts, assignment of accounts receivable) with a uniform and comprehensive Security Agreement and Financing Statement. The *SECURITY AGREEMENT AND FINANCING STATEMENT shows the debtor's name and address (cosigners and trade names would be included), the secured party's name and address (assignee), description and nature of the property used as collateral, and other items.*

Although the **Financing Statement** is subject to a Security Agreement, only the former is filed with the **Secretary of State in California**.

Only the brief, one-page Financing Statement, executed in quadruplicate, is required on file. Moreover, security transactions which involve consumer goods—personal, family, or household purchases—do not have to be filed.

The purposes for filing a Financing Statement with the "state" are similar to those for recording real property deeds with the county—to protect innocent purchasers and encumbrancers for value.

ENCUMBRANCERS are those who have a lender's interest in the property by virtue of having placed a lien on the property, acquired an easement against the property, imposed restrictions against it, or acquired any other interest which might be said to encumber the subject property.

By taking advantage of the UCC filing provisions, secured parties protect their current financial interests against those of subsequent purchasers.

In any transaction handled by an escrow agent, the transferee must deposit with the escrow the full amount of purchase price or consideration prior to any disbursement.

Not all escrow companies handle the sale of business opportunities. Not all brokers feel comfortable handling these business transactions and refer them out to another qualified company, for a fee.

D. COLLECTING SALES AND USE TAXES

Whenever a merchant engages in a business where sales of personal property at retail are made, he or she must secure a "Seller's Permit" from the State Board of Equalization.

The sale of a business opportunity is also subject to sales tax. Taxes are payable on the tangible personal property items only, and not on goodwill, patents, closes in action, and other intangibles. Thus, when a Business Opportunity (BO) is sold, sales tax must be charged on the furniture, trade fixtures, and equipment that are transferred. Until these taxes are paid, together with sales and use taxes owed by the seller to the state Board of Equalization, that agency will not issue its **CERTIFICATE OF PAYMENT OF SALES AND USE TAX**. *The issuance of this certificate releases the buyer from liability for the seller's unpaid sales and use taxes.* Without it, buyers will find themselves responsible for their payment, popularly referred to as **successor's liability**.

To guard against the possibility of unpaid taxes, the escrow agent is required to withhold from the purchase price a sufficient amount to cover any liability.

By filing and publishing the required notices of intent to sell, the buyer takes the business free of unfiled claims, and creditors who fail to file claims must look solely to the seller for payment.

As for taxation, the sovereign powers of the state are affected, and the successor to the business will still be liable until released.

E. BILL OF SALE

The **BILL OF SALE** *serves the same function in the transfer of personal property as the grant deed does for real property.*

F. ASSIGNMENT OF LEASE

Because few businesses transfer the underlying fee title (deed) to the land and improvements, one of the major reasons why businesses sell for comparatively less (in contrast to real property) is that only the personal property is being purchased, accompanied by an assignment of the lessee's interest in the realty (lease).

Obviously, a going concern is not as valuable without continued operation from a given location, particularly if a major reason for its success is its location. Many factors account for goodwill, not the least of which is the value of the location.

You should make sure that the business lease is assignable.

IX. Valuation of Business Opportunities

You should learn how to determine the value of different businesses—before you embark on your first listing. There is no magic formula to calculate the value of all business opportunities. There are industry-specific guidelines that help to establish the valuation of a business that is up for sale. More variables are involved, especially in establishing a true appraisal of the value of the leasehold.

A business opportunity may have one value to the lessor, but an altogether different value to the lessee.

Many differences of opinion inevitably exist because of the varying degrees of knowledge and skill of the appraisers and the approaches they utilize. When the business is large and involved, advise your seller to bear the expense of having it appraised by a trained specialist.

As might be expected, the value of goodwill is the most difficult to measure.

In establishing valuation for this intangible asset, consider the following: the length of time the business has been in existence, location, customer traffic, vehicle count, adaptability to change (if desired), present and future competition, continued use of a well-established and respected business name, the quality of service and dependability, provision for a noncompetition clause included in the sale, customer habits, personalities, and abilities of key personnel who will remain, and a variety of other factors.

You should visit an establishment on different days and at various times to visually determine business activities.

Based upon collection of data over many years, guidelines have been established to compute the value of a particular business. These guidelines may be said to be *NET MULTIPLIERS; that is, the amount that a business would sell for, based upon the multiplication of its annual net income by some standardized number, or multiplier. GROSS MULTIPLIERS are commonly used in valuations of income-producing real estate. Multipliers can also applied to the annual net income of businesses.*

You must be careful to obtain an accurate breakdown of income and expenses (income statement), as well as a correct count of the stock in trade. Assisting the transferor in the physical inventory may avoid misunderstandings.

Any agent who hopes to deal in business opportunities would be wise to take at least a basic course in financial accounting. Another valid option is to refer the client to a business opportunity broker and receive a referral fee.

X. Tax Consequences on the Sale of Business Opportunities

The income tax implications and applications in the sale of businesses differ from those in the sale of real property. The method of allocation of the various business assets has tax consequences to both seller/transferor and buyer/transferee.

A covenant not to compete is valid in California. Under the terms of a *COVENANT NOT TO COMPETE, the seller agrees that he or she will not open a competing business for a period of time within a specified geographical area.*

The amount paid for leasehold improvements is deductible by the buyer over the remaining term of the lease. It is a capital transaction to the seller, with capital gain consequences dependent upon the holding period.

The amount paid for goodwill is not deductible by the buyer and is a capital item that can be depreciated by the seller.

Amounts paid for fixtures and equipment are depreciable by the buyer and subject to income tax to the seller. Finally, inventory is generally priced at the seller's cost.

Always consult a CPA for tax purposes.

XI. Alcoholic Beverage Control Act

The *CALIFORNIA DEPARTMENT OF ALCOHOLIC BEVERAGE CONTROL (ABC) is charged with administration and enforcement of the Alcoholic Beverage Control Act, which regulates the issuance of liquor licenses.*

As a broker negotiating the sale of a business involving the sale and distribution of alcoholic beverages, you should be familiar with the legal controls and procedures for transfer of the liquor license or permit. In addition to federal statutes, many laws govern the manufacture, sale, and possession of alcoholic beverages in California. A detailed discussion of the subject is not essential for our purposes, but the reader who is interested in pursuing the matter is advised to consult the *CalBRE Reference Book* to obtain more information.

XII. Ancillary Activities and Specialty Roles

Inevitably, as a broker, you will be engaged in many activities which complement that of your main concern, general brokerage. A review of some of these activities follows.

A. REAL PROPERTY SECURITIES DEALER (RPSD)

Closely associated with loan brokerage is the activity of the real property securities dealer, who is regulated under Chapter 3, Article 6, of the Real Estate Law.

The essential difference between the real property securities dealer and the real property loan broker is that the mortgage loan broker is dealing with new loans in the primary mortgage (or money) market, while the *REAL PROPERTY SECURITIES DEALER (RPSD) is any person, acting as principal or agent, who, in the secondary market, engages in the business of: 1) Selling real property securities, or 2) Offering to accept or accepting funds for continual reinvestment in real property securities whereby the dealer implies that a return will be derived from a specific real property sales contract or promissory note secured directly or collaterally by a lien on real property.*

The statutes that regulate this area of real estate activity cover bulk transactions in trust deeds, real property sales contracts, and investment plans dealing with them.

To secure a CalBRE endorsement as a real property securities dealer, you must first have a real estate broker's license.

A real property securities dealer is defined as "any person, acting as principal or agent, who engages in the business of: (A) Selling real property securities to the public...." These are defined by Section 10237.1, subdivision (a) of the Business and Professions Code as investment contracts made in connection with the sale of a secured promissory note, or a property sales contract, wherein the dealer or his principal expresses or implies agreement to any kind of guarantee, payment, or repurchase of such investment contracts. The dealer might, for instance, guarantee the note or contract against loss or nonpayment of either principal or interest, guarantee a specific yield or return on the note or contract, agree to assume one or more payments in order to protect the security, or even to repurchase the note or contract.

Before selling real property securities to the public, the broker must obtain a permit from the California Bureau of Real Estate.

B. NOTARY PUBLIC SERVICES

A very significant part of every real estate transaction is the acknowledgement of a variety of documents used in the sale and purchase of real property. As you should be aware, such an *ACKNOWLEDGEMENT is a formal declaration before a duly authorized officer, by a person executing an instrument (that is, a formal document) that such execution is his or her act and deed.* **Its purpose is to entitle the document to be recorded so as to impart constructive notice of its contents.** Those who do not charge for such services perform them as an accommodation to the transaction. See Chapter 14 for more information.

XIII. Property Management Activities

As with the selling of insurance, the managing of properties for others is a natural addition to your general practice as a broker. Usually this is done on the basis of a percentage of gross rentals or for a flat fee. You are guided by the same principle here: As agent for the owner, you are obligated to obtain the most competitive rents and lower prices for your client when, for example, purchasing supplies and equipment for the property. This type of activity is excellent for future listing opportunities.

Specific functions and duties of the property manager are discussed in Chapter 13.

XIV. Escrow Activities

Another supporting service, which a large number of brokers offer, is that of escrow, discussed in detail in Chapter 10.

An *ESCROW is an impartial third party whose functions are to:*

1. *act as a depository of funds and documents placed with it;*

2. *prorate those charges and expenses between the parties to the escrow as instructed under the terms of the agreement for the sale and purchase; and*

3. *act as a clearinghouse for the exchange of monies and documents when the escrow is ready to close, that is, at the time when all the terms and conditions have been met.*

Under the Real Estate Law, a broker may act as an escrow agent in those transactions in which he or she represents the buyer or seller or both. See Chapter 10 for more information.

XV. Loan Brokerage (MLO Endorsement)

Being a broker or salesperson, as part of most real estate transactions, you may help your buyer fill out a loan application for a financial institution or arrange financing for your buyer. In either case, there are certain restrictions that apply to a real estate licensee acting as a loan broker in buying, selling, or exchanging loans. Most of these loans are in the form of a trust deed since it is the usual financing instrument in California (also see Chapter 9).

California law allows real estate licensees (with NMLS endorsement) who negotiate mortgage loans to receive compensation for their services (as arrangers, managers of loans, middlemen, or intermediaries).

They must obtain an MLO license endorsement from CalBRE.

XVI. Probate Sales

An executor possessing a power of sale under the terms of a will may sell directly or through one or more brokers.

If you are the broker, but don't have such power of sale, or you're a court-appointed administrator, you may also seek offers, providing you publish a legal notice advising that the property is to be sold on specified terms and conditions, and that offers from interested parties are invited.

Information concerning a sale is usually obtained from the attorney handling the estate or from a bank or trust company that is acting as executor or administrator. When the public administrator is in charge of the administration of an estate, inquiry is directed to that office.

Written offers to purchase must conform to statutory requirements and to the rules of the local superior court governing probate sales. The seller need not fill out a transfer disclosure statement, but the listing agent must provide the buyer with an abbreviated disclosure.

The initial offer must be for at least 90 percent of the inheritance tax appraisal value and should conform to the terms stated in any public notice. The personal representative may accept an offer, subject to court confirmation. The court sets the matter for a hearing and, at that time, anyone may bid more in open court, provided he or she increases the offer by at least 10 percent of the first $10,000, and 5 percent of the remaining portion of the original bid price. At the discretion of the court, the bidding may proceed on lesser raises, until the court declares a bid to be the highest and best obtainable, and thereby confirms the sale to the successful bidder. Not all probate sales need to be confirmed.

If you are the broker representing a bidder, you should attend the confirmation hearing and should be familiar with local court rules governing advance bidding, deposits required, and other matters. Normal escrow procedures are used to consummate the transaction, under terms and conditions approved by court.

Of course, as the broker, you should have a written agreement with the personal representative for payment of compensation. Commissions (5%) paid to participating brokers are governed by statute, and discretion is vested in the court as to distribution. **Generally, if more than one bid is made, half the selling commission goes to the broker representing the original bidder on the original amount, and the balance goes to the broker whose bidder submitted the higher bid, based on the higher amount.** You may also specify how commissions are disbursed in your listing agreement.

If the successful bidder is not produced by a bona fide agent, then the agent holding the contract is allowed a full commission on the amount of the original bid.

XVII. State of California Sales Opportunities

Occasionally, the state has real property for disposal, such as excess land acquired for easements that is no longer needed. The Department of Finance may authorize employment of a broker to affect sales when, after proper advertising, bids offered for such properties do not equal the appraised value.

A. SUBDIVISION SALES OPPORTUNITIES
1. Intrastate Sales

The division and subsequent sale of real property are governed by the Subdivision Map Act and the Subdivided Lands Act.

2. Interstate Sales

California licensees also have the privilege to sell real estate to purchasers outside the state. With such opportunities also come responsibilities.

Because of the massive scale of land promotions and abuses, Congress passed the *INTERSTATE LAND SALES FULL DISCLOSURE ACT. With certain exceptions, an offering for sale or lease of a subdivision of 25 lots or more through interstate commerce or by mail requires a permit from the Department of Housing and Urban Development. This permit is called a **PROPERTY REPORT**.*

B. REAL ESTATE INVESTMENT COUNSELOR

For the real estate broker who has considerable experience and superior education, there is another specialized field of real estate activity. The *REAL ESTATE INVESTMENT COUNSELOR is the broker's broker or consultant, doing for other brokers what those brokers cannot do for themselves, until their own knowledge and experience qualifies them for similar status.*

XVIII. Real Estate Brokerage — General vs. Specialization

The sale of residential property accounts for about three-fourths of sales made by the typical realty office.

After you've made a good start in general house selling, you may wish to specialize in a particular area of brokerage. You may become a specialist in one of the following areas of sales activities:

1. Homes in a defined **geographical section** of the city, usually within a radius of five to ten miles of your office.

2. Homes within a certain **price range**.

3. **Types** of property: condominiums, cooperatives, and townhouses; residential income; commercial and industrial; farms and acreage; motels; hotels; or business opportunities.

4. **Exchanges** of real property.

Similarly, once exposed to general brokerage activities, you may, after extensive experience, choose to enter one of the following fields of specialization, generally non-selling in nature:

Appraiser (licensed)	**Escrow**
Property manager	**Title insurance**
Mortgage loan broker	**Government**
Counselor	**Private**
Subdivider and **developer**	**Teaching**
Syndicator	

Note that general brokerage is the block upon which to stand, or it can become the stepping stone to specialization. As an ambitious person entering the field of real estate, it would be wise to carefully examine your interests, aptitudes, and limitations, and then plan your career accordingly.

XIX. Manufactured Housing and the Licensee

Although no longer referred to as "mobile homes," manufactured homes are what the original name implies; homes that can be moved. Like a vehicle, the *MANUFACTURED HOME is built on a steel chassis and equipped with wheels so that it can be pulled by truck from the factory to a dealer's lot and then to a site in a park or on private land. To be classed as a mobile home, a vehicle must be 8 feet wide (or more) and at 40 feet long (or more).*

A. MOBILE HOME DEALER VS. REAL ESTATE BROKER

New manufactured homes cannot be sold by real estate licensees.

Real estate licensees are not allowed to act as agents in the sale of mobile homes that can be used as vehicles on the highway. To mitigate against such practice, licensees are not even permitted to maintain any place of business where two or more mobile homes are displayed and offered for sale by such a person, unless the broker is also licensed as a vehicle dealer pursuant to the California Vehicle Code.

B. MARKETING

California specifically regulates manufactured home sales with a statute outlining rules and regulations permitting real estate brokers to sell the units.

Brokers may sell manufactured homes that have been registered with the Department of Motor Vehicles for at least one year and are larger than 8 feet in width and 40 feet in length.

Manufactured homes create greater title problems than ordinary real estate transactions. Before listing such property, you should demand and receive the owner's registration papers, indicating the true owner and outstanding loans, if any.

XX. CHAPTER SUMMARY

The number one objective of investing in real estate is to make money. An investor's capacity to handle the monthly cost of the investment, as well as the soundness of the investment, should be determined first. Some of the benefits of real estate investment are: the potential for tax sheltering or deferment, appreciation in value, and as a hedge against inflation. The rewards also include a monthly cash income, depreciation and operating expense deductions to reduce income taxes, and monthly principal deduction in the amount of trust deed loans.

To summarize, the four ways to make money on a real estate investment include:

1. cash flow
2. appreciation
3. depreciation
4. equity building

The three main sources of financing include **savings banks**, **commercial banks**, and **life insurance companies**. Financing may also be arranged from real estate syndicates and trusts, as well as sellers themselves. During tight money periods, sellers often become the only source of financing for raw land and special purpose projects through seller **carryback loans** and contracts of sales (**land contracts**).

Good sources of potential investment property buyers are the current tenants of the property, especially commercial tenants.

Brokers can be investment planners. Qualifying investment property buyers is similar to that of homebuyers, but additional consideration must be given to their financial

objectives. As such, details on the seller's property condition, tenants, rent schedules, vacancy factors, and more need to be gathered and analyzed.

An **income property statement** is used to prepare a comprehensive income and expense analysis of an apartment building. The analysis is based on estimated future operating income of the building. **Scheduled income** is the gross income a property would generate if there were no vacancies.

The steps involved in completing a property analysis include:

1. **Potential Gross Income**,
2. **Effective Gross Income**,
3. **Net Operating Income** to appraise using a rule of thumb (**Times Gross**), and with greater accuracy the process of **Capitalizing of Net Income**.

Operating expenses include fixed and variable expenses and replacement reserves. **MITUM** stands for maintenance, insurance, taxes, utilities, and management, which are all operating expenses. Loan payments, depreciation, and income taxes are not considered operating expenses.

Capitalization Rate (Cap Rate). The higher the cap rate, the lower the price.

The characteristics of a particular rental market can be comprised of:

1. income characteristics;
2. rent to income relationships;
3. current rental ranges;
4. current vacancy rates;
5. rent control; and
6. desired distribution of unit type and price class.

A **real estate syndication** is an association of two or more people combining their financial resources to purchase property. An **REIT** is a type of real estate investment trust company that sells ownership shares. If they distribute 90% of their income to the owner participants the trust pays no income taxes, only the recipients (no double taxation).

A **business opportunity (BO)** is the sale or lease of a business (inventory, fixtures, and equipment), as well as the goodwill of the existing business. Goodwill is the expectation of continued public patronage. The **State Board of Equalization** issues a **Certificate of Payment of Sales and Use Tax** to release the buyer from liability for the seller's unpaid sales and use tax.

As a sale of a business opportunity is considered the **transfer of personal property**, a **bill of sale** is used, which serves the same function as a grant deed for the transfer of real property.

Net multipliers and **gross multipliers** are often used as general guidelines to compute the value of a business.

A seller who agrees not to open a competing business for a period of time within a specific geographical area has entered into a **covenant not to compete**.

Real Property Security Dealers (RPSDs) are involved in the secondary mortgage (or money) market, and must have a broker's license as well as a **permit** issued by the Real Estate Commissioner.

In order to be recorded and give constructive notice, most real estate transaction documents require **acknowledgement** before a licensed notary public. In addition to notarial services, many brokers offer their clients **property management** and **escrow services**. **Licensees acting as escrow agents** must keep proper records and maintain all escrow funds in trust accounts subject to inspection by the Real Estate Commissioner.

Brokers can supplement their brokerage activities by lending their own money, or money of investors, as well as acting as representatives, agents, or correspondents for mortgage lending institutions **with the proper endorsement by CalBRE**. Brokers may focus on general housing sales or may choose to specialize in one particular area of brokerage, such as commercial properties, exchanges, syndication, escrow, teaching, and many more. However, remember that general brokerage is the foundation and stepping stone to specialization. Yet another avenue for business expansion is the marketing and sales of **probate property** (court-ordered sale of a deceased person's property or properties).

Finally, brokers may sell **manufactured (mobile) homes** that have been registered with the **Department of Motor Vehicles (DMV)** for at least one year, and are usually 8 feet wide (or more) and 40 feet long (or more). Brokers cannot sell mobile homes that can be used as vehicles on the highway, unless they are licensed vehicle dealers.

XXI. MATCHING VOCABULARY Fill in the blanks with the correct letter

A. Acknowledgement
B. Bill of Sale
C. Business opportunity
D. Capitalization rate
E. Cash flow
F. Corporation
G. Covenant not to compete
H. Down payment
I. Fixed expenses
J. Goodwill

K. Inflationary period
L. Interim use
M. Life insurance companies
N. Liquidity
O. Manufactured home
P. Mortgage loan originator (MLO)
Q. Onsite property manager
R. Operating expenses

S. Real Estate Investment Trust (REIT)
T. Real property securities dealer
U. Reserves for replacement
V. Savings bank
W. S Corporation
X. Vacancy factor

1. _____ During one of these periods, the cost of everything rises, including real estate.
2. _____ An individual who, for compensation or gain, or in the expectation of compensation or gain, takes a residential mortgage loan application or offers or negotiates terms of a residential mortgage loan.
3. _____ A formal declaration before a duly authorized officer, by a person executing an instrument that such execution is his act and deed.
4. _____ The Real Estate Law defines the sale of a business as a(n):
5. _____ In California, an apartment complex with 16 or more units requires a(n):
6. _____ An allowance for vacancies and uncollectible rents.
7. _____ The result of dividing the net operating income by the selling price.
8. _____ In a business with a good reputation, the customer base with the expectation of continued public patronage.
9. _____ This person is engaged in the secondary market, in addition to a host of activities that come under the definition of real property securities.
10. _____ A form of business entity legally defined as "an artificial being, intangible, invisible, and existing only in contemplation of law."
11. _____ The ease and rate with which an asset can be converted into cash.
12. _____ The amount the buyer is to pay towards the purchase price.
13. _____ This item serves the same function in the transfer of personal property as the grant deed does for real property.
14. _____ This type of corporation is taxed only once, on an individual income tax return.
15. _____ These expenses do not vary depending on the occupancy of the property.
16. _____ These funds are set aside for replacing short-lived components of the property.
17. _____ Under these terms, the seller agrees that he will not open a competing business for a period of time within a specified geographical area.
18. _____ A property temporarily generates rents for other than its future zoned use.
19. _____ This type of bank specializes in housing loans, particularly for single-family dwellings up to four units.
20. _____ This house is built on a steel chassis and equipped with wheels so that it can be pulled by a truck from the factory to a dealer's lot and then to the site in a park or on private land.
21. _____ These companies often invest in large commercial projects, like shopping malls, and serve markets far away from their home offices.

22. _____ These expenses include fixed and variable expenses, as detailed in the bottom half of the Income Property Statement.
23. _____ The difference between the income generated from an income property and the expenses associated with it, including taxes, mortgage payments, and operating expenses.
24. _____ A type of real estate investment company that sells ownership shares. The qualified company itself pays no income taxes if at least 90% of the income is distributed to the owners/participants.

See Page 610 for Answers

XXII. CHAPTER QUIZ

1. Which of the following is considered a benefit of real estate investment?

   a. Tax sheltering
   b. Appreciation potential
   c. Monthly income - cash flow
   d. All of the above

2. Which of the following is NOT a potential negative factor for real estate investors?

   a. Size of capital required
   b. Personal attachment
   c. Unfavorable financing conditions
   d. Fast and easy liquidation

3. Which of the following lenders is the most likely to finance the purchase of a large apartment complex?

   a. Savings bank
   b. Commercial bank
   c. Life insurance company
   d. None of the above

4. What type of income is most commonly used in determining the capitalization of net income?

   a. Net operating income
   b. Potential gross income
   c. Effective gross income
   d. Times gross

5. Which of the following is true concerning the cap rate?

   a. The higher the cap rate, the lower the price.
   b. The higher the cap rate, the higher the price.
   c. The lower the cap rate, the lower the price.
   d. None of the above.

6. When determining the characteristics of a rental market, the percentage of income a family can, or will, normally pay for shelter is:

    a. 5 to 10 percent.
    b. 10 to 20 percent.
    c. 25 to 40 percent.
    d. 50 to 60 percent.

7. In a probate sale, the first acceptable offer must be:

    a. 90 percent or more of the court appraisal.
    b. the same or more than the court appraisal.
    c. left to the discretion of the executor.
    d. none of the above.

8. A person with a CPM designation would most likely be engaged professionally in the field of:

    a. property management.
    b. property insurance.
    c. property appraisal.
    d. property financing.

9. A real estate syndicate can be a:

    a. corporation.
    b. partnership.
    c. trust.
    d. all of the above.

10. Before an individual real estate broker gets into the field of loan brokerage, he must obtain which license?

    a. Loan broker
    b. Real estate investment counselor
    c. Real property securities dealer
    d. MLO through NMLS

ANSWERS: 1. d; 2. b; 3. c; 4. a; 5. a; 6. c; 7. a; 8. a; 9. a; 10. d

Property Management: Managing and Leasing Properties

Before discussing your career in property management, it is extremely important to have a full understanding of the regulatory laws that govern the sensitive issues relating to **less-than-freehold estates**, also known as **leasehold estates**. If these laws are not closely adhered to, you (as the property manager) and the owner may be liable to high punitive fines and costly legal procedures.

A "leasehold estate" is a tenant's right to occupy real estate during the specific term of a lease.

I. Fair Housing Laws

California first passed the Unruh Civil Rights Act (no discrimination in business, including real estate agents' services) and then the Fair Employment and Housing Act (FEHA) (no discrimination in housing). These were later reinforced by the Federal Civil Rights Act of 1968 (expanded in 1988).

Figure 13-1 describes the different types of fair housing violations.

A. STATE LAW — UNRUH CIVIL RIGHTS ACT (No Discrimination in Business)

The Unruh Civil Rights Act was the first civil rights act in California. It prohibits "steering" and "blockbusting" as a real estate business practice.

California first passed the Unruh Civil Rights Act that declares:

> *"All persons within the jurisdiction of this state are free and equal, and no matter what their race, color, religion, ancestry, or national origin, they are entitled to the full and equal accommodations, advantages, facilities, privileges, or services in all business establishments of every kind whatsoever..."*

CHAPTER 13

Figure 13-1

Fair Housing Violations and Possible Remedies

REDLINING —————————————— The refusal of a loan or insurance based upon a property's location (zip code).

STEERING —————————————— Showing a client property in only one type of neighborhood, such as a Caucasian buyer in a Caucasian neighborhood, and the refusal to communicate the availability of housing in other neighborhoods.

OWNER (ILLEGALLY) TELLS AGENT NOT TO SHOW PROPERTY TO MINORITY —— The agent is relieved of the duty to show the property to "anyone," including a minority who has requested to see the property.

CONTRACT REFUSED TO BUYER BECAUSE OF RACE ————— ADVISE BUYER of the right to complain to the Department of Fair Employment and Housing (FEH) and WARN SELLER that he or she has violated fair housing laws.

RACE RESTRICTIONS ————————— Any race restriction is UNENFORCEABLE.

PANIC SELLING OR BLOCK BUSTING AND PANIC PEDDLING ————— An agent intentionally incites existing homeowners to sell their properties by saying that property values will fall because persons of a different race or religion have targeted a move into their neighborhood.

SALE OF PROPERTY—AGENT ASKED TO DISCRIMINATE ———————— Agent must REFUSE the listing.

As a real estate practitioner, you must be "color-blind" when it comes to selling and leasing properties.

B. STATE LAW - CALIFORNIA FAIR EMPLOYMENT AND HOUSING ACT (FEHA)

The California Fair Employment and Housing Act (FEHA) outlaws discrimination in housing. It also established the Commission of Fair Employment and Housing to investigate and take action against property owners, financial institutions, and real estate licensees who engage in discriminatory practices.

FEHA clearly defines **DISCRIMINATION** *as the refusal to sell, rent, or lease housing accommodations, including misrepresentation as to availability, offering inferior terms, and cancellations on the basis of race, color, national origin, religion, sex, familial status, and handicap.* It also outlaws sale or rental advertisements containing discriminatory information.

Owners of three single-family homes and owner-occupied buildings that are four units or less are exempt from Fair Housing Laws under the "Mom and Pop" provision.

Not so many years ago, buyers of child-bearing age, applying for financing on a purchase loan, were questioned about their use of birth control. We've come a long way since then!

C. STATE LAW - HOUSING FINANCIAL DISCRIMINATION ACT OF 1977 (No Redlining)

The Housing Financial Discrimination Act of 1977 prohibits financial institutions from engaging in the discriminatory loan practice called "redlining."

In remedying such violations, the state may force a landowner to proceed with the rental or sale in question, provide comparable housing accommodations if the original is no longer available, or pay punitive damages. Under the **Housing Financial Discrimination Act of 1977**, the practice of redlining is specifically outlawed. *REDLINING is the practice by financial institutions of denying loans or varying finance terms based on the location of a given property, regardless of the credit worthiness of the borrower.*

A grievance under this Act is directed to the lending institution or the California Bureau of Real Estate (CalBRE). Lending institutions in violation of the Housing Financial Discrimination Act may be required to pay for damages, limited to $1,000 for each offense.

D. FEDERAL LAW - FEDERAL CIVIL RIGHTS ACT OF 1968

Federal law prohibits discrimination on the part of owners of property and their agents based on the **U.S. Supreme Court case** *Jones v. Mayer* (which upheld the Civil Rights Act of 1866) and Title VIII of the Civil Rights Act of 1968.

At the federal level, the Federal Civil Rights Act of 1968 reinforced the California Unruh and Fair Employment and Housing Acts as follows:

1. Any discrimination in the two acts is prohibited.

2. It makes it illegal for real estate licensees to engage in discriminatory practices, regardless of any instructions the agent may have received from the seller or landlord. If asked to discriminate in the sale of a property, the salesperson must refuse to accept the listing.

3. It bars real estate boards or multiple listing services from discriminating by denying participation or restricting terms and conditions of membership.

4. It requires a fair housing poster to be displayed at all real estate offices and subdivision model homes. The poster (see **Figure 13-2**) must also be displayed at all financial institutions or by mortgage lenders who make loans to the general public.

The only time you, as an agent, can refuse to show a property to a buyer is when the owners have informed you that they will be out of town and, during their absence, have left instructions not to show the property to anyone.

A lender who charges an additional fee for processing loans to non-English speaking applicants (because the lender must hire non-English speaking employees) is practicing discrimination.

1. Federal Civil Rights Act Expanded in 1988 (HUD Can Initiate Housing Discrimination Cases)

A 1988 federal law allows the U.S. Government to take court action if it believes discrimination exists in home sales or apartment rentals. Landlords are explicitly forbidden from discriminating against families with children under 18 years of age. The only exemptions from this would be in retirement communities where most of the residents are more than 55 years of age.

This federal law also extends protections to handicapped homebuyers or tenants. Builders of all new apartment buildings are required to include ground floor rooms suitable for use by residents in wheelchairs.

The 1988 Fair Housing Amendments Act extended protection regarding familial status and the handicapped.

The Housing and Urban Development (HUD) Department is authorized to bring enforcement action against sellers and landlords who defy this law. Fines of up to $10,000 have been authorized for first time violators, up to $25,000 for a second offense within five years, and up to $50,000 for a third offense within seven years. Those accused of violating this tough statute would face an administrative judge unless they specifically requested a jury trial.

Complaints should be filed with Housing and Urban Development (HUD). Fair Employment and Housing will enforce any action.

Figure 13-2

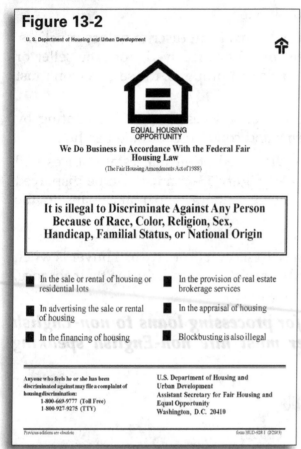

To sum up: Real estate licensees must not discriminate, and to that end should not accept restrictive listings or make, print, or publish any notice, statement, or advertisement with respect to a sale or rental of a dwelling that suggests discrimination.

II. Property Management

Few people possess sufficient knowledge, skill, and time to manage their own properties and, therefore, turn to property management specialists. Your reward for pursuing this specialty includes not only the additional revenue, but also the chance to meet your owners' complete real estate needs. As a property manager, you are in a better position to assess your clients' insurance needs, handle financing, offer timely suggestions on exchanging or sale opportunities, recommend other investment properties, obtain more referrals, and offer them a wide variety of other financial and estate-planning services. In short, you become a financial counselor. You are also in a good position to assist tenants when they decide to purchase real estate.

A. TYPES OF PROPERTIES

The basic types of income-producing properties include: 1) residential; 2) commercial office buildings; 3) retail property; and 4) industrial property.

Some types of property lend themselves especially well to the professional manager. Because **apartment buildings** are more common than other income-producing properties, they lead in the demand for management services.

Other properties requiring professional management are single-family houses, office buildings, retail stores and shopping centers, medical buildings, hotels, industrial parks, single-purpose structures, and even raw land.

B. TYPES OF PROPERTY MANAGERS

The principal goal of any property manager is to minimize expenses, maximize rents, and increase the long-term appreciation of the property.

Your prime objective as a professional property manager is to increase the net income (rents less operating expenses). Management, then, should not be a cost, but a completely recoverable fee, plus a profit to the property owner. In order to accomplish this objective, an owner may employ one or more managers. There are three classifications of real property managers.

1. Outside Manager (Does Not Reside on Property)

The category that concerns us most is that of professional outside manager. As part of their general brokerage operations, or as exclusive property management firms, *OUTSIDE MANAGERS represent more than one owner in more than one property*. They depict themselves as property managers, taking the place of the owners in order to meet the objective of profitability. They require no specific license other than the real estate broker license.

Because they make themselves available for numerous properties, outside (off-site) managers are often called "general managers."

Real Estate Investment Trusts (REITs) also offer outside management opportunities for managers; these are handled much the same way as mutual funds. The REIT usually contracts with a management company. However, most REITs form separate management companies to perform the managerial tasks, thus keeping the management fees within the company.

2. Resident Manager (Resides on Property)

RESIDENT MANAGERS live on the premises and are directly employed by the property owner or his agent. Resident managers do not need to be licensed. Of course, they cannot make themselves available to manage other properties without first obtaining a broker's or salesperson's license under a broker who engages in property management. They manage a single building and, therefore, may be referred to as **building superintendents**.

A resident (on-site) manager, as the title signifies, lives on the premises and does not need to be licensed.

For the protection and convenience of tenants, California law prescribes that when an owner does not reside in an apartment house containing 16 or more units, a resident manager, agent, or other responsible person must be hired to live on the premises.

For fewer than 16 units, with an exemption for fewer than five, the owner is required to post a notice stating the name and address of the owner or agent in a conspicuous place on the premises.

The California Apartment Association (CAA) offers the California Certified Residential Manager (CCRM) designation for qualified licensed real estate professionals and a certificate in residential management for qualified, on-site residential managers.

3. Institutional Manager (Works for Large Company)

The *INSTITUTIONAL MANAGER or BUILDING SUPERVISOR is also directly employed for a wage or salary, but by an institution*, such as the real estate management department of a bank, insurance company, government agency, REIT, trust, or endowment fund.

C. DUTIES AND RESPONSIBILITIES OF PROPERTY MANAGERS

A list of some important duties and functions of the manager follows. **No attempt is made to specify the type of manager who usually performs each duty.** (For example, as a resident manager, you and an outside manager may have overlapping responsibilities in accounting for funds.) As a manager, you may be required to:

1. Establish the rent schedule that will bring the **highest yield** consistent with sound economics principles.

2. Rent vacant units. Tenants need to know all rules.

3. Keep all plumbing, heating, and electrical in good working order.

4. Make sure roof is leak-free and that doors and windows are not broken and open and close properly.

5. Maintain the floors, stairways, and railings in safe and good condition.

6. Keep the premises clean and free of pests.

7. Qualify tenants through credit reports, eviction history, and character references.

The California Apartment Association (CAA) has many local associations to assist owners and managers with rental forms and credit checks.

As a property manager, it's a good practice to contact the tenant's past landlords for a fair portrayal of the renter's history. Too many moves should raise a red flag. A credit check should be used to determine a renter's ability to pay rent on time.

8. Prepare and renew leases and have them executed.

9. Collect rents and process them. Initiate eviction proceedings, if necessary, with the assistance of a real estate attorney.

10. Keep a separate trust account for rents and expense and maintain accurate bank records.

11. Submit monthly and annual statements to the owner in a timely fashion.

12. Order, supervise, and check all maintenance and repair work deemed necessary after securing estimates.

13. Advertise, prepare brochures, publicity releases, and correspondence.

14. Inspect properties periodically, particularly vacant space.

15. Interview, hire, fire, train, and supervise personnel.

16. Maintain necessary insurance (and upgrades when property value increases), including the basic fire and windstorm, liability, workers' compensation, errors and omissions, and consequential loss policies.

17. Pay taxes and recommend tax appeals when warranted.

18. Pay bills, including payments for loans, insurance, and all other authorized disbursements.

19. Estimate deferred maintenance, fixtures, and equipment, and establish reserve accounts for their ultimate replacement.

20. Prepare plans and specifications for alteration, rehabilitation, and remodeling.

21. Act as an advisor; recommend appraisers to determine **highest and best use** of the property. Analyze market trends and leasing arrangements that will enlarge the owner's net income or favorable times to refinance, sell, or exchange the property.

"Highest and best use" is the most profitable, physically possible, and legally permissible use for the property.

Some agents and brokers with investment properties often hire property managers (even if they manage other people's properties). It's a good idea to hire an outsider because it's too easy to get attached and personally involved. It's best to keep transactions at "arm's length."

1. The Tenant's Responsibilities

The tenant has the following responsibilities:

1. Keep the dwelling clean and sanitary.

2. Use all fixtures properly, keeping them clean.

3. Cause no damage to the property.

4. Use property as stated in the lease agreement.

5. Pay rent on time.

6. Give a 30-Day notice when vacating a month-to-month tenancy.

7. Return door and mailbox keys when vacating.

8. Leave unit in as clean a condition as taken at the start of the lease.

D. LANDLORD-TENANT TERMINATION LAWS AND ABANDONED ANIMAL LAWS
1. 30- and 60-Day Notices

A 30-day termination notice must be given when the possession of a rental unit is for less than one year.

A 60-Day Termination Notice must be given to a tenant who has been in possession of a rental unit for one year or more.

A landlord must provide a month-to-month periodic tenant with a 60-day notice to terminate the tenancy if the tenant has lived in the dwelling for one year or more, but a tenant who terminates a periodic tenancy may do so with a 30-day notice.

The following are situations where the 60-day notice is not required:

1. If the landlord enters into a fixed-term lease, such as a one-year lease agreement.

2. A **30-day notice** is sufficient for tenants who have lived in the property for **less than one year**.

3. Landlords selling their properties may give a **30-day notice** if all of the following conditions are met:

   a. The owner has entered into a contract to sell the dwelling or unit to a bona fide purchaser for value.
   b. The buyer is a natural person(s).
   c. The buyer, in good faith, intends to live in the property for at least one year after termination of the tenancy.
   d. The termination notice is given within 120 days of opening escrow.
   e. Notice has not been previously given to the tenant under this law.
   f. The owner has established an escrow with a licensed escrow officer or a licensed real estate broker.
   g. The dwelling or unit is alienable separate from the title to any other dwelling unit.

The ***THREE-DAY NOTICE TO PAY OR QUIT*** *states that the tenant has three business days to pay all past due rent or vacate the property or face an* ***unlawful detainer****. The* ***30-DAY*** *or* ***60-DAY NOTICE*** *is given when the landlord wants the tenant out of the property.* No reason needs to be given, unless the property is in a rent controlled city. Naturally a 30-day or 60-day notice cannot be given to a tenant with a bona fide lease.

The Three-Day Notice to Pay or Quit is a legal document requesting either the rent or a return of the premises. The document must be properly (legally) served.

It is important to remember that it is unlawful for the landlord or property manager to lock out tenants, take the tenants' property, remove doors, shut off utilities, or trespass.

2. Landlords and REO Lenders Must Take Charge of Abandoned Animals

Any person or private entity with whom a live animal has been "involuntarily deposited" must take charge of it, if able to do so, and immediately notify animal control officials so they can retrieve the animal.

E. SELECTION OF PROPERTY MANAGERS

Many considerations go into the choice of the right manager. He or she should be selected on the same basis as a manager of a firm. As a manager, you should have skills and talent in handling people, money, and a diversity of other responsibilities.

In general, as a professional manager, you should have a mind for details and knowledge of construction and mechanics, enjoy supervisory work, and possess above-average education, especially in real estate, accounting, general business, and even engineering. You should be tactful, be able to make sound judgments, have experience in supervising maintenance personnel, understand how to identify and solve problems, have an affinity for people, and know how to play the role of executive, operating the property as you would operate any important business.

1. Management Contract

Good business practice dictates that any agreement for the employment of a manager should be in writing. Standardized forms outlining the duties and responsibilities, as well as rights and benefits, are available through **apartment owners' associations**, realty boards, and office supply stores, or can be specially drafted by a lawyer. The California Association of REALTORS® has a comprehensive four-page Property Management Agreement (PMA) (**Figure 13-3**) that lists the broker's and owner's obligations, and can be adapted to typical situations. Included are provisions for marketing the space, leasing, collections, repairs and maintenance, fees to be paid when property is vacant, disbursements, periodic statements to owners, accounting for funds, and agent's compensation when renting and/or leasing the property.

As with real estate sales, property management compensation is always negotiable. As a loose rule of thumb, when managing a single-family residence, many brokers charge from 6% to 10% of the monthly income. When managing multiple units, this fee is usually somewhat reduced.

2. Compensation

Resident and **institutional managers** are customarily paid a straight salary. As an apartment resident manager, you may also receive rent-free quarters in lieu of salary, in whole or in part. Bonuses for extra jobs or for extraordinary performance are also common.

Outside professional managers are usually paid a percentage of the gross revenues, depending on the type of services, size of property, and other compensation. Besides the satisfaction of a job well done, a percentage of the gross rents should provide you with incentive to maintain high levels of occupancy; because the more space leased, the greater your income (as well as the owners'—property management should not cost the owner).

Figure 13-3

PROPERTY MANAGEMENT AGREEMENT

(C.A.R. Form PMA, Revised 11/13)

_____ Tony Seller, Ramona J. Seller _____ ("Owner"), and
_____ Sail Realty _____ ("Broker"), agree as follows:

1. **APPOINTMENT OF BROKER:** Owner hereby appoints and grants Broker the exclusive right to rent, lease, operate, and manage the property(ies)
   known as _____ 264 Beach Lane, Costa Mesa, CA 92627 _____

   _____ ,
   _____ and any additional property that may later be added to this Agreement ("Property"),
   upon the terms below, for the period beginning (date) _____ and ending (date) _____ , at
   11:59 PM. (If checked:) ☐ Either party may terminate this Property Management Agreement ("Agreement") on at least 30 days written notice
   _____ months after the original commencement date of this Agreement. After the exclusive term expires, this Agreement shall continue as a
   non-exclusive agreement that either party may terminate by giving at least 30 days written notice to the other.

2. **BROKER ACCEPTANCE:** Broker accepts the appointment and grant, and agrees to:
   A. Use due diligence in the performance of this Agreement.
   B. Furnish the services of its firm for the rental, leasing, operation and management of the Property.

3. **AUTHORITY AND POWERS:** Owner grants Broker the authority and power, at Owner's expense, to:
   A. **ADVERTISING:** Display FOR RENT/LEASE and similar signs on the Property and advertise the availability of the Property, or any part thereof, for rental or lease.
   B. **RENTAL; LEASING:** Initiate, sign, renew, modify or cancel rental agreements and leases for the Property, or any part thereof; collect and give receipts for rents, other fees, charges and security deposits. Any lease or rental agreement executed by Broker for Owner shall not exceed _____ year(s) or ☐ shall be month-to-month. Unless Owner authorizes a lower amount, rent shall be: ☐ at market rate; OR ☐ a minimum of $ _____ per _____ ; OR ☐ see attachment.
   C. **TENANCY TERMINATION:** Sign and serve in Owner's name notices that are required or appropriate; commence and prosecute actions to evict tenants; recover possession of the Property in Owner's name; recover rents and other sums due; and, when expedient, settle, compromise and release claims, actions and suits and/or reinstate tenancies.
   D. **REPAIR; MAINTENANCE:** Make, cause to be made, and/or supervise repairs, improvements, alterations and decorations to the Property; purchase, and pay bills for, services and supplies. Broker shall obtain prior approval of Owner for all expenditures over $ _____ for any one item. Prior approval shall not be required for monthly or recurring operating charges or, if in Broker's opinion, emergency expenditures over the maximum are needed to protect the Property or other property(ies) from damage, prevent injury to persons, avoid suspension of necessary services, avoid penalties or fines, or suspension of services to tenants required by a lease or rental agreement or by law, including, but not limited to, maintaining the Property in a condition fit for human habitation as required by Civil Code §§ 1941 and 1941.1 and Health and Safety Code §§ 17920.3 and 17920.10.
   E. **REPORTS, NOTICES AND SIGNS:** Comply with federal, state or local law requiring delivery of reports or notices and/or posting of signs or notices.
   F. **CONTRACTS; SERVICES:** Contract, hire, supervise and/or discharge firms and persons, including utilities, required for the operation and maintenance of the Property. Broker may perform any of Broker's duties through attorneys, agents, employees, or independent contractors and, except for persons working in Broker's firm, shall not be responsible for their acts, omissions, defaults, negligence and/or costs of same.
   G. **EXPENSE PAYMENTS:** Pay expenses and costs for the Property from Owner's funds held by Broker, unless otherwise directed by Owner. Expenses and costs may include, but are not limited to, property management compensation, fees and charges, expenses for goods and services, property taxes and other taxes, Owner's Association dues, assessments, loan payments and insurance premiums.
   H. **SECURITY DEPOSITS:** Receive security deposits from tenants, which deposits shall be ☐ given to Owner, or ☐ placed in Broker's trust account and, if held in Broker's trust account, pay from Owner's funds all interest on tenants' security deposits if required by local law or ordinance. Owner shall be responsible to tenants for return of security deposits and all interest due on security deposits held by Owner.
   I. **TRUST FUNDS:** Deposit all receipts collected for Owner, less any sums properly deducted or disbursed, in a financial institution whose deposits are insured by an agency of the United States government. The funds shall be held in a trust account separate from Broker's personal accounts. Broker shall not be liable in event of bankruptcy or failure of a financial institution.
   J. **RESERVES:** Maintain a reserve in Broker's trust account of $ _____
   K. **DISBURSEMENTS:** Disburse Owner's funds held in Broker's trust account in the following order:
      (1) Compensation due Broker under paragraph 8.
      (2) All other operating expenses, costs and disbursements payable from Owner's funds held by Broker.
      (3) Reserves and security deposits held by Broker.
      (4) Balance to Owner.
   L. **OWNER DISTRIBUTION:** Remit funds, if any are available, monthly (or ☐ _____), to Owner.
   M. **OWNER STATEMENTS:** Render monthly, (or ☐ Quarterly or ☐ _____), statements of receipts, expenses and charges for each Property.
   N. **BROKER FUNDS:** Broker shall not advance Broker's own funds in connection with the Property or this Agreement.

Owner's Initials (_____) (_____)   Broker's Initials (_____) (_____)

The copyright laws of the United States (Title 17 U.S. Code) forbid the unauthorized reproduction of this form, or any portion thereof, by photocopy machine or any other means, including facsimile or computerized formats. Copyright © 1991-2013, CALIFORNIA ASSOCIATION OF REALTORS®, INC. ALL RIGHTS RESERVED.
PMA REVISED 11/13 (PAGE 1 OF 4)

Reviewed by _____ Date _____

PROPERTY MANAGEMENT AGREEMENT (PMA PAGE 1 OF 4)

Agent: WALT HUBER	Phone:	Fax:	Prepared using zipForm® software
Broker: WALT HUBER REALTOR			

Owner Name: *Tony Seller, Ramona J. Seller* _____ Date: _____

O. KEYSAFE/LOCKBOX: ☐ (If checked) Owner authorizes the use of a keysafe/lockbox to allow entry into the Property and agrees to sign a keysafe/ lockbox addendum (C.A.R., Form KLA).

4. OWNER RESPONSIBILITIES: Owner shall:
   A. Provide all documentation, records and disclosures as required by law or required by Broker to manage and operate the Property, and immediately notify Broker if Owner becomes aware of any change in such documentation, records or disclosures, or any matter affecting the habitability of the Property.
   B. Indemnify, defend and hold harmless Broker, and all persons in Broker's firm, regardless of responsibility, from all costs, expenses, suits, liabilities, damages, attorney fees and claims of every type, including but not limited to those arising out of injury or death of any person, or damage to any real or personal property of any person, including Owner, for: **(i)** any repairs performed by Owner or by others hired directly by Owner; or **(ii)** those relating to the management, leasing, rental, security deposits, or operation of the Property by Broker, or any person in Broker's firm, or the performance or exercise of any of the duties, powers or authorities granted to Broker.
   C. Maintain the Property in a condition fit for human habitation as required by Civil Code §§ 1941 and 1941.1 and Health and Safety Code §§ 17920.3 and 17920.10 and other applicable law.
   D. Pay all interest on tenants' security deposits if required by local law or ordinance.
   E. Carry and pay for: **(i)** public and premises liability insurance in an amount of no less than $1,000,000; and **(ii)** property damage and worker's compensation insurance adequate to protect the interests of Owner and Broker. Broker shall be, and Owner authorizes Broker to be, named as an additional insured party on Owner's policies.
   F. Pay any late charges, penalties and/or interest imposed by lenders or other parties for failure to make payment to those parties, if the failure is due to insufficient funds in Broker's trust account available for such payment.
   G. Immediately replace any funds required if there are insufficient funds in Broker's trust account to cover Owner's responsibilities.

5. OWNER REPRESENTATIONS: Owner represents that unless otherwise specified in writing, Owner is unaware of: **(i)** any recorded Notice of Default affecting the Property; **(ii)** any delinquent amounts due under any loan secured by, or other obligation affecting, the Property; **(iii)** any bankruptcy, insolvency or similar proceeding affecting the Property; **(iv)** any litigation, arbitration, administrative action, government investigation, or other pending or threatened action that does or may affect the Property or Owners ability to transfer it; and **(v)** any current, pending or proposed special assessments affecting the Property. Owner shall promptly notify Broker in writing if Owner becomes aware of any of these items during the term of this Agreement.

6. TAX WITHHOLDING:
   A. If Owner is not a California Resident or a corporation or LLC qualified to conduct business in California, Owner authorizes Broker to withhold and transmit to California Franchise Tax Board ("FTB") 7% of the GROSS payments to Owner that exceed $1,500 received by Broker, unless Owner completes and transmits to Broker FTB form 589, nonresident reduced withholding request, FTB form 588, nonresident withholding waiver, or FTB form 590, withholding exemption certificate.
   B. If Owner is a nonresident alien individual, a foreign entity or other non-U.S. person, (Foreign Investor) Owner authorizes Broker to withhold and transmit to the Internal Revenue Service (IRS) 30% of the GROSS rental receipts unless Owner elects to treat rental income as "effectively connected income" by submitting to Broker a fully completed IRS form W-8ECI, Certificate of Foreign Person's Claim for Exemption From Withholding on Income Effectively Connected With the Conduct of a Trade of Business in the United States. A Foreign investor Owner will need to obtain a U.S. tax payer identification number and file a declaration with the IRS regarding effectively connected income in order to complete the form given to Broker. Further, the Foreign Investor Owner will be responsible for making any necessary estimated tax payments.

7. DISCLOSURE:
   A. LEAD-BASED PAINT
      (1) ☐ The Property was constructed on or after January 1, 1978.
      OR **(2)** ☐ The Property was constructed prior to 1978.
         (i) Owner has no knowledge of lead-based paint or lead-based paint hazards in the housing except: _____
         _____
         (ii) Owner has no reports or records pertaining to lead-based paint or lead-based paint hazards in the housing, except the following, which Owner shall provide to Broker: _____
   B. POOL/SPA DRAIN
      Any pool or spa on the property does (or, ☐ does not) have an approved anti-entrapment drain cover, device or system.
   COMPENSATION:

8. A. Owner agrees to pay Broker fees in the amounts indicated below for:
   (1) Management: _____
   (2) Renting or Leasing: _____
   (3) Evictions: _____
   (4) Preparing Property for rental or lease: _____
   (5) Managing Property during extended periods of vacancy: _____
   (6) An overhead and service fee added to the cost of all work performed by, or at the direction of, Broker: _____
   (7) Other: _____
   B. This Agreement does not include providing on-site management services, property sales, refinancing, preparing Property for sale or refinancing, modernization, fire or major damage restoration, rehabilitation, obtaining income tax, accounting or legal advice, representation before public agencies, advising on proposed new construction, debt collection, counseling, attending Owner's Association meetings or _____

If Owner requests Broker to perform services not included in this Agreement, a fee shall be agreed upon before these services are performed.

Owner's Initials (_____) (_____)   Broker's Initials (_____) (_____)

Copyright © 1991-2013, CALIFORNIA ASSOCIATION OF REALTORS®, INC.
PMA REVISED 11/13 (PAGE 2 OF 4)

Reviewed by _____ Date _____

EQUAL HOUSING OPPORTUNITY
CA RPA

PROPERTY MANAGEMENT AGREEMENT (PMA PAGE 2 OF 4)

Owner Name: *Tony Seller, Ramona J. Seller*   Date: _____

 C. Broker may divide compensation, fees and charges due under this Agreement in any manner acceptable to Broker.
 D. Owner further agrees that:
  (1) Broker may receive and keep fees and charges from tenants for: **(i)** requesting an assignment of lease or sublease of the Property; **(ii)** processing credit applications; **(iii)** any returned checks and/or (☐ if checked) late payments; and **(iv)** any other services that are not in conflict with this Agreement.
  (2) Broker may perform any of Broker's duties, and obtain necessary products and services, through affiliated companies or organizations in which Broker may own an interest. Broker may receive fees, commissions and/or profits from these affiliated companies or organizations. Broker has an ownership interest in the following affiliated companies or organizations:

_____

_____ .

  Broker shall disclose to Owner any other such relationships as they occur. Broker shall not receive any fees, commissions or profits from unaffiliated companies or organizations in the performance of this Agreement, without prior disclosure to Owner.
  (3) Other: _____ .

9. AGENCY RELATIONSHIPS: Broker may act, and Owner hereby consents to Broker acting, as dual agent for Owner and tenant(s) in any resulting transaction. If the Property includes residential property with one-to-four dwelling units and this Agreement permits a tenancy in excess of one year, Owner acknowledges receipt of the "Disclosure Regarding Agency Relationships" (C.A.R. Form AD). Owner understands that Broker may have or obtain property management agreements on other property, and that potential tenants may consider, make offers on, or lease through Broker, property the same as or similar to Owner's Property. Owner consents to Broker's representation of other owners' properties before, during and after the expiration of this Agreement.

10. NOTICES: Any written notice to Owner or Broker required under this Agreement shall be served by sending such notice by first class mail or other agreed-to delivery method to that party at the address below, or at any different address the parties may later designate for this purpose. Notice shall be deemed received three (3) calendar days after deposit into the United States mail OR ☐ _____ .

11. DISPUTE RESOLUTION:

 A. MEDIATION: Owner and Broker agree to mediate any dispute or claim arising between them out of this Agreement, or any resulting transaction before resorting to arbitration or court action. Mediation fees, if any, shall be divided equally among the parties involved. If, for any dispute or claim to which this paragraph applies, any party (i) commences an action without first attempting to resolve the matter through mediation, or (ii) before commencement of an action, refuses to mediate after a request has been made, then that party shall not be entitled to recover attorney fees, even if they would otherwise be available to that party in any such action. THIS MEDIATION PROVISION APPLIES WHETHER OR NOT THE ARBITRATION PROVISION IS INITIALED. **Exclusions from this mediation agreement are specified in paragraph 11C.**

 B. ARBITRATION OF DISPUTES:
 Owner and Broker agree that any dispute or claim in Law or equity arising between them out of this Agreement or any resulting transaction, which is not settled through mediation, shall be decided by neutral, binding arbitration. The arbitrator shall be a retired judge or justice, or an attorney with at least 5 years of residential real estate Law experience, unless the parties mutually agree to a different arbitrator. The parties shall have the right to discovery in accordance with Code of Civil Procedure §1283.05. In all other respects, the arbitration shall be conducted in accordance with Title 9 of Part 3 of the Code of Civil Procedure. Judgment upon the award of the arbitrator(s) may be entered into any court having jurisdiction. Enforcement of this agreement to arbitrate shall be governed by the Federal Arbitration Act. Exclusions from this arbitration agreement are specified in paragraph 11C.
  "NOTICE: BY INITIALING IN THE SPACE BELOW YOU ARE AGREEING TO HAVE ANY DISPUTE ARISING OUT OF THE MATTERS INCLUDED IN THE 'ARBITRATION OF DISPUTES' PROVISION DECIDED BY NEUTRAL ARBITRATION AS PROVIDED BY CALIFORNIA LAW AND YOU ARE GIVING UP ANY RIGHTS YOU MIGHT POSSESS TO HAVE THE DISPUTE LITIGATED IN A COURT OR JURY TRIAL. BY INITIALING IN THE SPACE BELOW YOU ARE GIVING UP YOUR JUDICIAL RIGHTS TO DISCOVERY AND APPEAL, UNLESS THOSE RIGHTS ARE SPECIFICALLY INCLUDED IN THE 'ARBITRATION OF DISPUTES' PROVISION. IF YOU REFUSE TO SUBMIT TO ARBITRATION AFTER AGREEING TO THIS PROVISION, YOU MAY BE COMPELLED TO ARBITRATE UNDER THE AUTHORITY OF THE CALIFORNIA CODE OF CIVIL PROCEDURE. YOUR AGREEMENT TO THIS ARBITRATION PROVISION IS VOLUNTARY."
  "WE HAVE READ AND UNDERSTAND THE FOREGOING AND AGREE TO SUBMIT DISPUTES ARISING OUT OF THE MATTERS INCLUDED IN THE 'ARBITRATION OF DISPUTES' PROVISION TO NEUTRAL ARBITRATION."

Owner's Initials _____ / _____	Broker's Initials _____ / _____

 C. ADDITIONAL MEDIATION AND ARBITRATION TERMS: The following matters shall be excluded from mediation and arbitration: (i) a judicial or non-judicial foreclosure or other action or proceeding to enforce a deed of trust, mortgage or installment land sale contract as defined in Civil Code §2985; (ii) an unlawful detainer action; (iii) the filing or enforcement of a mechanic's lien; and (iv) any matter that is within the jurisdiction of a probate, small claims or bankruptcy court. The filing of a court action to enable the recording of a notice of pending action, for order of attachment, receivership, injunction, or other provisional remedies, shall not constitute a waiver or violation of the mediation and arbitration provisions.

Owner's Initials (_____) (_____)   Broker's Initials (_____) (_____)

Copyright © 1991-2013, CALIFORNIA ASSOCIATION OF REALTORS®, INC.
PMA REVISED 11/13 (PAGE 3 OF 4)

Reviewed by _____ Date _____

PROPERTY MANAGEMENT AGREEMENT (PMA PAGE 3 OF 4)   CA RPA

EQUAL HOUSING OPPORTUNITY

Owner Name: _Tony Seller, Ramona J. Seller_ _____ Date: _____

12. **EQUAL HOUSING OPPORTUNITY:** The Property is offered in compliance with federal, state and local anti-discrimination laws.

13. **ATTORNEY FEES:** In any action, proceeding or arbitration between Owner and Broker regarding the obligation to pay compensation under this Agreement, the prevailing Owner or Broker shall be entitled to reasonable attorney fees and costs from the non-prevailing Owner or Broker, except as provided in paragraph 11A.

14. **ADDITIONAL TERMS:** ☐ Keysafe/Lockbox Addendum (C.A.R. Form KLA); ☐ Lead-Based Paint and Lead-Based Paint Hazards Disclosure _____ (C.A.R. Form FLD) _____

_____

15. **TIME OF ESSENCE; ENTIRE CONTRACT; CHANGES:** Time is of the essence. All understandings between the parties are incorporated in this Agreement. Its terms are intended by the parties as a final, complete and exclusive expression of their Agreement with respect to its subject matter, and may not be contradicted by evidence of any prior agreement or contemporaneous oral agreement. If any provision of this Agreement is held to be ineffective or invalid, the remaining provisions will nevertheless be given full force and effect. Neither this Agreement nor any provision in it may be extended, amended, modified, altered or changed except in writing. This Agreement and any supplement, addendum or modification, including any copy, may be signed in two or more counterparts, all of which shall constitute one and the same writing.

Owner warrants that Owner is the owner of the Property or has the authority to execute this Agreement. Owner acknowledges Owner has read, understands, accepts and has received a copy of the Agreement.

Owner _____ Date _____
Owner _Tony Seller_ _____
    Print Name
Address _264 Beach Lane_ _____ City _Costa Mesa_   Social Security/Tax ID # (for tax reporting purposes)
Telephone _____ Fax _____ Email _____ State _CA_ Zip _92627_

Owner _____ Date _____
Owner _Ramona J. Seller_ _____
    Print Name
Address _____ City _____ Social Security/Tax ID # (for tax reporting purposes)
Telephone _____ Fax _____ Email _____ State _____ Zip _____

Real Estate Broker (Firm) _Sail Realty_ _____ Cal BRE Lic. #: _00 000 000_
By (Agent) _____ _Carmen Caro_ Cal BRE Lic. #: _00 000 000_ Date _____
Address _227 Harbor Blvd._ _____ City _Costa Mesa_ _____ State _CA_ Zip _92627_
Telephone _____ Fax _(714) 616-2829_ Email _carmen@sailrealty.com_

THIS FORM HAS BEEN APPROVED BY THE CALIFORNIA ASSOCIATION OF REALTORS® (C.A.R.). NO REPRESENTATION IS MADE AS TO THE LEGAL VALIDITY OR ADEQUACY OF ANY PROVISION IN ANY SPECIFIC TRANSACTION. A REAL ESTATE BROKER IS THE PERSON QUALIFIED TO ADVISE ON REAL ESTATE TRANSACTIONS. IF YOU DESIRE LEGAL OR TAX ADVICE, CONSULT AN APPROPRIATE PROFESSIONAL.
This form is available for use by the entire real estate industry. It is not intended to identify the user as a REALTOR®. REALTOR® is a registered collective membership mark which may be used only by members of the NATIONAL ASSOCIATION OF REALTORS® who subscribe to its Code of Ethics.

Published and Distributed by:
REAL ESTATE BUSINESS SERVICES, INC.
a subsidiary of the California Association of REALTORS®
525 South Virgil Avenue, Los Angeles, California 90020

Reviewed by _____ Date _____

PMA REVISED 11/13 (PAGE 4 OF 4)

PROPERTY MANAGEMENT AGREEMENT (PMA PAGE 4 OF 4)

CA RPA

F. LEASING AND TENANT SELECTION

As a property manager, you're really a merchandiser of space. Therefore, the sensible selection of worthy tenants is extremely important. Unless rental applicants are carefully screened and the proper and latest rental agreements are used, the owner's investment may be seriously impaired. At the least, the cash flow will be less than expected.

Landlord and tenant laws change. It's important for you to stay up-to-date with these changes; use the most current forms available.

While idealistic owners or managers may view the investment as brick and mortar on a piece of mother earth they call their own, in reality, the tenants are their principal assets. A proper balance must be maintained between viewing tenants' requests as always unrealistic and believing the tenants are always right. Without qualified tenants, the owner-landlord's economic position will be weakened.

As a property manager in California, you may charge up to $30.00 per applicant as a nonrefundable tenant screening fee.

As a property manager, it's good practice to make a copy of the prospective renter's driver's license, social security card, and other pertinent information; keep them in a secure rental file.

Many forms for qualifying tenants are available, including the CAR® Application To Rent/Screening Fee (LRA) form shown in **Figure 13-4**. A copy is given to the applicant, who is less likely to falsify his or her credit and character references because the application is, after all, a contract that will be kept on file. Included in the application are employment data, bank references, address and telephone numbers, number of adults and children, and a stipulation regarding pets.

Landlords may not discriminate against residential tenants based on various characteristics, including age, disability, gender, medical condition, race, color, religion, marital status, sexual orientation, ancestry, national origin, or citizenship.

The application can easily be expanded to incorporate other questions, such as length of time at present address, reason(s) for leaving, auto, driver's license, outstanding debts, and other credit data. It is of utmost importance that you verify this information, particularly the applicant's reasons for vacating previous quarters. For instance, a quick check by telephone may reveal that he or she was asked to leave because of overdue rent, continued violations of house rules, or violations of other lease provisions. Remember that a landlord might confide things on the telephone that he or she would not disclose in a letter for fear of reprisal. A call to the tenant's landlord prior to the last reference quite often offers more information.

Figure 13-4

CALIFORNIA
ASSOCIATION
OF REALTORS®

APPLICATION TO RENT/SCREENING FEE
(C.A.R. Form LRA, Revised 11/13)

I. APPLICATION TO RENT

THIS SECTION TO BE COMPLETED BY APPLICANT. A SEPARATE APPLICATION TO RENT IS REQUIRED FOR EACH OCCUPANT 18 YEARS OF AGE OR OVER, OR AN EMANCIPATED MINOR.

1. **Applicant is completing Application as a (check one)** ☐ tenant, ☐ tenant with co-tenant(s) or ☐ guarantor/co-signor.
   Total number of applicants _____.

2. **PREMISES INFORMATION**
   Application to rent property at _____ *264 Beach Lane, Costa Mesa, CA 92627* _____ ("Premises")
   Rent: $ _____ per _____ Proposed move-in date _____

3. **PERSONAL INFORMATION**
   A. FULL NAME OF APPLICANT_____
   B. Date of Birth _____ (For purpose of obtaining credit reports. Age discrimination is prohibited by law.)
   C. Social Security No. _____ Driver's License No. _____
      State _____ Expires _____
   D. Phone Number: Home_____ Work _____ Other _____
   E. Email _____
   F. Name(s) of all other proposed occupant(s) and relationship to applicant _____
      _____
   G. Pet(s) or service animals (number and type) _____
   H. Auto: Make _____ Model _____ Year _____ License No. _____ State _____ Color _____
      Other vehicle(s): _____
   I. In case of emergency, person to notify _____
      Relationship _____
      Address _____ Phone _____
   J. Does applicant or any proposed occupant plan to use liquid-filled furniture? ☐ No ☐ Yes Type _____
   K. Has applicant been a party to an unlawful detainer action or filed bankruptcy within the last seven years? ☐ No ☐ Yes
      If yes, explain _____
   L. Has applicant or any proposed occupant ever been convicted of or pleaded no contest to a felony? ☐ No ☐ Yes
      If yes, explain _____
   M. Has applicant or any proposed occupant ever been asked to move out of a residence? ☐ No ☐ Yes
      If yes, explain _____

4. **RESIDENCE HISTORY**
   Current address _____ Previous address _____
   City/State/Zip _____ City/State/Zip _____
   From _____ to _____ From _____ to _____
   Name of Landlord/Manager _____ Name of Landlord/Manager _____
   Landlord/Manager's phone _____ Landlord/Manager's phone _____
   Do you own this property? ☐ No ☐ Yes Did you own this property? ☒ No ☐ Yes
   Reason for leaving current address _____ Reason for leaving this address _____
   _____ _____

5. **EMPLOYMENT AND INCOME HISTORY**
   Current employer _____ Previous employer _____
   Current employer address _____ Prev. employer address _____
   From _____ To _____ From _____ To _____
   Supervisor _____ Supervisor _____
   Supervisor phone _____ Supervisor phone _____
   Employment gross income $_____ per _____ Employment gross income $_____ per _____
   Other income info _____ Other income info _____

The copyright laws of the United States (Title 17 U.S. Code) forbid the unauthorized reproduction of this form, or any portion thereof, by photocopy machine or any other means, including facsimile or computerized formats. Copyright © 1991-2013, CALIFORNIA ASSOCIATION OF REALTORS®, INC. ALL RIGHTS RESERVED.

Applicant's Initials (_____) (_____)

Reviewed by _____ Date _____

EQUAL HOUSING OPPORTUNITY

LRA REVISED 11/13 (PAGE 1 OF 2)

APPLICATION TO RENT/SCREENING FEE (LRA PAGE 1 OF 2)

Agent: WALT HUBER	Phone:	Fax:	Prepared using zipForm® software
Broker: WALT HUBER REALTOR			

CHAPTER 13

Property Address: *264 Beach Lane, Costa Mesa, CA 92627*   Date: _____

6. CREDIT INFORMATION

Name of creditor	Account number	Monthly payment	Balance due

Name of bank/branch	Account number	Type of account	Account balance

7. PERSONAL REFERENCES

Name _____ Address _____
Phone _____ Length of acquaintance _____ Occupation _____
Name _____ Address _____
Phone _____ Length of acquaintance _____ Occupation _____

8. NEAREST RELATIVE(S)

Name _____ Address _____
Phone _____ Relationship _____
Name _____ Address _____
Phone _____ Relationship _____

Applicant understands and agrees that: **(i)** this is an application to rent only and does not guarantee that applicant will be offered the Premises; **(ii)** Landlord or Manager or Agent may accept more than one application for the Premises and, using their sole discretion, will select the best qualified applicant, and **(iii)** Applicant will provide a copy of applicant's driver's license upon request.

Applicant represents the above information to be true and complete, and hereby authorizes Landlord or Manager or Agent to: **(i)** verify the information provided; and **(ii)** obtain a credit report on applicant and other reports, warnings and verifications on and about applicant, which may include, but not be limited to, criminal background checks, reports on unlawful detainers, bad checks, fraud warnings, employment and tenant history. Applicant further authorizes Landlord or Manager or Agent to disclose information to prior or subsequent owners and/or agents.

If application is not fully completed, or received without the screening fee: (i) the application will not be processed, and (ii) the application and any screening fee will be returned.

Applicant _____ Date _____ Time _____

Return your completed application and any applicable fee not already paid to: _____
Address _____ City _____ State _____ Zip _____

II. SCREENING FEE

THIS SECTION TO BE COMPLETED BY LANDLORD, MANAGER OR AGENT.

Applicant has paid a **nonrefundable** screening fee of $ _____ , applied as follows: (The screening fee may not exceed $30.00, adjusted annually from 1-1-98 commensurate with the increase in the Consumer Price Index. A CPI inflation calculator is available on the Bureau of Labor Statistics website, www.bls.gov. The California Department of Consumer Affairs calculates the applicable screening fee amount to be $42.06 as of 2009.)

$ _____ for credit reports prepared by _____ ;
$ _____ for _____ (other out-of-pocket expenses); and
$ _____ for processing.

The undersigned has read the foregoing and acknowledges receipt of a copy.

_____   _____
Applicant Signature   Date

The undersigned has received the screening fee indicated above.

                     CalBRE Lic. # _____
_____   _____
Landlord or Manager or Agent Signature   Date

The copyright laws of the United States (Title 17 U.S. Code) forbid the unauthorized reproduction of this form, or any portion thereof, by photocopy machine or any other means, including facsimile or computerized formats. Copyright © 1998-2013, CALIFORNIA ASSOCIATION OF REALTORS®, INC. ALL RIGHTS RESERVED.
THIS FORM HAS BEEN APPROVED BY THE CALIFORNIA ASSOCIATION OF REALTORS® (C.A.R.). NO REPRESENTATION IS MADE AS TO THE LEGAL VALIDITY OR ADEQUACY OF ANY PROVISION IN ANY SPECIFIC TRANSACTION. A REAL ESTATE BROKER IS THE PERSON QUALIFIED TO ADVISE ON REAL ESTATE TRANSACTIONS. IF YOU DESIRE LEGAL OR TAX ADVICE, CONSULT AN APPROPRIATE PROFESSIONAL.
This form is available for use by the entire real estate industry. It is not intended to identify the user as a REALTOR®. REALTOR® is a registered collective membership mark which may be used only by members of the NATIONAL ASSOCIATION OF REALTORS® who subscribe to its Code of Ethics.

Published and Distributed by:
REAL ESTATE BUSINESS SERVICES, INC.
a subsidiary of the California Association of REALTORS®
525 South Virgil Avenue, Los Angeles, California 90020

LRA REVISED 11/13 (PAGE 2 OF 2)

Reviewed by _____ Date _____

APPLICATION TO RENT/SCREENING FEE (LRA PAGE 2 OF 2)

CA RPA

Remember: Should the property owner decide to sell the property during an existing, valid lease, the lease stays in effect.

1. Lease Contracts

Lease contracts vary with the kind of property being let (leased) and the requirements and preferences of the owners.

The CAR® Residential Lease or Month-To-Month Rental Agreement (LR) form (**Figure 13-5**) is designed primarily for the residential lease. There are innumerable forms used for different types of property. Select the lease that best fits the circumstances in each case.

Any rental agreement that ends over one year from the date of signing must be in writing. But it is a good idea to have all rental agreements in writing.

The standard form provides for the usual information. The preprinted paragraphs contain provisions for assignment and subletting, default proceedings, condition of premises, usage and occupancy, compliance with applicable laws and ordinances, liability for insurance, renewal rights, and waiver stipulations. Additional space is provided for insertion of items not specifically covered. Both lessor and lessee sign the lease, although technically, the tenant is accepting the lease by taking possession of the property.

Not shown here, a very specific room-by-room inspection form (CAR's® "Move In/Move Out Inspection"—MIMO) can be used if a more detailed description of the property condition is required by your owner or tenant. It would be filled out while walking the tenant through the property, before moving in and prior to moving out.

a. Types of Leasehold Estates

Prior to describing the five groups of leases, it is important to explain the four basic types of leasehold estates.

1. **Estate for Years.** This estate is a right of occupancy for a definite fixed period of time. This time frame could be for any specified length measured in days, weeks, or months.

2. **Estate from Period-to-Period.** The most common periodic tenancy is a month-to-month lease.

3. **Estate at Sufferance.** This estate is created when a tenant obtains possession legally, but then remains on the property, without the owner's consent, after the expiration of the terms. The landlord has the choice of evicting the tenant through court action, or accepting the tenant on the same terms and conditions of the previous occupancy.

In non-emergency situations, landlords must give the tenant a 24-hour notice, in writing, of the intent to enter the property. Entry must be during normal business hours, unless the tenant otherwise consents.

Figure 13-5

CALIFORNIA
ASSOCIATION
OF REALTORS®

**RESIDENTIAL LEASE OR
MONTH-TO-MONTH RENTAL AGREEMENT**
(C.A.R. Form LR, Revised 12/13)

Date _____, _____ _Tony Seller, Ramona J. Seller_ _____ ("Landlord") and
_____ _Walter Buyer, Debbie Buyer_ _____ ("Tenant") agree as follows:

1. PROPERTY:

  A. Landlord rents to Tenant and Tenant rents from Landlord, the real property and improvements described as: _264 Beach Lane, Costa_
  Mesa, CA 92627 _____ ("Premises").

  B. The Premises are for the sole use as a personal residence by the following named person(s) **only:** _____
  _____ .

  C. The following personal property, maintained pursuant to paragraph 11, is included:
  _____ or ☐ (if checked) the personal property on the attached addendum.

  D. The Premises may be subject to a local rent control ordinance _____

2. TERM: The term begins on (date) _____ ("Commencement Date"), **(Check A or B).**

  ☐ **A. Month-to-Month:** and continues as a month-to-month tenancy. Tenant may terminate the tenancy by giving written notice at least 30 days
  prior to the intended termination date. Landlord may terminate the tenancy by giving written notice as provided by law. Such notices may be
  given on any date.

  ☐ **B. Lease:** and shall terminate on (date) _____ at _____ ☐ AM/ ☐ PM.
  Tenant shall vacate the Premises upon termination of the Agreement, unless: **(i)** Landlord and Tenant have extended this Agreement in
  writing or signed a new agreement; **(ii)** mandated by local rent control law; or **(iii)** Landlord accepts Rent from Tenant (other than past due
  Rent), in which case a month-to-month tenancy shall be created which either party may terminate as specified in paragraph 2A. Rent shall be
  at a rate agreed to by Landlord and Tenant, or as allowed by law. All other terms and conditions of this Agreement shall remain in full force
  and effect.

3. RENT: "Rent" shall mean all monetary obligations of Tenant to Landlord under the terms of the Agreement, except security deposit.

  A. Tenant agrees to pay $ _____ per month for the term of the Agreement.

  B. Rent is payable in advance on the **1st (or** ☐ _____ **)** day of each calendar month, and is delinquent on the next day.

  C. If Commencement Date falls on any day other than the day Rent is payable under paragraph 3B, and Tenant has paid one full month's Rent in
  advance of Commencement Date, Rent for the second calendar month shall be prorated and Tenant shall pay 1/30th of the monthly rent per day
  for each day remaining in prorated second month.

  D. PAYMENT: Rent shall be paid by ☐ personal check, ☐ money order, ☐ cashier's check, or ☐ other _____ , to
  (name) _____ (phone) _____ at
  (address) _____ (or
  at any other location subsequently specified by Landlord in writing to Tenant) (and ☐ if checked, rent may be paid personally, between the hours
  of _____ and _____ on the following days _____). If any payment
  is returned for non-sufficient funds ("NSF") or because tenant stops payment, then, after that: (i) Landlord may, in writing, require Tenant to pay
  Rent in cash for three months and (ii) all future Rent shall be paid by ☐ money order, or ☐ cashier's check.

4. SECURITY DEPOSIT:

  A. Tenant agrees to pay $ _____ as a security deposit. Security deposit will be ☐ transferred to and held by the Owner
  of the Premises, or ☐ held in Owner's Broker's trust account.

  B. All or any portion of the security deposit may be used, as reasonably necessary, to: **(i)** cure Tenant's default in payment of Rent (which includes
  Late Charges, NSF fees or other sums due); **(ii)** repair damage, excluding ordinary wear and tear, caused by Tenant or by a guest or licensee of
  Tenant; **(iii)** clean Premises, if necessary, upon termination of the tenancy; and **(iv)** replace or return personal property or appurtenances.
  SECURITY DEPOSIT SHALL NOT BE USED BY TENANT IN LIEU OF PAYMENT OF LAST MONTH'S RENT. If all or any portion of the
  security deposit is used during the tenancy, Tenant agrees to reinstate the total security deposit within five days after written notice is delivered to
  Tenant. Within 21 days after Tenant vacates the Premises, Landlord shall: **(1)** furnish Tenant an itemized statement indicating the amount of any
  security deposit received and the basis for its disposition and supporting documentation as required by California Civil Code § 1950.5(g); and **(2)**
  return any remaining portion of the security deposit to Tenant.

  **C. Security deposit will not be returned until all Tenants have vacated the Premises and all keys returned. Any security deposit returned
  by check shall be made out to all Tenants named on this Agreement, or as subsequently modified.**

  D. No interest will be paid on security deposit unless required by local law.

  E. If the security deposit is held by Owner, Tenant agrees not to hold Broker responsible for its return. If the security deposit is held in Owner's
  Broker's trust account, **and** Broker's authority is terminated before expiration of this Agreement, **and** security deposit is released to someone
  other than Tenant, **then** Broker shall notify Tenant, in writing, where and to whom security deposit has been released. Once Tenant has been
  provided such notice, Tenant agrees not to hold Broker responsible for the security deposit.

5. MOVE-IN COSTS RECEIVED/DUE: Move-in funds made payable to _____
shall be paid by ☐ personal check, ☐ money order, or ☐ cashier's check.

Category	Total Due	Payment Received	Balance Due	Date Due
Rent from _____ to _____ (date)				
*Security Deposit				
Other				
Other				
Total				

*The maximum amount Landlord may receive as security deposit, however designated, cannot exceed two months' Rent for unfurnished premises, or
three months' Rent for furnished premises.

Tenant's Initials (_____) (_____)   Landlord's Initials (_____) (_____)

© 2013, California Association of REALTORS®, Inc.
LR REVISED 12/13 (PAGE 1 OF 6)

Reviewed by _____ Date _____

EQUAL HOUSING
OPPORTUNITY

RESIDENTIAL LEASE OR MONTH-TO-MONTH RENTAL AGREEMENT (LR PAGE 1 OF 6)

Agent: WALT HUBER	Phone:	Fax:	Prepared using zipForm® software
Broker: WALT HUBER REALTOR			

Premises: *264 Beach Lane*
Costa Mesa, CA 92627 _____ Date: _____

6. LATE CHARGE; RETURNED CHECKS:

    A. Tenant acknowledges either late payment of Rent or issuance of a returned check may cause Landlord to incur costs and expenses, the exact amounts of which are extremely difficult and impractical to determine. These costs may include, but are not limited to, processing, enforcement and accounting expenses, and late charges imposed on Landlord. If any installment of Rent due from Tenant is not received by Landlord within **5 (or ☐ _____) calendar days** after the date due, or if a check is returned, Tenant shall pay to Landlord, respectively, an additional sum of $ _____ or _____ % of the Rent due as a Late Charge and $25.00 as a NSF fee for the first returned check and $35.00 as a NSF fee for each additional returned check, either or both of which shall be deemed additional Rent.

    B. Landlord and Tenant agree that these charges represent a fair and reasonable estimate of the costs Landlord may incur by reason of Tenant's late or NSF payment. Any Late Charge or NSF fee due shall be paid with the current installment of Rent. Landlord's acceptance of any Late Charge or NSF fee shall not constitute a waiver as to any default of Tenant. Landlord's right to collect a Late Charge or NSF fee shall not be deemed an extension of the date Rent is due under paragraph 3 or prevent Landlord from exercising any other rights and remedies under this Agreement and as provided by law.

7. PARKING: (Check A or B)

    ☐ **A.** Parking is permitted as follows: _____
_____.
The right to parking ☐ is ☐ is not included in the Rent charged pursuant to paragraph 3. If not included in the Rent, the parking rental fee shall be an additional $ _____ per month. Parking space(s) are to be used for parking properly licensed and operable motor vehicles, except for trailers, boats, campers, buses or trucks (other than pick-up trucks). Tenant shall park in assigned space(s) only. Parking space(s) are to be kept clean. Vehicles leaking oil, gas or other motor vehicle fluids shall not be parked on the Premises. Mechanical work or storage of inoperable vehicles is not permitted in parking space(s) or elsewhere on the Premises.

  OR ☐ **B.** Parking is not permitted on the Premises.

8. STORAGE: (Check A or B)

    ☐ **A.** Storage is permitted as follows: _____
The right to separate storage space ☐ is, ☐ is not, included in the Rent charged pursuant to paragraph 3. If not included in the Rent, storage space fee shall be an additional $ _____ per month. Tenant shall store only personal property Tenant owns, and shall not store property claimed by another or in which another has any right, title or interest. Tenant shall not store any improperly packaged food or perishable goods, flammable materials, explosives, hazardous waste or other inherently dangerous material, or illegal substances.

  OR ☐ **B.** Except for Tenant's personal property, contained entirely within the Premises, storage is not permitted on the Premises.

9. UTILITIES: Tenant agrees to pay for all utilities and services, and the following charges: _____
except _____, which shall be paid for by Landlord. If any utilities are not separately metered, Tenant shall pay Tenant's proportional share, as reasonably determined and directed by Landlord. If utilities are separately metered, Tenant shall place utilities in Tenant's name as of the Commencement Date. Landlord is only responsible for installing and maintaining one usable telephone jack and one telephone line to the Premises. Tenant shall pay any cost for conversion from existing utilities service provider.

10. CONDITION OF PREMISES: Tenant has examined Premises and, if any, all furniture, furnishings, appliances, landscaping and fixtures, including smoke detector(s).

    (Check all that apply:)

    ☐ **A.** Tenant acknowledges these items are clean and in operable condition, with the following exceptions: _____

    ☐ **B.** Tenant's acknowledgment of the condition of these items is contained in an attached statement of condition (C.A.R. Form MIMO).

    ☐ **C.** **(i)** Landlord will Deliver to Tenant a statement of condition (C.A.R. Form MIMO) ☐ within **3 days** after execution of this Agreement; ☐ prior to the Commencement Date; ☐ within 3 days after the Commencement Date.
        (ii) Tenant shall complete and return the MIMO to Landlord within 3 (or ☐ _____) **days** after Delivery. Tenant's failure to return the MIMO within that time shall conclusively be deemed Tenant's Acknowledgement of the condition as stated in the MIMO.

    ☐ **D.** Tenant will provide Landlord a list of items that are damaged or not in operable condition within 3 (or ☐ _____) **days** after Commencement Date, not as a contingency of this Agreement but rather as an acknowledgment of the condition of the Premises.

    ☐ **E.** Other: _____

11. MAINTENANCE:

    A. Tenant shall properly use, operate and safeguard Premises, including if applicable, any landscaping, furniture, furnishings and appliances, and all mechanical, electrical, gas and plumbing fixtures, and smoke alarms, and keep them and the Premises clean, sanitary and well ventilated. Tenant shall be responsible for checking and maintaining all carbon monoxide detectors and any additional phone lines beyond the one line and jack that Landlord shall provide and maintain. Tenant shall immediately notify Landlord, in writing, of any problem, malfunction or damage with any item on the property. Tenant shall be charged for all repairs or replacements caused by Tenant, pets, guests or licensees of Tenant, excluding ordinary wear and tear. Tenant shall be charged for all damage to Premises as a result of failure to report a problem in a timely manner. Tenant shall be charged for repair of drain blockages or stoppages, unless caused by defective plumbing parts or tree roots invading sewer lines.

    B. ☐ Landlord ☐ Tenant shall water the garden, landscaping, trees and shrubs, except: _____

    C. ☐ Landlord ☐ Tenant shall maintain the garden, landscaping, trees and shrubs, except: _____

    D. ☐ Landlord ☐ Tenant shall maintain _____
    E. Tenant's failure to maintain any item for which Tenant is responsible shall give Landlord the right to hire someone to perform such maintenance and charge Tenant to cover the cost of such maintenance.

    F. The following items of personal property are included in the Premises without warranty and Landlord will not maintain, repair or replace them: _____

Tenant's Initials (_____) (_____)   Landlord's Initials (_____) (_____)

Premises: 264 Beach Lane
Costa Mesa, CA 92627 _____ Date: _____

12. NEIGHBORHOOD CONDITIONS: Tenant is advised to satisfy him or herself as to neighborhood or area conditions, including schools, proximity and adequacy of law enforcement, crime statistics, proximity of registered felons or offenders, fire protection, other governmental services, availability, adequacy and cost of any wired, wireless internet connections or other telecommunications or other technology services and installations, proximity to commercial, industrial or agricultural activities, existing and proposed transportation, construction and development that may affect noise, view, or traffic, airport noise, noise or odor from any source, wild and domestic animals, other nuisances, hazards, or circumstances, cemeteries, facilities and condition of common areas, conditions and influences of significance to certain cultures and/or religions, and personal needs, requirements and preferences of Tenant.

13. PETS: Unless otherwise provided in California Civil Code § 54.2, no animal or pet shall be kept on or about the Premises without Landlord's prior written consent, except: _____ .

14. ☐ (If checked) **NO SMOKING:** No smoking of any substance is allowed on the Premises or common areas. If smoking does occur on the Premises or common areas, (i) Tenant is responsible for all damage caused by the smoking including, but not limited to stains, burns, odors and removal of debris; (ii) Tenant is in breach of this Agreement; (iii) Tenant, guests, and all others may be required to leave the Premises; and (iv) Tenant acknowledges that in order to remove odor caused by smoking, Landlord may need to replace carpet and drapes and paint the entire premises regardless of when these items were last cleaned, replaced, or repainted. Such actions and other necessary steps will impact the return of any security deposit. The Premises or common areas may be subject to a local non-smoking ordinance.

15. RULES/REGULATIONS:
  A. Tenant agrees to comply with all Landlord rules and regulations that are at any time posted on the Premises or delivered to Tenant. Tenant shall not, and shall ensure that guests and licensees of Tenant shall not, disturb, annoy, endanger or interfere with other tenants of the building or neighbors, or use the Premises for any unlawful purposes, including, but not limited to, using, manufacturing, selling, storing or transporting illicit drugs or other contraband, or violate any law or ordinance, or commit a waste or nuisance on or about the Premises.
  B. (If applicable, check one)
    ☐ **1.** Landlord shall provide Tenant with a copy of the rules and regulations within _____ days or _____ .
    OR ☐ **2.** Tenant has been provided with, and acknowledges receipt of, a copy of the rules and regulations.

16. ☐ (If checked) **CONDOMINIUM; PLANNED UNIT DEVELOPMENT:**
  A. The Premises are a unit in a condominium, planned unit development, common interest subdivision or other development governed by a homeowners' association ("HOA"). The name of the HOA is _____ . Tenant agrees to comply with all HOA covenants, conditions and restrictions, bylaws, rules and regulations and decisions ("HOA Rules"). Landlord shall provide Tenant copies of HOA Rules, if any. Tenant shall reimburse Landlord for any fines or charges imposed by HOA or other authorities, due to any violation by Tenant, or the guests or licensees of Tenant.
  B. (Check one)
    ☐ **1.** Landlord shall provide Tenant with a copy of the HOA Rules within _____ days or _____ .
    OR ☐ **2.** Tenant has been provided with, and acknowledges receipt of, a copy of the HOA Rules.

17. ALTERATIONS; REPAIRS: Unless otherwise specified by law or paragraph 29C, without Landlord's prior written consent, **(i)** Tenant shall not make any repairs, alterations or improvements in or about the Premises including: painting, wallpapering, adding or changing locks, installing antenna or satellite dish(es) placing signs, displays or exhibits, or using screws, fastening devices, large nails or adhesive materials; **(ii)** Landlord shall not be responsible for the costs of alterations or repairs made by Tenant; **(iii)** Tenant shall not deduct from Rent the costs of any repairs, alterations or improvements; and **(iv)** any deduction made by Tenant shall be considered unpaid Rent.

18. KEYS; LOCKS:
  A. Tenant acknowledges receipt of (or Tenant will receive ☐ prior to the Commencement Date, or ☐ _____):
    ☐ _____ key(s) to Premises,   ☐ _____ remote control device(s) for garage door/gate opener(s),
    ☐ _____ key(s) to mailbox,   ☐ _____
    ☐ _____ key(s) to common area(s),
  B. Tenant acknowledges that locks to the Premises ☐ have, ☐ have not, been re-keyed.
  C. If Tenant re-keys existing locks or opening devices, Tenant shall immediately deliver copies of all keys to Landlord. Tenant shall pay all costs and charges related to loss of any keys or opening devices. Tenant may not remove locks, even if installed by Tenant.

19. ENTRY:
  A. Tenant shall make Premises available to Landlord or Landlord's representative for the purpose of entering to make necessary or agreed repairs, (including, but not limited to, installing, repairing, testing, and maintaining smoke detectors and carbon monoxide devices, and bracing, anchoring or strapping water heaters), decorations, alterations, or improvements, or to supply necessary or agreed services, or to show Premises to prospective or actual purchasers, tenants, mortgagees, lenders, appraisers, or contractors.
  B. Landlord and Tenant agree that 24-hour written notice shall be reasonable and sufficient notice, except as follows: (1) 48-hour written notice is required to conduct an inspection of the Premises prior to the Tenant moving out, unless the Tenant waives the right to such notice. (2) If Landlord has in writing informed Tenant that the Premises are for sale and that Tenant will be notified orally to show the premises (C.A.R. Form NSE), then, for the next 120 days following the delivery of the NSE, notice may be given orally to show the Premises to actual or prospective purchasers. (3) No written notice is required if Landlord and Tenant orally agree to an entry for agreed services or repairs if the date and time of entry are within one week of the oral agreement. (4) No notice is required: **(i)** to enter in case of an emergency; **(ii)** if the Tenant is present and consents at the time of entry; or **(iii)** if the Tenant has abandoned or surrendered the Premises.
  C. ☐ (If checked) Tenant authorizes the use of a keysafe/lockbox to allow entry into the Premises and agrees to sign a keysafe/lockbox addendum (C.A.R. Form KLA).

20. SIGNS: Tenant authorizes Landlord to place FOR SALE/LEASE signs on the Premises.

21. ASSIGNMENT; SUBLETTING: Tenant shall not sublet all or any part of Premises, or assign or transfer this Agreement or any interest in it, without Landlord's prior written consent. Unless such consent is obtained, any assignment, transfer or subletting of Premises or this Agreement or tenancy, by voluntary act of Tenant, operation of law or otherwise, shall, at the option of Landlord, terminate this Agreement. Any proposed assignee, transferee or sublessee shall submit to Landlord an application and credit information for Landlord's approval and, if approved, sign a separate written agreement with Landlord and Tenant. Landlord's consent to any one assignment, transfer or sublease, shall not be construed as consent to any subsequent assignment, transfer or sublease and does not release Tenant of Tenant's obligations under this Agreement.

Tenant's Initials (_____)(_____)   Landlord's Initials (_____)(_____)

LR REVISED 12/13 (PAGE 3 OF 6)

| Reviewed by _____ Date _____ |

RESIDENTIAL LEASE OR MONTH-TO-MONTH RENTAL AGREEMENT (LR PAGE 3 OF 6)

Premises: *264 Beach Lane*
Costa Mesa, CA 92627 _____ Date: _____

22. **JOINT AND INDIVIDUAL OBLIGATIONS:** If there is more than one Tenant, each one shall be individually and completely responsible for the performance of all obligations of Tenant under this Agreement, jointly with every other Tenant, and individually, whether or not in possession.

23. ☐ **LEAD-BASED PAINT (If checked):** Premises were constructed prior to 1978. In accordance with federal law, Landlord gives and Tenant acknowledges receipt of the disclosures on the attached form (C.A.R. Form FLD) and a federally approved lead pamphlet.

24. ☐ **MILITARY ORDNANCE DISCLOSURE:** (If applicable and known to Landlord) Premises are located within one mile of an area once used for military training, and may contain potentially explosive munitions.

25. ☐ **PERIODIC PEST CONTROL:** Landlord has entered into a contract for periodic pest control treatment of the Premises and shall give Tenant a copy of the notice originally given to Landlord by the pest control company.

26. ☐ **METHAMPHETAMINE CONTAMINATION:** Prior to signing this Agreement, Landlord has given Tenant a notice that a health official has issued an order prohibiting occupancy of the property because of methamphetamine contamination. A copy of the notice and order are attached.

27. **MEGAN'S LAW DATABASE DISCLOSURE:** Notice: Pursuant to Section 290.46 of the Penal Code, information about specified registered sex offenders is made available to the public via an Internet Web site maintained by the Department of Justice at www.meganslaw.ca.gov. Depending on an offender's criminal history, this information will include either the address at which the offender resides or the community of residence and ZIP Code in which he or she resides. (Neither Landlord nor Brokers, if any, are required to check this website. If Tenant wants further information, Tenant should obtain information directly from this website.)

28. **POSSESSION:**
    A. Tenant is not in possession of the Premises. If Landlord is unable to deliver possession of Premises on Commencement Date, such Date shall be extended to the date on which possession is made available to Tenant. If Landlord is unable to deliver possession within **5 (or ☐ _____) calendar days** after agreed Commencement Date, Tenant may terminate this Agreement by giving written notice to Landlord, and shall be refunded all Rent and security deposit paid. Possession is deemed terminated when Tenant has returned all keys to the Premises to Landlord.
    B. ☐ Tenant is already in possession of the Premises.

29. **TENANT'S OBLIGATIONS UPON VACATING PREMISES:**
    A. Upon termination of this Agreement, Tenant shall: **(i)** give Landlord all copies of all keys or opening devices to Premises, including any common areas; **(ii)** vacate and surrender Premises to Landlord, empty of all persons; **(iii)** vacate any/all parking and/or storage space; **(iv)** clean and deliver Premises, as specified in paragraph C below, to Landlord in the same condition as referenced in paragraph 10; **(v)** remove all debris; **(vi)** give written notice to Landlord of Tenant's forwarding address; and **(vii)**
    _____
    B. All alterations/improvements made by or caused to be made by Tenant, with or without Landlord's consent, become the property of Landlord upon termination. Landlord may charge Tenant for restoration of the Premises to the condition it was in prior to any alterations/improvements.
    C. **Right to Pre-Move-Out Inspection and Repairs: (i)** After giving or receiving notice of termination of a tenancy (C.A.R. Form NTT), or before the end of a lease, Tenant has the right to request that an inspection of the Premises take place prior to termination of the lease or rental (C.A.R. Form NRI). If Tenant requests such an inspection, Tenant shall be given an opportunity to remedy identified deficiencies prior to termination, consistent with the terms of this Agreement. **(ii)** Any repairs or alterations made to the Premises as a result of this inspection (collectively, "Repairs") shall be made at Tenant's expense. Repairs may be performed by Tenant or through others, who have adequate insurance and licenses and are approved by Landlord. The work shall comply with applicable law, including governmental permit, inspection and approval requirements. Repairs shall be performed in a good, skillful manner with materials of quality and appearance comparable to existing materials. It is understood that exact restoration of appearance or cosmetic items following all Repairs may not be possible. **(iii)** Tenant shall: **(a)** obtain receipts for Repairs performed by others; **(b)** prepare a written statement indicating the Repairs performed by Tenant and the date of such Repairs; and **(c)** provide copies of receipts and statements to Landlord prior to termination. Paragraph 29C does not apply when the tenancy is terminated pursuant to California Code of Civil Procedure § 1161(2), (3) or (4).

30. **BREACH OF CONTRACT; EARLY TERMINATION:** In addition to any obligations established by paragraph 29, in the event of termination by Tenant prior to completion of the original term of the Agreement, Tenant shall also be responsible for lost Rent, rental commissions, advertising expenses and painting costs necessary to ready Premises for re-rental. Landlord may withhold any such amounts from Tenant's security deposit.

31. **TEMPORARY RELOCATION:** Subject to local law, Tenant agrees, upon demand of Landlord, to temporarily vacate Premises for a reasonable period, to allow for fumigation (or other methods) to control wood destroying pests or organisms, or other repairs to Premises. Tenant agrees to comply with all instructions and requirements necessary to prepare Premises to accommodate pest control, fumigation or other work, including bagging or storage of food and medicine, and removal of perishables and valuables. Tenant shall only be entitled to a credit of Rent equal to the per diem Rent for the period of time Tenant is required to vacate Premises.

32. **DAMAGE TO PREMISES:** If, by no fault of Tenant, Premises are totally or partially damaged or destroyed by fire, earthquake, accident or other casualty that render Premises totally or partially uninhabitable, either Landlord or Tenant may terminate this Agreement by giving the other written notice. Rent shall be abated as of the date Premises become totally or partially uninhabitable. The abated amount shall be the current monthly Rent prorated on a 30-day period. If the Agreement is not terminated, Landlord shall promptly repair the damage, and Rent shall be reduced based on the extent to which the damage interferes with Tenant's reasonable use of Premises. If damage occurs as a result of an act of Tenant or Tenant's guests, only Landlord shall have the right of termination, and no reduction in Rent shall be made.

33. **INSURANCE:** Tenant's or guest's personal property and vehicles are not insured by Landlord, manager or, if applicable, HOA, against loss or damage due to fire, theft, vandalism, rain, water, criminal or negligent acts of others, or any other cause. **Tenant is advised to carry Tenant's own insurance (renter's insurance) to protect Tenant from any such loss or damage.** Tenant shall comply with any requirement imposed on Tenant by Landlord's insurer to avoid: **(i)** an increase in Landlord's insurance premium (or Tenant shall pay for the increase in premium); or **(ii)** loss of insurance.

34. **WATERBEDS:** Tenant shall not use or have waterbeds on the Premises unless: **(i)** Tenant obtains a valid waterbed insurance policy; **(ii)** Tenant increases the security deposit in an amount equal to one-half of one month's Rent; and **(iii)** the bed conforms to the floor load capacity of Premises.

35. **WAIVER:** The waiver of any breach shall not be construed as a continuing waiver of the same or any subsequent breach.

Tenant's Initials (_____) (_____)   Landlord's Initials (_____) (_____)

LR REVISED 12/13 (PAGE 4 OF 6) | Reviewed by _____ Date _____ |

RESIDENTIAL LEASE OR MONTH-TO-MONTH RENTAL AGREEMENT (LR PAGE 4 OF 6)

Premises: 264 Beach Lane
Costa Mesa, CA 92627   Date: _____

36. NOTICE: Notices may be served at the following address, or at any other location subsequently designated:
Landlord: _____   Tenant: _____
_____   _____
_____   _____

37. TENANT ESTOPPEL CERTIFICATE: Tenant shall execute and return a tenant estoppel certificate delivered to Tenant by Landlord or Landlord's agent within **3 days** after its receipt. Failure to comply with this requirement shall be deemed Tenant's acknowledgment that the tenant estoppel certificate is true and correct, and may be relied upon by a lender or purchaser.

38. REPRESENTATION:
A.   TENANT REPRESENTATION; OBLIGATIONS REGARDING OCCUPANTS; CREDIT: Tenant warrants that all statements in Tenant's rental application are accurate. Landlord requires all occupants 18 years of age or older and all emancipated minors to complete a lease rental application. Tenant acknowledges this requirement and agrees to notify Landlord when any occupant of the Premises reaches the age of 18 or becomes an emancipated minor. Tenant authorizes Landlord and Broker(s) to obtain Tenant's credit report periodically during the tenancy in connection with the modification or enforcement of this Agreement. Landlord may cancel this Agreement: **(i)** before occupancy begins; **(ii)** upon disapproval of the credit report(s); or **(iii)** at any time, upon discovering that information in Tenant's application is false. A negative credit report reflecting on Tenant's record may be submitted to a credit reporting agency if Tenant fails to fulfill the terms of payment and other obligations under this Agreement.
B.   LANDLORD REPRESENTATIONS: Landlord warrants, that unless otherwise specified in writing, Landlord is unaware of **(i)** any recorded Notices of Default affecting the Premise; **(ii)** any delinquent amounts due under any loan secured by the Premises; and **(iii)** any bankruptcy proceeding affecting the Premises.

39. MEDIATION:
A.   Consistent with paragraphs B and C below, Landlord and Tenant agree to mediate any dispute or claim arising between them out of this Agreement, or any resulting transaction, before resorting to court action. Mediation fees, if any, shall be divided equally among the parties involved. If, for any dispute or claim to which this paragraph applies, any party commences an action without first attempting to resolve the matter through mediation, or refuses to mediate after a request has been made, then that party shall not be entitled to recover attorney fees, even if they would otherwise be available to that party in any such action.
B.   The following matters are excluded from mediation: **(i)** an unlawful detainer action; **(ii)** the filing or enforcement of a mechanic's lien; and **(iii)** any matter within the jurisdiction of a probate, small claims or bankruptcy court. The filing of a court action to enable the recording of a notice of pending action, for order of attachment, receivership, injunction, or other provisional remedies, shall not constitute a waiver of the mediation provision.
C.   Landlord and Tenant agree to mediate disputes or claims involving Listing Agent, Leasing Agent or property manager ("Broker"), provided Broker shall have agreed to such mediation prior to, or within a reasonable time after, the dispute or claim is presented to such Broker. Any election by Broker to participate in mediation shall not result in Broker being deemed a party to this Agreement.

40. ATTORNEY FEES: In any action or proceeding arising out of this Agreement, the prevailing party between Landlord and Tenant shall be entitled to reasonable attorney fees and costs, except as provided in paragraph 39A.

41. C.A.R. FORM: C.A.R. Form means the specific form referenced or another comparable form agreed to by the parties.

42. OTHER TERMS AND CONDITIONS; SUPPLEMENTS: ☐ Interpreter/Translator Agreement (C.A.R. Form ITA);
☐ Keysafe/Lockbox Addendum (C.A.R. Form KLA); ☐ Lead-Based Paint and Lead-Based Paint Hazards Disclosure (C.A.R. Form FLD);
☐ Landlord in Default Addendum (C.A.R. Form LID)
_____
_____

The following ATTACHED supplements are incorporated in this Agreement: _____
_____

43. TIME OF ESSENCE; ENTIRE CONTRACT; CHANGES: Time is of the essence. All understandings between the parties are incorporated in this Agreement. Its terms are intended by the parties as a final, complete and exclusive expression of their Agreement with respect to its subject matter, and may not be contradicted by evidence of any prior agreement or contemporaneous oral agreement. If any provision of this Agreement is held to be ineffective or invalid, the remaining provisions will nevertheless be given full force and effect. Neither this Agreement nor any provision in it may be extended, amended, modified, altered or changed except in writing. This Agreement is subject to California landlord-tenant law and shall incorporate all changes required by amendment or successors to such law. This Agreement and any supplement, addendum or modification, including any copy, may be signed in two or more counterparts, all of which shall constitute one and the same writing.

44. AGENCY:
A.   CONFIRMATION: The following agency relationship(s) are hereby confirmed for this transaction:
Listing Agent: (Print firm name) _____ Sail Realty
is the agent of (check one): ☐ the Landlord exclusively; or ☐ both the Landlord and Tenant.
Leasing Agent: (Print firm name) _____ Ramos Realty
(if not same as Listing Agent) is the agent of (check one): ☐ the Tenant exclusively; or ☐ the Landlord exclusively; or ☐ both the Tenant and Landlord.
B.   DISCLOSURE: ☐ (If checked): The term of this lease exceeds one year. A disclosure regarding real estate agency relationships (C.A.R. Form AD) has been provided to Landlord and Tenant, who each acknowledge its receipt.
45. ☐ **TENANT COMPENSATION TO BROKER:** Upon execution of this Agreement, Tenant agrees to pay compensation to Broker as specified in a separate written agreement between Tenant and Broker.

Tenant's Initials (_____) (_____)   Landlord's Initials (_____) (_____)

Reviewed by _____ Date _____

EQUAL HOUSING OPPORTUNITY

LR REVISED 12/13 (PAGE 5 OF 6)

RESIDENTIAL LEASE OR MONTH-TO-MONTH RENTAL AGREEMENT (LR PAGE 5 OF 6)

Premises: *264 Beach Lane*
Costa Mesa, CA 92627 _____ Date: _____

46. ☐ **INTERPRETER/TRANSLATOR:** The terms of this Agreement have been interpreted for Tenant into the following language: _____ . Landlord and Tenant acknowledge receipt of the attached interpreter/translator agreement (C.A.R. Form ITA).

47. FOREIGN LANGUAGE NEGOTIATION: If this Agreement has been negotiated by Landlord and Tenant primarily in Spanish, Chinese, Tagalog, Korean or Vietnamese, pursuant to the California Civil Code, Tenant shall be provided a translation of this Agreement in the language used for the negotiation.

48. OWNER COMPENSATION TO BROKER: Upon execution of this Agreement, Owner agrees to pay compensation to Broker as specified in a separate written agreement between Owner and Broker (C.A.R. Form LCA).

49. RECEIPT: If specified in paragraph 5, Landlord or Broker, acknowledges receipt of move-in funds.

> Landlord and Tenant acknowledge and agree Brokers: **(a)** do not guarantee the condition of the Premises; **(b)** cannot verify representations made by others; **(c)** cannot provide legal or tax advice; **(d)** will not provide other advice or information that exceeds the knowledge, education or experience required to obtain a real estate license. Furthermore, if Brokers are not also acting as Landlord in this Agreement, Brokers: **(e)** do not decide what rental rate a Tenant should pay or Landlord should accept; and **(f)** do not decide upon the length or other terms of tenancy. Landlord and Tenant agree that they will seek legal, tax, insurance and other desired assistance from appropriate professionals.

Tenant agrees to rent the Premises on the above terms and conditions.

Tenant _____ Date _____
Address *100 Boat Avenue* _____ City *Marina del Rey* _____ State *CA* Zip *90292*
Telephone _____ Fax _____ E-mail _____

Tenant _____ Date _____
Address _____ City _____ State ___ Zip _____
Telephone _____ Fax _____ E-mail _____

☐ **GUARANTEE:** In consideration of the execution of this Agreement by and between Landlord and Tenant and for valuable consideration, receipt of which is hereby acknowledged, the undersigned ("Guarantor") does hereby: **(i)** guarantee unconditionally to Landlord and Landlord's agents, successors and assigns, the prompt payment of Rent or other sums that become due pursuant to this Agreement, including any and all court costs and attorney fees included in enforcing the Agreement; **(ii)** consent to any changes, modifications or alterations of any term in this Agreement agreed to by Landlord and Tenant; and **(iii)** waive any right to require Landlord and/or Landlord's agents to proceed against Tenant for any default occurring under this Agreement before seeking to enforce this Guarantee.

Guarantor (Print Name) _____
Guarantor _____ Date _____
Address _____ City _____ State ___ Zip _____
Telephone _____ Fax _____ E-mail _____

Landlord agrees to rent the Premises on the above terms and conditions.

Landlord _____ Date _____ Landlord _____ Date _____

Address *264 Beach Lane, Costa Mesa, CA 92627* _____
Telephone _____ Fax _____ E-mail _____

REAL ESTATE BROKERS:
A. Real estate brokers who are not also Landlord under this Agreement are not parties to the Agreement between Landlord and Tenant.
B. Agency relationships are confirmed in paragraph 44.
C. **COOPERATING BROKER COMPENSATION:** Listing Broker agrees to pay Cooperating Broker (Leasing Firm) and Cooperating Broker agrees to accept: **(i)** the amount specified in the MLS, provided Cooperating Broker is a Participant of the MLS in which the Property is offered for sale or a reciprocal MLS; or **(ii)** ☐ (if checked) the amount specified in a separate written agreement between Listing Broker and Cooperating Broker.

Real Estate Broker (Listing Firm) *Sail Realty* _____ BRE Lic. #*00 000 000*
By (Agent) _____ *Carmen Caro* BRE Lic. #*00 000 000* Date _____
Address *227 Harbor Blvd.* _____ City *Costa Mesa* State *CA* Zip *92627*
Telephone _____ Fax *(714)626-2829* E-mail *carmen@sailrealty.com*

Real Estate Broker (Leasing Firm) *Ramos Realty* _____ BRE Lic. #*00 000 000*
By (Agent) _____ *Joseph Ramos* BRE Lic. #*00 000 000* Date _____
Address *777 Newport Blvd.* _____ City *Newport Beach* State *CA* Zip *92663*
Telephone _____ Fax *(714)647-0001* E-mail *jr@ramosrealty.com*

© 2013, California Association of REALTORS®, Inc. United States copyright law (Title 17 U.S. Code) forbids the unauthorized distribution, display and reproduction of this form, or any portion thereof, by photocopy machine or any other means, including facsimile or computerized formats.
THIS FORM HAS BEEN APPROVED BY THE CALIFORNIA ASSOCIATION OF REALTORS® (C.A.R.). NO REPRESENTATION IS MADE AS TO THE LEGAL VALIDITY OR ADEQUACY OF ANY PROVISION IN ANY SPECIFIC TRANSACTION. A REAL ESTATE BROKER IS THE PERSON QUALIFIED TO ADVISE ON REAL ESTATE TRANSACTIONS. IF YOU DESIRE LEGAL OR TAX ADVICE, CONSULT AN APPROPRIATE PROFESSIONAL.
This form is made available to real estate professionals through an agreement with or purchase from the California Association of REALTORS®. It is not intended to identify the user as a REALTOR®. REALTOR® is a registered collective membership mark which may be used only by members of the NATIONAL ASSOCIATION OF REALTORS® who subscribe to its Code of Ethics.

Published and Distributed by:
REAL ESTATE BUSINESS SERVICES, INC.
a subsidiary of the California Association of REALTORS®
525 South Virgil Avenue, Los Angeles, California 90020

Reviewed by _____ Date _____

LR REVISED 12/13 (PAGE 6 OF 6)
RESIDENTIAL LEASE OR MONTH-TO-MONTH RENTAL AGREEMENT (LR PAGE 6 OF 6)

A court action called an "unlawful detainer" is used to evict a tenant who breaks the lease or stays past the expiration of a lease agreement.

4. **Estate at Will.** Termination may be made by either party, at any time, with as little as a one-day notice. Acceptance of rent by a landlord creates a periodic tenancy. A true tenancy at will is uncommon.

2. Establishing Rent Schedules

"Contract rent" is the current amount being paid, and "economic rent" is the amount the unit could make if available on the market today. As a good property manager, you should constantly work to bring contract rent up to economic rent.

Basic to the determination of a rental program is the market itself. As a property manager, you must assess the competition, which means determining how much space is available and the rents being charged—in short, the supply and demand factors. Other important considerations include terms of the lease and concessions allowed, the tenant's age, condition of the premises, amenities offered, distance to transportation and other conveniences, character of the neighborhood, including degree of economic and social obsolescence, and the form of lease.

Leases can be divided into five groups. Their names are derived from the way in which the rents are established. They include:

a. Flat Rental Lease

A *FLAT RENTAL LEASE provides for a fixed rate applied uniformly to the spaces being let.* It is determined by a square foot rental, by cubic footage, or so much per room, and so on.

b. Net Leases

A *NET LEASE requires the tenant to pay, in addition to rent, some or all of the property expenses that normally would be paid by the property owner (known as the "landlord" or "lessor").* These include expenses such as real estate taxes, insurance, maintenance, repairs, utilities, and other items. The precise items that are to be paid by the tenant are usually specified in a written lease.

In a *SINGLE NET LEASE, the lessee or tenant is responsible for paying property taxes.* In a *DOUBLE NET LEASE, the lessee or tenant is responsible for property tax and building insurance.* A *TRIPLE NET LEASE is a lease agreement where the tenant or leasee agrees to pay all real estate taxes, building insurance, and maintenance (the three "Nets") on the property in addition to any normal fees that are expected under the agreement (rent, utilities, etc.).* This type of lease is most fequently used for commercial freestanding buildings.

Net leases are used in shopping centers as well as office and commercial buildings.

c. Gross Lease

Under the terms of a *GROSS LEASE, the lessee (tenant) pays a flat amount each month*. Out of this amount, the lessor (landlord) pays for all the expenses of carrying the property. Residential leases are usually rented this way.

d. Percentage Lease

A *PERCENTAGE LEASE commonly provides for a minimum fixed rental plus a percentage of the lessee's gross business income*. The percentage lease might also include prohibitions to protect the landlord against the lessee's conducting unethical off-site *WAREHOUSE SALES, whereby tenants declare other sites for their operation in order to minimize their percentage lease rents.*

Additionally, a percentage lease may have a *RECAPTURE CLAUSE which provides that, should the tenant not obtain a pre-set minimum of sales, then the lessor has the right to terminate the lease.*

Percentage leases are most often used in malls and shopping centers, where each business complements other businesses in that center.

e. Graduated Lease

With a *GRADUATED LEASE, rents are increased at specified intervals, either for a fixed amount or at a fixed rate, which may be based on a percentage of the increased value of the leasehold*. Variations of this form include the *ESCALATOR LEASE CLAUSE, whereby the landlord is allowed to pass an increase costs on to the tenant,* and the *COST OF LIVING LEASE, whereby the rents are adjusted up or down according to fluctuations in the purchasing power of the dollar, as determined by price indices, such as the one published monthly by the United States Bureau of Labor Statistics or the 11th District Cost of Funds.*

G. ACCURATE RECORD KEEPING (A Must for Property Managers)

The following are some of the valid reasons for establishing and maintaining accurate records for the licensee who is engaged in the practice of property management:

1. The statutory requirements state that a **separate record must be kept for each managed property**.

2. The fiduciary capacity that requires you, as the agent, to operate with full and complete disclosure to your principal (owner).

The same agency disclosure forms used in a real estate sale are used in a lease agreement, as well as lead-based paint, water heater, and smoke detector disclosures.

3. Contractual obligations, such as the management agreement, will call for an accounting of all funds and financial data.

4. The owner will need substantiating records in order to file income tax and other returns.

5. A fifth reason for keeping records is for control. Accurate records will aid you in **evaluating income and operating expenses**, analyzing costs, and preparing and forecasting budgets for each property.

6. Records should be kept in the **broker's secure files**, so that you, the broker, or the agent, will have ready access to them whenever inquiries are made, problems arise, and so on.

7. The final reason for record keeping is to satisfy requirements of third parties (like tax assessors) who have an interest in the property. For example, if the rent schedule is the percentage lease, and you don't know how much the gross income was for a given period, a correct rental charge may be overlooked. Comparative records for similar periods help to disclose possible underreporting and shortages.

Specialized computer programs for property management are as varied as real property managers and the scope of their operations. Prices start at a few hundred dollars and go up from there. Many companies use a Microsoft Excel® program customized to their clients' needs, while others use professional software from Yardy Systems, Real Data, and other real estate software companies. QuickBooks® is an inexpensive accounting program used successfully by many small property management firms and their certified public accounts (CPAs).

1. Cash Journal

Figure 13-6 is a cash journal that can be used to report cash received from tenants. It includes the date when the rent was received and deposited in the bank, tenant's name, apartment number, period covered, amount received, overdue amounts, vacant rent schedule, and recapitulation. *RECAPITULATION is the **cash report** of the cash on hand (from the beginning of the period) and the cash received, from which all expenditures and the **manager's compensation** are subtracted.* The cash balance in the bank account is deposited into the broker's trust account or remitted directly to the owner, less the amount needed for petty cash expenditures, maintenance, and improvements for the ensuing period.

2. Activity Report

An activity report form for summarizing all revenues and expenses is shown in **Figure 13-7**. It is simple to read and understand, and it should be sent to the owner on a regular basis, at least monthly. It shows the bank balance for the owner, to which are added the rents that were detailed for each apartment in the cash journal.

Figure 13-6

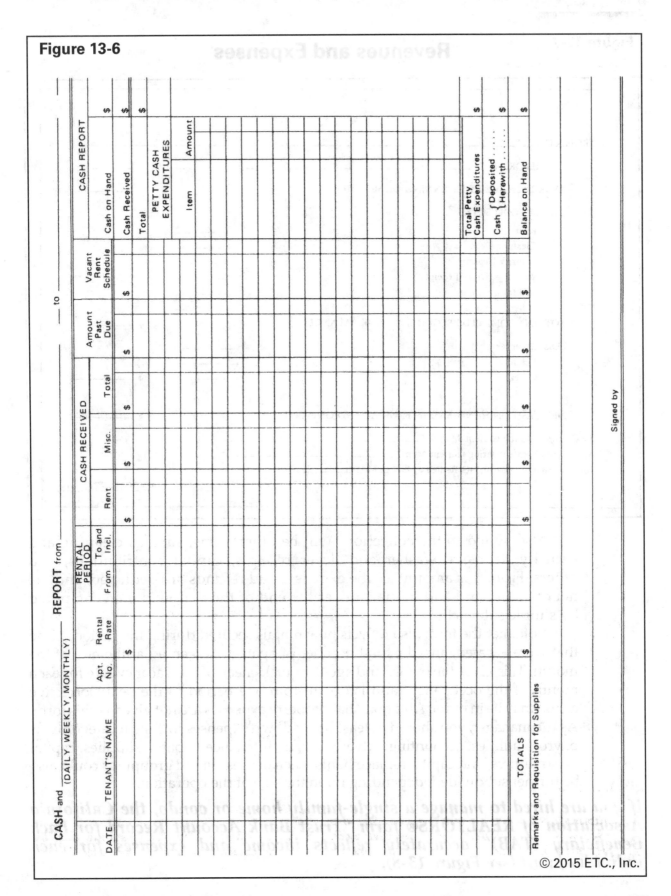

© 2015 ETC., Inc.

Figure 13-7   **Revenues and Expenses**

PROPERTY _____

ACTIVITY REPORT FOR _____ _____

    BANK BALANCE AT BEGINNING OF MONTH $ _____

    INCOME COLLECTED:

Rent	$ _____	
Cleaning Deposits	$ _____	
Security Deposits	$ _____	
Washer & Dryer Receipts	$ _____	
Capital Contributions	$ _____	
Other Income	$ _____	

    TOTAL INCOME PLUS BEGINNING BANK BALANCE $ _____

LESS: Expenses	$ _____	
Refunds	$ _____	
Other	$ _____	$ _____

    NET CASH ON HAND AND IN BANK AT END OF MONTH $ _____

New Rentals during Current Month _____

Apartments Vacated During Current Month _____

Total Number of Apartments Rented at End of Month _____ (%)

© 2015 ETC., Inc.

Also added to the collections will be other items, such as **cleaning** and **security deposits**, washer and dryer receipts, capital contributions, and others. From this amount all the expenses and refunds are deducted, and the net cash on hand and in the bank at the end of the period is then computed by simple subtraction.

Note that the form also reflects new rentals secured during the period, those that were vacated, and the total number of apartments rented at the end of the month. This gives the owner and agent a quick check of the vacancy rate for each month. If the occupancy ratio is down from one period to the next, corrective action may be in order. Also note that property expenses are not given in this form. As the manager, you should at least break down expenses into such categories as payroll, utilities, accounting, advertising, maintenance, repairs, supplies, capital expenditures, and capital replacements. Each of these broad groupings could also be further subdivided, depending upon the size of the operation.

If you are hired to manage a single-family home or condo, the California Association of REALTORS® form "Trust Bank Account Record for Each Beneficiary (TAB)" accurately reflects income and expenses for each individual unit (see Figure 13-8).

H. COMMON INTEREST DEVELOPMENT (CID) MANAGEMENT

Common interest developments (CIDs) are not only a type of real estate and form of ownership, but often a lifestyle as well. In addition to condominiums and "shared wall" apartment-type complexes, a growing number of CIDs include golf course communities, retirement villages, resort properties, timeshares, and lakeside subdivisions.

Common interest developments in California (as well as many other states) are increasing dramatically every year. As such, the need for professionals specializing in Homeowner's Association Management is also on the rise. Recognizing this explosive growth, the CalBRE now includes CID management in their required broker-related course options.

A *COMMON INTEREST DEVELOPMENT (CID) is a form of home ownership whereby individual owners are allowed the use of common property and facilities, the governing of which is controlled by a HOMEOWNER'S ASSOCIATION (HOA).* Membership in the association is automatic with the purchase of property in the CID. Members of the HOA usually elect a board of directors to operate the association and "preserve, enhance, and protect" the value of the common interest development.

The City of Irvine, California, is made up mostly of CIDs (usually condos) that pay for most of the private streets.

1. Duties of an HOA Manager

It is increasingly common for boards of directors to contract professional management companies to run the day-to-day affairs of the association. A management company acts as an agent for the association, taking direction from the board of directors. Your duties as an HOA manager will normally include the following:

1. Collecting assessments
2. Paying the association bills
3. Enforcing rules and addressing infractions
4. Hiring vendors to perform various services

Additional responsibilities may include assisting with the budget process, preparing meeting agendas and minutes, and acting as a neutral third party in disputes.

Ultimately, the board of directors (not the management company) is responsible for the management of an HOA. These obligations are set forth in the CC&Rs, Bylaws, the Corporations Code and the Davis-Stirling Common Interest Development Act (California Civil Code Sections 1350-1376).

CC&Rs (COVENANTS, CONDITIONS, and RESTRICTIONS) are the limitations on land use made compulsory by a deed, usually at the time the land was subdivided. It regulates building restrictions, density, and use for the benefit of other property owners.

Figure 13-8

CALIFORNIA
ASSOCIATION
OF REALTORS®

TRUST BANK ACCOUNT RECORD FOR EACH BENEFICIARY
(C.A.R. Form TAB, Revised 11/07)

Owner: _____

Address: _____

Remarks: _____

DATE	DEPOSIT (Received From)	OR	WITHDRAWAL (Paid To)	AMOUNT	BALANCE
					Forward from previous page $
	Name: _____ ☐ check ☐ cash ☐ _____ For: _____		Name: _____ Check # _____ For: _____	$	$
	Name: _____ ☐ check ☐ cash ☐ _____ For: _____		Name: _____ Check # _____ For: _____	$	$
	Name: _____ ☐ check ☐ cash ☐ _____ For: _____		Name: _____ Check # _____ For: _____	$	$
	Name: _____ ☐ check ☐ cash ☐ _____ For: _____		Name: _____ Check # _____ For: _____	$	$
	Name: _____ ☐ check ☐ cash ☐ _____ For: _____		Name: _____ Check # _____ For: _____	$	$
	Name: _____ ☐ check ☐ cash ☐ _____ For: _____		Name: _____ Check # _____ For: _____	$	$
	Name: _____ ☐ check ☐ cash ☐ _____ For: _____		Name: _____ Check # _____ For: _____	$	$
	Name: _____ ☐ check ☐ cash ☐ _____ For: _____		Name: _____ Check # _____ For: _____	$	$
	Name: _____ ☐ check ☐ cash ☐ _____ For: _____		Name: _____ Check # _____ For: _____	$	$
	Name: _____ ☐ check ☐ cash ☐ _____ For: _____		Name: _____ Check # _____ For: _____	$	$

THIS FORM HAS BEEN APPROVED BY THE CALIFORNIA ASSOCIATION OF REALTORS® (C.A.R.). NO REPRESENTATION IS MADE AS TO THE LEGAL VALIDITY OR ADEQUACY OF ANY PROVISION IN ANY SPECIFIC TRANSACTION. A REAL ESTATE BROKER IS THE PERSON QUALIFIED TO ADVISE ON REAL ESTATE TRANSACTIONS. IF YOU DESIRE LEGAL OR TAX ADVICE, CONSULT AN APPROPRIATE PROFESSIONAL.

This form is available for use by the entire real estate industry. It is not intended to identify the user as a REALTOR®. REALTOR® is a registered collective membership mark which may be used only by members of the NATIONAL ASSOCIATION OF REALTORS® who subscribe to its Code of Ethics.

The copyright laws of the United States (Title 17 U.S. Code) forbid the unauthorized reproduction of this form, or any portion thereof, by photocopy machine or any other means, including facsimile or computerized formats. Copyright© 1992-2007, CALIFORNIA ASSOCIATION OF REALTORS®, INC. ALL RIGHTS RESERVED.

Published and Distributed by:
REAL ESTATE BUSINESS SERVICES, INC.
a subsidiary of the CALIFORNIA ASSOCIATION OF REALTORS®
525 South Virgil Avenue, Los Angeles, California 90020

TAB REVISED 11/07 (PAGE 1 OF 1)

Reviewed by _____ Date _____

TRUST BANK ACCOUNT RECORD FOR EACH BENEFICIARY (TAB PAGE 1 OF 1)

Agent: WALT HUBER	Phone:	Fax:	Prepared using zipForm® software
Broker: WALT HUBER REALTOR			

2. Determining an HOA Budget

The budget of an HOA is determined by the amount of money required to operate and maintain the common area obligations of the CID. The association has the right to bill members for their fair share of the budgeted amount, in the form of an assessment.

"Regular assessments" cover the day-to-day operation and long-term maintenance costs of the association. One time "special assessments" are levied to cover major repairs, replacement, or new construction of the common area. HOA can't restrict local green conservation of water or landscape laws.

3. Managing Agent

A *MANAGING AGENT is a person or entity who, for compensation or in expectation of compensation, exercises control over the assets of a common interest development.*

If you're interested in a career in HOA management, check out *Homeowner's Association Management*, by Walt Huber and Kim Tyler, JD. This text covers the material required for the new broker course approved by the CalBRE.

4. Electric Vehicle (EV) Charging Station

Any restriction that prohibits or restricts the installation or use of an electric vehicle ("EV") charging station in a common interest development became void and unenforceable (Civil Code §1353.9(a)). If a homeowner wants to install an EV charging station in a common area or an exclusive use common area (his parking space), he must meet applicable health and safety standards and requirements imposed by state and local authorities as well as all other applicable zoning, land use or other ordinances, or land use permits. In addition, he/she must obtain HOA approval and agree in writing to the following:

1. Comply with the association's architectural standards.
2. Use a licensed contractor to install the station.
3. Within 14 days of approval, provide a certificate of insurance that names the common interest development as an additional insured under the homeowner's insurance policy.
4. Pay for electricity usage associated with the station.

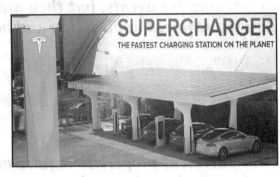

5. California Water Conservation

In order to conserve water during California's current historic drought, an HOA can't penalize members who conserve water by watering their lawns less often.

An HOA cannot impose a fine or assessment against a member for eliminating the watering of vegetation or lawns during any "Drought Emergency," nor can they prohibit "a water-efficient landscape."

 **http://ca.gov/drought**

I. PREPAID RENTAL LISTING SERVICE (PRLS)

You must pay for a Prepaid Rental Listing Service License (no exam required) for each location every two years, or have a real estate broker's license, in order to collect fees.

At one time, "advance fee rental agents" collected fees from prospective tenants before finding rental units for them, or by handing them a list of homes for rent, most of which were usually already rented. Some of these "locators" were not licensed, in violation of state law. Many of them did not even have a listing for any rental properties or any targeted properties to show to prospective renters, and the renters paid for a service they did not actually receive. As a result of these abuses, advanced fee rental agents must register with the California Bureau of Real Estate under the **Prepaid Rental Listing Service (PRLS)** licensing statutes, covered in the Business and Professions Code.

PRLS rules require, among other things, that licensees collecting fees from prospective tenants must have written or oral permission from owners to show the owners' properties, or to include such properties in a rental list.

There is no special examination or license, beyond a broker's license, required of advance fee agents, but they are required to register with the CalBRE and pay the required application and bonding fees for each location.

J. IMPROVING VALUE THROUGH BALANCED MANAGEMENT

In this section the role of the manager in apartment house investments is discussed, with special emphasis on how you, as a manager, maximize the **return to the owner** while **remaining sensitive to tenants** and to the community at large.

All apartment properties require management, whether rendered by separate professional services or by the owner-investors themselves.

Any manager of this type of property is going to be faced with the performance of many different functions in many different areas. Obviously, if the vacancy rate becomes excessive in the area, one of your main functions, as manager, will be to market the available space, while doing what's reasonable, under the circumstances, to minimize vacancies.

As the manager of large multiple-unit properties, you will have a **supervisory function** with regard to the number of employees, and you must be familiar with at least the basics of personnel management.

As a property manager, your responsibilities will include maintenance of the building, caring for mechanical equipment, and planning and implementing a "modernization" program.

This involves dealing with plumbers, electricians, and other trades, but also with professionals such as engineers and hazardous material professionals.

From time to time, as a property manager, you must deal with governmental bodies. In most communities, government, at one level or another, involves itself directly with zoning regulations, health and safety codes, taxation of property, and the application of building codes. Certainly, changes in taxation and regulation of rental properties, under the police power of the taxing authority, are of definite and continuing interest for the property manager.

Finally, the human relations aspects of your job as a manager are critical. In all activities relating to tenants, to professional, semiprofessional, and trades people, to governmental bodies, and to others within the real estate community, you will have to demonstrate a satisfactory level of **"reasonableness."**

Potential apartment owners must satisfy themselves that adequate plans are made and facilities are available for various and competent management.

1. To Spend or Not to Spend (Maintenance)

"Deferred maintenance" is delaying needed repairs considered necessary for the long-term maintenance of the property.

As a manager, you are usually trying to achieve **two objectives** for your investors that are, to a great degree, incompatible: (1) continually striving to correct and relieve the deterioration of the buildings due to normal wear and tear, while at the same time, (2) trying to refrain from spending money. To maintain the condition of an apartment house at an acceptable level obviously costs money. If these periodic outlays are not made, the annual net income from the rental operation may increase over the short run. However, such a process will result in deferred maintenance, eventually causing extraordinary expenditures to halt and correct structural deterioration.

Ideally, a structure should not be under maintained or over maintained, because either course will ultimately minimize the profitability of the property.

As the manager of a large property, you should consider hiring a professional real estate appraiser to advise you as to what improvements will be beneficial to increase the owner's net income in the long run. Part of your job description includes maximizing the resale value of a property.

Spending a little to maintain a property saves the owner a lot in the long run.

Your careful analysis of the market, and flexibility in responding to changes in market conditions, should satisfy your owner that his or her property is a useful and profitable investment.

As a property manager, you must be acutely aware of **changing conditions** in the real estate market, generally, and the apartment house rental market, specifically.

You should be flexible enough to experiment with the rental schedule in order to test the analysis of present rental conditions every time you rent a space. This means that the property owner must allow you a reasonable degree of latitude in rental policies. One of the most common errors of ownership is to restrict the manager's area of decision making so that you're really not able to manage.

Inflexible rental schedules are a prime cause of rent loss. It goes without saying that, once lost, rental income is gone forever, reducing your investor's satisfaction and income.

K. RENT CONTROL

Rent control discourages the building of more apartments, causing existing rents to go even higher, further damaging a city's housing affordability.

If you decide to become a residential property manager, you should be knowledgeable of any local rent control ordinances to ensure that rents and increases charged are not in violation of the law. Currently, in rent controlled cities in Los Angeles County, such as Los Angeles, Santa Monica, Beverly Hills, Malibu, and West Hollywood, when a unit **becomes vacant** you can increase the rent without limitation, but laws change. Different communities have different laws concerning rent control.

By California law, no governmental agency can adopt any rent control restrictions on nonresidential property.

L. LOW-INCOME HOUSING

If you're hired to manage lower income housing, you should become familiar with *SECTION 8, which is a county rent subsidy for qualified tenants who meet the required criteria.* The property must be approved by county inspectors for eligibility, and is checked for its condition at least once a year. The tenants usually pay a very low portion of the rent based on their income and familial obligations.

M. PROFESSIONAL ASSOCIATIONS FOR MANAGERS

Property managers have professional associations of their own. Most notable among these is the **Institute of Real Estate Management (IREM)**, a division of the National Association of REALTORS® (NAR). It was started by a group of REALTORS® who felt the need for an organized body of practitioners to promote the professional growth of what was a comparatively new field during the Great Depression, but has become an ever more profitable field.

Through professional associations, knowledge and experience can be shared, ethical standards established and maintained, and other benefits derived that could not be achieved by individuals alone.

A Code of Professional Ethics for the Institute of Real Estate Management was adopted by the institute and must be adhered to by any member of IREM applying for membership. *REALTORS® who qualify and are accepted into the institute are entitled to use the designation* **CPM (CERTIFIED PROPERTY MANAGER)** *after their names.* With the public's increasing awareness of the title, considerable prestige should be gained by the REALTOR® CPM. Similarly, the *firm that specializes in this field and has qualified for membership is entitled to use the designation* **AMO,** *or* **ACCREDITED MANAGEMENT ORGANIZATION.** One key executive, at least, must be a CPM, but the firm cannot use the CPM label, which is restricted to individuals alone.

A Certified Property Manager designation is considered the highest recommendation from an ethical, knowledge, and experience point of view.

7% FTB Tax for Out of State Landlords

Under California Franchise Tax Board (FTB) rules, property managers who manage residential properties for owners living outside of California are required to withhold seven percent of all distributions and payments associated with rent on a monthly basis and send it to the state quarterly. The withholding percentage would be higher for owners living outside of the United States.

Managers of commercial properties whose owners live outside of California must also withhold a percentage of rent and send it to the state, under a different schedule.

III. Going "Green" Made Easy

The CALGreen Act

The **CALIFORNIA GREEN BUILDING STANDARDS CODE,** or **CALGreen,** *is a green building code that imposes energy efficiency and other green standards on new construction in an effort to achieve reductions in natural resource consumption and greenhouse gas emissions.* Its first stage (Tier 1) includes voluntary measures, such as exceeding energy efficiency by 15 percent, achieving 30 percent water savings, reducing construction waste by 65 percent, using up to 10 percent recycled materials, and designating 10 percent of parking spaces for fuel efficient vehicles. That's just the beginning. Tier 2 is far more severe in its expectations for conservation.

The following is a short list of tips for a brokerage interested in using the least amount of energy and creating the least amount of waste:

1. **Energy Conservation** – Use energy efficient compact fluorescent or LED light bulbs. Set computers to go into sleep mode if not in use after a short period of time. Turn off lights and power strips that feed computers, printers, faxes, etc. at the end of the day.

2. **Paper Conservation** – Keep files on computers. Whenever possible, send emails instead of paper letters. Use recycled paper and print on both sides of the page when appropriate and use misprints as notepaper. Avoid color printing and print in draft mode whenever feasible.

3. **Gas Consumption** – Encourage office staff not in need of client transportation to carpool or use public transit. Offer incentives to your agents who use hybrid vehicles.

4. **Telecommuting** – Whenever possible, allow agents to send information via mobile phone or the Internet rather than make an unnecessary trip to the office.

5. **Recycling** – Make it a policy to place recycling bins in accessible, high-traffic areas and provide clear information about what can and cannot be recycled.

The following are some of the Green Building glossary terms from the NAR® Green Resources Council with which you should be familiar as a well informed property mamger. For the complete list of terms and information, see:

National Association of REALTORS® Green Resource Council
www.greenresourcecouncil.org/glossary.cfm

Green Building Glossary

Attic Fan – A fan typically mounted on the roof to create positive air-flow through an attic

Brownfields – A former industrial site, particularly one compromised by hazardous contaminants; examples are former dry cleaning establishments and gas stations.

Carbon Dioxide (CO_2) – The most prevalent of the greenhouse gases. Emitted by burning fossil fuels. Naturally occurring from sources such as human and animal respiration, ocean-atmosphere exchange, and volcanic eruptions.

Ceiling Fan(s) – Fans, set to push warm air into living spaces, can reduce winter heating bills, and they can cut cooling costs when they are used in lieu of air conditioners.

Climate Change – Also called climate destabilization or greenhouse effect, this term represents the possible adverse effects of greenhouse gasses on long-term weather patterns. ▼

Energy Efficient Light Fixtures – The fixture or the type of bulbs used in a fixture. Compact Fluorescent Lamps (CFLs) and Light Emitting Diodes (LEDs) are becoming more common in homes and buildings and they are more efficient and last longer than incandescent bulbs.

Fuel Cell – A clean fuel source that converts chemical energy from hydrogen to electrical energy. Yields zero emissions.

Greenhouse Gases – Emitted gases that are trapped in the atmosphere and contribute to climate change.

Low Flow Toilet – A toilet that combines efficiency and high performance. Design advances enable these toilets to save water with no trade-off in flushing power. Such toilets often have the EPA's WaterSense label.

On Demand Water Heater – A device that heats water rapidly as it is dispensed from the faucet. Eliminates the need for a conventional tank water heater.

Radon – A naturally occurring gas, colorless and odorless, that has been shown to cause adverse health effects. Radon gas often enters a structure by seeping through cellar walls and floors.

Rain Garden – A shallow, constructed depression that is planted with deep-rooted native plants and grasses. Rain gardens hold the water for a short period of time, allowing the water to naturally filter into the ground.

Renewable Energy Sources – Materials and natural resources that can be replaced, such as wind, solar, or hydroelectric power.

Retrofitting – The process of rethinking a development plan after completion to include newer features, such as green or eco-friendly features.

R-Value Upgrades – Improved or added insulation in the attic or exterior walls to improve the R-value of the building envelope. An R-value indicates an insulation's resistance to heat flow. The higher the R-value, the greater the insulating effectiveness.

Storm Windows – Single pane windows often installed on the interior of the main windows of home to improve insulation. When window replacement is cost prohibitive, adding storm windows can be an alternative for saving energy.

Sunscreen(s) – Awnings or window treatments which effectively block the sun's heat.

Tankless Water Heater – A system that delivers hot water at a preset temperature when needed, but without requiring the storage of water. Tankless water heaters have an electric, gas, or propane heating device that is activated by the flow of water.

Urban Infill – Redevelopment of sites, in the core of metropolitan areas, for commercial and residential purposes.

Windpower – Power supplied by an onsite wind turbine.

Zoned Heating – Heating systems with separate thermostat controls in different parts of a structure to allow for independent temperature control in each area.

IV. CHAPTER SUMMARY

State and federal laws deal with discrimination against prospective tenants. Fair Housing Laws prohibit landlords from discriminating by reason of race, religion, national origin, ancestry, color, sex, physical handicap, or marital status.

The California **Unruh Civil Rights Act** similarly bans discrimination, but is geared more toward "people in the business" of selling and renting properties. **Blockbusting** is the practice by unscrupulous agents of inducing panic selling of homes below market value.

The **California Fair Employment and Housing Act (FEHA)** provides an administrative remedy for the tenant who has been discriminated against.

The law does not prohibit the use of **reasonable standards** in the selection of tenants or buyers. Economic factors, family size, age, and many other criteria may be used.

The state **Housing Financial Discrimination Act of 1977** prohibits financial institutions from engaging in discriminatory loan practices called "**redlining**." This is the practice by lenders of denying loans or varying finance terms based on the property's location.

The federal **Civil Rights Act of 1968** similarly prohibits discrimination.

To terminate a rental agreement of less than one year, **Landlord/Tenant Law** requires landlords to give a tenant a **30-day notice**. If the tenant has been in possession of the unit for more than one year, the landlord must give the teant a **60-day notice**. The tenant still needs to give a 30-day notice to the landlord in either case.

There are **exceptions to the 60-day notice**. It does not apply to a fixed-term lease, or a tenant who has lived in the property for less than one year under a periodic tenancy.

A **3-Day Notice to Pay Rent or Quit** demands that the tenant pay the rent or vacate the property. It's unlawful to change locks, shut off the utilities, etc. **Unlawful Detainer** is the name of the legal action taken to physically remove a tenant.

The landlord must give the tenant a **24-hour notice to enter** (in writing), which must be performed during business hours, unless agreed to otherwise by the tenant.

Landlords may charge more for pets. Landlords/REO lenders are required to take charge of abandoned animals and notify animal control officials to retrieve the animal.

Property Management. Owners often don't have the time, and need the expertise of a real estate practitioner, to properly manage their investment property by minimizing expenses, maximizing profits, and increasing resale value. This should be a benefit, rather than a cost, for the investor.

Outside managers, or **general managers**, may manage as part of their general brokerage operations or as an exclusive management firm. They only require a real estate broker license, and they are usually paid a certain percentage of the rents they collect. **Resident managers** live on the premises. A resident manager is required if there are **16 or more units** and the owner does not reside on the property. **Institutional Managers** are employed by an institution, such as the real estate management department of a bank, and paid a salary.

Selection of Property Managers. Management Contracts should always be used in any agreement for the employment of a manager. There are varied contracts that can be used. The **CAR® Property Management Contract**, is included in this chapter. This spells out the duties of the manager and the responsibilities of the owner.

Tenant screening is very important. The manager should get proper identification, a current credit report, references, and verify all information, including eviction history.

A **lease contract** should be signed by all parties and include the date, the property address, the amount of rent and the terms of payments.

Flat Rental Lease is a flat fee charged for a unit, depending on its size. In a **net lease**, the tenant agrees to pay a fixed rent plus some of the expenses incurred by the property. There are different types of net leases. With a **single net lease**, the tenant agrees to pay property taxes. A **double net lease** requires a lessee to pay for property tax and building insurance. In a **triple net lease**, the lessee pays taxes, insurance, and maintenance.

A **percentage lease** is often used in shopping centers and includes a base rent plus a percentage of the tenant's gross receipts. With a **graduated lease**, rents are increased at specified intervals based on various cost of funds indices.

Record keeping is an important duty of the property manager. Each property managed must have a separate record or trust account.

Condominium Management is another opportunity for property management firms. Homeowner Associations (HOAs) often turn this task over to real estate brokers.

Prepaid Rental Listing Services (PRLS) charge prospective tenants for lists of rental properties. They must register with the California Bureau of Real Estate under the Prepaid Rental Listing Service licensing statutes.

Proper maintenance of a property is a balancing act on the part of a manager. Under maintaining or over maintaining ultimately minimizes profitability for an owner/investor.

Rent Control is the government regulation of the amount of rent a landlord may charge tenants. A city restricts, by percentage, annual increases in rental payments. Commercial, industrial, and luxury rentals are generally exempt.

Low-Income Housing. Property managers of lower income housing should become familiar with **Section 8** (HUD), which is a county rent subsidy for qualified tenants.

V. MATCHING VOCABULARY Fill in the blanks with the correct letter

A. 3 Day Notice to Pay
   or Quit
B. 60 days
C. CC&Rs
D. Certified Property
   Manager (CPM)
E. Common Interest
   Development

F. Discrimination
G. Estate at Sufferance
I. Estate from Period-
   to-Period
H. Estate for years
J. Graduated lease
K. Net lease
L. Percentage lease

M. Redlining
N. Resident manager
O. Section 8
P. Steering
Q. Unruh Civil Rights
   Act

1. _____ A tenant's right to occupy real estate for a definite fixed period of time.
2. _____ The first civil rights act in California that prohibits "steering" and "blockbusting" as a real estate practice.
3. _____ The refusal of a loan or insurance based upon a property's location (zip code).
4. _____ Showing a client property in only one type of neighborhood and refusal to communicate the availability of housing in other neighborhoods.
5. _____ The refusal to sell, rent, or lease housing accommodations on the basis of race, color, national origin, religion, sex, familial status, and handicap.
6. _____ This type of property managers live on the premises and are directly employed by the property owner or his agent.
7. _____ To terminate a periodic tenancy, how many days notice must be given to a tenant who has been in possession of a rental unit for one year or more.
8. _____ This notice states that the tenant has three business days to pay all past due rent or vacate the property or face an unlawful detainer.
9. _____ The most common periodic tenancy is a month-to-month lease.
10. _____ This estate is created when a tenant obtains possession legally, but then remains on the property, without the owner's consent.
11. _____ With this type of lease, the rents are increased at specified intervals, either for a fixed amount or at a fixed rate.
12. _____ This type of lease commonly provides for a minimum fixed rental plus a percentage of the lessee's gross business income.
13. _____ With this type of lease, the lessee pays for all maintenance, insurance, and property taxes.
14. _____ This is the most sought after designation for residential property managers.
15. _____ A term or category for a form of home ownership whereby individual owners are allowed the use of common property and facilities and the governing of which is controlled by a homeowner's association.
16. _____ The limitations on land use made compulsory by a deed, usually at the time the land was subdivided.
17. _____ This low-income housing subsidy allows qualified tenants in the county, who meet the required criteria, to pay a very low portion of the rent.

See Page 610 for Answers

VI. CHAPTER QUIZ

1. One of the prime objectives of professional property management is:

    a. to minimize expenses and to maximize profits.
    b. to make sure the tenants are not taking advantage of the owner.
    c. to maximize the return to the professional property management firm.
    d. to help society through private rental subsidies.

2. A person or firm hired to manage property by banks, insurance companies, government agencies, trusts, etc., is referred to as a(n):

    a. resident manager.
    b. freelance manager.
    c. institutional manager.
    d. none of the above.

3. What form of lease is increased at specified intervals?

    a. Net lease
    b. Gross lease
    c. Percentage lease
    d. Graduated lease

4. Which of the following is a reason for managers to keep accurate records?

    a. Compliance with statutory requirements
    b. Meeting the agent's fiduciary obligation to the client
    c. Substantiating records for filing income tax returns
    d. All of the above

5. With respect to balanced management, which of the following statements is correct?

    a. An effective manager tries to correct and relieve deterioration due to wear and tear, while trying to increase net income.
    b. If periodic outlays for materials and labor are not made, the annual income for the rental operation will be increased over the long run.
    c. It makes little difference whether a property is under maintained or over maintained, since either condition will maximize the profitability of the property.
    d. All of the above.

6. An on-site manager of an 18-unit apartment building:

    a. needs to have a real estate license.
    b. is directly employed by the property owner/property management company.
    c. usually manages several properties at once.
    d. all of the above.

7. Which of the following is an example of blockbusting?

  a. Installing new streets within a city block.

  b. Persuading property owners to sell by telling them minorities are moving into the neighborhood.

  c. Offering incentives to renters, like free utilities.

  d. Denying a loan to a qualified borrower based on location of a property.

8. It is important to analyze prospective tenants' backgrounds before renting them space in an apartment project. Which of these is NOT a consideration in the tenant selection process?

  a. Number of jobs held by the applicant within the past ten years.

  b. Number of times an applicant has been married.

  c. Number and amount of installment debts owed by the prospect.

  d. Number of times the applicant has moved within the last three years.

9. A property manager was instructed by his/her client to rent only to a married couple. Which is correct?

  a. The manager should screen the potential tenants to determine if they are married.

  b. The manager should rent to a couple and not tell the owner.

  c. The manager should inform the owner that he/she cannot violate Fair Housing Laws.

  d. None of the above.

10. After two years, a landlord wants to get a month-to-month tenant out of his rental. He or she has to:

  a. give the tenant a 3-day notice to pay or quit.

  b. give the tenant a 30-Day notice.

  c. change the locks when the tenant is at work.

  d. give the tenant a 60-day notice.

ANSWERS: 1. a; 2. c; 3. d; 4. d; 5. a; 6. b; 7. b; 8. b; 9. c; 10. d

Find Today's Value of Your Apartment Bldg

www.Apt.Value.com
CA. Dept. of Real Estate
Real Estate Broker

Company ds 200K

.COM busi-
for inven-
secured by

Commercial Property for Lease

Valley Village
1000 sq. ft., $2250.
Call 323-937-3966

esidential Income
erty

& Millichap

Long Beach
sh Style Bldg in
tion.
57.1231

OME

tviNewsRoom.com
Mag For Sale $800-795-1099

OWN YOUR own Medical
Alert Company. Be the 1st
and Only Distributor in You
area! Unlimited $ RETURN.
Small investment required.
Call toll free 1-844-225-1200
(CDCN)

MEDICAL DISPENSARY
Partnerships Available!
Opening in Many Locations
$10K min investment
Gold Rush! 310-557-6319

COMMERCIAL REAL ESTATE 1000

ENCINO MASTERPIECE 5
BDS 8 BAS - MASSIVE DIN
RM/PUB/LIB/MEDIA RM/
FAM RM/ INLAW UNIT W/
ELEV $2,750,000
Albert Foulad 818.906.1000

OPEN HOUSE

TARZANA Awesome single
level house on private street
south of Ventura Blvd. 3
large bedrooms, 3 bath-
rooms, den, Formal Dining
large living room with fire-
place.Central air and Central
vacuum. Private rear yard.
Close to all amenities and
walking distance to places
of worship. Easily con
to be wheelchair
Built in 1982
great

Premium Cigar Shop/Lounge
in prime Downtown LA area.
For info 213-675-2428

Real Estate Loans

$$$ LOANS $$$
BANK & PRIVATE MONEY
• CALL 24 HOURS •
$50,000 TO $50 MILLION
800.796.6630 • 818.366.9900
BKR CA BRE# 00831688

HOMES FOR SALE 1100

HOMES FOR SALE

LA COUNTY NORTH

San Fernando Valley,
Antelope Valley and
Santa Clarita Valley

HOMES FOR SALE
VACATION PROPERTIES

Sequoia Nat. Monument
Year-round custom home,
new in 2008, 4BR/3BA, Separate guest house, $350,000.
3 hours from LA
sequoiamountainhome.com
559-542-2032

ndcsales

NUSA

Trust Deeds. Sa

Investor Want

call 661

T. Chris +62
E. chris@nd

Real Estate Assistants: Time is Money

I. Assisting as a Career

There are only so many hours in the day to complete the necessary, time-consuming tasks required in real estate transactions. Therefore, having an assistant, licensed or not, comes in very handy and should be more than cost effective.

A real estate assistant with necessary digital skills can free the agent to perform activities that are more productive, such as "getting listings" and "making sales."

Real estate licensees have numerous career options from which to choose, including specializing in single-family home sales, investment property sales, property management, loan brokering and more. One of the fastest growing opportunities in the field is that of tech-savvy real estate assistant.

The more you know about social media plus any other online skills you have will make you more valuable to a time-constrained agent.

A. WHAT IS A REAL ESTATE ASSISTANT?

REAL ESTATE ASSISTANTS are helpmates and extensions of successful real estate agents. They are delegated a variety of duties that agents would normally be required to do in the course of a business day that takes them away from spending time in "the field." By definition, they may be licensed or unlicensed.

In this chapter, we deal exclusively with the characteristics and duties of professional real estate assistants who have already passed their salespersons' examinations from the California Bureau of Real Estate.

Real Estate Assistants may be expected to do several, if not all of the following duties:

CHAPTER OUTLINE

1. Maintain a paper and/or electronic filing system
2. Direct incoming calls
3. Solicit and make listing appointments
4. Prepare documents
5. Update client records
6. Write correspondence——letters, emails, and text messages
7. Communicate with clients
8. Input and remove expired listings from the MLS
9. Maintain and update company websites
10. Monitor listings (activity, price reduction, expiration)
11. Create newsletters, brochures, and direct mail (online and paper)
12. Meet with appraisers, home inspectors, and termite companies
13. Prospect for buyers and sellers (such as searching social media)
14. Assist and hold open houses
15. Create database and manage computer and paper files

1. Licensed vs. Unlicensed (Not Recommended)

Unlicensed assistants in the real estate industry are highly restricted from performing acts that require a real estate license such as quoting prices, terms, and property information with potential buyers. Unlicensed assistants are more often used as gophers for such functions as picking up documents, placing and retrieving lock boxes on properties, responding and communicating with clients, etc. Using an unlicensed assistant is, therefore, not recommended.

A licensed assistant, on the other hand, can be a very valuable asset to a seasoned and successful agent—according to NAR®, 10% of the top producers hire real estate assistants. Realistically, it is a win-win situation, where the assistant gains knowledge from a successful agent who has learned the pitfalls of real estate transactions. The agent, having delegated the "busy work" to the assistant, can now concentrate his or her efforts in obtaining a commitment for either a listing or a sale or even possibly both from the same client. The assistant, after making arrangements with the local board of REALTORS®, can help the agent in completing a market analysis, checking on available listings to show potential buyers, holding open houses, and communicating all leads to the employing agent, along with preparing the templates for various transactions, etc. These tasks will naturally evolve to additional tasks, depending the the assistant's willingness and ability to assist the employing broker/agent.

II. Who Hires Assistants?

The National Association of REALTORS® (NAR) conducted a survey among the most successful real estate brokerage firms in the country, and found that 10% of the top producers hired real estate assistants. Over 70% of those who employed assistant escrow coordinators felt that hiring those assistants contributed to their firms' increased profits. On average, the brokerages with over 50 agents employed seven assistants or more, and the most successful smaller firms employed at least one or two.

III. Getting the Job

Once you've decided to become a real estate assistant, you'll have to find the right brokerage or agent for you. As we discussed earlier, your long range goals and reasons for pursuing a career as an assistant should dictate where you intend to work. Before you're faced with the option of accepting or declining a job, you'll have to apply and interview for the position.

A. YOUR RÉSUMÉ

As in any profession, employees look for certain characteristics from a prospective employee. The following are all important aspects to include in your résumé:

1. **Consistency** – While a well-rounded background may be a plus in the real estate field, an employee who has jumped from job to job demonstrates unreliability. If you're a student, fresh from college, no one expects you to have an extensive employment history. If you're a more mature applicant, consider "trimming" your employment history to just those that reflect well on the type of experience that your position demands.

2. **People Skills** – The better you are at dealing with people, the better qualified you are to be involved in the real estate industry. This is particularly important if your goal is to eventually become an agent. Any experience you have with customer service or interpersonal skills should be accented. This is a people-business.

3. **Education** – Having a real estate license is always preferable to not having one. At the very least, your potential employer will know you possess the basic knowledge of the business, which means less training time and a lowered risk of liability. Your education level may also indicate your pay scale.

4. **Real Estate Background** – Any experience in the real estate field can be a plus. If you "got your feet wet" working as an agent, only to discover that you might be better suited to the role of assistant, don't be embarrassed to admit it! An agent looking for an assistant as a permanent employee, rather than an apprentice, will appreciate your decision-making process.

Retirees make exceptional assistants. All the knowledge and experience they've acquired can be hugely beneficial to an employer!

5. **Skills** – A variety of skills can enhance your value as a real estate assistant. Typing, dictation, and filing experience are always a plus. Computer and Internet skills, as well as a customer relations background, are even more appealing to employers.

> *While any and all computer skills are valuable, familiarity with one or more real estate programs (effectively use your MLS) give you an obvious advantage over other applicants. It's also important to know how to use zipForms® and various templates for different transactions.*

If you're just starting out in the business, a knowledge of Microsoft Word® and Excel® are your most valuable program skills. Knowing how to use an accounting spreadsheet program or financial management program (like Quickbooks®) is also beneficial.

Depending on your employer's needs, salary budget, and expertise expectations, a basic knowledge of computer and Internet skills may suffice. Understanding the computer as a tool indicates your ability to learn whatever program or programs your agent will need you to master. If, however, you're completely inexperienced with computers, you may severely limit your usefulness as an assistant and your employment potential.

Your ability to use social media sites and other mobile apps will be helpful.

6. **Recommendations** – Former employers with positive things to say about you are important to any job applicant. Even if your past employment had nothing to do with real estate, your reliability, integrity, personality, and adaptability are assets any agent values. As a new licensee, a glowing recommendation from your real estate professor(s) may influence your prospective employer, both in terms of your knowledge and dedication, but also as evidence of your people skills.

7. **Presentation** – It goes without saying that your personal appearance should be professional and pulled together. Your résumé should also be neat and orderly. Sentences should be well written, grammar and punctuation flawless, and the design attractive. All of these elements demonstrate your attention to details, and your ability to create an appealing and interesting written product—important skills if your job description includes writing newsletters and advertising copy, both print and online.

The more articulate and persuasive you are as a writer, the more likely you are to be trusted with your employing agent's creative responsibilities.

8. **Interests** – Any good résumé will include personal interests, like charity work, club memberships, and social interests. You might consider mentioning something truly personal about yourself, not only allowing your potential employer to know you a little better, but also to illustrate your willingness to share your life experiences—often a valuable asset when dealing with clients.

Hobbies count! If you like to surf, for example, you may have something in common with a client that your agent doesn't. This would be an opportunity for you to help direct your agent and his or her client toward a home that's within walking distance of a beach—one that also has a "good break" to the waves.

B. INTERVIEW QUESTIONS

You should expect to be asked a variety of questions by a prospective employer. The following is just a sampling of some typical interview questions.

1. Do you have your real estate license?
2. Why do you want to be an assistant?
3. What are your career goals?
4. What social media sites have you been using?
5. How fast do you type?
6. What computer and online skills do you have?
7. What were your responsibilities at your last job?
8. What about the real estate business most interests you?
9. What do you consider your greatest strengths/weaknesses?
10. What kind of experience do you have in real estate? (Have you ever bought or sold a home? Worked for an agent or as an agent?)
11. Where do you expect to be in five years?
12. Do you expect this to be a permanent position, or are you looking to advance?
13. Do you have any experience in escrow, title insurance, or lending?
14. Do you have a valid driver's license and a reliable car?
15. Do you have good organizational skills? Can you multi-task?
16. Do you have any experience in customer service, telemarketing, or advertising?
17. How flexible is your work schedule? Are you available full or part time? What about weekends or evenings?
18. Do you speak any other languages?
19. Are you related to or know anyone in the real estate industry?
20. Have you taken any additional courses, besides Principles, Practice, and one related course (if they have a license as we suggest they should), that might help you in this business? Do you intend to?
21. How would you handle an irate customer complaining on the phone?
22. Do you think of yourself as a problem-solver, or are you more comfortable behind the scenes, dealing with office details like filing, letter writing, etc.?

In addition to the face-to-face interview, you may be asked to take one or more tests to demonstrate your skills.

C. THE JOB OFFER

You've impressed your future employer with your professional résumé, charmed your way through the interview, passed the skills test with flying colors, and are offered the job as assistant. Now what?

1. Part-Time Employee

If you asked the right questions in the interview, you should know if your employer is looking for full or part-time help. It's not uncommon, however, for agents to be relatively flexible in terms of the commitment they're looking for, especially if they've never had an assistant before. Agents hiring their first assistants have obviously realized that they need help if they're going to maximize their potential, but may not know how much time that's going to require.

Your status as a full or part-time worker may be negotiable, depending on a variety of factors, including your employer's work load and willingness to delegate tasks, as well as your needs and expectations. After all, you may be pursuing this line of work because college or family obligations don't allow you to dedicate the long, unscheduled hours required to be a successful salesperson.

2. Full-Time Employee

While the option of part-time work is one of the perks of a career as an assistant, we've focused so far on the assumption that you have earned your salesperson's license and, therefore, made a commitment to the real estate industry as a career rather than just a job. If you're only available to work part-time, a firm may justifiably relegate you to the position of secretary, receptionist, administrative assistant, closing coordinator, or telemarketing assistant.

Armed with a license, computer knowledge, and the time to dedicate to your job, your desirability as an assistant will be dramatically improved.

As a licensed, full-time assistant, depending on your (negotiable) employment agreement, you can expect to work 35 to 40 hours a week, Monday through Friday, and be paid a weekly salary. If your employing agent or broker uses your licensed status to good advantage, he or she will probably expect you to be available some evenings and weekends, reflecting his or her own flexible hours. As such, the norm in the industry, by no means a guarantee, would be to pay you a base salary plus a percentage of commissions earned on transactions in which you're involved.

3. Employee or Independent Contractor

In terms of the employee versus independent contractor status, the relationship between assistant and agent is similar to that of salesperson and broker. An **EMPLOYEE** *works regular hours set by an employer, is paid a regular or hourly wage, and has a right to sick leave, insurance, retirement, and vacation benefits.* An employee works under the direct supervision of an employer, and his or her job definition is set by that employer.

An **INDEPENDENT CONTRACTOR** *pays his or her own taxes, works with a minimum of supervision, and, in general, sets his or her own schedule. He or she has some flexibility in determining the methods and procedures used to complete the job for which he or she was hired, and basically has more control over day-to-day activities than an employee.* (**Figure 14-1** shows CAR's® Personal Assistant Contract [PAC].)

By labeling an assistant an independent contractor, an employer may be attempting to avoid paying payroll taxes. Therefore, the IRS has strict regulations concerning who is or is not an independent contractor.

Reading over a Personal Assistant Contract will give you guidance!

Figure 14-1

CALIFORNIA ASSOCIATION OF REALTORS®

PERSONAL ASSISTANT CONTRACT
(Between Associate-Licensee and Licensed or Unlicensed Assistant)
(C.A.R. Form PAC, Revised 6/12)

This Agreement, dated _____ , is between _____
("Associate-Licensee") and _____ ("Assistant").
Assistant desires to work for Associate-Licensee, and Associate-Licensee desires to use the services of Assistant. In consideration for the covenants and representations contained in this Agreement, Associate-Licensee and Assistant agree as follows:

1. **ASSOCIATE-LICENSEE** is a California real estate licensee with a ☐ salesperson's, or ☐ broker's license. Associate-Licensee is licensed under _____ , ("Broker") or ☐ (if checked) works for him/herself.

2. **ASSISTANT REAL ESTATE LICENSE:** Assistant ☐ does, ☐ does not, hold a California real estate license. If Assistant does hold a real estate license, the license must be furnished to Broker immediately upon execution of this Agreement.

3. **EMPLOYER-EMPLOYEE RELATIONSHIP:** Assistant shall be an at-will employee of Associate-Licensee. This means either party may terminate this Agreement at any time with or without cause. As Assistant's employer, Associate-Licensee shall be responsible for compliance with all applicable local, state and federal laws including not limited to minimum wage and overtime pay, timekeeping requirements, income and employment tax withholdings, worker's compensation coverage and compliance with employment discrimination including harassment law. If Associate-Licensee and Assistant desire to enter into a different type of working relationship, such as independent contractor, a separate written agreement must be used. The classification of any person who performs services for an Associate-Licensee as an independent contractor has significant legal consequences for both the Associate-Licensee and the person who performs the services and can result in severe penalties and other adverse consequences if a person is misclassified as an independent contractor. Associate-Licensee and Assistant are advised to seek legal and accounting advice before considering classifying Assistant as an independent contractor.

4. **DUTIES:** Assistant shall assist Associate-Licensee in fulfilling Associate-Licensee's obligations under the Independent Contractor agreement (C.A.R. Form ICA, attached) between Associate-Licensee and Broker. Assistant shall comply with all obligations of Associate-Licensee imposed under the terms of that agreement and any office policy established by Broker. Associate-Licensee shall monitor the work and results of Assistant. If Assistant does not have a real estate license, Assistant shall not engage in any activity for which a real estate license is required. (Assistant may become more familiar with these limitations by reading the "DRE Guidelines for Unlicensed Assistants.") In addition, and more specifically, Assistant shall perform the following activities: _____
_____
_____

5. **COMPENSATION AND BENEFITS:**
   A. **Base Compensation:** Assistant's base compensation is $ _____ per **hour** payable in equal bi-weekly installments every other _____ (insert day of the week).
      OR ☐ (If checked) Assistant's base compensation is $ _____ per **hour** payable in equal semi-monthly installments on the 15th (or _____) and last (or _____) day of the month.
      OR ☐ (If checked) Assistant's base compensation is shown in Exhibit _____ attached hereto and incorporated as a part of this Agreement by reference.
   B. **Expenses:** Assistant shall be reimbursed for reasonable business expenses incurred by Assistant in performing Assistant's duties under this Agreement.
   C. **Advances:** Assistant shall not be entitled to any advance payment from Associate-Licensee upon future compensation, unless specified in a separate written agreement for each such advance. If Associate-Licensee elects to advance funds to Assistant pursuant to a separate written agreement, Associate-Licensee may deduct the amount advanced from any future paycheck due Assistant as specified in the separate written agreement.
   D. Deductions authorized by Assistant or required by law (including but not limited to FICA, Medicare and Federal and State income tax) will be with held from Assistant's pay.
   E. **Compensation Review:** Associate-Licensee shall review Assistant's base compensation annually. Associate understands and agrees that any such review is not an express or implied commitment to increase such compensation nor is there any express or implied commitment to maintain Assistant's compensation at any particular level in the future.
   F. **Timekeeping:** Associate-Licensee shall record Assistant's time on a daily basis including starting time, ending time and the beginning and ending time for all meal periods.
   G. **Vacation Policy:** Assistant shall be eligible to accrue vacation at the rate of ____ hours per pay period. The maximum unused vacation benefits Assistant may have at any one time shall equal two year's worth of vacation (or a total of _____ hours) **OR** ☐ as specified in Exhibit _____ , attached. If Assistant's earned but unused vacation reaches the maximum accrual amount, Assistant will cease to accrue additional vacation time until Assistant uses enough vacation to fall below the maximum accrual amount. All accrued and unused vacation will be paid to Assistant upon termination of this Agreement as required by law.

Associate Licensee's Initials (_____) (_____)   Assistant's Initials (_____) (_____)

The copyright laws of the United States (Title 17 U.S. Code) forbid the unauthorized reproduction of this form, or any portion thereof, by photocopy machine or any other means, including facsimile or computerized formats, Copyright © 1991-2012, CALIFORNIA ASSOCIATION OF REALTORS®, INC. ALL RIGHTS RESERVED.

Reviewed by _____ Date _____

EQUAL HOUSING OPPORTUNITY

PAC REVISED 06/12 (PAGE 1 OF 3)

PERSONAL ASSISTANT CONTRACT (PAC PAGE 1 OF 3)

Agent: WALT HUBER	Phone:	Fax:	Prepared using zipForm® software
Broker: WALT HUBER REALTOR			

6. **PROPRIETARY INFORMATION AND FILES:**
   A. Assistant acknowledge that as a result of Assistant's employment created by this Agreement, Assistant may given access to, make use of, create, acquire and/or add to non-public proprietary, confidential information of a secret, special and/or unique nature and value to Broker, including without limitation Broker's internal systems, procedures, manuals, confidential reports, client lists and client information, methods, strategies and/or techniques used by Broker, the equipment and methods used and preferred by Broker's clients, the fees paid by clients and any and all other confidential information of Broker (hereafter collectively and individually "Confidential Information"). Assistant further recognizes and acknowledges that all of Broker's Confidential Information which is now or may hereafter be in their possession is the property of Broker and that protection of this Confidential Information against unauthorized disclosure or use is of critical importance to Broker in order to protect Broker from unfair competition. As a material inducement to Associate-Licensee to enter into this Agreement, Assistant covenants and agrees Assistant will not at any time, either while this Agreement is in force or after it is terminated without the prior written consent of Broker make any independent use of such Confidential Information, or disclose the same, directly or indirectly, to any other person, firm, corporation or other entity, for any reason or purpose whatsoever, except as may be required by law provided that Assistant shall cooperate with Broker in taking all necessary and appropriate steps to assure the protection of such Confidential Information from unauthorized use or disclosure outside of any action, proceeding, inquiry or investigation, or except to the extent that any such Confidential Information shall be in the public domain other than by reason of Assistant's breach of this paragraph 6.
   B. All Confidential Information including without limitation files and documents pertaining to listings, leads, transactions and the operation of Broker's real estate brokerage are property of Broker. Assistant shall, on the termination of this Agreement for any reason, immediately surrender to Broker all such Confidential Information including without limitation all documents and files whether in paper or electronic format.
7. **INSURANCE:**
   A. **AUTOMOBILE:** Assistant shall maintain automobile insurance coverage for liability and property damage in the following amounts $ _____ /$ _____ , respectively. Associate-Licensee and Broker shall be named as additional insured parties on Assistant's policies. A copy of the endorsement showing the additional insured parties shall be provided to Associate-Licensee.
   B. **WORKER'S COMPENSATION:** Associate-Licensee's Worker's Compensation carrier is _____ . The contact information for this carrier is as follows: Address: _____ , Telephone: _____
   C. **ERRORS AND OMISSIONS INSURANCE:** Associate-Licensee represents that (check one):
      (i) ☐ Assistant is covered by errors and omissions insurance obtained by Broker.
      (ii) ☐ Assistant is covered by errors and omissions insurance obtained by Associate-Licensee.
      (iii) ☐ Assistant is not covered by errors and omissions insurance.
8. **COMPLIANCE WITH APPLICABLE LAWS, RULES, REGULATIONS AND POLICIES:** Assistant agrees to comply with all local, state and federal laws and regulations, and any office policy and procedures to which Associate-Licensee is subject as a result of engaging in real estate activity.
9. **NOTICE OF CLAIMS:** Assistant shall immediately notify Associate-Licensee or Broker in writing if Assistant is served with or becomes aware of any lawsuit, claim or proceeding relating to Associate-Licensee or Broker's brokerage business or the performance of this Agreement.
10. **DISPUTE RESOLUTION:** Associate-Licensee and Assistant agree to mediate all disputes and claims between them arising from or connected in any way with this Agreement before resorting to court action. If any dispute or claim is not resolved through mediation, or otherwise, Associate-Licensee and Assistant may agree to submit the dispute to arbitration at, and pursuant to the rules and bylaws of, the Association of REALTORS®.
11. **OTHER TERMS AND CONDITIONS AND ATTACHED SUPPLEMENTS:**
    ☐ Broker and Associate-Licensee Independent Contractor Agreement (C.A.R. Form ICA)
    ☐ Broker/Associate-Licensee/Assistant Three Party Agreement (C.A.R. Form TPA)
    ☐ Broker Office Policy Manual (or, if checked, ☐ available in Broker's office)
    ☐ BRE Guidelines for Unlicensed Assistants
    ☐ California Association of REALTORS® Real Estate Licensing Chart
    _____
    _____
    _____
12. **ATTORNEY FEES:** In any action, proceeding, or arbitration between Associate-Licensee and Assistant arising from or related to this Agreement, the prevailing Associate-Licensee or Assistant shall be entitled to reasonable attorney fees and costs.
13. **ENTIRE AGREEMENT:** This Agreement constitutes the entire Agreement between the parties. Its terms are intended by the parties as a final, complete, exclusive, and integrated expression of their agreement with respect to its subject matter, and may not be contradicted by evidence of any prior agreement or contemporaneous oral agreement. This Agreement may not be amended, modified, altered, or changed except in writing signed by Associate-Licensee and Assistant. If any provision of this Agreement is held invalid and legally unenforceable, the parties agree that such provision shall be deemed amended to the extent necessary to render it and/or the remainder of this Agreement valid and enforceable. Even after termination, this Agreement shall govern all disputes and claims between Associate-Licensee and Assistant connected with their respective obligations under this Agreement, including obligations and liabilities arising from existing and completed listings, transactions and services.

Associate Licensee's Initials (_____) (_____)   Assistant's Initials (_____) (_____)

The copyright laws of the United States (Title 17 U.S. Code) forbid the unauthorized reproduction of this form, or any portion thereof, by photocopy machine or any other means, including facsimile or computerized formats. Copyright © 1991-2012, CALIFORNIA ASSOCIATION OF REALTORS®, INC. ALL RIGHTS RESERVED.

PAC REVISED 06/12 (PAGE 2 OF 3)

Reviewed by _____ Date _____

PERSONAL ASSISTANT CONTRACT (PAC PAGE 2 OF 3)
Produced with zipForm® by zipLogix 18070 Fifteen Mile Road, Fraser, Michigan 48026 www.zipLogix.com Untitled

Associate-Licensee _____ Date _____
            Signature
Associate-Licensee _____
            Print Name
Address _____ City _____ State _____ Zip _____

Telephone _____ Fax _____ E-mail _____

Assistant _____ Date _____
          Signature
Assistant _____
          Print Name
Address _____ City _____ State _____ Zip _____

Telephone _____ Fax _____ E-mail _____

THIS FORM HAS BEEN APPROVED BY THE CALIFORNIA ASSOCIATION OF REALTORS® (C.A.R.). NO REPRESENTATION IS MADE AS TO THE LEGAL VALIDITY OR ADEQUACY OF ANY PROVISION IN ANY SPECIFIC TRANSACTION. A REAL ESTATE BROKER IS THE PERSON QUALIFIED TO ADVISE ON REAL ESTATE TRANSACTIONS. IF YOU DESIRE LEGAL OR TAX ADVICE, CONSULT AN APPROPRIATE PROFESSIONAL.
This form is available for use by the entire real estate industry. It is not intended to identify the user as a REALTOR®. REALTOR® is a registered collective membership mark which may be used only by members of the NATIONAL ASSOCIATION OF REALTORS® who subscribe to its Code of Ethics.

Published and Distributed by:
REAL ESTATE BUSINESS SERVICES, INC.
a subsidiary of the California Association of REALTORS®
525 South Virgil Avenue, Los Angeles, California 90020

Reviewed by _____ Date _____

PAC REVISED 06/12 (PAGE 3 OF 3)

PERSONAL ASSISTANT CONTRACT (PAC PAGE 3 OF 3)

Produced with zipForm® by zipLogix 18070 Fifteen Mile Road, Fraser, Michigan 48026 www.zipLogix.com

Untitled

IV. What Do Assistants Do?

As we stated earlier in this chapter, many of the responsibilities of real estate assistants will depend on the needs of the agent or broker who hires them. Regardless of your original duties, your employer's needs may change and you should be prepared to step in and take over increasing responsibilities, as needed. In this section, we will discuss the broad variety of duties that may be required of a licensed real estate assistant.

A. ALPHABETICAL FILING SYSTEMS

One of the most often used paper and electronic filing systems is the *ALPHABETICAL FORM*, *where files are organized alphabetically by street address and year.* Typically, files will be arranged according to the last name of your agent's client, usually the seller's name. Buyers and sellers generate numerous documents and different information. *Any document that has both buyers' and sellers' signatures is referred to as a* **SHARED DOCUMENT**, and should go into the client's file (see **Figure 14-2**).

Figure 14-2

Example of Documents in a Shared Document File

Sellers' Information	Purchase Agreement
Listings	Escrow Instructions
All Disclosures	Closing Statements
Buyers' Information	Lockbox Identification Number

The easier you make it for your agents to find documents, the more time you save them and the less risk of losing paperwork or computer files. Keeping different coding systems, like different "color file folders" for buyers and sellers, will help to simplify the filing system.

B. MASTER TRANSACTION FILE

A *MASTER TRANSACTION FILE contains all the documents a brokerage (broker) may require on a single completed transaction.*

The longer a company or agent stays in business, the more clients will come back for repeat business, generating different transaction files. If all the client's paperwork were to be filed in just one master transaction file, it could quickly become enormous.

C. COMPUTER FILING

Computerized office technology has put bulky metal file cabinets on the endangered species list. These space consuming dinosaurs are on the verge of becoming extinct in the modern real estate office.

For a variety of reasons, including your office policy, legal requirements, and the potential loss of data due to computer crashes, you should, at the very least, **keep a paper file containing signed copies and originals of documents for each transaction**. However, computer files are more convenient, less time consuming, take up less space and are more "green" than the "old school" method of saving every piece of paper generated by a real estate transaction.

For each client, open a new computer file and save everything related to this client in this file. This includes all emails you send and receive, and contracts, letters, and spreadsheets related to your agent's clients. Multiple listings entered or received on behalf of your agent's clients also go into the file. By scanning the hard copies of all your agent's documents, the computer filing system can include the entire transaction file.

D. UPDATING DATA (MLS and Office Info)

The MLS inventory of homes must be kept current. Most Multiple Listing Services penalize the listing agents with hefty fines when they do not report a property either pending or sold in a timely fashion (which is usually 48 hours). You, as the assistant, can take on this task and report the listings' status to the MLS as well as updating the office inventory book for the benefit of the other agents. Your agent's website also needs to be updated regularly. Articles that are time sensitive if not updated make the website lose its professional appearance.

As numerous homes come on and off the market on a daily basis, your agent may take advantage of MLS alerts that notify clients when homes become available that fit their needs. They will have filled out an MLS search form and checked a box okaying **automated alerts** be sent to them on either an hourly, daily, or weekly basis. These alerts will also be sent to the agent. One of your duties may include keeping track of the notifications or even following through with a phone call asking the buyers if they would like to set up an appointment to have your agent show them the property or properties to which they've been alerted. Working for a "top earner" means there may be a large number of these alerts sent out on a daily basis, so it's important that you keep close tabs on the progress of the alerts and whether or not potential buyers are getting the attention they deserve, by phone, email, or text!

Time is an extremely important commodity. No one can buy or rent more of it!

E. KEEPING AND ASSISTING WITH APPOINTMENTS

Another important assistant's task is reminding your agent of all appointments in a timely fashion. To a client, timeliness is everything! As such, it's important to know where and how to reach your agent at all times. Most agents carry smartphones, but if you both have Apple® or Android® devices, it will make this task even more efficient, as information is easily beamed from one device to another. We will discuss this handy real estate tool in more detail shortly.

A lost or delayed call, email, or text message can result in missed opportunities in listing or selling. Showing up late or missing an appointment can be disastrous!

As a trusted employee and licensee, you may assist your agent further by keeping some of his or her appointments yourself. For example, you may be asked (or volunteer) to meet with appraisers with favorable comparables, or accompany buyers on the final walk-throughs prior to closing.

Determine which documents (forms, brochures, electronic presentations) your agent prefers to take on listing or selling appointments. Prepare the appropriate packets in advance for your agent's appointments, whether electronically or in paper form.

F. STAYING IN TOUCH WITH YOUR AGENT'S CLIENTS - THE FASTER THE BETTER

Keeping your agent in constant contact with prospects is a very rewarding task for both of you.

Emails, text messaging, and social media connections are important.

Paper and electronic newsletters are an easy way to stay in touch with prospects and past clients. You can print your own cards with real estate computer software, but there are excellent and inexpensive professional cards being offered to the industry.

Although newsletters can be worthwhile, many agents no longer use them on a regular basis unless they have pertinent real estate news to convey. The shortness of a 140 charcter "Tweet" is often appreciated by busy clients.

Naturally, bulk mail is worthwhile if the agent/assistant does a lot of mailings. In our opinion, it is best to be selective and concentrate your mailing efforts on where they will do the most good.

G. TECHNOLOGY

You may be asked to take digital pictures of your agent's new listings.

Most Multiple Listing Services (MLSs) have the capability of entering ten pictures or more for each listing, but the first picture or video MUST be of the front of the house, or none of the pictures will be allowed.

When taking pictures, be careful that the garage door is closed, and that there are no trash containers in front of the property. Take the pictures from various angles to insure some good shots; take inside shots of the best features of the home. Edit these to make sure they are properly exposed; if you don't know how, take a class at a local association of REALTORS® or a community college. You'll make your agent look good to the real estate industry when there are several beautiful pictures of the listing. The pictures can be given to the advertising person in your office to be featured in the newspaper as the "house of the week," or on web or social media

sites. You'll also want to give email copies of the pictures and advertising to your clients to show them what's being done on their behalf.

Most MLSs will require a photo of the front of the house, but without a broker's sign visible.

1. Real Estate Software (Websites or Apps)

This is an excellent time to discuss real estate software. Most offices use Microsoft Word® for letter writing and Microsoft Excel® for income property spread sheets. Becoming proficient in these two programs is extremely important. As a smart assistant, you should take some classes at a community college or adult education to perfect these skills. If your broker is involved in property management functions, CAR's zipForms® has a user-friendly form for entering monies received and disbursed, thereby giving the property owner an accurate accounting of his or her investment on a monthly basis.

Take advantage of CARs® many seminars and online webinars to keep abreast of the latest technology!

Sophisticated real estate websites and apps can keep the agent's client databases on the Internet accessible to the agent, or to the assistant, from any location. So whether you are at the office, at home, or on a trip, online searches for clients and leads can be performed by first name, last name, street name, or even by city and category. Although it takes time to set a system up, once it's done, the rewards are great. Mass email mail-outs are as easy as a couple of clicks of the mouse; brochures and flyers can be professionally produced in color with pictures of the property, the agent, and the brokerage logo. Naturally, as an assistant who can maintain this system for your agent, you will earn his or her respect and gratitude.

a. Unique Market Analysis

With appropriate real estate software, you can also download MLS pictures and data into your system for a professional market analysis. Since sellers often interview more than one REALTOR®, it is important that your agent distances himself or herself from the crowd by using a detailed and unique, thorough presentation and marketing plan. This sophisticated software has a large library of letters for various occasions and extensive follow up; these letters can even be customized further for a better personal email and text communication. When properly used, your agent will have a distinct advantage over the other presentations that are all probably very similar.

Many real estate search engines share partial information from an MLS. However, only an MLS member has access to a full MLS listing, giving them an advantage over impersonal websites.

2. Mobile is the Way to Go!

CAR® forms are available on mobile devices.

There are a variety of real estate software programs and apps used in the industry for smartphones and tablets that allow mobile users automatic delivery of messages. These handy devices can be synchronized nightly with a computer and all hand-held devices. Also, all listings in the MLS can be searched by either price, city, or address. Naturally, it also contains the agent's clients and personal database with all current data. Mobile devices, programmed with the appropriate real estate software, can double up as a calculator, a programmer that opens lockboxes, note pad, appointment book, and calendar. Additionally, it can alert the owner in advance of appointments and important dates. As a competent assistant, you should become proficient in your agent's marketing software of choice in order to assist in all of the above tasks.

H. NOTARY PUBLIC

Being a notary public is extremely helpful in real estate and to your agent.

You, as an assistant, can perform this duty for your agent's clients. Just think, many buyers and sellers needing this mandatory service only have evenings and weekends to transact business, which makes it difficult to meet with escrow officers and lenders to have the necessary documents notarized. You can easily take care of this by becoming a notary.

1. Functions of a Notary Public (Thumb Print and ID Required)

A *NOTARY PUBLIC is a public official whose main powers include administering oaths and attesting to signatures, both important and effective ways to minimize fraud in legal documents.* Perhaps the most important duty of a notary public is attesting to signatures on documents. This duty is important because it aids in minimizing fraud; signature attestation must be done with the notary and the signatory in a face-to-face setting.

The process of notarizing a signature is simple. The person who wants his or her signature notarized must present sufficient evidence (such as driver's license or passport) to prove his or her identity and then sign the necessary document with the notary as a witness to the signing. The notary completes the process by stamping or sealing, dating, and signing the document. This face-to-face procedure helps ensure the authenticity of the signature.

2. Notary Journal

All notaries must keep a NOTARY JOURNAL that must include the following:

1. Date and time of signing
2. Type of notarization (usually acknowledgement)
3. Character or type of instrument (i.e., grant deed)

4. Name of signer (printed)
5. Satisfactory evidence of identity
6. Fee charged
7. Additional information (i.e., document dated 10/6 but acknowledged signing on 10/7)
8. Identification details (driver's license # and expiration date)
9. Signature (i.e., of "grantor")
10. Right thumbprint of signatore

Any person signing a grant deed, quitclaim deed, or trust deed is required to place a right thumb print on the notary's sequential journal. This is because of a high rate of fraud by the use of false deeds. Additionally, a notary must immediately notify the Secretary of State if the notary's sequential journal is stolen, lost, misplaced, destroyed, damaged, or otherwise rendered unusable.

 It might come in handy to tell a perspective employer that as a notary applicant you were checked out by the Department of Justice and FBI!

3. Eligibility

To be eligible for an appointment as a notary public, the California Secretary of State requires the person to:

1. Be a California resident (need not be a citizen unless serving on a military or naval reservation);
2. Be at least 18 years of age;
3. Complete a course of study approved by the California Secretary of State;
4. Pass a protored, closed-book examination; and
5. Pass a background test.

4. Official Seal of Notary Must Be Clear

Documents may be rendered unacceptable for recordation if a seal is placed over an integral part of the text or a signature; if the seal obscures the decorative or colored symbols or borders so that the seal is not photographically reproducible; if the seal has been altered with ink, typewriter, pencil, or whatever; or if an impression is made of a metal seal that has been inked too heavily and is not reproducible. If the notary's name is clearly shown in the seal, the name need not be typed or printed under his signature.

I. ESCROW COORDINATOR

Your agent may want you to assist with escrows. You need to have all the pertinent information on the transaction and a good understanding of the escrow process. Your agent should instruct you on what your responsibilities are. You can implement this information by talking to the escrow officer or his or her assistant. You need to find out if all the documents have been returned to escrow and what is still needed to close. Find out if all contingencies have been removed. Are all conditions met, such as termite clearance, home warranty, disclosures, etc.? It may be a good idea to visit the escrow office at least once prior to opening escrow. When escrow closes, the listing needs to be removed from the MLS, the file complete with all chronological documents properly secured, and the file placed in the office master file cabinet after the office manager or broker has initialed all pertinent documents. At this time, the commission check is issued to the agent. Also, don't forget to order the "For Sale" sign or take the "Sold" rider down.

J. FOLLOW-UP DETAILS

After sending out at least 200 "Just Sold" cards to neighbors in the immediate area of the sold property and following up with telephone calls, email, or texts within a few days (if this does not conflict with "cold call" procedures), this may be a good time to review this transaction with your agent. You both may decide to make some improvements in how to work your next transaction. This can be work in progress.

V. CHAPTER SUMMARY

A **real estate assistant** with a salesperson's license is not as limited as one who does not have a salesperson or broker license. **Assistants free up agents' time** to spend in the field, listing or selling. Their duties may include (among others) maintaining a filing system, soliciting appointments, preparing documents, maintaining the company website, meeting with appraisers and home inspectors, as well as assisting and holding open houses.

The more successful an agent becomes, the greater the need for an assistant. A NAR® survey found that **10%** of top producers hired real estate assistants, and were more successful as a result.

Finding the right broker for whom to work is an important decision. A **résumé** should include positive information concerning consistency, people skills, education, real estate background, skills, recommendations, and interests, presented in a professional manner. During the interview process, a prospective employer may ask about licensing, career goals, typing and computer skills, etc. Having a working car in good condition is important.

Employers hire both **part-time** and **full-time** assistants. An **employee** works regular hours set by the employer, is paid a regular or hourly wage, and has a right to sick leave, insurance, retirement and vacation benefits, and possibly a commission. An **independent contractor** pays his or her own taxes, works with a minimum of supervision and, in general, sets his or her own schedule, with more control over day-to-day activities. Most assistants work as employees rather than independent contractors.

Assistants are commonly asked to handle **office administration**, including a great deal of paperwork. An **efficient filing system** is necessary to keep track of shared documents, buyer's documents, seller's documents, and a **master transaction file**. This is frequently done alphabetically, with cross-referencing and an index of topics and may be kept digitally as well as in paper form.

Updating data is another important function of a real estate assistant. This includes reporting listing status of properties to the agent's MLS, and updating websites with the latest information.

A busy agent needs to be reminded of upcoming appointments and set up with a **listing or selling packet** to take on those appointments. An assistant may be able to step in and take over some of those meetings, like taking buyers on a walk-through before closing. Keeping the agent updated may require some technological know-how, including smartphones and tablets. Software produced specifically for the real estate industry can make this job a lot easier.

Becoming a **notary public** is one more way an assistant can save his or her employer time. A notary authenticates contracts, acknowledges deeds, and takes affidavits, among other things. A notary must keep an official record of all notarial acts, in a **notary journal**. All parties who sign a notarized document must place a right thumb print in the notary journal on all real estate-related documents. The **official seal of notary** must be clearly legible to be acceptable.

Assistants may be asked to assist with escrows, as well, making sure all contingencies have been removed, all conditions met, etc. After escrow is closed, signs must come down and the MLS notified. Finally, follow-up cards, emails, and calls should be made within a few days of closing.

VI. MATCHING VOCABULARY Fill in the blanks with the correct letter

A. Alphabetical form
B. A shared document
C. Auto alert
D. Employee
E. Independent
   contractor

F. Master transaction file
G. Mentors
H. Notarization
I. Notary journal
J. Notary public
K. Paperflow

L. Real estate assistant
M. Right thumb print

1. _____ Helpmates and extensions of successful real estate agents who do a variety of duties that allow the agent to spend more time in "the field."

2. _____ This person works regular hours set by an employer, is paid a regular or hourly wage, and has a right to sick leave, insurance, retirement, and vacation benefits.

3. _____ This person pays his own taxes, works with a minimum of supervision, and, in general, sets his own schedule. He has more control over day-to-day activities than an employee.

4. _____ An automatic email sent by an MLS notifying buyers and agents that a new property listing has come on the market.

5. _____ The path a document travels through an office.

6. _____ This file contains all the documents a brokerage may require on a single completed transaction.

7. _____ Any document that has both buyers' and sellers' signatures is referred to as this.

8. _____ This type of filing system organizes files alphabetically by street address and year.

9. _____ A person who is authorized to authenticate contracts, acknowledge deeds, take affidavits, and perform other official activities.

10. _____ A written statement, also called a certification, to which a notary public has affixed his or her official signature, seal, title, jurisdiction, commission, expiration date, and address.

11. _____ Notary public's maintain an official written record of his notarial acts in this book kept for such purposes.

12. _____ Due to fraud and forgeries, it is now necessary to have each person who signs the document, leave this impression in the notary's journal on all real estate-related documents.

13. _____ Professionals who are willing to take novices under their wings and not only teach them the basics, but share their experience and secrets to success.

See Page 611 for Answers

VII. CHAPTER QUIZ

1. An assistant:

   a. needs to have an assistant license.
   b. must have a real estate license.
   c. should preferably hold a real estate license.
   d. none of the above.

2. A "Notary Journal" must include:

   a. date and time of signing.
   b. signature.
   c. right thumbprint of signatore.
   d. all of the above

3. Who makes a good assistant?

   a. A retired person
   b. A person with a real estate background
   c. Licensed agents who prefer to work behind the front line
   d. All of the above

4. What are some of the duties of a licensed assistant?

   a. Assisting and holding open houses
   b. Preparing listing packages for his or her agent
   c. Making appointments for his or her agent
   d. All of the above

5. How does an assistant get paid?

   a. Usually a salary plus a percentage of the commission earned
   b. Hourly
   c. Base pay
   d. All of the above can be correct

6. Closed transaction files:

   a. may be taken home by the assistant.
   b. should be filed by the assistant in the office file cabinet.
   c. may be discarded when escrow closes.
   d. must be kept in the office for a minimum of 3 years.

7. Computer skills:

   a. are very important for an assistant.
   b. are not necessary.
   c. command a higher value to the assistant.
   d. both a and c.

8. A licensed assistant can:

   a. communicate with buyers and sellers quoting price.
   b. prospect for his or her agent.
   c. monitor a listing progress.
   d. all of the above.

9. An assistant's contract should:

   a. spell out how the assistant will be paid.
   b. spell out if the assistant is licensed or not.
   c. state who pays for the error and omission's insurance.
   d. all of the above.

10. An assistant:

   a. may be an independent contractor.
   b. must be an independent contractor.
   c. always gets paid by the broker.
   d. does not need to know the office policies.

ANSWERS: 1. c; 2. d; 3. d; 4. d; 5. d; 6. b; 7. d; 8. d; 9. d; 10. a

Licensing, Ethics, and Associations:

Acquiring and Maintaining Your License

I. California Bureau of Real Estate (CalBRE)

*Every state government regulates its own real estate brokerage activities by staff members who are collectively referred to as **REGULATORS**.* In California, all real estate agreements are under the jurisdiction of the *CALIFORNIA BUREAU OF REAL ESTATE (CalBRE), whose primary objective is to protect the public interest in offerings of subdivided lands, and the handling of real estate transactions by licensees. A standard of knowledge is measured by an examination given to potential real estate agents.*

The California Bureau of Real Estate is responsible for regulating real estate brokerage matters and the enforcement of real estate laws. These laws help protect both the individual citizen and the real estate profession. There are obvious benefits derived by shielding citizens from dishonest or incompetent real estate licensees. The reputation of the real estate profession is upheld by making sure that all practicing salespeople and brokers are both honest and capable of performing their jobs properly.

The California Bureau of Real Estate is governed by the Real Estate Commissioner. The Commissioner, who sets all the rules and regulations for the Bureau of Real Estate, receives his or her power from the state legislature. The legislature, in turn, used police power to create the position of Commissioner. *POLICE POWER is the right to enact and enforce laws beneficial to the health, safety, morals, and general welfare of the public.*

II. Real Estate License Requirements

As mentioned in the preceding section, the Real Estate Commissioner's main purpose is the regulation of the real estate business in the state of California. This regulation is accomplished by imposing mandatory licenses on those individuals who choose to work in the field of real estate. Who is required to have these licenses?

In short, any person who is actively involved in a real estate transaction at the service of another, in the expectation of receiving a commission, must be licensed. Fines for nonobservance are high.

CHAPTER OUTLINE

A. WHO MUST HAVE A LICENSE

A person is required to have a license if he or she:

1. sells or offers to sell, buys or offers to buy, and solicits buyers or sellers;
2. solicits or obtains listings;
3. negotiates the purchase, sale, or exchange of real property or business opportunities;
4. leases or rents, collects rents, or negotiates the sale, purchase, or exchange of leases;
5. assists in the purchase of leases on lands owned by the state or federal government;
6. negotiates loans, collects payments, or performs services for borrowers or lenders.

Any person found to be involved in such actions without a license may be guilty of breaking the Real Estate Law, under which stiff penalties can be imposed.

B. WHEN A LICENSE IS NOT REQUIRED

It should be noted that there are a few exceptions to these regulations. The following people, because of the nature of their work, are exempt from the licensing regulations (NO LICENSE REQUIRED):

1. Employees of lending institutions.

2. Lenders making federally insured or guaranteed loans.

3. Certain agricultural associations.

4. Personal property brokers.

5. Cemetery authorities.

6. Collectors of loans made on real property.

7. Certain clerical help.

An individual who is not a real estate salesperson or broker may solicit for the sale of real property as long as he or she is:

1. the owner;
2. holding power of attorney for the owner;
3. an attorney at law acting on behalf of the owner;
4. a receiver or court appointee; or
5. a trustee, selling under a deed of trust.

> The **Federal SAFE Act** requires all persons performing acts such as mortgage loan originations to be registered with and/or licensed through the **Nationwide Mortgage Licensing System and Registry (NMLS&R)**. CalBRE endorsement required.

C. OBTAINING THE FOUR-YEAR SALESPERSON'S LICENSE

To obtain a real estate salesperson license, you must first qualify for and pass a written examination. After passing the exam, a license application must be submitted to and approved by the California Bureau of Real Estate (CalBRE).

You are allowed to file your examination and license application at the same time.

1. **Age:** You must be 18 years of age to be licensed, but there is no age restriction for taking the exam.

2. **Residence:** Proof of legal presence in the United States is required. If you're not a California resident, refer to "Out-of-State Applicants" on the CalBRE website.

3. **Honesty:** Applicants must be honest and truthful. Conviction of a crime or failure to disclose **any** criminal violation or disciplinary action may result in denial of a license.

4. **Education:** Successful completion of the following college-level courses is required to become a real estate salesperson:

   a. Real Estate Principles
   b. Real Estate Practice
   c. One additional CalBRE-approved real estate course

For further information, use the CalBRE website (**www.calbre.ca.gov**), call, or write any district office of the Bureau of Real Estate. You can access the pamphlet, *Instructions to License Applicants* (see **Figure 15-1**) on the CalBRE website.

The salesperson exam (available electronically in all locations) takes three hours, fifteen minutes, has 150 questions, and requires a 70% correct score to pass.

See **Figures 15-2** and **15-3** for the salesperson's and broker's requirements.

Figure 15-1

California Bureau of Real Estate (CalBRE)

INSTRUCTIONS TO
LICENSE APPLICANTS

How to Obtain and Maintain:
California Real Estate Salesperson or Broker License
Prepaid Rental Listing Service License
Mortgage Loan Originator License Endorsement

Now Available Online Only!

CalBRE

PRINCIPAL OFFICE

SACRAMENTO
1651 Exposition Blvd.,
Sacramento, CA 95815
(877-373-4542)

www.calbre.ca.gov

| **All offices open 8-5 weekdays** |

DISTRICT OFFICES

LOS ANGELES Suite 350 (213-620-2072)
320 W. 4th St. Los Angeles, CA 90013-1105

OAKLAND Suite 702 (510-622-2552)
1515 Clay St., Oakland, CA 94612-1402

SAN DIEGO Suite 3064 (619-525-4192)
1350 Front St., San Diego, CA 92101-3687

FRESNO Rm. 3070 (559-445-5009)
2550 Mariposa Mall, Fresno, CA 93721-2273

PROOF OF LEGAL PRESENCE IN THE UNITED STATES

The **Personal Responsibility and Work Opportunity Act** (the "Act") requires states to eliminate a broad array of public benefits for illegal immigrants. The definition of a public benefit includes professional and occupational licenses issued to individuals by state agencies. For purposes of the Bureau of Real Estate, the term "public benefit" applies to original and renewal real estate salesperson and broker licenses, prepaid rental listing service licenses, and a payment from the Real Estate Recovery Account.

To implement the provisions of the Act, the Bureau has adopted Commissioner's Regulation 2718. This regulation requires **proof of legal presence in the United States from all applicants for a license**, and from applicants for payment from the Real Estate Recovery Account. This requirement applies to applicants for both original and renewal licenses.

Figure 15-2

EXAMINATION SUBJECT AREAS	SALESPERSON EXAM (APPROX.)	BROKER EXAM (APPROX.)
1. Property Ownership and Land Use Controls and Regulations	**15%**	**15%**

Classes of property; Property characteristics; Encumbrances; Types of ownership; Descriptions of property; Government rights in land; Public controls; Environmental hazards and regulations; Private controls; Water rights; Special categories of land

2. Laws of Agency and Fiduciary Duties	**17%**	**17%**

Law, definition, and nature of agency relationships, types of agencies, and agents; Creation of agency and agency agreements; Responsibilities of agent to seller/buyer as principal; Disclosure of agency; Disclosure of acting as principal or other interest; Termination of agency; Commission and fees; Responsibilites of agent to non-client third parties

3. Property Valuation and Financial Analysis	**14%**	**14%**

Value; Methods of estimating value; Financial analysis

4. Financing	**9%**	**9%**

General concepts; Types of loans; Sources of financing; Government programs; Mortgages/deeds of trust/notes; Financing/credit laws; Loan brokerage; Types of loan originators

5. Transfer of Property	**8%**	**8%**

Title insurance; Deeds; Escrow; Tax aspects; Special processes; Transfer through court supervision; Types of vesting

6. Practice of Real Estate and Mandated Disclosures (includes Specialty Areas)	**25%**	**25%**

Trust account management; Fair housing laws; Truth in advertising; Record keeping requirements; Agent supervision; Permitted activities of unlicensed sales assistants; CalBRE jurisdiction and disciplinary actions; Licensing, continuing education requirements and procedures; California Real Estate Recovery Fund; General ethics; Technology; Property management; Commercial/industrial/income properties; Specialty areas; Transfer disclosure statement; Natural hazard disclosure statements; Disclosure of material facts affecting property value; Need for inspection and obtaining/verifying information; Reports; Servicing Diverse Populations

7. Contracts	**12%**	**12%**

General; Listing agreements; Buyer broker agreements; Offers/purchase contracts; Agreements; Promissory notes/securities; Purchase/lease options; Advanced fee

Bureau of Real Estate
% of Exam Questions
Testing Emphasis

For more information:

www.calbre.ca.gov
California Bureau of Real Estate Home Page

www.calbre.ca.gov/Examinees/Preparing.html
Preparing for the Exam

Figure 15-3

SALESPERSON AND BROKER COURSES
(The statutory required college-level courses)

The statutory required college-level courses for people wishing to qualify for either the real estate salesperson or broker license examination are as follows:

APPLICANTS FOR THE SALESPERSON'S EXAM

To qualify to take an examination for a real estate salesperson's license, an applicant must have completed the **REAL ESTATE PRINCIPLES** and **REAL ESTATE PRACTICE** college-level courses, plus one additional real estate course from the following:

Real Estate Appraisal
Accounting
Business Law
Legal Aspects of Real Estate
Real Estate Finance
Real Estate Economics

Escrows
Property Management
Real Estate Office Administration
Mortgage Loan Brokering and Lending
Computer Applications in Real Estate
Common Interest Development

APPLICANTS FOR THE BROKER'S EXAM

1. An applicant for the broker's license examination must have completed eight courses in addition to the experience requirements. These eight courses must include the following five:

Real Estate Practice
Legal Aspects of Real Estate
Real Estate Finance

Real Estate Appraisal
Real Estate Economics (or Accounting)

2. The remaining three courses* are to be selected from the following:

Real Estate Principles
Business Law
Property Management
Escrows
Real Estate Office Administration
Mortgage Loan Brokering and Lending

Advanced Legal Aspects of Real Estate
Advanced Real Estate Finance
Advanced Real Estate Appraisal
Computer Applications in Real Estate
Common Interest Development

*If both Real Estate Economics and Accounting are taken, only two courses from the above group are required.

1. CalBRE and Electronic Exams

The CalBRE offers an electronic testing system at some CalBRE testing facilities. Check their website for more information.

The "Electronic Examination System" allows examinees to take the real estate salesperson and broker examination using an electronic method (now available in Fresno, San Diego, Los Angeles vicinity, Oakland, and Sacramento).

2. Salesperson's Examination

To pass, an applicant must achieve a score of at least 70 percent in the three-hour, fifteen minute salesperson's exam, which has 150 multiple-choice questions. Exams are usually scheduled during the morning or afternoon. A nonrefundable fee is required to take the test. If you fail, you may take the exam again as soon as possible, but you must pay for each exam. The applicant must successfully pass the examination within two years of the date the application is filed. If those steps are not completed within the two-year time limit, the application and fee will lapse.

The CalBRE website lists prohibited items at the state exam. An examinee must present a picture ID and printed test date notice.

3. Notification of Examination Results

If you took an electronic examination, your results were provided to you upon completion of the exam. In addition, qualified candidates who pass their examination can be issued a temporary license, which allows them to commence conducting licensed activities immediately. If you took a pencil and paper examination, examination results and/or related correspondence will be mailed to you, normally within five business days after your examination. You can also check your examination results through the eLicensing (**Figure 15-4**) online system (**https://secure.dre.ca.gov/elicensing**), or through the Interactive Voice Response system by calling toll free at 1-877-373-4542. Please wait at least five business days after you have completed your examination before calling.

There is no limitation to the number of re-examinations you may take during the two-year period following the date of the filing of the original application. If you wish to take additional examinations after the two-year period, you must complete a new application.

To speed up the process, you can apply and pay the fees for the broker/ salesperson examination AND broker/salesperson license at the same time.

4. Electronic Fingerprint Requirement (Salesperson and Broker)

Applicants for the salesperson's license must apply for a license within one year from the exam date.

Figure 15-4

eLicensing by the Bureau of Real Estate (CalBRE)

License information is now available online, using what the CalBRE refers to as eLICENSING. The CalBRE continues to upgrade its website capabilities, making the process of scheduling an exam date and obtaining the results a lot easier. Using eLicensing, look at the helpful information available to you:

1. Find out **which tests are being scheduled.**
2. Look up your **new test date.**
3. Get your **exam results.**
4. Find out if your **license has been issued yet.**

The CalBRE can also help licensees make changes online, including the following options:

1. Broker License Renewal.
2. Change Your Mailing Address Only.
3. Change Your Main Office Address Only.
4. Request a Duplicate License.
5. Change How You Receive the *Real Estate Bulletin.*
6. Status of Your Online Request.
7. Review Your License Application (requires Adobe Acrobat 5.0 or higher).
8. Change Your User Information.
9. Display Public License Information.

The general public can also obtain helpful information by accessing Internet CalBRE records, such as:

1. Licensee look up by name or license identification number.
2. Search for approved statutory (pre-license) real estate courses.
3. Search for approved real estate continuing education offerings.
4. Active prepaid rental listing service (PRLS) licensees.
5. Active Mineral, Oil, and Gas (MOG) broker licensees.

If you have taken Principles and Practice, plus one other required course and have passed the examination, you are qualified to apply for a four-year renewable license. You must pay $49 (paid to scan service provider—fee may vary) for the live scan set of your fingerprints.

Upon completion of the real estate license exam, a copy of *RE Form 237* (the Live Scan Service Request Form) will be mailed to all applicants. A list of providers of the live scan fingerprinting technique is available through the CalBRE website (www.**bre.ca.gov**). A complete list of Salesperson and Broker fees is shown in **Figure 15-5.**

Figure 15-5

California Bureau of Real Estate Examination and Licensing Fees		
Examination Fees		
	Salesperson	**Broker**
Original Examination	$60	$95
Re-Examination	$60	$95
First Rescheduled Exam	$15	$20
Subsequent Rescheduled Exam	$30	$30
Combination Examination and License Application		
Examination Fee	$60	$95
License Fee	$245	$300
Fingerprint Fee	*	*
Total Due to CalBRE with RE 436	$305	$395
Original License Fees		
License Fee	$245	$300
Fingerprint Fee	*	*
Total Due to CalBRE	$245	$300
Renewal Fees		
On Time Renewal	$245	$300
Late Renewal (within 2 years after license expiration date)	$367	$450

* Original license or examination applicants who reside in California will pay a $49 fingerprint processing fee directly to the live scan fingerprint service provider. Original license applicants who reside out of state should submit the $49 fingerprint processing fee to the CalBRE with their application and license fee.

Note: Examination and licensing fees are subject to change. Check the California Bureau of Real Estate website fo any changes (www.bre.ca.gov/Licensees/Fees.html).

D. OBTAINING THE BROKER'S LICENSE (Renewable Four-Year License)

A *BROKER'S LICENSE is required of any individual who wants to operate a real estate office.* The candidate for a real estate broker's license must:

1. be 18 years of age to apply for a license (no age restriction for taking the exam);
2. provide Proof of Legal Presence in the United States;
3. if not a California resident, refer to "Out-of-State Applicants" on CalBRE website;
4. have had two year's previous experience in the last five years or a bachelor's degree (major or minor in real estate);
5. complete the required eight broker courses;
6. be honest and truthful; and
7. pass the required CalBRE examination (governmental photo ID required).

1. Broker's Qualifying Experience (Two of the Last Five Years)

A candidate must also be able to prove that he or she has experience in real estate before applying for a broker's license. Generally, two years of full-time work (104 forty-hour weeks) as a salesperson within the five years immediately preceding the date of application is required. This two-year requirement (two of the last five years) may be replaced by an equivalent amount of part-time salesperson work.

Sometimes the State Real Estate Commissioner will accept experience in fields other than real estate sales. These fields include escrow or title officer or as a loan officer in a capacity directly involved in real estate. Also, real estate-related experience as a subdivider, contractor, or speculative builder, or real estate appraiser.

The education exemption to the experience requirement for applying for a new real estate broker's license is more stringent. The applicant, however, may petition the CalBRE for an exemption from the experience requirement if he or she graduated from a four-year college or university with "a major or minor in real estate."

University, College, and Community College students are encouraged to make sure they are real estate majors or at least real estate minors to help with their Education Petition.

But, all candidates must complete the eight required real estate courses, regardless of their educational degree.

All students are encouraged to submit an equivalency request with the Bureau of Real Estate. All decisions made by the Commissioner are final.

Four-year degree with a major or minor in real estate = 2 years of experience.

The broker's 200-question exam takes five hours to complete (100 questions in a 2 1/2-hour morning session and 100 questions in a 2 1/2-hour afternoon session). The applicant must answer 75% of the questions correctly to pass.

2. Broker's Required Education (Eight Courses)

Applicants for the real estate broker's license examination must have successfully completed the eight statutory-required, college-level courses. The required salesperson's courses can be found on the list of required broker's courses, but the number of required courses is different: three for the regular salesperson's license, and eight for the broker's license. An applicant's choice of eight (broker-required) courses must be taken by all broker candidates (refer back to Figure 15-3).

Members of the California State Bar are statutorily exempt from the college-level course requirements, but they must have at least two years real estate-related experience within the last five years.

E. OBTAINING THE CALBRE MORTGAGE LOAN ORIGINATOR (MLO) LICENSE ENDORSEMENT

To make California real estate loans and charge a fee, a salesperson or broker must obtain a CalBRE Mortgage Loan Originator (MLO) License Endorsement. This is part of the Mortgage Loan Originator NMLS/SAFE Act.

Anyone who acts as a mortgage loan originator (MLO) within California without having a proper CalBRE MLO license endorsement is guilty of a crime punishable by 6 months imprisonment, plus a $20,000 fine for individuals or $60,000 for corporations.

CalBRE charges a $300 fee annually for a MLO License Endorsement. See **http://mortgage.nationwidelicensingsystem.org** and **www.CalBre.ca.gov** for more important details.

In addition all licensees must report to the Bureau of Real Estate if they make, arrange, or service loans secured by residential property, 1- to 4-units, under the authority of a Bureau of Real Estate license.

F. RENEWAL OF LICENSE — EVERY FOUR YEARS (Salesperson and Broker)

If a real estate license is not renewed, the licensee has a two-year grace period and late renewal fees.

Once the license has expired, no licensed-required activity can be performed by the salesperson until the license has been renewed. The late renewal period (often referred to as the "grace" period) simply allows the licensee to renew on a late basis without retaking the examination; it does not allow the licensee to conduct license-required activity during the late renewal period. The license renewal fee for a salesperson is $245 if filed on time and $367 if filed late. A broker's renewal costs $300 if on time and $450 if late (refer back to Figure 15-5).

Whenever a real estate salesperson enters the employ of a real estate broker, or whenever the salesperson is terminated, the broker shall immediately notify the Bureau of Real Estate in writing.

G. CONTINUING EDUCATION (CE) REQUIREMENT
(45 Hours Every Four Years to Renew Your License)

The continuing education requirement (45 hours every 4 years for license renewal) is NOT the same as the requirement for statutory broker courses.

All real estate licensees are required to attend 45 clock hours of Commissioner-approved courses, seminars, or conferences during the four-year period preceding license renewal. First time renewal for both broker and salesperson requires five separate three-hour courses in the following subjects: Ethics, Agency, Trust Fund Handling, Fair Housing, and Risk Management; a minimum of 18 clock hours of Consumer Protection Courses, and the remaining clock hours related to either Consumer Service or Consumer Protection.

18 hours of Consumer Protection, including Agency, Ethics, Trust Fund Handling, Fair Housing, and Risk Management are all included in the required 45 hours of continuing education.

A "licensee in good standing" is one who holds an active license which has not been suspended, revoked, or restricted as a result of disciplinary action. Real estate licensees who submit satisfactory evidence to the Commissioner that they are 70 years of age or older and have been "licensees in good standing" for 30 continuous years in California are exempt from the continuing education requirements for license renewal.

H. PREPAID RENTAL LISTING SERVICE (PRLS) LICENSE

A *PREPAID RENTAL LISTING SERVICE (PRLS) license is required when running a business that supplies prospective tenants with listings of residential real property for rent or lease while collecting a fee for such service.* Negotiation of the rental of property is not a part of this activity. An individual may obtain, without examination, a two-year license to conduct PRLS activities.

Prior to issuance of the PRLS license, the applicant must submit, and have approved by the CalBRE, a contract to be entered into between the licensee and client (prospective tenant). Fingerprints and a $10,000 surety bond are required for each business location.

III. Real Estate Law and Regulations

California laws affecting real estate are included in several different acts and codes. The *CALIFORNIA REAL ESTATE LAW is the portion of the Business and Professions Code that refers to licensing and subdivisions.* On the other hand, the *COMMISSIONER'S REGULATIONS are rules that form part of the California Administrative Code established and enforced by the Commissioner of Real Estate.* All licensees should be familiar with the Real Estate Law, the Commissioner's Regulations, and the Subdivided Lands Act administered by the Commissioner.

A. REAL ESTATE COMMISSIONER (Appointed by the Governor)

The Governor appoints the Real Estate Commissioner, who is defended by the state Attorney General. The Real Estate Commissioner issues rules and regulations that have the force and effect of law.

www.ca.gov
State of California

The **REAL ESTATE COMMISSIONER** *is the chief executive of the California Bureau of Real Estate.* It is the Commissioner's duty, therefore, to mold the department's policy, create regulations (California Administrative Code), and to enforce Real Estate Law (found in the Business and Professions Code) so that both real estate purchasers and real estate licensed agents benefit from his or her rulings. The Commissioner's other duties include:

1. Deciding the business policy of the California Bureau of Real Estate (CalBRE).

2. Informing the Governor and other state officials as to what services the department can render to the state and providing them with descriptions of the department's licenses.

3. Recommending changes in policy that may have been deemed necessary for the good of the public and the business of real estate in California.

4. Regulating the sales of subdivisions.

5. Deciding if applicants for real estate licenses have met all the experience and education requirements.

6. Investigating complaints against allegedly incompetent license holders.

7. Investigating complaints against those performing acts without the required license.

The Commissioner does not take the place of a court of law, does not give legal advice, and does not settle commission (payment for real estate services) disputes. Commission disputes are settled by arbitration or civil lawsuits in local courts.

The Real Estate Commissioner has the power to call formal hearings to discuss any issue concerning an applicant for a license, a current license holder, or a subdivider. The Commissioner may subsequently suspend, revoke, or deny a license. He or she could also halt sales (desist and refrain order) in a subdivision. Remember: The Commissioner cannot take the place of a court of law.

A licensee can be disciplined by the Real Estate Commissioner, but the local "District Attorney" prosecutes for the Commissioner in a court of law.

B. ENFORCEMENT OF REAL ESTATE LAW

Licensing and regulatory law is effective only to the extent that it is enforced. The Commissioner, as the chief officer of the Bureau of Real Estate, is duty bound to enforce the provisions of the Real Estate Law. The Commissioner may, by his or her own choice, and must, upon a verified complaint in writing, investigate the actions of any person engaged in the real estate business or acting in the capacity of a licensee within this state. He or she has the power to suspend any real estate license, or to revoke it permanently. The Commissioner also has the authority to deny a license to an applicant if the applicant does not meet the full requirements of the law. If, through the screening process (including the fingerprint record) of an applicant for license, it is found that he or she has a criminal record or some other record that may adversely reflect on his or her character, an investigation is made by the Commissioner's staff. A formal hearing may be ordered to determine whether or not the applicant meets the requirements of honesty, truthfulness, and good reputation.

C. HEARINGS FOR LICENSE VIOLATIONS

One function of Real Estate Law is to hold a hearing when there is a question as to the rights of persons to obtain or keep their real estate licenses. The Bureau of Real Estate and other licensing agencies must conduct hearings with strict regard for the rules set forth in the **Administrative Procedure Act**. Before denying, suspending, or revoking any license, the licensee is served a statement, and the Commissioner acts as the complainant. The licensee, or respondent, as he or she is known in the hearing procedures, may appear with or without counsel. The hearing is conducted according to rules of evidence in civil matters.

A decision is made by the hearing officer, based upon his or her findings. The Commissioner makes the final decision regarding this decision.

After a license is revoked, the person affected may not apply for reinstatement until one year has passed.

D. LICENSES: REVOKE, RESTRICT, SUSPEND

The Real Estate Commissioner can revoke, restrict, or suspend the license of any real estate agent for misconduct.

REVOKE — take away the license.
RESTRICT — to limit the use of the license.
SUSPEND — to take away the license for a period of time.

1. Child Support Obligations (150-Day License)

Active licensees who appear on the list are given 150 days by the CalBRE to "get current," or have their licenses suspended. Furthermore, the CalBRE will not issue or renew full-term (four-year) licenses to otherwise qualified applicants who appear on the so-called "deadbeat" list. Instead, they will be issued

temporary 150-day licenses. No license will be issued, or suspension revoked, until a release is furnished from the District Attorney's office.

E. REAL ESTATE BULLETIN, AND OTHER BULLETINS

The **REAL ESTATE BULLETIN** *alerts real estate licensees to necessary current information and also gives the names, plus details, of any license violations.* The bulletin is published quarterly by the California Bureau of Real Estate (CalBRE). The *Real Estate Bulletin* is no longer printed and mailed to licensees; it's only available online at the CalBRE website (see **Figure 15-6**).

The other two bulletins made by the CalBRE are the *Mortgage Loan Bulletin* and the *Subdivision Industry Bulletin*. The *Mortgage Loan Bulletin* is published biannually for those who use their license to make or underwrite loans. This bulletin can be accessed online at the CalBRE website by brokers who are making loans. The *Subdivision Industry Bulletin* is published annually and is designed for those interested in subdivisions.

IV. Common Real Estate Law Violations

Section 10176 of the Business and Professions Code is the legal guideline for the licensee engaged in the practice and performance of any of the acts within the scope of the Real Estate Law. Section 10177 of the Business and Professions Code applies to situations where the licensee involved was not necessarily acting as an agent or as a licensee.

A. SECTION 10176: LICENSEE ACTING IN A LICENSEE CAPACITY

This section of the Real Estate Law covers violations by those licensees who are acting within the scope of their licenses (see **Figure 15-7**).

B. SECTION 10177: LICENSEE NOT NECESSARILY ACTING AS A LICENSEE

Section 10177 applies to situations where the affected party was not necessarily acting in the capacity of an agent or as a real estate licensee (see **Figure 15-8**). The vast majority of brokers and salespeople are honest and perform their services in a straightforward manner. Occasionally, a section of the Real Estate Law may be violated inadvertently and without intent. In such cases, the Commissioner would most likely consider restriction of the real estate license. On the other hand, a flagrant violation would most likely cause a revocation of the license.

It is "blind advertising" if an agent falsely gives the impression that he or she is the owner of the property for sale. The Real Estate Commissioner does not approve of pocket listings (kept within real estate offices)—they are not part of the professional code and guidelines and are usually used to benefit the listing company rather than the client.

Figure 15-6

Real Estate Bulletin

CALIFORNIA DEPARTMENT OF CONSUMER AFFAIRS • BUREAU OF REAL ESTATE

WINTER 2014

Vol. 73, No. 3

REAL ESTATE MATTERS!

Wayne S. Bell
Commissioner

Commissioner's Message

The Bureau's Resources "Toolbox" – For Real Estate Consumers, Licensees, and Those Interested in Residential Subdivisions

Consumers, real estate licensees, builders, and industry groups often inquire about what resources are available from and through CalBRE to (i) help consumers navigate through real estate issues, (ii) aid those persons involved with residential subdivisions better understand the Subdivided Lands Law (which is under CalBRE's jurisdiction and regulatory supervision) and subdivisions in general, and (iii) assist real estate licensees so they can meet the requirements of and stay compliant with an ever increasing and changing body of law.

We at the Bureau are mindful that laws regarding the sale, purchase, financing, and practice of real estate and the development of real property are complex and in a continual state of evolution. For that reason, among others, CalBRE has developed and is regularly creating and updating free resources and tools for constituencies it serves.

In the Fall 2013 Real Estate Bulletin, I discussed (among other things) the availability of CalBRE Real Estate Bulletin articles on a broad variety of practice-related and substantive topics, and the new and informative PowerPoint presentation on Trust Account Reconciliations for those licensees who handle trust funds through a bank account(s).

In this message, I want to highlight additional resources that are newly available and others that seem to or may be underutilized.

CalBRE is extremely pleased to announce the very recent publication and availability of *"A Guide to Understanding Residential Subdivisions in California"*, which we believe is a useful resource to, and a practical and valuable tool for, subdivision developers and builders, consumers who are interested in purchasing a home in a subdivision, owners of homes and units in subdivisions, real estate licensees, land use planners and other regional subdivisions staff, and anyone else who might be interested in residential subdivisions. This new tool discusses and addresses the mandate, operation, and substantive and procedural requirements of the Subdivided Lands Act. In addition, it provides important and significant information on common interest developments, homeowner associations, the Subdivision Map Act (which is the California enabling statute under which cities and counties enact local laws controlling the "subdivision" of land within their jurisdictions), and a variety of other issues pertaining to residential subdivisions in California.

(Continued on page 3)

www.calbre.ca.gov

Figure 15-7   **Business & Professions Code 10176**
(Real Estate Licensee <u>Acting</u> As Licensee)
Grounds for Revocation or Suspension

Misrepresentation - 10176(a)

The licensee must disclose to his or her principal all material facts that the principal should know. Failure to do so or lying is cause for disciplinary action. A great majority of the complaints received by the commissioner allege misrepresentation on the part of the broker or his or her salespeople.

False Promise - 10176(b)

A false promise is a false statement about what the promisor is going to do in the future. Many times a false promise is provided by showing the promise was impossible to perform and that the person making the promise knew it was impossible.

Continued and Flagrant Misrepresentation by Agents - 10176(c)

The right of the commissioner to discipline a licensee for a continued and flagrant course of misrepresentation or making of false promises through real estate agents or salespeople.

Divided Agency - 10176(d)

This section requires a licensee to inform all his or her principals if he or she is acting as agent for more than one party in a transaction.

Commingling - 10176(e)

Commingling takes place when a broker has mixed the funds of his or her principals with his or her own money. A broker should keep all funds separate.

Definite Termination Date - 10176(f)

A specified termination date, in writing, is required for all exclusive listing transactions.

Secret Profit - 10176(g)

Secret profit cases usually arise when the broker makes a low offer, usually through a "dummy" purchaser, when he or she already has a higher offer from another buyer. The difference is the secret profit.

Listing Option - 10176(h)

This section requires a licensee, when he or she has used a form which is both an option and a listing, to obtain the written consent of his or her principal approving the amount of such profit before the licensee may exercise the option. This does not apply where a licensee is using an option only.

Dishonest Dealing - 10176(i)

Dishonest dealing is a catch-all section used when the acts of the person required a license, but he or she did not have a license.

Signatures of Prospective Purchasers - 10176(j)

Brokers must obtain a written (business opportunities) authorization to sell from an owner before securing the signature of a prospective purchaser to the agreement.

Figure 15-8

Business and Professions Code 10177
(R.E. Licensee <u>Not Necessarily Acting</u> as a Licensee)
Grounds for Revocation or Suspension

Obtaining License by Fraud - Section 10177(a)

The Commissioner has the power to take action against a licensee for misstatements of fact in an application for a license and when licenses have been procured by fraud, misrepresentation, or deceit.

Convictions - Section 10177(b)

Proceedings against a licensee after a criminal conviction for either a felony or a misdemeanor which involves moral turpitude are permitted.

False Advertising - Section 10177(c)

Licensees who are parties to false advertising are subject to disciplinary action. The ban extends to subdivision sales as well general property sales.

Violations of Other Sections - Section 10177(d)

This section gives the Department authority to proceed against the licensee for violation of any of the other sections of the Real Estate Law, the regulations of the commissioner, and the subdivision laws.

Misuse of Trade Name - Section 10177(e)

Only active members of the national association or local associations of real estate boards are permitted to use the term "REALTOR®." This is a term belonging exclusively to such members.

Conduct Warranting Denial - Section 10177(f)

A general section of the Real Estate Law and almost any act involving crime or dishonesty will fall within it. A license applicant must be honest, truthful, and of good reputation.

Negligence or Incompetence - Section 10177(g)

Demonstrated negligence or incompetence, while acting as a licensee, is a just cause for disciplinary action. The department proceeds when the licensee is so careless or unqualified that to allow him or her to handle a transaction would endanger the interests of the clients.

Supervision of Salespersons - Section 10177(h)

Brokers are subject to disciplinary action if they fail to exercise reasonable supervision over the activities of their salespersons.

Violating Government Trust - Section 10177(i)

Prescribes disciplinary liability for using government employment to violate the confidential nature of records thereby made available.

Other Dishonest Conduct - Section 10177(j)

Specifies that any other conduct which constitutes fraud or dishonest dealings may subject the ones involved to license suspension or revocation.

Restricted License Violation - Section 10177(k)

Makes violation of the terms, conditions, restrictions, and limitations contained in any order granting a restricted license grounds for disciplinary action. ▼

Inducement of Panic Selling (Blockbusting) - Section 10177(l)

It is a cause for disciplinary action to solicit or induce a sale, lease, or the listing for sale or lease, of residential property on the grounds of loss of value because of entry into the neighborhood of a person or persons of another race, color, religion, ancestry, or national origin.

Violation of Franchise Investment Law - Section 10177(m)

Violates any of the provisions of the Franchise Investment Law or any regulations of the Corporations Commissioner pertaining thereto.

Violation of Securities Law - Section 10177(n)

Violates any of the provisions of the Corporations Code or any regulations the Commissioner of Corporations relating to securities as specified.

Violation of Securities Law - Section 10177(o)

Failure to disclose to buyer the nature and extent of ownership interest licensee has in property in which the licensee is an agent for the buyer. Also, failure to disclose ownership on the part of licensee's relative or special acquaintance in which licensee has ownership interest.

Importance of Section 10176 and Section 10177
REGULATIONS OF THE COMMISSIONER

The Real Estate Commissioner is empowered to adopt Regulations for the administration and enforcement of the Real Estate Law and the Subdivided Lands Law. Duly adopted regulations become part of the California Code of Regulations and, in effect, have the force and authority of the law itself. Therefore, all licensees, prospective licensees, and subdividers should be thoroughly familiar with the Real Estate Commissioner's Regulations.

10176. The Commissioner may, upon his or her own motion, and shall, upon the verified complaint in writing of any person, investigate the actions of any person engaged in the business or acting in the capacity of a real estate licensee within this state, and he or she may temporarily suspend or permanently revoke a real estate license at any time where the licensee, while a real estate licensee, in performing or attempting to perform any of the acts within the scope of this chapter, has been guilty of any act listed in this section.

10177. The Commissioner may suspend or revoke the license of any real estate licensee or may deny the issuance of a license to an applicant or may suspend or revoke the license of, or deny the issuance of a license to, a corporate applicant if an officer, director, or person owning or controlling 10 percent or more of the corporation's stock has done any of the acts listed in this section.

www.calbre.ca.gov
California Bureau of Real Estate

C. REGULATIONS OF THE REAL ESTATE COMMISSIONER (Found in the Administrative Code)

Real Estate Law (California Administrative Code) empowers the Commissioner to issue regulations to aid in the administration and enforcement of the law. These regulations, which are known formally as the Regulations of the Real Estate Commissioner, have the force and effect of the law itself. You should be familiar with these regulations. The California Bureau of Real Estate produces a factual law book entitled *Real Estate Law* (Real Estate Law—Business and Professions Code—and Regulations of the Real Estate Commissioner).

1. Broker Supervision (Regulation 2725)

A broker shall exercise reasonable supervision over the activities of his or her salespeople. Reasonable supervision includes, as appropriate, the establishment of policies, rules, procedures, and systems to review, oversee, inspect, and manage:

a. transactions requiring a real estate license;

b. documents which may have a material effect upon the rights or obligations of a party to the transaction;

c. filing, storage, and maintenance of such documents;

d. the handling of trust funds;

e. advertising of any service for which a license is required;

f. familiarizing salespeople with the requirement of federal and state laws relating to the prohibition of discrimination; and

g. regular and consistent reports of licensed activities of salespeople.

V. Real Estate General Fund

All the money collected from license and exam fees goes into the **REAL ESTATE GENERAL FUND**. Eighty percent of this money is used for the operating expenses of the Bureau of Real Estate. Twenty percent of the Real Estate General Fund is set aside as follows:

1. Eight percent to the Real Estate Education and Research Fund.
2. Twelve percent to the Recovery Fund.

The **RECOVERY FUND** *was established for the payment of damages and arbitration awards to people who have suffered financial loss due to the wrongful act of a licensee in a real estate transaction.* To qualify for these funds, plaintiffs must first obtain a judgment in civil court (or through arbitration) against a licensee on the grounds of fraud, misrepresentation, deceit, or conversion of trust funds. If, after reasonable effort, the judgment remains uncollected, a claim may be filed with the Commissioner's office.

A license is suspended until the fund is reimbursed (plus interest). The total liability of the recovery fund in any one transaction is $50,000, and the total series of judgments against any individual licensee is limited to $250,000.

California is one of the few states that actively helps protect the public against fraudulent acts by real estate licensees.

VI. Trade and Professional Associations

A *TRADE or PROFESSIONAL ASSOCIATION is a voluntary, nonprofit organization made up of independent firms in the same industry.* It is formed to promote progress, aid in solving the industry's problems, and enhance its service to the community. We will discuss the role of local boards of REALTORS®, the California Association of REALTORS® (CAR), the National Association of REALTORS® (NAR) and its Code of Ethics, and the term Realtist.

A "REALTOR®" is a member of the National Association of REALTORS® (NAR), a real estate trade association.

A. LOCAL REAL ESTATE ASSOCIATIONS

A *LOCAL ASSOCIATION OF REALTORS® is a voluntary organization of real estate licensees in a particular community.* A broker is entitled to full membership, a salesperson may be an associate member, and a non-REALTOR® (who is in a real estate-related field) may be an affiliate member. For example, an affiliate member might work for a title insurance company, an escrow company, a lender, or any other business having an interest in local real estate activities.

Local associations usually provide multiple listing services (MLSs) for their members so that all members can be equally informed. Most local associations provide services such as distribution of educational material, seminars, library services, and other worthwhile services for the local REALTORS®. MLSs often share information with numerous other real estate websites like Trulia.com® and Realtor.com®.

bhglaar.com
Beverly Hills/Greater Los Angeles Association of REALTORS®

B. CALIFORNIA ASSOCIATION OF REALTORS® (CAR) (www.car.org)

The *CALIFORNIA ASSOCIATION OF REALTORS® is the state division of the National Association of REALTORS®.* It is a voluntary organization whose membership includes local realty boards throughout the state and individual members who are not affiliated with any particular local board. With the exception of NAR, CAR is the largest REALTOR® organization in the United States, with over 150,000 members in California.

The objectives of the California Association of REALTORS® are:

1. to promote high standards and unite its members;
2. to safeguard the property-buying public;
3. to foster legislation for the benefit and protection of the real estate field; and
4. to cooperate in the economic growth and development of the state.

CAR® has many standing committees that meet at director's meetings, seminars, and annual conventions. These committees specialize in specific areas such as education, ethics, legislation, political affairs, real property taxation, professional standards, and many other areas. There are also many divisions of CAR®.

Most successful real estate salespeople in California are also members of the California Association of REALTORS®. You should become a member of this or some other trade association if you are serious about selling real estate.

C. NATIONAL ASSOCIATION OF REALTORS® (NAR) (www.realtor.org)

The *NATIONAL ASSOCIATION OF REALTORS® is the national trade association for all the state associations and local boards of REALTORS® in the United States.* NAR unifies the real estate industry at the national level. It encourages legislation favorable to the real estate industry and enforces professional conduct standards on behalf of its members across the nation.

1. Trade Name

Only active members of the National Association of REALTORS® (NAR) or the California Association of REALTORS® (CAR), through their local real estate associations, are permitted to use the term "REALTOR®." This is a term belonging exclusively to such members, and no licensee may advertise or present himself or herself to be a REALTOR® if not associated with such a group.

Use of the term "REALTOR®," without proper group affiliation, is grounds for revocation of your license.

The National Association of REALTORS® has affiliated institutes, societies, and councils that provide a wide-ranging menu of programs and services to assist members in increasing skills, productivity, and knowledge (see **Figure 15-9**).

Figure 15-9

NAR Affiliates

1. American Society of Real Estate Counselors (ASREC)
This division of NAR offers the CRE (Counselor of Real Estate) designation.

2. Commercial Investment Real Estate Institute (CIREI) www.ccim.com
CIREI enhances the professional development of those engaged in commercial investment real estate. Offers the CCIM (Certified Commercial Investment Member) designation.

3. Realtors® National Marketing Institute (RNMI)
RNMI promotes professional competence in real estate sales and brokerage and real estate brokerage management. It has two councils:

A. Council of Real Estate Brokerage Managers (CRB) www.crb.com
Recognized throughout the industry as the professional peer organization for managers of residential, commercial, industrial, relocation, appraising, and property management companies. The CRB designation is available for members who meet experience requirements and complete a series of courses. ▼

B. Counselors of Real Estate (CRE) www.cre.org

The Counselors of Real Estate is a professional membership organization established exclusively for leading real property advisors.

4. Council of Residential Specialists (CRS) www.crs.com

This designation is awarded to the top producing agents in the country who complete advanced training in selling and listing.

5. Graduate Realtor® Institute (GRI) www.edesignations.com

The GRI symbol is recognized nationwide, showing buyers, sellers, and other real estate industry members that you are a true professional, and have a solid grasp of real estate fundamentals. **It is the dominant real estate designation in California.**

6. Real Estate Buyer's Agent Council (REBAC)

REBAC (Real Estate Buyer's Agent Council) serves REALTORS® members who wish to devote all or part of their business to the practice of buyer's agency.

7. Society of Industrial and Office Realtors® (SIOR) www.sior.com

An international organization whose members specialize in a variety of commercial real estate activities. They offer the SIOR designation.

8. Women's Council of Realtors® (WCR)

WCR offers opportunities for developing leadership skills as well as a Referral and Relocation Certification (RRC). This is the only referral and relocation certification offered by NAR.

9. Professional Real Estate Executive (PRE) www.realtor.org

The PRE designation is available for corporate real estate executives who meet experience and course completion criteria.

10. Seniors Real Estate Specialist (SRES) www.seniorsrealestate.com

A Seniors Real Estate Specialist® (SRES) is experienced and knowledgeable in meeting the specific needs of clients 45 years or older. SRES has demonstrated requisite knowledge and expertise to counsel senior clients through major financial and lifestyle transitions involved in relocating, refinancing, or selling the family home.

11. The Institute of Real Estate Management (IREM) www.irem.org

This is an organization, within NAR, of professional property managers. They offer a number of designations including:

A. Certified Property Manager (CPM)
B. Accredited Resident Manager (ARM)
C. Accredited Management Organization (AMO)

12. Green Specialist

The National Association of REALTORS® has created a green designation and benefits program tailored for real estate agents. NAR's Green Designation provides advanced training in green building and sustainable business practices so that you can seek out, understand, and market properties with green features.

2. NAR Code of Ethics

The National Association of REALTORS® Code of Ethics (**Figure 15-10**) is given to all REALTORS®. These guidelines show not only how members should act, but how they must act, and may be obtained through the association or its website.

Every REALTOR® must swear to abide by the NAR Code of Ethics.

The National Association of REALTORS® and its state and local divisions form a composite organization of brokers whose objective is to forward the interests of brokers, encourage education of practitioners and the public, raise the standard of real estate practice, and increase the esteem in which brokers are held by their fellow citizens. To this end, a code of ethics has been formulated and adopted. It is the generally accepted code of ethics for real estate people.

"Under all is the land" are the beginning words of the NAR Code of Ethics.

a. NAR Ethics Course Required (Every Four Years)

The National Association of REALTORS® now requires all members to take a mandatory ethics course, or risk the loss of membership.

The **NAR ETHICS COURSE REQUIREMENT** *is a mandatory course, taken every four years, studying the NAR Code of Ethics and Standards of Practice.*
The NAR mandates that all REALTOR® members attend a training class on the Code of Ethics every four years. Failure to complete the required class results in suspension of membership until the training is completed. It is so important that the NAR also requires new member applicants to complete an Ethics Orientation Class within 60 days of their application date, or face automatic denial of membership and forfeiture of application fees. In California, the required ethics class fulfills this requirement.

Remember, if you've taken an ethics course for licensing purposes, it may not apply to the NAR requirement, unless it specifically covered the NAR Code of Ethics and Standards of Practice.

D. REALTIST DEFINED

"Realtist" is the name for a member of the National Association of Real Estate Brokers (NAREB). They have a social networking presence on Facebook, YouTube, Twitter, and LinkedIn.

The National Association of Real Estate Brokers, or "Realtist," is the oldest minority trade association in the United States. *Although composed principally of African Americans and other minority real estate professionals, the REALTIST organization is an integrated entity open to all practitioners who are committed to achieving "democracy in housing."*
The organization has local boards in the largest cities in most states. The organization in this state, called the California Association of Real Estate Brokers

CHAPTER 15

Figure 15-10

Code of Ethics and Standards of Practice
of the NATIONAL ASSOCIATION OF REALTORS®
Effective January 1, 2014

Where the word REALTORS® is used in this Code and Preamble, it shall be deemed to include REALTOR-ASSOCIATE®s.

While the Code of Ethics establishes obligations that may be higher than those mandated by law, in any instance where the Code of Ethics and the law conflict, the obligations of the law must take precedence.

Preamble

Under all is the land. Upon its wise utilization and widely allocated ownership depend the survival and growth of free institutions and of our civilization. REALTORS® should recognize that the interests of the nation and its citizens require the highest and best use of the land and the widest distribution of land ownership. They require the creation of adequate housing, the building of functioning cities, the development of productive industries and farms, and the preservation of a healthful environment.

Such interests impose obligations beyond those of ordinary commerce. They impose grave social responsibility and a patriotic duty to which REALTORS® should dedicate themselves, and for which they should be diligent in preparing themselves. REALTORS®, therefore, are zealous to maintain and improve the standards of their calling and share with their fellow REALTORS® a common responsibility for its integrity and honor.

In recognition and appreciation of their obligations to clients, customers, the public, and each other, REALTORS® continuously strive to become and remain informed on issues affecting real estate and, as knowledgeable professionals, they willingly share the fruit of their experience and study with others. They identify and take steps, through enforcement of this Code of Ethics and by assisting appropriate regulatory bodies, to eliminate practices which may damage the public or which might discredit or bring dishonor to the real estate profession. REALTORS® having direct personal knowledge of conduct that may violate the Code of Ethics involving misappropriation of client or customer funds or property, willful discrimination, or fraud resulting in substantial economic harm, bring such matters to the attention of the appropriate Board or Association of REALTORS®. *(Amended 1/00)*

Realizing that cooperation with other real estate professionals promotes the best interests of those who utilize their services, REALTORS® urge exclusive representation of clients; do not attempt to gain any unfair advantage over their competitors; and they refrain from making unsolicited comments about other practitioners. In instances where their opinion is sought, or where REALTORS® believe that comment is necessary, their opinion is offered in an objective, professional manner, uninfluenced by any personal motivation or potential advantage or gain.

The term REALTOR® has come to connote competency, fairness, and high integrity resulting from adherence to a lofty ideal of moral conduct in business relations. No inducement of profit and no instruction from clients ever can justify departure from this ideal.

In the interpretation of this obligation, REALTORS® can take no safer guide than that which has been handed down through the centuries, embodied in the Golden Rule, "Whatsoever ye would that others should do to you, do ye even so to them."

Accepting this standard as their own, REALTORS® pledge to observe its spirit in all of their activities whether conducted personally, through associates or others, or via technological means, and to conduct their business in accordance with the tenets set forth below. *(Amended 1/07)*

Duties to Clients and Customers

Article 1

When representing a buyer, seller, landlord, tenant, or other client as an agent, REALTORS® pledge themselves to protect and promote the interests of their client. This obligation to the client is primary, but it does not relieve REALTORS® of their obligation to treat all parties honestly. When serving a buyer, seller, landlord, tenant or other party in a non-agency capacity, REALTORS® remain obligated to treat all parties honestly. *(Amended 1/01)*

- **Standard of Practice 1-1**

  REALTORS®, when acting as principals in a real estate transaction, remain obligated by the duties imposed by the Code of Ethics. *(Amended 1/93)*

- **Standard of Practice 1-2**

  The duties imposed by the Code of Ethics encompass all real estate-related activities and transactions whether conducted in person, electronically, or through any other means.

  The duties the Code of Ethics imposes are applicable whether REALTORS® are acting as agents or in legally recognized non-agency capacities except that any duty imposed exclusively on agents by law or regulation shall not be imposed by this Code of Ethics on REALTORS® acting in non-agency capacities.

  As used in this Code of Ethics, "client" means the person(s) or entity(ies) with whom a REALTOR® or a REALTOR®'s firm has an agency or legally recognized non-agency relationship; "customer" means a party to a real estate transaction who receives information, services, or benefits but has no contractual relationship with the REALTOR® or the REALTOR®'s firm; "prospect" means a purchaser, seller, tenant, or landlord who is not subject to a representation relationship with the REALTOR® or REALTOR®'s firm; "agent" means a real estate licensee (including brokers and sales associates) acting in an agency relationship as defined by state law or regulation; and "broker" means a real estate licensee (including brokers and sales associates) acting as an agent or in a legally recognized non-agency capacity. *(Adopted 1/95, Amended 1/07)*

- **Standard of Practice 1-3**

  REALTORS®, in attempting to secure a listing, shall not deliberately mislead the owner as to market value.

- **Standard of Practice 1-4**

  REALTORS®, when seeking to become a buyer/tenant representative, shall not mislead buyers or tenants as to savings or other benefits that might be realized through use of the REALTOR®'s services. *(Amended 1/93)*

- **Standard of Practice 1-5**

  REALTORS® may represent the seller/landlord and buyer/tenant in the

NATIONAL
ASSOCIATION *of*
REALTORS®

same transaction only after full disclosure to and with informed consent of both parties. *(Adopted 1/93)*

- **Standard of Practice 1-6**

REALTORS® shall submit offers and counter-offers objectively and as quickly as possible. *(Adopted 1/93, Amended 1/95)*

- **Standard of Practice 1-7**

When acting as listing brokers, REALTORS® shall continue to submit to the seller/landlord all offers and counter-offers until closing or execution of a lease unless the seller/landlord has waived this obligation in writing. REALTORS® shall not be obligated to continue to market the property after an offer has been accepted by the seller/landlord. REALTORS® shall recommend that sellers/landlords obtain the advice of legal counsel prior to acceptance of a subsequent offer except where the acceptance is contingent on the termination of the pre-existing purchase contract or lease. *(Amended 1/93)*

- **Standard of Practice 1-8**

REALTORS®, acting as agents or brokers of buyers/tenants, shall submit to buyers/tenants all offers and counter-offers until acceptance but have no obligation to continue to show properties to their clients after an offer has been accepted unless otherwise agreed in writing. REALTORS®, acting as agents or brokers of buyers/tenants, shall recommend that buyers/tenants obtain the advice of legal counsel if there is a question as to whether a pre-existing contract has been terminated. *(Adopted 1/93, Amended 1/99)*

- **Standard of Practice 1-9**

The obligation of REALTORS® to preserve confidential information (as defined by state law) provided by their clients in the course of any agency relationship or non-agency relationship recognized by law continues after termination of agency relationships or any non-agency relationships recognized by law. REALTORS® shall not knowingly, during or following the termination of professional relationships with their clients:

1) reveal confidential information of clients; or
2) use confidential information of clients to the disadvantage of clients; or
3) use confidential information of clients for the REALTOR®'s advantage or the advantage of third parties unless:
   a) clients consent after full disclosure; or
   b) REALTORS® are required by court order; or
   c) it is the intention of a client to commit a crime and the information is necessary to prevent the crime; or
   d) it is necessary to defend a REALTOR® or the REALTOR®'s employees or associates against an accusation of wrongful conduct.

Information concerning latent material defects is not considered confidential information under this Code of Ethics. *(Adopted 1/93, Amended 1/01)*

- **Standard of Practice 1-10**

REALTORS® shall, consistent with the terms and conditions of their real estate licensure and their property management agreement, competently manage the property of clients with due regard for the rights, safety and health of tenants and others lawfully on the premises. *(Adopted 1/95, Amended 1/00)*

- **Standard of Practice 1-11**

REALTORS® who are employed to maintain or manage a client's property shall exercise due diligence and make reasonable efforts to protect it against reasonably foreseeable contingencies and losses. *(Adopted 1/95)*

- **Standard of Practice 1-12**

When entering into listing contracts, REALTORS® must advise sellers/landlords of:

1) the REALTOR®'s company policies regarding cooperation and the amount(s) of any compensation that will be offered to subagents, buyer/tenant agents, and/or brokers acting in legally recognized non-agency capacities;

2) the fact that buyer/tenant agents or brokers, even if compensated by listing brokers, or by sellers/landlords may represent the interests of buyers/tenants; and

3) any potential for listing brokers to act as disclosed dual agents, e.g., buyer/tenant agents. *(Adopted 1/93, Renumbered 1/98, Amended 1/03)*

- **Standard of Practice 1-13**

When entering into buyer/tenant agreements, REALTORS® must advise potential clients of:

1) the REALTOR®'s company policies regarding cooperation;
2) the amount of compensation to be paid by the client;
3) the potential for additional or offsetting compensation from other brokers, from the seller or landlord, or from other parties;
4) any potential for the buyer/tenant representative to act as a disclosed dual agent, e.g., listing broker, subagent, landlord's agent, etc., and
5) the possibility that sellers or sellers' representatives may not treat the existence, terms, or conditions of offers as confidential unless confidentiality is required by law, regulation, or by any confidentiality agreement between the parties. *(Adopted 1/93, Renumbered 1/98, Amended 1/06)*

- **Standard of Practice 1-14**

Fees for preparing appraisals or other valuations shall not be contingent upon the amount of the appraisal or valuation. *(Adopted 1/02)*

- **Standard of Practice 1-15**

REALTORS®, in response to inquiries from buyers or cooperating brokers shall, with the sellers' approval, disclose the existence of offers on the property. Where disclosure is authorized, REALTORS® shall also disclose, if asked, whether offers were obtained by the listing licensee, another licensee in the listing firm, or by a cooperating broker. *(Adopted 1/03, Amended 1/09)*

- **Standard of Practice 1-16**

REALTORS® shall not access or use, or permit or enable others to access or use, listed or managed property on terms or conditions other than those authorized by the owner or seller. *(Adopted 1/12)*

Article 2

REALTORS® shall avoid exaggeration, misrepresentation, or concealment of pertinent facts relating to the property or the transaction. REALTORS® shall not, however, be obligated to discover latent defects in the property, to advise on matters outside the scope of their real estate license, or to disclose facts which are confidential under the scope of agency or non-agency relationships as defined by state law. *(Amended 1/00)*

- **Standard of Practice 2-1**

REALTORS® shall only be obligated to discover and disclose adverse factors reasonably apparent to someone with expertise in those areas required by their real estate licensing authority. Article 2 does not impose upon the REALTOR® the obligation of expertise in other professional or technical disciplines. *(Amended 1/96)*

- **Standard of Practice 2-2**

(Renumbered as Standard of Practice 1-12 1/98)

- **Standard of Practice 2-3**

(Renumbered as Standard of Practice 1-13 1/98)

- **Standard of Practice 2-4**

REALTORS® shall not be parties to the naming of a false consideration in any document, unless it be the naming of an obviously nominal consideration.

- **Standard of Practice 2-5**

Factors defined as "non-material" by law or regulation or which are expressly referenced in law or regulation as not being subject to disclosure are considered not "pertinent" for purposes of Article 2. *(Adopted 1/93)*

Article 3

REALTORS® shall cooperate with other brokers except when cooperation is not in the client's best interest. The obligation to cooperate does not include the obligation to share commissions, fees, or to otherwise compensate another broker. *(Amended 1/95)*

- **Standard of Practice 3-1**

REALTORS®, acting as exclusive agents or brokers of sellers/landlords, establish the terms and conditions of offers to cooperate. Unless expressly indicated in offers to cooperate, cooperating brokers may not assume that the offer of cooperation includes an offer of compensation. Terms of compensation, if any, shall be ascertained by cooperating brokers before beginning efforts to accept the offer of cooperation. *(Amended 1/99)*

- **Standard of Practice 3-2**

Any change in compensation offered for cooperative services must be communicated to the other REALTOR® prior to the time that REALTOR® submits an offer to purchase/lease the property. After a REALTOR® has submitted an offer to purchase or lease property, the listing broker may not attempt to unilaterally modify the offered compensation with respect to that cooperative transaction. *(Amended 1/14)*

- **Standard of Practice 3-3**

Standard of Practice 3-2 does not preclude the listing broker and cooperating broker from entering into an agreement to change cooperative compensation. *(Adopted 1/94)*

- **Standard of Practice 3-4**

REALTORS®, acting as listing brokers, have an affirmative obligation to disclose the existence of dual or variable rate commission arrangements (i.e., listings where one amount of commission is payable if the listing broker's firm is the procuring cause of sale/lease and a different amount of commission is payable if the sale/lease results through the efforts of the seller/landlord or a cooperating broker). The listing broker shall, as soon as practical, disclose the existence of such arrangements to potential cooperating brokers and shall, in response to inquiries from cooperating brokers, disclose the differential that would result in a cooperative transaction or in a sale/lease that results through the efforts of the seller/landlord. If the cooperating broker is a buyer/tenant representative, the buyer/tenant representative must disclose such information to their client before the client makes an offer to purchase or lease. *(Amended 1/02)*

- **Standard of Practice 3-5**

It is the obligation of subagents to promptly disclose all pertinent facts to the principal's agent prior to as well as after a purchase or lease agreement is executed. *(Amended 1/93)*

- **Standard of Practice 3-6**

REALTORS® shall disclose the existence of accepted offers, including offers with unresolved contingencies, to any broker seeking cooperation. *(Adopted 5/86, Amended 1/04)*

- **Standard of Practice 3-7**

When seeking information from another REALTOR® concerning property under a management or listing agreement, REALTORS® shall disclose their REALTOR® status and whether their interest is personal or on behalf of a client and, if on behalf of a client, their relationship with the client. *(Amended 1/11)*

- **Standard of Practice 3-8**

REALTORS® shall not misrepresent the availability of access to show or inspect a listed property. *(Amended 11/87)*

- **Standard of Practice 3-9**

REALTORS® shall not provide access to listed property on terms other than those established by the owner or the listing broker. *(Adopted 1/10)*

- **Standard of Practice 3-10**

The duty to cooperate established in Article 3 relates to the obligation to share information on listed property, and to make property available to other brokers for showing to prospective purchasers/tenants when it is in the best interests of sellers/landlords. *(Adopted 1/11)*

Article 4

REALTORS® shall not acquire an interest in or buy or present offers from themselves, any member of their immediate families, their firms or any member thereof, or any entities in which they have any ownership interest, any real property without making their true position known to the owner or the owner's agent or broker. In selling property they own, or in which they have any interest, REALTORS® shall reveal their ownership or interest in writing to the purchaser or the purchaser's representative. *(Amended 1/00)*

- **Standard of Practice 4-1**

For the protection of all parties, the disclosures required by Article 4 shall be in writing and provided by REALTORS® prior to the signing of any contract. *(Adopted 2/86)*

Article 5

REALTORS® shall not undertake to provide professional services concerning a property or its value where they have a present or contemplated interest unless such interest is specifically disclosed to all affected parties.

Article 6

REALTORS® shall not accept any commission, rebate, or profit on expenditures made for their client, without the client's knowledge and consent.

When recommending real estate products or services (e.g., homeowner's insurance, warranty programs, mortgage financing, title insurance, etc.), REALTORS® shall disclose to the client or customer to whom the recommendation is made any financial benefits or fees, other than real estate referral fees, the REALTOR® or REALTOR®'s firm may receive as a direct result of such recommendation. *(Amended 1/99)*

- **Standard of Practice 6-1**

REALTORS® shall not recommend or suggest to a client or a customer the use of services of another organization or business entity in which they have a direct interest without disclosing such interest at the time of the recommendation or suggestion. *(Amended 5/88)*

Article 7

In a transaction, REALTORS® shall not accept compensation from more than one party, even if permitted by law, without disclosure to all parties and the informed consent of the REALTOR®'s client or clients. *(Amended 1/93)*

Article 8

REALTORS® shall keep in a special account in an appropriate financial institution, separated from their own funds, monies coming into their possession in trust for other persons, such as escrows, trust funds, clients' monies, and other like items.

Article 9

REALTORS®, for the protection of all parties, shall assure whenever possible that all agreements related to real estate transactions including, but not limited to, listing and representation agreements, purchase contracts, and leases are in writing in clear and understandable language expressing the specific terms, conditions, obligations and commitments of the parties. A copy of each agreement shall be furnished to each party to such agreements upon their signing or initialing. *(Amended 1/04)*

- **Standard of Practice 9-1**

  For the protection of all parties, REALTORS® shall use reasonable care to ensure that documents pertaining to the purchase, sale, or lease of real estate are kept current through the use of written extensions or amendments. *(Amended 1/93)*

- **Standard of Practice 9-2**

  When assisting or enabling a client or customer in establishing a contractual relationship (e.g., listing and representation agreements, purchase agreements, leases, etc.) electronically, REALTORS® shall make reasonable efforts to explain the nature and disclose the specific terms of the contractual relationship being established prior to it being agreed to by a contracting party. *(Adopted 1/07)*

Duties to the Public

Article 10

REALTORS® shall not deny equal professional services to any person for reasons of race, color, religion, sex, handicap, familial status, national origin, sexual orientation, or gender identity. REALTORS® shall not be parties to any plan or agreement to discriminate against a person or persons on the basis of race, color, religion, sex, handicap, familial status, national origin, sexual orientation, or gender identity. *(Amended 1/14)*

REALTORS®, in their real estate employment practices, shall not discriminate against any person or persons on the basis of race, color, religion, sex, handicap, familial status, national origin, sexual orientation, or gender identity. *(Amended 1/14)*

- **Standard of Practice 10-1**

  When involved in the sale or lease of a residence, REALTORS® shall not volunteer information regarding the racial, religious or ethnic composition of any neighborhood nor shall they engage in any activity which may result in panic selling, however, REALTORS® may provide other demographic information. *(Adopted 1/94, Amended 1/06)*

- **Standard of Practice 10-2**

  When not involved in the sale or lease of a residence, REALTORS® may provide demographic information related to a property, transaction or professional assignment to a party if such demographic information is (a) deemed by the REALTOR® to be needed to assist with or complete, in a manner consistent with Article 10, a real estate transaction or professional assignment and (b) is obtained or derived from a recognized, reliable, independent, and impartial source. The source of such information and any additions, deletions, modifications, interpretations, or other changes shall be disclosed in reasonable detail. *(Adopted 1/05, Renumbered 1/06)*

- **Standard of Practice 10-3**

  REALTORS® shall not print, display or circulate any statement or advertisement with respect to selling or renting of a property that indicates any preference, limitations or discrimination based on race, color, religion, sex, handicap, familial status, national origin, sexual orientation, or gender identity. *(Adopted 1/94, Renumbered 1/05 and 1/06, Amended 1/14)*

- **Standard of Practice 10-4**

  As used in Article 10 "real estate employment practices" relates to employees and independent contractors providing real estate-related services and the administrative and clerical staff directly supporting those individuals. *(Adopted 1/00, Renumbered 1/05 and 1/06)*

Article 11

The services which REALTORS® provide to their clients and customers shall conform to the standards of practice and competence which are reasonably expected in the specific real estate disciplines in which they engage; specifically, residential real estate brokerage, real property management, commercial and industrial real estate brokerage, land brokerage, real estate appraisal, real estate counseling, real estate syndication, real estate auction, and international real estate.

REALTORS® shall not undertake to provide specialized professional services concerning a type of property or service that is outside their field of competence unless they engage the assistance of one who is competent on such types of property or service, or unless the facts are fully disclosed to the client. Any persons engaged to provide such assistance shall be so identified to the client and their contribution to the assignment should be set forth. *(Amended 1/10)*

- **Standard of Practice 11-1**

  When REALTORS® prepare opinions of real property value or price they must:
  1) be knowledgeable about the type of property being valued,
  2) have access to the information and resources necessary to formulate an accurate opinion, and
  3) be familiar with the area where the subject property is located

  unless lack of any of these is disclosed to the party requesting the opinion in advance.

  When an opinion of value or price is prepared other than in pursuit of a listing or to assist a potential purchaser in formulating a purchase offer, the opinion shall include the following unless the party requesting the opinion requires a specific type of report or different data set:
  1) identification of the subject property
  2) date prepared
  3) defined value or price
  4) limiting conditions, including statements of purpose(s) and intended user(s)
  5) any present or contemplated interest, including the possibility of representing the seller/landlord or buyers/tenants
  6) basis for the opinion, including applicable market data
  7) if the opinion is not an appraisal, a statement to that effect
  8) disclosure of whether and when a physical inspection of the property's exterior was conducted
  9) disclosure of whether and when a physical inspection of the property's interior was conducted
  10) disclosure of whether the REALTOR® has any conflicts of interest *(Amended 1/14)*

- **Standard of Practice 11-2**

  The obligations of the Code of Ethics in respect of real estate disciplines other than appraisal shall be interpreted and applied in accordance with the standards of competence and practice which clients and the public reasonably require to protect their rights and interests considering the complexity of the transaction, the availability of expert assistance, and, where the REALTOR® is an agent or subagent, the obligations of a fiduciary. *(Adopted 1/95)*

- **Standard of Practice 11-3**

  When REALTORS® provide consultive services to clients which involve advice or counsel for a fee (not a commission), such advice shall be rendered in an objective manner and the fee shall not be contingent on the substance of the advice or counsel given. If brokerage or transaction services are to be provided in addition to consultive services, a separate compensation may be paid with prior agreement between the client and REALTOR®. *(Adopted 1/96)*

- **Standard of Practice 11-4**

  The competency required by Article 11 relates to services contracted for between REALTORS® and their clients or customers; the duties expressly imposed by the Code of Ethics; and the duties imposed by law or regulation. *(Adopted 1/02)*

Article 12

REALTORS® shall be honest and truthful in their real estate communications and shall present a true picture in their advertising, marketing, and other representations. REALTORS® shall ensure that their status as real estate professionals is readily apparent in their advertising, marketing, and other representations, and that the recipients of all real estate communications are, or have been, notified that those communications are from a real estate professional. *(Amended 1/08)*

- **Standard of Practice 12-1**

REALTORS® may use the term "free" and similar terms in their advertising and in other representations provided that all terms governing availability of the offered product or service are clearly disclosed at the same time. *(Amended 1/97)*

- **Standard of Practice 12-2**

REALTORS® may represent their services as "free" or without cost even if they expect to receive compensation from a source other than their client provided that the potential for the REALTOR® to obtain a benefit from a third party is clearly disclosed at the same time. *(Amended 1/97)*

- **Standard of Practice 12-3**

The offering of premiums, prizes, merchandise discounts or other inducements to list, sell, purchase, or lease is not, in itself, unethical even if receipt of the benefit is contingent on listing, selling, purchasing, or leasing through the REALTOR® making the offer. However, REALTORS® must exercise care and candor in any such advertising or other public or private representations so that any party interested in receiving or otherwise benefiting from the REALTOR®'s offer will have clear, thorough, advance understanding of all the terms and conditions of the offer. The offering of any inducements to do business is subject to the limitations and restrictions of state law and the ethical obligations established by any applicable Standard of Practice. *(Amended 1/95)*

- **Standard of Practice 12-4**

REALTORS® shall not offer for sale/lease or advertise property without authority. When acting as listing brokers or as subagents, REALTORS® shall not quote a price different from that agreed upon with the seller/landlord. *(Amended 1/93)*

- **Standard of Practice 12-5**

REALTORS® shall not advertise nor permit any person employed by or affiliated with them to advertise real estate services or listed property in any medium (e.g., electronically, print, radio, television, etc.) without disclosing the name of that REALTOR®'s firm in a reasonable and readily apparent manner. This Standard of Practice acknowledges that disclosing the name of the firm may not be practical in electronic displays of limited information (e.g., "thumbnails", text messages, "tweets", etc.). Such displays are exempt from the disclosure requirement established in this Standard of Practice, but only when linked to a display that includes all required disclosures. *(Adopted 11/86, Amended 1/11)*

- **Standard of Practice 12-6**

REALTORS®, when advertising unlisted real property for sale/lease in which they have an ownership interest, shall disclose their status as both owners/landlords and as REALTORS® or real estate licensees. *(Amended 1/93)*

- **Standard of Practice 12-7**

Only REALTORS® who participated in the transaction as the listing broker or cooperating broker (selling broker) may claim to have "sold" the property.

Prior to closing, a cooperating broker may post a "sold" sign only with the consent of the listing broker. *(Amended 1/96)*

- **Standard of Practice 12-8**

The obligation to present a true picture in representations to the public includes information presented, provided, or displayed on REALTORS®' websites. REALTORS® shall use reasonable efforts to ensure that information on their websites is current. When it becomes apparent that information on a REALTOR®'s website is no longer current or accurate, REALTORS® shall promptly take corrective action. *(Adopted 1/07)*

- **Standard of Practice 12-9**

REALTOR® firm websites shall disclose the firm's name and state(s) of licensure in a reasonable and readily apparent manner.

Websites of REALTORS® and non-member licensees affiliated with a REALTOR® firm shall disclose the firm's name and that REALTOR®'s or non-member licensee's state(s) of licensure in a reasonable and readily apparent manner. *(Adopted 1/07)*

- **Standard of Practice 12-10**

REALTORS®' obligation to present a true picture in their advertising and representations to the public includes Internet content posted, and the URLs and domain names they use, and prohibits REALTORS® from:

1) engaging in deceptive or unauthorized framing of real estate brokerage websites;
2) manipulating (e.g., presenting content developed by others) listing and other content in any way that produces a deceptive or misleading result;
3) deceptively using metatags, keywords or other devices/methods to direct, drive, or divert Internet traffic; or
4) presenting content developed by others without either attribution or without permission, or
5) to otherwise mislead consumers. *(Adopted 1/07, Amended 1/13)*

- **Standard of Practice 12-11**

REALTORS® intending to share or sell consumer information gathered via the Internet shall disclose that possibility in a reasonable and readily apparent manner. *(Adopted 1/07)*

- **Standard of Practice 12-12**

REALTORS® shall not:

1) use URLs or domain names that present less than a true picture, or
2) register URLs or domain names which, if used, would present less than a true picture. *(Adopted 1/08)*

- **Standard of Practice 12-13**

The obligation to present a true picture in advertising, marketing, and representations allows REALTORS® to use and display only professional designations, certifications, and other credentials to which they are legitimately entitled. *(Adopted 1/08)*

Article 13

REALTORS® shall not engage in activities that constitute the unauthorized practice of law and shall recommend that legal counsel be obtained when the interest of any party to the transaction requires it.

Article 14

If charged with unethical practice or asked to present evidence or to cooperate in any other way, in any professional standards proceeding or investigation, REALTORS® shall place all pertinent facts before the proper tribunals of the Member Board or affiliated institute, society, or council in which membership is held and shall take no action to disrupt or obstruct such processes. *(Amended 1/99)*

- **Standard of Practice 14-1**

  REALTORS® shall not be subject to disciplinary proceedings in more than one Board of REALTORS® or affiliated institute, society, or council in which they hold membership with respect to alleged violations of the Code of Ethics relating to the same transaction or event. *(Amended 1/95)*

- **Standard of Practice 14-2**

  REALTORS® shall not make any unauthorized disclosure or dissemination of the allegations, findings, or decision developed in connection with an ethics hearing or appeal or in connection with an arbitration hearing or procedural review. *(Amended 1/92)*

- **Standard of Practice 14-3**

  REALTORS® shall not obstruct the Board's investigative or professional standards proceedings by instituting or threatening to institute actions for libel, slander, or defamation against any party to a professional standards proceeding or their witnesses based on the filing of an arbitration request, an ethics complaint, or testimony given before any tribunal. *(Adopted 11/87, Amended 1/99)*

- **Standard of Practice 14-4**

  REALTORS® shall not intentionally impede the Board's investigative or disciplinary proceedings by filing multiple ethics complaints based on the same event or transaction. *(Adopted 11/88)*

Duties to REALTORS®

Article 15

REALTORS® shall not knowingly or recklessly make false or misleading statements about other real estate professionals, their businesses, or their business practices. *(Amended 1/12)*

- **Standard of Practice 15-1**

  REALTORS® shall not knowingly or recklessly file false or unfounded ethics complaints. *(Adopted 1/00)*

- **Standard of Practice 15-2**

  The obligation to refrain from making false or misleading statements about other real estate professionals, their businesses, and their business practices includes the duty to not knowingly or recklessly publish, repeat, retransmit, or republish false or misleading statements made by others. This duty applies whether false or misleading statements are repeated in person, in writing, by technological means (e.g., the Internet), or by any other means. *(Adopted 1/07, Amended 1/12)*

- **Standard of Practice 15-3**

  The obligation to refrain from making false or misleading statements about other real estate professionals, their businesses, and their business practices includes the duty to publish a clarification about or to remove statements made by others on electronic media the REALTOR® controls once the REALTOR® knows the statement is false or misleading. *(Adopted 1/10, Amended 1/12)*

Article 16

REALTORS® shall not engage in any practice or take any action inconsistent with exclusive representation or exclusive brokerage relationship agreements that other REALTORS® have with clients. *(Amended 1/04)*

- **Standard of Practice 16-1**

  Article 16 is not intended to prohibit aggressive or innovative business practices which are otherwise ethical and does not prohibit disagreements with other REALTORS® involving commission, fees, compensation or other forms of payment or expenses. *(Adopted 1/93, Amended 1/95)*

- **Standard of Practice 16-2**

  Article 16 does not preclude REALTORS® from making general announcements to prospects describing their services and the terms of their availability even though some recipients may have entered into agency agreements or other exclusive relationships with another REALTOR®. A general telephone canvass, general mailing or distribution addressed to all prospects in a given geographical area or in a given profession, business, club, or organization, or other classification or group is deemed "general" for purposes of this standard. *(Amended 1/04)*

  Article 16 is intended to recognize as unethical two basic types of solicitations:

  First, telephone or personal solicitations of property owners who have been identified by a real estate sign, multiple listing compilation, or other information service as having exclusively listed their property with another REALTOR® and

  Second, mail or other forms of written solicitations of prospects whose properties are exclusively listed with another REALTOR® when such solicitations are not part of a general mailing but are directed specifically to property owners identified through compilations of current listings, "for sale" or "for rent" signs, or other sources of information required by Article 3 and Multiple Listing Service rules to be made available to other REALTORS® under offers of subagency or cooperation. *(Amended 1/04)*

- **Standard of Practice 16-3**

  Article 16 does not preclude REALTORS® from contacting the client of another broker for the purpose of offering to provide, or entering into a contract to provide, a different type of real estate service unrelated to the type of service currently being provided (e.g., property management as opposed to brokerage) or from offering the same type of service for property not subject to other brokers' exclusive agreements. However, information received through a Multiple Listing Service or any other offer of cooperation may not be used to target clients of other REALTORS® to whom such offers to provide services may be made. *(Amended 1/04)*

- **Standard of Practice 16-4**

  REALTORS® shall not solicit a listing which is currently listed exclusively with another broker. However, if the listing broker, when asked by the REALTOR®, refuses to disclose the expiration date and nature of such listing, i.e., an exclusive right to sell, an exclusive agency, open listing, or other form of contractual agreement between the listing broker and the client, the REALTOR® may contact the owner to secure such information and may discuss the terms upon which the REALTOR® might take a future listing or, alternatively, may take a listing to become effective upon expiration of any existing exclusive listing. *(Amended 1/94)*

- **Standard of Practice 16-5**

  REALTORS® shall not solicit buyer/tenant agreements from buyers/tenants who are subject to exclusive buyer/tenant agreements. However, if asked by a REALTOR®, the broker refuses to disclose the expiration date of the exclusive buyer/tenant agreement, the REALTOR® may contact the buyer/tenant to secure such information and may discuss the terms upon which the REALTOR® might enter into a future buyer/tenant agreement or, alternatively, may enter into a buyer/tenant agreement to become effective upon the expiration of any existing exclusive buyer/tenant agreement. *(Adopted 1/94, Amended 1/98)*

- **Standard of Practice 16-6**

When REALTORS® are contacted by the client of another REALTOR® regarding the creation of an exclusive relationship to provide the same type of service, and REALTORS® have not directly or indirectly initiated such discussions, they may discuss the terms upon which they might enter into a future agreement or, alternatively, may enter into an agreement which becomes effective upon expiration of any existing exclusive agreement. *(Amended 1/98)*

- **Standard of Practice 16-7**

The fact that a prospect has retained a REALTOR® as an exclusive representative or exclusive broker in one or more past transactions does not preclude other REALTORS® from seeking such prospect's future business. *(Amended 1/04)*

- **Standard of Practice 16-8**

The fact that an exclusive agreement has been entered into with a REALTOR® shall not preclude or inhibit any other REALTOR® from entering into a similar agreement after the expiration of the prior agreement. *(Amended 1/98)*

- **Standard of Practice 16-9**

REALTORS®, prior to entering into a representation agreement, have an affirmative obligation to make reasonable efforts to determine whether the prospect is subject to a current, valid exclusive agreement to provide the same type of real estate service. *(Amended 1/04)*

- **Standard of Practice 16-10**

REALTORS®, acting as buyer or tenant representatives or brokers, shall disclose that relationship to the seller/landlord's representative or broker at first contact and shall provide written confirmation of that disclosure to the seller/landlord's representative or broker not later than execution of a purchase agreement or lease. *(Amended 1/04)*

- **Standard of Practice 16-11**

On unlisted property, REALTORS® acting as buyer/tenant representatives or brokers shall disclose that relationship to the seller/landlord at first contact for that buyer/tenant and shall provide written confirmation of such disclosure to the seller/landlord not later than execution of any purchase or lease agreement. *(Amended 1/04)*

REALTORS® shall make any request for anticipated compensation from the seller/landlord at first contact. *(Amended 1/98)*

- **Standard of Practice 16-12**

REALTORS®, acting as representatives or brokers of sellers/landlords or as subagents of listing brokers, shall disclose that relationship to buyers/tenants as soon as practicable and shall provide written confirmation of such disclosure to buyers/tenants not later than execution of any purchase or lease agreement. *(Amended 1/04)*

- **Standard of Practice 16-13**

All dealings concerning property exclusively listed, or with buyer/tenants who are subject to an exclusive agreement shall be carried on with the client's representative or broker, and not with the client, except with the consent of the client's representative or broker or except where such dealings are initiated by the client.

Before providing substantive services (such as writing a purchase offer or presenting a CMA) to prospects, REALTORS® shall ask prospects whether they are a party to any exclusive representation agreement. REALTORS® shall not knowingly provide substantive services concerning a prospective transaction to prospects who are parties to exclusive representation agreements, except with the consent of the prospects' exclusive representatives or at the direction of prospects. *(Adopted 1/93, Amended 1/04)*

- **Standard of Practice 16-14**

REALTORS® are free to enter into contractual relationships or to negotiate with sellers/landlords, buyers/tenants or others who are not subject to an exclusive agreement but shall not knowingly obligate them to pay more than one commission except with their informed consent. *(Amended 1/98)*

- **Standard of Practice 16-15**

In cooperative transactions REALTORS® shall compensate cooperating REALTORS® (principal brokers) and shall not compensate nor offer to compensate, directly or indirectly, any of the sales licensees employed by or affiliated with other REALTORS® without the prior express knowledge and consent of the cooperating broker.

- **Standard of Practice 16-16**

REALTORS®, acting as subagents or buyer/tenant representatives or brokers, shall not use the terms of an offer to purchase/lease to attempt to modify the listing broker's offer of compensation to subagents or buyer/tenant representatives or brokers nor make the submission of an executed offer to purchase/lease contingent on the listing broker's agreement to modify the offer of compensation. *(Amended 1/04)*

- **Standard of Practice 16-17**

REALTORS®, acting as subagents or as buyer/tenant representatives or brokers, shall not attempt to extend a listing broker's offer of cooperation and/or compensation to other brokers without the consent of the listing broker. *(Amended 1/04)*

- **Standard of Practice 16-18**

REALTORS® shall not use information obtained from listing brokers through offers to cooperate made through multiple listing services or through other offers of cooperation to refer listing brokers' clients to other brokers or to create buyer/tenant relationships with listing brokers' clients, unless such use is authorized by listing brokers. *(Amended 1/02)*

- **Standard of Practice 16-19**

Signs giving notice of property for sale, rent, lease, or exchange shall not be placed on property without consent of the seller/landlord. *(Amended 1/93)*

- **Standard of Practice 16-20**

REALTORS®, prior to or after their relationship with their current firm is terminated, shall not induce clients of their current firm to cancel exclusive contractual agreements between the client and that firm. This does not preclude REALTORS® (principals) from establishing agreements with their associated licensees governing assignability of exclusive agreements. *(Adopted 1/98, Amended 1/10)*

Article 17

In the event of contractual disputes or specific non-contractual disputes as defined in Standard of Practice 17-4 between REALTORS® (principals) associated with different firms, arising out of their relationship as REALTORS®, the REALTORS® shall mediate the dispute if the Board requires its members to mediate. If the dispute is not resolved through mediation, or if mediation is not required, REALTORS® shall submit the dispute to arbitration in accordance with the policies of the Board rather than litigate the matter.

In the event clients of REALTORS® wish to mediate or arbitrate contractual disputes arising out of real estate transactions, REALTORS® shall mediate or arbitrate those disputes in accordance with the policies of the Board, provided the clients agree to be bound by any resulting agreement or award.

The obligation to participate in mediation and arbitration contemplated by this Article includes the obligation of REALTORS® (principals) to cause their firms to mediate and arbitrate and be bound by any resulting agreement or award. *(Amended 1/12)*

- **Standard of Practice 17-1**

The filing of litigation and refusal to withdraw from it by REALTORS® in an arbitrable matter constitutes a refusal to arbitrate. *(Adopted 2/86)*

- **Standard of Practice 17-2**

Article 17 does not require REALTORS® to mediate in those circumstances when all parties to the dispute advise the Board in writing that they choose not to mediate through the Board's facilities. The fact that all parties decline to participate in mediation does not relieve REALTORS® of the duty to arbitrate.

Article 17 does not require REALTORS® to arbitrate in those circumstances when all parties to the dispute advise the Board in writing that they choose not to arbitrate before the Board. *(Amended 1/12)*

- **Standard of Practice 17-3**

REALTORS®, when acting solely as principals in a real estate transaction, are not obligated to arbitrate disputes with other REALTORS® absent a specific written agreement to the contrary. *(Adopted 1/96)*

- **Standard of Practice 17-4**

Specific non-contractual disputes that are subject to arbitration pursuant to Article 17 are:

1) Where a listing broker has compensated a cooperating broker and another cooperating broker subsequently claims to be the procuring cause of the sale or lease. In such cases the complainant may name the first cooperating broker as respondent and arbitration may proceed without the listing broker being named as a respondent. When arbitration occurs between two (or more) cooperating brokers and where the listing broker is not a party, the amount in dispute and the amount of any potential resulting award is limited to the amount paid to the respondent by the listing broker and any amount credited or paid to a party to the transaction at the direction of the respondent. Alternatively, if the complaint is brought against the listing broker, the listing broker may name the first cooperating broker as a third-party respondent. In either instance the decision of the hearing panel as to procuring cause shall be conclusive with respect to all current or subsequent claims of the parties for compensation arising out of the underlying cooperative transaction. *(Adopted 1/97, Amended 1/07)*

2) Where a buyer or tenant representative is compensated by the seller or landlord, and not by the listing broker, and the listing broker, as a result, reduces the commission owed by the seller or landlord and, subsequent to such actions, another cooperating broker claims to be the procuring cause of sale or lease. In such cases the complainant may name the first cooperating broker as respondent and arbitration may proceed without the listing broker being named as a respondent. When arbitration occurs between two (or more) cooperating brokers and where the listing broker is not a party, the amount in dispute and the amount of any potential resulting award is limited to the amount paid to the respondent by the seller or landlord and any amount credited or paid to a party to the transaction at the direction of the respondent. Alternatively, if the complaint is brought against the listing broker, the listing broker may name the first cooperating broker as a third-party respondent. In either instance the decision of the hearing panel as to procuring cause shall be conclusive with respect to all current or subsequent claims of the parties for compensation arising out of the underlying cooperative transaction. *(Adopted 1/97, Amended 1/07)*

3) Where a buyer or tenant representative is compensated by the buyer or tenant and, as a result, the listing broker reduces the commission owed by the seller or landlord and, subsequent to such actions, another cooperating broker claims to be the procuring cause of sale or lease. In such cases the complainant may name the first cooperating broker as respondent and arbitration may proceed without the listing broker being named as a respondent. Alternatively, if the complaint is brought against the listing broker, the listing broker may name the first cooperating broker as a third-party respondent. In either instance the decision of the hearing panel as to procuring cause shall be conclusive with respect to all current or subsequent claims of the parties for compensation arising out of the underlying cooperative transaction. *(Adopted 1/97)*

4) Where two or more listing brokers claim entitlement to compensation pursuant to open listings with a seller or landlord who agrees to participate in arbitration (or who requests arbitration) and who agrees to be bound by the decision. In cases where one of the listing brokers has been compensated by the seller or landlord, the other listing broker, as complainant, may name the first listing broker as respondent and arbitration may proceed between the brokers. *(Adopted 1/97)*

5) Where a buyer or tenant representative is compensated by the seller or landlord, and not by the listing broker, and the listing broker, as a result, reduces the commission owed by the seller or landlord and, subsequent to such actions, claims to be the procuring cause of sale or lease. In such cases arbitration shall be between the listing broker and the buyer or tenant representative and the amount in dispute is limited to the amount of the reduction of commission to which the listing broker agreed. *(Adopted 1/05)*

- **Standard of Practice 17-5**

The obligation to arbitrate established in Article 17 includes disputes between REALTORS® (principals) in different states in instances where, absent an established inter-association arbitration agreement, the REALTOR® (principal) requesting arbitration agrees to submit to the jurisdiction of, travel to, participate in, and be bound by any resulting award rendered in arbitration conducted by the respondent(s) REALTOR®'s association, in instances where the respondent(s) REALTOR®'s association determines that an arbitrable issue exists. *(Adopted 1/07)*

Explanatory Notes

The reader should be aware of the following policies which have been approved by the Board of Directors of the National Association:

In filing a charge of an alleged violation of the Code of Ethics by a REALTOR®, the charge must read as an alleged violation of one or more Articles of the Code. Standards of Practice may be cited in support of the charge.

The Standards of Practice serve to clarify the ethical obligations imposed by the various Articles and supplement, and do not substitute for, the Case Interpretations in *Interpretations of the Code of Ethics*.

Modifications to existing Standards of Practice and additional new Standards of Practice are approved from time to time. Readers are cautioned to ensure that the most recent publications are utilized.

Copyright 2014 NATIONAL ASSOCIATION OF REALTORS®

166-288-14 (01/14 VG)

For information about the Code's centennial go to: *www.realtor.org/coe100*

430 North Michigan Avenue • Chicago, IL 60611-4087
800.874.6500 • www.REALTOR.org

NATIONAL
ASSOCIATION *of*
REALTORS®

(CAREB), has thirteen board affiliations:

1. East County Association of Realist (ECAR), Antioch
2. Central Valley Realtist Association (CVRA)
3. Inland Empire Board of Realtist (IEBR)
4. Consolidated Realtist Board (CRB), Los Angeles
5. Associated Real Property Brokers (ARPB), Oakland
6. San Francisco Realtist Board (SFRB)
7. NLAR, Palmdale (NEW)
8. Richmond
9. Sacramento Realtist Association (SRA)
10. San Diego Realtist Democracy in Housing (SDRDH)
11. Orange County Association of Real Estate Brokers (OCAREB)
12. San Jose Association of Realtist (SJAOR)
13. The Solano Realtist Association (TSRA)

A Realtist must be a member of a local board as well as a member of the national organization. Both on the local and national levels, Realtists work for better housing in the communities they serve. In many instances, individuals are both REALTORS® and Realtists by virtue of dual membership.

E. NATIONAL ASSOCIATION OF HISPANIC REAL ESTATE PROFESSIONALS (NAHREP)

The ***NATIONAL ASSOCIATION OF HISPANIC REAL ESTATE PROFESSIONALS (NAHREP)*** *is a national non-profit trade association made up primarily of Hispanic members.* This association was created to establish a venue where members can congregate, exchange ideas, and formulate an agenda beneficial to the collective well-being of the Hispanic segment of the industry (**www.nahrep.org**).

F. ASIAN REAL ESTATE ASSOCIATION OF AMERICA (AREAA)

The ***ASIAN REAL ESTATE ASSOCIATION OF AMERICA (AREAA)*** *is a national trade association committed to enhancing business opportunities and success of real estate professionals serving the Asian American community.* AREAA is dedicated to promoting homeownership opportunities among the many Asian American communities throughout the nation (**www.areaa.org**).

G. INDEPENDENT ASSOCIATIONS

There are also several "independent" associations in California, some of which are large in membership and influential in their communities. Most of these boards are organized for some particular purpose, such as a multiple listing service. Many members of independent boards are also members of boards affiliated with CAR.

Examples of independent boards are:

1. Chinese American Real Estate Professionals Association of Southern California
2. Chinese Real Estate Association of America
3. Korean Real Estate Brokers of Southern California
4. Women in Real Estate (WIRE)

H. OTHER ASSOCIATIONS

In addition to the above-mentioned organizations, there are many trade associations and professional bodies that are related to the real estate business, such as:

1. American Bankers Association
2. American Savings and Loan Institute
3. Building Owners and Managers Association
4. Mortgage Bankers Association
5. National Association of Home Builders
6. National Association of Mutual Savings Banks
7. Prefabricated Home Manufacturers Institute

I. REAL ESTATE INSTRUCTOR AND LICENSING ASSOCIATIONS

Real estate instructor organizations and other professional bodies that are related to real estate education and licensing also play an important role in the real estate industry (see **Figure 15-11**).

J. NO AFFILIATION NECESSARY

Licensees need not be members of any trade or professional association. In this case, they are simply referred to as salespersons or brokers.

There is no compulsion for any licensee of the Bureau of Real Estate to join or affiliate with any local or state organization. That decision is strictly individual and personal.

K. OFFICE POLICY MANUAL

A *real estate OFFICE POLICY MANUAL spells out the company's ethical and professional expectations and requirements, including a mission statement, personnel policies, and general procedures.* A good policy manual expresses the office policy to attempt at all times to conduct business in the highest ethical, professional, and competent manner when dealing with clients, associates and employees in this office, REALTORS®, and other professionals. Some of the topics included in the policy manual should cover:

1. Company Mission Statement
2. Description of Broker/Associate Relationship
3. General Office Procedure

Figure 15-11

Real Estate Teacher's and Professional's Groups

Real Estate Educators Association (REEA)

The Real Estate Educators Association is a society of real estate education stakeholders (instructors, trainers, regulators, schools, authors, etc.). REEA's challenge is to continually give members the latest tools and techniques for effective adult education. REEA's goal is to make sure REEA members meet and exceed the high standards demanded in real estate's rapidly changing legal and professional environment.

Real Estate Educators Association (REEA)
7739 E. Broadway, #337
Tuscon, Arizona 85710
520-609-2380

 Real Estate Educators Association (REEA)
www.reea.org (REEA)
California Community Colleges Real Estate Education Center
www.ccsf.edu/NEW/en/educational-programs/school-and-departments/school-of-business/real-estate-education-center.html
Association of Real Estate License Law Officials - ARELLO
www.arello.org

CALIFORNIA COMMUNITY COLLEGES
REAL ESTATE EDUCATION CENTER

The California Community Colleges Real Estate Education Center is a real estate instructors' group sponsored by the California Bureau of Real Estate. The Center publishes a quarterly newsletter and sponsors educators' conferences three times a year in cooperation with the California Community College Chancellor's office. The newsletter, called *The Informer*, is a useful reference source to keep educators up to date on new laws and real estate practices. The conferences are held in the San Francisco Bay area, the Los Angeles area, and the San Diego area. For information about The Informer and Endowment Fund contact:

Carol Jensen, Director
California Community Colleges
Real Estate Education Center
City College of San Francisco - Downtown Campus
88 Fourth Street
San Francisco, California 94103
415-267-6550
cjensen@ccsf.edu

The Association of Real Estate License Law Officials (ARELLO) supports jurisdictions in the administration and enforcement of real estate license laws to promote and protect the public interest.

Association of Real Estate License Law Officials (ARELLO)
150 North Wacker Srive, Ste. 920
Chicago, Illinois 60606
312-300-4870

4. Sales Activities (Scope of Duties, Advertising Requirements, Proper Listing and Showing Procedures, etc.)
5. Dispute Resolution (Mediation Required, then Arbitration, if necessary).

VII. CHAPTER SUMMARY

A person who is actively involved in a real estate transaction at the service of another, in the expectation of receiving a commission, must be licensed by the **California Bureau of Real Estate (CalBRE)**, which is the regulatory agency for real estate in California. The CalBRE is governed by the **Real Estate Commissioner**, who is appointed by the governor and defended by the state Attorney General. The Commissioner does not settle commission disputes, take the place of a court of law, nor give legal advice, but the rules and regulations he or she issues do have the force and effect of law.

To obtain a **salesperson's license**, a candidate must: be 18 or over, honest and truthful, complete college-level Real Estate Principles and Practice courses plus one other course, and pass the state exam. The salesperson exam takes 3 hours and 15 minutes, has 150 questions, and requires a 70% or better to pass.

If you have a criminal record, you must disclose this information on your application, or you risk never getting your license.

Applicants must apply for a license within one year from passing the exam date, at which time he or she will have to submit an electronic fingerprint scan.

A **broker's license** is required to operate a real estate office. A broker must be 18 years old, have had two years previous experience or college education, complete the required 8 broker courses, be honest and truthful, and pass the required examination. The broker exam takes 5 hours, has 200 questions, and requires a 75% or better to pass. A four-year degree (B.S. or B.A) with a major or minor in real estate = 2 years experience, and a two year degree (A.A.) = one year of experience.

The **continuing education requirement** of 45 hours every four years for a license renewal includes three hours each of **Ethics, Agency, Trust Fund Accounting and Handling,** and **Fair Housing**.

California Real Estate Law is the portion of the **Business and Professions Code** that refers to licensing and subdivision. The **Commissioners' Regulations** are rules that form part of the **California Administrative Code** and are enforced by the Real Estate Commissioner. The Commissioner can revoke, restrict, or suspend the license of any real estate agent for misconduct.

All agents must adhere to Section 10176 (acting in a licensee capacity) and **Section 10177** of the **Business and Professions Code**, which have the force and effect of the law itself.

The Real Estate General Fund provides for the **Recovery Fund**, which pays damages and arbitration awards to people due to the wrongful act of a licensee in a real estate transaction. There is a limit of $50,000 per transaction, and a total of $250,000 against an individual licensee in a lifetime.

A **Trade** or **Professional Association** is a voluntary, nonprofit organization made up of independent firms in the same industry. A voluntary organization of real estate licensees in a particularly community is a **Local Association of REALTORS®**. They usually provide a multiple listing service for their members.

The **California Association of REALTORS® (CAR)** is the state division of the **National Association of REALTORS® (NAR)**. Only active members of NAR or CAR are allowed to use the term **"REALTOR®."** A REALTOR® must swear to and abide by NAR's **Code of Ethics**, governing his or her behavior.

The term **"Realtists"** refers to members of the **National Association of Real Estate Brokers (NAREB)**. Although primarily African American and other minorities, all practitioners are welcome to join. Other associations include the **National Association of Hispanic Real Estate Professionals (NAHREP)** and the **Asian Real Estate Association of America (AREAA)**, as well as local and independent boards associations such as the **Chinese American Real Estate Professionals Association of Southern California** and **Women in Real Estate (WIRE)**.

Real estate instructor organizations include the **Real Estate Educators Association (REEA)** and the **California Community Colleges Real Estate Education Center**, sponsored by the California Bureau of Real Estate. The **Association of Real Estate License Law Officials is known as (ARELLO)**. Licensees are not required to be a member of any trade or professional association.

VIII. MATCHING VOCABULARY Fill in the blanks with the correct letter

A. 150 days
B. 70%
C. 75%
D. Broker's license
E. California Bureau of Real Estate (CalBRE)
F. California Real Estate Law

G. National Association of REALTORS® (NAR)
H. Office policy manual
I. Police power
J. Prepaid rental listing service
K. Real Estate Commissioner

L. Real Estate License
M. Realtist
N. Recovery fund
O. Regulators
P. Restrict
Q. Revoke
R. Suspend
S. Trade association

1. _____ Every state government uses these staff members to regulate real estate brokerage activities.

2. _____ The primary objective of this state (California) agency is to protect the public interest in offerings of subdivided lands, and the handling of real estate transactions by licensees. A standard of knowledge is measured by an examination given to potential real estate agents.

3. _____ The right to enact and enforce laws beneficial to the health, safety, morals, and general welfare of the public.

4. _____ Any person who is actively involved in a real estate transaction at the service of another, in the expectation of receiving a commission, must have one of these.

5. _____ The salesperson's exam takes 3 hours and fifteen minutes, has 150 questions and requires this passing percentage of correct questions to pass.

6. _____ Any individual who wishes to operate a real estate office must have this.

7. _____ The broker's exam take 5 hours to complete, has 200 questions, and requires this passing percentage of correct questions to pass.

8. _____ This type of license is required when running a business that supplies prospective tenants with listings of residential real property for rent or lease while collecting a fee for such service.

9. _____ The portion of the Business and Professions Code that refers to licensing and subdivisions of real estate.

10. _____ The chief executive of the Bureau of Real Estate.

11. _____ To take away a real estate license.

12. _____ To limit the use of a real estate license.

13. _____ To take away a real estate license for a period of time.

14. _____ Any licensee who appears on the "deadbeat" child support list, is given this much time by the CalBRE to get current on their support payment, or have their license suspended.

15. _____ This fund was established for the payment of damages and arbitration awards to people who have suffered financial loss due to the wrongful act of a licensee in a real estate transaction.

16. _____ A voluntary, nonprofit organization made up of independent firms in the same industry.

17. _____ The national trade association for all the state associations and local boards of REALTORS® in the United States.

18. _____ A member of the National Association of Real Estate Brokers is called this.

19. _____ This guide spells out the company's ethical and professional expectations and requirements, including a mission statement, personnel policies and general procedures.

See Page 611 for Answers

IX. CHAPTER QUIZ

1. Who appoints the Real Estate Commissioner?

   a. The Governor
   b. The Legislature
   c. The Board of Governors
   d. Members of CAR

2. Who prosecutes for the Real Estate Commissioner?

   a. The Attorney General
   b. The District Attorney
   c. The Board of Governors
   d. The Real Estate Commissioner himself or herself

3. What is the minimum number of hours of Continuing Education required to renew a four-year license?

   a. 10
   b. 20
   c. 45
   d. 60

4. The broker's license examination process consists of:

   a. 200 multiple-choice question test.
   b. photo identification required for entry.
   c. two 2½ hour exam periods.
   d. all of the above.

5. The Real Estate Commissioner has the right to:

   a. revoke licenses.
   b. restrict licenses.
   c. suspend licenses.
   d. all of the above.

6. The name NAHREP stands for:

   a. National Association of Happy Real Estate Professionals.
   b. National Asian Homeowners Representatives and Estate Planners.
   c. National Association of Hispanic Real Estate Professionals.
   d. none of the above.

7. What is the lifetime ceiling the Recovery Fund will pay out for one licensee?

   a. $20,000
   b. $200,000
   c. $250,000
   d. None of the above

8. To acquire a broker's license, an applicant is required to:

   a. be 18 years old.
   b. be honest and truthful.
   c. pass the broker's exam.
   d. all of the above.

9. Every four years the National Association of REALTORS® requires members to take a course covering the:

   a. Code of Ethics.
   b. NAR Commission Plan.
   c. NAR Fair Housing Guidelines.
   d. none of the above.

10. To call yourself a REALTOR®, you must:

   a. belong to NAIFA.
   b. belong to the NAR.
   c. be an independent board member.
   d. be a member of ARELLO.

ANSWERS: 1. a; 2. b; 3. c; 4. d; 5. d; 6. c; 7. c; 8. d; 9. a; 10. b

APPENDIX 1

Chapter Websites

Chapter 1
Citrus Valley Association of REALTORS® *www.cvar.net*
Lyons & Associates, Inc. REALTOR® *www.lyonsandassociatesrltr.com*

Chapter 7
California Association of REALTORS® *www.car.org*

Chapter 8
Zillow *www.zillow.com*
Trulia *www.trulia.com*
Realtor.com *www.realtor.com*
LendingTree *www.lendingtree.com*
Quicken Loans *www.quickenloans.com*
Greenlight Loans *www.greenlightloans.com*

Chapter 9
Fannie Mae (FNMA) *www.fanniemae.com*
Ginnie Mae (GNMA) *www.ginniemae.gov*
Freddie Mac (FHLMC) *www.freddiemac.com*
U.S. Department of Housing and Urban Development (HUD) *www.hud.gov*
Department Of Veterans Affairs (VA) Home Loans *www.benefits.va.gov/homeloans*
Experian Credit Scores *www.experian.com/consumer/index.html*
TransUnion Credit Scores *www.transunion.com*
Equifax Credit Scores *www.equifax.com*
Stewart Title Insurance *www.stewart.com/title-insurance*
Federal Reserve Bank of San Francisco, 12th District *www.frbsf.org*

APPENDIX 1 - CHAPTER WEBSITES

Federal Deposit Insurance Corporation (FDIC) *www.fdic.gov*

Chapter 11

L. A. County Assessor *http://assessor.lacounty.gov*

List of Assessors *www.boe.ca.gov/proptaxes/assessors.htm*

Internal Revenue Service (IRS) *www.irs.ustreas.gov*

Franchise Tax Board (FTB) *www.ftb.ca.gov*

Chapter 13

National Association of REALTORS® Green Resource Council
www.greenresourcecouncil.org/glossary.cfm

Chapter 14

California Secretary of State - Notary Public Information *www.sos.ca.gov/business/notary*

Chapter 15

California Bureau of Real Estate (CalBRE) *www.calbre.ca.gov*

Preparing for the Exam *www.calbre.ca.gov/Examinees/Preparing.html*

California Bureau of Real Estate Licensees Fees *www.bre.ca.gov/Licensees/Fees.html*

State of California *www.ca.gov*

Beverly Hills/Greater Los Angeles Association of REALTORS® *bhglaar.com*

California Association of REALTORS® *www.car.org*

National Association of REALTORS® *www.realtor.org*

Real Estate Educators Association (REEA) *www.reea.org (REEA)*

California Community Colleges Real Estate Education Center
www.ccsf.edu/NEW/en/educational-programs/school-and-departments/school-of-business/real-estate-education-center.html

Association of Real Estate License Law Officials - ARELLO *www.arello.org*

A

Abandonment. Giving up any further interest in a thing or a right.

Abatement of Nuisance. The extinction or termination of an offensive activity; such as pollution of the atmosphere.

ABC Law (Alcoholic Beverage Control Law). Regulates the sale of alcoholic beverages. Encountered in connection with escrows handling the sale of a liquor license.

Absolute Ownership. (See **Fee Simple Estate**.)

Abstract. A brief summary; an abridgment.

Abstract of Judgment. A summary or condensation of the essential provisions of a money judgment in a civil action. When recorded, it creates a general lien on real property of the judgment debtor in the county where the abstract is recorded.

Abstract of Title. A summary of the condition of title to real property based on an examination of public records; includes a digest of the deeds or other transfers, encumbrances, and other instruments reflecting ownership of title or matters which may impair the title.

Abstraction. A method of valuing land. The indicated value of the improvement is deducted from the sale price.

Accelerated Cost Recovery System (ACRS). The system for figuring depreciation (cost recovery for depreciable real property acquired and placed into service after January 1, 1981 under the former federal income tax law).

Accelerated Depreciation. Allowing for a greater amount of depreciation of property in the earlier years of the life of the investment. Distinguished from **Straight-line Depreciation** (also see), which allows for equal amounts of depreciation each year.

Acceleration Clause. A provision in a note or deed of trust permitting the owner of the note to declare the entire unpaid balance due and payable earlier than the stated due date in the event of a default, such as failure to pay taxes or an installment when due, or in the event of the sale of the property.

Acceptance. Act indicating that the terms and provisions of a proposed contract are satisfactory and are agreed to; usually preceded by an offer by one contracting party, which is accepted by the other party; evidences a "meeting of the minds" that is an essential element of a contract. (See Counter Offer)

Access Right. The right of an owner to have ingress and egress (a means of entry and exit) to and from his or her property to a public street or way.

Accession. Acquisition of property by its incorporation or union (uniting) with other property. It may occur by the processes of **Accretion, Reliction, or Annexation**.

Accounts Payable. An aggregate or total of amounts owed to creditors; a liability.

Accounts Receivable. An aggregate or total of amounts due a creditor from his debtors; an asset.

Accretion. Increase of land on shore or bank of a river by the gradual deposit of sand or soil by natural action of the water.

Accrual Basis. Method of recording income and expenses in which each item is reported as earned or incurred without regard to when actual payments are received or made. Distinguished from **Cash Basis**.

Accrued. To be added or accumulated as a matter of periodic gain or advantage, as interest on money. Used variously, such as accrued dividends, accrued interest, or accrued depreciation.

Accrued Depreciation. The difference between the cost of replacement of a building new as of the date of a previous appraisal and the present appraised value.

Accrued Items of Expense. Those incurred expenses which are not yet payable. The seller's accrued expenses are credited to the purchaser in an escrow closing statement.

Acknowledgment. A form for authenticating instruments conveying property or otherwise conferring rights. A declaration before a notary public or other official by the party executing an instrument that it is his or her act and deed. Many instruments must be acknowledged before they are entitled to be recorded.

Acquisition. Act or process of acquiring or gaining title to or possession of property.

Acre. A measure of land equaling 160 square rods, 4840 square yards, or 43,560 square feet. A football playing field (300 x 160 feet) contains a little more than an acre of land.

Acre Foot. A unit volume of water in irrigation; the amount covering one acre to a depth of one foot, equal to 43,560 cubic feet.

Action. A court proceeding to enforce a right or redress (obtain satisfaction for) a wrong.

Act of God. Any unavoidable disaster which is a the result of natural causes, rather than manmade, such as earthquakes, violent storms (cyclones or tornadoes), lightning, or flooding.

Actual Authority. Authority expressly given by the principal or given by the law and not denied by the principal.

Actual Fraud. An act meant to deceive another, such as making a promise without intending to keep it, suppressing the truth, or making a false statement.

Actual Notice. Having actual knowledge of a fact, as compared with implied or inferred notice.

Adjustable Rate Mortgage (ARM). A mortgage loan with an interest rate that is subject to change during the term of the loan.

Adjusted Cost Basis. The cost basis of property with certain additions, such as the cost of improvements, and certain subtractions, such as depreciation in value.

Adjustments. In appraising, a means by which characteristics of a residential property are reflected by dollar amount or percentage to conform to similar, but not identical, characteristics of another residential property.

Administrator. A person appointed by a probate court as the representative of a deceased peron's estate where the decedent left no will. A woman appointed as the representative is called the administratrix.

Ad Valorem. According to the value; encountered in taxation of real property. An ad valorem tax assesses real property in relation to its value.

Advance Fee. A fee charged in advance for advertising or for preliminary expenses in connection with the sale of real estate or a business opportunity; regulated by statute.

Advances. Money advanced by the beneficiary under a trust deed to pay real estate taxes, hazard insurance premiums, or other items needed to protect the beneficiary's interest under the trust deed. Also refers to additional funds loaned under an open-end mortgage or trust deed.

Adverse Possession. A method of acquisition of title to property based on hostile use and occupation of another person's property for a continuous period of five years and payment of taxes.

Affidavit. A statement or declaration reduced to writing and sworn to or affirmed before some officer or official, such as a Notary Public, who has authority to administer an oath or affirmation.

Affidavit of Title. A written statement by a seller or grantor, made under oath and acknowledged before a Notary Public, in which seller or grantor identifies himself or herself and his or her marital status and certifies that, since the examination of title on the contract date, there are no judgments, bankruptcies, or divorces, no unrecorded deeds, contracts, unpaid repairs, or improvements, or defects of title known to sellor or grantor, and that he or she is in posession of the property.

Affirm. To state or assert that a statement made is true, but without oath; to confirm or ratify a judgment of a lower court by an appellate court; to ratify and accept an otherwise voidable transaction.

Affirmation. The statement or assertion that something is true; similar to an affidavit, except that the person making the statement, due to religious beliefs, does not take an oath but merely affirms. Many affirmations are specificallly made under penalty of perjury.

Agency. The relationship between principal and agent, whereby the agent represents the principal in dealings with a third party.

Agency, Apparent. When 3rd parties ar given the impression that someone who has not been to represent another is that person's agent. Also called Ostensible Agency.

Agent. A person who acts for another, who is called a principal.

Agent, Special. An agent with limited authority to do a specific thing or conduct a specific transaction.

Agreement. An expression of assent by two or more parties to the same object. The word actually ranges in meaning from a simple mutual understanding to a binding obligation, such as a formal contract.

Agreement of Sale. A written agreement or contract between a seller and purchaser of property in which they have reached a meeting of the minds on the terms and provisions of the sale.

Air Rights. The rights in real property to the reasonable use of the air space above the surface of the land.

Alien. An unnaturalized foreign resident; a foreigner; distinguished from citizen.

Alienate. To transfer or convey property to another.

Alienation. The voluntary parting with the ownership of real property; the transferring of property by the owner to another person; opposite of acquisition.

Alienation Clause. A clause in a note or trust deed permitting the payee or beneficiary to declare the entire unpaid balance immediately due and payable upon a subsequent transfer of the property. Also referred to as a due-on-sale clause.

Alienation, Involuntary. Transfer of an interest in property against the will of the owner, or without action by the owner, occurring through operation of law, natural processes, or adverse possession.

Alienation, Voluntary. Owner willingly transfers his/her interest to another.

All-Inclusive Deed of Trust. A trust deed that includes the amount due under another or other trust deed on the same property; also called a wraparound, or overriding deed of trust.

Allodial Tenure. A real property ownership system that can be complete ownership, except for rights held by the government. (For contrast, see **Feudal Tenure**.)

Alluvion. Soil or sand added by the process of accretion; i.e.; the gradual increase of land on the shore of a lake, sea, or ocean or on the bank of a river; also known as alluvium.

ALTA (American Land Title Association). The trade association of title insurance companies in the United States.

ALTA Owner's Policy. An extended policy that provides owners and buyers similar protection that lenders have with the ALTA policy.

ALTA Policy of Title Insurance. An extended coverage form of title insurance policy, which extends the coverage of a standard coverage policy to include various off-record risks, such as matters disclosed by a survey, or by an inspection of the land, or by inquiry of persons in possession of the land.

Amenities. Intangible benefits in real property ownership arising from such factors as pride of ownership, desirable social or cultural environment, architectural excellence, etc.; conditions of agreeable living.

Amortization. The liquidation or payment of a principal debt or financial obligation either on an installment basis or by creating a sinking fund; recovery over a period of time of cost or value.

Amortized Loan. A loan to be repaid by a series of regular payments, which are equal or nearly equal, over the life of the loan.

Annexation. The addition to property by adding or attaching other property to it, such as a fixture; the addition of unincorporated territory in a county to a city or town.

Annual Percentage Rate (APR). The actual cost of credit as determined under the Federal Truth in Lending Act.

Annuity. An amount of money payable yearly, or at other regular intervals, for a specified period of time.

Annul. To cancel or to make void and of no legal effect.

Anticipation, Principle of. Affirms that value is created by anticipated benefits to be derived in the future.

Antitrust Laws. Laws prohibiting any agreement that has the effect of restraining trade, including conspiracy.

Appellant. The party appealing a court decision or ruling.

Appraisal. An opinion or estimate as to the fair market value of property; may be made for various purposes, such as sale, condemnation, assessment, taxation, etc.

Appraise. To estimate or render an opinion as to the value of property.

Appraiser. A person qualified by education, training, and experience to estimate the value or real or personal property.

Apportionment. A division of property or liability allocated into proportionate parts, not necessarily equal parts.

Appropriation of Water. The taking of water flowing on the public domain from its natural course and the application of the water to some beneficial use to the appropriator.

Appurtenance. Something annexed to or made a part of another thing and transferred as an incident to it. This may be a dwelling or a garage or a barn or an orchard or other thing that becomes part of the land.

Appurtenant. Belonging to.

Arbitration. Submitting a disputed matter to a private party rather than ti the judicial system for resolution.

Architectural Style. Generally, the appearance and character of a building's design and construction.

ARM. Adjustable Rate Mortgage.

Arm's Length Transaction. A transaction in which there is no pre-existing family business relationship (as in a short sale).

Articles of Incorporation. An instrument setting forth the basic rules and purposes under which a private corporation is formed.

Artificial Person. A legal entity such as a corporation which the law treats as an individual.

Assess. To officially estimate the value of property as a basis for taxation.

Assessed Value. The value placed on property for the purpose of taxation.

Assessment. The valuation of property for the purpose of levying a tax; the amount of the tax levied. Assessments can also be imposed specially and locally upon property particularly benefited by a local work of improvement, such as sidewalks, curbs, lighting, sewers, etc.

Assessor. The official who has the responsibility for determining the assessed value of property. County tax assessors do not fix the amount of the property tax, nor do they collect the tax; these are responsibilities of other officials.

Assets. Items of ownership convertible into cash; things of value (opposed to liabilities).

Assign. To transfer one's interest in personal property, such as a contract or a leasehold estate.

Assignee. The person to whom property is assigned.

Assignment. A transfer by writing of a person's right, title, or interest in intangible property, usually of a chose in action (see **Choses**) such as a contract right.

Assignment of Rents. A usual provision in a mortgage or deed of trust that permits the lender, upon default, to collect the rents and apply them to the amount due.

Assignor. One who assigns or transfers his or her interest in property.

Assumption Agreement. Undertaking or adopting a debt or obligation primarily resting upon another person, such as the assumption by the purchaser of real property of a mortgage executed by the seller in favor of a third party lender. If the purchaser merely took subject to the mortgage, he or she would have no personal liability for the debt. By assuming the debt, he or she may become personally liable for payment.

Assumption Fee. A lender's charge for changing over and processing new records for a new owner who is assuming an existing loan.

Attachment. A seizure of property by judicial process while a court action is pending.

Attachment Lien. A lien on real property obtained prior to judgment in an action for money; obtained by levy of a writ of attachment.

Attest. To affirm or certify that a statement or document is true or genuine.

Attorney-in-Fact. An agent authorized to act for another person under a power of attorney.

Authority, Apparent. Authority to represent another that someone appears to have and that the principal is not allowed to deny although no actual authority has been granted.

Authorization to Sell. Formal name for a listing agreement under which a real estate broker is authorized to obtain a buyer for the owner's property.

Avulsion. The sudden removal of soil from an owner's property and its deposit on the property of another, as by a sudden change in the course of a river or other watercourse.

B

Backfill. The replacement of excavated earth into a hole or against a structure.

Bad Debt/Vacancy Factor. A percentage deducted from the potential gross income to determine the effective income, estimating the lost income due to vacancies and tenants who do not pay.

Balance. Used as a verb, this means to reconcile an account. Used as a noun, this represents the amount of loan still owed.

Balance Sheet. Statement showing assets, liabilities, and net worth as of a certain date.

Balloon Payment. The final installment payable on an installment note; it pays the note in full but is ordinarily considerably greater than the periodic installment payments called for by the note.

Bank. An institution for receiving, lending, exchanging, and safeguarding money and other things of value, and transacting other financial business. May be incorporated under state law or under federal law such as a national banking association.

Bankruptcy. A proceeding initiated under federal law whereby an insolvent debtor may obtain relief from payment of certain of his or her debts.

Bargain and Sale Deed. Any deed that recites a consideration and purports to convey the real estate.

Base and Meridian Lines. Imaginary lines used by surveyors to find and describe the location of land. A base line runs east and west, whereas a meridian line runs north and south. Their intersection forms a starting point for the measurement of land. There are three principal base and meridian lines in California, located on Mt. San Bernardino in San Bernardino County, Mt. Diablo in Contra Costa County, and Mt. Pierce in Humboldt County.

Base Price. See **Cost Basis**.

Basis. See **Cost Basis** and **Adjusted Cost Basis**.

Bearing Wall (or **Partition**). A wall or partition which supports a part of a building, usually a roof or floor above.

Bench Marks. A ground location indicated on a durable marker by surveyors and used to locate or describe real property.

Beneficiary. As used in a trust deed, the lender is designated as the beneficiary, i.e., the lender obtains the benefit of the security.

Beneficiary's Statement. Statement from a secured lender setting forth the unpaid principal balance and other information concerning the debt. Frequently obtained by an escrow agent during an escrow for the sale of real estate. Commonly referred to as a "Benny" statement.

Bequeath. To make a gift of personal property by will.

Bequest. A gift of personal property by will.

Betterment. An improvement upon property which increases the property's value; considered a capital asset, as distinguished from repairs or replacements where the original character or cost are unchanged.

Bid. An offer.

Bilateral Contract. A contract in which a promise is given by both parties; distinguished from a unilateral contract, which calls for an act by one party in exchange for a promise by the other.

Bill of Sale. A written instrument evidencing the transfer of title to tangible personal property, such as furniture and furnishings, as distinguished from a chose in action (see **Choses**), such as contract right. The latter is transferred by an **Assignment**.

Binder. An agreement to consider a downpayment for the purchase of real estate as evidence of good faith on the part of the purchaser and binds the parties; a notation of coverage on an insurance policy, issued by an agent, and given to the insured prior to the issuance of the policy.

Blanket Mortgage. A single mortgage or other encumbrance which covers more than one piece of real property; may describe "all real property" owned by the mortgagor in a designated county.

Blighted Area. A declining area in which real property values are seriously affected by destructive economic forces. May be caused by the infiltration of people from lower social and economic classes, by the rapid depreciation of the buildings, or by the inharmonious use of the property.

Blind Ad. An advertisement placed by a licensee that does not include the broker's name.

Blockbusting. The practice on the part of unscrupulous speculators or real estate agents of inducing panic selling of homes below market value, especially by exploiting the prejudices of property owners in neighborhoods in which the racial make-up is changing, or appears to be on the verge of changing. It is an actionable wrong.

Board of Equalization. A state or county board with the power and authority to adjust inequalities in tax assessments.

Bona Fide. In good faith; without fraud.

Bona Fide Purchaser. A person who buys property in good faith, for a fair value, and without notice of any adverse claims or rights of third parties.

Bond. A written promise of a surety, i.e., one who makes himself responsible for the faithful performance of an act by another person. Also, evidence of a debt or obligation owned by a governmental agency or other entity, such as a private corporation.

Book Value. Total cost of property minus total depreciation; the value of property as stated in a book of accounts (distinguished from **Market Value**).

Boot. In real estate exchange language, this represents cash, or something else of value, that is unlike the property in exchange. Applicable where the parcels being exchanged are not of the same value.

Boundary. Anything that indicates bounds or limits in the area or location of property.

Bounds. Boundaries; used with the word metes as Metes and Bounds, one of the principal methods for describing real property.

Breach. The violation of an obligation, or failure of duty, or the breaking of a law.

Broker. An agent who finds a buyer or seller of property for a principal on a commission basis; also may act as a loan broker in arranging loans on real property, or in other capacities; licensed by DRE.

Broker, Associate. A licensed real estate broker who is affiliated with another broker.

Broker, Designated. Broker is authorized to act as the company broker and is responsible for the agents' acts.

Brokerage. A real estate broker's business.

BTU (British Thermal Unit). The quantity of heat required to raise the temperature of one pound of water one degree Fahrenheit.

Building Code. A regulation of construction of buildings within a municipality established by ordinance or statute.

Building Line. Lines established by ordinance or statute, limiting how close an owner can build to the street; also referred to as setback lines (see **Setback Ordinance**).

Building, Market Value of. The amount of money a structure adds or subtracts from the value of the land it occupies; land valued on the basis of highest and best use.

Building Restrictions. Zoning regulations or deed provisions limiting type, size and use of a building.

Built-In. Cabinets or similar features built as part of the house.

Bulk Sales Law. State law regulating the sale of business establishments, including stock in trade; enacted for the purpose of protecting the interest of creditors of the business.

Bundle of Rights. The various interests or rights that owners have in their property.

Bureau of Land Management. A federal bureau within the Department of the Interior, which manages and controls certain lands owned by the United States.

Business Opportunity. As used in the Real Estate Law, refers to the sale or lease of the business and goodwill of an existing business enterprise or opportunity separate and apart from the real property.

Buydown. When discount points are paid to a lender to reduce the interest rate charged to the borrower which can be paid by seller/buyer.

Buyer's Market. The conditions which exist when a buyer is in a more commanding position as to the price and terms of sale, primarily because real property offered for sale is in plentiful supply compared to demand.

By-Laws. Rules governing the operation of the business and affairs of a corporation in addition to the rules set forth in its charter or articles of incorporation.

C

CalVet Loan. A loan made under the California Veterans Farm and Home Purchase Program as an aid to veterans in purchasing a home or farm at low financing costs.

CCIM. Certified Commercial Investment Member.

CC&Rs. Covenants, conditions, and restrictions.

Capacity. Legal qualification for entering into a contract; being capable.

Capital. Any form of wealth, whether money or other property, employed or capable of being employed in the production of more wealth.

Capital Assets. Assets of a permanent nature used in the production of income, such as land, buildings, machinery, and equipment. Under income tax law, it is usually distinguishable from inventory, which comprises assets held for sale to customers in the ordinary course of trade or business.

Capital Gains. Gains on the sale of property; under the income tax law there are tax advantages in long-term capital gains, i.e., gains on the sale of certain property held longer than a prescribed period of time.

Capitalization. In appraising, to determine the value of property by considering net income and the percentage of reasonable return on the investment.

Capitalization Rate (Cap Rate). The rate of interest which is considered a reasonable return on the investment, and used in the process of determining value based upon net income.

CAR. California Association of Realtors®.

Cash Basis. Method of recording income and expenses in which each item is entered as received or paid; distinguished from **Accrual Basis**.

Cash Flow. The measure of cash generated from income and depreciation after debt-servicing expenses.

Cause of Action. The basis for bringing a lawsuit; a ground for legal action; the matter over which a person goes to court. The party filing an action is the Plaintiff, who sets forth his or her cause of action in a pleading called a complaint.

Caveat Emptor. "Let the buyer beware." Usually, when a buyer examines the goods or property sold, he buys at his or her own risk, in the absence of misrepresentations.

Certificate of Eligibility. Certificate issued by the government evidencing an individual's eligibility to obtain a Veterans Administration (VA) loan.

Certificate of Reasonable Value. Certificate which informs a veteran under VA loan of the appraised value of the property and the maximum VA guaranteed loan a private lender may make.

Certificate of Sale. A certificate issued to the purchaser at a judicial sale, such as an execution sale. After the time for redemption has expired, the holder of the certificate is entitled to a deed.

Certificate of Taxes Due. A written statement in the form of a guaranty of the condition of the taxes on a particular property made by the County Treasurer of the County where the property is located.

Certificate of Title. A certification as to the ownership of land and the condition of title, based on an examination of the public records.

Chain. A unit of measurement used by surveyors; consists of 100 links equal to 66 feet.

Chain of Title. A chronological list of recorded instruments affecting the title to land, commencing with the document under which title was transferred from the government to private ownership, and ending with the latest document transferring title. In order to have marketable title, there must be an unbroken chain of title.

Change, Principle of. Holds that it is the future, not the past, which is of prime importance in estimating value. Change is largely the result of cause and effect.

Chattel. Personal property.

Chattel Mortgage. A mortgage of personal property to secure payment of a debt. Since the adoption of the Uniform Commercial Code, chattel mortgages are referred to as Personal Property Security Agreements.

Chattel Real. An interest in real estate less than a freehold, such as an estate for years.

Circuit Breaker. (1) An electrical device which automatically interrupts an electrical circuit when an overload occurs; may be used instead of a fuse to protect each circuit and can be reset. (2) In property taxation, a method for granting property tax relief to the elderly and disadvantaged qualified taxpayers by rebate, tax credits, or cash payments; usually limited to homeowners and renters.

Civil Action. A court action involving the civil law and private rights of parties, rather than the criminal law.

Civil Law. A body of law that is derived from the Roman system of law, rather than the common law of England. Often called **Statutory Law** in this country.

Civil Rights. Basic rights of freedom and liberty guaranteed to United States citizens by the 13th and 14th Amendments to the Federal Constitution and by later federal laws.

Civil Suit. A lawsuit in which a private party sues another private party.

Client. A real estate broker's client may be a seller or a buyer, landlord or tenant.

Closing. (1) Process by which all the parties to a real estate transaction conclude the details of a sale or mortgage. The process includes the signing and transfer of documents and distribution of funds. (2) Condition in description of real property by courses and distances at the boundary lines where the lines meet to include all the tract of land.

Closing Costs. The numerous expenses buyers and sellers normally incur in the transfer of ownership of real property.

Closing Statement. Statement furnished by an escrow holder to the principals at the time of closing an escrow, setting forth the charges and costs.

Cloud on Title. Any conditions revealed by a search of title, such as an ancient pipeline easement, which affect the marketability of title to property. Although sometimes seemingly unimportant, there may be a need to remove them by either a quitclaim deed or a court decree.

CLTA (California Land Title Association). The trade association of title insurance companies in California.

Code. A system of law. In California most of the statutes have been codified in a series of codes, such as the Civil Code and the Business and Professions Code.

Code of Ethics. A set of rules and principles expressing a standard of accepted conduct for members of a professional group.

Collateral. Something additional, such as collateral security, i.e., a separate obligation attached to a contract to guarantee its performance; the property subject to the security interest; in estate matters, collateral means descended from the same stock but in different line, i.e., not lineal. Example: a cousin is a collateral relative.

Collateral Loan. A loan secured by collateral, i.e., something of value to give greater assurance of payment.

Collateral Security. A separate obligation attached to a contract to guarantee its performance; the transfer of something of value to insure the performance of a principal agreement.

Collusion. An agreement between two or more persons to defraud another of his or her rights by going through the forms of the law, or to obtain an object that is forbidden by law, such as obtaining the property of a client by devious means.

Color of Title. That which gives the appearance of good title but is not title, in fact, because of some defect, such as an erroneous or insufficient legal description.

Commercial Acre. A term applied to the remainder of an acre of subdivided land after the area devoted to streets, sidewalks, curbs, etc., has been deducted from the acre.

Commercial Loan. A personal loan from a commercial bank, usually unsecured and for a short term, for other than mortgage purposes.

Commercial Paper. Drafts, notes, and bills of exchange used in commercial transactions.

Commingling. Unauthorized mixing of funds of a customer or client with one's own personal funds.

Commission. An agent's compensation for performing the duties of his agency. In real estate practice, commission represents a percentage of the selling price of the property, such as 6 percent, or a percentage of rentals collected, etc.

Commissioner. The legislature has created various commissioners, such as the Real Estate Commissioner and the Corporations Commissioner, to carry out the responsibilities of various state agencies, including the enforcement of the law.

Commitment. A pledge, promise, or firm agreement to perform an act, such as commitment to make a loan.

Common Area. An entire common interest subdivision except the separate interests therein.

Common Interest Subdivision. Subdivided lands which include a separate interest in real property combined with an interest in common with other owners. The interest in common may be through membership in an association. Examples: condominiums and stock cooperatives.

Common Law. Body of unwritten law, founded upon general custom, usage, or common consent, that developed in England "since the memory of man runneth not to the contrary." Prevails in England and most of the United States; sometimes referred to as **Case Law** in this country.

Common Stock. That class of corporate stock to which there is ordinarily attached no preference with respect to the receipt of dividends or the distribution of assets upon corporate dissolution.

Community Property. Property acquired by husband or wife or both during marriage when not acquired as separate property. Basically, property of a married person in California is either separate property or community property.

Co-Mortgagor. Someone who accepts responsibility for the repayment of a loan along with the primary borrower to help the borrower qualify for the loan.

Compaction. Whenever extra soil is added to a lot to fill in low places or to raise the level of the lot, the added soil is often too loose and soft to sustain the weight of improvements. Accordingly, it is necessary to compact the added soil by pounding it with appropriate tools so that it will carry the added weight of buildings without the danger of their tilting, settling or cracking.

Comparable Sales. Sales which have similar characteristics as the subject property and are used for analysis in the appraisal process. Commonly called comparables, they are recent selling prices of properties similarly situated in a similar market.

Comparison Approach. A real estate comparison method, which compares a given property with similar or comparable surrounding properties to determine value.

Competent. Legally qualified.

Competition, Principle of. Holds that profits tend to breed competition, and excess profits tend to breed ruinous competition.

Competitive Market Analysis. A comparison of homes that are similar in location, style, and amenities to the subject property in order to arrive at a realistic listing price. Similar to the sales comparison approach to value.

Compliance Inspection. A building inspection to determine whether building codes, specification, or conditions established after a previous inspection have been met before the loan may be made.

Component. One of the features making up the whole property.

Compound Interest. Interest paid on original principal and also on the accrued and unpaid interest which has accumulated.

Conclusion. The final estimate of value, realized from facts, data, experience, and judgment, set out in an appraisal. Appraiser's certified conclusion.

Condemnation. The exercise of the power of eminent domain, i.e., the taking of property for a public use upon payment of just compensation; also refers to condemnation of unsafe structures under the government's police power.

Condition. A qualification annexed to an estate upon the happening of which the estate is enlarged or defeated. It may be a condition precedent, which is a condition which must be fulfilled before an estate can vest. Or it may be a condition subsequent, which is a condition by the failure or nonperformance of which an estate already vested may be defeated.

Conditional. Not absolute, depending on a condition; made or allowed on certain terms.

Conditional Commitment. A commitment by an FHA lender of a definite loan amount on a specified property for some unknown purchaser of satisfactory credit standing.

Conditional Sales Contract. A contract for the sale of property where title remains in the seller until the conditions of the contract have been performed by the buyer.

Conditional Use Permit. Permitting a use of a parcel of property in contravention of zoning upon a finding that the permitted use is essential or desirable to the public convenience or welfare and is in harmony with the objectives of the master plan. Various conditions are imposed in granting such use permit.

Condominium. Ownership of a divided interest; i.e., an individually owned unit, in a multifamily or other structure, combined with joint ownership of the structure and the land. Sometimes referred to as a "horizontal" subdivision; involves both a vertical and a horizontal division.

Confirmation of Sale. Court approval of the sale of property by an executor, administrator, guardian, or conservator.

Conformity, Principle of. Holds that the maximum of value is realized when a reasonable degree of homogeneity of improvement is present.

Consent. To permit, approve, or agree.

Conservation. The process of utilizing resources in such a manner which minimizes their depletion.

Conservator. A person appointed by the probate court to take care of the person or property of an adult person needing such care; similar to a guardian.

Consideration. The inducement for entering into a contract; consists of either a benefit to the promisor, or a loss or detriment to the promisee. Anything of value given to induce entering into a contract. It may be money, personal services, or, in some cases, even love and affection.

Construction Loans. Loans, usually short term, made by a lender for the purpose of constructing homes or commercial buildings; funds are disbursed by the lender in stages after periodic inspections.

Constructive Notice. Notice given by the public records of a claim of ownership or interest in property. Generally, the law presumes that a person has the same knowledge of instruments properly recorded as if he or she were actually acquainted with them. The word "constructive" is frequently encountered in real estate. For instance, constructive eviction is applicable in the landlord-tenant relationship. Constructive possession may be involved in a claim of title based on adverse possession. And in the field of trusts, the courts may establish a constructive trust in property. Fraud also may be constructive or actual.

Consumer Goods. Goods used or bought for use primarily for personal, family, or household purposes. The term is used in the Commercial Code in connection with personal-property security agreements.

Contiguous. Adjoining or touching upon, such as contiguous parcels of land.

Contingent. Dependent upon an uncertain future event.

Constant. The percentage which, when applied directly to the face value of a debt, develops the annual amount of money necessary to pay a specified net rate of interest on the reducing balance and to liquidate the debt in a specified time period. Example: a 6% loan with a 20-year amortization has a constant of approximately 8.5%. Thus, a $10,000 loan amortized over 20 years requires an annual payment of approximately $850.00.

Constructive Fraud. A breach of duty, as by a person in a fiduciary capacity, without an actual fraudulent intent, which gains an advantage to the person at fault by misleading another to the other's prejudice. Any act of omission declared by law to be fraudulent, without respect to actual fraud.

Contract. An agreement by which a person undertakes or promises to do, or not to do, a certain thing; must be supported by **Consideration** to be enforceable.

Contract, Unilateral. A contract where the offeror promises to perform is and when the other party performs. The other party does not promise to perform and is only compensated upon performance of the required act.

Contract, Void. A contract that is not enforceable because of lack of a required element such as consideration.

Contract, Voidable. A contract that can be disaffirm without liability because of lack of capacity.

Contribution, Principle of. A component part of a property is valued in proportion to its contribution to the value of the whole. Holds that maximum values are achieved when the improvements on a site produce the highest (net) return, commensurate with the investment.

Conventional Loan. A mortgage loan which is not insured or guaranteed by a governmental agency, such as the FHA or VA.

Conversion. Change from one character or use to another; the unauthorized appropriation by a person of property belonging to another.

Conveyance. A written instrument transferring the title to land or an interest therein from one person to another.

Co-op. Community apartment projects owned as "stock cooperatives," where individual owners each acquire a share of stock in the corporation which owns the title, with each person owning the exclusive right to occupy a particular apartment.

Cooperative Sale. - A sale in which the buyer and the seller ware represented by agents working with different brokers.

Corner Influence. The increase in value of a corner lot due to its location.

Corporation. An artificial being, created by law, and possessing certain rights, privileges, and duties of natural persons. A corporation may acquire title to real property in its corporate name.

Corporation Sole. A corporation consisting of one person only and his successors in office, and incorporated by law in order to give some legal capacity not otherwise owned, such as ownership of property in perpetuity. Example: the Roman Catholic Archbishop of Los Angeles, who may acquire title to real property on behalf of the church in his name as a corporation sole.

Correction Lines. A system for compensating inaccuracies in the Government Rectangular Survey System due to the curvature of the earth.

Correlation. A step in the appraisal process involving the interpretation of data derived from the three approaches to value, leading to a single determination of value. Also referred to as **Reconciliation**.

Correspondent. An abbreviated term meaning mortgage loan correspondent. A mortgage banker who services mortgage loans as agent for the owner of the mortgage or investor. Also applied to the mortgage banker in his or her role as originator of mortgage loans for the investor.

Co-signer. A second party who signs a promissory note together with the promissory obligor (borrower).

Cost Approach. One of three methods in the appraisal process; an analysis in which a value estimate of a property is derived by estimating the replacement cost of the improvements, deducting them from the estimated accrued depreciation, then adding the market value of the land.

Cost Basis. A property value determined at the time of acquisition. The amount is dependent upon the method of acquisition, and subsequently serves as a base figure in determining profit or loss for income tax purposes.

Cost, New. Represents the present construction costs of a new building, including labor, material, and other expenditures.

Cost, Replacement. In appraisal, the current cost of constructing a building with the same utility as the subject property using modern materials and construction methods.

Counter Offer. A response to a contract, changing some of the terms of the original offer.

County. A political division of the state. There are 58 counties in California, each with a county recorder, tax collector, courthouse, and many other offices.

Covenants. Agreements contained in deeds and other instruments for the performance or nonperformance of certain acts, or the use or nonuse of property in a certain manner. Basically, a covenant is a promise to do or not to do a certain thing.

CPM (Certified Property Manager). A member of the Institute of Real Property Management of the NAR®.

Crawl Hole. Exterior or interior opening permitting access underneath a building, ordinarily required by building codes.

CRE (Counselor of Real Estate). Member of American Society of Real Estate Counselors.

Credit. A bookkeeping entry on the right side of an account, recording the reduction or elimination of an asset or an expense, or the creation of or addition to a liability or item of equity or revenue.

Creditor. A person to whom a debt is owed; any person extending credit to another person.

Creditor, Secured. A creditor with a security interest in something of value. If the debt is not repaid as per the contract, the creditor can repossess the property or foreclose in the case of real property.

CRV (Certificate of Reasonable Value). Used in connection with GI loans.

Cul-de-sac. A street, lane, or road closed at one end; a blind alley.

Curable Depreciation. Items of physical deterioration and functional obsolescence which are customarily repaired or replaced by a prudent property owner.

Current Index. With regard to an adjustable rate mortgage (ARM), the current value of a recognized index as calculated and published nationally or regionally. The current index value changes periodically and is used in calculating the new note rate as of each rate adjustment date.

Custodial Accounts. Bank accounts used for deposits of funds belonging to others.

Customer. Regarding real estate, a prospective buyer.

Cyclical Movement. The sequential and recurring changes in economic activity of a business cycle, moving from prosperity through recession, depression, recovery, and back again to prosperity.

D

Damages. The amount recoverable by a victim of the wrongful or negligent act of another.

Damages, Compensatory. Damages awarded to a plaintiff as compensation for injuries (financial, property damage, personal injuries) caused by the defendant acts or lack of.

Data Plant. An appraiser's file of information on real estate.

DBA (Doing Business As). Applicable where a person engages in business under a fictitious name, such as "John Smith, doing business as the Acme Building Company."

Debenture. Bonds issued without security; an obligation not secured by a specific lien on property.

Debit. A bookkeeping entry on the left side of an account; opposite of credit.

Debt. That which is due from one person to another; obligation; liability.

Debtor. A party owing money to another. Under the Uniform Commercial Code, the debtor is the party who "owns" the property subject to a security agreement, where previously this person was referred to as the mortgagor or pledgor.

Debt Service. The amount needed to make a periodic payment of principal and interest on an amortized loan.

Declaration of Homestead. The document which is recorded in order to obtain an exemption from forced sale of a person's home in satisfaction of certain types of creditors' claims.

Declining Balance Depreciation. A method of accelerated depreciation allowed by the IRS in certain circumstances. **Double Declining Balance Depreciation** is its most common form and is computed by using double the rate used for straight-line depreciation.

Decree of Distribution. An order of the probate court by which property of a decedent is distributed to his heirs or devisees.

Decree of Foreclosure. Decree by a court ordering the sale of mortgaged property and the payment of the debt owing to the lender out of the proceeds.

Dedication. A setting apart or donation of land by its owner for a public use. The dedication may be of the fee, perhaps for a park, or of an easement, such as a roadway.

Deed. Written instrument by which the ownership of real property is transferred from one person to another.

Deed in Lieu of Foreclosure. A deed to real property accepted by a lender from a defaulting borrower to avoid the necessity of foreclosure proceedings by the lender.

Deed of Trust. Written instrument by which title to real property is transferred to a third party trustee as security for a debt or other obligation owed to another person. Used in place of mortgages in many states, including California. Also called **Trust Deed.**

Deed Restrictions. (See **Restriction.**)

Default. Failure to fulfill a duty or promise or to discharge an obligation; the omission or failure to perform any act.

Default Judgment. A judgment entered against a party who fails to make an appearance in the action.

Defeasance Clause. The clause in a mortgage that gives the mortgagor the right to redeem mortgagor's property upon the payment of mortgagor's obligations to the mortgagee.

Defeasance Fee. Sometimes called a base fee or qualified fee. A fee simple absolute interest in land that is capable of being defeated or terminated upon the happening of a specified event.

Defendant. The party against whom a court action is brought.

Deferred Maintenance. Existing but unfulfilled requirements for repairs and rehabilitation of property.

Deferred Payment Options. The privilege of deferring income payments to take advantage of statutes affording tax benefits.

Deficiency Judgment. A personal judgment in a lien foreclosure action for the amount of the debt still remaining due after a sale of the security.

Delegation of Powers. The conferring by an agent upon another of all or certain of the powers that have been conferred upon the agent by the principal.

Delivery. Giving possession of a document, such as a deed, by one party (the grantor) to the other (the grantee) with the intent to convey title.

Deposit Receipt. Document used when accepting "earnest money" to bind an offer for property by a prospective purchaser; when properly filled out and executed by both parties, it may result in a binding contract. In California, more commonly referred to as a **Purchase Contract** by real estate professionals.

Depreciation. Loss of value in real property brought about by age, physical deterioration, functional or economic obsolescence, or any other cause.

Depth Table. A statistical table that may be used to estimate the value of the added depth of a lot.

Desist and Refrain Order. An order, which the Real Estate Commissioner is empowered by law to issue, directing a person to desist and refrain from committing acts in violation of the Real Estate Law.

Deterioration. Impairment of the condition or utility of property, brought about by wear and tear, disintegration, use in service, or the action of the elements. One of the causes of depreciation and reflecting loss in value.

Determinable Fee. An estate which will end on the happening of an event, which may or may not occur.

Devise. A gift of real property by will.

Devisee. One who receives real property by will.

Devisor. One who disposes of real property by will.

Directional Growth. The location or direction toward which the residental sections of a city are destined, or determined, to go.

Disclosure Statement. Statement required under the federal Truth in Lending Act, which sets forth the details of a loan transaction, including all finance charges.

Discount. To sell at a reduced price; to purchase or sell a note before maturity at a reduction based on the interest for the time it still has to run, or for market reasons.

Discount Points. The amount of money the borrower or seller must pay the lender to get a mortgage at a stated rate. This amount is equal to the difference between the principal balance on the note and the lesser amount which a purchaser of the note would pay the original lender for it under market conditions. **A point equals one percent of the loan**.

Divided Interest. Ownership of a particular piece or portion of a larger parcel of real property, such as a condominium; distinguished from an undivided interest.

Dividend. A sum of money paid to shareholders of a corporation out of earnings; also, anything received as a bonus or reward. In mathematics, the number divided by the divisor.

Document. An original or official paper relied upon as the basis, proof, or support of anything else. A more comprehensive word than instrument.

Documentary Transfer Tax. Counties are authorized to impose a documentary transfer tax to apply on transfers of real property located in the county; collected at the time of recording the document.

Dominant Tenement. The tenement (property) obtaining the benefit of an appurtenant easement.

Donee. A person to whom a gift is made.

Donor. A person who makes a gift to another.

Dual Agency. An agency relationship in which one agent acts concurrently for both of the principals in a transaction.

Due-on-Sale Clause. An acceleration clause granting the lender the right to demand full payment of the mortgage or trust deed upon a sale of the property. Also called an **Alienation Clause**.

Duress. Unlawful constraint or coercion, such as a threat of bodily harm, exercised upon a person, whereby he or she is persuaded to do some act against his or her will. Renders invalid a contract or other act entered into or performed under its influence.

DVA (Department of Veterans Affairs). The state agency that administers the California Veterans Farm and Home Purchase Program (CalVet loans).

E

Earnest Money. Something given as a part of the purchase price to bind a bargain.

Easement. A right, privilege or interest in the land of another existing apart from the ownership of the land, such as a right of way (a right to cross over another person's property). (See **Prescriptive Easement**.)

Easement by Implication. An easement that is implied or inferred from conduct or circumstances rather than being expressed.

Economic Life. The period during which a property will yield a sufficient return on the investment to justify maintaining it.

Economic Obsolescence. A loss in value due to factors not part of the subject property but adversely affecting the value of the subject property.

Economic Rent. The reasonable rental expectancy if the property were available for renting at the time of its valuation.

Effective Age of Improvement. The number of years of age that is indicated by the condition of the structure. Distinct from **Chronological Age**.

Effective Date of Value. The specific day the conclusion of value applies.

Effective Interest Rate. The percentage of interest that is actually being paid by the borrower for the use of the money. Distinct from **Nominal Interest**.

Egress. A means, or place, of going out.

Emblements. Crops produced annually, by labor and industry, as distinguished from crops that grow naturally on the land.

Eminent Domain. The power of the government to take property for a public purpose upon payment of just compensation.

Encroachment. The extension of an improvement or branch of a tree or other vegetation onto the property of another person.

Encumbrance. A lien or charge or burden on land (also spelled **"Incumbrance"**).

Endorsement. A writing on a negotiable instrument, such as a note, by which the instrument is transferred; a provision or rider added to an insurance policy to alter or enlarge the terms of the insurance contract. (Sometimes spelled **"Indorsement."**)

Enjoin. To prohibit or restrain by an injunction.

Equitable Title. Title of the purchaser under a contract of sale.

Equity. Value of an owner's interest in property in excess of mortgages and other liens; a system of jurisprudence or a body of doctrines and rules developed in England and followed in the United States, which series to supplement and remedy the limitations or inflexibility of the common law.

Equity Buildup. The increase of an owner's equity in property due to mortgage principal reduction and to value appreciation.

Equity of Redemption. The right which the mortgagor has of redeeming his or her property for a limited period of time after a foreclosure sale.

Equity Participation. A mortgage transaction in which the lender, in addition to receiving a fixed rate of interest on the loan, acquires an interest in the borrower's real property, and shares in the profits derived from the real property.

Erosion. The gradual wearing away of land by the action of the elements, such as tidal water or winds.

Escalator Clause. A clause in a contract providing for the upward or downward adjustment of specified items, such as interest or rent, to cover certain contingencies, such as higher or lower costs of living.

Escheat. Reverting of property to the state of California when an owner dies without a will and without heirs.

Escrow. The deposit of a deed or other instrument with a third party for delivery upon performance of a condition. Also, the transaction in which a third party acts as the agent for the buyer and seller or borrower and lender in carrying out the instructions of the parties and handling and disbursing the papers and funds. **Sales Escrow** is one relating to the sale of a parcel of property, as distinguished from a **Loan** or an **Exchange Escrow**.

Escrow Holder (Agent). The party who acts as the agent for the principals in an escrow transaction.

Estate. The degree, quantity, nature, and extent of the interest a person has in real estate, such as a fee or a life estate or lesser estate; refers to the property left by a decedent that is subject to probate administration, or the property of a bankrupt.

Estate at Sufferance. An estate arising when a tenant wrongfully holds over after the expiration of the term. The landlord has the choice of evicting the tenant (through court action) or accepting the tenant on the same terms and conditions of the previous occupancy.

Estate at Will. Occupation of lands and tenements by a tenant for an indefinite period of time; terminable by either party at any time on proper notice.

Estate for Life. An estate that continues for the duration of a person's natural life.

Estate for Years. An estate that continues for a specified period of time; usually created by a lease.

Estate From Period-to-Period. An interest in land where there is no definite termination date but the rental period is fixed at a certain sum per week, month, or year. Also called a **Periodic Tenancy**.

Estate of Inheritance. An estate which may descend to heirs, such as a fee estate.

Estimate. A preliminary opinion of value; to appraise; set a value.

Estimated Remaining Life. The period of time (usually years) it takes for the improvements to become valueless.

Estoppel. A doctrine which bars a person from asserting rights inconsistent with a previous position or representation.

Ethics. That branch of moral science, idealism, justness, and fairness concerned with the duties which a member of a profession or craft owes to the public, to his or her clients or patrons, and to fellow members of his or her profession or craft.

Eviction. Dispossession of a defaulting tenant or other person wrongfully in possession of property by bringing a court action.

Exception. In a deed, some part of a thing granted which is excluded from the conveyance and remains with the grantor. In zoning, it refers to an instance or case not conforming to the general rule.

Exchange. To transfer property for other property of equivalent value; to trade one parcel of property for another.

Exclusive Agency Listing. A written instrument giving one agent the right to sell property for a specified period of time but reserving the right of the owner to sell the property without payment of a commission.

Exclusive Right to Sell Listing. A written agreement between owner and agent giving the agent the right to collect a commission if the property is sold by anyone, including the owner, during the term of the agreement.

Execute. To sign a deed, or to perform or carry out a contract; to give effect or force to a law or decree of a court.

Executed. As used in contract law, this relates to a contract that has been fully performed.

Execution Sale. A sale of a judgment debtor's property by the sheriff to satisfy the judgment.

Executor. A person who is designated in a will as the representative of the decedent's estate.

Executory. As used in contract law, this relates to a contract that is yet to be performed.

Executrix. Feminine of executor.

Exemption. An immunity from some burden or obligation.

Expenses. Certain items which appear on a closing statement in connection with a real estate sale, chargeable to either buyer or seller.

Expressed. Something definitely stated rather than implied.

Extension Agreement. A grant of further time within which to pay an obligation.

F

Facade. Front of a building.

Fair Market Value. The highest price estimated in terms of money which a parcel of property will bring on the open market where neither buyer nor seller is under any compulsion to act.

False Pretenses. A deliberate misrepresentation of facts as a means of obtaining money or title to property.

Fannie Mae. See **Federal National Mortgage Association (FNMA)**.

Farmers Home Administration (FmHA). An agency of the Department of Agriculture. Primary responsibility is to provide financial assistance for farmers and others living in rural areas where financing is not available on reasonable terms from private sources.

Federal Deposit Insurance Corporation (FDIC). Agency of the federal government which insures deposits at commercial banks and savings banks.

Federal Home Loan Mortgage Corporation (FHLMC) "Freddie Mac." An independent stock company which creates a secondary market in conventional residential loans and in FHA and VA loans by purchasing mortgages. Now under conservatorship of the Federal Housing Finance Agency (FHFA).

Federal Housing Administration. (See **FHA**.)

Federal Housing Finance Agency (FHFA). Created in 2008 when the President signed into law the Housing and Economic Recovery Act of 2008. The Act created a world-class, empowered regulator with all of the authorities necessary to oversee vital components of our country's secondary mortgage markets – Fannie Mae, Freddie Mac, and the Federal Home Loan Banks.

Federal Land Bank System. Federal government agency making long-term loans to farmers.

Federal National Mortgage Association (FNMA) "Fannie Mae." A quasi-public agency converted into a private corporation, whose primary function is to buy and sell FHA and VA mortgages in the secondary market. Now under conservatorship of the Federal Housing Finance Agency (FHFA).

Federal Reserve System. The federal banking system of the United States under the control of a central board of governors (Federal Reserve Board) involving a central bank in each of twelve geographical districts with broad powers in controlling credit and the amount of money in circulation.

Fee. A charge for services, such as attorney's fees. See also **Fee Estate**.

Fee Estate. An estate of inheritance in real property, often referred to as a fee simple.

Fee Simple Absolute. The highest type of estate or interest a person may have in property. In modern usage, it expressly establishes the title to real property in the owner, without limitation or end. The owner may dispose of it by sale or trade or will as he or she chooses.

Fee Simple Defeasible. A fee estate that is subject to a qualification, condition, or limitation.

Fee Title. Ownership of a fee estate.

Feudal Tenure. A real property ownership system in which ownership rests with a sovereign who may grant lesser interests in return for service or loyalty. For contrast, see **Allodial Tenure**.

FHA (Federal Housing Administration). A federal agency, created by the National Housing Act of 1934, for the purpose of expanding and strengthening home ownership by making private mortgage financing possible on a longterm, low-down-payment basis. The vehicle is a mortgage insurance program, with premiums paid by the homeowner to protect lenders against loss of these higher-risk loans. Since 1965, FHA has been part of the Department of Housing and Urban Development (HUD).

FHA Insurance. An undertaking by FHA to insure the lender against loss arising from a default by borrower.

Fictitious Name. An assumed name; a name used for business which does not include the actual name of the owner, such as "Ace Lumber Company."

Fidelity Bond. A security posted for the discharge of an obligation of personal responsibility.

Fiduciary. One who holds a thing in trust for another person, or who acts in a trust capacity, such as an escrow holder.

Fiduciary Duty. That duty owed by an agent to act in the highest good faith toward the principal and not to obtain any advantage over the latter by the slightest misrepresentation, concealment, duress, or pressure.

Financial Intermediary. Financial institutions such as commercial banks, savings banks, mutual savings banks, and life insurance companies, which receive relatively small sums of money from the public and invest them in the form of large sums. A considerable portion of these funds are loaned on real estate.

Financing Process. The systematic five-step procedure followed by major institutional lenders in analyzing a proposed loan, which includes filing of application by a borrower, lender's analysis of borrower and property, processing of loan documentation, making the loan, and servicing (collection and record keeping).

Financing Statement. Evidence of a personal property security agreement that is filed or recorded to give public notice; replaced the term chattel mortgage (see **Security Agreement**).

First Mortgage. A legal document pledging collateral for a loan (see **Mortgage**) that has first priority over all other claims against the property except taxes and bonded indebtedness. A mortgage superior to any other.

First Trust Deed. A legal document pledging collateral for a loan (see **Trust Deed**) that has first priority over all other claims against the property, except taxes and bonded indebtedness. A trust deed superior to any other.

Fiscal Controls. Federal tax revenue and expenditure policies used to control the level of economic activity.

Fiscal Year. A business or accounting year as distinguished from a calendar year.

Fixity of Location. The physical characteristic of real estate that subjects it to the influence of its surroundings.

Fixture. A thing that was originally personal property but that has become attached to and is considered as part of the real property.

Flat Rental. Form of lease that provides a level or fixed amount of rent, as opposed to a variable amount.

FNMA (Federal National Mortgage Association). Popularly known as Fannie Mae.

Foreclosure. A proceeding to enforce a lien by a sale of the property in order to satisfy the debt.

Forfeiture. A loss of some right, title, estate, or interest in consequence of a default or failure to perform. Not readily enforceable, since the courts abhor a forfeiture. Liquidated damage clauses frequently have replaced forfeiture clauses in contracts of sale.

Franchise. A right or privilege conferred by law to carry on a business activity in a specified area, such as a franchise for a street railway; also, the permission granted by a manufacturer to a distributor or retailer to sell or service the manufacturer's product in a particular area or locale.

Fraud. The intentional and successful employment of any cunning, deception, collusion, or artifice, used to circumvent, cheat or deceive another person, whereby that person acts upon it to the loss of property and to legal injury. (**Actual Fraud:** A deliberate misrepresentation or representation made in reckless disregard of its truth or its falsity, the suppression of truth, a promise made without the intention to perform it, or any other act intended to deceive.)

Freddie Mac. See **Federal Home Loan Mortgage Corporation (FHLMC)**.

Freehold. An estate of inheritance or for life.

Frontage. A term used to describe or identify that part of a parcel of land or an improvement on the land which faces a street. The term is also used to refer to the lineal extent of the land or improvement that is parallel to and facing the street, e.g., a 75-foot frontage.

Front Foot. A method of property measurement for purposes of sale or valuation, usually of commercial property. The property is measured by the front foot on its street line or boundary and valued at so much a front foot.

Front Money. The minimum amount of money necessary to initiate a real estate venture, and get the transaction underway.

Full Reconveyance. A release of all the property covered by a deed of trust.

Full Release. A complete release of liability under a contract or other obligation.

Fully Indexed Note Rate. As related to adjustable rate mortgages, the index value at the time of application plus the gross margin stated in the note.

Functional Obsolescence. Loss of value of a structure due to adverse factors from within it, which affect its utility, such as old age, poor design, or faulty equipment.

Future Benefits. The anticipated benefits the present owner will receive from the property in the future.

G

Gain. A profit, benefit, or value increase.

Garnishment. A statutory proceeding whereby property, money, or credits of a debtor in possession of another are seized and applied to payment of the debt.

General Lien. A lien on all the property of a debtor.

General Plan Restrictions. Restrictions on the use of property imposed for the benefit of more than one parcel of property, usually a tract containing many lots.

GI Loan. Loans available to veterans of the armed services under a federal government program administered by the Department of Veterans Affairs.

Gift Deed. A deed where there is no material consideration; often given in consideration of "love and affection," especially between relatives.

GNMA (Government National Mortgage Association). Popularly known (for its initials) as Ginnie Mae. An agency of HUD, which functions in the secondary mortgage market, primarily in special housing programs.

Goodwill. An intangible, salable asset arising from the reputation of a business and its relations with its customers, distinct from the value of its stock in trade and other tangibles.

Government Survey. A method of specifying the location of parcels of land using prime meridians, base lines, standard parallels, guide meridians, townships, and sections.

Grade. Ground level at the foundation of a building.

Graduated Lease. A lease which provides for a varying rental rate, often based upon future determination, such as periodical appraisals; used mostly in long-term leases.

Graduated Payment Mortgage. Provides for partially deferred payments of principal at start of loan. There are a variety of plans; usually after the first five years of the loan term the principal and interest payments are substantially higher, to make up the principal portion of payments lost at the beginning of the loan. (See **Variable Interest Rate**.)

Grant. A transfer of real property by deed.

Grant Deed. A form of deed used in the transfer of real property; distinguished from a quitclaim deed.

Grantee. The person to whom a grant is made.

Grantor. The person who makes a grant.

Gratuitous Agent. A person not paid by the principal for services on behalf of the principal, who cannot be forced to act as an agent, but who becomes bound to act in good faith and obey a principal's instructions once he or she undertakes to act as an agent.

GRI. Graduate, Realtors® Institute.

Gross Income. Total income from property before any expenses are deducted.

Gross Margin. With regard to an adjustable rate mortgage, an amount expressed as percentage points, stated in the note which is added to the current index value on the rate adjustment date to establish the new note rate.

Gross National Product (GNP). The total value of all goods and services produced in an economy during a given period of time.

Gross Profit. What is left after a business pays all its bills excluding taxes. (See **Net Profit**.)

Gross Rate. A method of collecting interest by adding total interest to the principal of the loan at the outset of the term.

Gross Rent Multiplier. A number which, times the gross income of a property, produces an estimate of value of the property. Example: The gross income from an unfurnished apartment building is $200,000 per annum. If an appraiser uses a gross multiplier of seven percent, then it is said that, based on the gross multiplier, the value of the building is $1,400,000.

Gross Rental. Form of lease or rental arrangement in which the lessor/landlord pays out all expenses.

Ground Lease. An agreement for the rental of the land only; sometimes secured by improvements placed on the land by the tenant.

Ground Rent. Earnings of improved property credited to earnings of the ground itself after allowance is made for earnings of the improvements; often termed economic rent.

Guarantee. An assurance or undertaking as to the performance or quality or accuracy of a product.

Guaranty. A promise to answer for the payment of another person's debt or obligation.

H

Habendum. That clause in a deed which states, "to have and to hold to said grantee, his heirs, successors, and assigns, forever." Not required in California.

Hard Money Loan. Loan from a private lender through an intermediary; actual money loaned, secured by a trust deed, as distinguished from a purchase money trust deed in favor of a seller.

Hazard Insurance. Insurance of property against such risks as fire, wind, floods, etc.

Heirs. The persons designated by law to succeed to the estate of a decedent who leaves no will.

Highest and Best Use. An appraisal term meaning that type of use which will produce the greatest return to the land and improvements over a given period of time.

Holder in Due Course. A phrase encountered under the Negotiable Instrument Law; refers to a person who has taken a promissory note, check, or bill of exchange in due course before the due date, in good faith and for value, and without knowledge of any defects.

Holdover Tenant. Tenant who remains in possession of leased property after the expiration of the lease term.

Holographic Will. A will entirely written, dated, and signed by the testator in his own handwriting.

Homestead. A home upon which the owner has recorded a Declaration of Homestead under California law, which affords protection from creditors' claims up to a specified amount. Exemption may also be claimed in an action for money without recording a Declaration of Homestead under prescribed conditions. Also, under federal law, the limited right to claim a small tract of the public domain by establishing residence or making improvement on the land. The latter is sometimes referred to as a "jackrabbit homestead."

Housing Financial Discrimination Act of 1977. California Health and Safety Code Section 35800, et seq., designed primarily to eliminate discrimination in lending practices based upon the character of the neighborhood in which real property is located. (See **Redlining**).

HUD (Housing and Urban Development). An agency of the federal government.

Hundred Percent Location. A city retail business location which is considered the best available for attracting business.

Hypothecate. To give a thing as security without parting with possession.

I-J

Imperative Necessity. Circumstances under which an agent has expanded authority in an emergency, including the power to disobey instructions where it is clearly in the interests of the principal and where there is no time to obtain instructions from the principal.

Implied. Presumed or inferred, rather than expressed.

Impound Accounts. Funds retained in a special account by a secured lender to cover such items as taxes and hazard insurance on the property.

Improvement(s). Buildings and other structures on real property; a valuable addition made to the land.

Income Approach (Capitalization). One of the three methods of the appraisal process generally applied to income producing property. It involves a three-step process: (1) find net annual income, (2) set an appropriate capitalization rate or "present worth" factor, and (3) capitalize the income dividing the net income by the capitalization rate.

Income Tax. A tax imposed on gross income from a business or enterprise. Income tax laws (both federal and state) also apply to gains on real estate sales, and deductions are allowed for losses on such sales.

Incompetent. Unable to manage or incapable of managing one's own affairs, based on such factors as minority, illness, old age, insanity, etc.

Increment. An increase; most frequently used to refer to the increased value of land based on population growth and increasing wealth in the community. The term "unearned increment" is used in this connection, since values supposedly increase without effort on the part of the owner.

Incumbrance. (See **Encumbrance**.)

Indenture. Deeds or other instruments that are executed by both parties.

Independent Contractor. A person who acts for another but who sells final results and whose methods of achieving those results are not subject to the control of another.

Indorsement. (See **Endorsement**.)

Ingress. A means or way of entering onto property.

Inheritance. Property passing at the owner's death to his or her heirs; i.e., those entitled by law to succeed to the owner's estate.

Initial Note Rate. With regard to an adjustable rate mortgage, the note rate upon origination. This rate may differ from the fully indexed note rate.

Initial Rate Discount. As applies to an adjustable rate mortgage, the index value at the time of loan application, plus the margin, less the initial note rate.

Injunction. An order of a court of equity prohibiting some act, or compelling an act to be done.

In Propria Persona. "In his own person"; by himself, as in an action where the party acts as his or her own attorney (abbreviated as "pro per").

Input. Data, information, etc., that is fed into a computer or other system.

Installment Note. A promissory note providing for payment of the principal in two or more certain amounts at stated or periodic times.

Installment Reporting. A method of reporting capital gains, by installments for successive tax years, to minimize the impact of the totality of the capital gains tax in the year of the sale.

Installment Sales Contract. Commonly called "contract of sale" or **Land Contract**. Purchase of real estate wherein the purchase price is paid in installments over a long period of time, title is retained by seller, and upon default by buyer (vendee) the payments may be forfeited.

Institutional Lenders. A financial intermediary or depository, such as a savings and loan association, commercial bank, or life insurance company, which pools money of its depositors and then invests funds in various ways, including trust deed and mortgage loans.

Instrument. A writing, such as a deed, made and executed as the expression of some act, contract, or proceeding.

Insurance. Coverage by contract in which one party (the insurer) agrees to indemnify or reimburse another (the insured) for any loss or damage that may occur under the terms of the contract.

Intangible. Incapable of being perceived by the senses, as incorporeal or immaterial things; also, existing only in connection with something else, such as an intangible asset in the form of the good will of a business.

Interest. A share, right, or title in the ownership of land or the degree thereof; also, a sum paid or charged for the use of money.

Interest Rate. The percentage of a sum of money charged for its use.

Interim Loan. A short-term, temporary loan used until permanent financing is available, e.g., a construction loan.

Intermediation. The process of pooling and supplying funds for investment by financial institutions called intermediaries. The process is dependent on individual savers placing their funds with these institutions and foregoing opportunities to directly invest in the investments selected.

Interpleader. An action brought by a third party (such as an escrow holder) in order to determine conflicting rights between two or more other parties (such as the principals to the escrow).

Interval Ownership. A form of timeshare ownership. (See **Timeshare Estate**.)

Intestate. Without a will; a person who died without leaving a will.

Involuntary Lien. A lien not voluntarily created by the debtor, such as a judgment lien.

Irrevocable. Incapable of being recalled, revoked, or withdrawn; unchangeable.

Jarvis-Gann Initiative. (See **Proposition 13**.)

Joint Note. A note signed by two or more persons who have equal liability for payment.

Joint Tenancy. Title held by two or more persons in equal shares with right of survivorship, i.e., when one joint tenant dies, his interest vests in the surviving joint tenant or tenants.

Joint Venture. Two or more individuals or firms joining together on a single project as partners.

Judgment. The final determination by a court having jurisdiction over the parties and subject matter of the action, of a matter presented to it for decision.

Judgment Lien. A statutory lien created by recording an abstract or certified copy of a judgment for money in the county recorder's office.

Junior Lien. A subordinate or inferior lien; behind another lien.

Junior Mortgage. A mortgage recorded subsequently to another mortgage on the same property or made subordinate by agreement to a later-recorded mortgage.

Jurisdiction. The power of a court to hear and determine a matter.

K-L

Key Lot. A lot so located that one side adjoins the rear of another lot; usually near a corner and considered less desirable.

Land. The solid material of the earth and anything affixed permanently to it, including buildings, trees, minerals, water flowing on the land or beneath it, and air space above it.

Land and Improvement Loan. A loan obtained by the builder-developer for the purchase of land and to cover expenses for subdividing.

Land Contract. A contract often used when property is sold on a small down payment where the seller does not choose to convey legal title until all or a certain portion of the purchase price has been paid by the buyer; also referred to as a **Land Sales Contract**.

Landlocked. Shut in completely by adjoining land without a means of access to or from a public highway or road.

Landlord. An owner of real property who leases it to a third party, called the lessee or tenant.

Late Charge. A charge assessed by a lender against a borrower failing to make loan installment payments when due.

Latent. Hidden from view; concealed, such as a latent ambiguity in a document; distinguished from **Patent**.

Lateral Support. The support which the soil of an adjoining owner gives to a neighbor's land.

Lawful Object. Allowed or permitted by law; one of the requisites of a valid contract.

Lease. A contract for the possession of land for a designated period of time in consideration of payment of rent.

Leasehold Estate. A tenant's right to occupy real estate during the term of the lease. This is a personal property interest.

Legacy. A gift of money or other personal property by will.

Legal Description. A description satisfactory in law, i.e., one by which property can be definitely located on the ground by reference to a recorded map or government survey.

Lessee. The tenant under a lease.

Lessor. The landlord under a lease, i.e., the person who transfers the right to occupy property to another person by a lease.

Level-Payment Mortgage. A loan on real estate that is paid off by making a series of equal (or nearly equal) regular payments. Part of the payment is usually interest on the loan and part of it reduces the amount of the unpaid principal balance of the loan. Also, sometimes called an **Amortized Mortgage** or **Installment Mortgage**.

Leverage. Use of borrowed funds to purchase property in anticipation of substantial increase in value of the property; may produce a high return on a low down payment.

Levy. A seizure of property by judicial process, such as a levy under a writ of execution; a property tax is also a levy (collection of an assessment) under authority of law for governmental purposes.

Liability Insurance. Insurance covering the insured person against loss arising from injury or damage to another person or to property.

License. A personal privilege to enter upon or do some act on the land of another; also, authorization to engage in a business, an activity, or profession.

Licensee. A person to whom a license is issued or granted. In real estate, a person who has completed the requirements (including passing the examination) for a broker's or salesperson's license.

Lien. A charge upon property for the payment of a debt or performance of an obligation; a form of encumbrance. Liens include taxes, special assessments, and judgments, as well as mortgages. Additionally, there are mechanics' and material-men's liens for furnishing labor or materials to a work of improvement.

Life Estate. An estate in real property measured by the life of a natural person.

Limitations, Statute of. The commonly used identifying term for various statutes, which require that a legal action be commenced within a prescribed time after the accrual of the right to seek legal relief.

Limited Partnership. A partnership composed of one or more general partners and one or more limited partners. The contribution and liability of the latter are limited.

Lineal. In a direct line, such as a lineal descendant.

Linear. Involving measurement in one dimension only; pertaining to length, such as a linear measure, i.e., a foot, a yard, a meter, etc.

Liquidated Damages. Damages in an ascertained amount that may be recovered in a lawsuit.

Liquidated Damages Clause. A clause in a contract by which the parties, by agreement, fix the damages in advance for a breach of the contract.

Liquidity. Holdings in or the ability to convert assets to cash or its equivalent. The ease with which a person is able to pay maturing obligations.

Lis Pendens. A recorded notice of the filing of an action affecting real property.

Listing. An employment contract between a real estate broker (as agent) and a principal authorizing the broker to perform services in connection with the sale, purchase, exchange, or leasing of real property. There are various types of listing agreements, such as open, exclusive agency, option, etc.

Loan Administration. A general term encompassing those aspects of a mortgage lending operation that deal with the administration or servicing of loans after they have been put on the books, e.g., collection of monthly payments, accounting for payments, and handling of real estate taxes and hazard insurance.

Loan Application. The loan application is a source of information on which the lender bases a decision to make the loan; defines the terms of the loan contract, gives the name of the borrower, place of employment, salary, bank accounts, and credit references, and describes the real estate that is to be mortgaged. It also stipulates the amount of loan being applied for and repayment terms.

Loan Closing. When all conditions have been met, the loan officer authorizes the recording of the trust deed or mortgage. The disbursal procedure of funds is similar to the closing of a real estate sales escrow. The borrower can expect to receive less than the amount of the loan, as title, recording, service, and other fees may be withheld, or can expect to deposit the cost of these items into the loan escrow. This process is sometimes called "funding" the loan.

Loan Commitment. Lender's contractual commitment to make a loan on the appraisal and underwriting.

Loan Correspondent. One who acts as an agent for lenders; most often a large, incorporated mortgage banker representing institutional lenders such as eastern life insurance companies.

Loan Value. Value set on property to aid in determining the amount of a mortgage or trust deed loan to be made. Loan to value ratio is the percentage of a property's value that a lender can or may loan to a borrower. For example, if the ratio is 80 percent, this means that a lender may loan 80 percent of the property's appraised value to a borrower.

Lot. A plot of ground.

M

MAI - Member, Appraisal Institute. Designates a person who is a member of the American Institute of Real Estate Appraisers of the National Association of Realtors® (NAR).

Margin of Security. The difference between the amount of the mortgage loan or loans and the appraised value of the property.

Marginal Land. Land which barely pays the cost of working or using it.

Marketable Title. The status of a title when viewed in the light of whether or not it is in such a condition as to attract a purchaser; a title that is free from reasonable doubt in law and in fact.

Market Data Approach. One of the three methods in the appraisal process. A means of comparing similar type properties, which have recently sold, to the subject property. Commonly used in comparing residential properties.

Market Price. The price actually paid for property on the open market.

Market Value. The highest price estimated in terms of money which a property will bring if exposed for sale in the open market, allowing a reasonable time to find a purchaser with knowledge of the property's use and capabilities for use.

Marketable Title. Title which a reasonable purchaser, informed as to the facts and their legal importance and acting with reasonable care, would be willing and ought to accept.

Material Fact. Significant fact, which, for instance, an agent realizes is likely to affect the judgment of the principal in giving his or her consent to the agent to enter into a particular transaction of the specified terms. For example, the amount of income from rental property is a material fact.

Mechanic's Lien. A statutory lien in favor of laborers and material men who have contributed to a work of improvement.

Meridians. Imaginary north-south lines which intersect base (east-west) lines to form a starting point for the measurement of land.

Metes. Measurements.

Metes and Bounds. Measurements and boundaries; a term used in describing the boundary lines of land, setting forth all the boundary lines together with their terminal points and angles.

Mile. 5,280 feet.

Minor. All persons under eighteen years of age. Prior to March 4, 1972, minors were persons under twenty-one years of age.

Misplaced Improvements. Improvements on land which do not conform to the most profitable use of the site.

Misrepresentation. A false or misleading statement or assertion.

Mobilehome (Manufactured Housing). As defined in Business and Professions Code Section 10131.6(c), "mobilehome" means a structure transportable in one or more sections, designed and equipped to contain not more than two dwelling units to be used with or without a foundation

system; does not include a recreational vehicle, as defined in Section 18010.5 of the Health and Safety Code; a commercial coach, as defined in Section 18012 of the Health and Safety Code; or factory-built housing, as defined in Section 19971 of the Health and Safety Code.

Modular. A system for the construction of dwellings and other improvements to real property through the on-site assembly of component parts (modules) that have been mass produced away from the building site.

Monetary Controls. Federal Reserve tools for regulating the availability of money and credit to influence the level of economic activity, e.g., adjusting discount rates, reserve requirements, etc.

Monument. A fixed object or point designated by surveyors to establish land locations.

Moratorium. The temporary suspension, usually by statute, of the enforcement of liability for debts.

Mortgage. A written document executed by the owner of land by which the land is given as security for the payment of a debt or performance of an obligation.

Mortgage Banker. A company or individual engaged in the business of originating mortgage loans with its own funds, selling those loans to long-term investors, and servicing the loans for the investor until they are paid in full.

Mortgage Contracts with Warrants. Warrants make the mortgage more attractive to the lender by providing both the greater security that goes with a mortgage and the opportunity of a greater return through the right to buy either stock in the borrower's company or a portion of the income property itself.

Mortgage Guaranty Insurance. Insurance against financial loss available to mortgage lenders; in effect, guarantees payment of the debt; commonly referred to as **Private Mortgage Insurance (PMI)**.

Mortgage Investment Company. A company or group of private investors that buys mortgages for investment purposes.

Mortgage Loan Disclosure Statement. The statement on a form approved by the Real Estate Commissioner, which is required by law to be furnished by a mortgage loan broker to the prospective borrower of loans of a statutorily prescribed amount before the borrower becomes obligated to complete the loan.

Mortgagee. The party who obtains the benefit of a mortgage; the lender.

Mortgagor. The party who executes a mortgage; the borrower.

Multiple Dwelling. A dwelling that is designed for occupancy by two or more families.

Multiple Listing. A listing, usually an exclusive right to sell, taken by a member of an organization composed of real estate brokers (Multiple Listing Service - MLS), with the provision that all members will have the opportunity to find an interested client, and the commission will be shared by the listing broker and the selling broker; a form of cooperative listing.

Mutual. Reciprocal; possessed, experienced, understood, or performed by each of two or more persons. One of the requisites of a valid contract is mutual consent. Also, mutual mistake, either of a fact or law, may be grounds for avoiding a contract.

Mutual Savings Banks. Financial institutions owned by depositors, each of whom has rights to net earnings of the bank in proportion to his or her deposits.

Mutual Water Company. A water company organized by or for water users in a given district or area with the object of securing an ample water supply at a reasonable rate for its members who are issued shares of water stock.

N

NAR. National Association of REALTORS®.

NAREB. National Association of Real Estate Brokers.

Narrative Appraisal. A summary of all factual materials, techniques, and appraisal methods used by the appraiser in setting forth his or her value conclusion.

Natural Person. A person who is born and will die someday; distinguished from an artificial person, such as a corporation.

Naturalization. The conferring of the rights of citizenship upon a person who was an alien.

Negative Amortization. Occurs when monthly installment payments are insufficient to pay the interest accruing on the principal balance, so that the unpaid interest must be added to the principal due.

Negotiable. Capable of being negotiated; transferable in the ordinary course of business, usually by endorsement.

Negotiable Instrument. A promissory note or check or certificate of deposit or draft (bill of exchange) which under the Negotiable Instruments Law (now contained in the Commercial Code), entitles an endorsee to greater rights than an assignee, under certain prescribed conditions.

Net. Amount remaining after deduction of charges and expenses.

Net Income. Gross annual income less allowable expenses.

Net Lease. A lease requiring a lessee to pay certain charges against the property such as taxes, insurance and maintenance costs in addition to rental payments.

Net Listing. A listing agreement which provides that the broker may retain as compensation for his or her services all sums received over and above a net price to the owner.

Net Net Net Lease (Triple Net Lease). A term commonly used in connection with leases which means that all monies received by the lessor as rent are over and above all expenses of ownership, including taxes.

Net Profit. What is left after all bills and taxes are paid.

Net Worth. The difference between assets and liabilities.

Nominal Interest Rates. The percentage of interest that is stated in the loan documents.

Notary Public. A public officer or other person authorized to authenticate contracts, acknowledge deeds, take affidavits, etc.

Note. A signed, written instrument acknowledging a debt and promising payment.

Note Rate. Determines the amount of interest charged on an annual basis to the borrower; also called the **Accrual Rate**, **Contract Rate**, or **Coupon Rate**.

Notice. Being made aware. There are three types of notice: (1) **Actual Notice.** Express knowledge of a fact. (2) **Constructive Notice.** A fact, imputed to a person by law, which should have been discovered because of the person's actual notice of circumstances and the inquiry that a prudent person would have been expected to make, or implied or inferred from the public records. (3) **Legal Notice.** Information required to be given by law.

Notice of Cessation. A notice recorded under the mechanic's lien law after work has ceased for a period of time. Shortens the time for filing mechanics' liens.

Notice of Completion. A notice recorded under the mechanic's lien law after completion of the work of improvement. Shortens the time for filing mechanics' liens.

Notice of Default. Recorded notice that a default has occurred under a deed of trust and that the beneficiary intends to proceed with a trustee's sale.

Notice of Nonresponsibility. Notice recorded by an owner of real property to relieve the land from mechanics' liens which may result from an improvement on the property by a tenant or by a purchaser under a land sales contract.

Notice to Pay Rent or Quit. Notice to a tenant to either pay rent that is due or vacate the premises; also known as a three-day notice to quit.

Novation. The substitution of a new obligation in place of an existing one.

Null. Without legal force and effect; not valid.

O

Obligatory. Mandatory, such as obligatory advances under a deed of trust; compared with optional.

Obligor. One who places himself or herself under a legal obligation, e.g., a mortgagor or trustor under a deed of trust.

Obsolescence. Impairment of desirability and usefulness of property; one of the causes of depreciation in value of property. Economic obsolescence is due to changes in the character of the neighborhood. Functional obsolescence relates to the declining usefulness of the structure itself.

Offer to Purchase. The proposal made to an owner of property by a potential buyer to purchase the property under stated terms.

Offset Statement. Statement furnished to an escrow from a tenant regarding his or her right of possession (payment of rent, security deposits, etc.); also, by an owner of land subject to an encumbrance as to the unpaid balance.

Open End Mortgage. A mortgage which secures additional advances which the lender may make to the mortgagor; permits the mortgagor to borrow additional money without rewriting the mortgage.

Open Housing Law. Congress passed a law in April, 1968 which prohibits descrimination in the sale of real estate because of race, color, or religion of buyers. California has enacted comparable laws.

Open Listing. A nonexclusive listing; provides that the broker is to receive a commission if he or she is the first one to obtain a buyer ready, willing, and able to purchase the property on the seller's terms. Open listings may be given to any number of agents.

Operating Expenses. Expenses incurred in the operation of a business.

Option. A right given for a consideration to acquire property upon specified terms within a specified period of time.

Optional. Not obligatory; discretionary.

Optionee. The person who is given an option by the owner of property.

Option Listing. A type of listing which gives the broker the option to buy the property for a specified price.

Optionor. The person (owner) who gives an option to another person.

Oral. Spoken; verbal.

Oral Contract. A contract not in writing; ordinance; legislative enactment of a city or county.

Orientation. Placing a house on its lot with regard to its exposure to the rays of the sun, prevailing winds, privacy from the street, and protection from outside noises.

Original Contractor. Under the mechanic's lien law, a contractor who contracts directly with the owner of real property; others are designated as subcontractors.

Ostensible Authority. That authority which a third person reasonably believes an agent possesses because of the acts or omissions of the principal.

Overimprovement. An improvement which is not the highest and best use for the site on which it is placed by reason of excess size or cost.

Ownership. The right to the use and enjoyment of property to the exclusion of others.

P-Q

Package Mortgage. A type of mortgage used in home financing covering real property, improvements, and movable equipment/appliances.

Paramount Title. Title which is superior or foremost to all others.

Partial Reconveyance. A release of a part only of the property described in a deed of trust.

Partial Release Clause. A clause in a deed of trust that requires the beneficiary, under prescribed conditions, to cause a designated portion of the property to be released prior to payment in full of the obligation.

Participation. Sharing of an interest in a property by a lender. In addition to base interest on mortgage loans on income properties, a percentage of gross income is required, sometimes predicated on certain conditions being fulfilled, such as a minimum occupancy or a percentage of net income after expenses, debt service and taxes. Also called "equity participation" or "revenue sharing."

Parties. Persons who are involved in a lawsuit, designated as plaintiffs and defendants; also, those entities taking part in a transaction as a principal, e.g., seller, buyer, or lender in a real estate transaction.

Partition. An action which seeks to have property owned by two or more persons sold and the proceeds divided, or the property itself divided between the parties if physical division of the property is practical.

Partnership. A voluntary association of two or more persons to carry on as co-owners of a business for profit.

Party Wall. A wall for the common benefit and use of adjoining owners of property, their property being separated by the wall.

Par Value. Face value.

Patent. A conveyance of the title to public lands by the federal government. Also, when used as an adjective, it means something that is evident or obvious, such as a patent ambiguity in a document, and, as such, is distinguished from latent or hidden.

Payment Adjustment Date. With regard to an adjustable rate mortgage, the date the borrower's monthly principal and interest payment may change.

Payment Cap. With regard to an adjustable rate mortgage, this limits the amount of increase in the borrower's monthly principal and interest at the payment adjustment date, if the principal and interest increase called for by the interest rate increase exceeds the payment cap percentage. This limitation is often at the borrower's option and may result in negative amortization.

Payment Rate. With respect to an adjustable rate mortgage, the rate at which the borrower repays the loan—reflects buydowns or payment caps.

Penalty. A loss or forfeiture resulting from nonfulfillment of a contractual obligation, such as payment of an additional amount, called a late charge, if a note becomes delinquent.

Per Autre Vie. During the life of another. A life estate, for instance, may be measured by the life of a person other than the one who has the life estate, and would be referred to as a life estate per autre vie.

Per Capita. By the head. In the distribution of an estate, persons are said to take per capita when each one claims in his or her own right, based on an equal degree of kinship, an equal share of the estate. It is compared with the term "per stirpes," which means by right of representation (according to the roots). In the latter situation the children of a deceased heir would all take but one share and would not share equally with the other heirs in their own right.

Percentage Lease. A lease under which the rent is computed as a percentage of the gross receipts from the business of the tenant, with provision (usually) for a minimum rental.

Periodic Interest Rate Cap. With respect to an adjustable rate mortgage, limits the increase or decrease in the note rate at each rate adjustment, thereby limiting the borrower's payment increase or decrease at the time of adjustment.

Periodic Tenancy. Tenancy for specified periods, such as month to month, which can be terminated at any time by either party on proper notice.

Personal Property. Movable property; all property consisting of chattels as contrasted with real estate, e.g., furniture, car, clothing, etc.

Physical Deterioration. Impairment of condition; loss in value brought about by wear and tear, disintegration, use, and actions of the elements; termed curable and incurable.

Plaintiff. The party who brings a court action.

Planned Unit Development (PUD). A land-use design which provides intensive utilization of the land through a combination of private and common areas with prearranged sharing of responsibilities for the common areas. Individual lots are owned in fee with joint ownership of the open areas.

Planning Commission. The city or county agency that administers zoning regulations.

Plans and Specifications. Building plans with a detailed description of the requirements, dimensions, materials, etc., of the proposed structure.

Pledge. The depositing of personal property by a debtor with a creditor as security for a debt or other obligation.

Pledgee. One who is given a pledge as security.

Pledgor. One who gives a pledge as security.

Plottage Increment. The appreciation in unit value created by joining smaller ownerships into one large single ownership.

POB (Point of Beginning). The commencement point in a good and sufficient legal description of land.

Points. Additional charges for obtaining a loan computed like interest; i.e., one point is comparable to one percent interest.

Police Power. The power to enact laws and regulations deemed necessary for the common welfare.

Power of Attorney. A written authorization to an agent to perform specified acts on behalf of his or her principal. May be a general power or a limited power. Also, may be a durable power or a springing power.

Power of Sale. As used in a will, authorizes the executor to sell estate property without the necessity of publishing a notice of sale.

PRD (Planned Residential Development). Used interchangeably with PUD, planned unit development.

Precedent. As an adjective, means going before, such as a condition precedent, i.e., a condition or event which must first occur before an estate can be terminated.

Pre-Emption. Right to purchase before or in preference to others, such as a right of first refusal.

Prefabricated House. A house manufactured and sometimes partly assembled before delivery to a building site.

Preferred Stock. A class of corporate stock entitled to preferential treatment such as priority in distribution of dividends.

Prepaid Items of Expense. Prorations of prepaid items of expense which are credited to the seller in the closing escrow statement.

Prepayment. Provision made for loan payments to be larger than those specified in the note.

Prepayment Penalty. Penalty by way of an additional payment for the privilege of paying in full a mortgage or trust deed note prior to the due date.

Prescription. The obtaining of title to or a right in property by adverse possession, i.e., by occupying it openly, notoriously, and hostilely for a five-year period. By paying the real property taxes, the fee title can be claimed.

Present Value. The lump sum value today of an annuity. Example: a $100 bill to be paid to someone in one year is worth less than if it were a $100 bill to be paid to someone today. This is due to several things, one of which is that the money has time value. How much the $100 bill to be paid in one year is worth today will depend on the interest rate that seems proper for the particular circumstances. If 6% is the appropriate rate, the $100 to be paid one year from now would be worth $94.34 today.

Presumption. That which may be assumed as true without further proof. May be either a conclusive presumption or a rebuttable presumption.

Prima Facie. Presumptive on its face; assumed correct unless overcome by further proof.

Primary Money Market. A market where loans are made directly to borrowers by a lender who retains the loan in his portfolio rather than sell it to an investor.

Prime. Of the greatest commercial value, such as a prime building lot.

Principal. Used to mean the employer of an agent, or the amount of money borrowed, or the amount of the loan. Also, one of the main parties in a real estate transaction, such as a buyer, borrower, seller, lessor.

Principal Note. The promissory note which is secured by the mortgage or trust deed.

Principle. An accepted or professed rule of action or conduct.

Prior Lien. Earlier in point of time or right.

Priority of Lien. The state or quality of being earlier in point of time or right, as the priority of a first mortgage over a second mortgage.

Private Mortgage Insurance (PMI). Mortgage guaranty insurance available to conventional lenders on the first, high risk portion of a loan.

Probate Court. Department of the Superior Court which has authority over the estates of decedents, minors, incompetents, and missing persons.

Procuring Cause. The cause of originating a series of events that leads to the consummation of a real estate sale and normally entitles a broker to a commission.

Profit a Prendre. The right to take part of the soil or produce of land.

Progress Payments. Scheduled, periodic, and partial payment of construction loan funds to a builder as each construction stage is completed.

Progression, Principle of. The worth of a lesser valued residence tends to be enhanced by association with higher valued residences in the same area.

Promissory Note. A written obligation containing a promise to pay a definite amount of money at or prior to a specified time.

Property. Anything of which there may be ownership; classified as either real property or personal property.

Property Management. A branch of the real estate business involving the marketing, operation, maintenance and day-to-day financing of rental properties.

Proposition 13. A 1978 California initiative limiting amount of property taxes that may be assessed to one percent of market value.

Pro Rata. In proportion; according to a certain rate.

Proration. A proportionate division or splitting of taxes and other expenses and income from real estate between buyer and seller in a sales escrow transaction; usually computed as of date escrow closes.

Proximate Cause. That cause of an event which, in a natural and continuous sequence unbroken by any new cause, produced that event, and without which the event would not have happened. Also, the **Procuring Cause.**

Public Records. As used in a title policy, those records which impart constructive notice of matters relating to the land described in the policy.

Public Report. Report of the Real Estate Commissioner containing information about subdivided property.

PUD. Planned unit development.

Purchase and Installment Saleback. Involves purchase of the property upon completion of construction and immediate saleback on a longterm installment contract.

Purchase of Land, Leaseback, and Leasehold Mortgages. An arrangement whereby land is purchased by the lender and leased back to the developer with a mortgage negotiated on the

resulting leasehold of the income property constructed. The lender receives an annual ground rent, plus a percentage of income from the property.

Purchase and Leaseback. Involves the purchase of property by buyer and immediate leaseback to seller.

Purchase Money Mortgage. A mortgage (or trust deed) given as part or all of the purchase price of real estate.

Quiet Enjoyment. Right of an owner to the use of property without interference of possession.

Quiet Title. A court action to establish title to real property; similar in effect to an action to remove a cloud on title.

Quitclaim Deed. A deed which conveys whatever present right, title, or interest the party executing the deed may have.

R

Range. Part of a government survey; one of a series or divisions numbered east or west from the principal meridian of the survey and consisting of a row or tier of townships, each six miles square, which in turn are numbered north or south from a base line, e.g., Township 1 North, Range 3 East, SBBM (San Bernardino base and meridian).

Rate. The amount of a charge or payment, such as interest rate.

Rate Adjustment Date. With respect to an adjustable rate mortgage, the date the borrower's note rate may change.

Ratification. The adoption or approval of an act performed on behalf of a person without previous authorization.

Ready, Willing, and Able Buyer. One who is fully prepared to enter into the contract, really wants to buy, and unquestionably meets the financing requirements of purchase.

Real Estate. Real property; land and things affixed to land or appurtenant to land.

Real Estate Board. A local organization whose members consist primarily of real estate brokers and salespersons; affiliated with both the state association (CAR) and national board (NAR).

Real Estate Investment Trust (REIT). An association recognized under federal and state laws whereby investors may pool funds for investments in real estate and mortgages and avoid taxation as a corporation.

Real Estate Law. As codified in California, relates to the provisions of the Business and Professions Code creating the Department of Real Estate. Under this law, the Real Estate Commissioner has regulatory and disciplinary authority over real estate licenses, land sale transactions such as the sale of subdivided lands in or outside the state, and other related transactions.

Real Estate Settlement Procedures Act (RESPA). A federal law requiring the disclosure to borrowers of settlement (closing) procedures and costs by means of a pamphlet and forms prescribed by the United States Department of Housing and Urban Development.

Real Estate Syndicate. An organization of investors, usually in the form of a limited partnership, who have joined together for the purpose of pooling capital for the acquisition of real property interests.

Real Estate Trust. A special arrangement under Federal and State law whereby investors may pool funds for investments in real estate and mortgages and yet escape corporation taxes, profits being passed to investors who are taxed as individuals.

Real Property. Land and things attached to land or appurtenant to land; distinguished from personal property or chattels.

Real Property Loan Law. Article 7 of Chapter 3 of the Real Estate Law, under which a real estate licensee negotiating loans secured by real property within a specified range is required to give the borrower a statement disclosing the costs and terms of the loan and which also limits the amount of expenses and charges that a borrower may pay with respect to the loan.

Real Property Sales Contract. An agreement to convey title to real property upon satisfaction of specified conditions which does not require conveyance within one year of formation of the contract.

Realtist. A member of the National Association of Real Estate Brokers.

REALTOR®. A real estate broker holding active membership in a real estate board affiliated with the National Association of Realtors® (NAR).

Recapture. The rate of interest necessary to provide for the return of an investment (i.e., return of capital); distinguished from interest rate, which is the rate of interest on an investment (i.e., rate of return). May be more or less than the recapture amount.

Receipt. Written acknowledgment that money or other thing of value was received; as used in real estate practice, a deposit receipt when duly executed is also evidence of a contract between a buyer and seller.

Receiver. A person appointed by a court, such as a bankruptcy court, to take charge of a business or property of other persons, pending litigation.

Reconciliation. The act of bringing into harmony or agreement, such as reconciling an account, i.e., making it compatible or consistent.

Reconveyance. A conveyance to the landowner of the title held by a trustee under a deed of trust.

Record. An official writing or other document to be preserved; used as a verb, it means to make a public record of a document.

Recordation. Filing for record in the office of the county recorder.

Recovery Fund. A fund established by the Department of Real Estate from license fees to underwrite uncollectable court judgments against licensees based on fraud.

Redemption. Buying back one's property after a judicial sale, such as an execution or foreclosure sale.

Redemption Period. The time allowed by law during which the owner may redeem his or her property by paying, for instance, the amount of the sale on a foreclosed mortgage.

Redlining. A lending policy, illegal in California, of denying real estate loans on properties in older, changing urban areas, usually with large minority populations, because of alleged higher lending risks without due consideration being given by the lending institution to the creditworthiness of the individual loan applicant.

Refinancing. The paying-off of an existing obligation and assuming a new obligation in its place. To finance anew, or extend or renew existing financing.

Reformation. An action to correct a mistake in a deed or other document.

Regulate. To control or direct by a rule or law.

Regulation. A rule or direction prescribed under the authority of a statute, such as regulations of the Real Estate Commissioner.

Rehabilitation. The restoration of a property to satisfactory condition without drastically changing the plan, form or style of architecture.

Reinstate. To cure a default under a note secured by deed of trust.

Release Clause. A clause in a deed of trust providing for release of specified portions of the property upon compliance with certain conditions.

Reliction. Gradual recession of water from the usual water line or mark.

Remainder. A right to future possession after the expiration of a life estate.

Remainder Depreciation. The possible future loss in value of an improvement to real property.

Renegotiable Rate Mortgage. A loan secured by a long-term mortgage which provides for renegotiation, at pre-determined intervals, of the interest rate (for a maximum variation of five percent over the life of the mortgage).

Rent. Consideration paid for the use and possession of property under a rental agreement.

REO. Property which is in the possession of a lender as a result of foreclosure or forfeiture is known as Real Estate Owned (REO) property.

Replacement Cost. The cost to replace a structure with one having utility equivalent to that being appraised, but constructed with modern materials and according to current standards, design and layout.

Reproduction Cost. The cost of replacing the subject improvement with one that is the exact replica, having the same quality of workmanship, design and layout, or cost to duplicate an asset.

Rescission. An action to cancel or annul the effect of executing a contract or other document, based on fraud, mistake, etc.

Rescission of Contract. The abrogation or annulling of contract; the revocation or repealing of contract by mutual consent by parties to the contract, or for cause by either party to the contract.

Reservation. The creation on behalf of the grantor (in a deed) of a new right issuing out of the property granted, such as the reservation of a mineral interest.

Reserves. 1) In a common interest subdivision, an accumulation of funds collected from owners for future replacement and major maintenance of the common area and facilities. 2) With regard to mortgage loans, an accumulation of funds, collected by the lender from the borrower as part of each monthly mortgage payment; an amount allocated to pay property taxes and insurance when they are due.

Residual Cost. Accounting term for "book value"; the cost of a fixed asset, less any portion of the cost that has been treated as an expense, such as depreciation.

RESPA. (See **Real Estate Settlement Procedures Act**.)

Restriction. An encumbrance created by deed or agreement which limits the use and enjoyment of property; often created by a recorded Declaration of Covenants, Conditions and Restrictions (CC&R).

Return. A yield or profit from land or other property.

Return Premium. The refund of unearned advance premium resulting from cancellation of a hazard insurance policy prior to its expiration date or the date to which the premium has been paid.

Reversion. The residue of an estate remaining with a grantor after the expiration or termination of a lesser estate, such as an estate-for-years.

Reversionary Interest. The interest a person has in lands or other property upon the expiration or termination of a preceding estate.

Revocation. Nullification or cancellation or withdrawal, such as revocation of an offer to sell or an offer to buy a parcel of property.

Right of Redemption. The statutory right to buy back one's property after a judicial sale during a prescribed period of time, usually one year.

Right of Suvivorship. The distinguishing feature of joint tenancy, i.e., when one joint tenant dies, title vests automatically in the survivor without probate.

Right of Way. A right to cross or pass over, across, or under another person's land, for such purposes as ingress and egress, utility lines, sewer pipes, etc.

Right, Title, and Interest. A term used in deeds to denote that the grantor is conveying all of that to which the grantor held claim.

Riparian Rights. The right of a landowner to water located on, under, or adjacent to his or her land.

Risk Analysis. A study made, usually by a lender, of the various factors that might affect the repayment of a loan.

Risk Rating. A process used by the lender to decide on the soundness of making a loan and to reduce all the various factors affecting the repayment of the loan to a qualified rating of some kind.

S

SAFE Act. The **Secure and Fair Enforcement Mortgage Licensing Act** of the Housing and Economic Recovery Act of 2008 was signed into law on July 30, 2008 to enhance consumer protection and reduce fraud in mortgage loan transactions.

Sale. Transfer of property for money or credit.

Sale-Leaseback. A transaction where the owner of a parcel of property sells it to another person (buyer) and retains physical possession by leasing it from the buyer.

Sales Contract. A contract by which a buyer and a seller of property agree to the terms of a sale.

Sales Escrow. (See **Escrow**.)

Sales Tax. Tax on the sale of tangible personal property.

Salvage Value. In computing depreciation for tax purposes, the reasonably anticipated fair market value of the property at the end of its useful life, which must be considered with all but the declining balance methods of depreciation.

Sandwich Lease. A leasehold interest which lies between the primary lease and the operating lease; an in-between lease.

Satisfaction. Performance of the terms of an obligation.

Seal. An impression upon a document that lends authenticity to its execution.

Secondary Financing. A loan secured by a second mortgage or trust deed on real property.

Secondary Money (Mortgage) Market. A market in which existing mortgages are bought, sold or borrowed against, as distinguished from a primary market. The latter is made up of lenders who supply funds directly to borrowers and hold the mortgage until the debt is paid.

Section. One of the divisions employed in a government survey; measures one mile on each side and contains 640 acres of land.

Secured Party. The party having a security interest, such as a mortgagee, conditional seller, pledgee, etc.

Security. Something of value given or deposited to secure payment of a debt or performance of an obligation.

Security Agreement. Document now used in place of a chattel mortgage as evidence of a lien on personal property. A financing statement may be filed or recorded to give constructive notice of the security agreement.

Security Deposit. A deposit of money or other thing of value made to assure performance of an obligation; frequently required of lessees or tenants.

Security Interest. The interest of the creditor in the property of the debtor in all types of secured transactions.

Seisen. The possession of land under a claim of a freehold estate (also spelled **Seizen**).

Seller's Market. The market condition which exists when a seller is in a more commanding position as to price and terms because demand exceeds supply.

Senior Lien. A lien that is ahead of or prior to or superior to another lien on the same property. Distinguished from junior lien.

Separate Property. Property of a married person acquired before marriage, and property acquired during marriage by gift, devise, descent, or bequest; distinguished from community property.

Servicing Loans. Supervising and administering a loan after it has been made. This involves such things as: collecting the payments, keeping accounting records, computing the interest and principal, foreclosure of defaulted loans, and so on.

Servient Tenement. An estate burdened by an easement.

Servitude. A right in the nature of an easement in another person's property.

Setback Ordinance. An ordinance prohibiting the erection of a building or structure between the curb and the setback line.

Severalty Ownership. Sole ownership; owned by one person only, as compared with co-ownership, or ownership by two or more persons.

Shared Appreciation Mortgage. A loan having a fixed rate of interest set below the market rate for the term of the loan, which also provides for contingent interest to be paid to the lender on a certain percentage of appreciaton in the value of the property against which the loan is secured upon transfer or sale of the property or the replacement of the loan.

Sheriff's Deed. Deed given pursuant to an execution sale of real property to satisfy a judgment.

Short Sale. Where a lender accepts less than what is owed in the loan.

Simple Interest. Interest computed on the principal amount of a loan only, as distinguished from compound interest.

Sinking Fund. A fund created for the purpose of extinguishing an indebtedness, usually a bond issue; also, fund set aside from the income from property which, with accrued interest, will eventually pay for replacement of the improvements.

Slander of Title. False and malicious statements disparaging an owner's title to property and resulting in actual pecuniary damage to the owner.

Social and Economic Obsolescence. Reduction in value of property due to factors outside of the property; compared with functional obsolescence.

Sole Ownership. Ownership by one individual.

Special Assessments. Charges against real property imposed by a public authority to pay for the cost of local improvements, such as street lights, sidewalks, curbs, etc., as distinguished from taxes levied for the general support of the government (police and fire protection, etc.).

Special Power of Attorney. A written instrument whereby a principal confers limited authority upon an agent to perform certain prescribed acts on behalf of the principal.

Special Warranty Deed. A deed in which the grantor warrants or guarantees the title only against defects arising during grantor's ownership of the property and not against defects existing before the time of grantor's ownership.

Specifications. (See **Plans and Specifications**.)

Specific Performance. An action to compel performance of an agreement such as an agreement for the sale of purchase of land.

SREA. Designates a person who is a member of the Society of Real Estate Appraisers.

Standby Commitment. The mortgage banker frequently protects a builder by a standby agreement, under which banker agrees to make mortgage loans at an agreed price for many months into the future. The builder deposits a standby fee with the mortgage banker for this service. Frequently, the mortgage broker protects himself or herself by securing a standby from a long-term investor for the same period of time, paying a fee for this privilege.

State Contractors License Law. Law designed to protect the public against unqualified building contractors; establishes standards and requirements that must be met by contractors.

State Housing Law. State law which prescribes minimum building standards.

Statute. Federal laws enacted by Congress, and state laws enacted by the state legislature.

Statute of Frauds. State law which provides that certain contracts must be in writing to be enforceable, such as a contract for the sale of land, or a contract to pay a real estate broker a commission.

Statute of Limitations. Law which limits the time within which court action may be brought to enforce rights or claims.

Statutory Law. (See **Civil Law**.)

Statutory Warranty Deed. A short-term warranty deed which warrants by inference that the seller is the undisputed owner, has the right to convey the property, and will defend the title if necessary. This type of deed protects the purchaser in that the conveyor covenants to defend all claims against the property. If conveyor fails to do so, the new owner can defend said claims and sue the former owner.

Stock in Trade. Merchandise held by a business for sale to customers.

Straight-Line Depreciation. Definite sum of money set aside annually from income to pay cost of replacing improvements on property, without regard to interest it earns.

Straight Note. A promissory note that provides for repayment in a lump sum, as distinguished from installments.

Subagent. A person upon whom the powers of an agent have been conferred, not by the principal, but by an agent as authorized by the agent's principal.

Subcontractor. As used in the mechanic's lien law, a contractor hired by the general contractor rather than by the owner.

Subdivision. A parcel of property divided into lots for real estate development.

Subject to. The taking of real property subject to an encumbrance, such as a mortgage or deed of trust, is done without being personally liable to the holder of the note for payment of the debt; distinguished from **Assuming**.

Sublease. A lease given by a lessee to another person for a term less than his or her own. The lessee retains a reversion. Distinguished from an assignment.

Subordinate. To make subject to, or junior to, another encumbrance.

Subordination Agreement. An agreement under which a prior lien is made inferior to an otherwise junior lien; changes the order of priority.

Subpoena. Court process for the summoning of witnesses.

Subrogation. Replacing one person with another in regard to a legal right or obligation. The substitution of another person in place of the creditor, to whose rights he or she succeeds in relation to the debt. The doctrine is used very often where one person agrees to stand surety for the performance of a contract by another person; also, an insurer is subrogated to the rights of the insured against a third party causing a loss.

Subsequent. Occurring or coming later in time.

Suburb. An area lying immediately outside a city or town.

Subsidy Buydown. Funds provided, usually by the builder or seller, to temporarily reduce the borrower's monthly principal and interest payment.

Substitution, Principle of. Affirms that the maximum value of a property tends to be set by the cost of acquiring an equally desirable and valuable substitute property, assuming no costly delay is encountered in making the substitution.

Succession. The taking of property by inheritance.

Successor. One who acquires or succeeds to the interest of another person.

Summons. Court process which directs a defendant to make an appearance in an action filed against him or her.

Supply and Demand, Principle of. In appraising, a valuation principle stating that market value is affected by interaction of supply and demand forces in the market as of the appraisal date.

Surety. A person who binds himself or herself with another, called the principal, for the performance of an obligation; a guarantor.

Surplus Funds. Money obtained at a foreclosure sale in excess of the amount to satisfy or pay the obligation in full.

Surplus Productivity, Principle of. The net income that remains after the proper costs of labor, organization and capital have been paid, which surplus is imputable to the land and tends to fix the value thereof.

Survey. A map or plat containing a statement of courses, distances, and quantity of land, and showing lines of possession.

Syndicate. A pooling arrangement or association of persons who invest in real property by buying shares in an organization in the form of a partnership, joint venture, corporation, or other entity.

T

Take-Out Loan. The loan arranged by the owner or builder developer for a buyer. The construction loan made for construction of the improvements is usually paid in full from the proceeds of this more permanent mortgage loan.

Tangible Assets. Anything of value having form or substance, such as real estate, chattels, etc.

Tax. A levy, under authority of law, for governmental purposes.

Tax Base. The value of property for determining the tax. For property taxes, it is the assessed value; for income taxes, it is the net taxable income.

Tax Deed. A deed issued to the purchaser at a tax sale of real property.

Tax-Free Exchange. The trade or exchange of one real property for another without the need to pay income taxes on the gain at the time of trade.

Tax Sale. Sale of property by the tax collector for nonpayment of taxes.

Tax Shelter. Under income tax law, a situation where cost and depreciation equal income from property, hence no income tax is payable.

Tenancy in Common. Ownership of property by any two or more persons in undivided interests (not necessarily equal), without right of survivorship.

Tenant. One who occupies property of another person under an agreement to pay rent.

Tenements. All rights in land which pass with a conveyance of the land.

Tentative Map. Under the Subdivision Map Act, a subdivider initially submits this map to the local planning commission for approval.

Tenure. The manner in which title to land is held.

Term. Used variously in the real estate field; denotes any provision of a contract, or the period or provisions of a loan, or the period of a lease.

Termites. Ant-like insects that feed on wood.

Testate. Having made a will; as an adjective, "a person died testate."

Testator. A man who makes a will.

Testatrix. Feminine of testator.

Third Party. Persons who are not parties to a contract which affects an interest they have in the object of the contract, such as a third-party beneficiary.

Thirty-Day Notice. Notice to tenant to vacate the premises within a thirty-day period. No reason required.

Tidelands. Lands that are covered and uncovered by the ebb and flow of the tide.

Tight Money Market. A market in which demand for the use of money exceeds the available supply.

Time is of the Essence. A clause in a contract that requires strict compliance with the stated time limitations (within which a contracting party may perform).

Timeshare Estate. A right of occupancy in a timeshare project (subdivision), which is coupled with an estate in the real property.

Timeshare Project. A form of subdivision of real property into rights to the recurrent, exclusive use or occupancy of a lot, parcel, unit, or segment of real property, on an annual or some other periodic basis, for a specified period of time. (See **Subdivision**.)

Timeshare Use. A license or contractual or membership right of occupancy in a time-share project, which is not coupled with an estate in the real property.

Title. Evidence of a person's right or the extent of his or her interest in property.

Title Insurance. Assurances as to the condition of title; protects owner or other insured, such as a lender, against loss or impairment of title.

Title Plant. A physical collection of documents, maps, and other data, which may be pertinent to future title searches; maintained by title companies.

Title Report. A report which discloses condition of the title, made by a title company preliminarily to issurance of title insurance policy; usually called a preliminary report of title.

Topography. Nature of the surface of land, e.g., the topography may be level, rolling, mountainous, etc.

Tort. A wrongful act; violation of a person's legal right; a civil wrong not arising out of contract.

Townhouse. One of a row of houses usually of the same or similar design with common side walls or with a very narrow space between adjacent side walls.

Township. A part of a subdivision of the public lands of the United States; each township contains 36 sections.

Tract. A real estate development; an expanse or area of land.

Trade Fixtures. Articles of personal property, annexed to real property by a tenant, that are necessary to the carrying on of a trade and are removable by the owner of the fixtures upon termination of the tenancy.

Trade-in. A method of guaranteeing property owners a minimum amount of cash on sale of their present property to permit them to purchase other property. If the property is not sold within a specified time at the listed price, the broker agrees to arrange financing to purchase the property at an agreed-upon discount.

Trade Name. The name under which a firm does business.

Transaction. That which is conducted or processed as a business deal.

Transfer Fee. A charge made by a lending institution holding or collecting on a real estate mortgage to change its records to reflect a different ownership.

Transfer Tax. A tax payable upon the conveyance of property, measured by the consideration paid.

Trespass. An invasion of an owner's rights in his or her property; a wrongful entry upon the land of another person.

Trust. A fiduciary relationship in which one party (trustee) holds the title to property for the benefit of another party (beneficiary).

Trust Account. An account of property which is held in trust for another person; distinguished from personal account.

Trust Deed. (See **Deed of Trust.**)

Trustee. The person to whom property is conveyed in trust.

Trustee's Deed. Deed given by the trustee under a deed of trust when the property is sold under the power of sale.

Trustee's Sale. A foreclosure sale conducted by the trustee under a deed of trust after a default occurs.

Trust Funds. Money or other things of value received by a broker or salesperson to be held for the benefit of others.

Trustor. The person who conveys property in trust.

Truth in Lending. The name given to the federal statutes and regulations (Regulation Z) which are designed primarily to insure that prospective borrowers and purchasers on credit receive credit cost information before entering into a transaction.

Turnover. The number of times per year a given amount of inventory sells; change or movement of people, such as tenants, customers, etc.

U

UCC. (See **Uniform Commercial Code.**)

Underimprovement. An improvement which, because of its deficiency in size or cost, is not the highest and best use of the site.

Under Water (Upside Down). A property owner owes more on their loan than their property's worth.

Underwriting. Insuring something against loss; guaranteeing financially.

Undivided Interests. Nature of each owner's interest in property when owned as tenants in common or in joint tenancy.

Undue Influence. Taking fraudulent or unfair advantage of another person's weakness of mind or distress to induce him or her to do something he or she otherwise would not have done, such as disinheriting a close relative.

Unearned Increment. Increase in value of real estate due to no effort on the part of the owner; often due to increase in population.

Unenforceable. A claim or demand or agreement that cannot be sustained in court.

Uniform Commercial Code. Establishes a unified and comprehensive method for regulation of security transactions in personal property, superseding the existing statutes on chattel mortgages, conditional sales, trust receipts, assignment of accounts receivable and others in the field.

Unilateral Contract. A contract where one party makes a promise in exchange for an action on the part of the other contracting party; distinguished from a bilateral contract.

Unit-In-Place Method. The cost of erecting a building by estimating the cost of each component part, i.e., foundations, floors, walls, windows, ceilings, roofs, etc., (including labor and overhead).

Unities. As related to joint tenancy, there are four unities necessary to create a valid joint tenancy, namely, time, title, interest, and possession.

Unlawful Detainer. An action to recover possession of real property.

Unruh Act. A California act which, among other things, precludes discriminatory practices based on race, color, religion, national origin, or ancestry.

Unsecured. A loan that is not secured by a mortgage, pledge, or other security instrument.

Urban Property. City property; closely settled property.

Usury. Taking more interest than the law allows on a loan.

Utilities. Services rendered by public utility companies, such as light, gas, water power, telephone, etc.

Utility. The ability to give satisfaction and/or excite desire for possession; an element of value.

V

VA (Department of Veterans Affairs). The federal agency which administers GI loans. An independent agency of the federal government created by the Servicemen's Readjustment Act of 1944 to administer a variety of benefit programs designed to facilitate the adjustment of returning veterans to civilian life. Among the benefit programs is the Home Loan Guaranty program designed to encourage mortgage lenders to offer long-term low-down-payment financing to eligible veterans by guaranteeing the lender against loss on these higher-risk loans.

VA Guaranty. An undertaking by the federal government to guarantee the lender, subject to limitations, against loss arising from a default by the borrower under a GI loan.

Vacancy Factor. The percentage of a building's space that is unrented over a given period.

Valid. Sufficient in law; effective.

Valuation. The act or process of estimating value.

Value. The amount a property will command from a reasonable buyer in the open market.

Variable Interest Rate (VIRs or VMRs, Variable Mortgage Rates). An interest rate in a real estate loan which, by the terms of the note, varies upward and downward over the term of the loan depending on money market conditions.

Variance. A departure from the general rule; an exception.

Vendee. The buyer or purchaser under a contract of sale.

Vendor. The seller under a contract of sale.

Verification. An affidavit attached to a pleading or other document which states that the matters set forth are true.

Vest. To give an immediate, fixed right, title, or interest in property, with either present or future enjoyment of possession; also denotes the manner in which title is held.

Vested Interest. An interest in property that is fixed or determined.

Void. Having no legal effect; null.

Voidable. An instrument that appears to be valid, but is, in fact, lacking in some essential requirement.

Voluntary Lien. A lien voluntarily created by the debtor, such as a mortgage or deed of trust as contrasted with a judgment lien.

W-Z

Waive. To relinquish or abandon; to forego a right to enforce or require something.

Waiver. A relinquishment or abandonment of a right.

Warranty. An assurance or understanding that certain defects do not exist.

Warranty Deed. A deed containing express warranties of title and quiet possession; commonly used in other states, but not in California, since assurances are given by way of title insurance.

Warrenty of Authority. A representation by an agent to third persons that the agent has and is acting within the scope of authority conferred by the principal.

Water Table. Distance from surface of ground to a depth at which natural groundwater is found.

Wear and Tear. Depreciation of an asset due to ordinary usage.

Will. A disposition of property effective upon the owner's death; often referred to as "my last will and testament."

Witness. Used as a verb, means to see or know by personal presence and perception; as a noun, the person who sees or knows.

Wraparound Mortgage or Trust Deed. (See **All-Inclusive Deed of Trust**.)

Writ. A process of the court under which property may be seized or sold by the sheriff. Example: a writ of execution.

Yield. The interest earned by an investor on an investment (or by a bank on the money it has loaned). Also, called **Return** or **Profit**.

Yield Rate. The yield expressed as a percentage of the total investment. Also, called rate of return.

Zone. Area in a community set off by a zoning authority for specified uses, such as single-family residence.

Zoning. Governmental regulations by a city or county relating to the use of real property; imposes limitations regarding use.

APPENDIX 3 - INDEX

We strongly suggest that for better memory retention you fill in the Matching Vocabulary answers first, then correct your written answers by referring to this key.

Chapter 1

1. Y
2. M
3. Z
4. BB
5. L
6. R
7. P
8. D
9. V
10. W
11. O
12. N
13. DD
14. K
15. CC
16. X
17. H
18. U
19. E
20. G
21. AA
22. S
23. Q
24. F
25. EE
26. I
27. J
28. T
29. B
30. A
31. C

Chapter 2

1. C
2. N
3. K
4. O
5. H
6. G
7. B
8. A
9. D
10. I
11. E
12. L
13. M
14. F
15. J

Chapter 3

1. C
2. N
3. I
4. G
5. O
6. F
7. K
8. L
9. E
10. J
11. H
12. M
13. A
14. D
15. B

Chapter 4

1. H
2. J
3. I
4. C
5. K
6. A

7. G
8. D
9. E
10. B
11. F
12. L

Chapter 5

1. E
2. K
3. G
4. F
5. I
6. M
7. J
8. D
9. H
10. C
11. N
12. A
13. L
14. B

Chapter 6

1. G
2. I
3. O
4. E
5. M
6. D
7. A
8. B
9. F
10. C
11. H
12. J
13. L
14. N
15. K

Chapter 7

1. C
2. F
3. G
4. J
5. A
6. H
7. E
8. I
9. B
10. L
11. D
12. K

Chapter 8

1. F
2. L
3. D
4. B
5. A
6. K
7. N
8. P
9. O
10. M
11. C
12. H

13. I
14. E
15. G
16. J

Chapter 9

1. N
2. W
3. C
4. V
5. J
6. K
7. Q
8. P
9. H
10. I
11. L
12. M
13. R
14. S
15. F
16. B
17. G
18. O
19. T
20. E
21. D
22. X
23. A
24. Y
25. U

Chapter 10

1. H
2. L
3. J
4. M
5. G
6. I
7. O
8. R
9. D
10. S
11. N

12. F
13. P
14. C
15. E
16. A
17. Q
18. K
19. B

Chapter 11

1. T
2. B
3. F
4. G
5. S
6. P
7. V
8. M
9. Q
10. H
11. L
12. C
13. U
14. O
15. J
16. K
17. A
18. D
19. R
20. I
21. N
22. E

Chapter 12

1. K
2. P
3. A
4. C
5. Q
6. X
7. D
8. J
9. T
10. F

11. N
12. H
13. B
14. W
15. I
16. U
17. G
18. L
19. V
20. O
21. M
22. R
23. E
24. S

Chapter 13

1. H
2. Q
3. M
4. P
5. F
6. N
7. B
8. A
9. I
10. G
11. J
12. L
13. K
14. D
15. E
16. C
17. O

Chapter 14

1. L
2. D
3. E
4. C
5. K
6. F
7. B
8. A
9. J
10. H
11. I
12. M
13. G

Chapter 15

1. O
2. E
3. I
4. L
5. B
6. D
7. C
8. J
9. F
10. K
11. Q
12. P
13. R
14. A
15. N
16. S
17. G
18. M
19. H

New Laws Not To Be Ignored

(You Can't Hide From The Commissioner – More Transparency Required!)

A. USE OF BRANDS, "ASSOCIATES, GROUP OR TEAM" NAMES

A salesperson may be permitted to file an application on behalf of a responsible broker with a county clerk to obtain a fictitious business name. A "Doing Business As" (DBA) filling is required when a broker allows his or her agents to use a brand advertising name or term such as "associates, group, or team." All advertising must contain a team name in a conspicuous manner, in print or electronic media, and "for sale" signage along with their broker's name and CalBRE license number.

Your name as the broker and your CalBRE license number must be at least as large as the fictitious name (DBA) of the brokerage you represent. This includes brands (logos) that represent associates, groups, or teams!

An application must be delivered to the bureau, signed by the responsible broker, requesting the bureau's approval to use a county-approved fictitious business name that shall be identified with the broker's license number. Ownership of a fictitious business name that may be used subject to the control of a responsible broker must be maintained.

To add a DBA to your broker license, enter the name exactly as it appears on the **Fictitious Business Name Statement (FBNS)** as filed with the County Clerk. The DBA must be filed in the county of your main office address. Submit a copy with the "filed stamp" from the County Clerk's office.

To change application Information (update) – Salesperson's License. Use CalBRE RE 214. This form is to be used by salespersons only. Broker salespersons must use CalBRE RE 204.

B. REQUIRED: AGENT'S CURRENT CONTACT INFO

The Commissioner of Real Estate requires an agent's current office or mailing address, current telephone number, and current electronic mail address.

Even in this smartphone-heavy industry, you still must have a physical address (office or home) from which to do business. You also have to notify the Real Estate Commissioner within 30 days of changes to all contact information, including your email address!

Every licensed real estate broker or salesperson licensee must have and maintain a definite place of business in the state that serves as his or her office for the transaction of business, to display his or her license, and where he or she holds personal consultations with a client.

Every real estate broker and salesperson licensee must provide the Commissioner with his or her current office or mailing address, current telephone number, and current electronic mail address. All licensees must update this information no later than 30 days after making any change. CalBRE is not required to post or publish these electronic mail addresses or telephone numbers.

Textbooks From Educational Textbook Company

www.etctextbooks.com

Sometimes our textbooks are hard to find!

If your bookstore does not carry our textbooks, please send us a check or money order and we'll mail them to you with our 30-day money back guarantee.

Other Great Books from Educational Textbook Company:*

California Real Estate Principles - "Principles" Platinum Standard, 14th ed., by Huber. . .	$110.00 ____
California Real Estate Practice - "Practice" Gold Standard, 8th ed., by Huber & Lyons. . .	$110.00 ____
How To Pass The Real Estate Exam, 8th ed. - e-book (850 Exam Questions), by Huber. . .	$110.00 ____
California Real Estate Law, 8th ed., by Huber & Tyler.	$110.00 ____
Real Estate Finance, 8th ed., by Huber & Messick.	$110.00 ____
Real Estate Economics, 5th ed., by Huber, Messick, & Pivar.	$110.00 ____
Real Estate Appraisal – Principles and Procedures, 4th ed., by Huber, Messick, & Pivar. .	$110.00 ____
Residential Real Estate Appraisal, by Huber & Messick.	$110.00 ____
Mortgage Loan Brokering, 6th ed., by Huber, Pivar, Zozula.	$110.00 ____
Property Management, 6th ed., by Huber, Lyons, & Pivar.	$110.00 ____
Escrow I: An Introduction, 4th ed., by Huber & Newton.	$110.00 ____
Real Estate Computer Applications, by Grogan & Huber.	$110.00 ____
Homeowner's Association Management, by Huber & Tyler.	$110.00 ____
California Business Law, 4th ed., by Huber, McGrath, & Tyler.	$110.00 ____
Hubie's Power Prep 700 CD – 700 Questions, by Huber.	$110.00 ____

* <u>PRICES EXPIRE 1/1/2017</u>

Subtotal _____
Add shipping and handling @ $10.00 per book _____
Add California sales tax @ 9.75% _____
TOTAL _____

Allow 2-3 weeks for delivery

Name: _____

Address: _____

City, State, Zip: _____

Phone: _____

Check or money order: Educational Textbook Company, P.O. Box 3597, Covina, CA 91722

Books may be less expensive through your college bookstore. For faster results, order by credit card from the Glendale Community College Bookstore:
1-818-240-1000 x3024
1-818-242-1561 (Direct)
www.glendalebookstore.com